THIRD EDITION

THE PSYCHOLOGY OF
CRIMINAL CONDUCT

D.A. ANDREWS   JAMES BONTA
CARLETON UNIVERSITY   SOLICITOR GENERAL CANADA

anderson publishing co.
p.o. box 1576
cincinnati, oh 45201-1576
513-421-4142

The Psychology of Criminal Conduct, Third Edition

Copyright © 1994, 1998, 2003
Anderson Publishing Co.
2035 Reading Rd.
Cincinnati, OH 45202

Phone 800.582.7295 or 513.421.4142
Web Site www.andersonpublishing.com

Andrews, D. A. (Donald Arthur), 1941-
    The psychology of criminal conduct / D. A. Andrews, James Bonta. -- 3rd ed.
        p. cm.
    Includes bibliographical references and index.
    ISBN 1-58360-544-4 (pbk.)

Cover design by Tin Box Studio, Inc.

EDITOR Ellen S. Boyne
ACQUISITIONS EDITOR Michael C. Braswell

Preface to the Third Edition

The themes identified in the Preface to earlier editions remain important. (The previous preface is reprinted in this edition.) This third edition, however, was completed under conditions of some major changes in mainstream criminology. The psychology of criminal behavior is now readily evident in many mainstream textbooks and conferences. For example, there is a renewed interest in individual differences and an appreciation of the influence of personal, interpersonal, and structural factors. Developmental criminology continues to grow and contribute. Similarly, the literature on effective intervention including the effects of human service is becoming more sophisticated. The growing body of relevant research findings is represented throughout this third edition.

The text also includes some changes in organization of content. Chapter 2 now combines basic methodological concerns with overviews of the evidence regarding social origins and personality as covariates of criminal behavior. Chapter 2 also includes a brief narrative and quantitative overview of "what works" in terms of effective intervention. Systematic explorations of threats to validity are contrasted with more rhetorical approaches to criticism. Major theoretical approaches are now explored within only two chapters, with one chapter devoted to the general personality and social psychological perspective.

Applications of the psychology of criminal conduct remain a major focus in the third edition. Issues in practical prediction and effective intervention receive expanded coverage including the effects of official punishment and enhanced coverage of restorative justice models. Mentally disordered offenders, sex offenders, and psychopaths receive special attention along with domestic violence and substance abuse.

As in previous editions, the text concludes with consideration of contributions in the broader contexts of prevention, social change, and justice. The authors remain convinced that substantial progress is being made in understanding variation in the criminal behavior of individuals. At the same time, barriers to quality research and effective applications are a challenge.

Thanks to our editor Ellen Boyne for her thoughtful and careful review of the text and to our families for their continuous support and encouragement.

D.A. Andrews
J. Bonta
2002

Preface to the Second Edition

The content of this book reflects lecture notes and readings that were first compiled in the mid-1970s for an advanced undergraduate psychology course in criminal behavior. The course was designed with particular attention to understanding individual differences in criminal activity. The focus was on a conceptual and practical appreciation of the predictors of individual variation in criminal activity and of the effects of deliberate intervention on subsequent criminal activity. From the beginning, the authors have been involved as university-based instructors, as practicing psychologists in criminal justice settings and as consultants and researchers in human service and correctional agencies.

Our practice as psychologists, academicians, consultants and researchers served to support, strengthen and broaden our original conceptual and practical interest in understanding variation in criminal activity. Our experience as university-based instructors in the psychology of crime led us to extend our interests to include the social psychology of criminological knowledge. From the start, we were aware that mainstream sociological criminology and mainstream clinical/forensic criminology were not in tune with a general personality and social psychological approach to individual differences in criminal activity. We were not prepared, however, for the systemic nature and the depth and variety of the anti-differentiation, anti-prediction, anti-treatment and even anti-research bias that existed with the mainstream orientations.

With regard to mainstream sociological criminology, we quickly learned from our students who were exposed to sociology of deviance/crime courses that major portions of their learning involved denial of individual differences in criminality and denial of correlates of that variation. For example, many students entered our course believing that we are all equally criminal (that is, there is no variation in criminal behavior) and that any apparent variation was really a reflection of one's location in society (typically some variation on lower-class origins). Moreover, those students who had exposure to the sociology of deviance/crime already *knew* that deliberate intervention was not only criminogenic but morally deficient. These students *knew* that criminogenic processing also reflected too much processing (as they had learned from labeling theory) and too little processing (as they had learned from deterrence theory). Additionally, some of our students *knew* that the severity of criminal justice processing itself reflected not the seriousness of the offense but extralegal considerations such as the personality of the judge or the social location of the offender and victim (their age, gender, race/ethnicity, class and/or geography). The problem for us (and some of our students) was that the actual research findings regarding variation in criminal activity and its processing contrasted dramatically with what mainstream criminology was teaching. Thus, this text includes direct comparisons between the antipsychological assertions of mainstream sociological criminology and the actual research findings within the psychology of crime. This second edition of the text welcomes the major changes evident in the last few years, as several of the social location theories are being reformulated and turned into social psychological perspectives.

In regard to mainstream clinical criminology, this text compares the research findings in the areas of prediction and intervention with what the psychiatric/clinical psychological tradition would suggest. The text finds, for example, that the experience of personal distress (alienation, anxiety, low self-esteem) is as weak as lower-class origins in the prediction of criminal behavior. Furthermore, we find that high-risk, egocentric offenders were not dropped on earth from alien spaceships, although mental disorder may well contribute to criminality. Once again, this second edition welcomes some major developments in clinical criminology as social psychological perspectives are gaining strength.

For these reasons, this text takes some time to explore the facts regarding individual differences in criminal activity and makes a distinction between accounting for that variation and accounting for variation in aggregated crime rates, variation in processing and variation in processing institutions. We often use the phrase "a general psychology of criminal conduct" rather than "psychology of criminal behavior" in order to underscore the differences between the psychology in this text and the psychology of crime that is so often presented in a distorted manner in many criminology textbooks. For example, the lack of reference to Freud, the facile dismissal of Glueck and Glueck, the continuing tendency to equate "psychological" with "pathological," the outrageous promotion of sociology and the disregard for evidence so apparent in mainstream criminology is rejected in the psychology outlined in this book. Even today, in mainstream sociological criminology, we find general criminological theories that have individual differences at their base and yet continue to deny personality, prevention, rehabilitation and the dynamic nature of human behavior.

We think it is time for a truly interdisciplinary general psychology of criminal conduct that is open to the full range of potential correlates including the personal, interpersonal, familial, structural/cultural, political, economic and immediate situations of actions. Faith in the explanatory power of inequality in the distribution of social wealth and power has reached ludicrous levels, as has faith in official punishment and the denial of the evidence regarding the potential of direct human service. It is time to break free of a self-consciously sociological criminology that for too long has denied human diversity, human service and any thought or evidence that might threaten professional or ideological interests. One route is the exploration and development of a general psychology of criminal conduct. Thanks to some papers by Travis Hirschi, Ronald Akers, Michael Hindelang, Gwynn Nettler and Francis Cullen, we know that criminology is not a monolithic monster devoted exclusively to the promotion of the class-based theories of anomie, subculture, labeling and critical/Marxism or to the variations on themes of official punishment embodied within labeling, deterrence and just deserts theory. There is a window opening in which full-functioning human persons may be represented in criminological theory and research, represented as something more than hypothetical fictions whose only interesting characteristics reflect social location as indexed by age, gender, class, geography and race/ethnicity. By bringing the psychology of human behavior back into criminology, some of the extremes of the punishment and processing themes of current criminal justice may come to be viewed as the natural products of any "truly social theory" that denied psychology.

We continue to look forward to the future because all indications are that we will see an explosion of research on the psychology of crime, crime prevention and corrections. We also think that the social psychology of criminological knowledge will have demonstrated how the rational empirical traditions of unsparing criticism and respect for evidence may contribute to a fuller understanding of the criminal offender.

Although this book is a product of years of research, professional practice and countless discussions with students, colleagues and friends, its completion depended upon the patience and support of our families. For this we would like to acknowledge and thank our partners and children: to Catherine Carvell, and Karen, Donna, Vicky, Ashley, Rebecca and Adam, and to Christine Bonta and Carolyn and Mark, our deepest thanks.

D.A. Andrews
J. Bonta
1998

Table of Contents

Chapter 3
Understanding Through Theory: Toward Social Learning Through Psychodynamic, Social Location, and Differential Association Perspectives   101

Chapter 7
Prevention and Rehabilitation   273

Chapter 8
Getting Mean, Getting Even, Getting Justice: Punishment
and the Search for Alternatives   329

Chapter 1

An Overview of the Psychology of Criminal Conduct

The psychology of criminal behavior outlined in this book has certain values at its base. These values include a respect for human diversity and a respect for the complexity of human behavior. Respect for human diversity entails a respect for individual differences that extends well beyond the socially or biologically defined categories of ethnicity, race, gender, social class of origin, social class of achievement, or any other broader or more narrow definitions of social arrangements. Individual differences are apparent in biology, personality, cognition, behavioral history, and immediate associates in the domains of home, school, work, leisure, and community. It is considered possible in this psychology of criminal behavior that variation is evident within and among the socially and politically defined categories of ethnicity, gender, socioeconomic status, social structure, culture, and political economy. Respect for the complexity of human behavior means that this text is very suspicious of any account of human behavior that claims that individual differences in behavior may be attributed to any single type of variable, be it biological, psychological, or social. This psychology is particularly uneasy with tests of social structure and culture that are based on assessments of age, race, ethnicity, class, and gender at the personal level when it is obvious, but rarely acknowledged, that social contexts such as neighborhoods vary in their age, ethnic, and class compositions as well as in the roles, statuses, and supports available to members. Additionally, respect for complexity means that while we seek complete and total understanding, we value an enhanced, albeit incomplete, understanding.

This psychology of criminal behavior also respects unsparing criticism of theoretical assertions and research findings. Unsparing criticism is a major source of advancement. At the same time, all criticism, including criticism of theoretical and research-based assertions, is best combined with respect for evidence. Additionally, it views a reduction of the costs of both crime and criminal justice processing as highly desirable.

In the following pages, the psychology of criminal behavior (PCB) will be referred to as the psychology of criminal conduct (PCC). One reason is that "PCC" rings more positive than the letters "PCB," which imply toxicity. More important perhaps, the phrase "criminal conduct" more strongly implies the violation of deeply held and widely shared norms than does the phrase "criminal behavior." In brief, and for reasons that will become clear in the pages that follow, we want the psychology of crime explained in this text to stand separate from the weak psychology represented in mainstream sociological criminology and mainstream clinical/forensic psychology of the 1970s and 1980s. Notably, and positively for this third edition of *The Psychology of Criminal Conduct*, both mainstream sociological criminology and mainstream clinical/forensic psychology have continued to move in the direction of the values underlying PCC. This text continues to suggest that there exists a general personality and social psychology of criminal conduct (that is, a PCC) that has conceptual, empirical, and practical value within and across social arrangements, clinical categories, and various personal and justice contexts. The text closes with an assessment of that assertion.

The psychology of criminal conduct (PCC) seeks a rational and empirical understanding of variation in the occurrence of criminal acts and, in particular, a rational empirical understanding of individual differences in criminal activity. The first task of this chapter is to introduce this objective of PCC from the perspective of achieving a "rational empirical understanding." It will be found that rational empiricism seeks a variety of understandings of the phenomenon of interest. The second task is to locate PCC within the concerns of the broader fields of study represented by criminology, general human psychology, and criminal justice. The third task entails a brief look at the systematic challenges to a PCC that exist within mainstream sociological criminology. We will see that the rational empiricism of PCC has been under severe attack for years by criminologists who placed higher value on social theory and political ideology than on rationality and/or respect for evidence.

Objectives of the Psychology of Criminal Conduct (PCC)

The objective of the psychology of criminal conduct (PCC) is to understand variation in the delinquent and criminal behavior of individuals. First, the meaning of "variation in criminal behavior" is explored; then we review the meaning of the term "understand" in the tradition of rational empirical inquiry.

The Focus: Variation in Criminal Conduct

Criminal behavior refers to acts that are injurious and prohibited under the law, and render the actor subject to intervention by justice professionals. The specific acts included are many. They are subject to some temporal and cultural variation. Historical and cross-cultural research, however, reveals that most societies have formal procedures for the negative sanctioning of acts of theft, robbery, and physical assault. Variation in the occurrence of acts injurious to others is the primary focus of the psychology of crime, even though antisocial acts may not always be prohibited under the law and under some temporal and cultural circumstances may even be prescribed (for example, killing the enemy under the conditions of war).

The variation of interest is of two types. First, people differ in the number, type, and variety of criminal acts in which they engage. This variation is typically referred to as *interindividual* differences in criminal behavior. In addition, variation is found over time and across situations for particular individuals. This variation is called *intraindividual* variation. Some preliminary illustrations of these individual differences in criminal conduct will increase appreciation of what it is that the psychology of criminal conduct seeks to understand and explain. Examples of individual differences are presented below and they illustrate the variation in the *criterion* or *dependent variable* (i.e., criminal behavior) within PCC.

Casual Observation of Others. Casual observation will readily establish that, within almost any group, people may be differentiated according to their criminal histories. For example, within your circle of acquaintances and friends, you may be aware that some have been arrested, convicted, fined, placed on probation, or incarcerated, while others have not. Additionally, you may have information that some within your circle violate some laws rather regularly, while others do so much less frequently (if at all). Some may be particularly active in violating the laws governing the distribution of mood-altering substances, others may have difficulty conforming to laws governing property rights, while still others may violate laws designed to protect the dignity and integrity of the physical person of others.

Self-Observation. Reflecting upon your own behavioral history you may find that you have engaged in acts subject to the label "criminal." You may also find that your criminal activities were concentrated in a particular period of your life, or to have occurred under certain circumstances but not under others. For example, some people report that they are much more likely to violate rules when they have been drinking alcohol than when they are sober.

Systematic Observation. Systematic observation, as opposed to casual self-observation, yields more detailed (and, generally, more interesting) information on the criminal conduct of individuals. Chapter 2 is devoted to illustrations of individual differences in criminal conduct. These differences are found through systematic exploration of victim reports, self-reports, and reviews of official records. Here are a few introductory examples based on reviews of official records (these studies will be described in more detail in Chapter 2):

1. It was found that 23.1 percent (6,545) of the 28,338 people born
    in 1958 and residing in Philadelphia from age 10 to 18 years had
    an official record of arrest by age 18. Their total number of
    recorded offenses was 20,089. The delinquents with two or more
    offenses represented 12.1 percent of the total sample or 52.6 per-
    cent of the delinquent sample (3,440/6,545). This subsample of
    delinquents accounted for 16,984 recorded offenses. Thus, 12 per-
    cent of the subjects were responsible for 84.5 percent of the
    total number of recorded offenses (16,984/20,089).

2. It was found that 31 percent (1,968/6,347) of men born in 1953
    and residing in Stockholm in 1963 had an official record of
    delinquency by the year 1979. Twenty percent of the total sam-
    ple of men, those with a record of two or more offenses, account-
    ed for an estimated 88 percent of the delinquent offenses.

Types of Understanding Sought

The understanding of criminal behavior sought by PCC is empirical,
theoretical, and practical. In brief, this means that psychology seeks explanations of criminal conduct that are consistent with the findings of systematic observation, rationally organized, and useful to people with
practical interests in criminal behavior. These three interrelated aspects
of understanding criminal conduct are stressed throughout the text.

An Empirical Understanding. Empirically, PCC seeks knowledge
not only of the observable facts regarding the nature and extent of individual variation in criminal conduct, but also knowledge of the personal, situational, and social variables associated with or correlated with
criminal behavior. These are termed *covariates* and include the correlates
of individual differences in a criminal history and the predictors of the
criminal futures of individuals. For reasons related to a practical understanding (see below), the predictors are called risk factors, and when those
risk factors are dynamic (subject to change), they are called criminogenic
needs. Perhaps most importantly, PCC seeks knowledge of the causes of
the criminal conduct of individuals. *Causal* (or *functional*) covariates consist of observation-based knowledge that offers the potential to influence
the likelihood of a criminal act through deliberate intervention. Knowledge of causes come from experimental studies. These three types of
covariates—correlates, predictors, and causal or functional variables—
may be found in biology, personality, attitudes and beliefs, aptitudes and
skills, learning history, family, peer relationships, broader social arrangements, and the immediate situation of action.

As an illustration, gender is a well-known covariate of criminality. In
the Philadelphia 1958 birth cohort, as described above, 23.1 percent of
the total cases had an official record by the age of 18 years. However,
among males, the delinquency rate was 32.6 percent compared with 14.0

percent among females. This simple example illustrates an enhanced empirical understanding of criminal behavior. It appears that being male is a risk factor for delinquency. That is not to say, however, that all males were arrested at least once by age 18, nor that no females were arrested. A meaningful association or covariation may be established without it being perfect. Empirical knowledge that yields perfect prediction is an ideal to be sought, but empirical knowledge that yields an improvement in predictive accuracy over that achieved by chance is not to be devalued.

Resource Note 1.1 discusses the correlation coefficient as a general measure of the magnitude of covariation. The particular type of *correlation coefficient* most frequently employed in research and in this text is the Pearson Product Moment Correlation Coefficient (also known as *r*). The *r* statistic takes a value of 1.00 when the level of association or predictive accuracy is 100 percent. For example, if all men (100%) had a criminal record and no women (0%) had a record the correlation between gender and a criminal history would be 1.00. On the other hand, if the percent of men and women with criminal records were equal (for example: 20% and 20%, 50% and 50%, or 70% and 70%), the *r* would be 0.00. Generally, the magnitude of the *r* reflects the difference in percent criminal for one group relative to another—it reflects the simple difference in percentage values. In the paragraph above, that simple difference was 32.6 minus 14.0 (that is, 18.6 percentage points). All correlation coefficients may be interpreted as reflecting such a difference. Resource Note 1.1 reveals that the simple difference in percentage points provides a meaningful way of comparing the strength of association (or the level of covariation) among variables.

Resource Note 1.1

Measurement of Level of Covariation: The Pearson Product Moment Correlation Coefficient and Rosenthal's Binomial Effect Size Display

Covariation is important in this text. One of the most frequently used ways of quantifying level of covariation is the *Pearson Product Moment Correlation Coefficient* (or the Pearson *r*). Taking values between 0.00 and 1.00, *r* expresses the magnitude of a linear relationship between two variables. A linear relationship is one that may be described by a straight line: That is, for example, as the observed level of one variable increases so does the observed level of the other. The correlation coefficient will take a negative value if there is an inverse relationship: That is,

as the observed level of one variable increases, the observed level of the other variable decreases.

The correlation coefficient may be used to describe the findings of many types of studies. Often, the results of research on the potential covariates of criminal activity will be reported in terms of the percentage of one group (for example, men) who reoffend (no/yes) relative to the percentage of another group (for example, women) who reoffend (no/yes). Sometimes research results will be reported in terms of the covariation of a multilevel variable

Resource Note 1.1 *(continued)*

(such as verbal intelligence) and a multilevel measure of criminality (such as number of new offenses). At other times, research may be reporting how a two-level variable such as gender (men/women) is associated with the average number of offenses. The findings of all of these examples of research may be defined in terms of a Pearson Product Moment Correlation Coefficient (r).

Robert Rosenthal (1984) has shown how the findings from diverse studies may be compared. The *binomial effect size display* assumes that 50 percent of the cases are at one level of the potential covariate and 50 percent are at the other level (for example: 50 percent of the cases are men and 50 percent are women; 50 percent are below average in verbal intelligence and 50 percent are above average in verbal intelligence). Rosenthal's binomial effect size display additionally assumes that 50 percent of the cases are criminal (or had relatively many new offenses) and 50 percent are not criminal (or had relatively few new offenses). Under these conditions, the r is the simple difference in percentage points between the two groups. One group is assumed to be at higher risk for criminal behavior than the other. Thus, for example, if being female is considered lower-risk, and being male is considered higher-risk, the findings may be as follows:

If the correlation is 1.00:
Lower risk (being female)	000% criminal
Higher risk (being male)	100% criminal
	100-minus-000 = 100

If the correlation is 0.00:
Lower risk	050% criminal
Higher risk	050% criminal
	050-minus-050 = 000

If the correlation is 0.10
Lower risk	045% criminal
Higher risk	055% criminal
	055-minus-045 = 010

If the correlation is 0.60
Lower risk	020% criminal
Higher risk	080% criminal
	080-minus-020 = 060

An inverse relationship, looks as follows:

If the correlation is -0.60
Lower risk	080%
Higher risk	020%
	020-minus-080 = -060.

Given knowledge of the value of the correlation coefficient, it is an easy matter to compute the criminality rates for the lower-risk and higher-risk groups. Employing the binomial effect size display, the proportion criminal in the higher-risk group is 0.50 plus the r divided by two, and the proportion criminal in the lower risk group is 0.50 minus the r divided by two. For example, if the correlation is 0.40, then r divided by two is 0.20. Thus, with r = 0.40, the proportion criminal in the higher risk group is 0.70 (0.50 plus 0.20) and the proportion criminal in the lower-risk group is 0.30 (0.50 minus 0.20).

The binomial effect size display approach also may be employed to summarize the effects of experimental studies wherein, for example, equal numbers of cases are randomly assigned to treatment and control groups. For example, if success is reduced reoffending and the correlation between treatment and reoffending is 0.20, then the recidivism rate in the treatment group is 40 percent (50 minus 10) compared with 60 percent in the control group (50 plus 10).

By computing correlation coefficients, researchers are in a position to state not only whether they established covariation but also the level of covariation. Researchers are also in a position to compare the relative strength of various correlates. The binomial effect size display approach provides a convenient and easily interpretable representation of the magnitude of covariation.

Of course, correlation does not prove causation. As will be shown in Chapter 2, the correlational, predictive, or causal status of covariates, regardless of the level of covariation (or predictive accuracy) achieved, depends upon the way in which the observations are conducted. Because the differences among the types of covariates are so important, this text includes a review of the different research designs that yield information on different types of covariates. An empirical focus also suggests that PCC must be concerned with the reliability and validity of assessments of criminal behavior and the potential covariates of criminal conduct. Thus, the text will be attending to issues of the quality of measurement. Finally, PCC is concerned with the reliability and validity of any conclusions made regarding the nature and level of associations established between potential covariates and criminal conduct. Therefore, in Chapter 2, we review some standard threats to the validity of conclusions that may be drawn from systematic research.

A Theoretical Understanding. The search for theoretical understanding is a search for general, rational, simple, emotionally pleasing, and empirically accurate explanations of variation in criminal behavior. General explanations are ones that apply to a number of specific observations. For example, a general theory of criminal conduct will account for variation in both violent and nonviolent offenses, and will do so for men and women of different ages, races, nationalities, and socioeconomic origins.

Rational explanations are ones that withstand logical analyses, both internally and externally. A good theory is expected to be internally and externally consistent. *Internal consistency* refers to how well the assumptions and explanatory variables fit together within a theory. *External consistency* refers to how well a theory fits with other scientific theories. For example, a theory of criminal behavior may make internally consistent use of certain biological assumptions, but it would be less than satisfactory if those assumptions were at odds with reasonably well-established theory in the broader biological sciences.

Simple explanations are ones that make relatively few assumptions. Less objective, but not unimportant, "good" theories are also ones that make personal sense, provide a sense of unity, and give us the emotional "rush" often associated with great literature and other great works of art. It is also expected that the language of a "good" theory will respect human dignity and will not be disrespectful of individuals or groups.

The most important aspect of theoretical understanding, however, has to do with predictive accuracy. Empirically defensible explanations are explanations that are consistent with the findings of systematic research; that is, the correlates, predictors, and causal variables identified in the theory are validated by systematic observation. There are two major empirical tests of the adequacy of a theoretical understanding of criminal behavior. One involves the ability to predict accurately variation in criminal behavior. The second involves the potential to influence criminal activity by way of deliberate interventions that focus on the causal variables suggested by the theory.

A third aspect of empirical defensibility is research that supports the theoretically defined interrelationships among the predictor variables themselves. For example, a theory may suggest that family conflict and antisocial associates are risk factors and further suggest that family conflict contributes to association with delinquent peers. A fourth aspect of empirical defensibility links with the standard of a "general" understanding. In brief, does the research evidence regarding the ability to predict and influence criminal behavior generalize to people who differ in gender, ethnicity, or other personal and/or social considerations? PCC does not assume answers to such questions or declare the uniqueness of particular groups. Rather, PCC seeks out the evidence.

Resource Note 1.2 provides a very brief overview of theories of criminal conduct. This overview will render some of the research findings provided in the introductory chapters more theoretically meaningful, even before the middle chapters of the text outline the theories in more detail.

Resource Note 1.2

Overview of Theories of Criminal Behavior: A Brief Look Ahead to the Theory Chapters

The major theories of criminal activity have been classified in various ways by various authors. With some recognition of alternative classification systems, this text finds the following classification of value: psychodynamic, social location, differential association, and social learning/social cognition.

1. **Psychodynamic theory**, with roots in the psychoanalytic perspective of Sigmund Freud, is a source for much of current theory. The major contribution resided in Freud's description of the structure of human personality. The key structures of personality are ego and superego, which interact with the immediate environment and the demands of id for immediate gratification. Superego and ego develop as the child interacts with the environment and, for most children, that immediate environment constitutes the family. Psychological maturity involves a fully developed ego and superego and is characterized by the ability to delay gratification for longer-term gain, to love and be loved, and to be socially productive. A strong superego is the psychological representation of societal rules and a strong ego is a set of coping and defense skills by which demands

for immediate gratification may be delayed for longer term gain.

KEY THEORETICAL IDEA: Criminal behavior reflects psychological immaturity and particularly weak self-control in specific situations.

MAJOR RISK FACTORS: Impulsivity, disturbed interpersonal relationships, low levels of success in school and at work, weak superego (little guilt, reckless disregard for conventional rules and procedures, early misconduct, antisocial attitudes), weak ego (limited skill across a wide domain of skills), aggressive pleasure-seeking, readily angry, problems in the family of origin.

MAJOR IMPLICATIONS FOR PREVENTION: Strong on targets (see major risk factors above), weak on style and mode of service.

Psychodynamic theories are very much alive today, most notably in the form of social control theories such as those of Travis Hirschi (1969; Gottfredson & Hirschi, 1990). The most important development of psychodynamic theory, however, must be seen as

Resource Note 1.2 *(continued)*

the work of Sheldon Glueck and Eleanor Glueck (1950), who introduced the importance of temperament, attitudes, and family. To this day, multifactor theories are being developed that clearly reflect the work of Glueck and Glueck (1950).

The psychodynamic tradition is also evident in the development of frustration-aggression theory from the Yale school in the 1930s (Dollard, Doob, Miller, Mowrer & Sears, 1939) through the broadband social learning formulations of the 1970s and 1980s (Bandura, 1989) through the general personality and social psychology of the 1990s (see below).

2. ***Social location theories*** of crime suggest that criminal behavior reflects where one is located in the social system. Typically the importance of social location is said to reflect inequality in the distribution of societal wealth, power, and prestige. The typical indicators of social location are social class, age, race/ethnicity, and gender. Thus, being poor, being young, and being a member of a disadvantaged ethnic group may all contribute to motivation for crime. Being female, a position of disadvantage in a patriarchal society, however, apparently does not contribute to motivation for crime.

KEY THEORETICAL IDEA: Criminal behavior reflects personal distress (strain) that may be linked with socially structured inequality in the distribution of wealth and power.

MAJOR RISK FACTORS: lower-class origins, low levels of success at school and work, feelings of alienation (as opposed to feelings of anger), perception of limited opportunity in combination with desire for conventional success, being a gang member, adoption of lower-class values.

MAJOR IMPLICATIONS FOR PREVENTION: Opens up educational and vocational opportunities, but weak on how to do it.

Robert Merton's (1938) anomie theory asserted that crime was not the expression of untamed impulses (as in psychodynamic/control theory) but an innovative route to conventional success for those who found legiti-

mate routes blocked by virtue of their lower-class status. Subcultural developments within social location theories suggested that lower-class offenders were not innovating but conforming to criminal values and taking advantage of criminal opportunities.

Social location theories are in crisis today because the magnitude of the association between measures of inequality and individual criminal conduct is too slight to give the theories any serious consideration as a psychology of criminal conduct (see Chapter 2). Unfortunately, attention must be given because criminology textbooks continue to suggest that they remain important. Consider, however, the limited value of a near exclusive focus on young lower-class men who have been conventionally socialized and yet blocked in their pursuit of conventional success. Robert Agnew (1992) has severed ties to traditional strain theory and presents instead a general social psychology of criminal conduct reflecting the social learning models of anger and aggression.

3. ***Differential association theory***, like psychodynamic theory, actually has a powerful psychology of human behavior at its base. That psychology is symbolic interactionism, wherein what people think is very important, and any particular situation may be defined as one in which it is "OK" to violate the law. The attitudes, values, beliefs, and rationalizations that may support such a definition are learned through differentials in exposure to procriminal and anticriminal patterns. The major part of the learning occurs in association with others. Sutherland's (1939; Sutherland and Cressey, 1970) differential association theory was made stronger when Burgess and Akers (1966: Akers, 1973) reformulated it by introducing the principles of operant conditioning from behavioral psychology. Ronald Akers called that reformulation "social learning theory."

KEY THEORETICAL IDEA: Criminal behavior is an expression of differentials in the reinforcement and punishment of criminal and noncriminal alternative behavior.

Resource Note 1.2 *(continued)*

MAJOR RISK FACTORS: antisocial attitudes, antisocial associates.

MAJOR IMPLICATIONS FOR PREVENTION: Strong on intermediate targets but weak on how to do it.

4. *A general personality and social psychology* of human behavior of wide applicability has emerged in the late 1980s and 1990s. Criminal behavior is one class of behavior to whose analysis this general model appears particularly valuable. The general model is perhaps best described as a social learning/cognitive behavioral/social cognition theory. With the contributions of the Yale school (for example: Dollard, Doob, Miller, Mowrer & Sears, 1939), Albert Bandura (1989), and Donald Meichenbaum (1977), with contributions from general social psychology (for example: Ajzen and Fishbein, 1980) and with developments in understanding the major dimensions of personality (for example: Digman, 1990), it is possible for psychologists to suggest that if one is interested in predicting and/or influencing the occurrence of any particular human act, it is of value to assess and/or try to influence one or more of the following sets of variables—attitudes, associates, behavioral history, or personality. The "Big Four" themselves (i.e., attitudes, associates, his-

tory, and personality) may be influenced and or moderated by conditions in the major domains of family, school and work, leisure, and neighborhood.

KEY THEORETICAL IDEA: The chances of a criminal act (a) increase with the density of rewards signaled for criminal behavior and (b) decrease with the density of signaled costs of criminal behavior. These signaled rewards reflect personal control through antisocial attitudes, interpersonal control through the social support for crime provided by antisocial associates, nonmediated control established by a history of reinforcement of criminal behavior, and/or personal predispositions.

MAJOR RISK FACTORS: antisocial attitudes, antisocial associates, antisocial behavioral history, antisocial personality, problematic conditions in the domains of home, school, work, and leisure.

MAJOR IMPLICATIONS FOR PREVENTION: Strong on intermediate targets and strong on style and mode of service.

The general personality and social psychological approach, as demonstrated in Chapter 7, does still have a variety of competing perspectives on the essential causal variable (see Chapter 4).

A Practical Understanding. A practical understanding is guaranteed if the empirical and theoretical base of the psychology of criminal behavior is sound. Such a guarantee is possible because knowledge of predictors and causes brings with it the potential (although perhaps not the inclination) to influence the occurrence of criminal behavior in the context of corrections and prevention. In this sense, offenders and potential offenders, victims and potential victims, and all participants in prevention and criminal justice service may gain from a psychology of criminal behavior. In this text, special attention will be paid to those theories and empirical investigations that show the greatest practical potential.

Our overall conclusions will be relatively strong and encouraging with regard to research and theoretical development within PCC. Our conclusions will also be positive regarding practical applications of PCC. At the same time, references to the many gaps in knowledge within PCC will be encountered throughout the text. These gaps must be bridged if the above-stated objectives of PCC are to be reached. We will also stress the threats to validity associated with different types of research designs and how they are evident within particular studies. In other words, this text will underscore the healthy skepticism insisted upon by a rational empirical approach. As noted by Frederick Crews (1986), the characteristics of a community of rational empiricists include both unsparing criticism and respect for evidence.

Many irrational, anti-psychological, and anti-empirical impediments to the development of PCC are reviewed in this text. Interestingly, until very recently, the barriers to the development of PCC were most frequently encountered within the broad field of academic criminology itself. First, however, we locate PCC within the broader fields of psychology, criminology, and juvenile and criminal justice.

PCC and General Human Psychology

PCC is both a subfield of a truly interdisciplinary criminology and a subfield of human psychology. Being a subfield of psychology makes PCC a part of a vast scientific and professional discipline. As a science, psychology is concerned with producing empirically defensible explanations of behavioral phenomena. Professionally, psychologists are involved in the effective application of psychological knowledge at the individual, small group, organizational/broader community, and societal levels of action. Many psychologists combine professional and scientific interests because they have been trained according to a "scientist-practitioner model."

Criminal behavior has been a long-term (but not always mainstream) interest within psychology as a whole. In view of the great variety of interests and orientations within general human psychology, however, a psychological analysis of criminal behavior will be multifaceted. The many areas of interest in human psychology include human development, sensation and perception, learning and cognition, memory and information processing, motivation and emotion, personality and individual differences, assessment and evaluation, history and philosophy, clinical and applied, social and community, and biological and physiological psychology. This complex list includes areas of study sampled by almost all introductory textbooks in psychology. Thus, a psychology of criminal conduct seeks a richer and deeper understanding of criminal behavior than could possibly be found by concentrating on variables such as age, gender, race, and social class (until recently, the favored variables within sociological criminology). In brief, a psychology of criminal conduct will insist that the analysis of criminal behavior consider biological, personal, interpersonal, familial, and structural/cultural factors as well as consider the individual in particular situations and in their broader social context.

The theoretical orientations within human psychology are equally diverse. While this text emphasizes the contributions of social learning perspectives, this emphasis should not suggest that human psychology is successfully unified by that particular orientation. The psychology of human behavior in general, like the psychology of criminal behavior in particular, draws upon some combination of seven major orientations. These orientations to the exploration of human nature and individual differences are as follows:

1. *Biological* perspectives tend to emphasize relatively enduring soma-based predispositions (e.g., constitution and genetics), dynamic biological processes (e.g., the physiology of classical conditioning), the neuropsychology of emotion and self-regulation, and events with major somatic implications (e.g., the effects of alcohol on bodily functioning).

2. *Trait* perspectives tend to emphasize relatively enduring behavioral, cognitive, and affective predispositions (e.g., extraversion, intelligence, and emotionality) without necessarily requiring particular assumptions regarding the biological, psychological, or social bases of these traits.

3. *Psychodynamic* perspectives emphasize what many people still think of as the "truly psychological." Psychodynamic perspectives search for understanding through an appreciation of the personal psychological motivations and controls of overt behavior. The popular tendency to equate psychodynamic perspectives with psychology as a whole reflects the pervasive influence of Freudian theory on psychology and popular culture.

4. *Sociocultural* perspectives within psychology emphasize the effects of family, peers, and community on individual behavior. These theories tend to be socialization theories whereby individual differences in personal behavior, cognition, and emotions are linked to differences in the training provided by different families, peer groups, and social institutions. Other sociocultural perspectives place an emphasis on the contextual contributions of gender, class, and ethnicity.

5. *Radical behavioral* perspectives concentrate on how the immediate behavior-environmental contingencies are responsible for the acquisition, maintenance, and modification of individual behavior. The effects of the immediate environment depend very much upon how the environment reinforces, punishes, and ignores behavior.

6. *Humanistic* and *existential* perspectives may be differentiated from the above according to three concerns. The first is the emphasis placed upon "free choice" and "personal responsibility." The second is the emphasis placed upon perceptions of the self and the world as "perceived" and "interpreted" by the self. The third involves an attraction to the notion that the experience of interpersonal warmth, openness, and acceptance are associated with a pattern of personal "growth" that is both psychologically and socially positive.

7. *Social learning/cognitive behavioral/social cognition* perspectives may be differentiated from all of the above orientations by virtue of the additional emphasis placed upon learning by observation, the role of cognition, and the importance of considering the person in combination with particular situations. General social psychological perspectives tend to emphasize personal attitudes and beliefs, perceptions of the expectations of others, and the demands of particular situations.

8. Psychology is forever growing. Hence, in the near future, we may expect that PCC will be drawing upon developments in "positive psychology" and/or "post-modern" psychology and/or "feminist" psychology and/or "personal transformation" psychology and/or "culturally specific" psychology and/or "biologically universal" and/or "relational" psychology, and others not yet even on the horizon.

These interests and orientations within general human psychology are diverse. Fortunately, at least four unifying principles may be identified within this broad mix of interests and orientations:

1. *An interest in understanding the thoughts, emotions, and behavior of individuals.* The focus is on individuals with an interest in the full range of thought, feeling, and action.

2. *An openness to the full range of potential covariates of individual behavior, and to the full range of the moderators and mediators of those covariates* (i.e., soma, psyche, interpersonal, social, cultural, political, economic, and the immediate situations of action).

3. *Commitment to a rational empirical approach to knowledge construction.*

4. *The seeking of empirical knowledge, the construction of theoretical systems, and the application of psychological knowledge and opinion are subject to ethical and professional guidelines.*

Commonalities and Variation in the Behavior of Individuals.
Psychology, more than any other discipline, is called upon to recognize
the person and his or her behavior as a unit of analysis. Psychology, as
a science, is located between the biological and social sciences, and the
psychology of criminal behavior overlaps both the biological and social
sciences.

The biological sciences are concerned with the structures and
processes of the bodily system, how they relate to one another, and (sometimes) with how those parts and processes impact on the behavior of the
person. Biologically, the person is the sum total of biological structures and processes. The point of convergence between the interests of
biologists and psychologists is truly interdisciplinary. Some who work
in that area are biologists with an interest in psychology, while others
are psychologists with an interest in biology. That point of convergence
is described by terms such as biological psychology, physiological psychology, and neuropsychology.

Much of social science (sociology, economics, political science, geography, and history) is concerned with the parts and processes of social
systems and, sometimes, with how those parts and processes impact on
the behavior of the people who form or inhabit the social systems. A major
point of convergence between psychology and the social sciences is the
field of social psychology.

An Openness to the Full Range of Influences. Human psychology, as briefly described above, is too broad and too respectful of
diversity to restrict its concerns for the causes of crime to some narrow
set of variables reflecting social class, age, race, gender, or biology.
This characteristic of psychology may be difficult to understand for
some students of criminology. As noted above and below, mainstream
criminology tends to define psychology in terms of an interest in a personality and/or mental illness, when in fact the interests of psychology reflect the multiple orientations noted above. An interest in explaining individual differences in criminal behavior does not mean that
psychologists limit themselves to individual-level variables: Biology,
personality, personal attitudes, and interpersonal associations may be
important but so may be socially defined neighborhood and ecological
variables.

Understanding and Rational Empiricism. This element of the definition of psychology underscores the point that the theoretical understanding of individual behavior should be rational, that is, subject to
rejection on the grounds of an analysis of its logical structure. Second,
understanding must be subject to the findings of systematic observation;
that is, psychology is empirical.

Understanding in Ethical and Humane Ways. As a science
and as a profession, psychology has some established and developing
standards of conduct and practice. Thus, the pursuit and application of

knowledge is subject to ethical guidelines. For example, informed consent, confidentiality, and debriefing are elements of almost every piece of psychological research that involves direct contact between the psychological researcher and research participants. Similarly, professional psychologists are expected to describe their responsibilities and those of their clients in some detail prior to the full implementation of service. However, ethical issues are not always clear-cut. For example, clients of psychologists are deemed to have both the right to treatment and the right to refuse treatment. Moreover, major aspects of the supervision and treatment of offenders are mandated by the courts.

Thus, the following constitutes a working definition of a psychology of criminal conduct:

> As a science, the psychology of criminal conduct is an approach to understanding the criminal behavior of individuals through: (a) the ethical and humane application of systematic empirical methods of investigation, and (b) the construction of rational explanatory systems.

> Professionally, a psychology of criminal conduct involves the ethical application of psychological knowledge and methods to the practical tasks of predicting and influencing the likelihood of criminal behavior, and to the reduction of the human and social costs associated with crime and criminal justice processing.

So defined, a psychology of criminal conduct is, in part, an intellectual exercise in the use of general psychological principles and methods. Therefore, the psychology of learning and cognition and the general principles of human development may be applied to the analysis of illegal behavior. At the same time, studies of criminal behavior may contribute to knowledge in psychology generally. For example, the study of socialization is a major element of the psychology of crime and is also a major concern in developmental psychology.

This general description of the field makes two points that will be developed in more detail later in this chapter. In the first place, PCC does not encompass the wide variety of interests that psychologists have in the area of criminology. Nor does it cover the many roles that psychologists play in criminal justice. Many psychologists, including the authors, are interested in the behavior of victims, legislators, voters, and the public in general. Similarly, many psychologists are interested in the behavior of police, judges, jurists, prison guards, and probation officers (e.g., Bartol, 1996; Kassin et al., 2001; Trotter, 1999). Moreover, many psychologists in correctional practice probably spend more time dealing with the mental health needs of offenders than with criminality issues. All of these matters are interesting and important, but they are of concern in this text only insofar as they contribute to an understanding of individual criminal conduct.

Second, grounds have been established for making a distinction between psychology and the other disciplines and professions that share an interest in crime. Our focus is the criminal behavior of individuals. That focus is different from studies of bodily systems (biology), studies of variations in aggregate measures of crime rates and the structure of groups (sociology), and studies of the history and political economy of law and criminal justice. As important as these interests are for a general understanding of crime and criminal justice, they are outside the main focus of this text.

At the same time, many biologists, sociologists, political scientists, and economists share the interest in the psychology of criminal behavior. Their contributions to the psychology of criminal behavior are significant and will be represented throughout this text. Indeed, in the areas of the measurement of criminal behavior and in studies of the correlates of criminal behavior, many of the contributions of the last 20 years have been made by sociologists who conducted studies of the social psychological variety. A particular concern continues to be that social scientists so rarely actually explore community-level variables in relation to the criminal behavior of individuals. Let us look at mainstream criminology.

PCC and Criminology

Criminology is the broad interdisciplinary exploration of crime and criminal justice. As will be noted, however, textbook or official criminology has tended to be sociological. Until very recently, this sociological bent has tended to be explicitly antipsychological. These antipsychological themes will be developed, but for the next few paragraphs we present criminology as a truly interdisciplinary approach.

The outline and boundaries of the field of criminology have shifted somewhat over the last two decades. In the late 1960s, Donald Cressey and David Ward (1969:xii) prefaced their reader, *Delinquency, Crime, and Social Process*, with the following outline of the two key issues within criminology. One is the statistical distribution of criminal and delinquent behavior in time and space ("Why is the delinquency rate of this group, city, or nation higher than the delinquency rate of that group, city, or nation?"). The second issue is the process by which individuals come to behave criminally or in a delinquent manner ("How did Johnny happen to go wrong?").

By the end of the 1970s, it was clear that a third major focus of criminological study had emerged. There was a need to understand the broad historical, political-economic, social, and psychological factors that account for the emergence, maintenance, and modification of rules and laws, as well as the factors that account for the emergence, maintenance, and modification of societal reactions to the deviant act—that is, the study of criminal and social justice.

By the 1990s, yet another focus was apparent. The field of criminology had become so broad and mature that some scholars now focused on the sociology and social psychology of criminological knowledge. For example, this chapter's discussion of sociological criminology's reaction to the study of individual differences will illustrate an element of the fourth concern.

The second issue (explaining individual differences in criminal behavior) is the primary focus of PCC. The first issue (explaining aggregated crime rates) and the third issue (explaining criminal justice) are the primary focus of the social sciences, community psychology, and the psychology of criminal justice. The three central concerns of criminology, however, are not totally isolated from each other either rationally or empirically.

The defining element of PCC is the focus on individual criminal conduct, whereas the defining element of a social science of crime is a focus on aggregated crime rates. These focal concerns are not conflicting but simply different. Moreover, from a logical perspective, aggregated crime rates are direct reflections of individual differences in criminal conduct.

Aggregated Crime Rates as a Reflection of the Behavior of Individuals

Accurately measured variations in aggregated crime rates reflect real individual differences in criminal behavior. Logically, if true differences have been established in the crime rates of at least two different areas, one or both of two conclusions must be true regarding the criminal behavior of individuals:

1. Proportionally, more of the individuals in one area were committing criminal acts than were individuals in the other area(s);

2. Individual criminals in one area were committing more criminal acts than were individual criminals in the other area(s).

Thus, aggregate crime rates are a direct reflection of two major ways of expressing individual differences in criminal behavior. These two expressions are prevalence and incidence.

Prevalence refers to the number of criminals in a given area over a given time period (that is: number of criminals/population). *Incidence* refers to the number of crimes committed by the average criminal in that area over the period sampled (that is, number of crimes/criminal).

As expressed by James Q. Wilson and Richard Herrnstein (1985), the per capita crime rate reflects prevalence and incidence as follows:

$$\text{crimes/population} =$$
$$(\text{number of criminals/population}) \times (\text{number of crimes/criminal})$$

Jan Chaiken and Marcia Chaiken (1983:12) provided an illustration of these two key determinants of the crime rate in a community. If a city has 3,000 burglars per 100,000 population, and on average each committed two burglaries a year, the city's burglary rate would be 6,000 burglaries per 100,000 population—a very high rate. Alternatively, if the city has 300 burglars per 100,000 population, each committing on the average 20 burglaries per year, the burglary rate would also be 6,000 per 100,000 population.

The Chaiken illustration is particularly interesting because it reveals that while "true differences" in aggregated crime rates must reflect "true individual differences," "true" (i.e., accurately measured) similarities in aggregated crime rates do not imply regional similarities at the individual level of analysis. In other words, areas or historical periods with similar crime rates may differ considerably in terms of the prevalence and/or incidence of criminal conduct at the individual level. By definition, any variation in crime rates that does not reflect individual variations in criminal activity must reflect errors in the measurement of crime rates (e.g., differences in the reporting criteria of victims or police).

Ecological Fallacy

Enthusiasts of the social science approach sometimes assume that the regional or aggregated correlates of aggregated crime rates have something to say about the correlates of individual behavior. The *ecological fallacy* is the assumption that the aggregated correlates of aggregated crime rates imply knowledge of the correlates of individual behavior. The ecological fallacy is a particular threat when the aggregated correlate is a measure of the membership composition of the area: for example, areas may be differentiated according to some indicator of average income, average educational level, proportion of population unemployed, and so on. This discussion of the ecological fallacy does not suggest that social structural effects are unimportant. Rather, the point is that the effects of social structure on individual behavior are best established through studies of individuals in different social contexts. Otherwise, the ecological fallacy is a real threat.

Consider the issue of the relationship between income and crime. What we are calling a sociological investigation would involve an exploration of how mean income levels and crime rates might covary across neighborhoods of a city. For example, a widely accepted sociological "truth" is that crime rates are higher in low-income neighborhoods than they are in higher-income areas of a city.

Without debating the truth value of that "finding," the sociological investigation of an income-crime link may be compared with a psychological analysis of that link. A psychological investigation of an income-crime link would: (1) examine the criminal behavior of individuals, and (2) examine the criminal behavior of these individuals as a function of personal income and the average income level in the person's neighborhood. Psychologically, personal income and average income of the neighborhood are two distinct variables. Of the two variables, only the latter qualifies as a "social structural" variable or as a "social fact." A "social fact" is a measured property of a social system. Whether social facts actually impact on individual criminal behavior may be established only through psychological analyses wherein one disentangles the effects of personal facts (e.g., personal income) and social facts (e.g., neighborhood attributes) on individual behavior. To illustrate this point we draw upon Mayer's (1972) rational analysis of structural versus personal variables in relation to criterion variables. The illustrations contrast the interpretability of studies that focus on aggregate versus individual data.

Two quite different psychological findings are shown in Figures 1.1 and 1.2, yet both of the psychological findings are consistent with the hypothetical sociological finding that low-income neighborhoods have higher crime rates than do high-income neighborhoods.

In Figure 1.1, both lower-income and higher-income individuals tend to commit more crime when they live in lower-income areas. Here, with a focus on individuals, the psychological investigation was able to demonstrate that the "aggregate social fact" of below-average neighborhood income was impacting on both lower-income and higher-income individuals. The "social fact," a characteristic of the social environment, was a correlate of individual criminal conduct.

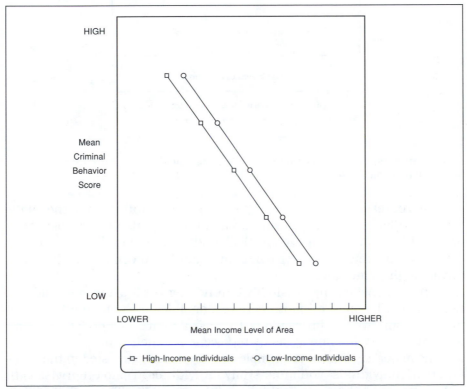

Figure 1.1
Criminal Behavior by Personal Income and Income Level of Neighborhoods:
A Hypothetical Illustration

In Figure 1.2, only the lower-income individuals who live in low-income areas show high levels of criminality. Here, the psychological investigation reveals that personal income is the important variable, but it is important only in low-income neighborhoods. In this illustration, the "social fact" was moderating the association between personal income and criminal conduct. That is, personal income was only important in neighborhoods that had low average incomes.

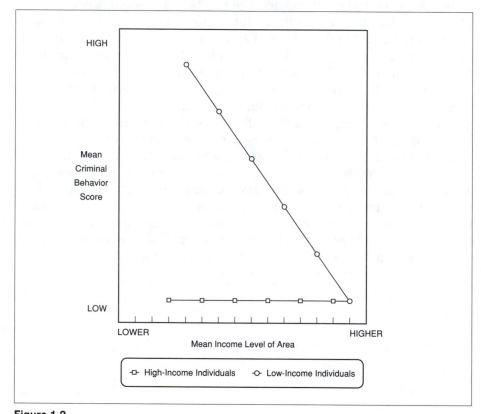

Figure 1.2
Criminal Behavior by Personal Income and Income Level of Neighborhoods:
A Hypothetical Illustration

Not represented in either figure is the possibility that the high-income individuals in low-income areas were responsible for most of the criminal activity. This psychological finding too would be consistent with the hypothetical sociological finding that low-income areas have relatively high crime rates.

Finally, consider the possibility that neither the low-income residents nor the high-income residents were responsible for the high crime rates in low-income areas. This would be the case if nonresident offenders were attracted to low-income areas as the scene for their crimes.

The major conclusion is a simple one. If you are interested in the criminality of individuals, you must study individuals. To do otherwise is to risk committing the ecological fallacy (Mayer, 1972). The ecological fallacy assumes that the aggregated correlates of aggregated crime rates imply knowledge of the correlates of individual behavior. An ecological linkage between income and crime is logically compatible with a number of possibilities at the individual level of analysis. In brief, ecological studies of aggregates are simply unable to establish the "facts" desired within PCC, whether those facts are personal or social.

We chose to illustrate the ecological fallacy with the income example because social-class explanations of criminal behavior are so widely assumed and because the data in support of a class-crime link are primarily of the aggregated variety. However, the "social facts" regarding the membership characteristics of social groups extend well beyond the issue of average income levels. For example, it is one thing to personally possess attitudes that are favorable to crime, and it is another to be a member of a group in which the dominant attitudes among group members are favorable to crime. Thus, both personal attitudes and the social facts regarding the dominant attitudes in groups are highly relevant variables in a psychology of crime. They, like income, must be independently assessed if their contributions to criminal behavior are to be understood.

There has been a strong tendency in sociology and social psychology to assign causal significance to group norms and group values. In the 1960s, much of criminology was dominated by subcultural theories of crime. According to this view, criminal behavior represented conformity to group norms that were antisocial. These norms were assumed to exist outside of and independently of the individual. Yet, in most studies, the existence of the norms was inferred from studies of the attitudes, values, and beliefs of individuals. Personal sentiment, like personal income, is not a proxy for a "social fact." The effect of the social fact can be established only by observing how variations at the group level are associated with the criminal behavior of individuals.

Consider how personal attitudes and social norms may relate to something like personal drug use. Using personal interviews or self-report, paper-and-pencil questionnaires, researchers are able to assess high school students according to whether the personal attitudes of the students are relatively favorable or unfavorable to the use of marijuana. If they have sampled widely enough, researchers also may be able to categorize schools according to the proportion of students with attitudes favorable to use of marijuana. Thus, schools too may be differentiated according to norms more or less favorable to use of marijuana.

Just as in the case of the income example, variations in personal use of marijuana may then be examined as a function of: (1) personal attitudes, (2) the normative context of the school that students attend, and (3) particular combinations of personal and contextual variables. A hypothetical finding is illustrated in Figure 1.3. The overall pattern of this hypothetical result will be evident in a number of studies reviewed in this text. That is, personal attitudes are more likely to be translated into personal action when the social context is favorable to that action (e.g., Andrews & Kandel, 1979).

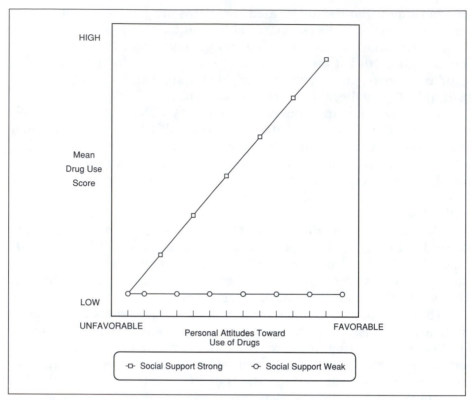

Figure 1.3
Drug Use by Personal and Social Support for Drug Use: A Hypothetical Illustration

A psychology of criminal conduct looks to social facts as well as other personal attributes and personal circumstances in the search for the sources of variability in individual criminal behavior. In developing a psychology of crime, we will not hesitate to draw upon the biological, social, and historical sciences when to do so truly informs the behavioral science of criminal conduct. As stated earlier, and as we shall see in later chapters, some of the best recent work on the psychology of criminal behavior has been completed by sociologists who conducted their work at the individual rather than the aggregate level of analysis.

In brief, knowledge of the correlates of aggregated crime rates tells us little regarding the sources of variability in the behavior of the individuals who are contributing to the prevalence and incidence rates. However, and as so well expressed by Cressey and Ward (1969), a sociology of crime rates and a psychology of criminal conduct will hopefully share the same theoretical models. An integrative perspective may be possible through a powerful social psychology of criminal behavior.

The thrust of this text will be to examine the research evidence regarding the factors associated with criminality, whether those factors or covariates reside under the skin, under the roof of the family home, on the streets, or within the broader social system. However, variables in the latter categories and their associations with criminal behavior should be assessed independently of assessments of other attributes of people and their circumstances. That is the only way in which the relative contributions of structure and culture and political economy may be shown to link with the criminal behavior of individuals.

We do not know how a convincing understanding of individual behavior could be achieved without studying the behavior of individuals. Nor do we know how it would be possible to come to a full interpretation of ecological or historical variations in crime rates without attending to the individuals who are responsible for the criminal acts that are tabulated across areas or over historical periods.

All of the disciplines and professions with an interest in crime are united in their commitment to the goal of improving the human and social condition. That we will assume. At the same time, it would be naive to expect consensus on the matter of what constitutes an improvement in the human condition or on which approaches will yield improvement.

Let our bias be clear: We believe that a major way in which psychology may contribute to the greater good is by systematically and ethically pursuing the development of empirically based knowledge. We are saying that the pursuit of a quantitative and empirically based psychology of crime is not only possible but is also highly desirable. The knowledge gained may be of value to all people, regardless of their personal, social, and political goals.

Social Context as a Moderator of Individual Differences

This text attends whenever possible to the social, political, economic, and historical contexts within which individual differences in criminal behavior are established. In particular, information on the generalizability of the correlates of individual differences in criminal behavior is sought. Although some correlates may be limited to particular social arrangements, we will find that many correlates are highly stable across social arrangements. A few preliminary examples follow.

Certain personality variables have proven to be relatively major correlates of the criminal conduct of adolescents even when social location varies according to geography, historical period, class of origin, race, age, and gender. John Hagan, A.R. Gillis, and John Simpson (1985) have shown that a propensity for risk-taking was a major correlate of the self-reported "common" delinquency of high school students in Toronto. Many other investigators have confirmed that risk-taking and sensation-seeking are correlates of a criminal history (e.g., Eysenck, 1977), but here we use the Hagan study to illustrate the general, versus limited, nature of this personal correlate of criminal conduct.

Hagan and his colleagues assessed a taste for risk-taking by look-ing at responses to two items on a self-report questionnaire. Students were asked to indicate their levels of agreement with the statements: "I like to take risks" and "The things I like to do best are dangerous."

They found that a taste for risk was associated with self-reported delinquency. More importantly, the study confirmed that an above-average taste for risk was associated with relatively high levels of crim-inal activity, regardless of the social class of family of origin or the gen-der of the young people studied. The positive correlation between a personal taste for risk and self-reported delinquent behavior was found among both the sons and daughters of owners, managers, workers, and the unemployed.

Hagan et al. also found that young men, regardless of their scores on the personality measure, reported more criminal activity than did young women. The effect of gender was evident among the offspring of owners, managers, and employees. This finding provides another exam-ple of the generality of correlates of delinquency. It, however, also appeared that the gender-delinquency link was not found among the chil-dren of the unemployed—at least not once a taste for risk was statisti-cally controlled. This very tentative qualification suggests that class of origin may moderate the correlation between gender and criminal behav-ior. This is an illustration, albeit weak, of how social class may influence the way other variables correlate with criminal conduct.

As weak as the moderating effects of social class were, the direct effects of social class on delinquent behavior were not only weak but also opposite in direction to that predicted by the class-based theories of crim-inal behavior. The adolescent offspring of managers, workers, and unemployed heads of household were not only statistically indistin-guishable from one another in their levels of criminal behavior, but their level of criminal activity was slightly lower than that of the sons and daughters of owners. This trend is in direct opposition to those class-based theories that suggest that lower-class origin is a major risk fac-tor for delinquency.

Stronger than the class-of-origin evidence noted above, and more in line with the evidence regarding the importance of a taste for risk, are the outstanding cross-cultural comparisons of delinquents and non-delinquents conducted with Gough's (1965) Socialization (So) scale from the California Psychological Inventory. The Socialization scale is a paper-and-pencil, self-report measure composed of items that tap a sensitivity to conventional rules and procedures. Low scores on this instrument are known to be associated with impulsivity and a general-ized disrespect for rules and convention.

Employing data pooled by Megargee and by Gough himself, Wilson and Herrnstein (1985) provided a rather dramatic summary of the abil-ity of So to distinguish between officially processed offenders and nonof-fenders in the United States. Inspection of Table 1.1 reveals the mag-nitude of the difference in the mean (i.e., average) So scores of American offenders and nonoffenders of both sexes.

Table 1.1
Mean Socialization Scores of Offenders and Nonoffenders by Gender

	NONOFFENDERS		OFFENDERS	
	Mean	SD	Mean	SD
Males	36.7 (N = 8,559)	5.7	28.6 (N = 845)	6.0
Females	39.5 (N = 9,687)	5.3	30.5 (N = 736)	6.9

Note. Low Socialization scores indicate a generalized disregard for conventional rules and procedures.

From Wilson & Herrnstein, 1985

In another study, Michael Hindelang (1972) showed that these differences were also evident in analyses of self-reported (unofficial) delinquency for a sample of American adolescents. Hindelang's findings confirmed that the socialization-criminality link was greater than—and independent of—class of origin, age, and race.

These studies, however, pale in comparison with Gough's cross-cultural study. Gough arranged for the administration of the So scale in eight languages in 10 countries to a total of 26,824 individuals. The total sample included 21,772 nonoffenders and 5,052 offenders. For both sexes in each language, the average socialization scores of the offenders were significantly lower than the average scores of the nonoffenders.

Additionally, consider the Eysenck and Eysenck (1978) report on the average personality scores on the Eysenck Personality Inventory measure of Psychoticism for British and Hungarian samples of offenders and nonoffenders. Within both the British (5.1 vs. 4.1) and Hungarian (7.1 vs. 4.3) samples, the mean psychoticism score of offenders was greater than the mean score of nonoffenders. In other words, psychoticism was a positive correlate of criminality in both countries. Interestingly, if there is any differentiation between countries, it is that personality was a more discriminating variable in what was, at the time, the less capitalistic system. Unfortunately, their results do not permit an analysis of the relative contributions of nationality and personality to individual behavior.

A final illustration of the interaction of social location and personal factors is an example of the recent rediscovery of the importance of neighborhood. Per-Olof H. Wikström and Rolf Loeber (2000) showed that variation in the socioeconomic neighborhood context had implications for the validity of assessments of risk that reflected impulsive personality, antisocial attitudes, antisocial associates, and problematic family relationships. The correlation of risk with serious youthful offending was approximately .70 within the more advantaged neighborhoods while the correlation was not statistically greater than .00 within the most disadvantaged neighborhood. Stated another way, even the young men who were at low risk for antisocial behavior according to their personality, attitudes, and immediate interpersonal environment were actually put at risk when they lived in a highly disadvantaged neighborhood. On the other hand, high-risk young people offended at relatively high rates regardless of socioeconomic context. Note, that the contributions of personal risk overall was much greater than the contributions of disadvantaged neighborhood overall (a correlation coefficient of .69 between personal risk and serious youthful offending compared to a correlation coefficient of .28 for neighborhood and serious youthful offending). The above noted correlation coefficients were gammas, and gammas yield somewhat higher values than Pearson *rs*.

In summary, PCC is interested in how social arrangements may moderate the personal correlates of criminal behavior. PCC also seeks knowledge of personal moderators of the effects of social context on individual behavior. Now we turn to PCC and the study and operation of criminal justice.

PCC and the Psychology of Criminal Justice

The offensive acts whose occurrence and processing are the preoccupation of criminology are widely condemned. This is demonstrated in Chapter 2. Given the high level and pervasive condemnation of criminal acts, elaborate and complex systems have developed to deter their occurrence, to detect their occurrence, and to identify, punish, and correct those who engage in the acts. Psychologists are involved in almost every facet of these justice systems. As John Monahan (1980) observed, a psychologist may have screened the police officer, provided training and counseling to the officer, assessed an accused's competency to stand for trial, provided treatment to a convicted offender, or advised a parole board on questions of release and supervision. Reflecting developments since 1980, psychologists may also have provided harm reduction/recovery services to the victims of crime; interpreted the criminal event for the press; provided expert opinion to the prosecution, the defense, or the court; or provided consultation services to the community at large.

Clearly, PCC involves but one small part of psychology's role in criminal justice. However, PCC may contribute in many ways to the creation and operation of a justice system that meets the public's expectations for effectiveness, ethical and humane treatment, efficiency, and ecological soundness.

An Effective System. The public expects the criminal and juvenile justice agencies to perform their duties effectively. The public wants crime control and victim services and believes that serious offenders should be identified and punished. Moreover, the public appears to be particularly offended by recidivism; that is, by the in-program and postrelease criminal activity of convicted offenders. The public also seems to take "correction" and "rehabilitation" seriously; that element of their concern is part of the domain of PCC. Traditionally, and with some pride, psychologists have been more concerned with effective rehabilitation than with efficient punishment. PCC does not deny the retributive and restorative aspects of justice but, as will be seen (and with a concern for reduced victimization), PCC seeks ethical, legal, decent, and humane ways of introducing human service into the justice context of sanctioning. It is through correctional treatment that re-offending is reduced.

An Ethical and Humane System. Recognizing the massive power that the state invests in the justice system, the public also insists that the justice system operate in fair, humane, and just ways while pursuing effectiveness. Thus, elaborate rules and procedures define the processes and limits of the labeling of acts and actors as criminal. In addition, applications of punishment and correction are subject to due process. The processes are so complex that criminal justice agents have been invested with considerable discretionary power. In part, these discretionary powers are a simple consequence of the fact that legislation, precedence, convention, and policy cannot possibly anticipate every possibility that may arise. More importantly, these discretionary powers are judged necessary if the system is to be fair and humane as well as effective. A mature PCC may contribute to guidelines that structure discretion in fair, ethical, just, and humane ways.

An Efficient System. A concern for efficiency is the third major expectation of the public. As important as the effective and fair control and punishment of crime may be, the system offends when it is wasteful of scarce resources and when it consumes more than it appears to be delivering. A PCC may assist in establishing systems that process offenders and control crime in efficient ways. Sometimes the contribution may be to suggest less costly alternatives to criminal justice processing.

A System that Fits with Other Systems. A fourth expectation of justice systems is that they connect appropriately with other societal institutions and social goals. This expectation may be called the ecological standard. For example, the justice system is a major employer and, as such, is of considerable interest to the educational system that produces lawyers and other professional and paraprofessional workers.

In addition, the operation of the educational, health, and welfare systems are of considerable interest within criminal justice. If the mental health and child welfare systems are unable to manage their clients, it is reasonable to expect that many of those clients will soon be in the courts and in the correctional system. At the other end, criminal justice officials are annoyed when the educational, health, welfare, and employment sectors are unable to respond to the needs of discharged offenders.

An intellectually mature PCC may provide, if nothing else, an empirically defensible knowledge base for the advocacy of the interests of individuals who become involved with the various service systems. The advocacy role is particularly important when bureaucrats battle with one another over their right to intervene (or to not intervene) in the affairs of selected individuals. Psychology, along with some other helping professions, has exercised the role of speaking out in the interest of the total and full-functioning person. This advocacy role is played out in the criminal justice arena.

A major source of tension and debate at the ecological level is the competition for resources among the various sectors and systems. A relatively recent addition to this debate has been a scholarly and practical concern with the apparently insufficient attention paid to "crimes" committed by business, labor, and government. Some scholars in criminology are now less interested in criminal justice than they are in social justice and human rights.

This broadening of the interests of criminologists is quite compatible with PCC. The psychology of criminal behavior has long recognized that "criminal acts" are but one component of a more general category of "antisocial acts." Antisocial acts are acts that are injurious to others. As we shall see, the same psychological principles that account for criminal acts will also account for noncriminal antisocial behavior and, indeed, for prosocial behavior.

PCC and the Psychology of Mental Health. The links between PCC and clinical psychology deserve a special notation because for years clinical psychology was more strongly linked with the forensic sciences than were many other parts of psychology. PCC, within general human psychology, has been developing for years. Unfortunately, the contributions of clinical psychologists have been primarily in terms of understanding how "mental disorder," "maladjustment," and such were associated with criminal conduct, and mainstream criminology appears to be aware only of these efforts. As will be seen in Chapter 9, the clinical contributions appear much stronger once combined with the contributions of the more general human psychology represented within PCC.

Objections to the Goals of PCC

Our brief description of the goals and methods of PCC may appear noncontroversial, and perhaps even rather mundane and banal. Who would argue against the importance of individual differences, and against rationality, regard for evidence, and practicality? Not many, one might think, because the alternatives would surely involve seeking an understanding of criminal conduct that is irrational, empirically false, useless, and dismissive of the characteristics of individuals. Nevertheless, many criminologists have argued—and a few continue to argue—in ways that are anti-person, irrational, anti-empirical, and anti-application. Consider the following assessments of mainstream sociological criminology of the 1970s and 1980s and even into the new millenium:

- Due to historic misfortune sociology captured the field in the 1920s. The contributions of biology and psychology have been minimized (Jeffery, 1979:7).

- In most sociological treatments of crime and delinquency, genetic explanations are either ignored or ridiculed (Rowe & Osgood, 1984:526).

- From the beginning, the thrust of sociological theory has been to deny the relevance of individual differences to an exploration of delinquency, and the thrust of sociological criticism has been to discount research findings apparently to the contrary. "Devastating" reviews of the research literature typically meet with uncritical acceptance or even applause, and "new criminologies" are constructed in a research vacuum (Hirschi & Hindelang, 1977:571-572).

- An objective of the psychology of crime is to understand personal covariates of criminal activity, whereas an objective of major portions of mainstream criminology is to discredit such an understanding (Andrews & Wormith, 1989:290).

- Sociology possessed a conceptual scheme that explicitly denied the claims of all other disciplines potentially interested in crime (Gottfredson & Hirschi, 1990:70).

- Advances in personality theory and assessment . . . have had little influence on research conducted by criminologists . . . Indeed, *Criminology* has published only four articles on the role of personality factors in crime since the journal was founded in 1964 (Caspi et al., 1994:165).

- The reason that most criminologists continue to resist the incorporation of biological factors into their understanding of criminal behavior is ideological. As part of their liberal academic tradition, criminologists tend to resist attempts to blame individuals . . . preferring instead to blame society and its institutions (Ellis & Hoffman, 1990:57).

- . . . [there is a] . . . skepticism within criminology and other social sciences about our ability to make accurate and reliable predictions of dangerousness and recidivism (Hannah-Moffat & Shaw, 2001:18)

The changes in mainstream textbook criminology and indeed in the content of the major criminology and criminal justice journals have bordered on astounding in the 1990s and into the new millenium. The two major empirical concerns of PCC—prediction and influence—are now mainstream. What were once called the major sociological theories of crime have almost uniformly been revised into social psychological theories. Within criminal justice, whole state, provincial, and even some national correctional systems have been transformed through attention to the principles of PCC. All of this will be explored in this text.

At the same time, some small portions of criminology and criminal justice are struggling openly with PCC and continue to advance the anti-prediction, anti-treatment, and anti-PCC themes. Some Marxist/critical criminologists, including even some "left realists," continue to assert that inequality in the distribution of social wealth and power is the major cause of crime. For example:

> After all, the United States is a nation characterized by gross economic inequality. . . . . The high rates of violent crime are major symptoms of these problems, and these crimes are committed mainly by . . . [the] underclass . . . In fact, social and economic inequality—not personality or biological factors—are the most powerful predictors of predatory violent crime (DeKeseredy & Schwartz, 1996:190).

This quotation provides an example of the irrationality within left-wing sociological criminology once the process of discounting PCC began. Briefly stated, the fact that nations differ according to their crime rates says nothing whatsoever about the causal roles of biology and/or personality. Within PCC, statements regarding the causal significance of any variables (be they biological, familial, or social) would be based on observations relevant to those variables. Within this critical/radical (albeit new left realism) criminology, however, evidence of international variations in crime rates may be asserted to signify the irrelevance of psychobiology and socialization experiences and to show clearly the importance of social inequality in the generation of crime. The evidence that predatory violent crimes are best predicted by social and economic inequality is reviewed in this text.

Notable in the quotation is the very restricted range of variables considered to be of interest. The two sets of variables are "social and economic inequality" and "personality and biological factors." This reflects a narrow vision of human behavior. Any student of introductory psychology and anyone with a personal awareness of their contacts with other human beings would know that the classes of variables associated with human behavior extend well beyond "inequality" and "personality/biology." Most of us have a sense that individual human beings—whatever their social/economic status and their personal/biological predispositions—may still be more interestingly differentiated according to their thoughts and emotions, their associates, their behavioral histories, and their satisfactions and dissatisfactions in major settings such as home, work, school, and neighborhood. Note also that PCC's agreed-upon openness to biology and socialization does not imply that "rents and tears" in the social fabric are unimportant in the analysis of crime.

The authors of this text and our students and colleagues cannot help but be amused when we are told by so many criminological scholars that they personally were never anti-prediction, anti-treatment, ideological, or blindly sociological ("not me"). The personal exoneration is often paired with the idea that perhaps Andrews et al., Ellis, Gottfredson, Hindelang, Hirschi, Hoffmann, Jeffery, Osgoode, Rowe, Wormith—and many other critics of sociological criminology not quoted several paragraphs above—were exaggerating the anti-psychological bias within criminology. Indeed, those who argue for PCC are sometimes accused of being "zealots," of making use of "smoke and mirrors," or of being "cult" members. There is a long history of negative labeling when criminologists are confronted with evidence overwhelmingly favorable to PCC (witness Sutherland's attacks on Glueck and Glueck; see Laub & Sampson, 1991).

Some critical post-modern feminist scholars go further and suggest that applications of PCC do not care enough about gender, race, ethnicity, and inequality (Bloom & Covington, 1998; Hannah-Moffat, 1999). Moreover, the construction of risk "evokes a white, middle-class male norm" and risk is "gendered and racialized." Moreover, it has been said that "nothing is a risk in itself: there is no risk in reality" and yet "anything can be a risk; it all depends on how one analyses the danger, considers the event." Moreover, "risk and the enterprise of risk management appears on the surface to be moral, efficient, objective, and non-discriminatory, but they are not" (Hannah-Moffat & Shaw, 2001:12). (Racist, sexist, unreal, immoral, inefficient, and discriminatory! Dear reader, do you dare to proceed any further in this text?)

This text suggests four major sources of the anti-psychological themes once so prominent in criminology and now virtually confined to a few groups. These groups include critical/Marxist theorists, some feminist and racial scholars, and some justice scholars preoccupied with the decency of punishment and the tyranny of correctional treatment (discussed in the punishment and treatment chapters). The four roots are historical/professional roots, moral roots, political roots, and the decline of positivism and emergence of theoreticism.

1. *Historical/professional.* The historical and professional roots of mainstream "social" criminology have been described by many observers, such as those cited above. The interdisciplinary field of criminology became a subfield of sociology in many North American universities in the 1920s and was firmly established as such in most universities by the 1940s. Robert Merton, one of the most important sociologists of all time, clearly rejected the psychology of the first 50 years of the century and proclaimed the understanding of crime to be essentially sociological. Edwin Sutherland, one of the most important sociological criminologists of the time, led this promotion of sociology through his now-discredited attacks on the work of Sheldon Glueck and Eleanor Glueck. These attacks are well-documented by John Laub and Robert J. Sampson (1991). Subsequent to the Sutherland attacks on PCC, individual differences research was considered antiso-

ciological (Hirschi & Hindelang, 1977). Moreover, not being anti-sociological obviously came to be judged as more important than being defensible on rational and empirical grounds.

2. *Moral.* The denial of individual differences was motivated in part to protect the "deviant" from charges of "being different." Being found different, it was thought, might be used as an excuse for abuse. We do not doubt that being different may be used to excuse abuse, but it is a strange social science that attempts to protect individuals by denying human diversity and overemphasizing social location (i.e., where people are situated in the social hierarchy). We think that respect for human diversity protects individuals, while fixations with social locators such as geography, race, and class promote genocide (Andrews & Wormith, 1989).

3. *The political crisis of the 1960s and 1970s.* The political context of the "disorder" or the "awakening" of the 1960s and 1970s is described elsewhere (Andrews, Zinger et al., 1990b; Cullen & Gendreau, 1989). A brief 10-year period saw the rise of conservative politics (and a focus on law and order), the decline of liberalism (and a disenchantment with the benevolence of the state), and the move of left-wing social science to the self-consciously "social" in the extreme (as it became enchanted with labeling and critical/Marxist perspectives of deviance). During this period, left-leaning social science withdrew active support for human science and human service delivery. The collapse of support for the ideal of rehabilitation cannot be attributed to the political "right"—they always supported punishment. It was due to the left adopting perspectives such as due process and critical/Marxist perspectives. To this day, left/feminist/sociological/radicals are in extraordinary states of confusion by the fact that PCC links variation in risk of recidivism to enhanced human service in the form of structured rehabilitation efforts, not to enhanced punishment (Hannha-Moffat & Shaw, 2001).

4. *The death of positivism and the rise of theoreticism.* The 1960s saw increased appreciation of certain intellectual truths. These may not be summarized easily but certain slogans from post-modern scholarship assist in making our points. Each of these slogans contained valuable truths. They suggested that all knowledge is partial (no single theory or single research study accounts for everything). Moreover, all knowledge is relative (no theory/research finding exists independent of time and social context) and all knowledge is socially constructed (theory and research reflect socially situated human imagination). Finally, all

knowledge is political (any theory or finding may serve the interests of one social group more than it serves another social group). These truths led rational empiricists to even more careful research and theory construction. However, these truths led major portions of criminology further away from a rational and empirical focus on crime and criminal justice, and toward the promotion of sociology, political-economy, and the political and personal interests of ideologues of the left and the right. In other words, large portions of criminology consciously adopted theoreticism as the sole method of seeking understanding. The search for these nonrational and nonemprical paths to knowledge is evident currently in some feminist approaches, in some transformative movements, in some aboriginal studies, in some restorative justice scholarship, and in some mainstream psychological studies of crime.

The essence of *theoreticism*, which is the alternative to a rational empiricism, is to adopt and discard knowledge insofar as it is personally or politically rewarding to do so, and to do so without regard for evidence (Crews, 1986). The theoreticists who were so dominant in mainstream textbook criminology of the 1960s, 1970s, and 1980s felt that they were the fortunate ones to whom "truth" had been revealed. Their visions were evident in three main ways:

1. Findings of systematic empirical investigations supporting their *a priori* positions were readily accepted and widely disseminated without critical review and qualification.

2. Research findings that were inconsistent with their *a priori* positions were ignored or discounted by essentially irrational appeals to what, when properly applied, are highly reasonable and well-known threats to the validity of the conclusions of systematic research.

3. The lack of research on many issues was treated not as a reason for caution but as a stimulus for the conversion of others to the revealed truths of a "superior" vision.

We have considered many ways of dealing with the anti-PCC and antiempirical elements of criminology briefly summarized in the above quotations and comments. We considered simply presenting the research and theory, assuming that students would reject the anti-PCC biases within criminology on their own. As sensible as this approach seemed, our years of research, teaching, and practice in criminal justice convinced us that it would be inappropriate simply to ignore the anti-PCC themes. These themes have been so prominent within criminology over the years that they must be addressed more directly. As implied in some of the quotations earlier, criminological audiences were more likely to applaud anti-PCC expressions than they were to display respect for evidence. As a result, we think it is important that the anti-PCC themes be faced directly in this text.

This text does two things. Most important, students are exposed to the reasonably solid theorizing, research, and applications that are highly relevant to PCC. In the process, students will also become aware of some glaring theoretical, empirical, and practical deficits within PCC. Thus, throughout, we will stress the knowledge construction aspects of rational empirical investigation. This involves an appreciation for the methods of research and for the many threats to valid conclusions that systematic research renders open to assessment. Additionally, when the correlates of crime are identified, we will attempt to provide concrete estimates of the magnitude of those correlations so that readers may assess the strength of associations with one set of covariates relative to some other set of covariates.

Second, students are asked to examine directly those elements of criminology and criminal justice that are actively hostile to a serious exploration of individual differences in criminal conduct. Here we will stress the destructive nature of theoreticism. It is important that students of PCC are able to recognize the rhetorical techniques employed by antipsychology and anti-person theoreticists. Systematic research approaches and challenges to rational empirical approaches are addressed directly in Chapter 2.

A Summary and Look Ahead

This discussion of criminology and criminal justice has provided an overview of the concerns of criminology, criminal justice, and corrections. Two summary points are notable:

1. Our particular concern in this text, the psychology of criminal conduct (PCC), is but one aspect of psychology's concern with crime, criminal justice, and antisocial behavior in general.

2. Psychology is not the only discipline with an interest in criminal behavior. However, when the focus is on the criminal behavior of individuals, the issue is one of primary concern within PCC.

Chapter 2 takes a closer look at criminal behavior, the criterion variable within PCC. Chapter 2 defines "criminal behavior" and provides detailed illustrations of the variability in criminal conduct that PCC seeks to "understand." Chapter 2 also develops the meaning of an "empirical understanding" of criminal conduct by providing a closer look at what an empirical understanding of criminal behavior entails. The terms *correlates*, *predictors*, and *causes* are defined according to the types of research designs used to establish them as covariates of criminal conduct. Chapter 2 takes a preliminary look at the multiple sources of variability in criminal behavior. In the context of correctional programming, the discussion stresses that "personal" and "social structural" variables are not in conflict for causal status but are analytically distinct variables that may be making independent and interactive contributions to the prediction of criminal conduct.

The Resource Notes in Chapter 2 show how the rhetoric of science may yield techniques that enable one to deny, discount, and dismiss the voluminous research on the relevance of personality to criminal behavior. In addition, criminology's attempts to discount the positive findings of personality research is underscored by its simultaneous inattentiveness to the dismal empirical performance of ideologically preferred variables such as social class. Similar attempts at knowledge destruction will be found in reactions to studies of the effectiveness of correctional counseling.

In Chapters 3 and 4, an overview of theoretical perspectives on criminal conduct is presented. These chapters emphasize the need for a truly human psychology of criminal conduct. We submit that the majority of perspectives on criminal conduct that are most favored in mainstream criminology reduce people to hypothetical fictions whose only interesting characteristics are their locations in the social system. Almost without exception among and within these theories, the causal significance of social location is presumed to reflect inequality in the distribution of social wealth and power. The latter is a major preoccupation of mainstream textbook criminology, even though such a focus has failed to make significant advances in the understanding of criminal conduct.

The social location perspectives contrast dramatically with classical psychoanalytic theory and with current social learning/social cognition models. These theoretical contrasts are drawn in rather bold print and, in the process, the theoretical biases evident throughout this text are clearly introduced. We take the following positions on criminological theory: (1) the contributions of psychoanalytic thought are appreciated; (2) the empirical and practical powers of social learning concepts and procedures are impressive; and (3) social location theories are a major impediment to progress in the social psychology of criminal conduct (even though we have seen how they may serve as minor moderator/mediator factors).

Chapter 5 takes a developmental perspective on delinquency and reviews various genetic, intellectual, and familial aspects of development. In this chapter, a fuller demonstration of the effectiveness of treatment programs is given by highlighting specific studies in the family therapy literature.

The remainder of the text moves beyond the establishment of the correlates and predictors of criminal conduct. Focal concerns become issues in the actual prediction (Chapter 6) and treatment (Chapter 7) of criminal conduct. Chapter 8 includes a review of the failure of punishment and deterrence policies in controlling criminal behavior, further accentuating the role of offender rehabilitation. This chapter concludes with a discussion of restorative justice as a new context for the delivery of offender treatment programs. Chapters 6 and 7, in particular, provide an empirical evaluation of the major theories according to their potential in the prediction and treatment of criminal conduct. Overall, the limits of the potential of social learning models are explored. We concentrate on practical applications of the psychology of criminal conduct, particularly applications in correctional programming.

Psychometrically sound assessments are required if we are to reach the upper levels of our ability to predict criminal behavior accurately. Throughout the text, but specifically in Chapter 6, reasonably well-validated assessment instruments are introduced that are useful in both the theoretical and practical analysis of criminal conduct. Chapter 7 is devoted to the issue of the effectiveness of correctional counseling and the value of case classification.

Chapter 9 involves a more specialized analysis of three "types" of offenders: the mentally disordered, the psychopath, and the sex offender. With these offenders we apply the principles of social learning theory and many of the ideas on effective assessment and intervention that are presented in Chapters 4, 6, and 7. Chapter 10 extends these applications to domestic violence, substance abuse, and community policing.

Finally, in Chapter 11, we conclude that a rational empirical approach to broader policy and justice issues is a serious alternative to the *a priorism* (reliance on a "known" or assumed cause as related to a specific effect) and theoreticism now rampant in the study of criminal justice. Certainly, the most intellectually serious and solid elements of current criminology may be directly attributed to the rational empiricism of a psychology of criminal conduct.

Chapter 2

Defining Criminal Behavior and Exploring Variability, Sources of Variation, and Major Findings Regarding Class, Personality, and Correctional Treatment as Covariates of Criminal Conduct

This chapter begins with explorations of definitions of criminal behavior. This discussion is located in the intellectual context of problematic definitions of crime that were so apparent in the 1960s and into the 1980s. We know, however, that issues of the definitions of crime are still very much with us, if not in psychology, then in criminal law, legal studies, critical criminology, radical criminology, and feminist criminology.

A detailed sampling of illustrations of individual differences in the prevalence and incidence of criminal conduct follows, as does a few operational definitions of "recidivism." The illustrations reveal individual differences under a variety of conditions of age, gender, poverty, and ethnicity as well as with criminal occurrences defined by victims, by self-report, and through official records of arrest and justice processing.

The covariates of criminal behavior are described as correlates, predictor variables, dynamic predictor variables, or functional variables, depending upon the structure of the research design (cross-sectional, longitudinal, multi-wave longitudinal, and experimental designs). Finally, meta-analyses (systematic quantitative reviews of the research literature) are used to summarize research on social class and crime, personality and crime, and the effectiveness of official punishment and correctional treatment in the control of criminal recidivism. These reviews not only introduce some major research findings within PCC but also provide the opportunity to explore the effects of potential errors of measurement and conceptualization. Rational empirical criticism and knowledge construction is compared with theoreticism and knowledge destruction.

Defining Criminal Behavior

"Criminal behavior" suggests a large number and variety of acts. Specific meanings vary according to the concerns of users of the phrase as well as with historical and social contexts (Mannheim, 1965). This text will draw upon four definitions of criminal behavior and will be most concerned with those acts that fit within the domains of all four definitions. These four definitions are as follows:

1. Legal: Criminal behavior refers to actions that are prohibited by the state and punishable under the law.

2. Moral: Criminal behavior refers to actions that violate the norms of religion and morality and are believed to be punishable by supreme spiritual beings.

3. Social: Criminal behavior refers to actions that violate the norms of custom and tradition and are punishable by the community.

4. Psychological: Criminal behavior refers to actions that may be rewarding to the actor but that inflict pain or loss on others. That is, criminal behavior is antisocial behavior.

Criminal acts, no matter which of the four above-noted definitions are employed, are part of a more general class of behaviors that social psychologists call "problem behavior" or "deviant behavior" (e.g., Jessor & Jessor, 1977; Ullmann & Krasner, 1976). Thereby, the essence of deviant acts is that their occurrence places the actor at risk of being targeted for interventions by figures of authority, control, regulation, and assistance. Problematic acts may occasion the intervention of parents, teachers, religious leaders, and neighbors. They may place the actor at risk of being attended to by mental health professionals, or by the relatively new army of regulators of business, labor, professional practice, government, and civil and human rights.

The psychological definition of crime as antisocial behavior is best combined with the broader definition of "problem behavior." If not so combined, some of the nondeviant practices of dentists, surgeons, and teachers would surely be judged criminal. Thus, with thanks to Ullmann and Krasner (1976), our working definition of criminal behavior is as follows:

> Criminal behavior refers to antisocial acts that place the actor at risk of becoming a focus of the attention of criminal and juvenile justice professionals.

No definition of criminal behavior is totally satisfactory. For example, the norm-based definitions have led to a number of dramatizations of certain trivial truths. In the 1960s, it was fashionable in some circles to note that we are all "criminal" because we all violate some rules some of the time. According to this position, criminality is not a variable but a constant; that is, we are all equally "criminal." Of course, the position was scientifically naive because not all rules are laws, and not all people violate the same rules (or laws) at the same rates or under the same circumstances.

At another extreme, the legal, moral, and social definitions imply that there would be no crime in the absence of legal, religious, and social norms. At a minor level, this is true. However, the injuries and losses suffered by victims would not be eliminated by the abolition of criminal codes and social norms. Two of the positive functions of the psychological definition (i.e., criminal behavior as antisocial behavior) is to prevent us from overdramatizing some of the trivial implications of norm-based definitions of deviance and to prevent us from losing touch with characteristics of offenders and the pain of victims.

"Acts of force or fraud in pursuit of self-interest," the psychological definition of crimes provided by Gottfredson and Hirschi (1990:15), is particularly interesting in this regard. These authors, as will be discussed in Chapter 3, develop their conception of the nature of criminal acts in such a way that the personality characteristics associated with criminal propensity follow directly from the nature of criminal acts. For example, criminal acts are said to provide immediate and easy gratification of desires; thus, weak self-control is an obvious personal source of variation in criminal activity.

The fact remains, however, that the behavioral content of the illegal, immoral, unconventional, and antisocial categories is neither temporally stable nor universal. The behavioral content of the domains varies over time and across cultures. Some acts may be deleted from the illegal domain (e.g., "wearing shorts in public"), while others may be added (e.g., "driving without a seat belt"). Similarly, the composition of the immoral and antisocial sets may vary. For example, the "physical punishment of children" and "cigarette smoking" are entering the antisocial set, while "homosexual acts" and "getting a divorce" are more acceptable. In the same vein, laws governing the distribution, sale, and consumption of drugs such as alcohol, tobacco, marijuana, heroin, cocaine, and amphetamines are a frequent topic of moral and legal debate in contemporary Western society.

A major task for philosophers, historians, and social and behavioral scientists in criminology is to understand more fully the definitional problems associated with "crime." In addition, many criminologists from various disciplines are interested in questions associated with the emergence, maintenance, operation, and modification of laws and the justice systems (Boyd, 1986; DeKeseredy & Schwartz, 1996; Mannheim, 1965; Nettler, 1989). As important and fascinating as these intellectual pursuits may be, they are not the focus of this text.

A serious problem remains. How can we claim to account for individual differences in a class of behavior that is, at the core definitional level, so subject to cross-cultural, subcultural, and temporal variability? How can we have a science of activities whose quality appears to be so dependent upon the evaluation of an audience? Indeed, how can we seek to account for individual differences in criminality when no act is intrinsically criminal? We will see that these issues have been found to be more threatening in rhetoric than in reality (e.g., Wellford, 1975).

As suggested in Chapter 1, the rhetoric was loud and intrusive in the 1960s and 1970s. Brian MacLean's (1986) edited collection on the political economy of crime provides some near definitive illustrations of these antipsychology themes:

> Some people's criminals may be other people's heroes. Underlying this dilemma is the problem that morality is variable, not absolute. Conceptions of "right" and "wrong" and "good" and "evil" vary from time to time, place to place, culture to culture, and group to group. This variation has led some criminologists to conclude that rules and laws are produced by "moral entrepreneurs" and their initiatives while other people remain less morally committed (Becker, 1963:47). Thus laws or rules reflect only the notions held by "moral entrepreneurs" (MacLean, 1986:4).

There is no question that criminals are seen as heroes by some people. People may view some criminals as heroes because they view some criminal acts as heroic acts. Indeed, sometimes the status of hero is totally dependent upon the commission of criminal acts. Would Bonnie Parker and Clyde Barrow be folk heroes if they had not robbed banks? We doubt it. Does their heroic status reflect a belief that it is "OK" to rob banks? We also doubt that. One may enjoy the stories of Bonnie and Clyde's bank robberies without believing that bank robbery should be legalized. Similarly, one may believe that banks are the products of an evil social system and should be abolished without believing that theft, robbery, and the killing of bank employees should be decriminalized.

Brian MacLean (1986) explains how traditional criminologists are mistaken in viewing crime as an event that constitutes the breaking of a rule, be it a rule of law or a rule of morality. "In actuality," proclaims MacLean (p.4), "crime is not an event" but a "social process":

> If we conceptualize crime as being an event, the violation of a law by an individual, then we run the risk of focusing on that individual at the expense of comprehending the entire process . . . criminology runs the risk of degenerating into what Taylor, Walton and Young [(1973:281)] have called "correctionalism" (p. 4-5).

Because the study of individual differences is said to place the whole field at risk of degeneration, the student of PCC had better read further on this "disease of correctionalism" (which was never defined). Turning to Taylor, Walton, and Young (1973:281-282), we learn that catching this disease is inevitable unless the scientist is committed "to the abolition of inequalities in wealth and power, and in particular of inequalities in property and life-chances."

> A fully social theory of deviance must, by its nature, break entirely with correctionalism . . . precisely because . . . the caus-es of crime must be intimately bound up with the form assumed by the social arrangements of the time . . . for crime to be abol-ished, then, those social arrangements themselves must also be subject to fundamental social change. . . . Men are now con-sciously involved . . . in asserting their human diversity. . . . The task is to create a society in which the facts of human diversi-ty, whether personal, organic or social, are not subject to the power to criminalize (pp. 281-282).

The disease, as they see it, is clear: By studying individual differences in criminal behavior, we will fail to advance the redistribution of wealth and power that will, in turn, create a society in which human diversity (i.e., individual differences) is not subject to punishment by the state. The major point here is that critical Marxists are not interested in understanding individual differences in criminal behavior.

Let us take a look at those aspects of human behavior that are sub-ject to the power to criminalize under various social arrangements. What organic, personal, or social aspects of human diversity, left unde-fined by Taylor et al. (1973), are subject to punishment over social space? What "notions" of the "moral entrepreneurs" lead to the pun-ishment of what aspects of human diversity? This question has been a focus of cross-cultural research and the answer need not be simply a mat-ter of ideology, polemics, or political slogans.

As early as the mid-1970s, Wellford (1975) showed that cultural rel-ativism, the possibility that crime is defined differently from one culture to the next, was not a threat to the study of individual criminal conduct. Anthropological inquiry suggests that some ethical principles are uni-versal and that the cross-cultural differences are relatively trivial. Accepting the fact of cultural relativism at the levels of customs and tra-ditions, Wellford concluded that universal condemnation was charac-teristic of those acts that have been the prime concern of criminology. These universally condemned acts were ones that involved violations of the physical integrity of the human organism; violations of property rights; violations of trust; murder, assault, and other acts of violence; rape and other forms of sexual assault; incest; robbery; theft; and destruc-tion of property. These acts represent points of convergence or areas of overlap among the domains of illegal, immoral, unconventional, and anti-social behavior. In other words, the criminal acts that rate a high con-sensus of disapproval tend also to be immoral, unconventional, and anti-social. The relative insignificance of cultural relativism when defining "core behavior patterns" that are deemed criminal remains true today (Ellis & Walsh, 1997).

The near universality of condemnation of "criminal behavior" was demonstrated by Graeme Newman (1976) in a sophisticated survey of opinion in seven nations. Newman did not suggest that he had drawn representative samples of the populations of these nations. For example, the United States respondents were all New Yorkers and the Italians were all Sardinians. New Yorkers are generally thought to represent a rather "liberal" lot and Sardinians are thought to represent the notion of a subculture of crime and violence. The Iranian sample was drawn before the revolution. The other nations sampled were Indonesia, India, and Yugoslavia.

Newman's study is rich and detailed. It is a significant contribution in many ways. It demonstrates the sophistication and potential of serious explorations of the dimensions of cultural relativism and provides a convincing legitimization of the focus of PCC. A sample of the questions posed and the answers given follows:

1. "Do you think this act should be prohibited by the law?"

    • Robbery (a person forcefully takes $50 from another person who, as a result, is injured and has to be hospitalized): 100 percent of the Sardinians and American respondents said yes. The lowest rate of condemnation was found in India, where 97.3 percent answered yes.

    • Appropriation (a person puts government funds to his or her own use): The condemnation rates varied from 100 percent (Sardinia) to 92.3 percent (USA).

    • Incest (a man has sexual relations with his adult daughter): The condemnation rates varied from 98.1 percent (Iran) to 71 percent (USA).

    • Factory pollution (a factory director continues to permit his factory to release poisonous gases into the air): The range of variability was 98.8 percent (India) to 92.8 percent (Yugoslavia).

    • Taking drugs (a person takes drugs; "heroin" in the United States, "soft" in Sardinia, "opium" in Iran, "gange" in India and Indonesia): The condemnation rates varied from 93.3 percent in Indonesia to 74.9 percent in India.

    • Much greater variability was evident within and across nations in terms of the prohibition by law of abortion, homosexuality, public protest, and not going to the assistance of someone in danger.

2. Respondents were asked to rate the seriousness of each act on a 12-point scale from 0 (not serious) to 11 (very serious). The acts were ranked in order of seriousness within each country and the rankings were compared among countries.

   - There was a high rate of agreement among nations concerning the relative seriousness of the acts. The highest correlation was .99 (India-Iran) and the lowest was .59 (Sardinia-USA).

   - The acts judged most serious were robbery, appropriation, incest, drug-taking, and factory pollution.

   - Within countries, the deviations from mean ratings tended to be lowest for the acts of robbery, incest, and appropriation.

   - We leave it to the reader to ponder some of the "deviant" responses of the New Yorkers. The New Yorkers questioned apparently consider drug taking to be more serious than incest, robbery, or appropriation. (We suspect that New Yorkers may know that heroin use is a major predictor of frequent and serious criminal activity in their neighborhoods.)

In summary, it appears that the aspects of human diversity subject to criminalization are such acts as assault, robbery, and theft. That many of these criminal acts are "high-consensus" ones, cross-culturally and subculturally, is also apparent. In brief, the psychology of criminal conduct has a criterion variable of generally recognized importance. Moreover, the fact is that psychology will continue to study antisocial behavior as it has from the beginning—whether the behaviors are high-consensus crimes or not. (It is comforting, however, to learn that many people from diverse social locations are not favorably disposed to sexual assault, robbery, and theft.)

What is also evident is that some social scientists, with an understandable and appreciated interest in social inequality and social control, have failed to make a major distinction between predictor variables and criterion variables. Human diversity is evident in behavior and in a variety of other organic, personal, and social variables. In the study of criminal behavior, the diversity evident in patterns of theft, assault, and pollution is the criterion variable.

Diversity in other areas that are not subject to the power to criminalize represents a host of potential predictor variables that may help explain the variability in criminal behavior. That is, the behavioral facts of human diversity that are judged criminal may well covary with other personal, organic, and social facts of human diversity.

Understanding those correlations is a focus of the psychology of criminal behavior. Readers are warned that they are at risk of catching the disease of "correctionalism" should they proceed any further. We will be looking well beyond inequality in the distribution of property and privilege in the search for an understanding of variations in criminal behavior.

The following section deals with the prevalence and incidence of the widely condemned and prohibited behaviors. The survey of the findings of various studies will render the nature and extent of variation on our criterion variables more concrete.

Exploring Variability in Criminal Behavior

Individual differences in criminal behavior are found within the histories of any sample of individuals. People differ according to the type, seriousness, variety, and number of criminal acts in which they have engaged. This variability in behavior is also evident when people are followed forward in time: some people become involved in more criminal activity and a greater variety of criminal activities than other people. Similarly, the number and variety of criminal activities in which particular individuals engage vary with immediate life circumstances and particular phases of the life span. Such are the variations that a psychology of criminal conduct seeks to understand through research, theory, and practice.

A few illustrations of the facts regarding variability in the criminal activity of individuals follow. The examples illustrate the extent and magnitude of the variation. We will also see that variability is found within most samples of individuals, be they male or female, black or white, young or old, upper-class or lower-class. In these examples, it will also be apparent that age (being young), gender (being male), and several other variables are major correlates and predictors of criminal behavior. Understanding these correlations—their magnitude and their causal and practical significance—is part of the focus of later chapters.

Inferring Individual Differences from Aggregated Crime Rates

The quality of centralized records of officially processed criminal activity may be questioned in many ways. However, national criminal justice statistics do provide a meaningful glimpse of the variation in types and frequency of criminal acts.

- The number of officially recorded murders was 542 for Canada in 2000 (Statistics Canada, 2001). This represents a rate of 1.8 based on 100,000 population. Unless we assume that a vast proportion of the Canadian population were accomplices to the 542 murders, it appears that in 2000 the act of murder was engaged in by relatively few Canadians.

- In 2000, approximately 1.3 million property crimes were recorded in Canada, yielding a rate of 4,070 per 100,000.

- Overall, 2,400,000 Canadian criminal code violations were recorded for a crime rate of 7,655 for 100,000 of the population in 2000.

- In sum, according to the national data banks that draw upon official records, relatively few Canadians were engaging in criminal activity in 2000. Certainly, in terms of having committed acts that contributed to the official counts for 2000, the vast majority of Canadians, but not all Canadians, would receive a criminal behavior score of zero.

Although the rates are higher in the United States, we still reach the same general conclusion: the vast majority of Americans, but not all Americans, commit few criminal acts. The rates per 100,000 persons as reported by the U.S. Department of Justice (2000) for various violent crimes in the United States in 1999 were as follows:

- 5.7 for homicide

- 32.7 for rape

- 150.2 for robbery

It is well known that official records provide underestimates of the overall level of criminal activity in the community. Thus, surveys of self-reported victimization are gaining some importance in criminology. Michael Hindelang (1981) studied the incidence of crime in the United States with data provided by the National Crime Survey. This survey involved interviewing all persons 12 years of age or older in a national sample of approximately 65,000 American households twice a year from 1973 to 1977. Interviewers asked questions regarding types of victimization in the last six months and inquired about the age, sex, and race of the offender in cases in which the offender had been seen by the victim.

Hindelang's (1981) report, although not the most recent, is interesting because he employed several weighing strategies in order to generate national crime rate estimates for various combinations of offender age, sex, and race. Personal crimes were defined as rape, robbery, assault, and theft from the person. The annual rates reflect the number of personal offenses occurring for every 100,000 potential offenders within 12 categories of age, sex, and race. A sample of the findings is reproduced in Table 2.1. ("Total" refers to the total number of personal crimes, not only to the numbers of rape and robbery).

Table 2.1 not only reveals substantial evidence of individual differences in criminal behavior but also shows that age, sex, and race are correlates of criminality in the United States. Taking all three risk factors into account, the rates reached levels of more than 84,000 offenses per 100,000 young black males between the ages of 18 to 20. On the other extreme, with the three risk factors absent, the rates for white women over 20 years of age were less than 300 per 100,000 such women.

Table 2.1
Estimated Annual Rates of Offending per 100,000 Potential Offenders

	MALES					
	White			Black		
Age	12-17	18-20	21+	12-17	18-20	21+
Rape	77	291	152	403	1,624	735
Robbery	1,203	2,245	463	16,663	35,030	7,000
Total	7,974	15,054	3,786	43,158	84,504	18,031
	FEMALES					
	White			Black		
Age	12-17	18-20	21+	12-17	18-20	21+
Rape	5	0	0	92	39	7
Robbery	212	71	33	1,307	703	164
Total	2,124	1,138	264	8,639	4,468	1,428

From Hindelang, 1981

Hindelang went on to show that the age, sex, and race differentials evident from the analyses of the reports of victims were also evident in the analyses of official records. For example, in the case of robbery, the correlation between victim-reported and officially recorded robberies across the categories of age, gender, and race was .95. The overall level of rate of crime may vary dramatically between victim reports (high) and official records (low), but the relative position of the rates of different groups may be very similar. In brief, while victim reports may be very high relative to officially recorded incidents, the correlates of criminal occurrence are quite similar.

Inferring Individual Differences from Surveys of a Criminal Past

The field of criminology can now draw upon a vast number of self-report surveys of a criminal past. We have chosen the Travis Hirschi (1969) survey because of its immense importance to the development of

PCC and criminology in general. Hirschi drew a stratified random sample of 5,545 students in 11 junior and senior high schools in Contra Costa County (California) in 1964. For 4,077 of the students, he was able to obtain both official (police files) and self-reported measures (questionnaires) of delinquency. For various reasons, Hirschi (1969) reported only on subsamples of this set of students. Thus, there are fluctuations in the composition of the samples referred to in the examples presented below. However, within each subsample there was evidence of the individual differences that constitute our main concern in this text.

- Within the subsample of 2,126 white boys: 68 percent had no police record, 8 percent had a record but no offenses had been recorded in the previous two years, 11 percent had one recorded offense in the last two years, 5 percent had two recorded offenses, and 8 percent had three or more recorded offenses.

- Within the subsample of 1,479 black boys: 43 percent had no police record, 12 percent had a record but no offenses had been recorded in the previous two years, 18 percent had one recorded offense in the last two years, 9 percent had two recorded offenses, and 18 percent had three or more recorded offenses.

Rick Linden and Kathy Fillmore (1981) compared the self-report data collected by Hirschi with the self-reported delinquent activity of young men and women who attended schools in Edmonton, Alberta. Their results are shown in Table 2.2. They reported extensive evidence of substantial individual differences in delinquent behavior.

- Fifty-three percent of the 1,264 California boys and 60 percent of the 571 Alberta boys admitted to theft of property worth less than $2.00. Seven percent of the California boys and 2 percent of the Alberta boys admitted to theft of property worth $50.00 or more. Forty-two percent of the boys in the California sample and 41 percent of the boys in the western Canadian sample admitted to having assaulted someone. Almost 24 percent (23.7%) of the California boys and 23.0 percent of the Canadian boys reported having committed three or more delinquent acts.

- The corresponding data for the 563 young California women and the 583 young Canadian women are presented in Table 2.2, along with the data for the boys. The tabled values refer to the percentage of cases admitting particular offenses.

Table 2.2
Percent of Young People Self-Reporting Criminal Activity
in California and Alberta by Gender

	MALES		FEMALES	
	California	Alberta	California	Alberta
N	1,264	571	563	583
Theft under $2	52.7%	60.1%	30.5%	33.3%
Theft $50 +	6.6%	2.4%	2.0%	0.2%
Auto theft	10.8%	5.9%	3.6%	0.7%
Damaged property	25.5%	40.3%	8.6%	16.0%
Assault	41.7%	40.9%	15.6%	8.1%
Three or more	23.7%	23.0%	5.1%	5.0%

Table 1, p. 346, from R. Linden & C. Fillmore (1981). A comparative study of delinquency involvement. *Canadian Review of Sociology and Anthropology, 18*, 343-361. Reprinted with permission.

Inferring Individual Differences from Prospective Longitudinal Studies

The extent of individual differences in criminal behavior is now well-established through a number of longitudinal studies in various countries and circumstances. These studies are so important to the development of the psychology of criminal behavior that several will be described in some detail here and will be referred to again throughout the text. A feature of some of these studies is that both incidence and prevalence were examined. That is, several of these longitudinal studies are able to report on both the number of offenders and the number of crimes committed by offenders.

The majority of the examples have been drawn from Katherine Van Dusen and Sarnoff Mednick's (1983) edited collection, *Prospective Studies of Crime and Delinquency*. That collection is recommended to all students of the social psychology of criminal behavior. Our sampling of findings will confirm that the social psychology of criminal conduct has much to explain.

The Philadelphia Birth Cohorts. Marvin Wolfgang (1983) and his colleagues have been reporting on two major samples of Philadelphia youths. The 1945 birth cohort includes 9,945 males born in 1945 who lived in Philadelphia from at least their tenth to their eighteenth birthdays. A 10 percent random sample (*N* = 975) of these boys was drawn and 567 of them were found and interviewed around the time of their twenty-fifth birthday. Not one of the men located refused to participate in the interview. The interview sampled various indicators of personal and social history, including self-reports of criminal behavior for which the boys were not arrested. Police records were subsequently reviewed up to age 30. The 1958 birth cohort includes 28,338 people, 13,811 males and 14,527 females, whose official records have been reviewed up to age 18.

- A total of 459 (47.3%) of the 1945 cohort had an officially record-ed arrest by age 30. Approximately 31 percent of the offenders had records of at least five offenses by age 30 (*N* = 144). These 144 "chronic offenders" had accumulated 1,683 offenses. Thus, approximately 15 percent of the individuals were responsible for 53 percent of all crime committed by the 1945 cohort.

- The official arrest records from age 10 to age 18 of the 1958 birth cohort revealed the following:

  1. Twenty-three percent of the 6,587 white males accounted for a total of 4,306 offenses. Among these offenses were four homicides, nine rapes, 103 robberies, 117 aggravated assaults, 217 other assaults, 454 break and enters, and 263 narcotic offenses. Slightly more than one-half of the offenses (50.9%) were committed by 499 "chronic delin-quents" (those who had records of arrest for five or more offenses). Thus, 7.6 percent (499) of the sample of white males accounted for more than one-half of the total amount of recorded criminal activity by white males.

  2. Forty-one percent of the 7,224 nonwhite males accounted for a total of 11,713 offenses. Among those offenses were 52 homicides, 96 rapes, 1,223 robberies, 459 aggravated assaults, 1,342 break and enters, and 474 narcotic offens-es. Almost 65 percent (64.7%) of the offenses were commit-ted by chronic delinquents who represented 17 percent of the total sample of nonwhite males.

  3. Similar trends were also found for the young women from the 1958 birth cohort. Overall, the repeat offenders (12.1% of 28,338) accounted for the vast amount of official delinquency (84.5% of 20,089 offenses) in the 1958 Philadelphia cohort.

 The Cambridge Study in Delinquent Development. David Farrington (1997) and his colleagues have been following a sample of 411 London working-class males since 1961-62, when the boys were about eight years of age. Data sources include interviews with parents, teach-ers, and the boys themselves, as well as reviews of official records of con-victions. Farrington's 1997 report is based on 404 of the men whose crim-inal records were complete up to age 40.

- Overall, 40.1 percent of the sample had a criminal conviction up to age 40. The most frequent of the offenses recorded were non-violent (a total of 643 nonviolent compared with 117 violent offenses).

- Six percent of the sample had six or more convictions. These "chronic offenders" accounted for one-half of the total number of convictions.

- Three percent of the boys were first convicted of a violent offense as children (age 10-16), 9.1 percent as young adults (17-24), and 7.9 percent as older adults (25-40).

- Ninety-six percent of officially convicted youths also self-reported convictions. In an earlier report (Farrington, 1983), fewer than 1 percent of the youths claimed convictions that were not officially recorded.

The Psykologisk Institut (Copenhagen) Adoption Files.
Sarnoff Mednick, William Gabrielli, and Barry Hutchings (1983) have described an analysis of the official records of all 14,427 nonfamilial adoptions in Denmark from 1924 to 1947. Court convictions for offenses committed by persons over 15 years of age were tabulated for male adoptees, female adoptees, and their biological and adoptive parents. Information was unattainable for some persons, but the Danish files provided a wealth of information on individual differences in officially recorded criminal activity. It was found that:

- 15.9 percent of 6,129 male adoptees had at least one criminal conviction and 6.9 percent had two or more;

- 2.8 percent of 7,065 female adoptees had at least one criminal conviction and less than 1 percent (0.8%) had two or more;

- 28.6 percent of 10,604 biological fathers had at least one conviction and 15.8 percent had two or more;

- 8.9 percent of 12,300 biological mothers had at least one conviction and 2.5 percent had two or more;

- 6.2 percent of 13,918 adoptive fathers had at least one criminal conviction and 1.6 percent had two or more; and

- 1.9 percent of 14,267 adoptive mothers had at least one criminal conviction and less than 1 percent (0.4%) had two or more.

The great value of this study resides in the possibility to examine the criminality of adoptees as a function of the criminality of biological and adoptive parents. The now famous Danish "cross-fostering" analysis found that criminality in the biological parents was associated with male adoptee criminality whether the adoptive parents were criminal (14.7% vs. 24.5%) or not criminal (13.5% vs. 20.0%).

The Psykologisk Institut (Copenhagen) 1944-1947 Birth Cohort. This cohort consists of all males born between 1944 and 1947 to mothers who were residents of Copenhagen and for whom criminal records were available ($N = 28,879$). Patricia Guttridge, William Gabrielli, Sarnoff Mednick, and Katherine Van Dusen (1983) reported upon the officially recorded criminal violence within this cohort up to the year 1974. Criminal violence included offenses of murder, rape, bodily injury, threats of violence, and robbery with violence. They found:

- 37.8 percent of the men had at least one arrest;

- 2.5 percent of the men were charged with at least one violent offense;

- 0.6 percent were charged with two or more violent offenses;

- the repeat violent offender accounted for 431 of the 993 violent offenses (i.e., 0.6% of the men accounted for 43.4 percent of the violent offenses that were recorded against the men); and

- the peak age for offenses in general was 17 years, while the peak age for violent offenses was 20 years of age.

The Swedish Project Metropolitan. Carl-Gunnar Janson (1983) and his associates worked with a sample of 15,117 boys and girls born in 1953 and registered as living in the Stockholm Metropolitan Area on November 1, 1963. The project records currently reflect the lives of the cohort members up to age 30. In addition to information from social welfare and justice records, the project team had access to self-report questionnaire data collected in 1966 and to interviews conducted with the mothers in 1968. Analyses are just beginning in the Swedish Project, but strong evidence of variation in criminal activity is already emerging. Table 2.3 reveals that individual differences in criminal activity are evident within and among several categories of early socioeconomic conditions. (For Table 2.3, we estimated the total number of offenses by assuming that the average number of offenses committed by those in the 2-4 category was 3 and by letting 5 represent the number of offenses for all cases within the 5+ category). Overall, 20 percent of the male cohort, those with two or more offenses, accounted for an estimated 88 percent (5,077/5,775) of the delinquent offenses.

Table 2.3
Official Delinquency Rates (%) of Males by Years on Welfare

	NUMBER OF DELINQUENT ACTS				
Number of Years on Welfare	0	1	2-4	5+	N
0	73	11	9	8	5,284
1	54	10	14	21	365
2 or 3	53	11	14	22	354
4 or more	46	12	16	26	344
Total Cases	69	11	10	10	6,347
Estimated # offenses	0	698	1,904	3,173	5,775

From Janson, 1983: Table 9.9

The Montreal 1960 Cohorts. Marc LeBlanc and his colleagues (LeBlanc, Ouimet & Tremblay, 1988) at the University of Montreal have been following two samples of males and females born during the years 1958-1962 (Table 2.4). One sample is composed of 3,142 young people who were attending school in Montreal in the early 1970s. The other is composed of 934 persons who had been identified officially as serious delinquents in the early 1970s.

Table 2.4
The Montreal Data (%)

	GENERAL SAMPLE			DELINQUENT SAMPLE		
	Males	Females	Total	Males	Females	Total
N	1,684	1,458	3,142	883	51	934
Education						
Secondary	59.8	67.1	62.6	2.2	0.0	2.0
Post-Secondary	24.5	27.2	25.7	0.3	0.0	0.3
Car Owner	51.1	22.8	38.0	21.6	3.9	20.7
Injured at Work	41.5	13.6	28.5	33.6	5.9	32.1
Welfare	14.2	13.3	13.8	55.8	37.3	54.8
Criminal Records						
Juvenile	4.4	2.6	3.6	75.8	56.9	74.7
Adult	11.2	3.6	7.7	70.2	33.3	68.2

From LeBlanc et al., 1986

The researchers reported on the achievements and adjustment of the youths from age 18 until they were about 23 years of age. Among other things, they reported on educational achievements (completion of high school and post-secondary diplomas), being the registered owner of an automobile, injuries at work, and official juvenile or adult records of offenses. Also examined were welfare records. A sample of the findings is shown in Table 2.4.

Most notably, the recidivism rates of the young male offenders were very high—more than 70 percent for both juvenile and adult reconvictions. In contrast, the official records of the young male students reveal official criminality for less than 12 percent of the cases. Recidivism on the part of the young female offenders was detected for more than 50 percent in juvenile court but only one-third of the cases registered adult criminal records. Among the young female students, an official criminal record was detected in less than 5 percent of the cases. The Montreal data are interesting too in that they indicate that a serious record of delinquency is strongly associated with poor educational achievement. Note that in this study it is a history of delinquency that is predicting poor educational performance as well as high levels of economic dependency.

A number of other birth cohorts will be introduced throughout the text. For now, it should be clear that a psychology of criminal conduct has much to explain. Variations in criminal behavior were found within groups of males and within groups of females, just as they were found within various racial and socioeconomic groups. At the same time, it is apparent that age, sex, and race are correlates of criminality. One of the tasks of the psychology of criminal behavior will be to explain these correlations.

It may also be apparent that those persons who come into contact with the criminal justice system are particularly interesting and that a relatively small number of official offenders appear to account for a large number of officially recorded criminal acts.

Some Longitudinal Studies of Recidivism in Correctional Samples

Recidivism rates are tabled below for several samples of male Canadian offenders. The rates are based on official reconvictions and convictions leading to incarceration over a two-year, postprogram follow-up period. Table 2.5 suggests, as later studies will show, that different levels of the correctional system serve groups who vary in their risk levels for recidivism. The table also reveals that the absolute level of recidivism within any sample depends upon the specific measure of recidivism employed. Not all persons who are reconvicted receive sentences of incarceration and still fewer receive prison sentences as long as two or more years. Table 2.6 explores gender differences in recidivism rates across a variety of definitions of recidivism. Obviously, men are more at risk for recidivism than are women.

In the Andrews, Friesen, and Kiessling (1980) follow-up (see Table 2.6), the 73 recidivists were responsible for a total of 194 new offenses, with 24 percent of the probationers who had two or more reconvictions responsible for 85 percent of the new crimes. Bonta and Motiuk (1986) followed both the prison conduct and the one-year post-release recidivism of Ontario male incarcerates. It is notable that less than 40 percent of the inmates were responsible for more than 60 percent of all misconducts and assaults within the prison. The same group included the majority of the cases who were reincarcerated for a new offense within a year of their release.

Table 2.5
Two-Year Recidivism Rates for Canadian Samples

Study	Rate (%)	Measure of Recidivism
Medium-Security Inmates	66.0	Reconviction
Cormier (1981)	49.0	Reincarceration
	15.8	Reincarceration (2 yrs +)
First Incarcerates	48.8	Reconviction
Gendreau & Leipciger (1978)	36.6	Reincarceration
	6.7	Reincarceration (2 yrs +)
Halfway House Residents	37.8	Reconviction
Holosko & Carlson (1986)	29.1	Reincarceration
	6.4	Reincarceration (2 yrs +)
Probationers	39.8	Reconviction
Rogers (1981)	25.3	Incarceration

Table 2.6
Recidivism Rates by Gender

Study	Sample	Male	Female	Outcome	Time (yr)
Canadian Centre for Justice Statistics (1992)	Inmates	49.0	35.8	Incarceration	3
Farrington & Morris (1983)	Arrestees	42.3	24.0	Arrest	2
Hoffman (1982) Hoffman et al. (1978)	Inmates	48.6	38.7	Arrest	3
Rogers (1981)	Probationers	39.8	16.1	Conviction	2
Andrews, Friesen & Kiessling (1980)	Probationers	45.0	17.1	Conviction	3
Andrews & Robinson (1984)	Probationers	33.0	22.0	Conviction	2.2

Criminal Careers

In view of the contributions of the Philadelphia cohort studies by Wolfgang and colleagues (as noted above), an interest emerged in understanding criminal careers. Here the interest is not in the facts of self-reported criminal acts or in the occurrence of an arrest, a conviction, or a conviction leading to less or more severe sanctions. Rather, the variable is the whole criminal career characterized, for example, as being a "chronic offender," a "nonchronic offender," or a "nonoffender." Frequency of offending over a specified developmental period (e.g., from age 14 to age 20) defines chronicity, but the number and nature of offenses needed to qualify as a "chronic offender" varies from researcher to researcher and from locale to locale when the distinction exists in legislation (Loeber, Farrington & Waschbusc, 1998). The latter authors report definitions as varied as five or more arrests, nine or more convictions, and three or more self-reported serious offenses. Some researchers further demand the persistence of offending over a specified period.

Rolf Loeber and David Farrington (1998) co-chaired a major project on serious and violent juvenile offenders. Serious offenders were those juveniles who had committed one or more of violent offenses (as defined below), felony larcency/theft, auto theft, fraud, dealing in stolen property, burglary break and enter, carjacking, extortion, forgery/counterfeiting, embezzlement, drug trafficking, arson (other than occupied dwelling), weapons violation, and firearms regulation/statutes. Violent offenders had committed one or more of homicide, aggravated assualt, robbery, kidnapping, voluntary manslaughter, rape or attempted rape, or arson of occupied building.

The Loeber and Farrington (1998) collection includes an appendix prepared by Howard N. Snyder. He examined the juvenile court careers of all 151,209 persons born between 1962 and 1977 who were referred at least once to the court in the Arizona county that includes the city of Phoenix. Snyder (1998) excluded referrals for status offenses such as running away, truancy, and underage drinking. He defined chronic offenders as those with four or more court referrals and he used the above-noted definitions of serious and violent careers. Fifteen percent of the young people were chronic offenders, 34 percent were serious, 30 percent were serious nonviolent, and 8 percent were violent. The majority of the young people (64%) were nonchronic with no serious offenses. Eighteen percent were nonchronic with at least one serious nonviolent offense. Three percent of the nonchronics had at least one violent offense and less than 1 percent of the chronics had at least one violent offense. Most notably, 60 percent of all those referred were referred only once (that is, an overall recidivism rate of 40%), and 83 percent of the young people charged with a violent offense never returned on a new violent offense (the violent recidivism rate of violent offenders was 17%). Only 1 percent of the 151,209 young people was charged with two or more violent offenses.

This brief survey of research has established a few of the basic facts regarding the criminal behavior of official offenders—facts that have been established in many areas of the world. Officially identified or not, the individual differences in criminal behavior are substantial. There is much to be understood. The remainder of the chapter provides an overview of the empirical ways of enhancing understanding and some summaries of the understanding achieved.

Empirical Knowledge of Covariates

Empirically, having established variation in the criterion of criminal conduct, PCC seeks knowledge of the covariates of criminal behavior. The covariates of interest in PCC are observable aspects of the universe, whether those aspects are "biological," "psychological," or "social." Again, we stress that it is an empirical focus on individual variation in criminal conduct that is the key to PCC, rather than disciplinary or political preferences regarding the potential covariates that ought to be observed. In the remainder of this chapter, we will stress certain research design issues as well as a few additional methodological concerns.

The covariates of criminal conduct may be of several types, depending upon how the observations of covariation are conducted. These types include the correlates, predictors, dynamic predictors, and causes of variability in criminal conduct. For reasons that will become clear, we will often refer to "causal" variables as "functional variables," or as variables of "functional significance."

This chapter continues with a review of these different types of covariates and provides some additional illustrations of some of the best-established covariates of criminal conduct. These particular risk factors, and others that will be identified in the text, ultimately will be linked to a theoretical and practical understanding. In this chapter, though, we concentrate upon the various ways that covariation may be documented.

At the end of this chapter, the reader will link correlates with cross-sectional research designs, predictors with longitudinal research designs, dynamic predictors with multiwave longitudinal research designs, and functional variables with experimental designs (see Table 2.7). The reader also will become aware of the importance of moderator variables. Moderator variables are variables that interact with covariates on criminal behavior. For example, as illustrated in Chapter 1, "Social Support for Drug Use" may interact with "Attitudes Favorable to Drug Use" in such a way that attitudes are strongly associated with drug use when social support for use is high but only weakly linked when social support for use is low. Moderator variables are a formal way of recognizing the complexity of human behavior—often, the correlates of criminal behavior "depend" upon other variables and/or the social context.

Table 2.7
Type of Covariate by Research Design and Criterion Variables

Covariate	Clinical Type	Research Design	Criterion
Correlate	Risk/Need Factor	Cross-sectional	Criminal past
Predictor	Risk Factor	Longitudinal	Criminal future
Dynamic Predictor	Need Factor	Multiwave Longitudinal	Criminal future
Functional	Intervention	Experimental	Criminal future

Note: Cross-sectional designs yield information on potential risk/need factors. Knowledge of true risk factors must be based on longitudinal studies and knowledge of need factors must be based on multiwave longitudinal studies.

This chapter focuses on the importance of the structure of research designs in the establishment of covariation and does not include a comprehensive review of the many potential sources of error in measurement, operationalization, and conceptualization. However, potential errors of measurement and conceptualization may inflate estimates of covariation, deflate estimates of covariation, or have no effect on level of covariation, depending upon the specifics of the threats.

The research approaches reviewed here are in the systematic quantitative tradition. Qualitative approaches to research also play important roles in PCC, such as building tentative models (initial conceptualization of variables and the relationships among variables). Once applied and tested through quantitative research, researchers may return to a qualitative study in order to explore whether the model possesses the "ring of truth." There is, for example, nothing like a good case study to inspire the feeling that we really understand the phenomenon of interest.

Although case studies frequently have been used as "proof" for favored theoretical positions, their methodological shortcomings are so severe that they provide little beyond generating hypotheses for experimentation or illustrating a phenomenon. When we provide a case study in this text, it is meant only to illustrate a finding already established by systematic research, not to serve as the research evidence itself. Thus, other than the more detailed discussion in Resource Note 2.1, we will say no more about case studies. Instead, we will continue with an elaboration of methodology and empirical knowledge.

Resource Note 2.1

Case Studies and Empirical Knowledge: The Case of the Necrophiliac

In 1978, Smith and Braun reported a case of a man convicted of homicide. Homicide is a relatively rare offense. However, in this situation, the murderer also reported that he had sexual intercourse with his victim after she was killed. Necrophilia (i.e., an erotic attraction to corpses) is extremely rare; paired with homicide, the circumstances become unique. In addition, the offender, called D.P. in the article, reported that this was not the first time he had sexual intercourse with a dead woman.

One of the explanations offered by Smith and Braun was drawn from psychoanalytic theory. To be brief, the necrophilia was the result of an unresolved Oedipal complex and castration anxiety. That is, D.P. sought the love and affection of his mother. Other women were symbols of his mother's affection and he sought their love (so far, a general explanation of a man's search for a woman who is like "the one that married dear old dad"). However, D.P. also feared that if his "father" discovered his intentions, "father" would punish him by castration. In psychoanalytic theory, these desires for love are instinctual (from

the id) and are always expressed either directly or indirectly.

In D.P.'s case, copulating with a dead woman who cannot inform his "father" fulfilled an instinctual desire while at the same time ensuring that he avoided castration.

Let us step back for a moment and examine this case from a methodological viewpoint. The hypothesis is that an unresolved Oedipal complex "caused" the necrophilia. Is this a valid conclusion? The answer is no; there are so many threats to the validity of this conclusion that we can say very little about the causes. These threats to validity are true for all case studies.

There are four major threats to the validity of the explanations found in most case studies. First, there is measurement bias. There is often little to guide the author(s) of a case study (other than their own theoretical orientation) in selecting what information to collect and how to collect the data. In the case of D.P., a tremendous amount of social history and personal material was collected without any controls preventing the selection of information based upon one's theo-

Resource Note 2.1 *(continued)*

retical position, and ignoring any contrary evidence. In addition, there was no direct measurement of the "causal" factor, castration anxiety, which according to psychoanalytic theory is unobservable anyway.

Second, is a sample of one representative of necrophiliacs in general? It is important to obtain a representative sample of the population in order to evaluate the generalizability of an explanation.

Third, other social history factors may be causal factors. That is, perhaps some unusual event in D.P.'s life may have caused the deviant behavior.

Fourth, perhaps maturational factors were the major influences. These last two threats to validity demand comparisons with other people who were exposed to similar social histories and maturational forces so we can rule out their influences. A case study, by definition, does not make use of comparison groups.

In closing, the second author of this text also had interviewed D.P. The explanation we prefer stems from social learning theory. Basically, D.P.'s behavior was maintained by the reinforcing effect of sexual intercourse. During sexual intercourse, D.P. would strangle his partner. Previous sexual partners saw this as a "sexual game" and would pretend unconsciousness, which heightened his arousal. Thus, there was a history of associating sex with the image of unconsciousness. Also, D.P. had reported that when he was a child he had observed his father having sexual intercourse with a corpse (modeling deviant behavior).

Which interpretation is correct? Perhaps neither. The social learning explanation may seem very plausible, but we still have only a case study with all its inherent threats to validity.

The Correlates of Crime: Differentiation Among Groups Known to Differ in their Criminal History

Knowledge of *correlates* comes from *cross-sectional observations* of individuals known to differ in their criminal history. Cross-sectional studies tend to be of two types: extreme groups and surveys.

In the *extreme groups approach*, individuals are selected for observation precisely because they are known in advance to differ in their criminal histories. For example, a sample of high school students may be compared with a sample of juvenile probationers, or a group of first offenders compared with a group of repeat offenders. The empirical issue here is to discover which of the potential covariates studied do, in fact, distinguish between offenders and nonoffenders. Alternatively, in the *survey approach*, a representative sample of individuals from some specified population is selected for systematic observation. One of the variables studied is the level and/or type of criminal activity in which the individuals have engaged. Other variables assessed are potential covariates of that criminal history. Here too, the task is to identify the variables that correlate with a criminal past. In brief, correlates are covariates of a criminal past.

The extreme groups and survey approaches have yielded information on a number of important correlates of criminal behavior. For example, assessments of individual characteristics variously labeled "antisocial personality," "psychopathic personality," or "weak self-control" are among the strongest and most consistent of the correlates of criminality. The correlations have been strong and consistent relative to, for example, those achieved by measures of social class or personal perceptions of limited conventional opportunity. These correlations have been established cross-culturally, subculturally, and for both sexes within various racial and ethnic groups.

One of the best-known of these personality measures is the Socialization (So) scale of the California Psychological Inventory (Gough, 1965), referenced in the first and second chapters. Another well-known assessment instrument is the Peterson, Quay, and Cameron (1959) measure of Psychopathy. Both of these instruments are self-report, paper-and-pencil questionnaires that ask respondents to respond to true/false items. High levels of criminal propensity are indicated by low scores on Socialization and by high scores on Psychopathy. Table 2.8 reveals that among Americans and Canadians, scores on these assessment instruments have distinguished between groups known to differ in their officially recorded histories of criminal activity. Recall from Chapter 1 that cross-sectional studies in many countries have yielded similar evidence.

Table 2.8
Mean Differences in Antisocial Personality Scores for American and Canadian Samples: Findings from Studies of Extreme Groups

	Nonoffenders	Offenders
American Samples on Socialization	38.1 (N = 18,246)	29.5 (N = 1,381)
Canadian Samples on Psychopathy	2.7 (N = 145)	6.7 (N = 376)

Note: American data drawn from Megargee (1972) and Gough (1965) and by Wilson and Herrnstein (1985). Canadian data from Andrews (1980).

Our two examples of survey studies are from Hindelang (1972) and Andrews, Wormith, and Kiessling (1985). As noted in Chapter 1, Hindelang explored the correlations between Socialization scores and self-reported delinquency among high school students in California. Correlations with the prestige ratings of father's occupation were also reported. The Canadian study (Andrews et al., 1985) surveyed the criminal histories of young adult male probationers. Both self-reported and official records of a criminal past were studied in the Canadian survey. Both surveys revealed that socialization and delinquency were negatively correlated (i.e., low scores on socialization were associated with high levels of criminal behavior), while social class showed no significant relationship with a criminal past (Table 2.9).

Table 2.9
Correlations of Social Class and Socialization with a Criminal Past in American and Canadian Samples: Survey Approach to The Study of Correlates

	Self-Reported	Official
Canadian Probationers (N = 131)		
Social Class		
Father's Occupation	.12 (ns)	.03 (ns)
Personality		
Socialization	−.29	−.23
American High School Students (N = 337)		
Social Class		
Father's Occupation	−.03 (ns)	na
Personality		
Socialization	−.51	na

ns = not statistically significant   na = correlation not available

Predictor Variables: True Prediction in a Longitudinal Design

Knowledge of predictors of criminal behavior comes from observations conducted within a longitudinal study. In a longitudinal study, hypothesized predictor variables are examined in relation to subsequent or future criminal activity. Relative to cross-sectional and survey studies, longitudinal research has the advantage of ensuring that the covariation established is truly prospective. That is, we may feel reasonably confident that the criminal behavior was not responsible for the covariation, because the assessment of criminal behavior was based on events that followed the predictor variables. Logically, "causes" must precede their "effects." In cross-sectional and survey designs, when we observe an association between two variables, we can never be sure what came first (e.g., does a muscular body type lead to criminal behavior or does criminal activity produce a muscular figure?).

Table 2.10 presents the predictive correlations found within longitudinal studies of two samples of adult Ontario probationers (Andrews et al., 1985). The correlations include those found between assessments of antisocial personality conducted during the period of probation and subsequent reinvolvement in criminal activity. The table extends our introductory sampling of potential covariates by also including information on three additional constructs that have been important in the history of PCC. These three additional factors are procriminal attitudes, a sense of alienation, and low levels of empathy.

Inspection of Table 2.10 reveals that assessments of antisocial personality and procriminal attitudes were predictive of future criminal behavior in both samples of probationers. The results also show that a sense of alienation (feelings of isolation and a perception of limited conventional opportunity) and low scores on interpersonal sensitivity (empathy) were relatively weak predictors of criminal activity.

Table 2.10
Predictive Correlations of Antisocial Personality, Procriminal Attitudes, Alienation, and Empathy with the Recidivism of Probationers

	Sample 1 (N = 149)	Sample 2 (N = 154)
Antisocial Personality		
Socialization	.26	.37
Psychopathy	.36	.51
Procriminal Attitudes	.37	.46
Alienation	.18	.29
Low Empathy	.04	.19

A PCC must appreciate in detail the meaning of such differential levels of covariation with criminal behavior. Issues such as these are a major focus of this text. However, discussions of concepts of antisocial personality, procriminal attitudes, and correlation coefficients may appear rather abstract at this stage in the text. For purposes of illustrating the practicality of longitudinal designs, a concrete example of the ability to forecast future crime follows.

Sally Rogers (1981) developed a simple, six-item risk scale that reflected certain well-known risk factors for criminal behavior. These six predictors (or risk factors) were: being male, being young (under 24 years of age), having a criminal record, having delinquent associates, aimless use of leisure time, and having a family that often relies on social assistance. Rogers worked with a representative sample of 1,104 Ontario probationers whose official reconvictions were monitored during probation and for two years after completing probation. On the basis of interviews while on probation, each probationer was assigned a score of "1" for each risk factor that was present. Thus, the risk scale could take values from "0" (no risk factors present) to "6" (all factors present). That official reconvictions increased with scores on the risk scale is obvious upon inspection of Table 2.11 The practical implications of such levels of predictive validity are an important focus of PCC.

Table 2.11
Reconviction Rates by Intake Risk Level

Risk Score	Recidivism Rate	N
6	94.2%	(of 17)
5	76.9%	(of 108)
4	62.7%	(of 109)
3	42.9%	(of 220)
2	24.2%	(of 397)
1	9.4%	(of 181)
0	5.6%	(of 36)
Total Sample	35.8%	(of 1,104)

From Rogers, 1981

Dynamic Predictors

Knowledge of dynamic predictors comes from *multiwave longitudinal studies*. Observations are made on at least three occasions in a multiwave longitudinal study. The first occasion involves the initial assessment of potential predictors, and the second involves a reassessment of these potential predictors. Some of the more dynamic aspects of body, psyche, and social arrangements may change over time. For purposes of establishing dynamic predictors, changes observed between the initial assessment and the reassessment are examined in relation to the third assessment, namely that of criminal conduct, which follows at some later date. Dynamic predictors are ones on which assessed change is associated with subsequent criminal behavior.

Some attributes of people and their circumstances are relatively fixed (for example, having criminal biological parents, being born male, and scores on fundamental temperamental variables such as emotionality). On the other hand, attitudes, values, and beliefs are highly personal cognitive-affective variables with relatively great potential for change.

As an illustration of dynamic predictors, Andrews and Wormith (1984) found that intake assessments of probationers on a paper-and-pencil measure called "Identification with Criminal Others" predicted criminal recidivism (this measure is a subcomponent of the procriminal attitudes shown in Table 2.10). With dynamic predictors, we are interested in the changes in scores between the first and second assessments and future recidivism. Andrews and Wormith found that probationers who identified with offenders to a moderate degree on intake and subsequently reduced their identification six months later had a recidivism rate of only 10 percent. Those who maintained moderate levels of identification with offenders (i.e., no change over the six months) had a recidivism rate of 38 percent. Those whose identification with offenders increased during probation had a recidivism rate of 57 percent. In summary, while all of these probationers were judged at moderate levels of risk for recidivism at intake, over a six-month period the risk levels decreased for some, remained the same for others, and increased for still others.

The identification of simple predictors in single-wave longitudinal studies shows that individuals may be reliably assigned to groups with different levels of risk for future criminal activity. The discovery of dynamic predictors confirms that risk levels are subject to change and that these dynamic predictors may serve as treatment goals. For example, in probation services, a primary objective is to provide treatment services and supervision to probationers in such a way that the lower-risk cases remain low-risk and that the higher-risk cases become lower-risk ones. Thus, the dynamic predictors may serve as a focus for a probation officer's efforts in bringing about change.

An understanding of dynamic predictors is very important within PCC, because a psychology of criminal behavior rejects outright an exclusive focus on the more static aspects of individuals and their situations. Indeed, when PCC practitioners and researchers uncover highly stable predictors, they immediately begin to think in terms of what may be the dynamic correlates of that stable predictor. For example, the historical fact that the family of origin included criminals does not mean that the more dynamic factor of antisocial attitudes is not subject to influence.

In practice, simple predictors are often called *risk factors*. Dynamic predictors of criminal conduct, on the other hand, are often called factors. The term "need" is used for the practical reason that it carries with it the hope that if *criminogenic need factors* are reduced, the chances of criminal involvement will decrease. However, our use of the term "need" is a highly specific one. We do not imply that all "unpleasant" conditions represent criminogenic need factors, nor that any or all of the covariates of crime are in any way "bad" or "unpleasant" on their own. Risk factors and need factors are simply predictors of future criminal conduct.

Just as predictors lead us closer to knowledge of causes than do simple correlates, so are dynamic predictors a still higher level of empirical understanding. PCC, however, seeks more than knowledge of dynamic predictors. PCC seeks an understanding that offers the potential not to simply forecast criminal events but to influence the chances of criminal acts occurring through deliberate intervention.

Causal/Functional Variables

The causes of crime are most convincingly established not through the determination of correlates and predictors, but through *functional variables*, demonstrations of the effects of deliberate interventions. As the conditions of intervention approximate experimental ideals, confidence in the functional status of any particular variable increases. The *classical experimental design* maintains control over variables that would compete for causal status. These controls are typically introduced by rendering the competing variables either constant or random, while examining the potential effects of the functional variable of primary experimental interest. Thus, PCC is concerned with the introduction of control groups, random assignment to groups, and the employment of other research techniques that increase confidence in conclusions regarding the causal significance of the covariates of criminal conduct (see Resource Note 2.2).

Approximations of the ideals of true experimentation are difficult to achieve even under highly controlled laboratory conditions with nonhuman animals. The difficulties are compounded when attempts are made to study human behavior that is as socially significant as criminal behavior. Certainly, psychologists are not about to play with increasing the chances of criminal conduct just to prove some theoretical point within PCC.

Resource Note 2.2

The Classical Experimental Design

Two research designs allow us to reach conclusions regarding functional (causal) validity: the A-B-A type of design (Hersen & Barlow, 1976) used in single-subject research and the classical experimental design (Campbell & Stanley, 1963). In the study of criminal behavior, the classical experimental design is most frequently used, typically in studies evaluating the effectiveness of intervention programs.

The central features of the experimental design are:

1. A minimum of two groups: An experimental group exposed to the hypothesized functional variable and a control group not subjected to the hypothesized functional variable.

2. Random assignment of subjects to groups.

3. Posttesting on the criterion variable of both groups at the same point in time.

Such a design controls for bias from subject selection factors through random assignment. The use of a control group and posttesting of experimentals during the same time period controls for maturation (i.e., growing older) and history factors (i.e., naturally occurring experiences between the intervention and posttests), because these factors would be expected to influence the control subjects in the same manner as the experimental subjects. Given that attention was also paid to objective measurement and experimenter bias, and that the results are tested for statistical significance, any difference found between the experimental and the control groups at posttest may be attributed to the intervention or the hypothesized functional variable.

Illustrating the power of the experimental design is an experiment by Michael Chandler (1973). Chandler evaluated a treatment program designed to teach role-taking skills to juvenile delinquents. He reasoned that the inability of some delinquents to take into account the perspective of another individual indicated a deficit in socialization and that this egocentricism resulted in social conflicts.

Forty-five delinquent boys, aged 11-13, were randomly assigned (controlling for subject selection) to one of three conditions. The experimental condition consisted of the treatment intervention. Treatment involved graduate students who trained the boys to write film skits that involved real-life social situations. The idea was to encourage the delinquents to think about the various perspectives of all the actors in the skits. Their skits were recorded and observed by the experimental subjects, and discussions about the viewpoints of the others were led by the graduate students.

The second group also wrote and filmed skits, but the skits were documentaries about their neighborhoods or cartoons. No attempt was made to encourage perspective-taking. This control group was intended to control for any possible effects from simply receiving special attention from the therapists (i.e., the graduate students). A third group received no treatment whatsoever.

All of the delinquents were administered a test of role-taking ability before any intervention. The three groups did not differ significantly in their scores on the perspective-taking test. A pretest provides the opportunity to test whether, in fact, random assignment procedures do result in experimental groups and control groups being equivalent on relevant variables at the time of the pretest. In this study, random assignment was effective in producing groups that were indistinguishable statistically in egocentricism scores.

At posttest (10 weeks later), the average test scores were 5.5 for the experimental group, 8.6 for the "attention" group, and 8.0 for the control group (the lower the score, the less egocentric). Statistical tests showed that the lower scores for the experimental group were not likely the result of chance.

Can we attribute the lower scores on the measure of egocentrism for the experimental group to some specific experience or maturational influences? Probably not, because we would expect similar influences to be operating on the other two groups. In this study, we can also discount the possibility that sim-

Resource Note 2.2 *(continued)*

ply giving attention to the experimental group, regardless of the content of the intervention, was a factor. Since the three groups differed only with respect to perspective-taking skills training, we can reasonably conclude that this training directly influenced egocentrism scores (i.e., functional validity).

Finally, we must ask the question whether changing perspective-taking skills is relevant to criminal behavior. Chandler followed the delinquents for a period of 18 months following the treatment.

At follow-up, police and court records showed that the average number of offenses for the "attention" group was 2.1; for the no treatment group, 1.8. These differences were statistically unreliable. However, the experi-

mental group differed significantly: they had an average of 1.0 offenses. Compared to their average number of offenses before treatment (1.9), this was a significant reduction. No similar reductions were found for the other groups.

Chandler demonstrated that perspective-taking skills have functional validity with respect to criminal behavior. By deliberately and systematically intervening (i.e., providing treatment), egocentrism decreased and so did delinquent behavior. In this manner, Chandler affirmed the vitality of correctional rehabilitation. The fact that some correctional treatment programs can "work" and that we can demonstrate this fact experimentally is one of the major themes of this text.

Some social agencies, however, are formally called upon to intervene in the lives of individuals with the expressed and socially approved purpose of controlling their criminal conduct. These agencies are also expected to perform their duties in effective, efficient, fair, and just ways (Chapter 1). It is this concern with the effective, efficient, and ethical control of criminal behavior that not only permits, but actually demands, active experimentation of the highest quality. Thus, throughout this text, contributions to the effectiveness of correctional and prevention programming are primary concerns. Controlled evaluations of practice are not only "practical," they permit a high-level exploration of the causes of crime.

In summary, much of our understanding of the covariates of criminal behavior is dependent upon the research methodology used in studies. This methodology limits our level of understanding and reminds us of the importance of empirical research to building knowledge. For all of this, the literature reviews conducted by Michael Gottfredson and Travis Hirschi (1990) suggest that the findings of cross-sectional studies and the findings of longitudinal studies have been highly compatible. That is, the validity of potential risk factors identified in cross-sectional studies of a criminal past have tended to be confirmed in longitudinal studies of risk factors.

On the other hand, the number of multiwave longitudinal studies of potential criminogenic need factors is so low that we are not yet in a position to assert with any degree of confidence that the potentially dynamic risk factors meet the required standards of dynamic predictive criterion validity. Moreover, as rare as multiwave longitudinal studies may be, ultimate tests of "criminogenic need" are even more rare, because these ultimate tests demand that "criminogenic need" be established within the structure of an experimental design. For the determination of criminogenic need, what we need to show is that: (1) deliberate interventions produce changes on the potential need factor, (2) deliberate interventions produce changes in criminal conduct, and (3) the magnitude of the association between intervention and criminal behavior may be reduced through the introduction of statistical controls for change on the potential need factor (Andrews, Bonta & Hoge, 1990). This point is developed below in a discussion of the sources of variation in the outcome of prevention and correctional programs.

Knowledge Through the Study of Practice

We have begun to see (and later chapters will confirm) that there is a substantial—even impressive—body of empirical knowledge in PCC regarding the correlates and predictors of criminal conduct. The empirical base for knowledge of dynamic predictors is not as well-developed, and there are few experimental demonstrations showing that changes regarding particular need factors are functionally significant in relation to criminal conduct. A challenge for PCC is to expand and refine research on criminal justice practice, particularly in the areas of prevention and corrections.

There are, in the English language, more than 400 controlled studies of correctional effectiveness (Lipsey, 1989). This literature will be explored in detail later, but here the focus is on the broad classes of variables that must be attended to if knowledge is to be maximized for purposes of understanding and practice. Active and deliberate interventions are occurring daily in the lives of offenders and people at risk for criminal activity, but very little use is being made of this from the perspective of knowledge development. These daily and numerous interventions represent lost opportunities for approximations of experimental studies of crime.

The task is to identify the major sources of variability in correctional outcomes and to gain reasonable levels of influence over the variables that make a difference. The intellectual and practical issues surrounding the effectiveness of correctional programs may be introduced with the assistance of an overview of the major classes of variables involved in the operation and evaluation of correctional programs. Because this text explores PCC, we begin with the ultimate objective of programming. That objective is to manage criminal offenders in such a way as to decrease their criminal activity. (Correctional programs are, of course, also concerned with cost-efficiency, fairness, ethicality, and consumer and public satisfaction, but these concerns are not unique to corrections.) In evaluation terms, the expectation is that offenders assigned to the "experimental" program will engage in less frequent and less serious criminal activity than offenders assigned to "comparison" programs.

Understanding corrections and the causes of criminal behavior may be facilitated by an introductory review of the major sets of variables that may contribute to variation in criminal recidivism. At least seven analytically distinct classes of variables contribute to the prediction of outcome (Andrews & Kiessling, 1980; Hoge & Andrews, 1986): (1) community and agency conditions surrounding the service, (2) preservice client characteristics, (3) preservice counselor characteristics, (4) the social structure and organizational characteristics of programs themselves, (5) particulars of the content and process of service, (6) the specific intermediate changes that occur in the person and/or circumstances of offenders over the course of the program, and (7) interactions among the preceding sets of variables. These classes of variables are summarized in Figure 2.1.

---

1) Surrounding Community and/or Agency Conditions

2) Preservice Client
Characteristics
(risk, need, responsivity)

3) Preservice Counselor
Characteristics
(training, relationship skills)

4) Program Characteristics
(sociocultural, economic)

5) Process and Content of Treatment Service
(relationship, direct training, advocacy)

6) Intermediate Treatment Goals
(gains and losses on need factors)

Ultimate Outcomes: Recidivism, Cost-effectiveness, Consumer Satisfaction

---

Figure 2.1
Some Major Elements for Correctional Program Evaluation

The major sources of variability in the outcomes of deliberate intervention may be summarized as follows:

1. *Surrounding community and/or agency conditions.* These broader social-structural, cultural, and political-economic conditions may place limits on who is served, who serves, the conditions of service, and outcomes. For example, during periods of economic restraint, agencies may "accept" fewer clients, hire fewer well-trained staff, and reduce the variety of programs offered. Similarly, broader labor market conditions may influence the apparent effectiveness of employment-oriented programming for offenders.

2. *Preservice client characteristics.* These variables include risk factors, need factors, and responsivity factors. Risk and need factors have already been described. Responsivity factors refer to the specific competencies, interests, or learning styles that a client must possess in order to benefit from particular types of programs. For

example, an offender who is inattentive to the wishes, feelings, and expectations of others is unlikely to benefit from a program whose success depends upon interpersonal sensitivity.

3. *Preservice counselor characteristics.* The characteristics of counselors may impact on outcomes in several ways. Two important variables are the skills needed to establish a warm interpersonal relationship and the direct training skills of the counselor. The interpersonal skill dimension determines how much influence a counselor may have (i.e., you have to like the person to heed his or her advice). The second set of counselor skills reflects a second, more general, dimension of interpersonal influence that is sometimes called the contingency, structuring, or normative aspect of interpersonal influence. This dimension determines the content of learning, what is learned, and whether the influence is procriminal or anticriminal.

4. *Program characteristics.* Programs may be described as miniature social systems with their own structure, culture, and economy. For example, programs may vary in the types of workers within the program (e.g., medical doctors, correctional officers, paraprofessionals) and the roles assigned to the staff (e.g., maintaining security in a maximum-security prison or doing therapy in a hospital). These structural and organizational aspects of a program may in turn influence the next set of variables: the process and content of intervention.

5. *Process and content of treatment services.* This set of variables refers to what actually goes on in treatment. For example, correctional counselors (who vary in interpersonal skills) and their clients may establish interpersonal relationships that vary in their intensity and quality. Similarly, counselors (who vary in their skillfulness in reinforcing appropriate behavior) may offer direct instruction and training to their clients that varies in focus and quality. It is these specifics of interaction that determine the effect of a program on intermediate gains or treatment goals.

6. *Intermediate treatment goals.* If correctional counseling or supervision impacts on criminal recidivism, it must be because it has influenced the attributes of clients and their circumstances that are of causal significance for criminal behavior. Using the language of "dynamic prediction," successful programs are those that reduce relevant needs, which in turn are associated with reductions in criminal recidivism. Alternatively, a program may be responsible for increased need levels; under those circumstances, increases in criminal recidivism may be expected. In a more neutral situation, a program may fail to influence need levels in any way that is relevant to future criminal conduct.

7. *Interactions among variable sets.* The preceding six sets of variables may be associated with the ultimate outcome (i.e., reduced criminal activity) in a number of ways. For example, sometimes "client-risk-by-type-of-program" interactions may emerge. An interaction, or the presence of moderator effects, indicates that the effects of one variable on outcome will differ depending upon some other variable. An example is provided in Resource Note 2.3.

Resource Note 2.3

Client Risk Interaction and Program Intensity

O'Donnell, Lydgate, and Fo (1971) evaluated a prevention program in Hawaii called the "Buddy System." Similar to programs that operate in many North American cities, youngsters judged at risk for delinquency were assigned nonprofessional companions who offered the youngsters companionship, academic tutoring, informal assistance, and recreational opportunities. The control youngsters did not receive this structured access to a companion. A *prior* arrest was a major risk factor with regard to postprogram arrests among the experimental and control subjects.

For the delinquents in the experimental group, those with at least one prior arrest (*n* = 50) had a rearrest rate of 56 percent (the 285 delinquents without a prior arrest had a rearrest rate of 22%). Similarly, for the control group, the rearrest rate was 78 percent for the 23 youngsters with at least one prior arrest and 16 percent for the 195 delinquents with no prior arrest.

This pattern of results is precisely what our discussion of "predictors" led us to expect. Risk factors may be operative within samples of clients in treatment.

However, the preservice client risk factor was associated with outcome not only directly within different types of service, but also in interaction with type of service. This interactive contribution of client-based risk factors

to the prediction of outcome is quite distinct from, and incremental to, simple predictive validity. This interaction is illustrated below through a slight rearrangement of the evidence just presented.

Recidivism Rates by Intake Risk Levels and Programming

| | BUDDY SYSTEM | |
Intake Risk Level	No	Yes
High (prior arrest)	78% (of 23)	56% (of 50)
Low (no prior arrest)	16% (of 195)	22% (of 285)
Total Sample	22% (of 218)	27% (of 335)

Inspection of the first row of the table suggests that the "Buddy System" was effective in reducing the criminal activity of high-risk youngsters. On the other hand, inspection of the second row suggests that the "Buddy System" was responsible for an increase in the delinquent behavior of low-risk children. We shall see that this pattern of results, what is called a *risk-by-treatment* interaction, is not unusual in corrections and prevention. In fact, many correctional agencies now take formal steps to reserve the highest levels of service for the higher-risk cases, and to assign the low-risk cases to the minimal levels of discretionary supervision. These formal steps follow the risk principle of case classification.

Illustrations of Observed Sources of Variability Through Meta-Analyses

Almost every student, and certainly every professor, is familiar with the "literature review." Scholarly journals are devoted to articles that review areas of interest, and every dissertation and research report begins with a review of the literature. The traditional literature review has been narrative in nature and the qualities of the reviews depend very much upon the expertise and thoroughness of the author(s). The reviewer is relatively free to select studies and unfettered to attend to those results viewed as relevant. Thus, it is not uncommon for two independent reviews of a particular literature to reach very different conclusions.

Meta-analytic reviews permit a more unbiased analysis of the literature and they provide a quantitative estimate of the importance of the results. Although meta-analyses have been used for more than 20 years, their use has exploded in the last 10 years. Many now regard meta-analysis as the standard approach for reviewing the literature. In essence, the results from individual studies are converted into a common metric or statistic commonly referred to as the effect size. The effect size allows more direct comparisons of the results from various studies and the averaging of effect sizes across studies.

As an illustration, let us take estimating the relationship between intelligence and crime. One study may report the results using a t test (a statistic measuring the differences between two groups), another may use the Pearson correlation coefficient (r) and a third study may report the percentage of low IQ and high IQ individuals in a group of offenders and nonoffenders. How can we best compare the results? In the traditional, narrative literature review, reviewers must make a judgment of the relative importance of the three studies. Reviewer A may emphasize the results from Study 2 and discount the results from the other two studies. Reviewer B may prefer the results based upon the t test and minimize the other statistics. We can see how this approach may lead to different conclusions.

In a meta-analysis, the results from the three studies would all be converted into the same statistic or effect size. Often the effect size used is the Pearson correlation coefficient (see Resource Note 1.1). In our illustration, the t score would be converted to r, as would the percentage differences (recall how easily percentage differences can be transformed using Rosenthal's binomial effect size display; Resource Note 1.1). Consequently, we can compare the effect sizes from the three studies and by averaging them, we can more accurately estimate the "true" relationship between intelligence and crime. Because many studies are conducted in various locations with different samples and time periods, the generalizability of the results from meta-analyses is enhanced.

At a number of points in the text, we will refer to the results from different meta-analyses. For the reasons outlined, we place more confidence in the results from a meta-analysis than from the traditional literature review.

This chapter concludes with summaries of meta-analytic investigations of the three issues that most differentiate sociological criminology from psychological criminology over the years. These issues are sociology's strong endorsement of the importance of lower-class origins, psychology's persistent interest in personality, and the "what works" position of psychology in regard to correctional treatment as opposed to the "nothing works" position of mainstream sociological criminology.

Some Meta-Analytic Studies of Social Class of Origin

No single variable has been more important in criminological theorizing than social class. According to most textbooks, no single fact was judged to be better established than a negative association between social class and criminal behavior (i.e., as one goes lower down in social class, the probability of criminal behavior increases). Many of the major sociological theories of crime and delinquency were theories of delinquency in the lower social classes. Crime was a direct reflection of being lower-class, of the deprivations associated with being lower-class, of poverty, of just trying to acquire what the upper classes have, and so forth.

Several reviews of the research literature speak to the role of social class in criminality. The first provoked a reexamination of the class-crime link. Charles Tittle, Wayne Villimez, and Douglas Smith (1978) made a major contribution to criminology and the psychology of criminal behavior. They noted that many forms of deviance and social pathology have been attributed to injustice or inequity in the distribution of societal resources such as wealth, prestige, and power. They provide a sophisticated meta-analysis of the research literature on the class-crime link, that is, a systematic quantitative review of the literature, a piece of research on research findings.

Tittle et al. reviewed studies that examined the class-crime link at the individual level, thus avoiding the ecological fallacy. Studies that characterized individuals in traditional measures (personal or familial, occupational, educational, and income) of socioeconomic status (SES), as well as the class structure of their areas of residence, were included. They found a mere 40 studies of the class-crime link in the research literature. Generally, it had been assumed that the evidence in support of a substantial negative relationship between class and crime was voluminous and comprehensive.

Thirty-five studies reported data in such a form that gamma coefficients could be calculated in order to estimate the magnitude of the association between class and crime. Gamma is a measure of covariation that exists in an ordinal contingency table. The important question is whether decreases in SES categories are associated with increases in the proportion of criminals. Gamma is interpreted in the same way as a Pearson correlation coefficient. It takes the value zero when there is no relationship and takes a value of one (1) in the case of a perfect 1:1 relationship. The sign of the gamma, minus or plus, indicates the type of relationship. Minus (–) signals an inverse association and plus (+) signals a positive association.

Whenever possible, separate gammas were computed for men and women, whites and nonwhites, youths and adults, self-report and official measures of criminality, and different types of offenses. In this way, the 35 studies yielded 363 separate gammas for various combinations of sex, race, and other factors.

The overall mean or average gamma was –.09. The means for studies of men, women, and mixed groups were –.08 (N = 198), –.11 (N = 83), and –.10 (N = 82). The means for whites, nonwhites, and mixed groups were –.07 (N = 130), –.01 (N = 36), and –.12 (N = 197), respectively. Overall, with mean gammas of such trivial magnitudes, it appeared that the evidence was at best slight for a class-crime link.

Tittle and his associates (1978), however, went further. They recognized that some of the gammas were strong and negative even though the average gammas were weak. Similarly, some gammas were actually positive in sign, suggesting that under some circumstances, increases in SES were associated with higher, rather than lower, levels of criminality. The latter finding was opposite to that predicted by class-based theories.

Using gamma as the criterion variable (the variable to be explained), Tittle et al. conducted several statistical analyses in an attempt to discover any variables that might account for the variations evident among the 363 gammas. We have already seen that mean gamma values did not vary with sex or race. Differences attributable to offense type also were slight—and effectively disappeared when other variables were held constant.

The magnitude of the class-crime link did seem to vary with how criminality was measured (self-report versus official records) and with the decade in which the study was completed (i.e., a type of measure-by-period interaction). The mean gamma from the self-report studies was small (–.06) but was larger (–0.25) for studies of official records. The relatively large gamma found with official records was traced to studies conducted before the 1970s. The mean gammas based on official records over four decades (before 1950, 1950-59, 1960-69, after 1970) were –.73, –.43, –.22, and +.04, respectively. On the other hand, the gammas based on self-reported criminality were relatively constant over time and trivial in magnitude (ranging from –.03 to –.11). According to Tittle et al., there is today essentially no relationship between class and criminality in the United States. One may have existed in the past, but even the early links between class and official criminality may have reflected processing effects rather than criminality.

Tittle et al. were open to the possibility that their approach to reviewing the literature may have missed the fact that some studies, or particular gammas based on certain measures of class and crime obtained under particular conditions of measurement, may have provided better estimates of the "true" class-crime link than others. In addition, they were open to the possibility that future research might be able to demonstrate that particular measures of social class and particular measures of criminality do covary in substantial and inverse ways under certain conditions. However, they thought that the most reasonable interpretation of their findings was that class-based theories of criminal behavior rest on empirically weak premises.

John Braithwaite (1981) provided a response to the Tittle et al. challenge. It was very lively and applauded by many, but in the end, it was not very helpful to class-based theory. His review demonstrated that studies of aggregated crime rates supported the class-crime link (although that was not the issue being addressed), that personal educational/vocational achievement was linked with crime (which is something everyone, including psychodynamic theorists, agrees on), and that there was a minor link between class of origin and criminal activity (which is exactly what Tittle et al. [1978] had demonstrated).

Subsequently, Charles Tittle and Robert Meier (1990) reviewed the evidence published since 1978 and found support for the class-crime link in less than 20 percent of the tests explored. Tittle and Meier (1991) have taken another look at the class-crime issue. This paper reports on nearly 500 tests of a class-crime link conducted under a variety of "social contexts." These contexts include the overall socioeconomic level of the home community (see the discussion in Chapter 1 on personal income and average income of neighborhood as separate variables) and the variety of levels of class represented in the home community (heterogeneity). In brief, their analysis failed to find any condition under which lower-class origins were linked consistently with delinquency.

Loeber and Stouthamer-Loeber (1987) also conducted a systematic review of the literature on the predictors of delinquency. They limited their studies to those that could be summarized in the form of two-by-two prediction tables (see Chapter 6), and the accuracy of prediction was summarized by the statistic "Relative Improvement Over Chance" (RIOC). The median RIOC for six tests of the predictive accuracy of lower-class origins was very low: 18 percent (range of 11%-31%). In comparison, general problem behavior yielded a median RIOC of 28 percent (15 tests with a range of 4% to 83%), and the median RIOCs for parental criminality and parental supervision were 31 percent and 51 percent, respectively. Once again, the class-delinquency link was found to be minor.

Additional meta-analyses of the predictors of criminal offending provide yet another series of tests of the class-crime link (Gendreau et al., 1992: see Resource Note 2.4). So far, this review of the literature has generated more than 1,700 Pearson correlation coefficients as summaries of the magnitude of association between various risk/need factors and recidivism. To date, 97 of these tests of the predictability of recidivism have involved lower-class origins as the potential predictor variable. The mean of these 97 correlation coefficients was .06, once again revealing a very modest class-crime link. The predictive validity of personal academic/vocational achievement, once more, was stronger than class of origin (mean correlation = .12 in 129 tests). The predictive validity of lower-class origins was weak for males ($r = .04$ in 58 tests) and females (.03 in 12 tests), for blacks (.07 in 7 tests) and whites (.05 in 20 tests), for young offenders (.06 in 71 tests) and adult offenders (.06 in 23 tests), and for self-reported crime (.02 in 35 tests) and officially recorded crime (.08 in 59 tests). Various other controls have been introduced in these ongoing explorations of a class-crime link, but everything leads to the conclusion that lower-class origin is a relatively minor risk factor for delinquency and crime (relative, that is, to other potential risk factors such as personal socioeconomic achievement, family functioning, personal attitudes, associates, and personality).

The meta-analytic evidence now extends well beyond the 1992 review summarized in Resource Note 2.4. Linda Simourd (Simourd & Andrews, 1994) drew a fresh sample of studies focusing exclusively on the correlates of juvenile delinquency within samples of young men and young women. Once again, class of origin was a minor risk factor (38 separate estimates yielded a mean r of 0.05). Additionally, Paul Gendreau, Tracy Little, and Claire Goggin (1996) examined the predictors of adult criminal recidivism; once again, lower-class origin was found to be a minor risk factor (the mean of 24 estimates was 0.06).

Overall, the conclusion must be that the theoretical dominance of class of origin in mainstream sociological criminology from the 1960s on was not based on evidence. When the social psychology of criminological knowledge is finally written (and that text is close to becoming a reality, as witnessed by the work of Gottfredson and Hirschi [1990] and Andrews and Wormith [1989]), the theoreticism of mainstream sociological criminology in regard to social class may well become one of the intellectual scandals of science.

There have been many attempts to rescue social class in recent years. There are too many social scientists with too much invested in the concept for it simply to fade away. Some of the attempts to rescue social class are semantic from the point of view of theory. For example, the knowledge regarding the importance of personality variables is gradually making its way into the official textbooks under the guise of "inequality in the distribution of biological and psychological resources," "inequality in social capital," and even inequality in distribution of "untalented individuals" (Vold & Bernard 1986:203). Similarly, the over-representation of blacks and natives in prison is being used as a proxy for a class-crime link. By all means, the field should be concerned with racism, but surely the field is sophisticated enough to distinguish race and ethnicity from class of origin. There was also a distinctly sentimental and nostalgic literature building around the themes of "the poverty of a classless criminology" (Hagan, 1992) and the negative nature of "corrections without class" (Hastings, 1991).

Some responses are simply social science by assertion, without presentation of evidence:

> . . . social inequality is the main cause of crime . . . . (DeKeseredy & Schwartz, 1996:463)

Resource Note 2.4

The University of New Brunswick/Carleton University Meta-analysis of Predictors of Criminal Behavior: Highlights of Findings

This ongoing project (Gendreau, Andrews, Goggin & Chanteloupe, 1992) involves a survey of all studies of the correlates of crime published in the English language since 1970. The studies were uncovered through automated library searches, surveys of key review articles, and follow-ups on reference lists of the studies in hand.

Approximately 1,000 studies had been listed, 700 studies located, and 372 studies subjected to content analysis and meta-analysis. These 372 studies yielded more than 1,770 Pearson correlation coefficients, each of which reflected the covariation of some potential correlate of individual criminal conduct with some measure of criminal conduct.

Reflecting the general social psychological perspective underlying this text, particular risk/need factors were assigned to seven categories. These categories were: (1) lower-class origins as assessed by parental educational and occupational indices and neighborhood characteristics, (2) personal distress indicators including "psychological" measures of anxiety, depression, and low self-esteem as well as more "sociological" assessments of anomie and alienation, (3) personal educa-

tional/vocational/economic achievement, (4) parental psychological status and functioning as well as family cohesiveness and parenting practices, (5) antisocial temperament, personality, and behavioral history, (6) antisocial attitudes and antisocial associates, and (7) other variables not obviously fitting within the first six categories.

The mean correlation coefficients for each of the first six categories of risk/need factors were as follows (with number of coefficients in parentheses):

1. Lower-Class Origins   .06   (97)
2. Personal Distress
   Psychopathology   .08   (226)
3. Personal Education/
   Vocational Achievement   .12   (129)
4. Parental/Family Factors   .18   (334)
5. Temperament/Misconduct/
   Personality   .21   (621)
6. Antisocial Attitudes/
   Associates   .22   (168)

The rank ordering of the six sets of risk/need factors has proven to be very robust across various types of subjects (differentiated according to gender, age, and race) and across

Mean Correlation Coefficient by Type of Risk/Need Factor and Various Control Variables (N)

Type of Risk/Need Factor

	1		2		3		4		5		6	
Overall	.06	(97)	.08	(226)	.12	(129)	.18	(334)	.21	(621)	.22	(168)
Gender												
Male	.04	(58)	.09	(157)	.11	(180)	.16	(180)	.18	(461)	.21	(113)
Female	.03	(12)	.08	(19)	.13	(7)	.16	(43)	.23	(38)	.23	(12)
Age												
Juvenile	.03	(49)	.09	(66)	.10	(40)	.18	(151)	.22	(142)	.23	(63)
Adult	.05	(49)	.09	(105)	.12	(60)	.11	(64)	.18	(301)	.19	(50)
Race												
White	.05	(20)	.09	(102)	.10	(56)	.20	(148)	.19	(235)	.24	(77)
Black	.07	(7)	.05	(6)	.17	(5)	.12	(22)	.22	(23)	.29	(10)
Measure of Crime												
Self-reported	.00	(28)	.08	(31)	.10	(19)	.14	(94)	.20	(58)	.25	(42)
Official	.06	(40)	.10	(140)	.12	(81)	.18	(121)	.19	(385)	.19	(71)
Design												
Longitudinal	.11	(47)	.08	(152)	.14	(89)	.17	(179)	.21	(423)	.20	(118)
Cross-sectional	.03	(50)	.08	(74)	.08	(40)	.19	(156)	.19	(198)	.27	(50)

1) LOWER-CLASS ORIGINS   4) PARENTAL/FAMILY FACTORS
2) PERSONAL DISTRESS/PATHOLOGY   5) TEMPERAMENT/MISCONDUCT/PERSONALITY
3) PERSONAL EDUCATION/VOCATIONAL ACHIEVEMENT   6) ANTISOCIAL ATTITUDES/ASSOCIATES

In summary, the research findings reveal that lower-class origins and personal distress are *minor* risk factors for criminality relative to indicators of antisocial propensity drawn from assessments of family, personality, attitudes, and interpersonal association patterns.

Resource Note 2.4 *(continued)*

methodological variables (such as self-report versus official measures of crime and longitudinal versus cross-sectional designs). The robustness of these findings is illustrated in the following table:

1. Lower-Class Origins	.05	(38)
2. Personal Distress/ Psychopathology	.07	(34)
3. Family Structure/ Parent Problems	.07	(28)
4. Minor Personality Variables	.12	(18)
5. Poor Parent-Child Relations	.20	(82)
6. Personal Education/ Vocational Achievement	.28	(68)
7. Temperament/Misconduct/ Personality	.38	(90)
8. Antisocial Attitudes/ Associates	.48	(106)

We will come to speak of antisocial attitudes, antisocial associates, a history of antisocial behavior, and an antisocial personality set as the "Big Four" risk factors.

Some responses border on the continuation of theoreticism:

> The linkage of poverty and crime is inexorable, despite the inability of researchers to establish it at the individual level (Short, 1991:501).

What James Short may mean in the above-noted quotation is that sociological criminologists (and behavioral psychologists, for that matter) will continue to have an interest in poverty, in crime in lower-class areas, and in redistributing societal wealth and power. Those interests, however, do not depend upon there being an inexorable link between class and crime.

Other responses will involve case studies regarding inner-city crime. Recognizing a weak class-crime link does not dismiss the real problems of the poor, nor does it deny the existence of high-crime neighborhoods. What the recognition of a weak class-crime link does do is remind students, scholars, and policymakers that the socioeconomic context makes, at best, a minor contribution to variation in crime, relative to a host of other personal, interpersonal, familial, and structural/cultural variables, including the immediate situations of action. Delbert Elliott, William Julius Wilson, David Huizinga, Robert Sampson, Amanda Elliott, and Bruce Rankin (1996) provide a particularly promising look at how truly ecological factors, such as neighborhood disadvantage, may be assessed by looking beyond poverty to include indicators of neighborhood organization such as social support and informal social control. Still, as Delbert Elliott and colleagues acknowledge, the effects of the ecological factors are slight. Recall also the brief discussion of disadvantaged neighborhoods in Chapter 1.

Attempts are being made to specify the conditions under which a class-crime link is found through the search for moderator variables, but so far the findings (e.g., Tittle & Meier, 1991) have been discouraging for class-based theory. Another approach entails focusing upon the levels

of disposable income actually available to individuals at particular periods of time. In essence, what are the implications of having some loose
change in your pocket or purse? Some American (e.g., Cullen, Larson &
Mathers, 1985) and British (e.g., West & Farrington, 1977) data already
suggest that relative wealth in the immediate sense is a correlate of juvenile delinquency. Delinquent kids tend to have more money than nondelinquent kids. Having money may indeed give one power, including the
power to remove oneself from parental control and enabling one to do
what one wants to do, including acting in illegal ways (Hagan, 1989).

Another line of research also takes the concepts of power and privilege seriously. It treats power as a "social fact" that may impact upon
the behavior of individuals in social circumstances. For example, consider the concept of social power with respect to the "ruling class" versus the rest of society. We are talking about "capitalist" territory here.
These owners control production and employees and they buy labor. The
laborers include the "managers," who are nonowners but who supervise
"workers," as well as the "workers," who have no control over other
workers. The "surplus population" refers to nonowners who have been
unable to sell their labor.

Hagan, Gillis, and Simpson (1985) analyzed the self-reported delinquency of 485 high school students from Toronto families in which the
head of household (gender not specified) was an owner, a manager, a
worker, or unemployed. The information on class structure was obtained
not from the students but from telephone interviews with the parents.
Nine percent of the students were from homes of owners, 44 percent from
homes of managers, 38 percent from homes of workers, and 9 percent
from homes with an unemployed head. Conventional measures of social
class (i.e., occupational prestige ratings) were unrelated to delinquency and, overall, there were no differences in the self-reported delinquency
of the youths from the four Marxist categories. However, when the children of owners were compared with the three other groups, a mild correlation emerged (r of approximately +.11). The kids of the powerful were
engaging in slightly more delinquency than the kids of the less powerful. To Hagan et al. this indicated that the offspring of the most powerful are most free to be delinquent.

We strongly endorse the study of crime at all levels of class of origin,
class of achievement, and relationship to the means of production. Yet,
one troubling response to the current state of knowledge was provided
by Hartnagel (1992:119-120), who criticized Tittle et al. (1978) for suggesting that criminologists should give up on class-based theories of criminal conduct. Rather, Hartnagel suggested, even greater attention to class-
based theories is required. The focus of class-based theories should be
on the absolute extremes of the class structure, concentrating on the least
powerful and the most powerful. Clearly, by urging us to concentrate on
what is perhaps only the 20 percent of the population located at either

extreme of the class distribution, the efforts of some sociological criminologists really are not about understanding criminal conduct but about studying social class.

Those interested in "social origins" would be well-advised to consult Glueck and Glueck's (1950) classic analysis of delinquent behavior (see Chapter 3). In addition to providing evidence regarding the predictive potential of assessments of various personal characteristics, Glueck and Glueck also clearly suggested that "social origins" is a trivial variable compared to "the familial bio-social legacy." The major familial correlates of delinquency were not parental levels of education or occupation but parental attitudes toward employment, not having been on welfare but reliance upon welfare, not the socioeconomic circumstances of the family but intergenerational emotional, intellectual, and conduct problems that may impact upon parenting. Indeed, with careful attention to sustained states of disadvantage and sustained involvement in street crimes, at least modest class-crime links are found (Farnworth et al., 1994).

It is likely to be suggested that, no matter what the studies may be showing, we all know that our prisons are filled with members of the lower classes. There is no question that low levels of personal educational achievement and high levels of personal unemployment are correlates and predictors of criminal conduct. The fact, however, remains that social origin is a minor predictor of criminal conduct.

For example, a survey of the social origins of male inmates of Canadian federal prisons by Ed Zamble and Frank Porporino (1988) found that three of the 133 inmates were sons of the chronically unemployed, while five were sons of professionals. The majority of the inmates were sons of workers—the sons of blue-collar workers being slightly overrepresented. Even when we examine the social origins of prisoners residing in settings reserved for the most serious and frequent of offenders, what is found is only a minor inverse relationship between class of origin and criminality. This conclusion, however, is not inconsistent with the opinion of some that our prisons will become filled with persons of lower-class origins if, as a matter of social policy, we choose to attempt to solve the problems of lower-class, high-crime neighborhoods by locking up the young people who reside in those neighborhoods. Indeed, the "war on drugs," with its selective focus on crack cocaine use in the inner city, does appear to have contributed to an overrepresentation of young African-American men in prison in the United States (Tonry, 1994).

Reviews of Personality and Crime

We now turn to direct rather than incidental investigations of the variable: personality. Personality refers to characteristic patterns of thinking, feeling, and acting that may be evident among individuals within any particular social location that may be defined according to age, gender, race, ethnicity, or geographical area. What will be found is that the research evidence has been voluminous and overwhelmingly supportive of personality as a correlate of crime. We saw that social class was promoted in mainstream textbooks even though the evidence was weak. We will see that the personality evidence was denied and discounted by theoreticists. The next section will also document how the discounting process worked and will expose the pseudoscientific nature of the process of knowledge destruction.

We begin with a summary of a few of the classic reviews of the personality literature. Please note in advance that the majority of studies involved cross-sectional designs in which groups of offenders and nonoffenders were compared in terms of their scores on personality inventories and tests. The issues of predictive and functional validity will be discussed later.

Schuessler and Cressey (1950)

A total of 113 studies were reviewed and 42 percent of the studies reported a difference in the personalities of offenders and nonoffenders. Schuessler and Cressey concluded that the combined results did not support the hypothesis that personality and criminality were linked. Their conclusion is appreciated because most of the studies were crude. Of the 30 different personality tests employed in the 113 studies, only four were of sufficient psychometric quality to warrant their use in the 1960s (Quay, 1965). In view of this fact, however, an interstudy hit rate of 42 percent looks quite impressive (particularly because we now know that the more favored variable of social class had a hit rate of less than 20%).

Waldo and Dinitz (1967)

Waldo and Dinitz reviewed 94 studies published after the Schuessler and Cressey (1950) review (i.e., 1950-1965). Eighty-one percent of the studies found a personality-criminality link. However, Waldo and Dinitz reached a negative conclusion regarding an association between personality and criminal behavior (as did the reviewers before them).

Tennenbaum (1977)

Tennenbaum found 44 studies of personality and crime published between 1966 and 1975. He noted that the methodological quality of the studies had improved and that a wider range of personality tests were being explored than in the earlier years. Eighty percent of the 44 studies reported a personality-crime association.

Across all three reviews, there was considerable consensus regarding the aspects of personality that were most strongly associated with criminality. Most notably, assessments of antisocial personality consistently differentiated between offender and nonoffender samples. The concepts of antisocial personality and psychopathic personality will be developed in later chapters but for now the notions of a generalized disregard for conventional rules and procedures and a reckless, callous, egocentric, adventurous, and impulsive pleasure-seeking style captures the content of these measures.

The specific inventories and personality tests that most consistently differentiated between offender and nonoffender samples were the Socialization (So) scale from the California Personality Inventory (CPI), the Psychopathic Deviate (Pd) scale from the Minnesota Multiphasic Personality Inventory (MMPI), and the Porteus Maze Test. The first two inventories are self-report, paper-and-pencil questionnaires. The MMPI in particular will be described in more detail in Chapter 9. The Porteus Maze Test is a performance measure that requires, among other things, sustained concentration and a lack of impulsivity. The MMPI, particularly the Pd scale, significantly distinguished between offender and nonoffender samples 90 percent of the time (37/41). The CPI, particularly the So scale, had an interstudy hit rate of 86 percent (12/14). The interstudy hit rate with the Porteus Maze was 100 percent (7/7).

Overall, there is an abundance of information here. Measures of antisocial personality were found to bear consistent and clear linkages with criminality. These scales are well-validated and have been the focus of volumes of research. Scores on So and Pd are known to correlate with familial and biological variables, measures of self-management skills and impulsivity, and measures of deviance that extend well beyond the issue of the legality of conduct. The scales are also well-constructed. In addition to their known correlations with theoretically relevant measures, the items that compose the scales were deliberately selected according to their documented criterion validity. In brief, during the construction of the Pd and So scales, items were deleted if they failed to distinguish between groups who differed in their levels of conduct problems. This empirical approach to scale construction is intended to ensure that the scale will indeed correlate with criterion variables of interest.

Returning to Tennenbaum's (1977) paper, one might think that he must have reached the conclusion that, as a minimum, the evidence supports a serious exploration of the nature of the personality-criminality linkage. However, the conclusion was that personality testing had not differentiated criminals from noncriminals. We noted that Tennenbaum engaged in a classic example of knowledge destruction. The process was as follows:

1. He first commented that he found it "disconcerting" that personality tests are no better predictors of criminality now than they were 10 years ago.

    Comment. He has told us that he is concerned, but about what? The interstudy hit rate was 42 percent in 1950, 81 percent in 1967, and 80 percent in his own review of 1977. Does he think an interstudy hit rate of 100 percent is required? We think he has here engaged in a major aspect of knowledge destruction: to plant a vague suspicion or sense of uneasiness in the minds of the readers.

2. Recognizing that the assessments of antisocial personality have consistently demonstrated concurrent criterion validity, that achievement is then described as mere "surface validity." In Chapter 4, various types of validity—including functional validity, predictive validity, and concurrent validity—will be discussed. What is "surface validity"?

    Comment. Again, the reader is being emotionally prepared for an exercise in knowledge destruction. Note how initially we are alerted to a vague sense of negative concern. Now our negative feelings not only have been reinforced by the term "surface" but, in addition, they have been linked directly with science through a pairing with the term "validity."

3. Finally, we reach the core of Tennenbaum's effort at knowledge destruction: Because the So and Pd were constructed so that they might successfully distinguish between offender and nonoffender samples, their success in actually doing so in one study after another is a hollow achievement. More specifically, Tennenbaum states that the measures of antisocial personality provide "no information not obtainable simply by procuring a list of offenders."

    Comments. Let us consider some of the possible meanings of Tennenbaum's last statement:

    A. Nothing is known about scores on the So and Pd scales beyond their correlation with criminality. He cannot mean this because there are few (if any) assessment instruments in the human and social sciences that have been so exhaustively explored and linked with such a wide variety of criterion variables (e.g., family variables, self-management skills) as those scales.

    B. The items on the So and Pd scales include references to deviant behavior; hence, the validity of these scales is nothing more than a proxy for a criminal history. It is granted that a few of the items from the Pd and So scales are direct indicators of criminal behavior. For example, the Pd scale has items such as "I have never been in trouble with the law" and the So scale has items such as "A lot of times it's fun to be in jail." However, most of the items are not obvious measures of criminal conduct (e.g., "I am neither gaining or [sic] losing weight," from the Pd scale) and yet these items contribute to the differentiation of offenders and nonoffenders. Moreover, the scales have predicted future criminal behavior in samples in which everyone had a criminal record.

C. A personality measure is important only if the measure correlates more strongly with the criterion than the criterion does with itself. The new standard is that a personality measure must give us more information about the criterion than we could gain "simply by procuring a list of offenders" in advance. That is, sorting people into offender and nonoffender groups on the basis of their personality scores must be as accurate or more accurate than sorting them into those groups on the basis of advance knowledge of the groups to which they belonged. If this is what he meant, Tennenbaum has set a standard for criterion validity that no measure, no matter how constructed, could hope to achieve.

The reviews of the literature convincingly establish the fact that the majority of studies of psychopathy have differentiated between offenders and nonoffenders. However, the magnitude of that covariation has not been demonstrated.

This section of the chapter takes a brief look at the Simourd, Bonta, Andrews, and Hoge (1991) meta-analysis of the predictive criterion validities of three measures of psychopathy, including Pd, So, and the Hare Psychopathy Checklist. David Simourd and his colleagues used the Pearson correlation coefficient as a summary measure of the magnitude of covariation between personality and crime; hence, these summary values may be compared directly with some of the results from studies in which social class was the risk factor under investigation.

The first finding confirmed that type of research design was a major source of variation in the magnitude of the estimate of covariation. Extreme group studies were defined as those that involved comparisons between officially defined offenders and nonoffenders and/or those studies that selected subjects according to extreme scores on either the assessment of psychopathy (e.g., excluding the middle-range people and comparing only the upper one-third with the lower one-third) or the assessment of criminal behavior (e.g., comparing first offenders with offenders with four or more offenses, and excluding the middle range of offenders). Extreme group studies yielded higher validity estimates than did studies with more representative samples of subjects for each of the three measures of psychopathy.

The major finding of Simourd et al.'s (1991) study, however, was that the predictive validity of each of the assessments of psychopathy was significantly greater than zero (and obviously greater than the average predictive validity estimate previously reviewed for social class). The mean predictive validity of even the weakest of the three measures (the MMPI Pd measure) was impressive relative to the estimates previously reviewed for social class. The mean correlation of Pd scores with criminal behavior was .19 ($N = 27$) overall and varied from a low of .16 (when statistically adjusted for both an extreme groups design and studies of young versus adult offenders) to a high of .20 (when adjustments were made for research design and for sample size or violent/nonviolent recidivism). The mean predictive validity estimates for So and the Hare checklist were statistically indistinguishable from each other. However, they were clearly stronger than zero, than the average estimates for social class (as previously reviewed), and than the mean estimates for MMPI Pd. The mean predictive validity estimates for So and the Hare Checklist varied within the narrow range of .34 to .39 as statistical controls were introduced for extreme group designs, for cross-sectional versus longitudinal designs, for age of sample, and for violent recidivism.

Referring once again to Resource Note 2.4, note how measures of temperament, personality, and early misconduct relate to criminal behavior. In the 621 tests summarized by Gendreau et al. (1992), the mean r was 0.21. Linda Simourd (Simourd & Andrews, 1994) differentiated between major personality variables such as socialization/psychopathy (mean $r = 0.38$ in 90 tests) and minor personality variables such as below-average intelligence or general extraversion (mean $r = 0.12$ in 18 tests). The mean r for the prediction of adult criminal recidivism was 0.18 in 62 tests (Gendreau et al., 1996). We will return to the concept of psychopathy in later chapters, but for now, in our view, the reviews of the research clearly demonstrate the importance of personality in understanding crime. In brief, mainstream sociological criminology ignored the negative evidence regarding the importance of social class and denied and discounted the positive evidence regarding personality.

A very real criticism of the personality-crime literature entails the idea that the field has not explored the issue across the major domains of personality that are identifiable through systematic factor analytic work. Factor analysis involves attempts to identify the fundamental dimensions of personality as they are evident across methods of measurement and other circumstances. An important example of a study with one of the new generation of approaches to the assessment of personality was provided by Caspi, Moffitt, Silva, Stouthamer-Loeber, Krueger, and Schmutte (1994). A renowned team of researchers employed the Multidimensional Personality Questionnaire in an exploration that looked for personality crime relationships across countries, genders, races, and methods.

The two dimensions of personality that linked with criminal behavior under a variety of conditions were Constraint and Negative Emotionality. The elements of Constraint are traditionalism (endorses high moral standards), harm avoidance (avoids excitement and danger), and control (reflective, planful). Offenders scored lower on Constraint than did nonoffenders. The elements of Negative Emotionality are Aggression (causes discomfort for others), Alienation (feels mistreated), and Stress Reaction (anger and irritability). Offenders scored higher on Negative Emotionality than do nonoffenders. Offenders and nonoffenders did not differ on measures of Positive Emotionality. The elements of Positive Emotionality are achievement (enjoys demanding projects), social potency (forceful and decisive), well-being (happy, feels good about self), and social closeness (sociable).

Incidentally now, but to be developed throughout the text, exploration of Resource Note 2.4 shows that the meta-analyses of risk factors for criminal behavior suggest that the major correlates of criminal behavior are clearly personal: for example, antisocial attitudes (attitudes, values, beliefs, rationalizations, cognitions, and cognitive-emotional states supportive of criminal behavior), a history of antisocial behavior, antisocial associates (immediate social support for crime), antisocial personality, and problematic functioning in the domains of home, school, and work. Even within the family of origin, it is parent-child relations rather than the structure of the family that relates most strongly to criminal conduct. A broad-band social learning perspective on criminal behavior will be presented in this book wherein broad and more narrow social arrangements will be linked to individual conduct through their impact on the immediate contingencies of action, but those immediate contingencies of action are themselves primarily a reflection of immediate personal, interpersonal, and situational factors.

How could a discipline continue to dismiss personality in the face of such evidence? Here are a few of the knowledge destruction techniques that were applied (with thanks to Michael Gottfredson, 1979):

1. Note that researchers and theorists with an interest in individual differences and the personal correlates of crime are portrayed as "not nice people." Note that such interests perhaps indicate an "authoritarian personality" (as did Matza, 1964:15), that "bogeyman theories" slur over the existence of upperworld criminals and focus on the underclass (wait a minute Don Gibbons, 1986:509, is it not the sociologists who focus on class of origin?). When really up against the wall, just note that such people are anti-sociological.

2. Declare that, in fact, prediction is impossible. Matza (1964) *knew* that the risk factors suggested by diverse theories were "almost always" empirically undemonstrable. Taylor, Walton,

and Young (1973:58) *knew* "the enterprise is doomed to failure: inconsistent results abound." Schur (1973:154) *knew* that "so-called delinquents" are not different from nondelinquents "except that they have been processed by the juvenile justice system." According to Lab and Whitehead (1990), false predictions exceed 50 percent "and some go as high as 99 percent" (they didn't say that if you are wrong 99% of the time, all you have to do is reverse your prediction formula and you will be correct 99% of the time).

3. When it is obvious that prediction is possible, ask "so what?" Sutherland and Cressey (1970) noted that "almost everything in the universe has been found to be associated in some direct or indirect manner with criminality." Cohen (1985) appeared just to be bored with it all: "Testing, testing" (p 183), "it is ritualistic" (p. 187).

4. When it is obvious that prediction is possible, declare that it all "really" reflects social class. Thus, for Taylor, Walton, and Young (1973), "differential reinforcement histories" (p. 52), "personality" (p. 57), and "parenting" (p. 64) may be "class-based value differences. For Gibbons (1986:510), the extraordinarily high rates of violence and crime in the United States were "clear indicators that the causes of crime lie not in biology or faulty socialization but in economic and social inequality, the lack of meaningful jobs... and other rents and tears in the social fabric of America."

5. Declare that prediction is theoretically naive. Taylor, Walton, and Young (1973:58) *knew* that significant "correlations where they occur merely result in false imputations of causality." Johnson (1979:10) knew that biology and psychology as "general explanations" lacked support. Vold and Bernard (1986:121-122), at the very moment in time when PCC was just about to overtake nearly all sociological perspectives, declared the following:

> It seems the best conclusion to draw is that the differences that appear between criminals and noncriminals on personality tests do not seem to have any theoretical relevance to understanding the causes of criminal behavior.

The latter conclusion is interesting. It is because of irrelevance of personality in mainstream sociological criminology that most of the theories then dominant were themselves about to be found empirically inadequate and woefully incomplete explanations of criminal behavior.

Experimental Studies of the Dynamic Validity of Risk Factors and General Applicability

As the preceding reviews show (in combination with information from some later chapters), it now makes sense to refer to the "Big Eight" risk factors. These are the best-validated risk factors in the research literature: antisocial attitudes, antisocial associates, a history of antisocial behavior, antisocial personality pattern, problematic circumstances at home (family/marital), problematic circumstances at school or work, problematic leisure circumstances, and substance abuse. The first four are also known as the "Big Four." The ability to predict criminal behavior increases with the number and variety of major risk factors assessed (multi-domain assessment) and with the number of different sources of information employed (multi-method assessment: for example, interviews and review of case files).

The number of multiwave longitudinal studies of dynamic risk factors are too few to allow meta-analytic reviews. Similarly, we have few experimental studies in which effects on recidivism may be explored as a function of changes on intermediate targets. We, however, do have a large number of experimental studies in which the intermediate targets of change were identified, and that identification may be linked with the effects of treatment on recidivism (Andrews, Dowden & Gendreau, 1999). These studies yielded 374 tests of the effects on recidivism of setting particular intermediate targets of change.

The targets set were grouped according to the "Big Eight." Thus, the targeting of antisocial attitudes and self-control deficits formed one set of criminogenic needs. The targeting of antisocial associates (reducing association with criminal others and enhancing association with anticriminal others) was one aspect of interpersonal criminogenic targets. Another aspect of the interpersonal consisted of family practices aimed at enhancing quality of relationship in combination with improved monitoring and supervision. Some programs targeted academic and vocational enhancements and a few targeted substance abuse. The less promising targets were a focus on low self-esteem, increasing fear of official punishment, and targeting aspects of family functioning other than affection/supervision.

Inspection of the first row of Table 2.12 reveals that in 26 percent of 374 tests of correctional treatment, the intermediate targets set included personal targets such as antisocial attitudes, self-control, and problem-solving deficits. When the targets were something else, as they were in 277 tests, the mean effect size was a very low: .04. The effect size was a correlation coefficient (or a phi coefficient) reflecting the recidivism rate in the comparison condition compared to the recidivism rate in the treatment group. When the intermediate target was a personal criminogenic need, the mean effect size was .21 in 97 tests. Using the Binomial Effect Size Display, the mean effect size translates into a recidivism rate of 60.5 percent in the comparison group $(50 + 2^1/_2)$ compared to 39.5 percent in the treatment group $(50 - 2^1/_2)$. The strength of the association between targeting personal criminogenic needs and reduced recidivism was .39. Finally, the first row shows that two independent raters agreed 90 percent of the time in judging whether a particular program targeted a personal criminogenic need.

Table 2.12
Criminogenic Needs Rank Ordered by Magnitude of Correlation with Effect Size: Percentage of Tests with Need Targeted, Mean Effect Size When and When Not Targeted, Correlation with Effect Size, and Inter-Rater Agreement Rates

Need Area Targeted	%	Mean Effect Size (k)		r with effect size	Inter-rater % Agree
		Not a Target	Targeted		
Personal Criminogenic Targets: Antisocial Cognition and Skill Deficits					
	26	.04 (277)	.21 (97)	.39***	90
Antisocial Cognition	21	.04 (296)	.21 (78)	.36***	80
Self-Control Deficits	16	.05 (315)	.22 (59)	.33***	90
Interpersonal Criminogenic Targets: Family and Peers					
	19	.05 (302)	.22 (72)	.37***	100
Family Process	08	.06 (344)	.29 (30)	.33***	100
Antisocial Associates	14	.06 (323)	.21 (51)	.28**	100
Matched Individualized Need	17	.06 (313)	.21 (61)	.30**	97
School / Work	24	.06 (286)	.15 (88)	.21**	90
Substance Abuse	10	.08 (338)	.11 (36)	.06ns	97

Notes: k = number of studies
*** p < .001; ** p < .01
ns = nonsignificant
Components of Antisocial Cognition: Antisocial Attitudes (r = .23**), Anger (r =.32**).
Components of Family Process: Affection (r = .29**), Supervision (r = .31**).
Components of Antisocial Associates: Increase contact with Prosocial (r = .26**), Decrease contact with Antisocial (r = .11**).
Components of School / Work: School (r = .21**), Vocational Skills (r = .04 ns), Vocational Skills plus Obtaining Work (r = .24**).
Components of Substance Abuse: Treatment (r = .03 ns), Information (r = .08 ns).

The other criminogenic need areas reflect previously noted risk factors except for that described in Table 2.12 as Matched Individualized Need. That set of targets reflects studies in which it was noted that particular risk areas were targeted on an individual basis but the specific need areas were not reported. Overall, with the exception of substance abuse, the targeting of criminogenic needs was associated with reduced reoffending.

In contrast, the targeting of noncriminogenic needs was associated with null effects of treatment or even increased reoffending (see Table 2.13). Note in particular that programmed attempts to increase fear of officials actually yielded a mild average increase in recidivism of five percentage points (mean effect size of –.05 in 43 tests of treatment).

Table 2.13
NonCriminogenic Needs: Percentage of Tests with Need Targeted, Mean Effect Size When and When Not Targeted, Correlation with Effect Size, and Inter-Rater Agreement Rates

Need Area Targeted	%	Mean Phi (k) Not a Target	Targeted	r with effect size	Inter-rater % Agree
Personal Non-Criminogenic Targets					
	46	.11 (203)	.04 (171)	-.18**	93
Fear of Official Punishment					
	11	.10 (331)	-.05 (43)	-.25**	100
Personal Distress	27	.09 (273)	+.08 (101)	-.08ns	
	93				
Physical Activity	12	.08 (331)	+.08 (43)	.00ns	100
Conventional Ambition	08	.08 (345)	+.08 (29)	.00ns	100
Interpersonal Noncriminogenic Targets					
	12	.09 (329)	.01 (45)	-.13*	100
Family: Other	07	.09 (348)	+.02 (26)	-.10ns	100

Notes: k = number of studies.
ns = nonsignificant
** p < .001; * p < .05
Components of Personal Distress: Self-Esteem (r = -.08, ns), Other Distress (r = -.04, ns).

How general are these differential effects of targeting criminogenic rather than noncriminogenic needs? Inspection of Table 2.14 reveals that the correlation between targeting criminogenic needs and reduced reoffending is found in treatment studies with young offenders, with female offenders, and with minority group members. The only finding notably different from the overall pattern was the failure of a focus on school and or work to link with reduced reoffending with female offenders. We do not know why.

Table 2.14
Percentage of Tests of Treatment with Need Areas Targeted and Correlation of Need Area Targeted with Effect Size by Subpopulation

Need Area	Total %	r	Young %	r	Female %	r	Minority %	r
Criminogenic Needs Targeted								
Personal Criminogenic Targets: Antisocial Cognition and Skill Deficits								
	26	.39	33	.39	18	.32	29	.33
Interpersonal Criminogenic Targets: Family and Associates								
	19	.37	23	.33	31	.45	15	.34
Individualized Matching with Need (Specific criminogenic needs not identified)								
	17	.30	19	.30	07	.26	12	.28
School / Work								
	24	.21	26	.23	16	–.08ns	21	.10ns
Substance Abuse								
	10	06ns	03	.04ns	11	–.01ns	08	–.02ns
Noncriminogenic Needs Targeted								
Personal Noncriminogenic Targets (Personal distress, Physical activity)								
	46	–18	45	–.20	24	–.03ns	40	–.18
Interpersonal Noncriminogenic Targets (Family process not affection/supervision)								
	12	–25	17	–.20	13	–.23	13	–.16ns

Note. ns = nonsignificant

Multi–Domain Assessments of Major Risk Factors and General Applicability

The chapter on practical prediction and correctional classification introduces a number of assessment instruments with documented reliability and predictive validity. One of those instruments is the Level of Service Inventory–Revised (LSI-R: Andrews & Bonta, 1995). It is completed on the basis of interviews with offenders and collateral information and reviews of case files. A revised LSI-R now in use in the province of Ontario, Canada, concentrates on the "Big Eight" risk factors to yield an overall risk/need score. Total scores represent the number of risk indicators present for a given offender and the scores are grouped into five levels of risk/need from Very Low through Very High. These risk scores then may be linked to the recidivism rates found when other offenders with similar scores were followed for a standard time period such as one, two, or three years. Do standardized assessments of the major risk factors correlate with reoffending? And is that predictive validity evident with different types of people in different social contexts?

Inspection of Table 2.15 reveals how the risk/need scores of 561Ontario probationers were associated with three-year post-probation recidivism rates. The recidivism rates are presented as proportions at each level of risk need for the total sample and for each level of age (young offenders/adult offenders), gender (women/men), and poverty (reliance on social assistance/those who are less financially dependent on the state). Examining the first row, it is evident that 9 percent of the 151 probationers scoring very low risk recidivated, 20 percent of the 169 low-risk cases recidivated through to 100 percent of the two very-high-risk cases. The recidivism rate was clearly increasing with risk/need level and the overall risk-recidivism correlation was .44. The correlation coefficients for each of the eight components of risk need and recidivism were .41 (antisocial personality pattern), .28 (antisocial attitudes), .32 (antisocial associates), .24 (criminal history), .20 (family/marital), .34 (school/work), .27 (leisure), and .19 (substance abuse).

Table 2.15
Recidivism Rates by Risk-Need Level for 561 Probationers (n)

Group/Subgroup	Risk-Need Level				
	Very Low	Low	Medium	High	Very High
Total Sample	.09 (151)	.20 (169)	.48 (196)	.77 (43)	1.00 (2)
Young males relying on SA	.00 (1)	.00 (0)	.73 (11)	1.00 (3)	.00 (0)
Young females relying on SA	.00 (1)	.00 (1)	.33 (3)	1.00 (2)	.00 (0)
Adult males relying on SA	.17 (6)	.38 (13)	.46 (48)	.67 (15)	.00 (0)
Adult females relying on SA	.00 (3)	.10 (10)	.30 (10)	1.00 (2)	.00 (0)
Young males	.13 (23)	.34 (32)	.61 (33)	.88 (8)	1.00 (2)
Adult males	.09 (84)	.15 (97)	.44 (80)	.50 (8)	.00 (0)
Young females	.00 (7)	.17 (6)	.25 (4)	.67 (3)	.00 (0)
Adult females	.08 (26)	.10 (10)	.57 (7)	.50 (2)	.00 (0)

What happens when controls are introduced for age, gender, and poverty? These three variables are not only risk factors on their own, they are also highly valued variables in critical/Marxist/feminist/sociological criminology. Indeed, the validity of the major risk factors has been severely challenged by some scholars. The suggestion is that the intersection of such variables may be a particularly special context.

First, note that being young (under 18 years of age), being male, and being in a state of poverty (reliance on social welfare) are each risk factors with predictive validity estimates (correlation coefficients) of .15, .09, and .16 respectively. (The latter is at the high end for tests of a social class–crime link.) Once the total risk/need score was entered, the contributions of gender and poverty were reduced to nonsignificant levels and the r for age and reconviction was reduced to .11. On the other hand, controlling for age, gender, and poverty had little impact on the predictive validity of overall risk need (the correlation coefficient dropped to .40 from .44). It appears that the contributions of age, gender, and poverty to criminal recidivism can be understood through their contributions to attitudes, associates, and so on. The LSI-R predictive validity estimates were .37, .49, .51, and .64 for the adult men, adult women, young men, and young women, respectively.

Second (summarizing a tremendous amount of information), Table 2.15 reveals that recidivism rates increased with LSI-R risk/need levels for every combination of age, gender, and poverty. Not tabled are the findings from the same sample of offenders that the predictive validity of LSI-R scores were maintained with mentally disordered offenders, the frequently unemployed, those living in high-crime neigborhoods, violent offenders, and those with and those without a prior criminal record. There is no evidence that the LSI-R is invalid for women and no evidence that there is any special contextual impact on the validity of the LSI-R as a function of being both female and on welfare. This finding does not deflate the importance of gender and poverty. It just reveals that in this study, offending reflected the "Big Eight" risk factors in the variety of contexts generated by consideration of age, gender, and poverty.

The risk-recidivism relationships presented in Table 2.15 reflect the experiences and correctional outcomes of more than 400 provincially (Ontario) sentenced adult women (Rettinger, 1998; Andrews, Dowden & Rettinger, 2001). Once again, intake risk levels linked with reoffending in all contexts surveyed. The overall predictive validity of the LSI-R was .63. Of the contextual variables, only frequent unemployment contributed significantly over and above LSI-R risk level.

In sum, the meta-analyses of risk factors and two particular LSI-R studies support the general value of the major risk factors.

Experimental Investigations of the Effectiveness of Correctional Treatment: A Quick Look at What Works

The issue of the effectiveness of correctional programs has been a controversial one. Within criminology, many have taken the position that, simply put, "nothing works." These criminologists appear to have known *a priori*, without evidence, that a focus on individual offenders could not work. Hence, they endorsed without criticism program evaluations that failed to establish the effects of human service and criticized studies that appeared to find evidence in support of particular approaches to counseling or supervision. For mainstream criminology, human service could be rejected outright *a priori* because it was inconsistent with their myths.

Having rejected direct human service, many in mainstream criminology and criminal justice fell into the active endorsement of official punishment in controlling the criminal conduct of individuals. They did so by way of four routes. First, labeling theory suggested that official processing (legal sanctions and correctional treatment) was associated with increased recidivism through the stigma produced by processing. Second, deterrence theory suggested that official punishment was associated with decreased recidivism through the fear of future punishment induced by a severe sanction. Third, some criminologists endorsed the incompatible positions of labeling and deterrence theory by suggesting that the best punishment is that which strikes a balance between minimal stigma and maximum fear of punishment (Chapter 7). Fourth (and here we reach a peak of anti-treatment bias), there is the just deserts theory, which asserts that all we are morally entitled to do is to make sure that the punishment fits the crime, and we should not worry about whether it changes future criminal activity. The just deserts theorists reject labeling, deterrence, and psychological theory by asserting that the control of recidivism through official processing is not only impossible but also immoral. They merged the labeling and deterrence concerns regarding how much punishment is administered into a position in which the concern is that offenders receive a dose of punishment that is matched in a precise way with the seriousness of the offense and the culpability of the offender. For the just deserts theorists, rehabilitation concerns must be discarded because they may result in offenders not receiving that precise dose of punishment they deserve. According to these theorists, deviations from just deserts will result in nonoffenders becoming offenders through vigilante activity—and then we will see the breakdown of the rule of law.

Here we take just a brief look at the cumulative findings of the treatment effectiveness literature. First, note that we have been unable to find any review of experimental studies that reveals systematically positive effects of official punishment on recidivism (that is, there is no evidence that official punishment reduces recidivism). In contrast, studies of direct service (offered under a variety of conditions of judicial sanctioning such as diversion, probation, and custody) have demonstrated reduced recidivism in 40 to 80 percent of the studies. The reviews of controlled studies of human service programs in corrections began to appear in the literature in the 1950s.

In a review published in 1954, Bernard Kirby was able to locate only four studies of correctional counseling that approximated experimental ideals. Three of the four studies produced findings that were favorable to the notion that direct and controlled interventions were responsible for decreases in criminal behavior. By 1966, Walter Bailey was able to find 100 studies of correctional effectiveness in the research literature; nearly 60 percent (13 of 22) of the better controlled studies found evidence in support of the idea that type of intervention was related to outcome. In 1972, Charles Logan reviewed the literature. Our inspection of his tables showed that at least 18 studies focused on counseling procedures, involved the use of experimental and control groups, and employed objective outcome indices. At least 50 percent of these studies found evidence in support of counseling.

Martinson (1974) and Lipton, Martinson, and Wilks (1975) examined more than 230 studies. A minimum of 40 percent and up to 60 percent of the studies yielded results consistent with a conclusion that some treatments work. Reporting in 1979, Paul Gendreau and Bob Ross found 95 reasonably well-controlled studies published between 1973 and 1975. Eighty-six percent of the studies reported some significant levels of reduced criminal behavior as the result of treatment. Again, in 1987, they reached essentially the same conclusions based upon studies published between 1981 and 1987. In 1989, Mark Lipsey reported on the findings of more than 400 studies of correctional effectiveness, wherein 60 percent reported positively.

How could "nothing works" prevail and punishment be promoted when, at a minimum, the research evidence suggested that at least some programs appeared to be working for some offenders under some circumstances? The evidence was not consistent with the myths of sociological criminology. The myths were: (a) the roots of crime are buried deep in structured inequality, (b) individual differences and personal variables are trivial or just a reflection of social class, and (c) correctional treatment/rehabilitation cannot possibly work because the psychology of criminal behavior is misguided. The problem is theoreticism—accepting or rejecting knowledge not on the basis of evidence but on the basis of personal and professional interests and political ideology.

We turn now to the meta-analyses that have proved to be less readily dismissed than the narrative reviews. The Carleton University meta-analyses of effective correctional treatment and many other meta-analyses will be reviewed in detail later (in Chapters 7 and 8). For now, we present a brief summary to give an overview of the findings and to see how research design, methodological issues, and knowledge destruction approaches may be explored in meta-analyses. Resource Note 2.5 summarizes the antirehabilitation themes that allowed dismissal of the positive pattern of results evident even in the narrative reviews.

Resource Note 2.5

A Sample of Some Anti–Rehabilitation Themes: How to Destroy Evidence of the Effectiveness of Correctional Treatment

(Adapted from Andrews, 1989; Gottfredson, 1979).

1) Enthusiastically endorse the findings of studies that fail to uncover treatment effects, and promote those findings as scientifically sound evidence that rehabilitation does not work. Do not cast a critical eye on this set of studies.
2) Note that crime is socially functional in that it helps define the boundaries of acceptable conduct for society as a whole, and hence the pursuit of of effective rehabilitation programs threatens the very existence of society.
3) Assert that rehabilitation, even when it works, is inherently evil and ideologically incorrect, and that it promotes both severe sentences and unwarranted sentencing disparity (relative to the dignity of just desert and radical nonintervention).
4) Discount rehabilitation because it involves, by definition, more social control than does absolute freedom.
5) Discount rehabilitation because it involves, by definition, less social control than does absolute social control.
6) Discount rehabilitation because any program, upon close inspection, may be found to include elements of sexism, racism, elitism, and/or homophobia.
7) Discount rehabilitation programs because they are not primary prevention programs (or some other personally favored program).
8) Discount evidence of reduced recidivism because it is not evidence of improvement in the bigger picture of criminal justice, or the even bigger picture of social justice, or a cure for cancer.

9) Discount evidence of reduced recidivism because it is not evidence of effects on community-wide (aggregated) crime rates.
10) Discount evidence of effects on officially recorded crime because it is not evidence of effects on self-reported crime.
11) Discount evidence of effects on self-reported crime because it is not evidence of effects on officially recorded crime.
12) Discount evidence of effects on any measure of recidivism by asserting that the program failed to increase self-esteem or to make the offender a better person in some other way.
13) Discount the positive evidence by asserting that rehabilitation is nothing but a state-sponsored attempt to make lower-class persons more acceptable to higher-class persons.
14) Discount positive evidence because criminals were being judged by middle-class morality.
15) Discount positive evidence by noting that it is a shame that offenders get access to quality programs (they deserve just punishment).
16) Discount reduced recidivism over a one year follow-up period because it is not evidence of effects over a two-year follow-up; discount reduced recidivism over a two-year follow-up period because it is not evidence of effects over a three-year follow-up; discount. . . .
17) Assert that rehabilitation can't possibly work because criminology has proven that the human science of criminal conduct is nonsense.
18) Assert that we all know, from prior experience, that rehabilitation does not work.

Resource Note 2.5 *(continued)*

19) Regardless of the quality of the design or the magnitude of the treatment effect, suggest some ambiguity regarding what *really* caused the effect, and then note the absurdity of claiming effectiveness when the *true* cause of reduced recidivism remains unknown.

20) Regardless of the quality of the study, note that experimental designs are the patriarchal tools of criminology's male-dominated, paternalistic, and positivistic past, and the mere playthings of ritualistic positivists (we don't know what this means, but arguments like this are readily found in some sections of criminology).

21) Reject positive findings because it is immoral that the comparison clients did not have access to it.

22) Reject a treatment program that has been found to be effective with some types of offenders under specific circumstances because it doesn't work for everyone under all circumstances. (A complex and differentiated world is inconsistent with the universally applicable and morally supe-

rior visions of truth to which theoreticists have been privileged.)

23) No matter what number and types of offenders were studied, note that the study failed to work with a sample of all types of offenders that one could possibly imagine. (That's fine, but what about the special contextual uniqueness at the nexus of age, gender, poverty, race, ethnicity, sexual orientation, personal history, and physical ability.)

24) Question the motives and objectivity of scholars and practitioners who speak in favor of human service in a justice context.

25) Be very bored with the whole issue. "Who cares? Testing. Testing. Research. Research. All those research assistants running around. I am interested in the big picture of what the whole world would be like if only my vision was shared."

26) THE ULTIMATE KNOWLEDGE TECHNIQUE: Remind readers that studies that report positively on treatment "are based upon the conclusions of the authors of the reports themselves."

Most recently, the Carleton University databank (Andrews, Dowden & Gendreau, 1999) includes information on 374 controlled experimental tests of the effects on recidivism of various judicial and correctional treatment interventions. Every test represents an approximation of the ideals of the true experimental design (Resource Note 2.2) in that there is an intervention and a comparison group, and group members are followed forward in time for a specified time period. A measure of recidivism is taken on the intervention and comparison group in each study and the differences computed within the many studies are expressed by a common measure of effect size (in our case, the Pearson correlation coefficient, which is also known as the *phi* coefficient when two groups are compared on a binary outcome such as no-yes in regard to reconvictions). Variability in effect sizes may be explored through investigation of study, methodological, and treatment variables as potential sources of variability.

Overall, the 374 tests yielded a mean effect size of .08, with a dramatic range of effect sizes varying from –.43 (a 43 percentage-point increase in recidivism, according to the Binomial Effect Size Display, Resource Note 1.1,) to .83 (an 83 percentage point reduction in recidivism). What can we do in the face such variability? First, note that, on average, the least valid conclusion is that nothing works. Rather, in 374 tests, the mean effect is not .00 (no effect on average) and it is not a negative value, which would indicate, on average, an increase in reoffending. What was found, on average, was a mild *decrease* in reoffending. Using the Binomial Effect Size Display, on average, the recidivism rate in the intervention group was 46 percent (50 – 8/2) and 54 percent (50 + 8/2) in the comparison group. The mild positive effect encourages exploration of the sources of variability in effect size. What can account for the more negative, the more neutral, and the more positive findings represented in the research literature? Only a small sampling of variables are explored here because later chapters focus on official punishment and human service/treatment in more detail.

The Effects of Severity of Sanctions. Among the 374 tests were 101 tests of the effects of increases in the severity of official punishment. These tests compared, for example, longer versus shorter periods of community supervision, longer versus shorter periods of incarceration, a custody disposition versus a community-based disposition, and formal arrest versus a warning. The overall mean effect of increases in the severity of the penalty was a very mild increase in reoffending ($r = -.03$, range –.32 to .22, 95% confidence interval: –.05 to –.03). Once again, there is considerable variability, but 95 percent of the time the true mean value resides in the narrow negative range of –.03 and –.05.

The Effects of Correctional Treatment. Among the 374 tests were 273 tests of the effects of human service in the justice contexts of community supervision, custody, and diversion from the justice system. The human service programs studied included academic and vocational programs, skill-building programs, family therapy, substance abuse treatment, and anything that identified itself as a correctional treatment program as opposed to an official punishment. (The mean effect size was .12, range –.43 to .83, 95% confidence interval: .09 to .14.) The value of .12 is mild but positive, and the confidence intervals do not even overlap with those for official punishment. On average, employing the Binomial Effect Size Display, the average recidivism rate for the treated offenders was 44 percent (50 – 12/2) and 56 percent for the comparison group, a 12 percentage point difference.

The Effects of Clinically Relevant and Psychologically Informed Human Service. Using the general personality and social learning model (Chapter 4), certain principles of effective correctional treatment were derived. The principles support delivering human service to higher-risk rather than lower-risk cases (risk principle), targeting dynamic risk factors (criminogenic need principle, as noted above), and using generally powerful influence and behavior change strategies (general responsivity principle: use behavioral / social learning / cognitive behavioral strategies rather than unstructured, nondirective, or "getting tough" approaches). When human service is delivered in corrections and that service adheres to the principles of risk, need, and general responsivity, the mean effect size is .26 in 60 tests of treatment. When only two of the three human service principles are met, the mean effect size drops to .18 (in 84 tests). With conformity to only one of the three principles, the mean effect size is .02 (106 tests). When no human service is introduced and/or human service is delivered in a manner inconsistent with each of risk, need, and responsivity principles, the mean effect size is −.02 (124 tests).

Table 2.16
Mean Effect Size by Treatment and by a Selection of Control Variables (k)

	Inappropriate Treatment	Appropriate Treatment			Correlation with Effect Size
Conditions:	0	1	2	3	
Random Assignment to Treatment and Control Groups					
Yes	−.03 (36)	.02 (40)	.21 (40)	.24 (29)	.61
No	−.02 (88)	.03 (66)	.15 (44)	.28 (31)	.56
Evaluator Involved in Design / Delivery of Service					
Yes	−.05 (3)	.07 (12)	.24 (33)	.31 (30)	.48
No	−.02 (121)	.02 (94)	.14 (51)	.21 (30)	.49
Small Sample Studies: N < 100					
Yes	−.03 (29)	−.01 (30)	.27 (33)	.30 (42)	.63
No	−.02 (95)	.04 (76)	.12 (51)	.17 (18)	.47
Community-Based versus Custody-Based					
Yes	.00 (95)	.03 (74)	.22 (50)	.35 (30)	.61
No	−.10 (29)	.01 (32)	.12 (34)	.17 (30)	.59
Number of Major Control Variables Favorable to Large Effect					
None / One	−.09 (27)	−.02 (28)	.07 (23)	.11 (13)	.48
Two	−.01 (88)	.03 (55)	.17 (25)	.22 (21)	.56
Three/Four	.04 (9)	.06 (23)	.25 (36)	.38 (26)	.60

Notes: k = number of tests; ns = nonsignificant. Correlations with effect size all at p < .001
Conditions: Adherence to the principles of effective treatment (risk, need, responsivity)

It appears that the promotion of punishment and the delivery of treatment services inconsistent with the principles of the psychology of criminal conduct are actually contributing to increased criminal recidivism relative to the effects of clinically and psychologically appropriate treatment. This is a serious conclusion and needs to be subjected to critical review. What about the basic coding according to human service, risk, need, and general responsivity? The inter-rater agreement rate on the coding of the four-level variables was 86 percent, which is an acceptable level of reliability.

Inspection of Table 2.16 reveals that the effects of appropriate correctional treatment were evident in both randomized groups designs and approximations of randomized groups design. An involved evaluator was a major source of variability in the magnitude of effect sizes, but inspection of Table 2.16 once again reveals that psychologically appropriate treatment was found in studies with and without involved evaluators. Thus, controlling these two indicators of internal validity did not weaken the conclusion that psychologically appropriate treatment yields more positive effects than tests of alternative treatments. Similarly, controls for small sample studies did not threaten the conclusions of the meta-analyses. Moreover, the positive effects of psychologically appropriate treatment were evident in both community correctional settings and custodial correctional settings. It is noteworthy that the effects of increases in the severity of custodial sanctions were associated with a mean effect size of –.10, an average 10 percentage-point higher recidivism rate in the more severe punishment conditions. Note as well that the magnitude of the average positive effect of psychologically appropriate treatment was smaller in custodial corrections (.17) than in community corrections (.35). Correctional setting was a moderator of the effect of psychologically appropriate treatment.

Many additional potential control considerations were explored (and will be reviewed in the Chapter 7). Four variables contributed to the prediction of the magnitude of effect size over and above the contributions of clinically relevant and psychologically informed human service. These variables were: involved evaluator (internal validity issue), community-based setting (external validity), and non-justice ownership and justice referral (both reflecting organizational issues). The important finding to date is that the effects of psychologically appropriate treatments are evident even when all other conditions favor a low effect size (Table 2.16). Under conditions in which only one or fewer of the four control variables favored a large effect size, the mean effect sizes for the four levels of psychologically appropriate treatment were –.09, –.02, .07, and .11. Under conditions in which at least three of the four critical control variables favored a large effect size, the corresponding mean effect sizes for psychologically appropriate treatment were .04, .06, .25, and .38. It appears that when appropriate human service is delivered under hostile conditions, the magnitude of the effect is reduced but still exceeds the effects of alternative interventions.

The above paragraphs reveal high levels of general applicability for appropriate correctional treatment under the extreme conditions most favorable versus least favorable to a large effect size. What about generality under the conditions of variability in age, gender, and ethnic/racial minority status? In the total sample of 374 tests, the correlation of clinically appropriate treatment and reduced recidivism was .55. In the sample of tests with young offenders, it was .46, and it was .56 with female offenders and .46 with members of minority groups. A conclusion of general applicability is supported by the meta-analytic evidence.

In closing, we return to the Pearson correlation coefficient as a means of quantifying the level of empirical knowledge, and we do so in relation to the three myths of sociological criminology. The average correlation between social class of origin and crime is in the area of 0.07 at a maximum. In other words, the empirical support for Myth #1 ("Crime is truly a social phenomenon reflecting inequality") is mild at best. The average correlation between antisocial personality and crime is in the area of .20 at a minimum and approaches or exceeds .30 at a maximum. Thus, there is no empirical support for Myth #2 ("Personal correlates of criminal conduct are trivial"). The average correlation between official processing and reduced recidivism is in the area of .08, even when punishment and treatment are not distinguished. Thus, the research evidence regarding the effectiveness of undifferentiated intervention is at least equal to the very modest effect of being lower-class. When intervention is differentiated according to the principles of PCC, the average (negative) effects of official punishment are in the same modest range of the effects of lower-class origins, while the magnitude of the average effect on recidivism of psychologically appropriate treatment is in the area of the average effects of criminogenic personality. Thus, Myth #3 ("Correctional treatment doesn't work") receives no empirical support unless the "nothing works" perspective is limited to the effects of variations in punishment.

Summary

With the end of Chapter 2, our introduction to PCC is complete. Readers now know that PCC is but one small part of the vast discipline and profession of psychology and but one part of a broader interdisciplinary field of criminology and criminal justice (Chapter 1). The relationship between psychological criminology and sociological criminology has not always been mutually supportive, but PCC is committed to a truly interdisciplinary general personality and social psychology of individual differences in criminal conduct (Chapter 2). Individual differences in criminal activity are substantial across and within categories of age, gender, ethnicity, class, and geography, as well as across measurement approaches and across definitions of crime.

We have seen how the correlation coefficient may be used to summarize the magnitude of covariation in the search for both correlates and treatment effects (Resource Notes 1.2 and 2.4; Tables 2.12 to 2.16). We also have seen that there is a substantial body of research in the domains of both prediction and influence, and that these two bodies of research have been subjected to meta-analytic review. It is already apparent that a rank ordering of risk factors is possible and that the promise of reduced offending resides more in prevention and treatment than in variations in official punishment.

In Chapter 2, we differentiated among correlates, predictors, dynamic predictors, and variables with functional significance. Several important points were made. First, knowledge of the different types of covariates of criminal conduct is generated by different types of research designs. Second, these different types of covariates may be further differentiated according to the extent to which they approach the conditions under which causal effects may be inferred with a reasonable degree of confidence. Third, our introductory review has introduced the concept of moderator variables. Correlates and predictors, like program variables, may have their moderators. In the human sciences, it is to be expected that many statements of covariation must be qualified by references to the conditions under which the covariation is found. We have seen many examples of the general applicability of knowledge of risk factors and knoweldege of what works.

Considerable emphasis was placed on the many sets of variables that may be associated with the outcomes of correctional programs. Simply recognizing that these different sources of variability may be analytically and operationally distinguished is an important step toward the design of effective programs and useful evaluations.

For some readers, the introduction of so many technical terms may appear to represent an unnecessary glorification of jargon. However, by the end of this text, we think the value of these differentiations among types of covariates will be appreciated. The failure to distinguish among them has caused many problems in criminology—problems that could easily have been avoided had more careful attention been given to the details of research design. Now we can turn to theory, and then to policy and practical prediction and intervention in justice settings.

Chapter 3

Understanding Through Theory: Toward Social Learning Through Psychodynamic, Social Location, and Differential Association Perspectives

The major sources of theoretical development in criminology have been—and continue to be—psychological. A theory of criminal conduct is weak indeed if uninformed by a general psychology of human behavior. We will see this most clearly when the self-consciously "social" class-based theories are reviewed. The psychological base for the more empirically defensible theories of crime and delinquency include the psychodynamic perspective of Sigmund Freud, the radical behavioral perspective of B.F. Skinner, and the cognitive behavioral perspectives of Albert Bandura, Walter Mischel, and Donald Meichenbaum. More recently, a general cognitive social psychology is emerging that reflects, for example, the symbolic interactionism of George Herbert Mead, the self-efficacy work of Albert Bandura, and general developments in the social psychology of attitudes and behavior. By the end of Chapter 3, we will have found that theoretical and research studies of crime and delinquency are converging on a general personality and social psychological framework that is empirically rich, and of some practical value to those interested in reducing the harm caused by criminal conduct.

The outlines of this high-consensus theoretical framework were drawn in Europe by the 1900s and the outline was significantly advanced in the 1940s in the United States (e.g., Glueck & Glueck, 1950). The framework continues to develop in Australia (e.g., Mak, 1990), the United Kingdom (e.g., Farrington, 1995), Canada (e.g., LeBlanc, Ouimet & Tremblay, 1988) and the United States (e.g., Sampson & Laub, 1990). The converging constructs are found in general psychodynamic and control models (Glueck & Glueck, 1950; LeBlanc et al., 1988), integrated differential association/behavioral perspectives (Akers, 1973, 1985), bonding perspectives (Hirschi, 1969; Linden, 1987), and general social learning perspectives strongly influenced by Bandura (Jessor & Jessor, 1977; Patterson, 1982; Ross & Fabiano, 1985).

Empirically, the weakest of the theories were based on psychopathology and social location perspectives. Psychodynamic perspectives, historically, are at the heart of empirically defensible criminological theory. We begin, however, with psychopathological perspectives. Quite frankly, we want this discussion out of the way so that we may move directly to the progress evident in the psychodynamic, symbolic interaction, behavioral and social learning /cognitive behavioral pathways toward an empirically defensible theories with considerable practical value.

Psychopathological Perspectives

Psychopathological perspectives perform very poorly when evaluated according to the standards of an adequate theory. Rarely is there a rationally organized set of principles that may be evaluated according to their internal consistency, external consistency, parsimony, and so on. In fact, we cannot find an example that we think even approximates the minimum standards of a theory. Rather, in clinical forensic mental health (clinical psychology, clinical psychiatry, and social work), there has simply been the position that assessments of mental disorder conducted by clinical professionals will assist in understanding criminal behavior. Typically, this understanding would be evident by the ability to predict recidivism and violent offending in particular.

How well do clinicians do in their unstructured clinical judgments of the probability of antisocial outcomes? As will be reviewed in the chapter on exceptional offenders, the mean predictive validity estimates (correlation coefficients) for clinical judgment are in the area of .03 to .09. Systematic structured assessment instruments not concentrating on psychopathology readily yield mean predictive validity estimates of .30 and higher. In regard to the ability to influence antisocial outcomes through deliberate programs, the evidence is equally bleak. Recall from Chapter 2 (and to be developed in more detail in Chapter 7), the effective intervention programs were those consistent with the principles of human service, risk, need, and general responsivity. None of these conditions need make any use of psychopathological perspectives.

Forensic mental health has recently undergone a revival because of the demonstrated predictive validity of the Hare Psychopathy Checklist-Revised (PCL-R: Hare, 1990; see Chapters 2 and 9). Recall from Chapter 2, and as you will see in more detail later, the PCL-R does predict recidivism and violent offending at levels well above that achieved by unstructured clinical judgment. However, how does the PCL-R do relative to assessments of the "Big Eight" as introduced in Chapter 2? As a risk/need scale, PCL-R is an assessment instrument that focuses on antisocial personality pattern and a history of antisocial behavior. The quick answer is easy: The mean predictive validity estimate for the PCL-R is .23 while the mean predictive validity for the LSI-R (a survey of the Big Eight factors) is .37 (Gendreau, Goggin & Smith, 2002). The corresponding values for the prediction of violent recidivism are .21 and .26.

The more prolonged answer requires attention to the construction of the Violence Risk Assessment Guide (VRAG: Quinsey et al., 1998; Chapter 9 of this volume). The detailed clinical records and psychosocial histories of various selected samples of more than 600 mentally disordered offenders were subjected to exhaustive review. In addition, quantitative indices were explored in relation to violent recidivism. The major predictors were not psychiatric history, clinical diagnoses, or clinical symptoms. The major risk factors were early involvement in crime, criminal history, alcohol abuse, aggression, impulsivity, trouble in school and at work, psychopathy (PCL-R) and other personality disorders, and scores on the Level of Service Inventory-Revised (LSI-R). VRAG is a weighted composite of PCL-R scores, elementary school maladjustment, being young at time of index offense, nonviolent offense history score, separated from either parent when under age 16, never married, alcohol abuse, meeting criteria for any personality disorder, and failure on prior conditional release. Finally, three items were surprising to some people. Meeting the American Association of Psychiatry's Diagnostic and Statistical Manual-III (DSM-III) criteria for schizophrenia is scored as a protective factor (that is, it is negatively correlated with violent recidivism), as is serious victim injury (from the index offense) as well as being a female victim in the index offense. The predictive validity estimate for the VRAG was an r of .45.

The performance of the three "protective" factors noted above helps us to understand why clinical judgments have performed so poorly in forensic mental health. Briefly put, clinicians tended to make their judgments on the basis of the seriousness of psychiatric disorder and the seriousness of the offense that brought the individual to the attention of the court and/or clinic.

What about the PCL-R and personality disorder items? Do they support the mental health perspective? Well, not really. We have already noted that the PCL-R may be considered a high-quality assessment of a history of antisocial behavior as well as an assessment of antisocial personality pattern (impulsivity, restless aggressive energy, easy to anger). Moreover, Vernon Quinsey and his associates have already proposed that the PCL-R may be replaced by an eight-item survey of child and adolescent indicators including elementary school maladjustment, teenage alcohol problems, childhood aggression rating, history of school suspension/expulsion, an arrest under age 16, parental alcoholism, and living with both parents to age 16 (except for death of parents), and more than three Conduct Disorder symptoms as defined in DSM-III. The items of the DSM-III could be replaced without reference to formal mental disorders. We also expect that with a host of nonclinical risk factors available, the VRAG references to "schizophrenia," "personality disorder," and "female victims" could easily be replaced without damaging predictive validity.

Psychodynamic Conceptions of Human Behavior

Freud's perspective on human behavior was rich, detailed, and deeply human, and we encourage everyone to take the time to read his introductory lectures on psychoanalysis (Freud, 1953). It is a highly literary perspective—one informed by biology, anthropology, and an appreciation of Western culture and the arts. The theory was also very speculative. Many of Freud's specific ideas have not survived systematic empirical exploration, and yet, in its broader outlines, as will be shown, Freudian theory anticipated almost all elements of current theory.

Freudian theory postulates that behavior is a function of four main "structures." One of the structures is external to the individual (the immediate situation of action) and three of the structures are internal. The internal structures are id, ego, and superego. Behavior in any particular situation is to be understood in terms of how the ego manages the external situation, the forces of the id, and the demands of the superego.

Freud offered many suggestions regarding how the ego and superego developed and functioned. Basically, the emergence of the ego and superego depends upon the interaction of biologically determined growth patterns within the environment. The most crucial developmental periods are early and middle childhood, and the major determinants reside in the context of familial relationships.

Id. According to Freud, human beings have strong aggressive and sexual drives that are biologically based. The psychological storehouse of this aggressive-sexual energy is the id, and the id operates according to the pleasure principle. The pleasure principle summarizes human nature in the form of the seeking of immediate gratification. Gratification always means the maximization of pleasure and the minimization of pain in the immediate situations of action. Aggression is particularly evident when basic needs (e.g., to suck, eat, and experience warmth and sexual relief) are frustrated. This basic frustration-aggression hypothesis contributed to important behavioral and social learning theories (as reviewed later in this chapter).

In Freudian theory, the motivation of all behavior reflects the sexual and aggressive forces of the id. In this sense, Freudian theory is a prototype for what criminologists call "control theory" or "containment theory." The motivation for rape, murder, suicide, and theft is within us all. For all practical purposes, however, individual differences in criminal behavior are not a reflection of basic motivation. Rather, individual differences in criminal behavior are (indeed, all behavior is) the result of the differences in the external realities faced by individuals and in the abilities of the ego and the superego to perform their control functions. As the person matures, the internal structures of the ego and the superego emerge from the id.

Ego. The ego emerges from id as the developing child confronts an external environment that selectively reinforces, punishes, or ignores certain behavioral expressions of basic needs. The fully developed ego has the capacity to consciously (and unconsciously) regulate or manage the demands of id in accordance with the demands of the immediate external situation. That is, the ego operates in accordance with the reality principle, which prescribes that gratification may be delayed for longer-term gain.

The child learns that unbridled biting and expulsion of feces are not appreciated by the immediate environment. In fact, most everything the infant/child finds delightful is subject to the judgments of a highly selective environment. Eating and drinking are dependent upon the presence and will of others to nourish (and increasingly only at certain times of day). Urination and defecation are judged proper only in certain locations. Limits are placed on access to the physical warmth of parents, and playing with one's genitals becomes so problematic that such play comes to be restricted to only the most private settings.

Selective environments (i.e., "training" experiences) like these are frustrating for the child. The natural response, according to Freud, is to protest and act aggressively. However, these displays of aggression also are subject to a selective environment. Parents do not like being hit and they do not enjoy temper tantrums. Fortunately, the selective environment is interested in more than placing limits on highly pleasurable behavior. The training also involves encouraging children to master their environment, to be independent, and to cooperate with others.

Through such training, the executive and coping skills of the ego begin to emerge. The ego's task is to maximize pleasure and minimize discomfort while balancing the demands of the id and the external situation. Conscious ego functions include rational analysis of the situation, consideration of alternative courses of action, and the selection of a course of action that maximizes pleasure and minimizes pain. Ego, unlike id, recognizes that sometimes the delay of immediate gratification is associated with long-term gains.

The many unconscious functions of the ego, the "defense mechanisms," are highly important. They are unconscious because the ego does not recognize that the "justified" behavior is in fact an attempt to satisfy the sexual or aggressive needs of the id. The process must be unconscious; otherwise the satisfaction of the id would be impossible. Thus, for example, rape is possible because "she wanted it" (defense mechanism of "rationalization") or because "she wanted me" (a "projection").

Superego. An additional task of the ego is to manage the demands of the superego. The superego emerges from the ego as a result of the selective reactions of the environment to certain behaviors, and through identification with intimate authority figures. For Freud, this identification process is the single most important determinant of moral conduct, and it is largely determined by the age of six or seven. The superego consists of two elements: the conscience and the ego-ideal. The conscience contains internalized representations of conduct that are subject to punishment. The ego-ideal is the mental representation of conduct that is positively valued by the environment.

For boys, identification with the father is the solution to the "Oedipal" conflict. Faced with a desire for intimate contact with their mothers and recognizing that their fathers are quite powerful, being "just like daddy" may one day earn them a privileged relationship with someone like mommy. Girls are faced with the "Electra" conflict. Aware, like their mothers, that they do not have a penis (which they desire), girls identify with their mothers in the hope that, because they are just like mommy, someone like daddy will eventually come along.

With these Oedipal and Electra conflicts resolved through identification with the same-sex parent, the developing person enters the latency period. The child is able to get on with the tasks of developing basic social and life skills, and acquiring knowledge of the world. The basic sources of energy are sublimated so that sexual and aggressive drives are channeled into socially constructive ways. Thus, with the development of the superego, the opportunity arises for still further strengthening of the ego.

In sum, the id operates according to the pleasure principle, while the ego operates according to the reality principle. The superego operates according to a severe moralistic principle whereby moral lapses of commission or omission are subject to the experience of intense guilt. The ego thus manages the demands of the id, external reality, the conscience, and the ego-ideal.

Adolescence represents a particularly risky period for criminal activity because, with puberty, the sexual instincts are reawakened and remain at relatively high levels until dampened by advancing age. By puberty, however, a more mature ego has developed that can manage both the id and the superego.

Psychological Maturity. If the developmental process proceeds well, a mature adult emerges. For Freud, maturity is reflected in the ability to delay immediate gratification, to love and be loved in the context of long-term sexual relationships, and to be socially productive. Without question, Freud's conception of the mature person coincides with what is often called "middle-class morality." This coincidence may not, however, rule it out of order. One may place a high value on personal creativity and self-actualization without dismissing the relevance of "conventional" concerns for other people—and the protection that rules may provide for the integrity of others.

Value judgments put aside, the empirical fact is that each of Freud's three indicators of "maturity," when absent in individuals, are risk factors for criminal conduct. That is, weak self-control, marital instability, and an unstable employment record are each well-established predictors of criminal conduct in adult samples.

There is another side to Freud's conception of maturity that is often missed in discussions of psychoanalytic theory. One of the consequences of a strong superego is a hyperconventionality, which, while often incompatible with criminal conduct, produces high levels of personal misery. Freudian theory is explicit on the point that the very socialization experiences that may control criminal conduct may also be responsible for neurotic misery. In other words, Freudians are as much, if not more, concerned with freeing individuals from conventional controls as they are with controlling violations of conventional codes.

The extraordinary significance that Freud assigned to weaning, toilet training, and early sexual advances toward opposite-sex parents are among the features of Freudian theory that have not survived systematic research. However, Freudian notions of the importance of moment-to-moment, day-to-day, and more sustained environmental conditions have received some consistent empirical support. These notions are developed below.

Environmental Barriers to Development

In classical Freudian theory, the development of a mature ego and superego depends upon conditions of warmth, care, and attention, in combination with supervision, direct training, and direct modeling for purposes of both skill development and moral development. In Freudian theory, a number of conditions are associated with problematic development. One is extreme neglect and the outright abuse of the developing child. Neither a strong ego nor a strong superego may be expected to develop under such conditions.

A second problematic condition is that of extreme permissiveness or unconditional warmth and affection. While a strong ego may evolve, the superego will be weak except insofar as the parents have incidentally modeled clear conceptions of "right" and "wrong."

A third problematic developmental condition involves patterns of child rearing in which the moral training occurs without a background of warmth and affection. Children from these families may be oriented to rules but may not possess a positive orientation to people. These are just some of the variations in early childhood experience that a Freudian perspective suggests may be important.

The Immediate Environment, the Situation of Action, and the Psychological Moment

One strength of the general personality and social psychological perspectives is that they recognize the importance of both: (1) the person in the immediate situation of action, and (2) background predispositional factors. Attention to the immediate situation of action suggests the immediate causes of human behavior, while the background dispositional factors suggest what leads some people to circumstances in which the probability of a criminal act may be high. Background dispositional factors attempt to account for "criminality," that is, to identify the factors responsible for variation in criminal conduct over a broad time frame. This variation, however, reflects a history of particular people in a variety of immediate situations of action.

In psychodynamic theory, the immediate causes of crime are both situational and personal. Criminal acts are to be understood in the context of the person in immediate situations. Figure 3.1 presents a summary of the immediate causes of antisocial behavior according to psychodynamic theory, wherein the person is represented by the superego, the ego, and the id. The immediate environment may be distinguished according to the temptations they provide and the external controls present.

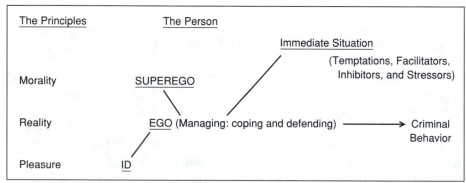

Notes: SUPEREGO (Internalized Societal Standards): Conscience plus ego-ideal.
        EGO: Coping, defending, *and* "interpreting."
        ID: An antisocial constant in Freud.
        SITUATION: In part selected by the person, in part a function of family of origin, and in part a function of broader social arrangements.

Figure 5.1
The Psychological Situation (or Psychological Moment)
in Traditional Psychodynamic Theory

Thus, understanding and predicting individual criminal conduct requires a knowledge of superego strength (e.g., attitudes, values, and beliefs regarding rule violations), a knowledge of the self-regulation/self-control and problem-solving skills and processes possessed by the ego, and knowledge of the facilitating and inhibiting aspects of the immediate environment.

The psychodynamic perspective also has much to say on background predispositional factors. These are reviewed below as a variety of routes to crime and as a psychodynamic typology of offenders.

Types of Offenders in Psychoanalytic Theory

Freudian theory suggests many different routes to crime. Here we sample some of the more frequently traveled routes, drawing upon the work of Mannheim (1965). Our sampling also provides an introduction to the correlates and predictors of criminal behavior that extend well beyond age, sex, race, and social class. This summary of types of offenders does not cover the most inclusive of the Freudian types because they have already been described. Recall that the psychologically immature are characterized primarily by impulsivity and the inability to delay gratification as well as instability in both their family and vocational lives. The psychologically immature present some combination of what is described below as weak superego and weak ego.

The Weak Superego Type. Some people engage in frequent and serious criminal behavior because they lack internalized representations of those behaviors that are punished and reinforced in conventional society. Thus, their behavior, whether prosocial or antisocial, is subject only to the need for immediate gratification and the demands of the immediate external situation. These indicators of a weak superego may be defined independently of the criterion of criminal behavior and include the following:

1. Reckless disregard for conventional rules and procedures;

2. Antisocial cognitions/procriminal sentiments (lack of conscience);

3. Little evidence of a life plan and weak conventional ambition (lack of an ego-ideal);

4. Little evidence of guilt (lack of a conscience);

5. The early appearance of persistent and generalized conduct problems (the superego is supposedly formed by the age of eight);

6. Expressions of bravado, flirtatiousness, and exhibitionism (early conflicts stemming from the seduction of the opposite-sex parent are unresolved);

7. Conflict with authority figures (again, early conflicts and frustrations have not been resolved);

8. A basic separateness from other people that reflects essential isolation, lovelessness, and a desperate loneliness.

Perhaps the best known description of a "weak superego" type comes from Hervey Cleckley's *The Mask of Sanity* (1982), which is a classic work in the psychiatric/clinical tradition. It has been so influential and so closely tied to the image that there has come to be known a "Cleckley checklist for psychopathy." These characteristics, which will be reviewed in Chapter 9, are: superficial charm; good intelligence (not retarded); absence of delusions and other signs of irrational thinking (not psychotic); absence of nervousness (not neurotic); unreliability; untruthfulness and insincerity; lack of remorse or shame; inadequately motivated antisocial behavior; poor judgment and failure to learn from experience;

pathological egocentricity and incapability for love; general poverty in major affective relations; specific loss of insight; unresponsiveness in general interpersonal relations; fantastic and uninviting behavior with drink (and sometimes without); impersonal, trivial, and poorly integrated sex life; and failure to follow any life plan. The Hare Psychopathy Checklist-Revised (PCL-R), an objective measure of psychopathy, will be reviewed in detail in Chapter 9.

It should not be a surprise that systematic empirical research consistently supports the predictive validity of assessment instruments that tap into the content described above for weak superego and psychopathy. Controversy continues, however, about what is actually being measured.

The Weak Ego Type. A weak ego implies immaturity, poorly developed social skills, poor reality testing, gullibility, and excessive dependence. In psychoanalytic terms, the weak ego types are less under the control of superego than of the id and the immediate environment. For weak ego types, criminal behavior may represent stumbling into trouble (misreading the external environment), having a temper tantrum, or following the leader.

The "Normal" Antisocial Offender. These offenders have progressed through the psychosexual stages of development without any particular problems. Psychologically, they match the ideal of the full-functioning mature adult. However, a mismatch with the ego-ideal is evident. The superego is procriminal as a result of identification with a criminal parent and the ego has incorporated a mastery of criminal skills.

The Neurotic Offender. Freudian theory suggests a number of ways in which neurotic conflicts may translate into criminal behavior. The "criminal from a sense of guilt" is the most interesting, though perhaps not the most frequent. This type is driven by an unconscious desire to be punished for past crimes. An overactive superego may be seeking punishment for prior sins that, even if not actually committed, were either contemplated or the focus of a wish-fulfilling fantasy.

Frequently represented in samples of neurotic offenders are people who use criminal acts as a means of managing specific frustrations or emotional disturbances, or as a way of impacting on disturbed family relations. For example, some "neurotics" may use criminal activity to gain the attention of, or to punish, their parents.

Many clinicians have noted that the offenses of some offenders have elements that appear to exceed those necessary for the achievement of certain concrete goals. For example, obtaining money is an obvious explanation of the behavior of a purse snatcher. Yet, understanding this behavior may benefit from a deeper analysis when the stealing is associated with increases in sexual arousal.

Other Types. The psychoanalytic perspective recognizes a number of other routes to crime. Among those routes are the following:

1. The psychotic and mentally retarded are at risk for violations of the law. This may be a logical extension of the incapacities that underlie definitions of being psychotic or being retarded. If one is out of contact with reality or so intellectually disadvantaged as to be unable to manage one's affairs, illegal acts may occur as just another of many transgressions of conventional rules.

2. The situational offender responds to extreme and isolated circumstances such as having stumbled upon the infidelity of a trusted spouse or being confronted with some other particularly "unjust" or "enraging" situation.

3. The perception of injustice is a particularly interesting route to crime within psychoanalytic theory. Those who are persistently criminal as a result of a sense of injustice also possess a hatred of their fathers. In brief, the state has been equated with the hated father.

4. Psychoanalytic thinkers, like most others who have attempted to map the routes to crime, have attended to the role of alcohol and drug use (and abuse). Some drugs for some people may enhance motivation for crime and reduce internalized controls.

5. The accidental offender may have stumbled into crime because of particularly unlucky circumstances. Within psychoanalytic theory, even crimes of negligence or "slips" may reflect unconscious motivation.

According to psychoanalytic theory, the possible routes to crime are many and diverse. With respect for another medical father of criminology, we will take a brief look at the typology of Lombroso, who was a physician in Italian prisons during the late 1800s. Lombroso was not a Freudian, but he and Freud had similar intellectual backgrounds. Freud saw all human beings as born criminals, with most of us socialized out of it before coming of age. Lombroso was interested in offenders in particular and thought that the observation and measurement of individual offenders should be an important component of criminology. His ideas, as summarized by Gould (1981), were heavily influenced by evolutionary theory, but shifted over his working life toward an emphasis on environmental factors in response to criticism, further observation, and reflection.

The vast majority of criminals, according to Lombroso, were of the "occasional" type: the pseudocriminal who is essentially nonevil and relatively harmless, who is either responding to extreme socioeconomic pressures or whose acts are crimes of passion. Lombroso also identified a group of habitual offenders whose criminal activity reflected a procriminal upbringing as well as association with criminals, and another group whose criminality reflected mental disease or insanity. Lombroso, however, is best known for his work on the atavistic or "born" criminal. The born criminal, said to represent about 35 percent of all criminals, was described as a genetic throwback to primitive human or prehuman evolutionary types. The psychology of the born criminal had both motivational and control elements in the form of exceptionally strong animalistic drives and exceptionally weak internal controls, respectively. In psychoanalytic theory, there is little interesting variation in the desire to achieve pleasure and avoid pain (it is a basic part of human nature) and almost all of the variation of interest resides on the control side (and depends upon the interaction of the biopsychological organism and the environment).

For Lombroso, the atavistic criminal could be distinguished from the noncriminal and from other criminals by certain physical features (such as abnormal brain size, receding forehead, long arms, large ears, and bushy eyebrows). There are tremendous individual differences in most any bodily measure that might be taken. However, Lombroso was wrong on his basic points (Gould, 1981). First and foremost, extremes on normal distributions of physical measures do not imply atavism. Second, there is no convincing evidence regarding the covariation of these physical characteristics and criminality.

Lombroso also provided a list of psychosocial factors associated with born criminality. Many of the items on the "Lombroso checklist" bear a strong resemblance to the psychoanalytic concept of the superego (and to the content of questionnaires and rating scales currently used in the prediction of recidivism): moral immaturity, cruelty, idleness, vanity, high tolerance for physical pain, use of criminal argot, and the wearing of tattoos.

The intellectual base for a vigorous pursuit of the variety of routes to crime had been established by the 1920s through the work of Freud and Lombroso. Two intellectual giants, both medically trained, one preoccupied with psychology and the other with biology, had each suggested that understanding criminal conduct would be significantly advanced through the development of perspectives that recognized the importance of both the egocentric pursuit of gratification and the development of internal controls. The perspectives of each also noted that some criminal activity may reflect benign psychological inadequacies, atypical situational pressures, conformity within a criminal subculture, and even self-righteous and deliberate responses to a perceived social injustice. Freud and Lombroso may have disagreed in regard to the importance of variation in the pursuit of pleasure, but they agreed on the importance of variation in control. Recall, however, from Chapters 1 and 2, the problematic status of biology and psychology in mainstream sociological criminology:

> Due to historic misfortune sociology captured the field in the 1920s. The contributions of biology and psychology have been minimized (Jeffery, 1979:7).

> In most sociological treatments of crime and delinquency, genetic explanations are either ignored or ridiculed (Rowe & Osgood, 1984:526).

These promising leads were systematically missed for years in criminology. Later we will review the most explicitly antipsychological of criminological theories (the class-based anomie, subcultural, labeling, and conflict/Marxist perspectives) and they are found to be the least empirically defensible theories in the whole of PCC. Chapter 4, with a focus on social learning theory, will outline differential association theory, which was sociological in conception but did not become empirically defensible or of any practical value until integrated with social learning and social cognition theory. The remainder of this chapter concentrates upon developments of the psychodynamic perspective. However, readers are reminded that the authors of this text do not believe that classic psychoanalytic thought represents the current state of psychological knowledge.

Psychodynamic Thought and Recent Psychological Advances

As we shall see here and in later chapters, current psychology has concepts and procedures that have significantly advanced, altered, and successfully replaced the psychoanalytic perspective. Several of these advances are briefly noted:

1. Freud, in contrast to Lombroso, did not hypothesize individual differences in the innate strength of the id or in the capacity for ego or superego development. Yet, current personality theorists who conceptualize individuals as having enduring personality characteristics or traits have drawn upon convincing evidence that children vary in their propensity for rule violations and their ability to learn. Some psychologists (e.g., Digman, 1990) talk of the "Big Five" temperamental or trait dimensions of personality: Introversion-Extraversion, Friendly Compliance-Hostile Noncompliance, Will to Achieve, Emotional Stability, and Intellect.

2. Behavioral genetics and physiological psychology have pointed to the importance of inheritance, cortical arousal, the classical conditioning of anticipatory fear responses, and the neuropsychology of self-regulation. The avoidance-learning models of socialization (e.g., Eysenck, 1977; Eysenck & Gudjonsson, 1989) appear to be particularly relevant to some types of persistent and serious criminal behavior.

3. There have been advances in theory and research on the impor-
    tance of environments in the selection of acts that are rein-
    forced, punished, or ignored. Principles of learning (e.g., operant
    conditioning) are better understood now than they were in
    Freud's time.

4. Current theory and research in social learning and cognition has
    much to offer regarding the variables associated with modeling,
    identification, and learning by way of observation.

5. Current social learning and cognitive theory specifies some of the
    processes of behavioral self-control. Research has detailed the
    specific skills of self-control and recognized the importance of per-
    sonal standards of conduct. That is, self-regulation may be guid-
    ed by attitudes, values, and beliefs that are either anticriminal
    or procriminal.

6. Developments within social psychology include perspectives on
    how attitudes, values, and beliefs supportive of a specific action
    may combine with perceived social support for that action, and
    thereby yield highly accurate predictions of specific behavioral
    acts.

7. Freud emphasized that the person must always deal with the
    external environment, but he thought that the major elements of
    personality were formed very early. While not denying the impor-
    tance of early learning and experience, social learning theory con-
    siders the person in the contemporaneous environment to be of
    overriding behavioral significance.

In summary, the Freudian model of human behavior, for all of its
speculative components, encompasses many people's notions of what it
is to be human. Human beings seek pleasure and avoid pain, and that
pursuit is governed by the demands, constraints, and opportunities of
the immediate situation and by the internal controls that are developed
through socialization experiences.

Reformulations of Psychodynamic Theory

The most important development in a psychodynamic theory of
delinquency and crime must be that of Sheldon Glueck and Eleanor
Glueck (1950). Their "tentative causal formula," reflecting Freudian
theory as well as their empirical findings, is among the best validated of
all predictive models of criminal behavior.

Glueck and Glueck thought the roots of criminality were more deeply and personally rooted than either 1940s practice or theory recognized. They accepted that underprivileged urban neighborhoods were criminogenic for young males, but they also expected that the families and individuals residing in underprivileged areas were far from being uniform in their attitudes and abilities:

> The varieties of the physical, mental, and social history of different persons must determine, in large measure, the way in which they will be influenced by social disorganization, culture conflict, and the growing-pains of the city (p. 6).

Arguing for a fair sampling of the various aspects of a complex biopsychosocial problem, Glueck and Glueck proposed that research and theory should focus upon personal and environmental variables. This focus was fundamental to psychoanalytic thinking, according to which all human behavior is to be understood in terms of "the point of contact between specific social and biologic processes as they coalesce, accommodate, or conflict in individuals" (p. 7). Quoting from Freud's introductory lectures:

> Economic conditions . . . can do no more than set their [people's] instinctual impulses in motion—their self-preservative instinct, their love of aggression, their need for love and their impulse to attain pleasure and avoid pain (p. 9).

Glueck and Glueck had a clear idea regarding the environmental and situational factors that might be criminogenic. They explicitly noted the many exciting opportunities and the lack of controls in some neighborhoods. Their "tentative causal formula" emphasized weak internal controls (a weak superego) resulting from poor parenting practices and parental modeling, and temperamental/constitutional predispositions toward the expression of aggressive energy and the pursuit of self-interest. Perhaps it is best if Glueck and Glueck (1950: 281-282) provide their own summary of their perspective on male delinquency:

> Physically: Delinquents are essentially mesomorphic in constitution (solid, muscular).
>
> Temperamentally: restlessly energetic, impulsive, extroverted, aggressive, destructive.
>
> Attitudinally: hostile, defiant, suspicious, stubborn, adventurous, unconventional, nonsubmissive to authority.
>
> Cognition: direct and concrete rather than symbolic, less methodical in problem-solving.

> Familial: reared in homes of little understanding, affection, stability, or moral fiber by parents usually unfit to be effective sources for emulation needed for the construction of a well-balanced and socially normal superego.

In the exciting, stimulating, but little-controlled and culturally inconsistent environment of the underprivileged area, such boys readily give expression to their untamed impulses and their self-centered desires by means of various forms of delinquent behavior.

Some of the language used by Glueck and Glueck is offensive, but readers are reminded that they were committed to reducing behavior harmful to others and to enhancing the quality of services for those at risk for antisocial behavior. They were disturbed by the differential in societal resources devoted to the punishment of offenders relative to the resources devoted to the reduction of harm.

Note that Glueck and Glueck's causal formula did not make reference to two of the strongest correlates of delinquency in their research: delinquent associates and misconduct in school. For them, patterns of companionship and behavior problems in school were expressions of more fundamental personal and familial variables. School and community, however, were viewed as major settings for intervention by Glueck and Glueck.

In addition to developing psychodynamic theory, the Glueck data suggested that certain theories of delinquency were simply not capable of accounting for much of the variability in officially defined delinquent behavior within disadvantaged urban neighborhoods:

1. Culture conflict: Intergenerational culture conflict was uncovered in more than 50 percent of the families but culture conflict was unrelated to delinquency.

2. Social class: Within the narrow range sampled, economic circumstances, educational levels of parents, and occupational levels of parents were all incapable of accounting for much of the variability in delinquency. Economic considerations were not even a major emotional issue for the boys.

3. Limited access to services: The families of delinquents had more, not fewer, contacts with social service agencies. Quality of service, as our review of the treatment literature will reveal, is more important than number of services.

4. Physical health: Physical and general health problems were not associated with delinquency.

5. Conventional ambition: Conventional ambitions on the part of parents and the boys were negatively, not positively, associated

with delinquency. It was clear that personal or parental endorsements of conventional success standards could not account for delinquency.

6. Feelings of failure in conventional pursuits: Preoccupation with personal and academic failure was more characteristic of non-delinquents than of delinquents. Indeed, delinquents disliked school because it was confining and controlling, while it was the nondelinquents who disliked school because of feelings of failure. Emotional conflicts regarding school, future prospects, finances, and material surroundings occurred with a low frequency within both groups of boys and generally were weakly associated with delinquency.

7. Marxist/conflict perspectives: Overall, those confined in the "prisons" of convention (family, church, school, and work) were less likely to be delinquent than were "nonprisoners" of convention. Clearly, delinquency was most evident among those who were most free of such "prisons," who took to the streets and unsupervised playgrounds, who ventured outside of their neighborhoods and who rejected age-based norms regarding smoking, sexual conduct, and school attendance. The price paid by the prisoners of conventional morality was suffering an increased risk for neurotic misery and hyperbanality.

8. Psychopathology: Glueck and Glueck were clear that the major personality correlates were not simply pathological traits. Rather, the correlates were impulsiveness, a strong taste for adventure, a lack of conscientiousness, hostility, and antiauthority attitudes. Psychopathological antisociality was slightly more evident within the delinquent sample, while psychopathological neuroticism was slightly more evident within the nondelinquent sample of boys.

9. Personal distress theories of delinquency were not supported by Glueck and Glueck. The Glueck data suggested that many young people harbor feelings of insecurity, anxiety, powerlessness, and of not being appreciated or loved. These near constants of the human condition, however, were unrelated to delinquency.

Overall, Glueck and Glueck recognized multiple routes to illegal conduct, and any of the potential causes implied in Theories 1 through 9 may well apply to some individuals on some occasions. Their "tentative causal formula," however, was more widely applicable. According to them, some delinquency may be explained by any one of the major psychological, familial, and neighborhood factors, but the probability of delinquency increases as the various contributors are combined.

The theoretical contributions of Glueck and Glueck rest solidly on their psychodynamic underpinnings and on their research findings. Their 1950 study is the classic piece of cross-sectional research in the whole of criminology. At the very least, the flavor of their approach and their data should be appreciated. The research study involved comparisons between 500 delinquent boys recruited from two training schools in the Boston area and 500 nondelinquent boys recruited from schools in the same neighborhoods. The delinquents and nondelinquents were matched on age (generally from 10 to 17 years, mean age of 14), IQ, and ethnic origin.

Data were collected through social history interviews with the boys, their relatives, and others (such as social workers and teachers). Social welfare, court, and correctional records and school files were reviewed, as well as medical examinations, psychiatric interviews, psychological tests, anthropometric analyses of photographs of the boys, and teacher-completed checklists.

The findings of Glueck and Glueck are selectively summarized in Tables 3.1, 3.2, and 3.3. Table 3.3 may most usefully be perused with attention to our nine-point summary of variables that were not highlighted in Glueck and Glueck's causal formula.

Table 3.1
Temperament/Personality, Cognitive Skills, Antisocial Attitudes, Antisocial Associates and School: Percent of Delinquents and Nondelinquents with a Factor Present

	Delinquents	Nondelinquents	Difference
Temperament/Personality			
Mesomorphy dominant	60	31	29
Extreme restlessness	60	30	30
Inattention	48	19	29
Vivacity, liveliness	51	23	28
Self-control	39	66	-27
Conscientiousness	9	54	-45
Cognition			
Mean Verbal IQ	88.6	92.0	ns
Common sense: Marked	29	39	-10
Methodical approach to problems: Absent	79	65	14
Antisocial Attitudes			
Marked submissiveness	27	80	-53
Defiance	50	12	38
Ambivalence to authority	41	20	21
Conventional ideas, behavior	8	32	-24
Adventurousness	55	18	37
Hostility	80	56	24
Antisocial Associates			
Gang member	56	1	55
Chums largely with delinquents	98	7	91
School			
Poor grades	41	8	33
School misbehavior	96	17	79
Never truant	5	89	-84
Persistently truant	63	0	63
Mean grade in which first misbehavior occurred	4.36 (of 478)	7.38 (of 86)	

ns = not significant

From Glueck & Glueck, 1950

Table 3.2
Family and Parenting: Percent of Delinquents and Nondelinquents with a Factor Present

	Delinquents	Nondelinquents	Difference
Family of Origin			
Mother's family of origin			
Criminality	55	36	19
Father's family of origin			
Criminality	40	32	12
Mother's history			
Mental retardation	33	9	24
Criminality	45	15	30
Father's history			
Emotional disturbances	44	18	26
Criminality	66	32	34
Siblings' history			
Criminality	65	26	39
Stability of Living Arrangements with Parents			
Raised continuously by one or both parents	54	88	-34
Out-of-home placements	71	9	62
Affective Quality of Family Life			
Cohesiveness of family			
Marked	16	62	-46
Affection of father for boy			
Warm	40	81	-41
Affection of mother for boy			
Warm (even if overprotective)	72	96	-24
Supervision/Discipline/Standards of Conduct			
Poor conduct standards	90	54	36
Supervision of children by mother suitable	7	65	-58
Mother's discipline of boy firm but kindly	4	66	-62
Father's discipline of boy firm but kindly	6	56	-50
Social service agency involvement (mean)	11.7	6.9	***

From Glueck & Glueck, 1950

The Glueck causal formula is sometimes criticized because those variables that actually differentiated between delinquents and nondelinquents were identified as causal. Since 1950, however, many other researchers have conducted independent tests of similar models of proposed causal significance (e.g., Laub & Sampson, 1988; Sampson & Laub, 1990). Perhaps the best known of the theories derived from the psychodynamic model are the control theories of Walter Reckless and of Travis Hirschi. The next section of this chapter explores these variations on psychodynamic themes.

Variations on Psychodynamic Themes in Control Theories

Control or containment theories produced by sociological criminologists concentrate upon explaining why people do not commit crimes rather than explaining why people do commit them. Following Freudian theory, control theories are socialization theories. They are theories that focus upon how people come to develop strong ties to convention and resist the temptations to steal and aggress.

Table 3.3
Other Factors Suggested by Other Theories: Percent of Delinquents and Nondelinquents with a Factor Present

	Delinquents	Nondelinquents	Difference
Socioeconomic Class of Origin			
Economically Dependent	29	12	17
Reasons for Financial Assistance			
Illness of breadwinner	16	16	ns
Recession/seasonal unemployment	39	59	-20
Unwilling to assume responsibility	45	25	20
Reason First Left Home			
Delinquency	32	0	32
Ran away	31	0	31
Death/separation/divorce	14	55	-41
Financial problems	8	17	-9
Sources of Emotional Conflict			
Lack of monetary resources	4	2	ns
Material surroundings	3	0	ns
Father	23	5	18
Mother	15	2	13
Problems of identification with adult male	30	12	18
Anomie/Strain/Personal Distress/ Powerlessness			
Sources of Emotional Conflict			
Educational expectations	10	7	ns
General prospects	5	2	ns
Reasons for Marked Dislike of School			
Unable to learn	33	50	-17
Feels inferior	14	28	-14
Resents restriction or control	24	5	19
Lack of interest	22	10	12
Shyness	10	19	-9
Uncritical of self	29	11	18
Fear of failure and defeat	44	63	-19
Enhanced feeling of insecurity/anxiety	14	29	-15
Feeling of helplessness and powerlessness	42	54	-12
Feeling of resignation	5	3	ns
Depressive trends	3	1	ns
Feeling of being able to manage own life	73	64	9
Feeling of not being taken seriously or not counting	59	64	-5
Feeling of not being wanted or loved	92	97	-5
Marked vague/unconscious feeling of insecurity/anxiety	89	96	-7
Psychopathology			
Psychopathic	24	6	18
Neurotic	25	36	-11

ns = not significant

From Glueck & Glueck, 1950

Walter Reckless (1967) followed Freudian theory in suggesting that there were both inner and outer sources of control. The external controls were social pressures to conform, and the strength of these controls would increase with a sense of belonging to anticriminal groups. These groups include the family, social clubs, schools, and religious organizations. "Inner containment" is Reckless's term for what psychologists call self-control, conscience, or superego. Reckless listed five indicators of inner control:

1. Positive self-concept that involves not only self-esteem but also seeing one's self as conventional as opposed to criminal;

2. A commitment to long-range, legitimate goals;

3. Setting realistic objectives;

4. High tolerance for frustration;

5. Identification with lawfulness and respect for the law.

Reckless's list fails to incorporate certain key indicators, such as guilt and generalized disregard for conventional rules, and misses completely the restless energy and aggressive pursuit of self-interest that the psychodynamic image contains. From the perspective of sociological theorizing, the major theoretical significance of Reckless's theory was that the social networks of young people constituted something more than class and subcultural membership. He also gave ascendancy to internal control and to the recognition of individual differences in socialization.

Travis Hirschi's *Causes of Delinquency* (1969), a classic cross-sectional study, contained his variation on the psychodynamic/Glueck themes. The present summary will focus upon a selection of the theoretical issues explored by Hirschi. Comparisons will be made with Glueck and Glueck's *Unraveling Juvenile Delinquency* (1950), because both books are important in the understanding of criminal behavior.

There are a number of theoretical points of convergence between the two studies. Most notably, both studies are grounded in control theory. In both *Unraveling* and *Causes*, it is accepted that the crucial explanatory issue is "why *don't* we violate the law?" rather than "why *do* we violate the law?" In brief, it is conformity rather than deviance that must be explained.

Psychoanalytically, Glueck and Glueck accepted that antisocial behavior was an expression of basic sexual and aggressive energy. Thus, delinquency was an expression of untamed impulses, or of immorality in the absence of external controls. Hirschi saw little value in postulating an id, but was quite willing to assume that there are individual differences in morality without concerning himself with the nature of criminal motivation.

For Hirschi, the moral ties consist of attachment, commitment, involvement, and belief in the validity of the law:

1. Attachment to (or caring about) the opinions of family, teachers, and peers is the social psychological version of the "ego ideal" portion of the superego.

2. Commitment to conventional pursuits involves increasing the risk of losing one's investment should deviance be detected. Thus, commitment serves the same theoretical role as does the ego, that is, the operation of the reality principle in the control of rule violations. The Freudian ego, however, involves the operation of self-regulation skills, problem-solving, and various conscious and unconscious processes.

3. Involvement in conventional pursuits reduces delinquency simply by the limited time available for deviant pursuits. Similarly, the development of absorbing moral substitutes for crime was a particular recommendation within Glueck and Glueck's list of principles of prevention programming.

4. Belief in validity of the law refers to individual differences in the extent to which people believe they should obey the rules. Thus, belief serves the same theoretical function as the superego and antisocial attitudes (the "conscience" portion of the superego).

The second point of convergence between the Hirschi study and the Glueck study involves rejection of the central causal significance of social class. The Glueck theory drew upon Freud, to whom class meant little unless individual differences entered the prediction formula. Able to draw upon the post-1940s research evidence, Hirschi "knew" that class was at best a weak correlate of delinquency. He also was aware that the logical structure of social class theories was very weak.

Third, both the Hirschi and Glueck theories were underwhelmed by differential association theory. We have already seen that Glueck and Glueck chose not to include delinquent associates (the single strongest correlate of delinquency that their work had uncovered) in their list of causal variables. Similarly, Hirschi's downplaying of the role of delinquent associates proved to be the empirically weakest of his theoretical positions. (Reanalyses of Hirschi's data have confirmed that having delinquent associates is a major correlate of delinquency; Matseuda, 1982).

In terms of research, *Causes* illustrates the methodological advances that had occurred since *Unraveling*. Hirschi surveyed both official and self-reported delinquency. He carefully selected a representative sample of delinquents and nondelinquents by working with a high school cohort from a community. Most of Hirschi's delinquents were not persistent and serious official offenders. Typical of a limitation of much of the cross-sectional research in the 1960s and 1970s (with only a few exceptions), assessments of potential correlates of delinquency were totally dependent upon self-reports provided on paper-and-pencil questionnaires. A comparison of the findings of *Causes* and *Unraveling* is interesting in view of the conceptual overlap and the dramatic differences in methods of inquiry.

Table 3.4 reveals that Glueck and Glueck's findings regarding the empirical importance of (1) parental supervision, (2) the boy's identification with his father, and (3) delinquent companions were each supported by Hirschi's study. Similarly, findings regarding the importance of verbal intelligence and attitudes toward school were replicated and extended by Hirschi in 1969. Hirschi did not include traditional assessments of personality beyond sampling a few of what the Glueck analysis had called "adventurous activities" and some attitudinal/belief items (e.g., involvement with smoking, alcohol, and girls correlated with delinquency).

In addition, Table 3.4 reveals that egocentric attitudes toward law violations, deficits in self-control, disrespect for authority, and boredom were each associated with delinquency. While these data were not presented, Hirschi also noted that mesomorphs (self-described as "well-built," as opposed to fat, skinny, or average) were more likely to have committed delinquent acts.

Table 3.4
Delinquency Rates by Family Characteristics

Predictor/Question	% Delinquent	N
Mother's Supervision (Does your mother know where you are/whom you are with when you are away from home?)		
0 Never	55	11
1	41	29
2	29	236
3	20	252
4 Usually	12	698
Affectional Identification with Father (Would you like to be the kind of person your father is?)		
0 Not at all	38	138
1	22	172
2	17	387
3	11	404
4 In every way	16	121
Delinquent Companions (Have any of your close friends ever been picked up by the police?)		
0 Four or more	45	208
1	44	62
2	21	99
3	21	164
4 None	7	520
Verbal Aptitude Scores (DAT)		
0 Very High	10	21
1	13	140
2	14	319
3	22	452
4 Very Low	21	224

From Hirschi, 1969

Table 3.4 *(continued)*
Delinquency Rates by Family Characteristics

Predictor/Question	% Delinquent	N
Attitudes Toward School (Do you like school?)		
0 Dislike	49	72
1	25	101
2 Like	9	580
Educational Aspirations (How much schooling would you like to get eventually?)		
0 Less than college	56	172
1	47	240
2 College graduation	40	825
Age at which Cigarette Smoking Began		
0 Before age 13	48	154
1 Age 13-15	32	117
2 After age 15	28	29
3 Don't smoke	12	952
Involvement in Adult Activities (smoking, drinking, dating)		
0 Smokes, drinks, dates	78	154
1	65	17
2	62	149
3	61	73
4	40	270
5 Not one of the 3	25	535
Feeling Bored (Do you ever feel that "there's nothing to do"?)		
0 Often	51	313
1	43	619
2	40	246
3 Never	38	78
Attitude Toward the Law: (It is all right to get around the law if you can get away with it.)		
0 Strongly agree	41	49
1	45	93
2	29	219
3	15	493
4 Strongly disagree	9	426
Lack of Self-Control (I can't seem to stay out of trouble no matter how hard I try.)		
0 Strongly agree	63	46
1	66	104
2	49	176
3	44	621
4 Strongly disagree	25	251
Respect for Authority (I have a lot of respect for the police.)		
0 Strongly agree	45	89
1	33	98
2	22	325
3	13	496
4 Strongly disagree	12	273

From Hirschi, 1969

Overall, the correlates were highly consistent with the image of delinquents provided by *Unraveling*: energetic and easily bored, mesomorphic, below average in verbal aptitude, lacking in self-control, exhibiting a generalized violation of age-based norms, and having dislike for school, poor family relations, poor parental supervision, procriminal and antiauthority attitudes, weak conventional ambitions, and delinquent associates. The importance of the near identical pattern of results in the two studies cannot be overemphasized. Critics of the Glueck findings noted that they reflected the correlates of frequent and serious crime committed by serious criminals, and hence were not of general significance. Critics of the Hirschi findings noted that they reflected the correlates of minor and trivial antisocial acts committed by schoolchildren, and hence were not of general significance. Unless you are not all interested in individual differences in youthful crime, these strikingly similar findings from two dramatically different studies are impressive.

As we shall soon see, however, Hirschi's four-factor theory places an overemphasis on ties to convention, an underemphasis on ties to crime (only antisocial attitudes are included and antisocial associates are excluded) and relegates the temperamental/personality variables such as self-control, taste for adventure, and aggressivity to background factors with unspecified linkages with ties to either crime or convention.

Recent Variations on Psychodynamic Themes

In 1990, in collaboration with Michael Gottfredson (Gottfredson & Hirschi, 1990), Travis Hirschi have returned once again to basic psychodynamic principles (the Glueck work is cited, but Freud is not mentioned at all). Ties to convention are minimized and procriminal attitudes are minimized; what is emphasized is what Freud called psychological maturity, that is, self-control or the ability to avoid the temptations of the moment. Gottfredson and Hirschi's (1990) "general theory of crime" suggests that low self-control is the personality variable that accounts for stable individual differences in criminal behavior. They flirted with the construct of "criminality," but felt that the word connoted compulsion rather than lack of restraint. They also considered the construct "conscience," but decided that "conscience" was too connected to the notion of compulsive conformity (in Freudian theory, it is the construct of ego-ideal, not conscience, that connects with allegiance to "doing good"). More generally, on several occasions they note their discomfort with constructs such as "aggressivity" or "psychopathy."

It is fascinating to read how Gottfredson and Hirschi dealt with what has always been the most serious problem in psychodynamic (and behavioral) perspectives on crime: Is there a single construct underlying the undeniable predictive validity of the set of personality variables identified, for example, by Glueck and Glueck (1950) and reviewed in the personality section of Chapter 2? If there is, what is it? Can it be assessed in a manner independent of assessments of the criterion of criminal behavior and, more generally, how can we best measure it? If there is not a single construct that will serve the function of capturing "psychological immaturity" or "psychopathy" or "weak ego/weak superego," how many different constructs are involved and how do we best assess them?

Gottfredson and Hirschi took on this task in a brave and somewhat innovative manner. The least innovative, but still courageous, aspect of their approach is that they actually make a choice and declare that there is only one construct: "self-control." The choice of the term "self-control" is a brave one because the task of describing the construct and building a single-assessment approach that would tap it in a reliable and valid manner represents a major unresolved set of problems in psychology to this day (cf. Webster & Jackson, 1997). Innovatively, perhaps, they purport to derive the elements of self-control directly from the nature of criminal acts. Interestingly, too, a majority of elements of their self-control construct coincide with some of the empirically best established correlates of criminal conduct.

The elements of their construct of low self-control are as follows:

1. The tendency not to defer immediate gratification. They speak of a "tendency" rather than an "ability." Hence, they appear willing to operationalize this element of self-control by assessments of a behavioral history of deferment as opposed to an analysis of the process of deferment. The link with criminal acts is said to be the fact that criminal acts provide immediate gratification.

2. The tendency to lack diligence, tenacity, or persistence in a course of action. Once again, behavioral history rather than an analysis of process (in this case, of conscientiousness) is suggested to be sufficient for assessment of an element of self-control. The link with criminal acts is said to be the fact that criminal acts provide easy/simple gratification of desires.

3. Tending to be adventuresome, active, and physical (as opposed to cautious, cognitive, and verbal). Criminal acts are described as exciting, risky, or thrilling.

4. A history of unstable commitments to work, marriage, family, and friends. We think shortsightedness is being referred to here, but once again it appears that the construct is assessed through behavioral history rather than directly. In order to link these aspects of behavioral history with criminal acts, criminal acts are said to provide few or meager long-term benefits.

5. Minimal cognitive, academic, and manual skill, and devaluation of cognitive, academic, and manual skill. Criminal acts are said to require little skill or planning.

6. Being self-centered and indifferent or insensitive to the suffering and needs of others. This is said to link with criminal acts because criminal acts are antisocial acts (i.e., harmful to others).

There are a number of interesting issues here. First, although this was an opportunity to introduce antisocial attitudes, values, and beliefs as a trait, Gottfredson and Hirschi chose not to do so. Rather, they chose to work with the constructs of empathy and egocentrism. Interestingly, they entered one of the ongoing debates in psychology: in brief, to what extent are the constructs of egocentrism, callousness, and emotional empathy in any sense overlapping? Also interesting is that Gottfredson and Hirschi were careful to qualify this element of low self-control by noting that people with low self-control may well be charming and generous because they have learned how easily such behavior generates rewards. This qualification recalls ongoing debates regarding the defining elements of psychopathy, that is, dealing with the fact that some offenders are interpersonally "nice" and some are "not nice."

The above-noted six factors appear to be the defining elements of Gottfredson and Hirschi's (1990) construct of self-control. In a summary statement (p. 90), they characterize people with low self-control as impulsive (#1 above), insensitive (#6), risk-taking (#3), shortsighted (#4, we think), physical as opposed to mental (#3 and/or #5, perhaps), and nonverbal (#3 and #5 again, perhaps). Within our understanding of the elements of their construct of self-control and their summary of that construct, Element #2 (conscientiousness) does not even appear in their summary statement, and there is ambiguity with regard to what traits fit within which categories. This, of course, is the classic problem that personality-oriented researchers and theorists have always faced.

A major source of variation in self-control suggested by Gottfredson and Hirschi is ineffective child-rearing. Indicators of ineffectiveness follow the Glueck research findings and "tentative causal formula" to a close degree: weak attachment of parent to child, poor parental supervision, poor conduct standards (parents' failure to recognize deviance), and ineffective punishment. The authors of the general theory recognize, like Glueck and Glueck, that not all children are equally lovable or equally subject to supervision, but they leave individual differences of the temperamental/constitutional variety an open question.

In this first statement of their general theory, Gottfredson and Hirschi (1990) did not present original research. Nor did they review the psychological literature on the construct of self-control, the assessment of self-control, or even the links between assessments of self-control and criminal conduct. Thus, the conceptual and measurement problems noted in our outline of their elements of self-control have yet to be faced. They did make it clear, however, that the massive body of empirical research on personality (Chapter 2) is consistent with their theory but does not meet their standards of relevant evidence. In particular, they are concerned that some of the personality measures (e.g., socialization and psychopathy scales) reflect content that directly samples a history of antisocial conduct (see Chapter 2). They are not yet ready to suggest that early and diverse misconduct is a theoretically meaningful construct in the forecasting of a criminal future.

We have already seen that assessments of antisocial personality pattern were among the strongest of risk factors in several meta-analyses (Chapter 2). Directly relevant to low self-control theory, Travis Pratt and Francis T. Cullen (2000) revealed meta-analytically not only that antisocial attitudes and antisocial associates were risk factors in addition to low self-control but that they made incremental contributions to the prediction of criminal behavior. The effect size (correlation coefficient) was .44 with only indicators of low self-control entering the prediction formula but increased to .59 with the addition of antisocial attitudes and antisocial associates. In regard to the theory being "general," the measures of low self-control correlated with the delinquency of males and females, the younger and older, general samples and offender samples, and with both delinquent and nondelinquent antisocial behavior.

Perhaps the most highly developed of the new generation of psychodynamic theories of crime is that of Marc LeBlanc, Marc Ouimet, and Richard Tremblay (1988) and others at the University of Montreal. This model attempts to integrate Hirschi's control theory with psychodynamic theory. It does this by taking personality seriously. The model includes four major sets of variables called Social Ties, Adolescent Role, Social Constraints, and Psychological Functioning. Social Class is a background variable that may impact through Social Ties and Psychological Functioning, and Sex is an additional variable that may impact on delinquency directly or through one of four major sets of variables.

The particular variables within each set are as follows:

1. Social Ties: (a) attachment to parents and other authority figures, and (b) involvement in school, work, church, and so on.

2. Social Constraints: (a) external, relating to supervision and control from parents and school, and (b) internal, relating to adhesion to norms, risk-taking, and neutralization.

3. Adolescent Role: (a) school adaptation, and (b) delinquent peers.

4. Psychological Functioning: (a) social maladjustment, (b) aggression, (c) insecurity/alienation, and (d) psychoticism (Eysenck's measure).

The content of the first three sets is obvious from our previous discussions, even though we would prefer to see antisocial/procriminal attitudes (which, in the University of Montreal system, is part of Social Constraints) and antisocial/procriminal associates (Adolescent Role) examined on their own in relation to criminal conduct. As the Montreal perspective now stands, the contribution of antisocial attitudes to the prediction of crime is potentially confounded with the contribution of parenting variables, and the contribution of antisocial peers is potentially confounded with adjustment to school. Antisocial attitudes and antisocial associates are more meaningfully treated as theoretically distinct variables that are correlated. When social learning perspectives are reviewed in the next chapter, it becomes clear that almost every study that has included measures of both attitudes and associates has found them to be among the strongest correlates of criminal behavior (challenged only by assessments of the types of personality measures reviewed in Chapter 2 and suggested by the Freudian and Glueck theories). The issue of personality is explored here.

LeBlanc et al. (1988) use the term "egocentric personality" to best capture the essence of what they mean by a personality-based predisposition for delinquency. The Montreal scholars are working in the psychodynamic tradition and are not referring to simple emotional skills or interests. Rather, they are referring to psychic development from the more primitive to the more rich. Second, they are drawing directly upon prior research that links personality and crime. This research directs attention to an insensitivity to conventional rules (low socialization) as opposed to an insensitivity to people (low emotional empathy).

LeBlanc et al. (1988) describe the egocentric personality as a combination of four traits. First, "social maladjustment" (measured with the Jesness Inventory) refers to difficulty coping with the demands and constraints of social life. The second core trait they linked with egocentricity was "negativeness" or a hostile attitude toward others. Their measure for this was Manifest Aggression from the Jesness Inventory (which is clearly consistent with the aggressiveness and hostility described by Glueck and Glueck). Third, "insecurity" reflects malaise and strong feelings of discomfort. This was measured with the Alienation scale from the Jesness Inventory, which taps feelings of resentment and anger and which should not be confused with measures of anxiety, depression, or powerlessness that do not involve acting out. Finally, "primitivity" is described as a rudimentary manner of functioning with a strong priority given to personal needs (measured with the Eysenck Psychoticism scale).

The elements of the model are linked to criminal conduct as indicated in Figure 3.2, where Social Constraints and Adolescent Role are represented as the most immediate "causes" of crime. Findings from their cross-sectional and longitudinal studies with two different sets of Montreal boys and girls (aged 12-16) supported the overall perspective. With multiple correlations hovering above .70, delinquency was most strongly and consistently linked with the sets predicted to be most directly relevant, while psychological functioning tended also to make an incremental contribution to the prediction of delinquency.

Yet another integration of psychodynamic and control theory has appeared recently in the form of Anita Mak's (1990, 1991, 1996) psychosocial control theory. Mak, like Hirschi himself (Gottfredson & Hirschi, 1990), thought that Hirschi's (1969) control theory overemphasized ties to convention and neglected the personal control variables of impulsiveness and empathy.

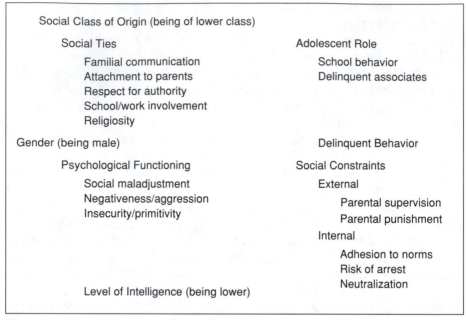

Figure 3.2
Integrative Psychodynamic and Control Theory

From LeBlanc, Ouimet & Tremblay, 1988

For Mak, a more complete account of delinquency could not be accomplished without a consideration of individual differences in thinking through consequences, a preference for immediate gratification, poor planning, and a lack of patience. While not cited by Mak (1990), this constellation of traits recalls the temperament/personality variables that Glueck and Glueck (1950) linked to persistent and serious delinquency, and it introduces one element that Gottfredson and Hirschi (1990) think needs a reintroduction into control theory.

In a cross-sectional survey of nearly 800 Australian high school students, Mak (1990) indeed found that the Eysenck and Eysenck (1978b) measure of impulsiveness was a correlate of delinquency. The correlation with delinquency was approximately .50 (males and females together). The only variable to outperform impulsiveness was Mak's measure of antisocial attitudes, which tapped the young people's perceptions of the seriousness of delinquent acts (the correlation was .62). Combining these two key variables from the psychodynamic perspective yielded an R square of .45. The R square increased to .51 with the addition of age, gender, attachment to school, and broken home variables, but nearly 50 percent of the explained variance was attributable to impulsivity and antisocial attitudes.

The findings for empathy (assessed with the Eysenck measure) were far less positive. Empathy was not reliably associated with delinquent behavior. If there are substantial effects of empathy, they may reside in interactions with other variables. Emotional empathy, we think, is not the risk factor; rather, it is egocentricism and callous disregard for others.

Summary to This Point

The psychodynamic perspective has been promising for criminology from its beginnings in Freudian psychoanalytic theory. The underlying model of human nature fits well the task of explaining antisocial behavior. The classic research of Glueck and Glueck (1950) was our starting point for systematic empirical explorations of psychodynamic theory and subsequent refinements of psychodynamic conceptions of criminal conduct. The psychoanalytic perspective is so broad and diverse that it affords a large variety of reasonable routes to persistent criminal conduct. The most obvious routes are weak internal controls (in terms of ego and superego functioning), which in Freudian theory are directly linked to family process and parenting.

Sheldon Glueck and Eleanor Glueck attended to these concerns and conducted a comprehensive survey of additional variables suggested by the biological, human, and social sciences of their day. Their findings were strong and clear. The major correlates of persistent and serious delinquency were antisocial attitudes, antisocial associates, a complex set of indicators of an antisocial personality pattern (restless energy, aggressiveness, impulsivity, callousness), a set of problematic family conditions (psychologically disadvantaged parents, weak affection, poor parenting, structural instability), and problematic circumstances in school and the broader community. These variables functioned well relative to financial and scholastic worries, indicators of personal distress, and culture conflict or feelings of helplessness. They developed a tentative causal formula that was dismissed and/or denied by much of mainstream sociological criminology (see the account Sampson & Laub, 1990), but was carefully read by Travis Hirschi.

Hirschi (1969) offered a milder, more "socialized" statement of the Glueck theory by emphasizing ties to convention (that is, crime reflects weak attachment to conventional others, institutions, and pursuits). He maintained the causal status of "antisocial attitudes" but, just as Glueck and Glueck had done, he hesitated to offer causal status to "antisocial associates." Hirschi then moved (Gottfredson & Hirschi, 1990) toward emphasizing the self-control element of Glueck and Glueck's complex of personality, downplaying what was the strongest correlate in his 1969 theory (belief in the validity of the law). Other researchers are retaining causal status for antisocial attitudes, the personality complex, the bonding set (family in particular), and antisocial associates. The importance of associates is examined in the next section, in which additional contributions of psychodynamic theory are found.

Toward Social Learning via Frustration–Aggression, Class–Based, and Differential Association Theory

From Freud to Social Learning: Frustration–Aggression

A recurring theme in the psychology of crime has been the frustration-aggression hypothesis. At first, Freud's hypothesis was integrated with radical behavior theory and the conditioning models of socialization. Subsequently, the principles of observational learning and the cognitive models of self-control were incorporated. In these later models, the frustration-aggression link is still evident but no longer dominant. What has emerged is a model of human behavior that appreciates human diversity and complexity and that includes an active, organizing individual.

The beginning of modern conceptions of aggression and criminality can be dated to 1939 at Yale with the publication of *Frustration and Aggression*, by Dollard, Doob, Miller, Mowrer, and Sears. These psychologists and sociologists linked Freudian concepts with the methods and concepts of an emerging behavioral perspective on human behavior:

1. Aggression is always a consequence of frustration. All aggression is preceded by frustration, and frustration is always followed by some form of aggression.

    Frustration is interference with a behavior sequence that has a valued goal-response.

    Aggression is an act that has the goal of injuring another person.

2. The strength of instigation to aggression (i.e., the amount of frustration) increases with:

    a)   the strength of instigation to the frustrated response;

    b)   the degree of interference with the frustrated response;

    c)   the number of frustrations.

3. The strength of inhibition of any act of aggression increases with the amount of punishment anticipated as a consequence of that act.

4. The instigation to aggress is strongest against the agent perceived to be responsible for the frustration.

5. The greater the degree of inhibition specific to the frustrating agent, the more probable the occurrence of indirect aggression and/or displaced aggression.

6. The occurrence of an aggressive act is followed by a temporary reduction in the instigation to aggress (catharsis).

Dollard and his colleagues were well aware of the many problems associated with the state of knowledge in criminology in the 1930s. However, upon reviewing that knowledge base, they proposed that the frustration-aggression hypothesis could account for the majority of "facts" regarding criminal behavior. They viewed the correlates of criminality as indicators of frustration and/or as indicators of the inhibitors of criminal behavior. The frustration-aggression hypothesis also had a major influence in the development of social learning theory.

The Rise of Social Learning Theory

In 1962, Berkowitz published a major update and revision of the frustration-aggression hypothesis called *Aggression: A Social Psychological Analysis*. The work reflected the tremendous amount of research that had been conducted in the quarter century since the publication of the original Yale monograph. Most notable was the introduction of more sophisticated learning principles, the introduction of cognitive-emotional mediators, and the increased attention paid to the concept of aggressive personalities.

For Berkowitz (1962), and for Buss (1966), there is an important distinction between instrumental aggression and angry aggression. Instrumental aggression is aggression primarily oriented toward some goal other than doing injury (e.g., the acquisition of money as a goal of armed robbery). The learning of instrumental aggression follows the principles of operant conditioning. On the other hand, angry aggression is a response to a specific frustration, and the goal is injury.

A frustration creates a predisposition to aggression by arousing anger. Anger is a drive that leads to drive-specific behaviors (i.e., aggression) in the presence of appropriate cues or releasers. A person displays violence if anger is high and/or if violent behavior has been reinforced in the past. The aggressive person has learned to interpret a wide variety of persons and situations as threatening or frustrating and has learned habits of aggression to these cues.

The aggressive personality will differ from less aggressive people in the following ways:

1. The number and variety of events defined as a threat and that arouse anger.

2. The level of affective-physiological arousal, and the cognitions supportive or not supportive of violence.

3. The specific forms of aggressive behavior that have been rein-forced in the past, and the availability of alternative nonaggres-sive responses.

This model, which we have only sketched here, is the basis for treatment programs that target the control of anger (e.g., Novaco, 1975).

Megargee's Algebra of Aggression

Megargee (1982) provided a framework that incorporates the vast majority of the elements of current psychological research on aggression and criminality. The variables associated with criminal violence are represented within the following broad categories:

1. Instigation to aggression (A). The sum of all internal motivators. Some examples are personal gains such as money, anger in response to frustration, and jealousy.

2. Habit Strength (H). Behavioral preferences learned by rewarded experience and observation.

3. Inhibitions against aggression (I). The sum of all internal factors opposing an aggressive act, including conditioned fear of pun-ishment, learned attitudes and values, and identification with the victim.

4. Stimulus factors in the immediate environment that may facili-tate (S_a) or inhibit (S_i) violence.

5. Response competition. Other possible responses are subject to their own algebra and nonaggressive responses may have a more favorable cost-benefit ratio than the aggressive response.

The occurrence of an aggressive act, then, depends upon the following formula:

$$A + H + S_a > I + S_i$$

Stated differently, the motivational factors must outweigh the inhibitory factors.

We have traced the evolution of psychological thought through the development of the Freudian hypothesis of frustration-aggression. The links with Freud remained clear in the early behavioral reformulations. However, as general psychology was influenced by radical behaviorism and highly cognitive social learning theories, aggression and criminality were increasingly seen to be complex functions of facilitators, inhibitors, prior learning, and the immediate situation. This appreciation of human diversity and complexity contrasts dramatically with the class-based sociological theories of criminal conduct.

Class–Based Sociological Theory: Social Location, Social Reaction, and Inequality

In Chapters 1 and 2, we showed examples of antipsychological bias in mainstream sociological criminology. To understand the professional roots of this bias, it helps to appreciate that in the 1930s and 1940s, psychiatry, psychology, and, in particular, psychoanalytic thought were dominant, while the fledging discipline of sociology was struggling to find a unique voice and some recognition. We have seen how the Yale school (Dollard et al., 1939) accepted the challenge by trying to build a general psychology of human behavior that was not only informed by psychoanalytic and sociological thought but that would serve the interests of all human and social science. The approach was different at Columbia and Chicago. In the Chicago tradition, as will be seen later in this chapter, Edwin Sutherland chose the symbolic interactionism of George Herbert Mead over Freudian theory, developed the strong cultural tradition at Chicago, and turned his theory of differential association into a framework that glorified sociology and sociological contributions to criminology. Things were also different at Columbia, where Robert Merton helped create an independent sociology by adopting aspects of Durkheim's anomie theory and by turning psychoanalytic assumptions "on their head." With the rise of labeling and conflict/Marxist perspectives in the 1960s and 1970s, not only were psychology and human diversity denied but systematic empirical research itself became suspect.

The class-based sociological perspectives on delinquency and crime entail anomie/strain theory, subcultural theory, labeling theory, and conflict/Marxist theory. These theories, in their social psychological versions, each purport that social class of origin is a major source of variation in illegal conduct at the individual level. The research evidence (as reviewed in Chapter 2) has shown that such an assumption is empirically indefensible in that class of origin is at best a minor risk factor. None of the class-based sociological theories are capable of providing images of crime and offenders that can even begin to approach the predictive validity of the psychodynamic and general personality and social psychological models (recall Chapter 2 and Glueck & Glueck, 1950; Hirschi, 1969; Johnson, 1979; Mak, 1990; Tittle, Villimez & Smith, 1978).

Remaining open to new evidence, it must be stressed that several of the class-based theories are so poorly specified that ideological commitments are bound to remain powerful. For example, some statements of anomie/strain theory suggest simultaneously that (a) too much conventional ambition causes crime, (b) too little conventional ambition causes crime, (c) frustrated conventional ambition causes crime, and (d) conventional success may produce uncontrolled conventional ambition (and greed, in turn, causes crime). In other words, there is no way that any finding regarding conventional ambition, conventional success, or conventional failure does not relate to crime in a way that may be supported by anomie theory. Indeed, revisions of anomie theory are now appearing in which individual differences of the psychodynamic variety are being reformulated as "socially structured inequality" in the distribution of psychological resources (e.g., Passas & Agnew, 1997; Vold & Bernard, 1986). For all of this, the fact remains that social class of origin is a distal and minor correlate of crime and delinquency.

It is valuable to review these theories because they did contribute to the research that ultimately brought them down. Moreover, they should be reviewed so that we may avoid inadvertently starting down the same roads in the future. Some of the ideas are powerful and attractive, and the theories themselves may even have some causal significance in studies of aggregated crime rates and criminal justice processing. Most importantly, however, the descriptions of the content of subculture that came out of subcultural theory have proved to be quite valuable in the specification of personal attitudes, values, and beliefs supportive of criminal activity.

Anomie/Strain Theory

According to Robert Merton (1938, 1957), social structures exert a pressure upon certain persons to engage in deviant behavior. This text includes examples of the fact that certain social structures are indeed criminogenic. The core assumption of Merton's theory, however, was that lower-class persons were more likely to engage in criminal behavior than middle- and upper-class persons. Thus, position in the socioeconomic system (that is, social location) was said to account for a major portion of variability in criminal behavior. Social location could be assessed by parental education, occupation, and income, as well as by the socioeconomic characteristics of neighborhoods.

Deviant behavior occurs when conventional aspirations exceed the levels of achievement that are possible by way of legitimate behavior. In America, the dominant aspiration to which all people are socialized (or which people come to share) was said to be "success" (money, property, and prestige). Anyone can grow up to be President and the legitimate route to success is working hard in school and on the job. The power of this aspect of the theory is clear because it is nothing less than the "American dream." Counter to the dream, however, is the fact that access to the conventional routes to success is blocked for many members of the lower class. Thus, criminal behavior was conceptualized as an innovative route to the same rewards that conventional employment would bring if only legitimate channels were available.

Here is where Merton turned psychoanalytic images of crime and criminals upside down and provided sociology with a socialized theory of crime. Crime was not the unsocialized expression of unbridled sexual-aggressive energy but rather an expression of socialized conventional ambition. Offenders were not "deviants" but "innovators."

The notions of anomie and strain enter as mediating variables between the disjunction of legitimate means and the pursuit of illegitimate means. Merton reformulated psychoanalytic thought in sociologically acceptable ways. We have already discussed the frustration-aggression hypothesis wherein anger is a primary psychological mediator between frustration and aggression. For traditional strain theorists, the psychological mediator is anomie (i.e., feelings of alienation). Thus, it is not anger, hate, resentment, defiance, the search for adventure, or even too much conventional ambition (greed) that causes criminal activity. Rather, criminal behavior reflects awareness of limited opportunity and feelings of alienation, isolation, powerlessness, normlessness, and personal distress.

Strain or personal distress theories are not unknown in psychology, and a few of the psychodynamic routes to crime explicitly involved personal distress (recall the Freudian types of offenders earlier in this chapter). Since Glueck and Glueck (1950), however, the emphasis has been on ego and superego functions. Psychology also has self-esteem and mental health perspectives that attend to feelings of self-worth, anxiety, depression, and such, but to our knowledge, none of these perspectives have ever approached the status of an empirically defensible theory of criminal conduct. Generally, in psychodynamic and social psychological theory, feelings of low self-esteem, worry, depression, helplessness, and so forth, decrease rather than increase the chances of aggressive pursuit of self-interest (recall the Glueck finding). Indeed, the differential effects of anger and other negative emotional states (e.g., depressed, insecure, worried, disappointed) were clear in a self-report study of undergraduates by Lisa Broidy (2001). In this study, anger was associated with increased criminal behavior while other negative emotional states were associated with less criminal behavior.

Interestingly, Merton suggested that there were different modes of adaptation to anomie and that innovation (i.e., crime) was only one such mode. Here too, Merton drew upon the frustration-aggression hypothesis. The other adaptations to limited opportunities were retreatism (mental disorder and substance abuse among the real "down and out" of society), rebellion (attempts to create a new social order on the part of the more able and intellectual within the lower class), and ritualism (the mindless grinding away of the working poor who have transferred the dream to that of their children "making it"). No matter how questionable the underlying psychology and no matter how potentially offensive the image of the poor (drunks, drug addicts, criminals, the mentally disordered, mindless ritualists), anomie theory is a politically powerful statement that has fascinated social scientists and the public for years.

In summary, anomie/strain theory attempted to rid criminal motivation and criminals of all that "rude psychoanalytic stuff." Psychologically, a social location translation of frustration-aggression theory homogenized the abilities and diversity of human beings and created a banal image of the person. Not surprisingly, even with the connections to social class weakened, anomie theory is empirically indefensible as a general theory of criminal conduct. Consider the following study conducted by Johnson (1979).

Johnson (1979) administered a self-report, paper-and-pencil questionnaire to 734 tenth-grade students in three schools situated in lower-class (but not slum) areas of Seattle, Washington. Slum areas were not sampled because Johnson could not find any in Seattle and because he was aware that little could be expected from simple measures of parental education and occupational status. Johnson took a number of steps toward a more powerful conceptualization and measurement of social origins by defining the "underclass" in terms of below-average income, any unemployment, having been on welfare, and having less than a college education. Contrast this notion of the "underclass" with Glueck and Glueck's (1950) notion of a "negative biosocial legacy," specifically intergenerational mental retardation, psychopathology, alcoholism, criminality, and intergenerational reliance upon social service and welfare agencies.

Johnson set up a causal chain in which underclass membership was to impact on delinquency through negative associations with love/concern of parent for child, success in school, and attachment to parents. Initially, Johnson accepted as empirically well-established the link between underclass membership and problems in school and listed a number of possible reasons for such a link. The possible, but unmeasured, reasons include low intelligence, poor academic aptitude, social incompetence, attitudes unfavorable to progress in school, low achievement motivation, deficits in specific skills relevant to school success, and the middle-class bias of the school system. Note that 30 years after Glueck and Glueck's *Unraveling Juvenile Delinquency* (1950) demonstrated the relative power of direct assessments of a negative "biosocial legacy" and its products, sociologists continued to assume that socioeconomic indicators provide a satisfactory proxy.

Similarly, Johnson (1979) listed the many reasons why one may expect a link between class and family relations, which in turn would mediate a class-delinquency link. These were: underclass parents are unable to inspire the respect, love, or concern of their offspring; they are incapable of offering their children love and supervision; they make excessive use of physical punishment; and they do not have the time to invest in the child's need for self-esteem. We can see that a rather negative view of the socioeconomically disadvantaged was still alive in sociology in the late 1970s.

Johnson found that underclass membership was unrelated to delinquency either directly or through the paths of family relations, school performance, and attachment to school. Similarly, underclass membership
was unrelated to several complex measures of future-oriented occupational strain. There was one minor exception: an educational aspirations-
achievement discrepancy was slightly greater for underclass young people. Overall, Johnson delivered multiple blows to the validity of anomie
theory:

1. A class-crime link was not found;

2. Class did not link with strain;

3. Worrying about a future occupation was positively (not negatively)
   associated with school attachment;

4. High educational aspirations were negatively (not positively)
   associated with delinquency, and were so correlated whether educational expectations were low or high.

Robert Agnew (1992) severed the ties of anomie theory to the political and professional ideology surrounding social class; replaced the
structural anomie-alienation-innovation path with the original psychodynamic, social-learning path of frustration-anger-aggression; and rela-
beled the now massive evidence regarding the link between crime and difficulties at home, school, and work as indicators of a strain-crime link.
He appears to have adopted what we call a general personality and
social psychological perspective that has virtually nothing to do with traditional strain/anomie theory. Agnew calls his perspective General
Strain Theory (GST) and the sources of negative affect (that is, anger
rather than alienation) extend well beyond an aspiration-achievement discrepancy in the arena of conventional success.

The work on GST by Robert Agnew and his colleagues and students
has brought a new energy to the annual meetings of the American Society of Criminology, at which many new directions are being explored. For
example, the multiple potential motives for crime are being explored
(Agnew, 1995): (a) moral evaluations of crime (unconditional approval as
in "theft is not that wrong," conditional approval as in "a hungry person
has the right to steal," moral imperative as in "people who disrespect me
must be hurt"; (b) systematic review of the multiple potential rewards and
costs; and (c) negative affect (cognitive-emotional states with an emphasis on anger). With GST, anomie theory is no longer anomie theory but
a general social psychology of criminal behavior with a particular interest in negative affect. The multiple findings from the general psychology of aggression are being brought into mainstream criminology in a
strong manner.

Studies of recidivism from correctional psychology (Zamble & Quinsey, 1997) and forensic mental health facilities (Quinsey et al., 1997) are revealing that proximal indicators of negative emotionality upon discharge from a prison or hospital may greatly enhance the predictability of criminal recidivism. General Strain Theory, as a general social learning perspective, may both gain empirical status and inform practical parole, probation, and relapse prevention programming.

Other developments are apparent. Scott Menard (1995) provided a vigorous retest of Mertonian anomie theory and concluded that his findings, based on a careful reading of Robert Merton, support anomie theory. Menard suggested that more careful attention should be afforded individual responses (modes of adaptation) to blocked opportunities. According to Menard, most tests of anomie theory measure variation in acceptance of cultural goals (conventional success is valued) and then measure acceptance of legitimate means as a route to those goals. The traditional notion is that innovation (crime) is a function of goal acceptance in combination with low expectations for the success of legitimate means. The results of traditional tests of anomie did not support the theory and, according to Menard, there was no reason to expect support.

Rather, suggested Menard (1995), the aspirations-opportunities discrepancy exists at the structural level in Merton's theory. At the social psychological (individual) level of analysis, meaningful individual differences in modes of adaptation should be assessed by attention to aspirations and acceptance not of legitimate routes but of illegitimate routes. Thus, in a large sample of adolescents ages 11 to 17 years, one question posed was "How important is it to you to have a good job or career after you have finished?" (very important versus somewhat important versus not important at all). This was the measure of aspirations. The second question asked how wrong it was to commit a variety of delinquent acts (very wrong or wrong for all acts versus a little bit wrong or not wrong at all for one or more acts).

With this assessment approach, the innovators (high aspiration/not wrong to commit delinquent acts) and the retreatists/rebels (low aspiration/not wrong to commit delinquent acts) self-reported more delinquent acts than did the conformists and the ritualists, who thought it was wrong to commit delinquent acts. This is no surprise. The importance of antisocial attitudes, values, and beliefs in the prediction of delinquency is well established. If Scott Menard's interpretation of Merton on modes of adaptation becomes widely accepted, then the uniqueness of Merton's anomie theory is greatly reduced and it is no longer apparent that Robert Merton turned Freudian theory upside down. Rather, it appears that the motivation for crime is no longer conventional but clearly anti-conventional even in Merton. Glueck and Glueck in 1950 had shown the world that antisocial cognition was strongly associated with delinquency, and that has been replicated and/or extended in virtually every study of antisocial attitudes ever conducted (recall the meta-analyses in Chapter 2). We are now asked to believe that anomie theory of 1938 really meant that the motivation for crime was not conventional but explicitly anti-conventional.

We think we can predict the next step in Menard's analysis: now that antisocial attitudes are in, bring in antisocial associates, then an early history of antisocial behavior, and then (if he dares) antisocial personality. Why stop with the "Big Four"? If Menard really wants to rescue anomie theory, he should look beyond class, gender, and school achievement and bring in quality of parenting. Over and over again, the social location theories are being rewritten to render them consistent with risk factors identified in psychodynamic theory.

Sociologists were aware of problems with anomie theory well before Agnew's (1992) and Menard's (1995) return to a more informed social psychology. In the early years, the response was to embrace subcultural theory and the idea that criminal behavior was conformity to the norms and values in opposition to mainstream, middle-class society. Furthermore, these deviant norms and values were shared mainly by the disenfranchised segments of society. Thus, our review of subcultural theory proceeds in two steps. First, the sociological (and antipsychological) elements of subcultural theory are underscored because one of the professional functions of these theories was to promote sociology. Second, the subcultural theories are reviewed from the perspective of a social psychology and, from this vantage, we find a gold mine for the psychology of criminal conduct.

Subcultural Perspectives in the Bold Sociological Mode

Subcultural theorists spoke primarily of young, urban, lower-class men who conformed to the urban, lower-class culture in which they were located. This culture devalued conventional routes to success and valued hedonism and destruction. Merton's people were not allowed to be "deviant," but at least they were allowed to "innovate." Within subcultural theory, though, criminal behavior is conformity. Stealing was conforming with the criminal subculture, doing drugs was conforming to the retreatist subculture, and fighting was conforming to the conflict subculture. The nonconformists in the deviant subculture (the nonoffenders) were the real deviants.

Matza (1964) was among those social scientists who became concerned that subcultural theories were: (1) overpredicting delinquency among the young lower-class males, and (2) not even attempting to account for the delinquency of occupants of other social positions. In addition, it was clear that the delinquent cultures were difficult to identify except by examining personal attitudes and personal behavior. One obvious solution to this problem was to give credit to personal attitudes and values. Instead, however, it was hypothesized that there was a "subculture of delinquency" not bound by the limits of geography, age, sex, race, or class. Therefore, we are all surrounded by a subculture of delinquency.

Why then are there individual differences in criminal behavior? Matza provided a vague answer. He refers to an "impetus" that realizes the criminal act. This impetus comes from being pushed around, which then leads to a mood of fatalism and a feeling of desperation. Not everyone is exposed to and affected by this impetus, but for those affected, engaging in delinquent behavior serves to overcome these feelings and provide a sense of control and power. Matza warns us, however, not to test his ideas because the subcultural delinquent is no different from other boys. Indeed, he says, the lack of a difference between delinquent and nondelinquent persons is "precisely the point" of his theory. (We thank Hirschi, 1969, for underscoring Matza's point—this theory actually makes its empirical untestability a point of pride.)

Labeling and Marxist Perspectives in the Bold Sociological Mode

As if the denial of human diversity apart from social location was not sufficiently dehumanizing, the labeling theorists (Becker, 1963; Schur, 1973) even denied people their criminal behavior. "Criminal" was not an aspect of the behavior of people but a status conferred upon the actor by the more powerful. Indeed, there are no "true criminals" beyond those created by the criminal justice system. These "true criminals" were allowed a criminal sense of self, but that self grew out of their interaction with the official control agents of the state.

The powerful make criminals of the less powerful in three ways. First, they set the rules that, when violated, may result in official processing. Second, we all engage in rule-violating behavior ("primary deviance"), but it is the less powerful among us who are selected for official processing. Thus, social location—as indexed by age, race, gender, and class—causes social reaction (i.e., processing). Third, social reaction sets up stigmatization and other social psychological processes that produce people with criminal attitudes, values, and beliefs, who then engage in "true crime" ("secondary deviance"). Thus, it is societal reaction that causes persistent and serious crime.

The psychology of criminal conduct (PCC) has no difficulty with the notion that variation in social reaction (criminal justice processing and correctional treatment) may be associated with criminal recidivism. Why would treatment not have effects if "processing" affects criminogenic factors that are functionally related to future criminal conduct? But why would these effects necessarily be negative (see the treatment section of Chapter 2 and Chapter 10) when "processing" is far from uniform?

According to labeling theory, the powerful create criminals because it serves their interests. A minor variation on the labeling theme was introduced by the Marxist and conflict theorists. In this variation, the social locations of the "criminals" and the "victims" are reversed. The powerful are the criminals and the less powerful are the victims. These theorists look to statistics that show that more people die under the knives of surgeons than by stabbings on the street (e.g., Reiman, 1979). In addition, we are exposed to daily newspaper clippings that reveal the evils of the ruling classes. These evils include the Ford Pinto, the Corvair, breast implants, the Love Canal, and the sale of infant formula to populations with contaminated water supplies (e.g., Henry, 1986). It appears that the conflict theorists have been shocked to discover that accidents cause harm and that antisocial behavior is not limited to the lower classes. (However, they still say that all crime is to be understood as a reflection of capitalism.)

The psychology underlying the bold outlines of class-based theories reveals contempt for human diversity and contempt for the complexity of human behavior. The social locationists were only minimally interested in the criminal behavior of individuals. They were primarily interested in promoting their visions and building an ideologically and professionally acceptable social theory (Andrews & Wormith, 1989).

Uncovering Social Psychological Value in Sociological Criminology

To cut through the ideology and professional rhetoric that has infused discussions of theory in many mainstream criminological textbooks of the past, we will accept these theories as social psychologies and ignore the rhetoric around social class and culture. We are not particularly interested in how subcultures develop (blocked opportunities are claimed to be the cause). Our interest is in whether membership in certain socially or ecologically defined groups impacts on criminal behavior, and in what particular attitudes, values, beliefs, skills, and situational supports are associated with criminal conduct.

Theories of the Motivational Variety: Subcultural Versions

Cloward and Ohlin (1960) increased the sophistication of Merton's class-based theory by recognizing that the values supportive of frequent, serious, and persistent criminal activity were not at all conventional. Indeed, these values were explicitly anticonventional and procriminal. Through direct links with differential association theory (to be reviewed later in this chapter), they suggested a number of variables that had not been developed in strain/anomie theory. These additions have proven to be more important within the social psychology of crime than the correlates suggested by strain/anomie theory.

A major contribution of subcultural theory was to suggest that there may be important individual differences in degree of access to illegitimate means. While Merton emphasized differentials in the availability of socially prescribed means, Cloward and Ohlin said that the criminally-prone have been exposed to and have internalized a different set of rules and beliefs. Cloward and Ohlin, similar to Merton, were not particularly interested in the possibility that personal factors might be responsible for the differentials in opportunity.

For purposes of a psychology of criminal conduct, it is important that certain personal sentiments and behavioral preferences can be shown to relate to criminal behavior. A bonus would be to find that being a member of groups in which certain values were dominant actually impacted on criminal behavior in a manner independent of the values of the individual (recall this point from Chapter 1).

The Content of Criminal Subcultures

Initially, the content of the values and norms said to be dominant in deviant subcultures was examined. Cohen (1955) was explicit in suggesting that criminal subcultures shared procriminal sentiments in direct opposition to the middle-class values of reason and verbalization, delayed gratification, and respect for property. That is, the major values were hostility and aggression, immediate gratification and short-term hedonism, and destruction. Interestingly, just as Merton called upon Freud in his specification of reactions to frustration, so did Cohen call upon the Freudian mechanism of reaction formation to account for the development of oppositional values supportive of delinquency. Thus, dropping out of school and not working were acts of defiance toward middle-class values. Cohen can then account for the fact that some hostile and destructive acts often accompany break-and-enter offenses.

Miller (1958) was still more informative in his specification of the content of procriminal sentiments. We do not need to view the following "focal concerns" as peculiar to the lower classes in order to appreciate their potential role in criminal behavior: trouble (generalized difficulty), toughness (physical prowess, "masculinity," daring), smartness (outsmarting others, "con"), autonomy (independence, not being bossed), fatalism (luck), and excitement (thrills, danger).

Within the "gang," major concerns have to do with belonging and status; both are achieved through demonstrations of toughness, smartness, and the other focal concerns. With reference to status within a group of male adolescents, Miller was explicit on the point that early expressions of adulthood were highly valued (recall the Glueck findings that delinquents would smoke, drink, and engage in sexual behavior at an earlier age). Finally, the establishment and maintenance of the reputation of the gang often provided the motivation for delinquent activities such as gang fights.

Here, antisocial or procriminal attitudes, values, and beliefs, which in psychodynamic theory are a primary (albeit not total) reflection of a lack of socialization, are being externalized as properties of cultures. In turn, then, these external "values" are internalized. In addition, something else is happening. What the subcultural theorists and researchers are doing is giving PCC a new, more extensive, more grounded, and more complete vocabulary to be included in any theoretical representations of the cognitive processes that lead to criminal activity. Sykes and Matza (1957) made an outstanding contribution to the analysis of the cognition of crime.

Sykes and Matza (1957) were less inclined than subcultural theorists to accept the image of the delinquent as one committed to criminal values. They suggested that relatively few people would endorse the position that it was "OK" to steal or to inflict pain upon another person deliberately. The important variable was not so much delinquent subcultures but a subculture of delinquency.

The subculture of delinquency is characterized by a set of verbalizations that function to say that, in particular situations, it is "OK" to violate the law. Further, in some situations, violating the law is the only appropriate action. These verbalizations have been referred to as "techniques of neutralization," "rationalizations for law violations," and "a vocabulary of motives for illegal action" (Hartung, 1965). Note that they may be used prior to action and are considered causal. Their use is not limited to deflecting blame or controlling guilt after an offense has occurred. In social learning/social cognition theory, these types of cognitions are called "exonerating mechanisms" or processes of "moral disengagement" (Bandura et al., 1996; see the discussion of personal control in Chapter 4).

For Sykes and Matza, the verbalizations are not at all discontinuous with patterns of belief evident in everyday living—deviant as well as nondeviant. Many are extensions of the aggravating and mitigating factors that play a formal role in legal decisionmaking. In fact, most people use them to make behavioral choices in moral situations. The subcultural perspective suggests, however, that offenders may make more extensive use of them, and may apply them more widely. The techniques by which guilt is neutralized (or the rationalizations for law violations) include each of the following:

The denial of responsibility: "I couldn't help it," "The devil made me do it," "It's not my fault," "It was an accident." If delinquent acts are due to factors beyond the control of the individual, then the individual is guilt-free and also free to act. Many of these rationalizations have the apparent support of social science: living in a slum, coming from a broken

home, having been the victim of abuse, bad companions, having an exceptionally strong sex drive, drinking too much, and so forth.

The denial of injury: "I didn't hurt anyone," "I borrowed the tape
recorder," "We just took the car for a ride around town." In employing
these rationalizations, the delinquent admits responsibility for the act
but not for any serious injury.

The denial of the victim: In situations in which responsibility and/or
injury are difficult to deny, one can deny a victim by reversing the offender and victim roles. The victim "had it coming to him" or "deserved what
she got." Thus, homosexuals, disobedient wives, nasty kids, and unfair
teachers are appropriate candidates for abuse and harassment. There is
no end to the list of "offenders" whose "punishment" is justifiable in the
eyes of some—from corrupt politicians to the "fat cats" in business.

Condemnation of the condemners: With this type of rationalization,
those who would disapprove of the offender's actions are defined as
immoral, hypocritical, or criminal themselves. Thus, one hears "lawyers
are no good," "courts can be fixed," the "police are brutal," and "everyone has their own racket." Have sociologists not proven that criminal justice processing reflects not the criminality of the accused but the social
power of the accusers? Did Marx not show that the major institutions of
society function to serve the interests of the powerful, while keeping the
oppressed down?

Appeal to higher loyalties: "I didn't do it for myself." Rather, one was
being loyal to a brother or sister, to a friend, or to the gang. The demands
of the larger society were sacrificed for the demands of more immediate
loyalties. While not illustrated by Sykes and Matza (1957), presumably
appeals also may be made to the longer-term good, such as burning a
video shop in order to interfere with the distribution of pornography or
taking hostages in order to publicize a social wrong.

The pool of procriminal sentiments suggested by subcultural theorists has not been exhausted in our brief discussion. Nor have we been
careful in making distinctions among attitudes, values, beliefs, norms,
rationalizations, or neutralizations. This is saved for an examination of
the specific psychological processes involved in the cognitive control of
behavior. However, we are now in a position to summarize the potential
predictors suggested by the social psychology of subcultural theory:

1. Personal association with delinquents or with groups within
    which procriminal sentiments are endorsed;

2. Personal endorsement of antisocial/procriminal sentiments;

3. Having acquired the skills necessary to conduct some criminal
    acts and/or having access to the necessary materials or resources
    such as a drug supplier, a "fence" for stolen goods, or access to
    weapons.

These three correlates of delinquency and crime are of unquestioned empirical significance (although the third has been less well-studied than the first two). They are in no way incompatible with psychodynamic or control theory. In view of the findings of Glueck and Glueck (1950), why did we not have a high-consensus, general personality and social psychology of crime as early as 1960? In view of the findings of Hirschi (1969), why did we not have a high-consensus, general PCC by the mid-1970s? You know part of the answer by now: Mainstream sociological criminology was professionally and ideologically opposed to a general PCC. More narrowly, why were Glueck and Glueck (1950) and Hirschi (1969; Gottfredson & Hirschi, 1990), researchers and theorists so obviously open to consideration of personal and structural variables, not willing to offer causal status to antisocial associates? Let us take a look a differential association theory before attempting an answer.

From Differential Association to Social Learning

Admitting our bias from the start, we are favorably disposed to differential association (DA) theory (Andrews, 1980), just as we were favorably disposed to early psychodynamic thought (Andrews & Wormith, 1989). In our opinion, there is much of immediate value within DA theory, as there was in early psychodynamic theory. Our presentation of DA theory will not delve into some nagging irritants or ambiguities in the theory for the same reasons that we did not concentrate on the difficulties and flights of fancy within classic psychoanalytic thought. When a theory rings true and identifies powerful correlates of criminal conduct that are readily validated empirically, we believe it deserves serious attention. (Resource Note 3.1 outlines the principles of DA.)

Interest increases further when the theory has obvious practical value for purposes of prediction and prevention (Andrews, 1980). In addition, as we did in the case of Freud, we encourage readers to consult the original statements of DA theory by Edwin Sutherland (1939; Sutherland & Cressey, 1970). In the case of Sutherland, however, we alert readers to the fact that the man who produced one of the most powerful PCCs is the same man who helped make antipsychological bias part of the institution of mainstream sociological criminology (Andrews & Wormith, 1989; Gottfredson & Hirschi, 1990; Laub & Sampson, 1991).

An attractive aspect of DA theory is the inclusion of two of the best validated correlates of criminal conduct in the whole of PCC: antisocial attitudes and antisocial associates. This text has already shown that assessments of antisocial/procriminal attitudes have consistently proved to be meaningful correlates of a criminal past and predictors of a criminal future. We have even seen evidence that changes in procriminal sentiments are predictive of future criminal activity. This evidence is highly relevant to DA because a central causal assumption of DA is that criminal acts reflect cognitions favorable to criminal activity: A person becomes delinquent because of an excess of "definitions" favorable to violation of law over "definitions" unfavorable to violations of law (Sutherland, 1947). Remember also that every perspective on crime we have reviewed would give causal status to antisocial attitudes. Even Merton's original statements regarding structurally induced anomie were qualified by a footnote to the effect that alienation would not lead to criminal acts if there were internalized prohibitions against law violation (see the above discussion of Menard's reinterpretation of Mertonian anomie theory).

Resource Note 3.1

The Principles of Differential Association Theory
Edwin Sutherland (1939, 1947; Sutherland and Cressey, 1970)
[With Some Minor Modifications]

1. Criminal behavior is learned.

2. Criminal behavior is learned in interaction with other persons in a process of communication.

3. The principal part of the learning occurs within intimate personal groups.

4. The learning includes techniques of crime and the specific direction (procriminal vs. anticriminal) of motives, drives, rationalizations, and attitudes.

5. The process of learning by association with criminal and anticriminal patterns involves all of the mechanisms that are involved in any other learning.

6. A person becomes delinquent because of an excess of definitions favorable to violation of law over definitions unfavorable to violations of law.

7. Differential associations may vary in frequency, duration, priority, and intensity.

Behavioral Reformulations

Criminal behavior is learned according to the principles of operant conditioning.

Learning occurs both in nonsocial situations and social interaction.

Second, antisocial associates are a major correlate of antisocial behavior even though Glueck and Glueck (1950) and Hirschi (1969; Gottfredson & Hirschi, 1990) did not assign it the causal significance that the findings of their research would suggest was reasonable. From the earliest explorations of the empirical validity of antisocial associates (e.g., Short, 1957) through to the latest reviews of a now vast empirical literature (Resource Note 2.4), it is clear that assessments of antisocial associates are able to distinguish between offenders and nonoffenders with a level of accuracy rivaled only by assessments of antisocial personality and antisocial attitudes, or by a very broad sampling of risk factors in the home, school, work, and the broader community. Within DA, the importance of antisocial associates resides in a fundamental theoretical principle: Criminal behavior is learned by associations with criminal and anticriminal patterns, and the principal part of that learning occurs in interaction with other persons in a process of intimate communication (Sutherland, 1947).

Thus, the fundamental causal chain in classical DA theory is from antisocial associates to the acquisition of antisocial attitudes to antisocial behavior in particular situations. With the development of behavioral reformulations of DA theory (Andrews, 1980; Burgess & Akers, 1966) and the impressive background of empirical research, a more powerful causal model is one that allows antisocial associates some direct causal significance unmediated by antisocial attitudes. With this model, antisocial attitudes and antisocial associates not only influence each other but may each contribute to the definitions of particular situations that are favorable to criminal activity.

Another positive feature of DA theory, as in the case of early psychodynamic and behavioral/social learning theory, is that it actually reflects a psychology of action based on the person in immediate situations. Moreover, the immediate psychology of action underlying DA theory is not very different from the psychology underlying early psychodynamic perspectives—or for that matter the immediate psychology of Megargee's (1982) algebra of aggression noted earlier in this chapter. In psychodynamic theory, criminal behavior reflected the ego's resolution of the id, superego, and immediate situational variables in the interest of maximizing pleasure and minimizing pain. In radical behavioral terms, behavior in a particular situation is determined by the discriminative properties of the situation whereby the probability of a particular act is a function of the reinforcement history of the act in similar situations. Our understanding of symbolic interactionism, on which DA theory is based, suggests a similar psychology of action. People behave in accordance with their cognitive "definitions of situations." A particular behavior occurs in a particular situation when that behavior is defined as appropriate or "OK." That behavior will not occur when the definitions of the situation are unfavorable to engaging in that particular behavior.

This perspective on the immediate situation of action fits neatly with one of the best validated models of human behavior in the whole of social psychology. This well-validated model is Ajzen and Fishbein's (1980) theory of reasoned action. (We appreciate the irony that the psychodynamic/control theories of crime place such a heavy emphasis upon impulsive action, that is, unreasoned action and weak self-control.) According to Ajzen and Fishbein, people behave in accordance with their intentions. The behavioral intentions reflect attitudes favorable to the act, perceived social support for the act, and perceived barriers to enactment. This model of the immediate situation of action also fits well with Albert Bandura's emphasis on the immediate causal significance of self-efficacy beliefs, according to which people engage in those behaviors that they believe will be rewarding and successfully enacted. This general model is developed further in Chapter 4.

Cross-sectional studies of DA variables have delivered an image of delinquency and criminality that is remarkably consistent from study to study, cross-culturally, and across a variety of measures of deviance. The latter point has been well demonstrated in the studies conducted by Jessor and Jessor (1977), by Ronald Akers (1985), and by Delbert Elliott and colleagues (Elliott, Huizinga & Ageton, 1985). Jessor and Jessor, as well as Akers, have consistently taken the position that the principles that yield high levels of differentiation between criminals and noncriminals may also yield high levels of differentiation between alcoholics and non-alcoholics, and between marijuana users and nonusers.

Ronald Akers and John Cochran (1985) reported on a direct comparison of the abilities of social learning, anomie, and social control theories to account for variability in the use of marijuana within a sample of students in midwestern United States schools, grades 7 through 12. They obtained self-report questionnaire responses from 67 percent (N = 3,065) of the target population. Several measures of anomie and alienation, based on Merton's theory, could account for only 3 percent of the variability in marijuana use. Measures derived from the social control theories (e.g., parental attachment, grade point average, commitment to school, and the valuing of education) accounted for no more than 30 percent of the variability in drug use.

However, measures derived from the behavioral reformulations of differential association theory (that is, the social learning variables) accounted for 68 percent of the variability in drug use. The most potent variables within the social learning set included the following: (1) personal attitudes favorable to the use of marijuana; (2) having close friends who use marijuana; and (3) having close friends who approve of one's use of marijuana.

The addition of the anomie and control variables to the prediction formula was unable to increase the R square significantly above the 68 percent level achieved by the social learning variables on their own. In brief, these results strongly support the position that, in cross-sectional studies, the most important variables are the personal endorsement of delinquent values in combination with close delinquent associates who approve of one's engaging in delinquency.

The body of theoretically relevant work completed by Ronald Akers (1994) and his colleagues is truly impressive. They have demonstrated the power of attitudes and associates across a wide rang of criterion variables, including general delinquency, general criminality, alcohol use, marijuana use, and violence against women. The wide applicability of Akers's version of social learning theory is evident in an analysis of computer crime among college students (Skinner & Fream, 1997). Computer crimes such as piracy of computer software and illegal access were clearly a reflection of personal cognitions favorable to such crime as well as associations with friends favorable to such crime. As will become apparent in the next chapter, we look forward to Ronald Akers taking an interest in intervention studies because the behavioral reformulation of

DA theory not only suggests major predictors but directs attention to the powerful influence strategies of modeling and reinforcement in the context of prevention and treatment.

With such an impressive empirical track record, why are the psychodynamic and control theorists so insistent about keeping antisocial associates out of the causal formula? The evidence on the importance of criminal associates is consistent in the juvenile delinquency literature, and when the literature from adult corrections is considered, there remains no doubt as to its significance. For all of the empirical power of DA theory, Sutherland's variables have been held out to be the necessary and sufficient causes of crime, rendering all other variables scientifically uninteresting.

According to Glueck and Glueck (1950), DA theory—and the variable antisocial associates in particular—represented a "roof without a house." They thought that "birds of a feather flock together" was something to be explained rather than an explanation of delinquency. As noted earlier in the chapter, Glueck and Glueck saw the association with delinquent others as a reflection of the more fundamental personal and familial factors that were the causes of crime. Gottfredson and Hirschi (1990) continue this line of thought and additionally argue that the cross-sectional correlations of delinquent peers and delinquency are inflated by a host of problems in the measurement of delinquent associates.

There are a number of important methodological and conceptual considerations. First, "delinquent behavior occurs in the company of others." It is now well-established that many of the offenses of young offenders occur in the company of others. Thus, high correlations between delinquent associates and concurrent criminality are a part of the criterion variable and not, in any sense, a covariate of any causal significance. Being a member of a team does not account for participation in team activities—they are the same thing.

Second, "birds of a feather flock together." Directly reflecting the position of Glueck and Glueck, the fact that delinquents happen to associate primarily with other delinquents is a phenomenon to be explained. It is not an explanation of delinquency. Indeed, the findings of Glueck and Glueck and of Hirschi are consistent with the view that the personal attitudes and behavioral propensities of deeply involved delinquents are such that nondelinquents would avoid them, and vice versa.

Third, the predictive validity (as opposed to concurrent validity) of delinquent associations is relatively weak or, more accurately phrased, underinvestigated. Lee Robins (1966) found that children with severe conduct disorders were more likely to be members of gangs than were less disturbed children. This is the typical finding of cross-sectional studies. However, upon long-term follow-up, it was not early gang membership that predicted serious antisocial conduct in adulthood. Rather, adult antisocial behavior was better predicted by childhood antisocial behavior, regardless of gang membership as a child.

Fourth, many predictors (perhaps including some with incremental predictive validity) clearly predate differential peer associations. The findings displayed above are consistent with the many studies (e.g., Farrington, 1997; Loeber & Dishion, 1983) that confirm the predictive importance of early conduct problems. The most dramatic of these studies is that of Rowe and Osgood (1984). They found, as expected, that the correlation between the self-reported delinquent behavior of high school students and self-reported delinquent peer associations was .50 for boys and .58 for girls. Rowe and Osgood, however, had sampled twins, both identical and fraternal. Thus, they were able to separate the variance shared by delinquent associates and delinquent behavior into that portion likely due to genetics and that portion due to environment. The results were clear. In both the male and female samples, more than 60 percent of the variance shared by peer associations and delinquent conduct was traced to the genetic component.

Rowe and Osgoode (1984) suggested that this linkage may reflect the operation of one or more of a number of biologically based mediators. For example, variations in verbal intelligence, psychopathic personality, impulsivity, and predisposition to anger have all been linked to biology. All or some combination of such characteristics may impact upon the types of associates that are mutually acceptable.

Fifth, Travis Hirschi (1969; Gottfredson & Hirschi, 1990) objected to the motivational/conformity and subcultural elements of DA theory, and there is much to object to on these points. That is why we took a general social psychological approach in our discussion of subcultural theory and explicitly ignored the theoretical rhetoric about class, culture, and the transmission of cultural values. For example, it is reasonably well-established that lower-class origin is as weak a predictor of antisocial attitudes and procriminal associates as it is of criminal behavior. The predictors of antisocial associates and antisocial attitudes are the same personal, interpersonal, and familial variables that predict antisocial behavior. The issue is the extent to which antisocial attitudes and associates mediate the influence of the background variables on criminal conduct.

In our view, the social psychology of DA does not demand that offenders be viewed as conforming to antisocial values. The construct of antisocial sentiments refers to those dynamic cognitions (attitudes, values, beliefs, techniques of neutralization) that are explicitly supportive or nonsupportive of criminal activity. The construct of antisocial sentiments does not require the learning of antisocial values (motivational/subcultural theory) any more than it requires that antisocial sentiments reflect a failure of socialization (as in psychodynamic/control theory). Stated another way, the general social psychological perspective on DA is as open to the view that some of the *inhibitors* of criminal behavior are learned as it is to the view that some of the *facilitators* of criminal behavior are learned.

In pure DA terms, antisocial attitudes include expressions favorable to violation of the law and expressions unfavorable to violation of the law. In DA theory, criminal behavior reflects an excess of definitions favorable to the act over definitions unfavorable to the act. Sutherland's use of the phrase "excess" is problematic only if one works in absolute terms. However, scientifically, we can have a measure of overall attitudinal support for a particular act that allows meaningful interindividual and intraindividual predictions to be made (Andrews, 1980).

The general social psychological perspective, liberated from the sociological structural/cultural rhetoric, has no need to adopt the accounts of some subcultural theorists wherein delinquent boys are represented as "just folks," possessing similar skills and drives as the middle-class boys who direct their energies to collecting Scout badges. The personal characteristics of friendliness, sociability, and loyalty are not needed in order to humanize delinquents and, empirically, such traits are not characteristic of delinquents.

Travis Hirschi objects in particular to the DA principle that much of the learning of procriminal patterns occurs within the context of relatively intimate interpersonal communication. He knows from his own data that delinquents have less respect for their friends than do nondelinquents, and he knows additionally that association with delinquents is a correlate of delinquency. There is no difficulty here for the social psychological version of DA theory. Although delinquent peer groups tend to be composed of individuals with little respect for others, association with delinquents is an additional important risk factor. Those who associate with delinquents and who lack respect for others are more at risk for delinquency than those who score low on both risk factors or who score high on only one. In fact, delinquent associates are a much more powerful risk factor than is the quality of peer relationships.

The social learning and general social psychological perspective will be developed further in Chapter 4. Resource Note 3.2 summarizes a series of experimental tests of behavioral reformulations of certain principles of differential association. In the next chapter we will see additional experimental evidence in support of behavioral reformulations of DA theory and find real value in a general personality and social psychological approach that recognizes that the causes of criminal conduct are situational, circumstantial, personal, interpersonal, familial, and structural/cultural.

Resource Note 3.2

Some Experimental Investigations of Principles of Differential Association (DA) Through Manipulation of the Social Structure of Miniature Social Systems
(based on Andrews, 1980)

By the end of the 1970s, there was already near massive cross-sectional and longitudinal support for the predictive validity of assessments of one or both of antisocial attitudes and antisocial associates. Experimental evidence, however, was virtually zero. In two of the leading collections of the day (Cressey & Ward, 1969; Rubington & Weinberg, 1973), only one experimental study was found in a sample of more than 100 studies.

In 1955, Donald Cressey presented an interesting rationale for the application of the theory of differential association to "changing criminals," but it did not generate many controlled program evaluations. Guided group interaction (GGI) programs certainly emphasized using delinquent peers as change agents in a programmed manner. As noted in the treatment chapter, however, this self-described "clinical sociology" did not employ structured cognitive change or skill-building strategies and appeared to want the "group" to adopt anticriminal values on their own without staff prompting. Such passivity was apparent because attitudes were thought of as properties of groups and not really properties of individuals, and because active modeling on the part of staff might promote "rejection of the rejectors." For all of this, LaMar Empey (with Erickson, 1972; with Rabow, 1961) and Stephenson and Scarpitti (1974) were very important leaders in introducing approximations of experimental ideals into criminology and corrections. Briefly, GGI programs did no better than community-based probation supervision (although sometimes clearly better than incarceration).

During the 1970s, a research program involving Carleton University and the Ontario Ministry of Correctional Services explored the treatment implications of a behavioral reformulation of differential association. A behavioral /social learning approach not only helps make sense of the predictive validity of risk factors suggested by DA theory but prevents treatment programs from relying on passive and weakly supported influence strategies. Notably, behavioral and social learning theory provide the powerful influence strategies of modeling and reinforcement and also are specific about self-management processes.

Three key principles of DA were recast into two broad sets. One set has to with the conditions that promote criminal learning, and the other with the conditions that promote the translation of criminal learning into criminal behavior. The principles relating to promotion of criminal learning are the contingency principle and the relationship principle. The contingency principle reflects the importance in DA of differentials in exposure to criminal and anticriminal patterns. Behaviorally, the contingency principle directs attention to what patterns are being modeled (or demonstrated)—if you want to get a behavior going, demonstrate that behavior. The contingency principle also directs attention to the immediate consequences of criminal and anticriminal expressions—the immediate consequences of interest are reinforcing consequences and punishing consequences, the former increasing the chances of a behavior recurring, the latter decreasing the chances of a behavior recurring. The contingency principle is also called the normative principle and sometimes the structuring principle. The contingency principle influences the direction of learning or the direction of interpersonal influence. For anticriminal learning, look for vivid expressions of anticriminal alternatives to procriminal patterns of thinking, feeling, and acting, for differential reinforcement of anti-criminal alternatives, and for differential disapproval of expressions of procriminal patterns.

The relationship principle reflects the importance in DA of differentials in exposure occurring within intimate personal groups. The principle may also be called the socioemotional principle or the control principle. It

Resource Note 3.2 *(continued)*

directs attention to what influences the amount of learning or the amount of interpersonal influence. A high density of powerful rewards and costs is found within "intimate" personal groups. We define "intimacy" in terms of open, warm, understanding, sensitive, caring, nonblaming, enthusiastic, respectful, and frequent communication. Under these conditions, attention and warmth are strong reinforcers, mutual liking and caring increases the chances of modeling, frequency increases the opportunity for reinforced practice, and settings within which such interactions are apparent are approachable environments rather than ones to be avoided. In addition, even cost contingencies such as disapproval are more powerful in a pleasing environment (behaviorists speak of the "4 to 1 rule," at least four rewards for every punishment delivered).

Potentially, these are powerful principles that may guide assessments of the primary prevention/rehabilitative potential of naturally occurring and/or deliberately-designed treatment environments. They may also guide the selection, training, and supervision of correctional and clinical staff. But let us return to the research program.

The third principle is called the self-management principle. It reflects the DA position that criminal behavior occurs when there is an excess of favorable definitions. In social learning terms, attitudes translate into behavior through self-control. In brief, attitudes, values, beliefs, rationalizations, and cognitive emotional states such as anger and resentment provide the standards that influence self-management through comparisons of behavior with the standard. In addition, self-approval, self-disapproval, and self-instructions to proceed or cease a behavior sequence are emitted. In brief, people talk to themselves and that talk (and imagining) may support or not support criminal behavior depending on antisocial attitudes and self-management skill.

The principles were explored in a series of studies in prison and probation settings. The first few studies focused on the criminal learning and the later ones on the self-management principle. Consistent with DA's applauded ability to serve at the structural and individual levels, the experimental manipulations of relationship and contingency dimensions of interpersonal influence were conducted at the structural level of miniature service systems. Structurally, we varied the composition of groups and the roles assigned to group participants.

Rideau Correctional Center was a medium-security custody setting established to contain short-term adult recidivists and, in a separate facility on the same grounds, young first-time incarcerates. It was a rural facility that actually operated a farming enterprise (and during some growing seasons, the crops were actually brought in without contracts being set with local farmers). A systematic offender-based need survey had established that there was a need for a variety of programs at Rideau. A host of short-term structured groups were introduced. Many programs were subjected to experimental evaluations as student research and thesis projects. While controlled evaluations revealed effects on a variety of short-term outcomes, including internal rule violations, social skills, and knowledge of community post-release resources, one outcome was not achieved over and over again. Shifts in antisocial thinking were not being accomplished. It appeared that a way was required in which to introduce the exposure of real alternatives to antisocial styles of thinking, feeling, and acting.

The prison chaplain, Jerry Brown, had introduced an interesting program in which citizen volunteers (typically elderly and Christian) visited the prison one night a week and met with inmates in groups to discuss current affairs or whatever consensus suggested as the topic of the night. Discussions with Brown led to the introduction of Community Groups, in which citizen volunteers and prisoners were co-participants in weekly discussion groups. The discussion groups were composed of eight to 14 participants that met one night a week for eight weeks. The leaders of the groups initially were clinical staff of the prison and then other staff such as shop instructors and ultimately nonoffender graduates of earlier groups. The leaders encouraged open, warm, honest, and enthusiastic talk, and structured that talk around issues

Resource Note 3.2 (continued)

of rules, rationalizations for law violations, and self-management processes. The Community Group became very attractive, the number running increased, and the citizen volunteer participants were supplemented by undergraduates from Carleton University.

Study One: The effects of participation in Community Groups. Prisoner volunteers and citizen volunteers were assigned randomly to Community Groups or to a waiting list. Pre-group and post-group assessment were conducted on the same paper-and-pencil questionnaire measures of antisocial attitudes that had been unable to show change in earlier programs. [A little aside: Among sociological criminologists at Carleton University at the time, the "bet" was that citizen volunteers and prisoners would not differ in antisocial attitudes (remember, it was the 1970s).] In fact, compared to the citizen volunteers, at pretest, the prisoners presented with more negative attitudes toward the law, courts, and police, with higher levels of identification with criminal others, and with greater acceptance of rationalizations for law violations. At posttest, and for the first time in our research, and consistent with the contingency principle, prisoner participants showed reduced antisocial thinking compared to prisoner non-participants. Notably, and consistent with the contingency principle, but not anticipated, the participating citizen volunteers showed increased antisocial thinking. Pleased with evidence supporting the contingency principle, we introduced additional service programs for evaluation. Not so pleased with the effects on citizen volunteers, we enhanced the pre-service training and the debriefing of citizen volunteers.

Study Two: The effects of participation in Community Groups versus Recreation Groups. Recreation Groups do not involve structured opportunities for exposure to the anticriminal patterns of citizen volunteers. Rather, citizens and prisoners play cards or other board games. In brief, reduced antisocial attitudes were found only in the Community Group. It appeared that the effect was due to differentials in exposure to anticriminal patterns rather than simple exposure to anticriminal others. An unanticipated finding emerged in

that inmates who were in the recreation condition showed increases in self-esteem while inmates in the Community Groups did not. Fortunately, we had a waiting list control group and they too showed increases in self-esteem. It began to appear that increases in self-esteem were a routine consequence of incarceration that was blocked by exposure to Community Groups.

Study Three: The effects of enhanced interpersonal relationships within Community Groups. Prior to participation in Community Groups, the interpersonal relationship skills of citizen volunteers were assessed. Community Groups were then formed with some groups including citizens who were above average in their relationship skills and other groups in which the citizen volunteers were below average in their interpersonal skills. Please note that as a group, citizen volunteers score well above average in their relationship skills as compared to nonvolunteers. Thus, even the low relationship group included relatively high-functioning citizens. The actual results were not as clean as the findings we had begun to expect. It was only low-anxiety inmates who responded best to the high-functioning volunteers. It appeared that interpersonally anxious offenders did better with lower-intensity volunteers.

Study Four: The effects of discussion groups with and without citizen participants. This study was conducted with long-term incarcerates in the Canadian federal system. The findings depended on considering how inmate-rated relationship conditions were associated with reduced antisocial thinking. Within inmate-only groups, open communication was associated with increased antisocial attitudes. Within the Community Groups, open communication was associated with decreased antisocial attitudes. This pattern of findings supports the theoretical position that a high-quality relationship promotes influence and that the direction of that influence depends upon what is being modeled and reinforced.

Study Five: The relationship, contingency, and self-management principles in probation as explored in the Canadian Volunteers in Corrections study (CaVIC). In this study, 190 probationers were randomly assigned to profes-

Resource Note 3.2 *(continued)*

sional probation officers or to citizen volunteers who were assistants to professional probation officers. The volunteer program was directed by Jerry Kiessling, a senior probation officer in Ottawa, Ontario. Jerry was so respected by his colleagues and citizen volunteers that the university-based researchers and students were allowed to conduct personality assessments of the probation officers and probationers and to ask both groups to report on their impressions of the supervision process and short-term outcomes. Additionally, some supervision sessions were audio-taped with the consent of both probation officers and probationers.

Many assessment instruments were administered but the basic ones for our purposes were Empathy, Socialization, and anti-social attitudes. Officer Empathy scores were positively associated with probationer and officer ratings of the quality of the interpersonal relationship. Officer Socialization scores were positively associated with probationer and officer ratings of the help received. Officer Empathy scores were unrelated to tape-based assessments of modeling and reinforcement, but officer Socialization scores were positively correlated with anticriminal modeling and anticriminal reinforcement.

Summary

Psychodynamic theory led to early social learning theory via the frustration aggression route as early as the 1930s through the Yale school. Differential association theory was reformulated in behavioral terms; in criminology, it is called social learning theory. Traditional strain theory has returned to its roots in frustration-aggression and thereby profited from the social learning and social cognition perspectives on anger and aggression. Once again, there is social learning theory.

In the middle of this chapter, we questioned why, given such a wealth of empirical knowledge of the correlates of crime, a high-consensus, general personality, and social psychology of crime has not developed as yet. Our answer is that the residuals of the anti-PCC elements of mainstream sociological criminology prevented many of us from seeing that Sheldon Glueck and Eleanor Glueck (1950) offered a general theory that may be rendered less "tentative" by replacing their psychodynamic model of the immediate psychological moment of action with one more in tune with differential association theory and behaviorism.

Chapter 4

The General Personality and Social Psychological Approach: A Personal, Interpersonal, and Community–Reinforcement Perspective

This book opened with the objective of describing and assessing the empirical, theoretical, and practical status of the psychology of criminal conduct (PCC). Even without having yet reviewed detailed knowledge within developmental psychology (Chapter 5) and the evidence in regard to practical prediction (Chapter 6) and practical treatment (Chapter 7), it is already becoming clear that there is a reasonably strong empirical base to PCC.

PCC has a highly meaningful criterion variable in that substantial individual differences are found in both "primary" and "secondary" deviance, whether defined by self-reports, victim reports, or official records, and when measured within any of the typical categories of social location (Chapter 2). Knowledge of the correlates and predictors of individual criminal conduct is sufficiently strong to assert that the best-established risk factors for criminal conduct within almost any sample are *antisocial cognition*, *antisocial associates*, a *history of antisocial behavior*, and a complex of indicators of *antisocial personality* (recall Resource Note 2.4). These indicators of antisocial personality include restless energy, adventuresomeness, impulsiveness, poor problem-solving skills, hostility, and a callous disregard for other people and responsibilities. In the middle range of predictive validity reside assessments of family and parenting, indicators of personal school/employment achievement, and leisure/recreation. Substance abuse also enters the middle set. In the lower range of predictive validity are lower-class origins, low verbal intelligence, and personal distress.

Accepting all of the above, empirical knowledge is still weak on many issues. First, psychology has yet to deliver a way of organizing the various indicators of antisocial personality into a single construct or set of interrelated constructs that is agreed upon by audiences either within or outside of the discipline of psychology (however, see the work of

Patricia Van Voorhis in the prediction chapter and the work of Avshalom Caspi and his colleagues in Chapter 2). Second, the specific moderators of the covariates of criminal conduct (e.g., variation in the risk/need factors depending upon the stages of human development and/or with type of offense) remain an issue. Third, the impact of broader social arrangements on individual criminal conduct is poorly documented (recall from Chapter 2 that even the best of efforts to link ecology of neighborhoods to individual criminal conduct yield minor effects). Social science rhetoric aside, interesting and convincing demonstrations of the impact of broad structural/cultural factors on variation in individual criminal conduct are few. Fourth, limits placed upon particular constructs because of choice of research design or because of errors of measurement and/or conceptualization are known (recall Chapter 2) but not fully considered. Finally (and obviously), empirical knowledge can reflect only the findings of studies that have already been conducted and reported upon. Empirical knowledge is not only relative, political, and socially constructed, but it is also partial and incomplete.

Recognizing these problems, if a theory is to meet the criterion of empirical defensibility, it must deal with the empirical findings noted in the second paragraph of this chapter. For purposes of empirically derived theory, the obvious choice is to select the major causal variables from the list of the strongest correlates. We would choose antisocial attitudes, associates, behavioral history, and personality. We are unaware of any cross-sectional or longitudinal study in which at least one of the "Big Four" was not singled out from other potential predictors in the construction of an efficient and effective predictive model. Moreover, cross-sectional (e.g., Akers & Cochran, 1985; Johnson, 1979) and longitudinal (e.g., LeBlanc et al., 1988) research reveals that two or more of the four will be selected within the most potent and efficient prediction formula. Our own work with adjudicated offenders convinces us that the most empirically defensible theories will be those that assign causal significance to at least two of the four. Why we choose all four will become clear, but note now that the reasons are theoretical rather than "dustbowl empirical."

Building theories on the basis of existing data may be characterized as "dustbowl empiricism" at the extreme. Limitations admitted, the radical empirical approach to building theoretical understanding at least has the potential of organizing knowledge in a rational manner. Some sociological criminologists complain that Glueck and Glueck's (1950) "tentative causal formula" was nothing but a list of admittedly powerful correlates of delinquency simply organized according to psychoanalytic principles. We may remind them that the variables left out of the Glueck causal formula included those empirically indefensible variables that class-based sociological theories continued to promote for decades. Given the choice of choosing causal variables through consideration of evidence as opposed to professional and ideological interests, rational empiricism within PCC prefers even a radical empiricism over theoreticism.

It is not enough, however, for radical empirical approaches to simply be better than theoreticism. Theories should also be fruitful. They should organize empirical knowledge in a rational and attractive manner and also assist in the search for new empirical understandings that lead to a deeper theoretical appreciation of criminal conduct. Moreover, we expect theories to be practically useful in decreasing the human and social costs of crime. A good theory also will be consistent with other strong theories in the broader domain of the biological, human, and social sciences.

The latter two concerns lead to the next steps in the empirically informed construction of a general personality and social psychology of criminal conduct. First, we seek an organizing set of assumptions that is consistent with the best-validated and most promising of psychological perspectives of human behavior. This means that we seek a general psychology that is *empirically defensible* and promising in terms of understanding variation in human behavior. Second, we seek a *clinically relevant* underlying theory of human behavior. No matter how professionally strong and moral our interests in aggregated crime rates, our interest in criminal justice processing, and/or our interest in political correctness, clinical relevance requires PCC to provide meaningful assistance in the design and delivery of direct services that reduce antisocial behavior and/or reduce costs of processing. If we find that prevention and rehabilitation through direct service are wasted efforts, so be it. The point is that a clinically irrelevant PCC is less valuable than a clinically relevant PCC.

Is there a human psychology that may serve the interests of PCC better than alternative psychologies of action? Our answer is that there are several such human psychologies, some clearly better than others. One of these promising psychologies was psychodynamic theory. The psychodynamic psychology of the person in immediate situations was outlined in Chapter 3, and the predictive validity of Glueck and Glueck's psychodynamic interpretation of risk factors has proved impressive on all counts except for their dismissal of antisocial associates as a major variable.

Glueck and Glueck were aware of the importance of the immediate environment in psychoanalytic theory but, for some reason, they failed to view antisocial associates as an indicator of the facilitative versus inhibiting effects of many immediate situations of action. More generally, with the post-Freud and post-Glueck advances in human science, we can now do better than a psychology of action that depends on operationalizations of the very broad and nondynamic constructs of ego and superego. Stable traits are required when the task is predicting behavior over the long term, but more dynamic characteristics are required for shorter-term prediction and for clinical relevance. In regard to clinical relevance, Glueck and Glueck themselves were not satisfied with psychoanalysis as a treatment model. Moreover, we find few examples of successful psychodynamic treatment to this day.

Radical behaviorism offers a detailed and well-validated analysis of the determinants of action in particular situations. It is of demonstrated clinical value and has been integrated with psychodynamic theory (e.g., frustration-aggression theory). The result of the integration is most often called social learning or social cognition theory. These labels are also applied to that which emerged when behavioral principles were integrated with the symbolic interactionism underlying differential association (DA) theory.

Symbolic interactionism offered a potentially powerful psychology because of the emphasis on the cognitive control of behavior and the key causal significance assigned to attitudes, beliefs, and interpersonal interactions. Differential association theory, however, had little to say about the background predictors of persons in particular situations. Clinically, symbolic interactionism fared poorly in directing clinical effort. Thus, once again, integration with behavior theory was indicated.

Although the term "integration" is used loosely, rather than debate the issue, let us look at the immediate psychology of action in a general personality and social psychological perspective on criminal conduct. Figure 4.1 shows that immediate causal significance is assigned to constructs akin to definitions of situations favorable to criminal acts. Some theorists speak of "behavioral intentions," others of "self-efficacy beliefs," the "algebraic solution," or "personal choice"; some use phrases such as "the balance of rewards and costs." It remains to be seen whether operational distinctions among assessments of these variables may be differentiated in construct validity studies. We expect not; the main problem for the field may be to settle on a common vocabulary. So far, assessments of behavioral intentions and self-efficacy beliefs have impressive predictive validities in many different situations (Ajzen, 1996; Ajzen & Fishbein, 1980; Bandura, 1989; Bandura et al., 1996; Fishbein, 1997).

An internal dialogue is being assumed here. Many acts of fraud and force do occur on the spur of the moment and are so "easy" (in the language of Gottfredson and Hirschi, 1990) that almost anyone could reach that stage of self-efficacy at which they believed that they were skilled enough to engage in the act. Not everyone, however, would assess the situation as one in which that behavior would be appropriate. The major sources of variation in judgments of appropriateness are: (a) characteristics of the immediate environment, (b) the attitudes, values, beliefs, and rationalizations held by the person with regard to antisocial behavior (how wrong it would be, discounting of any objections), (c) social support for antisocial behavior, most often in the form of perceived support from others for that action but also including direct assistance, (d) a history of having engaged in antisocial behavior, (e) relatively stable personality characteristics conducive to antisocial conduct, and (f) self-management and problem-solving skills. Self-management and problem-solving skills are in parentheses in Figure 4.1 because they have contributed heavily to that particular person being in that particular situation; any additional contribution may only be in the form of moderator variables in interaction with attitudes or social support.

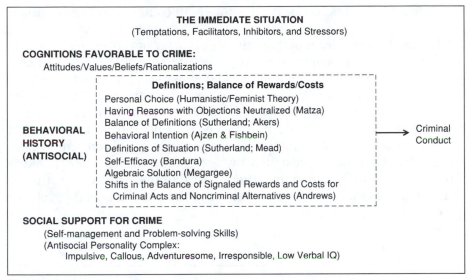

Figure 4.1
The Psychological Situation (or Psychological Moment) in a General Personality and Social Psychology of Criminal Conduct

Psychodynamic theory and social learning theory suggest, however, that the psychological moment should incorporate some understanding of "ego skills" such as problem-solving and self-regulation. Here the emphasis is not on *what* we think (as in the case of antisocial attitudes) but on *how* we think. For some theorists, these skills and cognitive processes are accepted as given. For example, David Matza (1964) recognized that young people may engage in active rationalization wherein any anticipated guilt over rule violations is neutralized in advance by verbalizations such as "I couldn't help it" or "the 'victim' deserved it." At the same time, however, Matza was committed to the view that young offenders and nonoffenders could not be differentiated according to their propensity to or their ability to engage in these rationalizations. Today, cognitive skills are a major focus of research in developmental and cognitive psychology, and there is no question that there are major individual differences in both the "how" and "what" of thinking/interpreting/coping (e.g., Ross & Fabiano, 1985).

Consideration of cognitive skills may be of particular value in studies of young offenders because developmental delays in cognitive functioning may be of exceptional importance in the study of antisocial behavior (see the Chapter 5). In addition to self-regulation and problem-solving skills, there are several other candidates for inclusion in the psychological moment that are focused on in current research and theoretical debate. Intoxication through substance abuse is an obvious one in that it may disrupt normal controls. Similarly, particularly stressful circumstances and depressive or psychotic states may weaken normal controls. An ongoing concern is the extent to which combinations of variables are particularly crucial. For example, antisocial attitudes may translate into antisocial behavior most strongly in combination with antisocial associates.

Figure 4.2 provides a path analytic summary of routes to the occurrence of particular people being in particular circumstances. It incorporates the more distal or background dispositional factors that shape both the person and the immediate context of action. It is similar to the empirically impressive model independently derived by Marc LeBlanc and colleagues (1988; presented in Chapter 3), but Figure 4.2 does not group the variables according to adolescent role or social constraint. Similar models have been presented by Jessor and Jessor (1977), Akers (1973, 1985, 1994), and many others, but like the Montreal group, we think that personality is best brought into the general social psychology of crime.

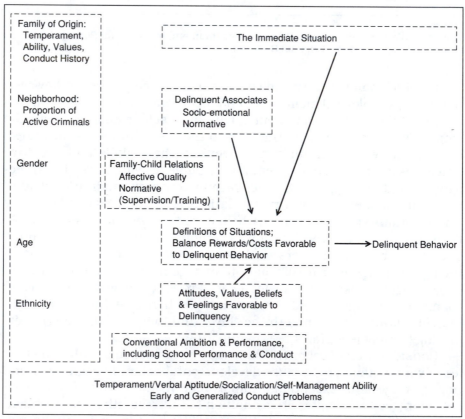

Figure 4.2
A General Personality and Social Psychological Perspective on Criminal Conduct

The model recognizes that there are multiple routes to involvement in illegal conduct, but suggests that antisocial attitudes and criminal associates are particularly strong risk factors. The model does not assume, for example, that all young offenders are temperamentally restless or aggressive, or that all young offenders are weakly tied to home and school. The chances of illegal conduct increase dramatically as the number and variety of the more proximal set of predispositional factors increase.

Where do political economy, social structure, and culture fit into this general personality and social psychology of crime? Because they are constants, they are distal background contextual conditions that cannot account for variation in individual conduct within particular social arrangements. Figure 4.3 shows the various classes of variables that may impact on individual behavior ordered from the broadest structural level down to the person in an immediate situation. Structure and culture have important roles to play in establishing the fundamental contingencies that are in effect within each particular social arrangement. A personal, interpersonal, and community-reinforcement perspective of deviant behavior attempts to account for this role within a model that seeks to explain individual differences in criminal conduct.

A Personal, Interpersonal, and Community-Reinforcement (PIC-R) Perspective on Criminal Conduct

The principles of one example of the general personality and social psychological approach [a Personal, Interpersonal, and Community-Reinforcement (PIC-R) perspective on deviant behavior (Andrews, 1982a)], are outlined in Resource Note 4.1. Incidentally, the outline of the principles of PIC-R was prepared in the decade before publication of the meta-analytic findings regarding the relative strength of different risk factors (for example: Chapter 2) and the characteristics of effective prevention.

As a broad social learning perspective on human conduct, PIC-R attempts to be both comprehensive and flexible. It considers factors that actively encourage or discourage deviant activity. In this sense, PIC-R incorporates elements of both motivational and control theories. It emphasizes control elements, because of the nature of criminal activity and its consequences, rather than *a priori* theoretical preferences. In addition, it explicitly recognizes factors at the personal, interpersonal, and community levels of analysis. PIC-R also stresses that the specific factors governing the conduct of persons are many, that they may be highly individualistic, and that their importance may vary over time and situations. Due to its comprehensive nature, PIC-R helps organize and locate what other less comprehensive theories attended to, as well as what they minimized.

THE BROAD CONTEXT: POLITICAL, ECONOMIC, CULTURAL, SOCIAL-STRUCTURAL

Dominant Values and Distribution of Wealth and Power
Legislation/Policy/Convention

Labor Market   Competitive Individualism

MORE IMMEDIATE SOCIAL STRUCTURAL AND CULTURAL FACTORS

Family of Origin, Membership   Neighborhood: Membership Composition
Composition: Personality,   (e.g., Proportion of Active Criminals)
Ability, Values, Mental Health,   and Roles and Statuses
Conduct History (Crime/Substance Abuse),
Educational, Occupational,
Parenting Skills and Resources

Community Settings:
School/Work/Recreational/Mental Health/Social Service Agencies
The Justice System: Police, Courts, Formal Agencies

THE INTERPERSONAL: PROCESS AND CONTENT OF INTERACTION

Family-Child Relations: Ties to Anticriminal Others
Affection/Supervision/
Neglect/Abuse
Interaction with Agencies   Ties to Criminal Others
(i.e., processing and service)

THE PERSONAL

Biological Given: Temperament/Aptitude/Verbal Intelligence
Age/Gender

Early Conduct Problems: Personality:
Lying, Stealing, Aggression   Socialization/Psychopathy in particular

(Self-regulation skills/problem-solving style)
(Internal/external monitoring for standards of conduct)

Conventional Ambition and Performance   School Performance and Conduct

Cognitions Favorable to Crime: Perceived Social Support for Crime
Attitudes, Values, Beliefs,
Rationalizations, Neutralizations,
and Feelings

History of Criminal Behavior

THE PERSON IN IMMEDIATE SITUATIONS

Immediate Situation: Signaled Outcomes
Facilitators, Inhibitors,   ⟶   Favorable to   ⟶   Criminal Acts
Stressors   Criminal Activity

Figure 4.3
A Personal, Interpersonal and Community-Reinforcement Perspective on the Multiple Classes of Relevant Variables in the Analysis of Criminal Behavior

PIC-R recognizes that an understanding of deviant behavior must draw upon knowledge from the biological, human, and social sciences in general, but emphasizes behavioral and social learning principles because of their demonstrated functional power in applied settings. The practical and clinical utility of PIC-R will reside in its ability to encourage comprehensive assessments and to assist in planning reasonable and effective interventions. Its value to policy will depend on its ability to allow crime control policies to reach down to people in immediate situations of action.

Resource Note 4.1

Principles of Behavioral Analysis

The key concepts of the learning perspectives are summarized here.

- Classical (or respondent) conditioning: The process by which a previously neutral stimuli comes to control a conditioned response through pairing with an unconditioned stimulus. The conditioned response is often some fraction or component of the unconditioned response to the unconditioned stimulus.

- Instrumental behaviors (or operants): Behaviors that operate upon the environment or that are instrumental in bringing about changes in the environment.

- The consequent control of operants: The changes in the chances of an act recurring that are due to the relatively immediate environmental consequences of an act.

- Rewards (or reinforcers): The immediate environmental changes produced by operants that are associated with an increased chance of the act recurring.

- Costs (or punishers): The immediate environmental changes produced by operants

that are associated with a decreased chance of the act recurring.

- Modeling: Learning through observation and imitation (or, if the model: demonstrating a behavior).

- Antecedent control: Variations in the chances of an act occurring due to the immediately preceding stimulus conditions.

Some important antecedents include: other people as models; other people as potential sources of rewards or costs; self-talk; images and thoughts; affective states; the physical resources or aids necessary for the completion of an act; discriminative stimuli that, through experience, set the occasion for an act; unconditioned stimuli; conditioned stimuli, intentions or definitions of situations; beliefs regarding one's ability to perform; and the consequences of performance.

- An alternative act or an alternative response: In any situation, more than one act is under the influence of antecedent and consequent control. Those other acts are called alternatives.

PIC-R draws upon radical behaviorism for its most fundamental principles in that the factors responsible for variation in human conduct are found in the immediate situation of action. Specifically, these include rewards and costs and those antecedents to behavior that signal the delivery of either rewarding or costly consequences for particular acts. These fundamental principles of behavioral analysis are summarized in Resource Note 4.1. The theoretical principle is that the variation in the immediate contingencies of action are responsible for the acquisition, maintenance, and modification of human behavior. Behavioral principles are not limited to learning but are fundamental principles of performance. Even what Gottfredson and Hirschi (1990) call the "easy and simple" criminal acts are under behavioral control within the PIC-R perspective.

PIC-R draws upon the concepts of personality and the social sciences. While the immediate contingencies of action account for variation in human conduct, it is the personal, interpersonal, and community factors that are responsible for the development, maintenance, and modification of these contingencies. Stable contingencies account for stability in behavior over time and across situations. Thus, for example, we will see how stability in personal attitudes and choice of associates, as well as personal temperament, may maintain relatively high chances of deviant conduct across situations.

Some contingencies may be or become relatively automatic, given the nature of some acts (theft produces property; ingestion of a drug produces sensory change); others are personally mediated (self-management through self-instruction and self-reward); and still others are interpersonally mediated (e.g., other persons may explicitly approve or disapprove of one's actions). In addition, the political economy and social structure of broader social systems will produce and maintain certain contingencies that may involve personal and/or interpersonal mediation. In clinical and policy practice, intervention at the level of immediate contingencies is less likely and less efficient than intervention at the level of the personal, interpersonal, and community roots of those contingencies. Without altering the personal, interpersonal, and community sources of rewards and costs, long-term behavior change is unlikely.

Finally, the contingencies in effect for nondeviant alternative behaviors are important in the analysis and practical modification of deviant behavior. When nondeviant alternative behaviors are highly rewarded, the motivation for some forms of deviance may be reduced. Thus, while there is some room for anomie theory, the psychological process is dramatically different from that proposed in the sociological and psychological strain theories. The potential for reduced criminal behavior resides not so much in reduced motivation for crime but in the potential for dramatic increases in the costs of crime through increases in the subtractive costs of crime. As the rewards for "noncrime" increase, the individual has more to lose.

Antecedent and Consequent Control

Resource Note 4.2 provides a summary of the PIC-R principles. At this point, we will expand upon these principles and provide a fuller explanation.

Principle 1 holds that occurrences of deviant and nondeviant behavior are under the control of antecedent and consequent events.

Principle 2 holds that interindividual and intraindividual variations in the probability of occurrence of a given class of behavior (deviant or nondeviant) are due to variation in the signaled rewards and costs for that class of behavior.

Resource Note 4.2

The Principles of PIC–R

1. Occurrences of deviant and nondeviant behavior are under antecedent and consequent control.

2. Inter- and intraindividual variations in the probability of occurrence of a given class of behavior (deviant or nondeviant) are due to variations in the signaled rewards and costs for that class of behavior.

3. Antecedents and consequences are of two major types: additive events (stimuli are introduced, extended, or augmented) and subtractive events (stimuli are withdrawn, postponed, or diminished).

4. The controlling properties of antecedents and consequences are acquired through the interaction of the person with the environment. The principles governing the acquisition, maintenance, and modification of the controlling properties of stimulus conditions include those of genetic and constitutional disposition and capability; biophysical functioning; cognitive functioning; human development; behavioral repertoire; state conditions; and respondent and operant conditioning, including observational learning, rule learning, symbolic control, and role enactment.

5. Antecedents and consequences arise from four major sources: (1) the actor (personally mediated events), (2) other persons (interpersonally mediated events), (3) the act itself (nonmediated or automatic and habitual events); and (4) other aspects of the situation of action.

6. Variations in the probability of occurrence of a given class of behavior are a positive function of the signaled density of the rewards for that class of behavior and a negative function of the signaled density of the costs for that class of behavior.

7. The magnitude of the effect of any one signaled reward for any class of behaviors depends upon the signaled density of other rewards for that class of behaviors. Generally, the magnitude of the effect of any one reward is greatest at some intermediate level of density, and the magnitude of the effect of any one reward is diminished at the lowest and highest levels of density. Similarly, the magnitude of the effect of any one cost for any class of behaviors is greatest at some intermediate level of density of costs.

8. The magnitude of the effect of the signaled density of the costs for any class of behaviors depends upon the signaled density of the rewards for that class of behaviors. Generally, the effect of density of costs is greatest at some intermediate level of density of rewards and diminished at the lower and higher levels of density of rewards.

9. Variations in the signaled rewards and costs for one class of behavior (deviant or nondeviant) may produce variations in the probability of occurrence in another class of behavior. The magnitude of the effect is a function of interconnecting contingencies and schedules for deviant and nondeviant behavior. The rewards for nondeviant behavior approach their maximum impact on the chances of deviant behavior under the following conditions:

   a) when and where relatively noncostly and nondeviant behaviors produce a relatively high density of rewards, including rewards similar to those produced by deviant behavior;

   b) when and where the costs for deviant behavior include a reduction, postponement, omission, or interruption in the delivery of those rewards produced by nondeviant behavior; and

   c) when and where nondeviant behavior is incompatible with deviant behavior.

10. Historical, geographic, and political-economic factors influence individual behavior primarily by way of the contingencies that they produce within settings and communities.

Resource Note 4.2 *(continued)*

11. Setting and community factors include physical, environmental, and cultural variables, as well as the structure of social systems; these influence individual behavior through the reward-cost contingencies they maintain within the settings.

12. Two basic dimensions for the analysis of the effects of systems on the deviant and nondeviant behaviors of its members are the normative and the control dimensions. The normative dimension includes behavioral prescriptions and proscriptions and their distribution according to one's position within the system. The control dimension includes the visibility of normative and deviant behavior to persons who control resources (including potential rewards and costs); the quantity, variety, quality, and magnitude of potential rewards and costs; the immediacy, frequency, and regularity with which rewards and costs are delivered; and the maintenance of interconnecting contingencies for deviant and nondeviant behavior.

13. Variations in the probability of occurrence of any given behavior within each of the deviant and nondeviant classes of behavior may be understood or produced by the application of the preceding principles to that specific behavior.

14. The predictability of behavior and its amenability to influence increase with individualized assessment of the signaled reward/cost contingencies.

15. The human and social value of any perspective on human conduct is in some part a function of predictive efficiency and the ability to influence events. For the most part, its value is a function of ethical and humane applications.

Antecedent stimuli are stimulus events that precede and (as opposed to neutral stimuli) control the behavior. They constitute the "A" in the A-B-C (antecedent-behavior-consequence) of behavioral analysis. Antecedent control implies that changes in stimulus conditions alter the probability of the behavior occurring. For example, the presence or absence of a police officer will affect the probability of jaywalking, and the presence of a handgun affects the likelihood of a murder.

Antecedent stimuli gain control over behavior through the processes of classical conditioning, vicarious learning, and discrimination learning. When antecedent stimuli gain behavioral control through classical conditioning, there is almost an automatic quality to the stimulus-response relationship. Often the behavior is described as emotional behavior. For example, the sight of a syringe may elicit pleasurable emotions for a heroin addict. Modeling is a strong principle of antecedent control, whereby a demonstration of a behavior increases the chances of the behavior occurring. When antecedent stimuli gain behavioral control via other learning processes, they function by providing information regarding the outcome of certain behavior. That is, antecedent stimuli serve to signal the rewards and costs that will follow a given behavior.

Consequent control (or outcome control) refers to the effect of the consequences of an act on the chances of a behavior recurring. Consequences that increase the probability of a behavior recurring are called reinforcers or rewarding consequences (i.e., rewards). The process is called reinforcement. Consequences that decrease the probability of a behavior recurring are called costs, and the process is called punishment. This time, human nature's tendency to seek pleasure and avoid pain is found at the heart of behavioral principles. This should warm the hearts of psychodynamic theorists and control theorists alike.

Principle 3 holds that antecedents and consequences are of two major types: additive events (stimuli are introduced, extended, or augmented) and subtractive events (stimuli are withdrawn, postponed, or diminished).

Additive, or positive, rewards are consequences that add something pleasing to the environment (e.g., delivering praise to a child contingent upon a particular act). Subtractive, or negative, rewards are consequences that remove something unpleasant (e.g., the chances of an assault recurring will increase if the assault was successful in stopping someone from making derogatory comments). A clinical illustration is provided in Resource Note 4.3.

Resource Note 4.3

Case Study: The Simultaneous Operation of Additive and Subtractive Rewards

Julia was sentenced to 30 days in jail for prostitution and possession of drugs. She was 19 years old and this was her first time in jail. Upon entry to jail, Julia was processed like all the other offenders: fingerprints were taken, a medical check-up completed, and a brief social history recorded. Nothing out of the ordinary was noted.

On the first check of the nightly rounds, a correctional officer found Julia semiconscious and bleeding from the forearms. Earlier that day she had asked for a razor to shave her legs. The razor was not collected and she used it that night to cut her forearms. Julia was given prompt medical attention. Except for a few stitches, the physical harm Julia inflicted upon herself was minor.

The next day Julia was interviewed by the psychologist for a suicidal assessment. Julia was somewhat surprised that the staff thought she was suicidal and denied any intention of killing herself. "It was just one of those things," she said. That night, once again, she was found bleeding, having cut her arm with her eyeglasses (she took the glass out of the rim). Even though the cuts were superficial, staff members were alarmed. She was placed in the hospital ward under 24-hour nursing care.

Frequently, behavior such as Julia's is seen as a "call for help" or a "search for attention." Suicidal gestures often bring a great deal of attention from others and, for someone who is terribly lonely, the reinforcing properties can be powerful. When Julia was seen again by the psychologist, the working hypothesis was that the slashes to the forearm produced "interpersonal additive rewards."

What was surprising was that the behavior also brought subtractive rewards (i.e., the removal of unpleasant stimuli). On the second interview, Julia was more relaxed and open. She revealed a life of physical and sexual abuse, extreme poverty, and addiction to alcohol. She also reported that she had, in the past, cut her forearms when feeling particularly anxious. As painful as this was, it created a distraction from her problems. While watching the blood ooze out of her cut, for the moment her mind was not dwelling on her horrendous life. As the blood continued to flow, she felt a sense of relaxation and peacefulness (no doubt brought on by the gradual loss of blood). Finally, she could drift off to a sleep that would re-energize her to face a new day when she awoke.

Similarly, costs may be additive or subtractive. Thus, the principles of consequent control encompass both additive (positive) punishment and subtractive (negative) punishment. Admonishing a child's behavior is an example of additive punishment. Removing a positive aspect of a situation (e.g., withholding attention) is an example of subtractive punishment. The additive-subtractive distinction will be found to be very important in distinguishing among existing theories. Subtractive punishment in particular will be found to have value in the design of effective intervention programs (Hunt & Azrin, 1973).

Jumping ahead to Principle 6, we see that variation in the probability of occurrence of a given class of behavior is a positive function of: (1) the signaled density of the rewards for that class of behavior, and (2) a negative function of the signaled density of the costs for that class of behavior.

Many forms of deviant behavior are multifunctional in that they produce multiple payoffs. Therefore, PIC-R stresses the density of the rewards and costs. "Density of reinforcement" refers to the number, variety, quality, and magnitude of rewards as well as the immediacy, frequency, and regularity with which they are delivered. The chances of an act occurring increase with the density of the rewards and decrease with the density of the costs. The appeal of the behavioral principles is that they focus directly upon the matter of interest, that is, variation in behavioral events. The concept of "density" is important because it encourages a comprehensive assessment of current and potential rewards and costs, rather than a fixation upon specific types of rewards or costs.

The concept of density also leads to a set of PIC-R principles that suggest that the background density of rewards or costs is important in understanding the relative importance of any specific reward or cost. For example, adding one specific reward to the situation of action may have little effect on behavior when the background density is very high or very low. However, that additional reward may have a great impact on behavior when the background density is at some intermediate level (see Principles 7, 8, and 9 in Resource Note 4.2).

Finally, with regard to Principle 4, there are many "physical" and cognitive characteristics of the person that influence the capability to respond and learn. Sometimes these person factors are permanent (e.g., brain damage), sometimes they are transitory (e.g., developmental and maturational changes), and sometimes they are acute (e.g., intoxication). Principle 4 accents PIC-R's departure from radical behaviorism and invites knowledge from biological and cognitive psychology. In particular, this principle alerts us to the possibility that an individual's sources of control may vary with developmental changes (something that we will see in the next chapter).

Sources of Control

Principle 5 (again see Resource Note 4.1) holds that antecedents and consequences arise from four major sources: (1) the actor (personally mediated events), (2) other people in the situation of action (interpersonally mediated events), (3) the act itself (nonmediated or automatic and habitual events), and (4) other aspects of the situation of action.

Consideration of the sources of the controlling stimuli expands the analytic and practical value of a behavioral perspective. We have located the source of these stimuli in the behavior itself (e.g., the pleasure that automatically derives from the injection of heroin) and in other people within the immediate environment. This perspective is similar to that of radical behaviorism.

PIC-R, however, adds another source of control: personally mediated control, that is, individuals have the potential to exercise control over their own behavior. Here direct contact is made with symbolic interactionism and the explosion of knowledge that began with Bandura's writings on social cognition theory and Meichenbaum's (1977) cognitive behaviorism. Radical behaviorism remains important because the analytic and technical power of the fundamental principles of behavior continue to serve well in applied settings, and the best of the cognitive approaches are antecedent and consequent-oriented approaches (see Chapter 7).

A particularly important aspect of the social learning concept of self-control is the ongoing specification and empirical validation of self-regulation processes. It is no longer necessary for self-control to be operationally defined by observations of its presumed effects (e.g., a history of impulsive acts, a history of pleasure-seeking, etc.). The more important point is the promise that these "skills" can be developed through direct training. This is something that parents of restlessly energetic children (and the children themselves) may find attractive. The processes of self-regulation may include, for example, the setting of standards of conduct, planning activities, choosing activities, self-monitoring, and even self-consequation in terms of delivering rewards and costs to oneself after self-evaluation of behavior. Here we are deliberately using a language consistent with radical behaviorism, but the process is pure social learning/social cognition in the tradition of Albert Bandura.

Albert Bandura (with colleagues such as Barbaranelli, Caprara, and Pastorelli, 1996) has made major contributions to understanding how personally mediated control operates. These authors describe in detail the mechanisms of moral disengagement through which self-punishment for immoral acts may not only be avoided but also diverted into expressions of self-reward. Similar to Sykes and Matza's techniques of neutralization (Chapter 3), these mechanisms of moral disengagement include all of the following:

1. *Moral justification*: "It is all right to fight/lie/steal in order to protect your friends/to take revenge for your family."

2. *Euphemistic language*: "It is all right to fight/steal/take drugs when you are just joking/giving someone a lesson/just borrowing property/ doing it once in a while."

3. *Advantageous comparison*: "It is all right to fight/lie/steal when others are doing worse/other acts are worse."

4. *Displacement of responsibility*: "You can't blame me, if I live under bad conditions."

5. *Diffusion of responsibility*: "You can't blame me, when the whole gang was involved/friends asked me to do it."

6. *Distorting consequences*: "No one was really hurt."

7. *Attribution of blame*: "If I misbehave, it is the fault of my teachers/parents."

8. *Dehumanization*: "It is all right to hurt those who deserve it."

The immediate examples above represent examples of the content or the "what" of thinking. Other scholars and clinicians have been focusing on the "how" of thinking. Carefully defined deficits in cognitive skills have been linked with criminal conduct, and many clinicians and researchers are pushing the cognitive skill approach to the limits (e.g., Goldstein & Glick, 1994; Goldstein et al., 1978; Platt & Prout, 1987; Ross, 1995; Ross & Fabiano, 1985). Clinically, depending upon the criminogenic needs identified in particular individuals, a skill curriculum (Goldstein, 1986; Goldstein & Glick, 1987, 1994) might target interpersonal skills, including both the behavioral and cognitive elements of "starting a conversation," "apologizing," "expressing affection," "responding to failure," and "setting a goal." These skills range from basic interpersonal skills through the development of specific alternatives to aggression. Anger control management in the Goldstein and Glick system entails "identifying triggers," using self-statements and relaxation techniques to lower arousal, and using self-reinforcement to control anger. Other relevant need areas include problem-solving training and social perception training.

The behavioral, cognitive behavioral, and social learning approaches have the overriding value of being active, experimental, and pro-intervention. The basics of skill training are well-understood in terms of defining the skill, modeling the skill, and arranging plenty of opportunity for reinforced practice in the context of role playing. The review of the intervention literature later in the text indicates that society and PCC cannot afford not to take social learning theory seriously. Some alternative theories may be able to account for the correlates and predictors of crime and incorporate personality. None, however, have the demonstrated applicability of social learning theory. The ultimate test of a theory is the ability to influence the phenomenon of interest. So far the social learning approach has virtually no competitors in that regard.

Relationship to Other Theories

Figure 4.4 provides a summary of principles through a cross-classification of types and sources of consequences. Behavior—both criminal and noncriminal—is under the control of antecedent and consequent events; in order to alter behavior, the antecedent and consequent conditions that govern the behavior must be altered. These controlling conditions can be additive or subtractive in nature, and they can be non-mediated, interpersonally mediated, and/or personally mediated. Many of the traditional theories of criminal behavior are limited in scope and weak in their underlying psychology of human behavior. A powerful theory will be open to the full diversity and complexity of human behavior.

Note how the major social psychological theories of deviance distribute themselves across Figure 4.4. The motivational theories fall in the first two columns (the rewards), while the control theories fall in the last two columns (the costs). Motivational theorists emphasize the potential rewards for deviant behavior, whereas control theorists emphasize the potential costs of—or the factors that deter—deviance. Anomie theory emphasizes the material rewards of money and property and makes some additional reference to enhanced power and prestige. While such outcomes may function as additive rewards, there is the distinct sense in Merton's writings that such events also serve as subtractive rewards. That is, they function to produce relief from a sense of frustration and alienation. The classic psychoanalytic and frustration-aggression theories (Berkowitz, 1962; Dollard et al., 1939) suggest that crime may serve an escape/avoidance function such as that proposed in the stress reduction model of alcoholism (Sobell & Sobell, 1972) and Lindesmith's (1947) perspective on opiate addiction.

Some valued end states may be more readily affected by deviant rather than nondeviant acts: for example, excitement and thrills (Miller, 1958; Quay, 1965), independence (Jessor, Jessor & Finney, 1973; Miller, 1958), or a demonstration of contempt for the existing social order or an affirmation of commitment to a new order (the conflict theorists). Depending upon the orientation of one's self and one's friends, deviant activity may also bring about the approval of the self and others.

Sources of Consequences or Antecedents	Rewards		Costs	
	Additive	**Subtractive**	**Additive**	**Subtractive**
(Some typical descriptions of any concomitant emotional states.)	("Pleasure")	("Relief")	("Pain")	("Frustration"/ "Disappointment"/ "Grief")
A. Personal: Self-Mediated				
(Thoughts, images, self-talk, anticipation of the reactions of others.)	i) **Events:** Positive self-labeling. Personal approval. Self-instructions to proceed.	Self-removal of negative labels. Avoiding or discounting negative labels.	Negative self-labeling. Personal disapproval. Self-instructions to cease.	Self-removal of positive labels. Recognition of potential losses.
(An "active," "conscious," "deliberate," "self-managing" person is assumed.)	ii) **Examples:** "This is great." "This is fun." "What a stone!" "I am at one with the universe." "I am free, independent, powerful." "That was one of the cleanest B & Es I have ever accomplished." "Wait until I tell Joe about this."	"I am not a wimp/coward." "This is relaxing." "This is exciting, it was so boring before." "Finally, some energy." "The drug laws are stupid anyway." "The SOB deserves it."	"I feel sick" "This is wrong, in my eyes, in the eyes of my mother, in the eyes of God." "This guy might fight back."	"Am I the type of person who would steal/hurt other people/leave my kids out in the rain while I buy a pack of cigarettes?" "If my mother says this...." "I am losing control."
Some general psychological perspectives on self-regulation: Bandura; Meichenbaum; Kanfer; Mahoney; Carver & Scheier.	Glaser Differential Identification	Lindesmith; Sykes & Matza	Reckless: Hirschi; Piliavin; Freud	
		Subcultural and labeling theorists with an emphasis on symbolic interaction	Control theorists with an emphasis on symbolic interaction	
			Differential Association Theory: with an emphasis on symbolic interaction	
B. Automatic: Nonmediated	i) Sensory/physiological effects and affective stimulation. "Pleasure." The "stone," "rush," "high," "buzz." Arousal jag.	"Relief": from boredom; [Quay] frustration; [Anomie: Frustration, Aggression] anxiety/tension/guilt; [Stress-reduction theories] withdrawal distress; [Lindesmith] from a dry, scratchy throat.	"Pain" Nausea [Some interventions such as negative practice and "rapid smoking" exaggerate the naturally aversive consequences of specific behaviors.]	"Frustration" Loss of physical coordination. Removal of pleasant affective or sensory status.
	ii) Conditional emotional responses "Hope"	"Relief"	"Fear"	"Frustration"
	The behavioral versions of Lindesmith	Eysenck; Hare; Lykken, Schachter & Latané		
	iii) External events tied in an intimate manner to specific types of acts such as theft and aggression. Money, property. Sexual satisfaction. Signs of pain/submission.	Removal or destruction of a frustrating agent.	The possibility of retaliation; signs of conquest by another.	Interference with ongoing activities. Hunt & Azrin Loss of money (gambling).
C. Interpersonally Mediated	**Events:** i) Direct evaluation of expressions of others. Approval, affection, attention.	Reduction of disapproval.	Disapproval.	Reduction of approval, attention.
	ii) Behavioral opportunities involving other person. Opportunity to engage in "valued" activities. The approval of others and group membership brings the opportunity for a variety of social, recreational, and sexual activities.	Opportunity to escape/ avoid "disliked" activities (such as work and authority; family responsibility; or being alone, bored, generally frustrated.) Opportunity to engage in otherwise very costly behaviors (in the sense that intoxication may reduce the costs of aggressive/sexual displays).	Forced to engage in disliked activities (for example: having to listen to the same old stories told by drinking buddies; having to interact with disliked others).	Lost opportunity to engage in "valued" activities. Reduced approval, affection and attention.
Some relevant general social-psychological perspectives on interpersonal influence: group dynamics theory; social learning theory; the relationship and contingency dimensions.	Subcultural and labeling theorists, with an emphasis on the interpersonal contingencies. Matza ("Sounding")		Control Theorists, with an emphasis on the interpersonal contingencies. Reckless; Hirschi; Piliavin, Hunt & Azrin	

Figure 4.4
A Cross-Classification of Type and Sources of Consequences

Subcultural and labeling theorists emphasize some of the afore-mentioned personal values and social norms, though they tend to ignore the process by which norms guide behavior. In contrast, PIC-R shows the process and specifies that control will be evident at both the personal and interpersonal levels. As suggested by Burgess and Akers (1966) and Sykes and Matza (1957) years ago, and now endorsed by so many (e.g., Agnew, 1994), techniques of neutralization (i.e., rationalizations for deviance) are verbalizations that serve to avoid, escape, or deflect negative labeling by oneself or by others. Gottfredson and Hirschi (1990) suggest that some behavioral reformulations of cultural deviance theories sound as if they are merely reformulations of the old notion of deviance as conformity. However, that is not what a broad social learning perspective purports. PIC-R incorporates the general rewards suggested by the narrower motivational theories of deviance, but it is not limited to them. Furthermore, PIC-R does not negate the possibility that for some individuals, under some circumstances, the motives for deviant behavior can be highly idiosyncratic (e.g., the pain of others, as in the case of sadism; or sexual attraction for children, as in the case of pedophilia). PIC-R also says that no matter what the rewards, the costs remain relevant.

Differential association theory (Sutherland & Cressey, 1970)—one of the more conceptually and empirically satisfying of the general perspectives (Akers & Cochran, 1985; Andrews, 1980; Johnson, 1979) when not read as a cultural theory (Akers, 1996)—appears sensitive to both rewards and costs. However, the original statement of differential association may have placed an overemphasis on the symbolic (or personal) level of control. The available empirical literature, with a few exceptions, suggests that peer support and personal sentiment measures make independent contributions to the predictability of indices of deviant behavior (Andrews & Kandel, 1979; Andrews & Wormith, 1984; Jenson, 1972; Johnson, 1979). In essence, deviant associates increase the chances of deviant activity above and beyond the influence they have on personal beliefs regarding deviance. Social support involves interpersonally mediated approval as well as the possibility of increased resources for particular actions, such as access to a "fence" or to drugs.

Control theorists emphasize the costs of deviance but differ among themselves in terms of the types of costs given the most theoretical attention. Eysenck (1977) emphasized deficits in conditioned fear responses. Some researchers (cf., Harpur & Hare, 1990) have found specific correlates of psychopathy at the autonomic level and are exploring the neuropsychology of emotion. Others emphasize ties to conventional moral codes and affective ties to conventional others (Hirschi, 1969; Piliavin, Hardyck & Vadum, 1968; Reckless & Dinitz, 1972). When a person is strongly tied to convention, deviant activity occurs at the risk of personal and interpersonal disapproval as well as the loss of affection and esteem.

The *personality* correlates of criminality also may be located within Figure 4.4. When high value is placed upon excitement and thrill-seeking, the probability of exploring crime increases. As noted, some valued consequences are simply more readily achieved through deviance. Egocentrism suggests a reduction in the controlling potential of the reactions (anticipated or actual) of others to one's deviant acts. Even measures of psychic discomfort (such as anxiety, low self-esteem, and alienation) may be related to criminality under particular circumstances. Certain forms of deviance may reduce psychic distress (a subtractive reward), and with a background of low levels of self-satisfaction, the subtractive costs of deviance will be relatively low. Low scores on measures of social power and personal competence suggest that a person is unlikely to receive many rewards for nondeviant pursuits; hence, the subtractive costs of deviance may be slight and the motivation for crime increased.

The construct of *antisocial attitudes* has a crucial role in PIC-R. It is these attitudes, values, and beliefs—i.e., procriminal versus anticriminal sentiments—that determine the direction of personally mediated control. They contribute to the standards of conduct that determine whether personally mediated control favors criminal over noncriminal choices. They also represent the pool of justifications and exonerating statements that the person has available in any particular situation. The content of thought may well be more important than the functions of cognitive control.

The construct of *antisocial associates* is also very important. Antisocial associates (including parents, siblings, peers, and others in the immediate situation of action) influence the procriminal versus anticriminal nature of modeling in the situation of action as well as govern the rules by which rewards and costs are signaled and delivered. Antisocial significant others also impact on antisocial attitudes, which in turn may influence personally mediated control even in the absence of others.

The construct of a *history of antisocial behavior* is also theoretically relevant. It increases self-efficacy beliefs with regard to being able to complete the act successfully and serves as a measure of habit strength in the tradition of behaviorism. Empirically, rationally, and (as we shall see in Chapters 6 and 7) practically, the "Big Four" factors are central to PIC-R and PCC in general.

Summary

The general personality and social psychological approach to building a predictive understanding of criminal conduct has made considerable progress. In order to move into the realm of demonstrated causal significance, PCC needs an approach that is linked with a general psychology of human behavior that has demonstrated functional value. We used social learning theory as the underlying psychology, presenting the outline of PIC-R. PIC-R is a broad perspective that encompasses the contributions of many theories. Criminal behavior reflects not just particular motivations or particular costs but also the density of signaled rewards and costs. The implications of the perspective will be explored in the following chapters.

Chapter 5

Developmental Aspects
of Criminal Behavior

In the previous chapter, we presented a general theory of criminal behavior: PIC-R. PIC-R, a personal, interpersonal, and community-reinforcement perspective, is an empirically based theory that draws upon a general psychology of human behavior. It recognizes the multiple pathways to crime depending upon the specific controlling personal and environmental conditions that affect each individual. Principle 4 of PIC-R (see Resource Note 4.1) calls attention to biological, maturational, and developmental factors that moderate the influence of rewards and costs on behavior. In this chapter, we pursue in more detail the empirically and clinically relevant knowledge base regarding developmental influences on criminal conduct.

A concern to students of human development is understanding change and stability in individual behavior. Within criminology there has been a resurgence of interest in explaining how some children grow into crime and grow out of it. The interest is so widespread that a subdiscipline has emerged referred to as *developmental criminology* (Le Blanc & Loeber, 1998; Loeber & Le Blanc, 1990). Developmental criminology attempts to explain the different pathways or "trajectories" that lead to criminal behavior and the factors that contribute to a certain pathway (Loeber & Stouthamer-Loeber, 1996). It also assumes that the correlates of crime change as a function of age. For example, Bartusch, Lynam, Moffitt, and Silva (1997) found that poor verbal ability and hyperactivity were strongly related to childhood antisocial behavior (ages 5-11), whereas delinquent peers was the more important correlate among 13- to 15-year-olds.

Part of the impetus for a developmental criminology comes from a need to explain a number of facts about crime. First, many youths, especially boys, will engage in delinquent activities at some point during adolescence but not continue into adulthood. If we plot crime rates as a function of age, we find that crime gradually increases, peaking around age 20 and then diminishing gradually. Explaining this age-crime curve has generated considerable debate (cf., Tittle & Grasmick, 1998), but it does suggest that youth enter and leave the delinquent role at different times. Understanding the precursors to the onset and desistance of criminal behavior is a major goal of developmental criminology.

The age-crime curve also points to a second fact: the stability of criminal behavior. Although the majority of male youths who engage in crime eventually desist by early adulthood, for some, entry into a delinquent pathway means the development of a criminal career (Blumstein et al., 1986; Moffitt, 1997). For these offenders, delinquency turns into chronic adult criminality. Considering both the age effect and the stability of delinquent behavior, developmental criminologists have suggested that there is a need to explain the rise of two general types of offenders.

The first type of offender is referred to as the "experimenter" (Loeber & Stouthamer-Loeber, 1996) or the "adolescent-limited" (Moffitt, 1993). This type represents the majority of youthful offenders who account for most of the age-crime peak seen in late adolescence. They are hypothesized to begin their experimentation in antisocial behavior in adolescence but soon give way to more conventional pursuits. In addition, it appears that the behavior of these youths may be characterized as "rebellious" acts (e.g., arguing with teachers, cheating on tests) rather than more serious, aggressive acts such as hitting a teacher or carrying a weapon (Piquero & Brezina, 2001). The second type is the "persister" or "life-course" delinquent. This type never "grows out of it." They are the chronic offenders who exhibit antisocial behavior in childhood and continue into adulthood, often escalating in the seriousness of their acts. Understanding the factors that govern the development of persistent offenders has important implications for social policy and crime prevention. An overview of these factors constitutes the body of this chapter.

Children are not born completely ready to be molded by experience. They begin life with certain inherent capabilities and predispositions that mediate the influence of the environment. These biological capabilities and predispositions can and do change through interactions with the environment. One of the most exciting aspects of developmental criminology is its dynamic nature.

This chapter begins with a summary of some of the biosocial factors that underlie the child's abilities and his or her responsiveness to the environment. We will see a biological basis not only in cognitive development but also in personality development. Some of the traits and styles of behavior observed in adults are evident in infancy. Knowing the difference between right and wrong (moral reasoning) and behaving appropriately also requires caring about others and learning appropriate interpersonal skills. Sensitivity and concern toward others arises from healthy child-adult attachments and positive family, school, and peer experiences. Because there are multiple pathways to crime, we discuss a variety of topics (intelligence, moral reasoning, egocentrism, temperament, attachment). However, we end with two of the most important developmental factors—peers and the family.

The Biological Basis of Criminal Behavior

There has been a long-standing interest in the behavioral and biological sciences of the relative influence of biological and environmental factors on the expression of behavior. Fifty years ago, the research was portrayed as a battle between nature explanations versus nurture explanations of behavior. Today, most scientists believe that *both* nature and environment shape behavior. Our discussion of the development of criminal behavior begins with the biological underpinnings of criminal conduct.

Genetics and Crime

That crime runs in families has been a high-consensus inference of casual observers for years. Almost anyone who has worked in a criminal justice setting can provide vivid examples of intergenerational criminality. A famous, early study of the inheritability of criminal traits is Richard Dugdale's (1877/1970) analysis of the Juke family. Beginning with the children of Max Juke (circa 1750), Dugdale traced the Juke lineage to 1870. From the 709 descendants, nearly 20 percent were criminals and slightly more than 40 percent were dependent upon the state for financial support. Dugdale concluded that the high rate of criminality and "pauperism" was evidence for the inheritability of criminality and poor social adjustment. A more recent example comes from the Cambridge Study. In this longitudinal study, the correlation between the father's criminality and the son's criminality was quite high ($r = .43$; Rowe & Farrington, 1997), although the criminal careers of the sons were about four years shorter than the fathers' career (Farrington, Lambert & West, 1998). However, these findings may not so much reflect some genetic transmission of criminality as the fact that antisocial individuals tending to mate with similar individuals ("assortative mating"; Krueger et al., 1998). In the Cambridge Study, 83 percent of the boys in the study grew up and married women who also had criminal records (Farrington, Barnes & Lambert, 1996). In addition, a major problem in attributing the children's criminality to heredity is that the children have common or shared environments that are dysfunctional in nature. Most investigations of heredity depend on the study of twins and adopted children rather than the analysis of family lineage.

Twin Studies. In the first study of twins and criminality, Lange (1929) identified 13 pairs of monozygotic (MZ) twins and 17 pairs of dizygotic (DZ) twins from birth registries in Germany. Monozygotic twins (identical twins) originate from one egg and one sperm and therefore are genetically the same. Dizygotic twins (fraternal twins) originate from two eggs and are genetically different. If genetics plays a role, then the behaviors of MZ twins should show more similarity or concordance than is found in the behaviors of DZ twins. Lange found that the concordance rate for MZ twins with respect to criminality was 77 percent; it was just 12 percent for DZ twins. That is, for 10 of the 13 pairs of MZ twins, both siblings had histories of incarceration, whereas only two pairs of the 17 DZ twins had joint histories of incarceration.

While the magnitude of the effect was impressive, Lange's study and others conducted during the same period were suspect for a number of reasons. Certainly, social scientists in Britain and North America were not about to be impressed by a report originating from Germany during the rise of Nazism. The early studies also were plagued by serious methodological problems. For example, Lange grouped the twins with respect to zygoticity by examination of pictures, and the groupings were done with knowledge of the outcome. That is, the investigator knew beforehand whether the twins were involved in criminal activity, and this may have accounted for the high concordance rate for MZ twins.

Christiansen (1977) attempted to control for many of the earlier criticisms of twin studies. Drawing from the Copenhagen birth registry, he located a large sample of twins (3,586) that could be reliably identified as MZ or DZ. Criminal activity was defined according to official records. He also reported the concordance rates for both same-sex and different-sex DZ twins. This is an important comparison because the base rate for criminal behavior is higher among male-male twins than among male-female twins. For MZ twins, the concordance rate was 35 percent; it was 12 percent for DZ twins.

As twin studies have become more sophisticated, the concordance rate for MZ twins has decreased from 77 percent in Lange's study to 26 percent reported by Dalgaard and Kringlen (1976). Only two studies do not fit the general findings. Rowe (1983) found very high concordance rates for male MZ twins (74%) *and* for DZ twins (69%) drawn from the state of Ohio. The high rates may be due to two factors. First, a self-report scale measuring relatively minor delinquency was used (e.g., lying about age, starting a fight, shoplifting). Because such behaviors are frequent among adolescent males (recall the "experimenters" in the age-crime curve), the high base rate limits the ability to differentiate groups. Second, inner-city schools were excluded from the study, which may have further limited the sampling of more serious forms of delinquency. The other unusual findings reported by Gurling, Oppenheim, and Murray (1984) were that DZ twins had a higher concordance rate than MZ twins (14% vs. 7%). However, the sample size ($n = 14$) was quite small.

Despite a couple of unexpected results, general reviews and meta-analytic summaries of the twin literature show a relationship between genetics and crime. Carey and Goldman (1997) found six of seven "modern" (post-1968) studies showed a genetic effect. Walters's (1992) meta-analysis of 18 twin studies found a phi coefficient (a measure of association similar in meaning to a correlation coefficient) of .21. In a meta-analysis that used a broad definition of antisocial behavior that included aggression and a diagnosis of antisocial personality, Mason and

Frick (1994) found an almost identical correlation of .23 between twin studies and antisocial behavior (r was calculated from Cohen's d statistic of .48).

Although the results from twin studies point to a role for heredity, the fact that all of the studies used twins reared together is problematic. A frequently noted criticism has been that identical twins are treated more alike by their social environments and they influence each other more than fraternal twins (Carey, 1992; Carey & Goldman, 1997). Thus, the high concordance may be inflated by environmental influences (Brennan & Mednick, 1993). An "ideal" twin study would involve MZ twins separated at birth and raised in completely different environments. However, we are aware of only one such study of MZ twins reared apart. William Grove and his colleagues (Grove et al., 1990) followed 32 pairs of MZ twins who were separated before the age of five (one-half were separated within the first few months of birth). In adulthood (median age of 43), the twins were assessed using the Diagnostic Interview Schedule, a standardized method for formulating a clinical diagnosis. The concordance rate for antisocial personality disorder was 29 percent, about the range found by most twin studies on crime. The sample size may be small, but the findings by Grove et al. (1990) lend credence to the view held by some behavior geneticists (e.g., Carey, 1992; Plomin, 1989) that the shared environments of twins may not be as important as earlier thought. To address some of the difficulties with the twin approach, researchers have conducted adoption studies that more clearly separate the influence of environment and genetics.

Adoption Studies. Adoption studies use a method commonly called the cross-fostering design. This design requires an analysis of children who are separated soon after birth from their biological parents and raised, or fostered, by nonrelatives. In adoption studies, the criminal futures of adopted children are analyzed in relation to: (a) criminal history of the biological parents, (b) criminal history of adoptive parents, and (c) particular combinations of criminality in the biological and adoptive parents. The assumption is that if the rate of criminality among adopted children is higher for those who have a biological parent with a criminal record than for the adoptees with a noncriminal biological parent, then heredity has an effect.

An impressive databank has been created in Denmark that includes social history information on more than 14,000 children who were adopted between 1924 and 1947 (some of these findings were described in Chapter 2). Working with this databank, Mednick, Gabrielli, and Hutchings (1984) tabulated the convictions of male adoptees in relation to the criminal convictions in the biological and adoptive parents. Inspection of Table 5.1 finds that the evidence is mildly consistent with a genetic effect (r = .03). Note that adoptees raised by noncriminal parents but who had criminal biological parents were at a higher risk to be convicted (20% vs. 13.5%).

Table 5.1
Cross-Fostering Analysis of Criminality in Male Adoptees by Criminality of Biological and Adoptive Parents

| Criminal adoptive parents? | CRIMINAL BIOLOGICAL PARENTS? | |
	Yes	No
Yes	24.5% (of 143)	14.7% (of 204)
No	20.0% (of 1226)	13.5% (of 2492)

From Mednick et al., 1984

Is There a Genetic Basis to Serious and Chronic Criminal Behavior? The evidence for a heritability factor in criminal behavior, not unexpectedly, has raised expectations that genetics may be especially important in the development of violent and chronic criminal behavior. Evidence of a genetic-violence crime link is not only important for theory development and prevention efforts but it would also have significant legal implications. A genetic argument could be used as evidence for a "compulsion" to act and therefore serve as a defense against criminal punishment (Coombs, 1999; Dinwiddie, 1994).

To this point, geneticists have identified very few disorders that can be traced to a single gene (e.g., Down's syndrome, Huntington's disease). For most complex medical and behavioral disorders, such as heart disease, schizophrenia, or alcoholism, scientists agree that many genes come into play in the expression of complex behaviors. Nevertheless, this has not stopped the search for a single "crime gene" (Tehrani & Mednick, 2000). The most notable example of this search is the XYY chromosome anomaly.

Each human cell has 23 pairs of chromosomes (each parent provides 23 chromosomes). A chromosome is a complex biochemical structure composed of many genes. Genes are the basic units of heredity and control the manufacture of proteins and hormonal and enzymatic processes. One of the 23 chromosomal pairs determines sex, with males having an X chromosome paired with a Y chromosome and females having two X chromosomes. It is the Y chromosome that carries the genes associated with male features (e.g., height, male genitalia development, hair distribution). The fact that males far outnumber females in crime has led some to hypothesize that criminal behavior may be partially attributed to the Y chromosome.

Chromosomal mutations, either through spontaneous means or through accident (e.g., X-ray exposure), do occur. One such mutation is the XYY chromosomal aberration first reported in 1961 by Sandburg, Koepf, Ishihara, and Hauschka. This individual with the extra Y chromosome was a nonoffender and of average intelligence. More reports followed, but this time the individuals were linked to excessive aggressiveness (Jacobs et al., 1965). They were described as tall, intellectually slow, and violent. In brief, the description reinforced the layperson's idea of the violent criminal as a product of some biological defect. Emotional reactions to these findings contributed to such extreme programs and laws as screening male infants and high school students for the XYY chromosome (Katz & Chambliss, 1995). However, a careful analysis of the early findings indicated that the generalizations were limited because all of the reports were on physically and intellectually handicapped males, most of whom were in institutions (Jarvik, Klodin & Matsuyama, 1973).

There have been two large-scale studies on sex chromosome abnormalities and crime involving thousands of participants. (Goetz, Johnstone & Ratcliffe, 1999; Witkin et al., 1976). Herman Witkin and his colleagues studied all males born in Copenhagen, Denmark, between 1944 and 1947; Michael Goetz and his colleagues (1999) studied men born between 1967 and 1979 in Edinburgh, Scotland. Both studies found very few men with an XYY chromosomal abnormality. Witkin et al. (1976) found only 12 with the XYY aberration and Goetz et al. (1999) found 17 (less than 1% of each sample). The researchers then compared the XYY men to men who had an additional X chromosome rather than a Y chromosome. Witkin et al. (1976) identified 16 XXY males (i.e., Klinefelter's syndrome characterized by male genitals but often with sterility, breast enlargement, and intellectual retardation). Goetz et al. (1999) found 17 XXY men. In both studies, XYY men had more criminal convictions than normals (XY men), but most of the offenses were for property crimes. There were no differences in violent offending between the two chromosomal abnormal groups. Thus, not only is the existence of the XYY anomaly extremely rare, but, more importantly, it links weakly with criminality and not at all with violence.

In another investigation of the possible link between heredity and more serious forms of criminal behavior, Mednick, Gabrielli, and Hutchings (1987) conducted additional analysis of the Danish adoptee data set previously described. They focused on chronic offenders who were defined as having at least three prior convictions. The chronic offenders represented 4 percent of the sample but were responsible for 69 percent of all the crimes recorded by the adoptees. The biological parents were also categorized according to their convictions (from 0 to 3 or more). As the number of convictions for the biological parents increased, so did the number for the adoptees. These results, however, held for property offenses only and *not* for violent offenses. However, in a more recent analysis of another Danish data set, an association with violence was found when parental psychiatric hospitalization was added to criminal history (Tehrani et al., 1998). Thus, available data suggests that genetic factors may be important for chronic offending, but it is still unclear whether they are limited to the nonviolent type (Tehrani & Mednick, 2000; Moffitt, 1987).

In summary, the research findings to date require the inclusion of genetic factors in any full explanation of delinquent and criminal behavior. Returning to the previous reviews of the literature, Carey and Goldman (1997) found that all six of the adoption studies in their review showed a genetic effect. In the meta-analysis by Walters (1992), the weighted phi coefficient was .07 for the 21 adoption studies (Mason and Frick, 1994, found an effect size of .25, but only three studies were used for the adoption analysis). Those who conduct behavior genetic research are convinced that no matter "how much variance is accounted" by genetics, this research tells us more about the importance of the environment than nature. For example, Michael Lyons and his colleagues (Lyons et al., 1995) found in a study of 8,000 male twins that environment explained six times more of the variance in juvenile antisocial traits than heredity. Even in adoption studies, families are selective and choose children to adopt who best fit in to their environments (Stoolmiller, 1999). As Anthony Walsh (2000) puts it, genes control biochemical reactions—not thoughts, feelings, and beliefs. It is the environment that controls the content of these psychological processes. The important area of research for behavior geneticists is to identify and understand what psychosocially inheritable attributes increase the risk for crime. We now turn our attention to some of these factors.

The Energetic, Impulsive, Sensation-Seeking Temperament

Temperament describes the individual's usual way of responding to environmental stimuli. It forms the biological basis for certain personality traits that remain relatively stable throughout life (Halverson, Kohnstamm & Martin, 1994; Rothbart & Ahadi, 1994; Svrakic, Svrakic & Cloninger, 1996). Personality is a more general construct that encompasses temperament, structure (e.g., Freud's id, ego, and superego), and motivation (e.g., Freud's instinct or Carl Rogers's self-actualization tendency). Temperamental traits such as impulsiveness and sensation-seeking are observable very early in life with some evidence of a genetic component (Saudino et al., 1995; Zukerman, 1993). Moreover, temperament appears related to the five-factor model of personality currently in vogue (Costa & Widiger, 1994; Digman, 1990). Criminology's interest in the relationship between temperament and delinquency has been sporadic (e.g., Glueck & Glueck, 1950). However, the recent longitudinal findings and theorizing from Terri Moffit and her colleagues has refocused attention on this important construct.

The origin for today's research in temperament can be traced to the studies by Alexander Thomas, Stella Chess, and their colleagues (Chess & Thomas, 1990; Thomas & Chess, 1977; Thomas et al., 1963). In the original research, 133 newborn infants were assessed along nine categories (e.g., activity level, quality of mood, distractibility, intensity of reaction). The categories were further clustered into three types: "easy," "slow to warm," and "difficult." Our interest is in what Chess and Thomas (1984) called the "difficult" child, a category that comprised 10 percent of the 133 children. The difficult child was described as intense in his or her reactions to stimuli, generally negative in mood, slow to adapt to change, and irregular in sleep, hunger, and other bodily functions. Following the children into early adulthood (age 24), there was significant stability, especially along the easy and difficult dimensions (Chess & Thomas, 1984). For example, at age 10, the difficult child had a varied sleep schedule, showed difficulties adjusting to school, threw tantrums when frustrated, and cried when he or she could not solve homework problems. In adolescence, 10 of 12 cases diagnosed with a behavior disorder were temperamentally difficult children.

Regardless of the number of dimensions and the terminology used by researchers, some form of a "difficult" temperament is common to almost all classification schemes. We will continue to use the term "difficult" because it conveys well the potential problems these children can create. A difficult temperament, as characterized by high energy levels, impulsiveness, and poor adaptation to novel stimuli, would certainly tax many a parent. Although all children begin life with no self-control skills, most gradually do learn self-management skills. The highest rate of physically aggressive behavior is actually among three-year-olds, not older adolescents or young adults (Tremblay, 2000). Learning nonaggressive behaviors to achieve goals and delay gratification are skills dependent upon learning experiences. Children with a difficult temperament, we would expect, would have a more arduous time learning these skills.

High energy, impulsiveness, low self-control, and sensation-seeking are major personality characteristics of adult offenders, and they form what we broadly define as the antisocial personality pattern. This pattern represents one of the "Big Four" correlates of criminal conduct. These personality traits are also common among juvenile delinquents (e.g., Luengo et al., 1994; Tinklenberg et al., 1996) and in young, behaviorally disordered children. Childhood hyperactivity is a predictor of persistent, frequent, and violent delinquency (Dalteg & Levander, 1998; Lahey & Loeber, 1997) and in a meta-analysis, hyperactivity yielded an average correlation of .13 with antisocial behavior (Hawkins et al., 1998). Childhood attention-deficit/hyperactivity disorder now plays an important role in many developmental theories of antisocial behavior (Farrington, 1998; Moffit, 1993).

A difficult temperament in infancy has predicted childhood aggressive behavior and adolescent delinquency. Schwartz, Snidman, and Kagan (1996) followed young children from 21 months and 31 months of age until the age of 13. Difficult ("Uninhibited") temperament predicted self-reported delinquency and aggressiveness as reported by the parents. A Norwegian study of 759 twin pairs, age seven to 17, found "emotionality" associated with the Delinquent Behavior and Aggressive Behavior scales of Achenbach's Child Behavior Checklist (Gjone & Stevenson, 1997). The correlations ranged from .11 to .51, depending on the gender and outcome (girls tended to have lower correlations on the Delinquent scale). Terri Moffitt and her colleagues found a difficult ("Lack of Control") temperament as early as age three to be predictive of self-reported and officially reported antisocial behavior at age 21 (Caspi et al., 1996; Henry et al., 1996; Krueger et al., 1994).

If a child is born with a difficult temperament, how does this temperament translate into the development of criminal behavior? As we have suggested, parenting such a child is demanding. A positive outcome for the child could result if the child has the "right" parent(s) (caring, patient, and flexible in adapting to the child's behavioral pattern). However, if there is a "poorness of fit" (Chess & Thomas, 1990) between parenting styles and the child's temperament, then parent(s) who find it difficult to cope may distance themselves emotionally from the child (Shaw & Vondra, 1995) or resort to inflexible and inappropriate disciplinary techniques. Gerald Patterson (Dishion & Patterson, 1997; Patterson, DeGarmo & Knutson, 2000), for example, hypothesized that hyperactivity is the first stage on the road to chronic delinquency. The child's hyperactivity interferes with effective discipline and consequently contributes to an early onset of delinquency. When a child with a difficult temperament is matched with impatient, impulsive, and hostile parents, the consequences could be unfortunate.

In the PCC, temperament is an ever-present characteristic of the individual. For the development of criminal behavior, a temperament characterized by impulsivity, high activity levels, and negative emotionality can be an important factor. We portray temperament as a risk factor and the "how" of personality. Therefore, the difficult temperament tells us something about how the child tends to respond to the environment. Temperament is one of the biological foundations to the Responsivity Principle of effective treatment (discussed in more detail in Chapter 6). Socialization efforts and treatment effectiveness are enhanced when the service provider or socialization agent (clinician, parent, or teacher) is sensitive to the personality characteristics of the individual that affect his or her responsiveness to social reinforcements and costs.

Underlying the energetic, impulsive, sensation-seeking temperament is neurophysiological arousal (Raine, 1997). The state of neurophysiological arousal may be monitored by measuring the electrical activity of the brain or central nervous system (CNS) or the physiological activity external to the brain (i.e., the Autonomic Nervous System, ANS). An electroencephalogram (EEG) measures the frequency and amplitude of various brain waves and gives an indication of the level of cortical arousal. ANS activity is monitored by measuring heart and respiration rates, eye pupil dilation, and sweating.

Neurophysiological underarousal is central to the theories of Hans Eysenck, Sarnoff Mednick, and Herbert Quay. Eysenck (1977; Eysenck & Gudjonsson, 1989) and Quay (1965) postulated that there is a biological basis to the personality traits of extraversion, neuroticism (or emotional instability), and psychoticism (described as an impersonal, aggressive, and impulsive style). Criminals are underaroused; in order to bring some physiological balance to their system, they seek out stimulation and excitement. Paired with impulsivity and poor self-control, this combination of personality characteristics inevitably brings them into conflict with the law.

Another aspect of neurophysiological underarousal is the role it plays in learning self-control (or as Eysenck writes, a "conscience"). In Sarnoff Mednick's (1977) biosocial theory, self-control is learned through a combination of instructions, modeling, and the reinforcement of prosocial alternatives and the punishment of inappropriate behaviors. Normally, punishment elicits fear, which is a biologically based emotion as indicated by increased heart rate, blood pressure, and sweating. Inhibiting the inappropriate behavior (i.e., self-control) avoids the unpleasant fear reaction.

Thus, critical inhibitory learning requires that: (1) antisocial behavior is punished, and (2) the child has the capacity to learn to inhibit antisocial behavior. The antisocial behavior of some people may be traced to the fact that they did not receive the training. That is, they have normal neurophysiological arousal patterns but either their parents did not monitor their behavior, were unable to distinguish moral and immoral behavior, and/or simply failed to punish. The antisocial behavior of others may be traced to a breakdown in the biological ability to learn self-control.

The learning of inhibition emphasizes the importance of "fear reduction" and passive avoidance learning (learning *not* to act in order to avoid punishment). Passive avoidance learning proceeds in this manner:

1. The child contemplates an aggressive act.

2. Previous punishment produces fear in the child.

3. Fear causes the child to inhibit the aggressive response.

4. The child no longer entertains the aggressive impulse and the fear dissipates.

5. The immediate reduction of fear reinforces the inhibition of the antisocial act.

In addition to requiring a socialization agent to deliver the original lessons through punishment, the process requires that the child display an adequate fear (ANS) response, possess the ability to acquire the fear response, and show a fast dissipation of fear in order to receive the natural reinforcement for inhibition. Several studies (reviewed by Venables, 1987) have found evidence that antisocial personalities show relatively diminished ANS responses to aversive stimuli, and once fear is aroused, ANS activity is slow to dissipate (Hare, 1978; Raine et al., 2000).

The extent to which neurophysiological underarousal is prevalent among general offender samples and children with difficult temperaments needs further exploration. The hypotheses and few studies that relate underarousal to impulsivity and poor self-control skills are enticing. A deficit in passive avoidance learning may, however, be caused by factors other than a fear deficit. For example, some psychopaths may have the potential to feel fear but simply do not attend to the stimuli that provoke fear (Hare, 1982; Newman, 1989).

Within the context of PIC-R, neurophysiological underarousal and the need for stimulation highlight the automatic, nonmediated reinforcement potential of criminal behavior. That is, some offenders may engage in criminal acts not so much because of peer approval or some type of self-reinforcement strategy but because the act itself feels good (here we are referring to nonsexual offenses). Compared to nonoffenders, criminals tend to score higher on measures of sensation-seeking (Gottfredson & Hirschi, 1990; Zuckerman, 1984) and will readily report a feeling of a "high or rush" when committing crimes (Wood et al., 1997). Thus, the neurophysiological arousal hypothesis provides a plausible explanation for antisocial behavior in the absence of interpersonal or personally mediated controls.

Other Biological Correlates of Criminal Behavior

There are many correlates of crime that have biological origins. Note that three predictors of crime—age, sex, and race—are biological as well as social psychological variables. Researchers have identified a variety of biological correlates of criminal and violent behavior. Neurochemicals such as serotonin and testosterone (Booth & Osgood, 1993), cerebral hemispheric asymmetry (Moffitt, 1990), and hypoglycemia (Virkkunen, 1987) have been linked to criminality. Prenatal exposure to drugs (including cigarette smoking) and alcohol can affect neurophysiological functioning and cognitive ability (Brennan, Grekin & Mednick, 1999; Coles & Platzman, 1993; Kaemingk & Paquette, 1999) and temperament (Schuler, Black & Starr, 1995), which in turn increase the risk for criminal behavior.

In the Dunedin Multidisciplinary Health and Development Study (New Zealand), approximately 1,000 children born between 1972 and 1973 have been tested on a range of factors every two years (Moffitt, Lynam & Silva, 1994). At age 13, they were administered neuropsychological and IQ tests; and at age 18, delinquency was assessed. Terri Moffitt and her colleagues found many of the neuropsychological tests predicted delinquency at age 18. Tests that measured verbal abilities, as opposed to tests measuring visual-motor abilities, showed the highest correlations with future delinquency. The researchers found that poor neurological functioning was associated only with the chronic or "life-course-persistent" male delinquents. This was a very small group (12% of the male sample) but they accounted for 59 percent of all convictions. For those whose delinquency was "adolescent-limited," neuropsychological functioning was not predictive of outcome.

Debra Denno (1990), however, found that although delinquents scored lower on verbal IQ and attentional and memory tasks than non-delinquents, these tests did not differentiate the chronic and violent offenders from the more typical offender. Her data was taken from a 10-year follow-up of 987 black subjects selected from Philadelphia's Collaborative Perinatal Project. The differences in the results reported by Denno may be an artifact of the tests used and when they were administered. In another study using a sample drawn from the same project, Stephen Tibbetts and Alex Piquero (1999) found that neurospsychological deficits did predict early onset of offending.

The findings from the Dunedin Study speak to one of the major questions asked by developmental criminology: What are the factors that lead youths into stable, chronic criminality? The Moffitt et al. (1994) findings suggest that neuropsychological factors have some importance in explaining persistent criminal behavior. Together with the evidence reviewed on heredity and temperament, explanations of chronic, persistent offending must include biological factors. This is not to say that chronic and serious offending cannot occur in the absence of biological correlates. Socialization experiences also can shape the development of persistent offenders. For the persisters, though, biological variables appear to increase the risk of offending.

We wish to emphasize that the relationship between biological factors and crime is not direct and simple. The consistent findings are poor verbal/language skills, inhibitory deficits, and poor attentional and planning abilities. Whether these deficits have direct effects or are mediated by other factors (such as family and school environment) is an unresolved question (Moffitt, 1990). Generally, it appears that genetic and psychophysiological contributions to criminal conduct will be greatest when the social milieu is least supportive of crime. For example, the genetic and neuropsychological effect is greater when the more serious rather than less serious crimes are sampled (Mednick et al., 1986; Moffitt et al., 1994), greater among women than among men (Cadoret & Cain, 1980), and greater when the subjects live in a disadvantaged environment (Tibbetts & Piquero, 1999). Under conditions in which crime is relatively infrequent and/or is subject to the highest levels of control, the biopsychological factors emerge most strongly.

Although we agree with those who argue that a comprehensive theory of criminal behavior must include biological and genetic factors (e.g., Ellis & Walsh, 1997; Walsh, 2000), we must keep these factors in perspective. Walters's (1992) meta-analysis found that the strength of the gene-crime relationship varied with the type of study and the quality of the research design. Family pedigree studies (i.e., examining the criminal behavior of parents and relatives in relation to the child's criminal activity) showed the largest association (phi = .26), while the more sophisticated adoption studies showed the smallest association (phi = .07). Furthermore, in a study involving 192 families with twins, 60 percent of the variance was attributed to poor parenting practices (Reiss et al., 1995).

Finally, there is some recent evidence suggesting that environment and genes may have different influences depending upon the *type* behavior. Criminal behavior is a product of the biological predisposition and rewards and costs associated with criminal behavior *and* prosocial behavior. Robert Krueger, Brian Hicks, and Matt McGue (2001) have completed the only study that evaluated the genetic influence on altruistic (prosocial behavior). Two hundred and seventy-six male twins born in Minnesota between 1961 and 1964 were located and asked to complete a number of measures (average age of 33 years). The questionnaires included a self-report of criminal history and a self-report altruism scale. There were two important findings. First, altruism and antisocial behavior were uncorrelated. That is, criminality and altruism were not the extreme ends of one dimension; one can be antisocial and also have a helpful orientation to people. Second, antisocial behavior showed a genetic effect (MZ correlation of .51 and DZ correlation of .28), while altruism did not show a genetic effect (MZ correlation of .38 and DZ correlation of .31, nonsignificant). In other words, altruistic, prosocial behavior was explained by environmental factors.

Plomin's (1989) comments on the heredity-behavior literature are instructive and worth quoting:

> These same data (genetic research) provide the best available evidence of the importance of the environment . . . they also indicate that nongenetic factors are responsible for more than half of the variance for most complex behavior. (p. 108)

Cognitive Development

When speaking of cognition, most people tend to think of attention, memory, thinking, planning, and problem-solving. However, congruent with recent views of cognition, this book will use a broader definition to include social cognition (understanding the behavior of other people) and language/communication skills. In criminology, relatively little attention has been directed to intelligence and almost none to social cognition and language. The cognitive abilities of a child are important for many reasons. They affect his or her responsiveness to socialization efforts by parents and other significant adults. Poor cognitive abilities impact on the likelihood of success in school and may also interfere with the learning of life skills needed for everyday interpersonal interactions. On many fronts, cognitive and intellectual abilities reflect a generalized ability to adapt to the environment (Sternberg, 1986).

Intelligence as a Correlate of Crime

That criminal offenders are less intelligent than nonoffenders is a notion that has been with us since Lombroso's description of the atavistic man (Goodard, 1920). Popularizations of "degenerate" families such as the Jukes (Dugdale, 1877/1970) fed the view that criminals and other social misfits were all mentally retarded. However, Denkowski and Denkowski (1985) found that mentally retarded persons (IQ score of less than 70) are not overrepresented in prison populations. (There have been no estimates of the prevalence of mentally retarded offenders in probation and parole settings.) Mental retardation, especially at the low end of IQ scores, does not appear to be an important risk factor. Kenneth Day (1993) did find relatively high rates of reconviction for mentally retarded offenders, but the recidivism was for minor offenses. Anne Crocker and Sheilagh Hodgins (1997) found that *non*institutionalized mentally retarded men and women had conviction rates similar (not higher) to non-mentally retarded individuals followed from birth to the age of 30 (institutionalized mentally retarded offenders were not examined).

Two meta-analytic reviews have found IQ moderately related to crime, with offenders scoring approximately five to 10 IQ points lower than nonoffenders. Travis Hirschi and Michael Hindelang (1977) reviewed eight studies of the IQ-crime relationship conducted between 1959 and 1973 and found IQ correlated with delinquency in the range of .16 to .31. Gendreau et al.'s (1996) more recent review found an average correlation of .07. Both reviews found IQ to be a stronger correlate of delinquency than social class and race. In addition, it appears that intelligence explains variation in criminal behavior independent of race and class. For example, Donald Lynam, Terri Moffitt, and Magda Stouthamer-Loeber (1993) asked 411 boys to complete self-report measures of delinquency, categorized into levels of seriousness at the ages of 12 and 13. The boys were selected from the Pittsburgh Youth Study, a longitudinal study of fourth-grade boys who were administered a battery of tests, including IQ measures. First, they found that the delinquent boys scored 10 to 11 points lower on Full Scale IQ (FIQ) and eight points lower on Verbal IQ (VIQ) than nondelinquents (many IQ tests measure verbal and nonverbal abilities such as spatial perception and manual dexterity). There were no differences in Performance (nonverbal) IQ (PIQ) scores. Table 5.2 summarizes the results with controls for the effects of class and race.

Table 5.2 shows that FIQ and VIQ were related to delinquency regardless of race and class and that both IQ measures were correlated with the seriousness of delinquency. Noteworthy was the finding that PIQ was related to the seriousness of delinquency for blacks. More will be said about the VIQ–PIQ relationship later. Nevertheless, most studies of IQ and crime agree that offenders perform poorly compared to nonoffenders. The questions now is: What does this mean, and is the relationship sufficiently significant to influence policy and practice?

Table 5.2
Delinquency and IQ Scores Adjusted for Race and Class

| Measure/Race | Seriousness of Delinquency | | |
	No/Low	Medium	High
FIQ			
White	109	105	103
Black	97	93	90
VIQ			
White	107	98	96
Black	96	92	89
PIQ			
White	110	109	109
Black	99	97	93

No/Low Group: 18 minor delinquents and 223 nondelinquents.

From Lynam et al., 1993

Interpreting the IQ-Crime Relationship

The relationship between intelligence and crime has important policy implications (see Resource Note 5.1) depending on how one interprets the relationship. One popular interpretation of the IQ-crime relationship is that the less intelligent are more likely to be apprehended. This would then account for why low-IQ individuals are overrepresented in adjudicated populations. Yet, self-report measures of delinquency also show the IQ-delinquency link (Hirschi & Hindelang, 1977; Moffitt & Silva, 1988). Another argument suggests that the lower IQ scores are the result of a delinquent lifestyle. That is, the impulsive, thrill-seeking, and risky lifestyle of the delinquent damages or interferes with the cognitive abilities measured by IQ tests. This interpretation is highly unlikely because many longitudinal studies show that IQ measured prior to the onset of delinquency predicts future criminality (Elkins et al., 1997; Farrington, 1998; Fergusson, Horwood & Nagin, 2000). Paul Lipsitt, Stephen Buka, and Lewis Lipsitt (1990) found in a cohort of more than 3,000 children that IQ scores measured as early as age four predicted delinquency. Stattin and Klackenberg-Larsson (1993) found that IQ scores at age three predicted future criminal behavior.

How then does IQ affect delinquency? A widely suspected mediator is school performance and adjustment (Hirschi & Hindelang, 1977; Ward & Tittle, 1994). That is, low IQ hinders academic achievement, which in turn impacts upon other factors more directly linked to criminal behavior (e.g., employment success, peer associations). There is, however, some question as to the universality of the school performance hypothesis. For example, Lynam et al. (1993) found that school performance mediated the IQ-delinquency relationship for blacks but not for whites. Low IQ would most certainly contribute to school failure, but low IQ is also correlated with childhood behavioral problems. There is evidence suggesting that it is early antisocial behavior rather than school problems that is most related to adolescent delinquency (Fergusson & Horwood, 1995; Tremblay et al., 1992).

Resource Note 5.1

Theory and Application to Practice
How Important is IQ?

In a provocative book, *The Bell Curve*, Richard Herrnstein and Charles Murray (1994) argued that IQ is a major determinant of crime and that the cognitively deficient are overrepresented among chronic and serious offenders. Taking this view and applying it to social policy, Herrnstein and Murray (1994) proposed simplifying laws to make them more understandable. In addition to simplification of the penal code, they recommended that punishment be administered in a clear and unambiguous manner. Presumably, mitigating and aggravating circumstances would confuse this class of intellectually challenged criminals and dilute the deterrent effect of punishment.

Herrnstein and Murray's (1994) analysis and thesis have been sharply criticized. Richard Darlington (1996) questioned whether the IQ test used in the study really measured intellectual aptitude or whether it gauged, more precisely, academic achievement. Francis Cullen and his colleagues (Cullen, Gendreau, Jarjoura & Wright, 1997) re-analyzed the data used by Herrnstein and Murray and found that IQ accounted for, under the best conditions, 3.4 percent of the variance in criminal behavior. To further place the relative importance of IQ among other potential predictors, the results of four meta-analyses on the predictors of criminal behavior were examined. An inspection of their data showed that the maximum correlation between IQ and crime was .10 for adults and .17 for juveniles. Compared to other predictors, measures of intelligence were in the middle range, eclipsed by the "Big Four" (criminal history, antisocial attitudes, peers, and personality). The findings on the IQ-crime relationship must be considered in relation to other correlates of crime. When IQ is compared to other criminogenic factors, the policy suggestions recommended by Herrnstein and Murray lose their force.

Another possible interpretation comes from the finding that delinquents score significantly lower than nondelinquents on VIQ. Early research produced conflicting results on the relative importance of verbal abilities and nonverbal, PIQ (see Baxter, Motiuk & Fortin, 1995). However, a number of recent studies call for continued research on verbal cognitive abilities. In a sample of nearly 1,800 adult inmates and 513 juvenile delinquents, Anthony Walsh (1992) found lower VIQ compared to PIQ correlated with delinquent activity even after controls were implemented for socioeconomic status and overall IQ. Moffitt et al. (1994) found poor verbal ability predicted chronic and violent offending in the Dunedin sample. In another New Zealand longitudinal study (the Christchurch Health and Development Study), Fergusson et al. (2000) found that 51.1 percent of the chronic offenders at age 18 scored in the lowest quartile on IQ tests at age eight whereas only 20.3 percent of the nonoffenders scored in the lowest quartile. And finally, Lynn Kratzer and Sheilagh Hodgins (1999) followed a Swedish cohort of nearly 14,000 children into adulthood. They found that early-onset delinquents scored lower on verbal intelligence measures than delinquents who started late and desisted from crime. The importance of verbal abilities is reflected in the following comments by Moffitt et al. (1994:296):

> Children who have difficulty expressing themselves and remembering information are significantly handicapped. *Dysfunctional* communication [italics added] between a child and his parents, peers, and teachers may be one of the most critical factors for childhood conduct problems that grow into persistent antisocial behavior in young adulthood.

The above quotation suggests that a language deficiency would be related to delinquency. Those who work directly with offenders are quite familiar with offenders who have difficulty expressing themselves and who have a limited and concrete-oriented vocabulary. These observations are usually attributed to school-achievement failure (Hinshaw, 1992), but it is possible that these language difficulties may have been evident before starting school. One study by Hokan Stattin and Ingrid Klackenberg-Larsson (1993) provided predictive evidence for a language-crime association. They followed 122 boys from birth to age 30. Assessments of language skills were conducted at a number of intervals between three months and five years of age. Assessments of babbling and vocalizations as early as six months predicted official criminality ($r = -.16$). In addition, the mothers of the offenders reported more difficulties in understanding their children at four years of age than mothers of nonoffenders (17.5% vs. 5.9%). More research along these lines is strongly encouraged.

Targeting Academic Achievement in Treatment

Although the school performance and adjustment mediational model does not adequately explain the IQ-crime link, this does not mean that what happens in school is unimportant. Poor academic performance and adjustment in itself can hinder knowledge and skill development, thereby diminishing one's access in employment markets and interfering with the development of prosocial values and behaviors. Moreover, academic achievement and prosocial bonding to school can be independent of each other. For example, a child may not have an A average on a report card but may nevertheless develop strong attachments to students and teachers. Travis Hirschi's control theory clearly emphasizes the prosocial bonding opportunities offered by schools. From an intervention perspective, the two processes would suggest that improving academic performance and attachment to school should decrease the likelihood of criminal behavior.

Early intervention programs aimed at improving academic performance and cognitive abilities have shown improvements in cognitive performance, but findings on the impact on delinquency have been mixed. Operation Headstart and similar programs provide formal school programs for prekindergarten children from impoverished families. Evaluations of these programs often used academic achievement and IQ as the outcome criteria, but a few studies examined the impact of these programs on delinquent behavior (Haskins, 1989). One exemplary program is the Perry Preschool Project (Berrueta-Clement et al., 1987; Schweinhart & Weikart, 1995).

The Perry Preschool Project randomly assigned low-SES children with IQs between 60 and 88 to either an experimental group or a control group. The 58 experimental children participated in a daily preschool program, and the teachers visited the family once per week. The 65 children in the control group did not attend preschool. All the children were four years of age at entry and they were followed up to the ages of 19 (Berrueta-Clement et al., 1987) and 27 years (Schweinhart & Weikart, 1995). At follow-up, school, police, and court records were reviewed, as well as interviews with 98 percent of the sample. The experimental group had fewer arrests and was more likely to be employed. IQ scores were higher at early follow-ups for the preschool group, but by middle childhood, the IQ advantage had disappeared. At age 27, 71 percent of the experimental children completed high school, compared to 54 percent of the controls. Only 7 percent of the treated children had five or more arrests; this was considerably less than the nontreated children (35%). The results of the Perry Preschool Project suggest that for some high-risk children early educational intervention may prevent future delinquency. It works, suggest the authors, because it prevents school failure and facilitates positive responses from the teachers.

Early preschool interventions may not be effective for all at-risk children. Stevens Clarke and Frances Campbell (1998) found no effect on adult crime for impoverished African-American children who attended the Abecedarian childhood intervention program. Canadian researchers in Montreal evaluated a preschool program for socially disadvantaged children with a history of birth complications (Pagani et al., 1998). Birth complications may increase the risk for neuropsychological problems and delinquency. More than 400 boys comprising four groups (with/without birth complications and attending/not attending preschool) participated in the study; at ages 11 and 12, they completed a self-report delinquency scale. Surprisingly, the researchers found that attendance in the preschool program actually benefited the children who did *not* have perinatal complications.

Drawing upon Hirschi's theory, Denise Gottfredson (1986) evaluated a program aimed at increasing attachment to school, decreasing school failure, and improving self-concept. School staff was trained in classroom management, students and staff met in extracurricular activities, and vocational programming was enhanced. In other words, schools were made more pleasant in order to enhance student attachment to the school. For "marginal" or high-risk students, intensive academic programming was also provided. In general, an increased attachment to school was associated with fewer disciplinary problems and self-reported delinquency. Although, educational attainment improved for the "marginal" (i.e., high-risk) students, the intervention failed to impact upon their delinquency. That is, a commitment to school may be more associated with reduced delinquency than improvements in academic achievement.

The importance of school bonding also comes from research on dropping out of school. Although school dropouts show higher rates of delinquency, poor academic achievement may not be the main culprit. Rather, the antecedent disruptive behavior of many dropouts (e.g., school suspensions, substance abuse on school property) is more closely associated with delinquency than school achievement (Jarjoura, 1993).

Denise Gottfredson's findings that the school environment is related to antisocial behavior confirm many earlier conclusions on the importance of "warm but restrictive" school climates (Coleman, Hoffer & Kilgore, 1982; Rutter et al., 1979). Warmth and restrictiveness tap into two fundamental sets of factors that influence behavior. Not many people would be in favor of our schools reducing the value placed on intelligence. However, finding alternatives to delinquency for the low-IQ offender is an important task for schools and for society in general.

Social, Practical Intelligence

IQ tests are very good at predicting success in school (with an average $r = .50$). They do not predict other socially relevant outcomes as well. When predicting job success, the correlations drop to the .20 range (Wigdor & Gardner, 1982), and they fall further to the .07 range when we consider criminal behavior (Gendreau et al., 1996). In the last 20 years, a distinction has been made between academic/school-related intelligence and what Robert Sternberg calls "practical intelligence" (Sternberg et al., 1995). Practical intelligence requires knowledge and ability to cope with everyday problems and people. It requires an understanding of why doing something is important for the actor and an ability to exercise self-control in order to reach personal goals. Practical intelligence also includes sensitivity to the motives of others and an ability to work with others in order to achieve goals.

In the field of criminology, there is only now emerging a recognition of the importance of practical intelligence. There are pockets of research that may be subsumed under the umbrella of practical intelligence. We have introduced the possible role of language, the basic communication process for social interaction, in the development of criminal behavior. We close our discussion of cognitive abilities with a brief overview of moral reasoning (understanding why it is important to act in a certain way) and interpersonal cognitive skills (exercising self-control and understanding others).

Moral Reasoning: Thinking about Right and Wrong. Lawrence Kohlberg (1958) described moral reasoning as progressing along six stages of development. The stages have a biological basis, but they are also influenced by environmental factors. The stages and associated levels are summarized in Table 5.3.

Table 5.3
Kohlberg's Theory of Moral Development

Level	Stage	Description
I Preconventional	1. Punishment and obedience	Egocentric
	2. Instrumental hedonism	(What happens to me?)
II Conventional	3. Approval of others	Social expectations
	4. Authority maintaining morality	(What do others expect of me?)
III Principled	5. Democratically accepted law	Universality (What is best for all?)
	6. Principles of conscience	

Most reviews of the literature conclude that moral reasoning is correlated with antisocial behavior (Blasi, 1980; Jennings, Kilkenny & Kohlberg, 1983; Palmer & Hollin, 1998). Where stage information is provided, the majority of offenders functioned at Stages 1 and 2 (Arbuthnot & Gordon, 1986; Craig & Truitt, 1996; Gibbs et al., 1984; Lee & Prentice, 1988). Gender differences in moral reasoning may be a factor. Carol Gilligan (1982) has hypothesized that female moral development is governed more by a concern for the other, whereas male morality is guided by rules that allow men to pursue utilitarian goals even if others are hurt in the process. Some empirical support for an "ethic of care" among female delinquents has been observed (Watt et al., 2000), but more research is needed to clarify the concept. In another study of gender differences, Daniel Mears, Matthew Ploeger, and Mark Warr (1998) found that females were less influenced by delinquent peers than males because of differences in moral values. Females consistently rated the offenses more "wrong" than the males, and this functioned as a protective factor against the influence of antisocial peers. Despite the association, we must be clear that we cannot conclude that low moral reasoning causes delinquency (if it did, then all young children would be delinquent). Instead moral reasoning is likely a contributing factor that, together with other personality and situational factors, leads to delinquency.

There have been a number of efforts to accelerate the rate of moral development for offenders who function at the preconventional level. One approach is to teach moral reasoning skills by encouraging "what if" thinking and estimating future consequences to behavior (Hayes & Walker, 1986; Morash, 1983). Another approach is to present moral dilemmas that challenge the subject with a higher stage of moral reasoning. In general, these intervention efforts have focused on adult offenders in prisons. Typically, the studies have shown changes in moral reasoning and prison adjustment (Craig & Truitt, 1996; Hickey, cited in Jennings et al., 1983; MacPhail, 1989; Putnins, 1997), but recidivism has been evaluated in only one adult study. Gregory Little and Kenneth Robinson (1989) followed up adult offenders who completed a "Moral Reconation Therapy" and found a significant correlation between their moral reasoning scores and new arrests (however, the average follow-up period was only eight months).

Only two studies report on the impact of teaching moral reasoning on recidivism. Jack Arbuthnot and Donald Gordon (1986) randomly assigned 48 male and female youths described by their teachers as behaviorally disordered to either a moral dilemma discussion group or a no-treatment control group. At the end of treatment (in-program recidivism), the moral dilemma group had fewer police and court contacts compared to the control group. One year later, however, neither group had any contact with the police or courts. John Gibbs (1995) randomly assigned institutionalized juvenile delinquents to a treatment program that included a moral educational component or to one of two control groups. A 12-month follow-up showed a recidivism rate of 15 percent for the treatment program and 41 percent for the control groups combined. Although the differences are impressive, the results could have been due to the anger management and social skills training given to the treatment group.

In summary, a relationship between delinquency and moral reasoning exists but is small. It is important to remember that there are significant proportions of offenders who score at the conventional and even the principled levels of moral development (Blasi, 1980). Furthermore, interventions that challenge moral reasoning can influence movement to a higher developmental level, but convincing links with reduced criminal behavior are few (Mears et al., 1998; Priest, Kordinak & Wynkoop, 1991; Smith & Brame, 1994). The mixed findings underscore a major area of research for the future. In brief, the developmental stages of moral development need to be more clearly differentiated from the construct of antisocial attitudes. From the perspective of a PCC, we expect that specific attitudes, values, beliefs, and rationalizations supportive of crime are much more strongly correlated with criminal conduct than are the stages of moral development. We look forward to what future research will show.

Interpersonal Cognitive Skills. Earlier we made a distinction between cognitive skills that involve academic intelligence and those that involve practical intelligence. Practical intelligence includes the abilities to exercise self-control and to relate constructively with others. Offenders show deficits not only in academic intelligence but also in the cognitive skills needed to deal effectively in social situations.

In order to get along with others, an individual must be able to understand the point of view of others, as well as their expectations and desires. Through this understanding, one can avoid the interpersonal costs associated with upsetting or hurting others. In addition, an interpersonal sensitivity facilitates appropriate conduct and can gain the individual interpersonal rewards. Achieving such an understanding is no small feat; parents spend endless hours teaching children to think of others before they act, to share their toys, help others, and the like. Success in teaching social understanding varies tremendously, and a failure results in interpersonal discord.

The development of interpersonal sensitivity requires a departure from an egocentric perspective of the world. Egocentrism involves an inability to consider the perspective of others both cognitively and emotionally. Empathy and role-taking are also some of the specific factors that contribute to an egocentric stance toward others. Targeting egocentrism, role-taking, and empathy may be expected to impact on criminal behavior. One of the classic interventions targeting egocentrism is found in Michael Chandler's 1973 study. This study was presented from a methodological point of view (in Resource Note 2.2); here we describe it in the context of interpersonal sensitivity.

Chandler asked nondelinquent and delinquent boys (ages 11-13) to describe a series of cartoons from two different perspectives. The boy was first asked to describe a cartoon sequence that began with the main character performing a number of actions and then introduced a second character halfway through the story. In the second telling of the story, the child was asked to describe the story beginning when the second character enters the sequence. Thus, in the second description, the story must be told pretending to have no knowledge of what has previously happened.

For example, one cartoon sequence shows a little boy playing baseball in a field. He hits the ball and the ball accidentally breaks the window of a car. The boy runs home and is seen gazing out of a window with a distressed look on his face. An adult enters the cartoon sequence at this point, there is a knock at the door and the little boy runs away while the adult looks on in puzzlement. Egocentric individuals were expected to show difficulty in describing the story when the adult enters without making reference to "privileged information" (i.e., information from the pictures prior to the introduction of the adult). The results were as expected. The delinquent children had significantly higher egocentrism scores than the nondelinquents.

In the treatment phase of the study, the experimental group members were guided by the research staff in role-taking skills and were asked to write skits around real-life events. These skits were acted out and videotaped, with the participants taking turns playing each role. The control group also produced films, but the films were of a documentary or cartoon nature and specific direction in role-taking was not provided. The experimental group showed the greatest decrease in egocentrism at the end of the 10-week program. Eighteen months later, police and court records were reviewed. The average number of official contacts was 1.0 for the treated juveniles and 2.1 for the control group.

Norma Feshbach's (1984, 1989) Empathy Training Program for aggressive children consists of a series of training exercises. The exercises teach children to identify emotional states (e.g., identifying the emotion of a person in a photograph), increase perspective-taking (e.g., imagining the world from the viewpoint of another), and increase emotional responsiveness (e.g., by role-playing several characters of a play). Feshbach randomly assigned teacher-rated aggressive children to one of three groups: (1) Empathy Training Program, (2) problem-solving skills, and (3) a nontreatment control. Both the Empathy Training and problem-solving groups showed decreases in classroom aggression. However, the Empathy Training group also showed increases in prosocial behavior (cooperation and altruistic behavior).

Exercises enhancing the identification of emotional states and responsiveness to these cues, as well as facilitating perspective-taking, are not limited to young, classroom-aggressive children. Viki Agee (1979, 1986) has applied many of these principles to her work with chronic and serious delinquents. In her early work in Colorado she worked with juvenile delinquents who were seen as untreatable (adolescents who had murdered, raped, assaulted, or escaped from other institutions). A major aspect of treatment consisted of developing an understanding of the victim's perspective. For example, she may take a juvenile who had murdered someone to the victim's gravesite and ask the delinquent to imagine the feelings of the victim's parents, friends, and so forth.

There are two other therapeutic interventions dealing with social cognition that are worthy of note. These are George Spivack and Myrna Shure's (1982) Interpersonal Cognitive Problem-Solving Skills (ICPS) program and Robert Ross and Elizabeth Fabiano's (1985) more broadbased interpersonal cognitive program.

The ICPS program teaches the following six cognitive skills:

1. generation of alternative solutions

2. consideration of the consequences of social acts

3. means-ends thinking (steps needed to reach a goal)

4. social-causal thinking (understanding that an individual's present situation is the result of past events)

5. sensitivity to social problems

6. dynamic orientation (perspective-taking)

Much of the research with the ICPS has been conducted with young children, usually in a classroom setting (Shure, 1993, 1997; Spivack & Shure, 1982, 1989; Webster-Stratton & Hammond, 1997). However, there is some evidence that a deficit in ICPS is related to delinquency.

George Spivack and Norma Cianci (1987) followed 660 children in Philadelphia from kindergarten to the age of 15. They found that the children who demonstrated involvement with police showed an early high-risk pattern of behavior marked by impulsiveness and self-centeredness, some of the behaviors targeted by an ICPS program. We are somewhat surprised that given the face validity of the program, there is only one outcome evaluation (with positive results) with offenders (Platt, Perry & Metsger, 1980). It is interesting that Shure (1988, 1997) also contends that teaching individuals "how" to think and not "what" to think will lead them toward making the right decision. We are less inclined to this view, but direct comparisons of the validity of assessments of antisocial attitudes and social/moral reasoning are not available to our knowledge. Certainly, the predictive validity of antisocial attitudes and weak socialization greatly exceed the predictive validity of emotional empathy.

Robert Ross and Elizabeth Fabiano (1985) have developed a more broad-based cognitive model for intervention. Their model utilizes many of the ICPS components, but also teaches perspective-taking skills, self-control, empathy training, and aspects of moral reasoning (Ross & Ross, 1995). Like ICPS, the emphasis is on *how* people think rather than *what* thy think (Robinson & Porporino, 2001). In the first evaluation of this treatment program, high-risk probationers were randomly assigned to either intensive probation, intensive probation with life skills training, or intensive probation with interpersonal cognitive skills training (Ross, Fabiano & Ewles, 1988). Nine months later, the recidivism rate was 69.5 percent for the intensive probation condition, 47.5 percent for the life skills condition, and 18.1 percent for the cognitive skills group.

There have been a number of replications of the Ross et al. (1988) findings (these studies are summarized by Robinson and Porporino, 2001). Although many of the studies had relatively small sample sizes, used weak research designs, and/or found small effects, the results were consistent in showing that interpersonal cognitive skills treatment can be effective. For example, a one-year follow-up of probationers in the United Kingdom showed a recidivism rate of 35 percent for the treated group and 40 percent for the control subjects (Raynor, Sutton & Vanstone, 1995; Raynor & Vanstone, 2001). In a large-scale evaluation of more than 2,000 Canadian federal parolees, the reincarceration rate for those who completed the cognitive skills program was 44.5 percent and 50.1 percent for a control group (Robinson, 1995).

One interesting role for interpersonal cognitions in criminal behavior has to do with the offender's use of rationalizations or techniques of neutralization. Recall from Chapter 3 that Sykes and Matza described various cognitions that offenders may use to avoid censure for their antisocial actions—that is, to "neutralize" the potential punishment that may be delivered by others (e.g., "It's not my fault I killed my parents, they failed to raise me properly"). Results from research on neutralizations draw our attention to the role of cognitive processes in "disarming" inhibitory prosocial cognitions. An individual may learn all the morally right things to do from structured intervention programs. However, well-intentioned programs may come to naught if neutralizing techniques are used to "short circuit" moral reasoning and moral values. In addition, there is the possibility that continued antisocial behavior leads to a "desensitization" to moral values and a greater "excuse" acceptance (McCarthy & Stewart, 1998). Moral reasoning, empathy, and egocentrism are but components of a more complex cognitive understanding of social relationships. Furthermore, interpersonal cognition is just one general factor that combines with situational, personality, and biological factors to produce criminal behavior.

To summarize our review of intelligence and other cognitive factors, recent research has shown that intelligence is a factor that requires consideration in theory and that it is more than a simple by-product of class and race. The data are clear: delinquents tend to score lower on standardized measures of intelligence than nondelinquents. In addition, intelligence represents more than academic knowledge. It involves a complex of cognitive skills ranging from verbal/language facility to moral reasoning to interpersonal problem-solving. Many intervention programs center around the cognitive skills described, with some programs showing more promise than other programs. Studies with young children have shown mixed results. For example, a review of the results from 19 randomized experiments of interpersonal skills training with children concluded that "the value of interpersonal skills training is limited" (Taylor, Eddy & Biglan, 1999:175). Programs targeting interpersonal cognitive skills with adults have been more successful. Despite the importance of these thinking skills, learning to behave prosocially also requires healthy emotional attachments to socializing agents. We now turn to an examination of the development of such bonds.

Interpersonal Attachments and the Development of Social Bonds

Given the behavioral roots of PIC-R, the probability of an act occurring was said to increase with the number, variety, quality, and immediacy of signaled rewards for that act and to decrease with the density of the costs. Interpersonally mediated signals of rewards and costs are significant for two reasons. First, they are important because so much of human behavior occurs in the presence of others. Second, other people (family, friends, teachers, and therapists) strongly influence the acquisition of behavior and the attitudes and values that bring behavior under personally mediated control. These personally mediated controls may even reflect anticipated or imagined reactions of significant others.

The interpersonal environment shapes, elicits, and maintains the behavior of an individual by selectively modeling, reinforcing, and punishing behavior. One factor that impacts strongly on the degree of interpersonal influence is the quality of the relationship between any two (or more) people. When the model and source of rewards and costs is a person who is highly valued, loved, cared about, interesting, enthusiastic, and respected, that model/source will be attended to and the reactions of that model/source will have powerful reward/cost implications. Without a strong relationship or attachment, interpersonally mediated rewards and costs have little influence. Why change for someone whom you do not care for or value?

Understanding the nature of social attachments is important not only for understanding the insensitivity of some to the immediate control of others, but also for understanding behavior in the absence of others. In addition to self-regulation, some theorists view social attachment as the basis for the more grand traits of egocentricism, empathy, and moral development, which imply a generalized interpersonal stance toward others (Fonagy et al., 1997; van Ijzendoorn, 1997). Finally, attachment to parental figures sets the parameters for all future social relationships.

Attachment theory has its roots in the work of John Bowlby (1971, 1988). Bowlby studied the nature of social attachments by observing the distress shown by the child when separated from the mother. In his early writings, Bowlby viewed attachment as instinctive or biological, with the mother being the natural target for attachment. Disagreeing with Freud's view that forming a bond to the mother served as a drive reduction (mother fed the child and reduced a biological need), the critical function of attachment was that it provided the infant security to explore the environment and develop independence. The mother was the safe haven to return to when the world was frightening. Finally, the mother-child bond was the prototype for all social attachments.

Bowlby's ideas about the importance of mother-child attachment and its influence on personality development and future social relationships stimulated a great deal of research. The results from the research also led Bowlby to modify his views in 1988. Two important modifications were: (a) primary attachment need not be with the mother; any consistent caregiver who meets the infant's needs for security is sufficient; and (b) it is not critical, though it is desirable, to have a healthy parent-child attachment within the first two years of life; that is, after age two, it is still not too late to form healthy social attachments.

With the parent-child bond seen as the foundation for all future love relationships, disruption of the bond would herald difficulties in attachment to other adults, peers, and symbols of authority (teachers, employers, the social order, etc.). Thus, Bowlby's work focused upon analyzing what happened when a mother-child bond was disrupted, even briefly. One result of a mother-child bond disruption is detachment. Detachment refers to a lack of interest in the adult. Bowlby's contention was that lengthy and frequent disruptions lead to a situation in which children "stop altogether attaching (themselves) to anyone" (p. 50) and develop a "superficial sociability."

One of the common causes of separation between parent and child is divorce. Studies of children from divorced parents or "broken homes" show small to moderate relationships with future child maladjustment. However, it appears that the difficulties evidenced by the children are partly attributable to the emotional conflicts within separating families rather than the loss of a parent. Heather Juby and David Farrington (2001) found higher delinquency rates for boys raised in disharmonious families than boys who lost a parent through death. In addition, boys from "broken homes" had rates of delinquency similar to boys from intact, high-conflict families. Wells and Rankin (1991) conducted a meta-analysis of 44 studies of "broken homes" and found a correlation of .15 between coming from a "broken home" and delinquency. A meta-analysis by Mark Lipsey and James Derzon (1998) compared nine studies of "broken homes" experienced between the ages of six to 11 as well as 13 studies of separation between the ages 12 to 14. The outcome variable was *violent* behavior. At the younger age, the average effect size was .06; it was .10 for the older children (the differences were not significant).

Joseph Rankin and Roger Kern (1994) found in their analysis of the National Survey of Youth database that a positive attachment to the caregiver in the single-parent family could not replace positive attachments to two parents in intact families. Hirschi (1969) suggested that a "broken home" would have no effect on delinquency if the child had a strong bond to one of the parents. To a certain extent, Hirschi was right. Single-parent families with a positive emotional parent-child attachment had lower rates of self-reported delinquency than families with poor parent-child bonds, but not as low as in intact families in which there were positive attachments with both parents (Cookston, 1999; Griffin et al., 2000).

Attachment is not an all-or-nothing affair. There are different degrees of attachment, ranging from secure and independent to angry and disorganized (Main, 1996; van IJzendoorn, 1995). Disorganized attachments and avoidant attachment patterns have been associated with a variety of behavioral maladjustments, including childhood aggression (Lyons-Ruth, 1996), pedophilia (Sawle & Kear-Colwell, 2001), and adolescent substance abuse and antisocial behavior (Allen, Hauser & Borman-Spurrell, 1996; Rosenstein & Horowitz, 1996).

Travis Hirschi (1969) used the concept of attachment to his advantage in his study of delinquency. Attachment to parents is central for control theory and Hirschi evaluated this concept by asking 4,000 high school students about their parents. Before we look at his results in more detail, it is noteworthy that Hirschi found age of parental separation (before or after the age of five) unrelated to delinquency. However, recent research has found that age becomes important when it is considered along with the frequency of "transitions" (i.e., separation and remarriage). In the Montreal cohort of 427 boys, those who experienced remarriage in the family between the ages of 12 and 15 were at a greater risk for delinquency (Pagani et al., 1998). Returning to Hirschi's study, attachment was defined as supervision by the parent (e.g., Does your mother/father know where you are when you are away from home?), communication with parents (e.g., Do you share your thoughts and feelings with your mother/father?), and affectionate identification (e.g., Would you like to be the kind of person your mother/father is?). All of these measures were predictive of delinquency. Furthermore, these measures of attachment were related to delinquency regardless of the youth's race or social class.

What remains to be understood are the mechanisms through which attachment leads to prosocial behavior. A number of scholars (Haapasalo & Pokela, 1999; Waters et al., 1986) have proposed parental identification as an important mediator between attachment and prosocial behavior. The operationalization of identification has two major components: (1) imitation of parental behavior, and (2) responsiveness to parental control. Poor parenting practices and child abuse may also interfere with attachment and lead to poor identification and distance the child from the parent(s). Although the model has not been verified by direct tests, it does appear to be consistent with the data. Among male delinquents, attachment to parents reduced the severity of delinquency (Anderson, Holmes & Ostresh, 1999), and family attachment was associated with belief in the law (Sokol-Katz, Dunham & Zimmerman, 1997).

Parents are likely sources for identification because they are proximal, frequent, and have control over a wide range of rewards and costs. That is, they have functional significance. The necessary ingredients for vicarious learning are also present. The extent to which learning takes place and what exactly is learned depends upon the parent-child relationship, what is modeled, and child-rearing techniques. Fonagy et al.'s (1997) and Bolen's (2000) reviews of the literature find that attachment and prosocial behavior is enhanced when parents are emotionally warm and fair disciplinarians. Another important feature of identification is the internalization of parental values and behavior.

A final comment on attachment and delinquency trajectories comes from a hypothesis proposed by Fonagy et al. (1997). They hypothesized that adolescence is marked by a fundamental change in attachment patterns from parent-child bonds to more general adult and social bonds. In addition, there is a "moment of detachment when neither old [nor] new (attachment) patterns are fully active" (p. 241). This "moment of detachment" is a normal process but also a point at which controls are loosened. This transition period may contribute to the increase in delinquency among "experimenters." Correspondingly, the hypothesis would suggest that a smooth transition to new prosocial models is not only preventive but also may help in desistance. In fact, this is typically what is reported. For example, Born, Chevalier, and Humblet (1997) found that institutionalized delinquents who desisted from further delinquency showed successful attachment to other prosocial people. In an analysis of data from the New Zealand Dunedin Study, prosocial ties were associated with reduced self-reported and officially documented crime for low self-control individuals (Wright et al., 2001). Although attachment to family and others is important, in our view, the most powerful of the familial correlates of delinquency is parenting practices.

Parenting Practices, Family Interventions, and Delinquency

The family is the child's first socializing agent. Few would dispute this statement and there is ample cross-sectional data available indicating the importance of family factors. Many of these factors also appear to have cross-cultural significance (Zhang & Messner, 1995). Predictive studies of family factors and crime have been summarized by Loeber and Dishion (1983) and Loeber and Stouthamer-Loeber (1986). In the Loeber reviews of the family literature, the parental family management techniques exceeded the predictive validities of other predictors of delinquency including SES and educational achievement.

From a social learning perspective, the family operates along two major dimensions. There is a *normative* dimension, in which the parents' role is to convey and instill prosocial norms, values, and beliefs, as well as the skills to succeed in society. Inconsistent monitoring and disciplining and the absence of prosocial models are seen as critical in this regard. Then there is a *relationship* dimension that facilitates the learning of these norms and promotes an attachment to the members of society. Parental neglect and maltreatment are the family factors that impact on the relationship dimension. There is considerable evidence from longitudinal studies that the use of physical punishment and other harsh disciplinary practices and emotional neglect lead to delinquency and violence (Dembo et al., 1998; Haapasalo & Pokela, 1999; Smith & Thornberry, 1995; Straus, 1991; Widom & Maxfield, 2001). Both of these dimensions were evident in our discussions of attachment theory, moral development, and egocentrism. At this juncture, we would like to provide an overview of the evidence from the family literature that addresses the learning of norms and the role of familial relationships in criminal conduct.

Although the two dimensions—(1) the learning of norms, and (2) familial relationships—are analytically independent, it is often difficult to separate them in a particular study. Our outline serves as a model to organize the literature in a coherent scheme. Families that clearly promote prosocial norms and are characterized by strong emotional attachments are predicted to have the lowest rates of delinquency. Families that fail to provide clear training in social convention and that are characterized by weak affective bonds would be expected to evidence the highest rates of delinquency. Finally, families may show other combinations of the normative and affective dimensions (e.g., high prosocial norms and low attachment).

Neighborhood Context and Crime

There are two other major sources of variation in the "outcomes" of family life and parenting: the neighborhood and the child. Neighborhood factors that facilitate criminal behavior are recognized in theory (see Figure 4.2) and in the empirical literature (Hawkins et al., 1998). The relationship between neighborhood context and crime, however, is complex.

One of the theories underlying the relationship between neighborhood characteristics and crime is called the "broken windows" thesis. The idea is that disorder in a neighborhood (e.g., graffiti, public drunkeness, litter in the streets) signals a social environment in which no one cares and, therefore, antisocial activity is permitted to occur unchecked. The typical response to dealing with such neighborhoods has been police crackdowns on minor crimes and efforts to mobilize the community to make neighborhoods more visually appealing. However, the relationship between neighborhood decay and crime is indirect. Robert Sampson and Stephen Raudenbush (2001) analyzed crime in 196 Chicago neighborhoods and interviewed 3,800 residents. They found that informal social controls ("collective efficacy") were far more important factors than the physical look of the neighborhood.

The importance of the social environment in controlling criminal behavior has been found in a number of studies. This is not to say that impoverished neighborhoods with few resources have absolutely no effect on the delinquent behavior of youths who live in these neighborhoods. Housing experiments in which families in low-income neighborhoods were moved into housing developments built in middle-class neighborhoods resulted in lower delinquency rates compared to families who remained in low-income neighborhoods (Leventhal & Brooks-Gunn, 2000). However, the effects of neighborhood residence appears to be small, accounting for approximately 5 percent of the variance in childhood outcomes (Leventhal & Brooks-Gunn, 2000).

Per-Olof Wikström and Rolf Loeber (2000) investigated the interaction between "kinds of individuals" (parental supervision, guilt, peer associations, school motivation) and "kinds of context" (neighborhood poverty, unemployment levels, ethnic composition). They found that highly disadvantaged neighborhoods, where the temptation and opportunities for crime were relatively high, seemed to have affected youths differentially, especially as they entered adolescence. Adolescents with some feelings of guilt, satisfactory parental supervision, and so on had more difficulty avoiding delinquency in disadvantaged neighborhoods than youths in well-off neighborhoods (unfortunately, Wikström and Loeber did not specify the relative influence of family supervision). Youths with poor parental supervision, school motivation, and the like, were more likely to engage in serious delinquent behavior regardless of the neighborhood conditions.

In another study by Donald Lynam and his colleagues (Lynam et al., 1999), an interaction between impulsivity and neighborhood context was found. Analyzing data from the Pittsburgh Youth Study, impulsive children from the most impoverished neighborhoods were more likely to self-report delinquency than youths from better neighborhoods. Nonimpulsive youths from poor and well-off neighborhoods posed equal risk for delinquency.

Family and social support for dealing with a difficult neighborhood context appears to be an important protective factor. Children with low levels of parental support and who live in neighborhoods with high levels of violence evidenced a range of psychological problems, whereas children with good caregiving had more positive adjustment (Kliewer et al., 1998). Parents who recognize the danger of the neighborhood ("be careful out there") and monitor closely their child's activities are also less likely to have children that become delinquent (Leventhal & Brooks-Gunn, 2000).

In a longitudinal study by Emmy Werner (1987), a significant number of children from impoverished backgrounds and with other risk factors present did not become delinquent. What made them, to use her term, "resilient" to these risk factors? Two sets of factors were identified. The first was temperament. Mothers of "invulnerable" children described them as being easy to love and nourish. They posed few caretaking difficulties and made reasonable and easy adjustments throughout life. The second set of factors dealt with the caretaking environment. The resilient children came from extended families that provided supervision, discipline, and emotional supports. That is, factors that other studies found absent among delinquents (warm parental bonds and supervision) also protected the children from future delinquency when risk factors were abundantly evident. To quote Werner:

> [C]hildren with "difficult temperaments" who interacted with distressed caretakers in disorganized, unstable families had a greater chance of developing delinquent behavior than children who were perceived as rewarding by their caretakers and who grew up in supportive homes (p. 40).

When Families Lose Control: The Influence of Delinquent Peers

Poor familial relationships and inadequate monitoring and control are important precursors to criminal conduct. Dysfunctional family environments increase the risk for delinquency in two ways. First, children are not socialized properly. Aggressive and other antisocial behaviors (e.g., lying, stealing) are left unchecked while prosocial values and behaviors (e.g., respect for social institutions, motivation to achieve in school) are inconsistently encouraged. Second, as the child becomes older and begins to spend more time outside of the home, opportunities to develop delinquent friends increase. If the parents do not know or do not care with whom the child associates, then involvement with delinquent peers and even joining a delinquent gang become all the more likely (Lahey et al., 1999; Simons et al., 1998). The aggressive and other antisocial behaviors established within the family context will restrict the type of social network. Well socialized children (and their parents) will not accept the friendship of antisocial children. In this section, we enter into a discussion of the influence of antisocial peers and delinquent gangs.

The breakdown of parental monitoring and exposure to delinquent peers may be particularly important in the development of early-onset, chronic offending. One of the results of associating with delinquents is the increased opportunity to learn a variety of criminal behaviors, particularly "covert" antisocial behaviors. Gerald Patterson sees the development of chronic offending progressing from the overt, aggressive behavior evident at a young age to a growth in covert antisocial behaviors such as stealing and drug abuse (Patterson & Yoerger, 1999). Furthermore, antisocial peer groups are responsible for this transition. Thus, the chronic offender becomes quite versatile demonstrating both physically aggressive and other deviant behaviors. Although, there is evidence that some forms of antisocial behavior (i.e., physical aggression) vary by gender and age (Leschied et al., 2001; Tomada & Schneider, 1997), it appears that early-onset, chronic delinquent girls also follow a trajectory of versatility similar to boys (Mazerolle et al., 2000).

Reviews of the literature consistently place antisocial peers as one of the strongest correlates of criminal behavior (Gendreau et al., 1996). As expected, the influence of delinquent peers increases with age. In the meta-analysis by Lipsey and Derzon (1998), the average effect size for antisocial peers was .12 for children ages six to 11 years and .43 for children ages 12 to 14. The question that researchers have been grappling with is the interpretation of the relationship. Two hypotheses have been presented. The first, originally proposed by Glueck and Glueck (1950), is that the youths have already established antisocial behaviors and attitudes before joining delinquent social networks ("birds of a feather flock together" hypothesis). Thus, associating with other delinquents does not really increase the chances of criminal behavior; the youths would engage in crime regardless of with whom they associate.

The second hypothesis follows a general personality and social learning explanation. Delinquent youths may be attracted to each other, but once they form association and friendship bonds, interpersonal reinforcements for antisocial behavior would augment the risk for criminal behavior. That is, they directly model and reinforce antisocial behavior and discourage expressions of prosocial attitudes and behavior. Direct observations of social interactions among delinquents provide unequivocal support for this effect (Buehler, Patterson & Furniss, 1966; Dishion et al., 1996). Antisocial peers strongly encourage antisocial attitudes and behaviors and punish prosocial behavior. In addition, it appears that antisocial peers increase criminal behavior beyond personal characteristics and behavioral history (Matseuda & Anderson, 1998; Wright et al., 2001), lending support to treating antisocial peers as a unique contributory factor to crime.

In the last 10 years, the media and the academic community have paid special attention to the role of delinquent gangs. Delinquent gangs have always been an interest to the general public, but they tended to be romanticized (e.g., *West Side Story*, James Dean's portrayal of "the rebel"). They are no longer seen this way. Gangs are portrayed, at least in the media, as well organized, well armed, and highly dangerous. Criminologists have a long history of trying to understand the formation and maintenance of antisocial groups (e.g., Cloward & Ohlin, 1960; Cohen, 1955), and this interest has flourished with professional journals entirely devoted to the study of gangs (e.g., *Journal of Gang Research*).

The first challenge faced by researchers studying gangs is defining their target of study. What makes a gang? Do two delinquents who regularly associate with each other count as a gang or do you need more than two? Do members have to commit all the crimes together or can they go off individually to commit crimes? Is participation in criminal activity required or is simple association sufficient (the "gang wannabes")? Must there be some concrete symbol such as a colored kerchief indicating their affiliation? Fortunately, there is a growing consensus of what constitutes a criminal gang and the questions raised may reflect different levels of commitment to a gang. Most researchers view participation in crime and some level of organization (i.e., leadership) as essential features of a gang (Esbensen et al., 2001). Furthermore, asking the simple question, "Do you belong to a gang?" appears to identify the same individuals that law enforcement officials use to ascertain gang membership (Curry, 2000).

Using self-report methods, it is estimated that there are more than 23,000 youth gangs in the United States, with the majority concentrated in urban areas (U.S. Department of Justice, 1997). As predicted from social learning theory, gang membership increases the likelihood of criminal activity even beyond having delinquent friends (Battin et al., 1998). Ronald Huff (1998) interviewed 140 gang members and a group of 145 "at risk" youths from four United States sites. Gang members were identified by a combination of self-reports and police and social service agency referrals. The "at risk" group was identified by social service agencies as being "at risk" to joining a gang. Reporting on the data from Cleveland, Ohio, gang members were significantly more likely than "at risk" youths to be involved in assaults, drive-by shootings, and drug trafficking.

Not all self-reported gang members engage in criminal behavior. Some males are peripheral to the gang and some young women "hang out" with the gang rather than directly engage in crime. Delinquents who join gangs appear to have different backgrounds and characteristics than nongang delinquents. As we hypothesized earlier, greater gang involvement is associated with lower levels of parental monitoring. Esbensen et al. (2001) used five definitions of gangs, each definition becoming increasingly limiting (definitions varied from "ever in a gang" to "core members"). Nine hundred and ninety-four middle-school students reported currently being a gang member or a member in the past. As the definition of a gang became more restrictive, levels of parental monitoring decreased. In addition, participation rates in criminal activity increased; core members reported six times more violent offenses than nongang members.

The risk factors for gang membership are similar to the risk factors for chronic delinquency. Being an ethnic/racial minority, having a childhood conduct disorder, and coming from a dysfunctional family and criminal neighborhood have been associated with gang membership (Esbensen et al., 2001; Hill et al., 1999; Lahey et al., 1999). Among psychological variables, antisocial attitudes and a broadly defined antisocial personality have been related to gang membership both in Canada and the United States. Marc Le Blanc and Nadine Lanctôt (1998) compared 190 boys who admitted gang membership to 406 nongang delinquents from Montreal. The gang members evidenced a greater degree of antisocial attitudes and were more emotionally callous, adventurous, and impulsive. In a longitudinal study of 808 children from Seattle, Hill et al. (1999) found antisocial attitudes and an "externalizing" personality (i.e., aggressive, inattentive, overreactive) to be predictive of gang membership. In addition, these risk factors were the same for both girls and boys.

Although an antisocial personality pattern has been indicative of gang membership, psychopathy does not appear to be a major element among gang members (despite mass media portrayals). Avelardo Valdez, Charles Kaplan, and Edward Codina (2000) administered the screening version of Psychopathy Checklist-Revised (PCL-R) to 50 gang members and a matched sample of 25 nongang members. More will be said about the PCL-R in the next chapter, but for now all the reader needs to know is that the PCL-R is an objective assessment instrument used to aid in the diagnosis of psychopathy. They found that only 4 percent of gang members were psychopaths while 24 percent of the *non*gang members were assigned a diagnosis of psychopathy. The lower prevalence of psychopathy among gang members may indicate that these individuals have such low affectional bonds to others that they prefer to operate on their own rather than with others.

Intervention efforts have focused on suppression or prevention of gang membership, with only a couple of programs trying to disrupt antisocial peer groups. Suppression programs are police "get tough" approaches in which police patrols are increased in gang areas and gang activities are aggressively prosecuted. Not surprisingly, the "get tough" approach has not demonstrated much success (Klein, 1995).

One well-known preventive program is the Gang Resistance Education and Training (GREAT) program. GREAT is modeled after a drug prevention program called DARE (discussed in more detail in Chapter 10). Uniformed police officers speak to seventh-grade students about the negative aspects of gang membership, drugs, and conflict resolution. The goal is to give youths the skills to resist peer pressure and the temptation to join a gang. In a large-scale evaluation of the program, Finn-Age Esbensen and Wayne Osgood (1999) compared 2,629 students who completed the program to 3,207 students who did not complete it. Thirty-three outcome measures were assessed. GREAT completers showed favorable differences on 14 of the 33 variables. They reported lower rates of drug use, fewer delinquent friends, and more negative attitudes toward gangs. Esbensen and Osgood (1999) concluded that GREAT produced "modest short-term benefits" but cautioned against placing too much confidence in the results. The results were based on a retrospective research design and self-reports of subjects. Furthermore, the participants were too young to allow researchers to conduct a follow-up about actual entry into gangs.

Another gang intervention program is EQUIP, a peer-group therapy that teaches prosocial skills and attempts to change the social-cognitive distortions found among delinquents. Male juvenile offenders were randomly assigned to EQUIP and to two other control groups. A one-year follow-up found a recidivism rate of 15 percent for the EQUIP group and 40.5 percent for the control subjects (Gibbs et al., 2001).

In summary, one consequence of a family environment that demonstrates poor emotional bonds, monitoring, and disciplining practices is that the child is more likely to associate with other delinquent children. Social support for crime is theoretically and empirically one of the most important correlates of criminal behavior. From a preventive perspective, effectively intervening at the family level would not only benefit families directly but also impact on the associational patterns that the child develops. We now turn to a review of efforts to help families deal with conduct-disordered and delinquent children.

Have Family Interventions Been Able to Reduce Subsequent Delinquent Behavior?

Family treatment is one of the more frequently evaluated forms of prevention and correction in the criminological literature. There have been two meta-analytic reviews of the family treatment literature and delinquency. In a review of 27 family treatment studies and recidivism, the overall mean effect estimate was $r = .21$ (Gordon et al., 1992). Jeff Latimer (2001) reviewed 35 studies and found an average correlation of .15. These estimates indicate a meaningful reduction in recidivism following family treatment and may be contrasted with the small increase in recidivism found when criminal justice processing without treatment services was studied ($r = -.07$). The literature becomes even more promising when differences among the studies are considered. Treatments that used behavioral methods of intervention yielded significantly greater reductions in recidivism than did less structured and directive treatments of the psychodynamic or client-centered variety. Descriptions of the more promising family therapies follow.

Gerald Patterson and his colleagues in Oregon, James Alexander and company in Utah, and Scott Henggeler's group (Tennessee, South Carolina, and Missouri) have made outstanding contributions in understanding what needs to be changed in families with behaviorally disruptive, antisocial children. Working mostly with conduct-disordered and hyperactive children and their families, the Oregon researchers found that the parents and children were locked in a coercive process of control (Patterson, 1982, 1997). The children learned at a very young age that behaving in an aversive and annoying manner resulted in reinforcement, for example, when the parent gives in to the child's temper tantrum. Consequently, treatment focused on disrupting the coercive cycle by teaching parents to reinforce positive behavior and to ignore (extinguish) negative behavior.

The Oregon program has been successful in changing family interactions and parental disciplining practices. However, most of the efforts have been with young children (ages 3–12); there have only been a few applications of the treatment program to adjudicated delinquents. A study by Bank, Marlowe, Reid, Patterson, and Weinrott (1991) randomly assigned delinquents (average age of 14) to the Oregon Social Learning Center (OSLC) treatment ($n = 28$) and to a community treatment program ($n = 27$). The average number of prior offenses for the adolescents was eight. While in treatment, the OSLC group showed significantly less delinquent activity than the control subjects, but the differences disappeared over the course of a three-year post-program follow-up. The only enduring difference was that the OSLC treatment group spent fewer days incarcerated, producing an estimated cost savings of $100,000.

The failure of this highly structured behavioral program to decrease long-term recidivism is puzzling and not at all in line with the findings of other behavioral approaches. Chamberlain suggested that for extremely dysfunctional families treatment might better be conducted in foster homes and residential settings. Even with residential care, however, the impact on recidivism has been negligible (Chamberlain, 1996; Chamberlain & Friman, 1998; Chamberlain & Reid, 1994).

Despite the limited impact on recidivism, the family intervention program developed in Oregon is extremely valuable. Its significance lies in its potential as a preventive program. More recent research by Patterson and his colleagues suggests that hyperactivity and conduct disorder is the first stage on the path to chronic delinquency (Patterson et al., 2000). The critical mediating variable between early childhood behavioral problems and delinquency is parental discipline. If parents can be trained to monitor and discipline these children appropriately, then the risk for delinquency is diminished. The family intervention program developed in Oregon has been quite effective in managing younger behavioral-disordered children.

If the behavioral skills training approach from the OSLC did not significantly impact on older children, then what is needed to reduce delinquent behavior within these families? One possible explanation is that the focus on the normative dimension may be insufficient. What may be needed is a more comprehensive approach that includes targeting the relationship dimension.

James Alexander and his Utah colleagues have placed a greater emphasis on the relationship dimension. They targeted family communication and cohesiveness and focused on solving particular family irritants before looking at the reinforcement contingencies that may be facilitating or failing to deter delinquent behavior. Their approach, developed over 20 years of research, is called Functional Family Therapy, or FFT (Barton & Alexander, 1980). The research was based in Salt Lake City and, as such, the majority of the subjects have come from a middle-class community that is 70 percent Mormon. However, the families investigated had officially identified "delinquents" as opposed to Patterson's conduct-disordered children.

There is little doubt that families with a delinquent child differ from nonproblematic families in terms of emotional warmth and positive communications. Videotaped analysis found family interactions varying along the dimensions of supportive and defensive communication (Alexander, 1973). Supportive communication was demonstrated when a family member responded empathically, provided helpful information or waited until the other person finished talking before interrupting. Defensive communication was evidenced when a family member showed indifference, placed unreasonable demands, or was highly critical of the other family member. In nondelinquent families, supportive communication was reciprocated and defensive communication ignored. If the child said something positive, then the parent responded in a warm and encouraging manner while negative communications were ignored. In delinquent families, the patterns were opposite; defensive communication was reciprocated by harsh and angry communications and supportive communications ignored. The reader is alerted that these communications are not the only types that differentiate delinquent families from nondelinquent families. For example, delinquent families also tend to have more "rule-breaking talk" and rationalizations for deviance (Dishion & Poe, 1993).

Proceeding from these observations, Parsons and Alexander trained family members to use less defensive communication and more reciprocal supportive communication. This brought delinquent family processes more in line with normal family process. Training in more effective communication was then integrated with training in behavioral parenting techniques that was similar to the approach used by the OSLC (a modified Patterson behavior modification manual was given to the parents, but Alexander reported that few families read the manual). Evaluations of FFT with delinquents have been consistently positive.

In the first outcome study, families were randomly assigned to one of four groups (Alexander & Barton, 1976; Alexander & Parsons, 1973). All of the families had a child involved in minor delinquent activity (e.g., runaway, truant, "ungovernable"). The delinquents ranged in age from 13 to 16 years and included males and females. Forty-six families received FFT from graduate students in clinical psychology under the supervision of experienced therapists. Nineteen families were assigned to a client-centered family therapy program, 11 to a psychodynamic-oriented family therapy program, and 46 to a no-treatment control group. In addition, there was a comparison sample of cases that went through the courts in Salt Lake County. Juvenile court records were reviewed 18 months following the end of treatment.

The client-centered program was nondirective and focused on family feelings and attitudes. The psychodynamic family therapy was provided through a community program offered by the Mormon Church. The goal of treatment was described as providing "insight." The control group was composed of families who had no court orders for formal treatment.

First, we look at the results with respect to family process measures. At the end of treatment, the FFT group showed the greatest equality in conversation, the most activity (e.g., less silence), and the fewest interruptions. However, the following comment was made:

> The trained researcher may marvel at an array of significant F's [sic] (a statistical test of significance) to be found in the summary tables, while harried parents, court officials, and police officers wonder how these findings translate to reducing juvenile delinquency (p. 177).

The results of the follow-up are summarized in Table 5.4. The data is drawn from Alexander and Parsons (1973) and a report by Alexander and Barton (1976) that included a replication of the FFT group. The findings clearly indicated that FFT reduced future delinquency. The FFT group showed a recidivism rate that was one-half the rate for those receiving no treatment. The client-centered treatment had no impact on future delinquent behavior. This is not to say that client-centered therapy was ineffective in changing family interactions. This program either did not target the critical family interaction variables or lacked the strength to bring changes in delinquent behavior. Finally, the psychodynamic, insight approach actually increased the recidivism rate (73%).

In another study, the amount of therapy and the characteristics of therapists were related to family process changes and success (Alexander et al., 1976). Twenty-one families were randomly assigned to different FFT-trained therapists. Each therapist was evaluated on eight characteristics (ability to relate affect to behavior, humor, warmth, directiveness, self-confidence, self-disclosure, blaming, and clarity in communication). The success of treatment was rated on a four-point scale of how long the families stayed in therapy (1 = dropped out after first session,

2 = attended several sessions, 3 = continued to end of project but could still use more treatment, and 4 = terminated and judged successful by both therapist and family). The data on the therapist variables were partitioned into a relationship dimension (the first five characteristics) and a normative or "structuring" dimension (the last three characteristics). Analysis indicated that relationship skills accounted for 44.6 percent of the variance; adding the normative skills increased the variance to 59.7 percent. The effective therapists used *both* directive and relationship skills to keep families in treatment and promote change (skills that are important in motivational interviewing and working with resistant clients).

Table 5.4
Family Intervention and Recidivism

Group		N	% Recidivated
FFT:	1st group	46	26
	2nd group	45	27
Client-centered		19	47
Psychodynamic		11	73
Control:	Testing Only	6	50
	No Treatment	46	48
	County Base Rate	2,800	51

From Alexander & Parsons, 1973; Alexander & Barton, 1976

FFT has also impacted upon the siblings of the target children. Nanci Klein, James Alexander, and Bruce Parsons (1977) searched juvenile court records for information on the clients seen in the intervention programs described earlier. They tabulated the percentage of siblings who were in contact with the court after treatment and found that for the no-treatment control group, 40 percent of the siblings had official court records. The rate for the client-centered group was 59 percent and for the psychodynamic group it was 63 percent. The rate of sibling contacts with the courts for the FFT group was 20 percent.

Finally, Barton, Alexander, Waldron, Turner, and Warburton (1985) provided FFT to 30 families of "hard-core" incarcerated delinquents (an average history of 22 offenses). On average, 30 hours of FFT was provided. For some families, the therapy started in the institution prior to the release of the youth to the family. This group was compared to 44 offenders from the same training school who attended various community treatment programs. The two groups were matched for age, educational level, ethnicity, and the severity and number of prior offenses. At a 15-month follow-up, 60 percent of the FFT group and 93 percent of the comparison group had received additional charges. Furthermore, for those who did recidivate, the number of new offenses was less for the FFT group (there was no difference in terms of severity).

Can FFT be effectively implemented outside of Utah? The answer to date is yes. Don Gordon and his colleagues have been training family therapists in FFT and evaluating programs throughout North America (Gordon, 1995; Gordon, Jurkovic & Arbuthnot, 1998). For example, FFT was provided to families of delinquents from a rural and depressed area of Ohio (Gordon et al., 1988). Psychology graduate students were trained in FFT and supervised on a weekly basis. A 28-month follow-up found a recidivism rate of 11 percent for the treated delinquents and 67 percent for a nontreated probation sample. An extended three-year follow-up of these youths into adulthood yielded an 8.4 percent conviction rate for the treated sample and 40.9 percent for the control group (Gordon, Graves & Arbuthnot, 1995).

Recall that the client-centered and psychodynamic interventions were ineffective, perhaps because of their reliance on relationship and the neglect of active structuring. The need for both relationship skills and active direction in therapy is both commonsensical and may be particularly relevant to families of delinquents. Many parents of delinquents are in a state of marital discord. Unhappy parents may not only influence communication patterns within the family but may also interfere with effective monitoring and supervision of the children (e.g., Griffin et al., 2000). For example, Mark Dadds, Steven Schwartz, and Matthew Sanders (1987) randomly assigned parents who had conduct-disordered children and who suffered marital discord to one of two treatment programs. One treatment consisted of parenting skills training only. The other program was a combination of both skills training (the structuring dimension) and partner-support training (relationship dimension). For the distressed parents who received the skill training only, all treatment gains were lost at the six-month follow-up. Only the parents who received the combined treatment maintained their skills.

FFT is not the only effective treatment for delinquent families. There are a number of effective family intervention programs and they all share a common, cognitive-behavioral, skills-oriented approach (McCord et al., 1994; Webster-Stratton & Hammond, 1997). However, one family treatment program has gained prominence. Scott Henggeler has developed what is to date the most comprehensive family-based program for the serious delinquent (Henggeler et al., 1998; Swenson, Henggeler & Schoenwald, 2001). The program, Multisystemic Therapy (MST), has a core family therapy component ("family preservation") that teaches parents the skills needed to deal with adolescent problems (normative) and to reduce conflict within the family (relationship). In addition, MST enlists the school, peers, and other key community agents in order to maintain treatment benefits and increase generalization (see Resource Note 5.2). Evaluations have found positive outcomes for delinquents who committed serious felonies (Henggeler, Melton & Smith, 1992) and even for adolescent sex offenders (Borduin et al., 1990; Swenson et al., 1998).

Resource Note 5.2

Theory and Application to Practice
Multisystemic Therapy
(Henggeler et al., 1998)

Multisystemic therapy (MST) is today's most effective intervention for high-risk delinquents. Much of the success of MST in changing the behavior of difficult youths may be due to the comprehensive nature of the intervention. Scott Henggeler and his colleagues have drawn heavily on family systems and social ecological theories. The individual is part of a broad social context that includes family, peers, school, and community. This approach is consistent with the theoretical formulations of PIC-R. The effective interventions predicted from both models are similar. That is, high-risk individuals with many needs require multiple interventions that change the reward-cost contingencies associated with antisocial behavior.

MST attempts to promote positive changes in the family both through direct intervention and arranging community supports that help families maintain the benefits of family therapy. Youths are given assistance with school performance and social adjustment, including the development of prosocial friends. Finally, individual counseling is provided to meet the unique needs presented by the delinquent. All of these services are given in a highly professional context with extraordinary efforts to maintain treatment integrity.

At the family level, therapists work directly with families observing their interactions. Strengths are noted and serve as building blocks to more effective family functioning. The family is viewed as a social system in which changes in one family member can alter the behavior of the other members. Family members are often asked to monitor their behavior and the behavior of other family members. After the initial assessment stage, parents are taught to change their discipline strategies and use rewards and punishments more effectively. MST therapists are also especially attentive to the personal problems that parent(s) may have. If a psychiatric disorder is evident, for example, then the appropriate community treatment is secured. If the parent needs help in monitoring a child, then a neighbor may be enlisted to help. The value of community resources in helping families is taken very seriously by MST.

As the therapist works with the family, efforts are made to diminish associations with deviant peers. Therapists try to understand issues of prosocial peer rejection and teach parents to monitor their children's social interactions. Parents are taught to communicate more effectively to their children the harm that results from antisocial peer associations (e.g., they should not berate the child's delinquent peers, as it may only harden the child's resolve to associate with them). During individual counseling with the child, discussion of peers and the teaching of interpersonal skills are common.

The school is an important part of the social ecology of the high-risk delinquent. The youth is given assistance with academics, parents are supported in monitoring their children's school activities, and teachers are enlisted as agents of change. MST leaves no stone unturned in identifying the immediate social and community supports that can increase the rewards for prosocial behavior and interfere with the social forces that support antisocial activity.

A carefully controlled evaluation of MST can be found in the Missouri Delinquency Project (Borduin, Mann et al., 1995). Families with adolescents who have had at least two prior arrests were randomly assigned to either MST ($n = 92$) or individual therapy ($n = 84$). The individual therapy was a mix of behavioral, client-centered, and psychodynamic therapies. The MST therapists had a minimum of two months training and received three hours of supervision per week, reflecting a high degree of program integrity. MST was associated with decreases in adolescent problem behavior and improved family relationships, whereas no such association was found for the individual therapy group. A four-year follow-up found a recidivism rate of 26.1 percent for MST and 71.4 percent for individual therapy. These differences in treatment effect were also found for violent crimes.

MST is presently being applied to many different problems and samples. MST has been demonstrated to reduce drug use (Borduin et al., 1995; Henggeler et al., 1992, 1998) and delinquent activity among violent youths with lengthy criminal records (Henggeler et al., 1993). Recently, Scott Henggeler and his colleagues (Henggeler et al., 1998) have reported work with teenage parents, abused children, and parents who use drugs. Early results from an evaluation of MST with high-risk youths in Canada is also reporting positive results (Leschied & Cunningham, 2001).

There are two important conclusions that we can draw from the family intervention studies. First, behavioral treatment approaches can and do change family interactions along the normative and relationship dimensions, and these changes are associated with decreases in delinquent behavior. There is absolutely no evidence that nondirective, insight-oriented, and cathartic interventions work with distressed families, any more than there is evidence that intrusive and insensitive introduction of behavioral technologies work.

Second, the reasons for the success of family programs and other programs that incorporate family components (e.g., Kumpfer, Molgaard & Spoth, 1996) go beyond attention to relevant intermediate targets, relationship and structuring in interpersonal influence, and the use of behavioral techniques. They are all closely tied to university-based training and research units (Dembo et al., 1999; Henggeler, Schoenwald & Pickrel, 1995). They each involve detailed attention to program integrity—particularly with regard to specifying a relevant model and providing systematic training and supervision of therapists according to that model (Edwards et al., 2001). These programs take extraordinary steps to minimize treatment dropout rates by going to the home (Gordon, 1995), enlisting foster parents (Chamberlain, 1996), and involving teachers and peers (Henggeler et al., 1995). In one study (Henggeler et al., 1996), 98 percent of families assigned to MST completed treatment, whereas only 22 percent of families assigned to regular community services received any treatment. Program effectiveness depends upon appropriate and intensive strategies being carried out with integrity.

Summary

There is a substantial body of knowledge on the development of criminal behavior. In this chapter, we have seen a wide array of variables correlated with delinquency—variables that, for the most part, have been ignored or depreciated by mainstream criminology. Heredity, temperament, cognitive development, and the origins of interpersonal attachment often garner no more than a few pages in many criminology textbooks, and they are rarely integrated with theory. The evidence on family factors contributing to delinquency is particularly robust. There is not one longitudinal study that does not find inconsistent and harsh parenting to be related to delinquency.

The research on developmental aspects of delinquency and crime has exploded in the past decade (Glueck and Glueck would pleased). Criminologists are now trying to incorporate the evidence from the developmental studies into their general theories. Some of these efforts are hardly distinguishable from social-psychological theory. Consider, for example, Robert Agnew's (1997) attempt to stretch strain theory into a developmental framework. "Strain" and its effects are described as follows:

> Negative relationships increase the likelihood that individuals
> will experience negative affect, with anger being an especially
> important reaction. This negative affect creates a pressure for
> corrective action, and crime is one possible response. Crime may
> be a method for alleviating strain, seeking revenge, or manag-
> ing negative affect (through illicit drug use) (p. 103-104).

We have come a long way to find a sociological criminologist giving such prominence to individual emotions and reactions. Also, consider the possibility that if we did not tell you the quotation is from Agnew, you may have guessed that it was taken from Dollard et al.'s (1939) *Frustration and Aggression*. Strain is used to explain both the young criminal experimenters (adolescence is marked by extensive "negative relations" and frustrations) and the criminal persisters (the early learning of aggressiveness to deal with frustrations continue through life). The potency of social-psychological and personality constructs is becoming widely accepted.

What do we know about the development of criminal behavior? Table 5.5 provides a brief summary of the developmental risk factors of delinquency reviewed in this chapter. More detailed and comprehensive summaries are available elsewhere (Elkins et al., 1997; Loeber & Farrington, 1998; Le Blanc & Loeber, 1998). Furthermore, the findings are consistent across countries and continents (e.g., Fergusson et al., 2000). Chronologically, we begin with predispositional factors. There is sufficient evidence to conclude that heredity plays at least a minor role, although the mediating mechanisms are far from clear. However, plausible mediators are neurophysiological arousal and a difficult temperament. Related to these biological risk factors is intelligence. Intelligence is broadly defined, and specific aspects of intelligence that are related to social adaptation are stressed more so than academic intelligence. Thus, poor verbal skills affect interpersonal communication, and concrete thinking patterns affect egocentric thought and moral reasoning.

From a societal and policy level, the persisters are the most problematic. The potential for the development of the persistent delinquent is probably evident very early in life and can been seen in the predispositional and intelligence factors shown in Table 5.5. However, our view, and that of others (Taylor et al., 1999), is that it is the family environment that is pivotal to the trajectory of a persistent offender. A family environment characterized by emotional neglect, inconsistent supervision, and harsh disciplining is, to recall Chess and Thomas's label, a "poorness of fit." By the time the child enters school, aggressive and "wild" behavior is well established and explains the early age of onset for persistent delinquents. The trajectory continues: teachers find it difficult to manage the child, and the parents have increasingly less control over the child as he or she becomes older. In early adolescence, the persistent delinquent has acquired antisocial "sticky friends" (Warr, 1993) and a strong behavioral antisocial history.

Table 5.5
Developmental Risk Factors for Delinquency

Risk Factor	Age Evident

Predispositional
    Biological criminal parent
    Difficult temperament: energetic, impulsive,
        sensation-seeking
    Neurophysiological arousal
	0 - 3

Intelligence
    Low verbal IQ/poor language skills
    Concrete, egocentric thinking style,
        delayed moral reasoning
    Poor interpersonal cognitive skills
	2 - 7

Family Factors
    Emotional neglect—lack of attachment
        to others
    Poor monitoring and supervision
        —learning of aggressive/disruptive behavior
        —failure to acquire anticriminal verbalizations
	0 - 7

School Factors
    Lack of commitment to school
    Academic failure
    Dropout
	5 - adolescence

Antisocial Peers
    Social support for antisocial behavior
    Learning of antisocial attitudes and
        techniques of neutralization
	adolescence

As presented in Table 5.5 and found in the most recent studies of childhood development and crime (Ayers et al., 1999; Herrenkohl et al., 2001), many factors influence the delinquent trajectory. There is some "good news" from the research literature. There are some innovative programs that can make a difference in preventing delinquency and reducing the recidivism of established offenders. Delivering some of these programs is becoming easier with the aid of technology. For example, Don Gordon (2000) has placed a family training program on CD-ROM. Most importantly, there are a number of family intervention programs that have been highly effective with predelinquent, conduct-disordered children and the more serious offenders. Together, the research suggests that we can better identify the high-risk children who require intervention and that we have effective interventions at our disposal.

A number of important challenges remain. Foremost is the need to rank-order the developmental predictors of crime. Heredity, neuropsychological deficits, temperament, and moral reasoning are probably not as important as family socialization experiences, but we would like to be more specific. Meta-analytic reviews are now giving us more precise estimates (e.g., Lipsey & Derzon, 1998). We know, for example, that family variables are more important than intelligence, but because these variables are broadly defined, we cannot say whether, for example, emotional neglect is a more important risk factor than egocentrism.

Second, we need to have a better understanding of the interaction between biological/maturational factors and the environment. Principle 4 of PIC-R (see Resource Note 4.2) emphasizes this interaction and alerts us to the changing patterns of deviant behavior that vary with the development of the individual. PCC provides a broad outline of how the influence of rewards and costs are dependent on cognitive, biological, and temperamental predispositions. Continued investigations on this interaction and the development of highly specific models of behavior is encouraged (for a noteworthy example, see Conger & Simons, 1997).

Finally, developmental criminology is making important contributions to describing the specific trajectories or pathways. Of primary interest is the formation of the persisters or (to use Terri Moffitt's term) the "life-course persistent-offender." For this group of offenders, biological and cognitive factors may play a more salient role, compared to the experimenting adolescent. Rolf Loeber (1991) describes a "stacking" process wherein an infant comes into this world with a difficult temperament, may then become hyperactive as a toddler, show school difficulties in the elementary grades, begin to associate with delinquents in junior high school, and become actively delinquent in early adolescence. With development, the correlates and predictors may change and identifying these factors is an important challenge for research in the twenty-first century.

Chapter 6

Prediction of Criminal Behavior and Classification of Offenders

Every day, whether we are psychologists, police officers, economists, students, or what have you, we make predictions to guide our behavior. Sometimes this prediction task uses information that is purely physical. For example, when we see thunder clouds gathering in the distance, we predict a storm approaching. We then may decide to postpone starting the barbecue until the clouds pass. At other times, our prediction task involves the gathering of information about people and their behavior. For example, in a job interview, information about the applicant's past employment is used to make a judgment on how the applicant may behave if hired for the new job. In this chapter, our interest falls on the later prediction task. Namely, can we—and how do we—assess and predict future criminal behavior? Even more important is determining the basis of that prediction information and the outcomes of those actions.

The prediction of criminal behavior is perhaps one of the most central activities in the criminal justice system. From it stems community safety, prevention, treatment, ethics, and justice. Predicting who will reoffend guides police officers, judges, prison officials, and parole boards in their decisionmaking. Knowing that poor parenting practices lead to future delinquency directs community agencies in providing parenting programs to families. As we shall see later, treatment programs may be most effective with offenders who are likely to reoffend. Ethically, being able or unable to predict an individual's future criminal behavior may weigh heavily upon the use of dispositions such as imprisonment and parole.

These decisions have implications for the public. The economic costs of managing various penalties (e.g., probation, prisons) are significant. Should the decisions appear to yield disparity, then public perceptions of the criminal justice system might shift away from those of a fair and just system and move closer to oppression. The decisions may influence the general deterrence function of criminal justice (e.g., "given my background and community ties, the most I would get is five months and I can expect to be on parole in two months").

The various issues raised by prediction are relevant to the concerns of citizens as a whole because the human, social, and economic costs of prevention are not trivial and because the power that criminal justice professionals have over people who are arrested, detained, convicted, probated, or incarcerated is extraordinary. The issues are of immediate interest to those who become entrapped in the process of criminal justice by way of being a victim, an offender, or a criminal justice professional. Whatever our current role might be—concerned citizen, offender, victim, or involved professional—we all share an interest in prediction. Thus, we all have a right to insist upon knowledge of the following aspects of prediction:

1. Demonstrations of the extent to which criminal behavior is predictable (the issue of predictive accuracy);

2. Clear statements regarding how the predictions are made so that the information used in making predictions may be evaluated on ethical, legal, sociopolitical, economic, and humanitarian criteria (the issue of normative validity);

3. Demonstrations of the extent to which the ways of making predictions actually facilitate criminal justice objectives (the issue of utility);

On the assumption that general knowledge (and hence, service) are enhanced through an integration of theory, research, and practice, a fourth issue is notable:

4. We may expect that predictions and the actions based on them be recorded, monitored, and explored empirically in a way that increases our understanding of crime and criminal justice (i.e., the enhancement of theory and practice through research).

Assessing Predictive Accuracy

To this point, we have been content to limit the meaning of prediction to the magnitude of the association of variables measured at one point in time with an assessment of future criminal activity. Thus, the preceding chapters have made frequent references to statistically significant associations between predictors (information collected at Time 1) and the criterion (criminal behavior measured at Time 2). The phrase "statistically significant" refers to an observed level of association that exceeds chance or is significantly different from a correlation coefficient (r) of .00. For example, we have seen that lower-class origins and criminal conduct were correlated with one another at the level of approximately .05. This level of correlation, when the sample size is large, may be statistically different from .00, but it represents a low level of association. Predictive correlations of antisocial personality and antisocial attitudes with criminal behavior have reached the level of .30 and greater. When the sample size is sufficiently large, an r of .30 is not only significantly greater than zero but is significantly different from an r of .05 between lower-class origins and crime. On the basis of such findings, we may conclude that variables are (or are not) predictive of future criminal conduct, and that one type is more predictive of a criminal behavior than another type.

Correlation coefficients and similar statistical measures of association are valuable for research and theory. However, when it comes to everyday, practical situations, more meaningful measures of predictive accuracy are needed. Take, for example, the problem faced by a parole board that must decide whether to release an inmate. Many factors weigh on the minds of board members. There is the likelihood of making a correct decision that encompasses both a safe release and the denial of parole for a highly dangerous individual. In addition, there is consideration of the costs of making a mistake either by releasing someone who commits another crime or denying parole to someone who is unlikely to commit another crime. As we will soon show, prediction is never perfect and the parole board members in our example must make decisions based on a reasonable balance between making a correct decision and making a mistake. To add to the difficulty in decisionmaking, the value placed on correct decisions and mistakes are usually socially defined. For example, for some, releasing someone who commits another crime is more serious then denying parole to an inmate who does not reoffend.

This practical problem is illustrated by what researchers call the two-by-two (2 x 2) prediction accuracy table (see Part A of Table 6.1). Inserted in each cell is the language of prediction. There are four possible outcomes: (a) True Positive—"I am positive he will reoffend (predicted yes) and it turns out to be true"; (b) False Positive—"I am positive he will reoffend but he doesn't" (prediction was false); (c) False Negative—"Negative, he will not reoffend but he does" (prediction was false); and (d) True Negative—"He will not reoffend and he does not." Note that Cells (a) and (d) are correct predictions and Cells (b) and (c) are errors. Obviously, we want to maximize the numbers in (a) and (d) and minimize the numbers in (b) and (c).

[handwritten margin note: False positive (false Alarm)]

[handwritten margin note: P.T.O.]

In addition to the four outcomes that are generated from the 2 x 2 table, we can calculate the following indices of predictive accuracy:

1. the overall proportion of correct predictions (true positives plus true negatives divided by the total number of predictions): $(a + d)/(a + b + c + d)$;

2. the proportion of cases judged to be at risk who did recidivate: $a/(a + b)$;

3. the proportion of cases judged not to be at risk and who did not recidivate: d/(c + d);

4. the proportion of recidivists correctly identified: a/(a + c);

5. the proportion of nonrecidivists correctly identified: d/(b + d);

Table 6.1
Two-by-Two Prediction Accuracy Tables

A: Two-by-Two Prediction Accuracy Table

Predict Recidivism?	Actually Recidivated?	
	Yes	No
Yes: High-Risk	(a) True Positive	(b) False Positive
No: Low-Risk	(c) False Negative	(d) True Negative

B: Two-by-Two Prediction Accuracy Table (Phi = .15)

Predict Recidivism?	Actually Recidivated?			
	Yes	No	N	Rate
Yes: High-Risk (male)	109	345	454	24.0%
No: Low-Risk (female)	3	59	62	4.8%
N	112	404	516	21.7%

Part B of Table 6.1 presents real data from our research files. The risk factor was being male and the outcome measure was officially recorded reconvictions over a two-year period. The phi value, a statistic similar to r, was a moderate .15. What can be said about predictive accuracy in this case depends, in part, upon how we choose to report on the findings:

1. The recidivism rate of males (the "high-risk" cases) was five times that of females (24% vs. 4.8%);

2. Classifying males as high-risk identified 97.3 percent of the recidivists (109/112). A total of 112 cases were reconvicted; of these, 109 were males predicted to recidivate;

3. The true negative rate was 95.2 percent (59/62) in that 59 of the 62 cases that we predicted would not recidivate did not recidivate (and thus, the false negative rate was only 4.8 percent [3/62]);

4. However, the overall rate of correct predictions was only 32.6 percent: (109 + 59)/516;

5. The true positive rate was only 24 percent (109/454) and thus the false positive rate was 76 percent (345/454).

For assessing predictive accuracy, the lesson to be learned is that more information is required than any one of the above statements provides on its own. Imagine a parole board making decisions based on gender. In our example, many inmates would remain incarcerated unnecessarily and at great financial costs. For a more complete appreciation of predictive accuracy, one needs to be able to recreate the full 2 x 2 prediction table.

In Part B of Table 6.1, the outstanding accuracy achieved in capturing recidivists (97.3%) was due in large part to the fact that our risk assessment (gender) assigned a very large proportion of the cases to the category predicted to reoffend. That is, 88 percent of the cases were male (454/516). The proportion of cases assigned to the high-risk group (or to the category of people we predict will reoffend) is called the *selection ratio*. Because the selection ratio was high (88%), our hit rate for recidivists was high, but our hit rate for nonrecidivists was low (14.6% or 59/404). When the selection ratio is high, the false positive rate will also tend to be high—particularly when relatively few people actually do recidivate. The number of cases that actually do recidivate is called the *base rate*, which in our example was a fairly low 21.7 percent (112/516).

The rates of false positives, false negatives, true positives, and true negatives, as well as the magnitude of the association between the risk predictor and criminal behavior, are all influenced by base rates and selection ratios (Smith & Smith, 1998). In assessing the predictive accuracy of different approaches to risk assessment, examining the 2 x 2 tables they generate is the ideal. In practice, however, the risk assessment approach that yields the greatest number of overall correct predictions may not always be chosen. For example, one may be willing to tolerate a few more false positives in order to maximize the number of recidivists correctly identified—or there may be a situation in which it is judged more important to minimize false positives.

How many false positives and false negatives there are depend on the: (1) accuracy of the risk measure itself, (2) selection ratio, and (3) base rate. Most of this chapter deals with the accuracy of risk measures, but further comments on the effect of the selection ratio and base rate on errors are warranted. In our example of gender defining risk, the selection of high-risk cases is clear. If male, then high-risk; if female, then low-risk. Many offender risk scales however, have more than one risk factor and produce a range of scores. For example, the Level of Service Inventory–Revised, an offender risk scale that we will present in more detail later in the chapter, produces scores from 0 to 54. Thus, low risk can be defined as "0 to 7," or "0 to 14," or "0 to 30." Changing the "cut-off" score, or the selection ratio, will affect how many offenders are defined as low-risk or high-risk and therefore will influence the number of correctly identified recidivists and nonrecidivists and the proportion of errors.

One should also avoid getting caught in a situation in which prediction is no problem at all. These situations exist when the base rate for criminal behavior is either very low or very high. Take, for example, a situation in which the base rate of a certain type of criminal behavior, such as a sadistic sexual murder, is close to zero (e.g., 5%). Prediction is easy and risk assessments are not needed because the best strategy is to predict that no one will recidivate; in this case, you will be correct 95 percent of the time. Likewise, when the base rate is close to 100 percent (e.g., 96%), if you predict that everyone will recidivate, you will be correct 96 percent of the time. Most of the time, however, the base rates for most criminal behavior (e.g., property offenses, assaults, drug violations) fall in the 20 to 80 percent range. Thus, prediction through risk assessment can make a significant contribution.

We have been emphasizing the importance of considering the 2 x 2 tables for evaluating predictive accuracy. We have also observed that base rates and selection ratios can influence predictive accuracy as measured by statistics such as r and phi. There are however, statistical measures of predictive accuracy that are hardly affected by base rates and selection ratios. One important measure is the Receiver Operating Characteristic (ROC). ROC is usually presented in the form of a graph; an example is given in Figure 6.1. Along the vertical axis we have the proportion of true recidivists or "hits," and along the horizontal axis we have the proportion of false positives. The diagonal line going from the bottom left to the top right represents chance level, where the hits equal the false positives. Most quantitative offender risk instruments have a range of scores and therefore we can plot for each score the proportion of hits and the proportion of false positives.

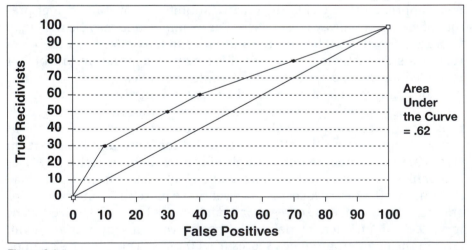

Figure 6.1
An ROC Curve for a Risk Scale

In Figure 6.1, we plotted an imaginary four-item risk scale. Each item can be scored 0 or 1. For example, one item could be gender and we would assign females a score of 0 and males a score of 1. As a result, our four-item risk scale will have scores ranging from 0 to 4 and, assuming that we did a follow-up of a group of offenders, we can calculate the proportion of true recidivists (hits) and false positives associated with each score. Figure 6.1 is based upon the following data:

Risk Score	Hits	False Positives
0	1.0	1.0
1	.8	.7
2	.6	.4
3	.5	.3
4	.3	.1

In interpreting the data given above and displayed in Figure 6.1, consider a risk score of 2. Fifty percent of offenders with a score of 2 recidivated and 30 percent did not reoffend (shown as the second data point in the graph). Thus, for each score from our imaginary risk scale, we can plot five data points and draw a (rough) curve through the data points. From this ROC curve we can make two statements. First, we can evaluate whether our risk scale is better than chance. In Figure 6.1, the curve is above the diagonal indicating that the scale predicts better than chance. Second, we can calculate the "area under the curve" (AUC). An AUC of 1.0 would represent perfect prediction; all recidivists would be correctly identified without errors. An AUC of .50 (the diagonal line) is chance. In our example, the AUC has a value of .62. An easy way of interpreting this value is to say that there is a 62 percent chance that a randomly selected recidivist would have a higher score than a randomly selected nonrecidivist. The larger the area, the better the overall predictive accuracy of the scale (more hits and fewer false positives). Calculating the AUC for different risk scales would allow us to compare the predictive accuracy of the various scales, controlling for the effects of base rates and selection ratios.

ROCs have been used sporadically in the prediction of criminal behavior (e.g., Fergusson, Fifield & Slater, 1977; Serin & Lawson, 1987). However, in the past few years, there has been a significant renewal of interest in the use of this simple and valuable method for evaluating approaches to risk assessment (Bonta et al., 1996; Grann, Belfrage & Tengström, 2000; Mossman, 1994; Rice & Harris, 1997; Ward & Dockerill, 1999). When we describe some of the methods evaluating offender risk later in this chapter, we will try to provide (when possible) the AUCs so the reader can judge the relative merits of different approaches to offender assessment.

Before proceeding, we wish to emphasize the unreasonableness of demanding perfect predictive accuracy from criminal justice and forensic professionals. Perfect prediction is an impossibility, and we extend our sympathy to those criminal justice professionals who have to work under conditions in which senior managers or colleagues expect it.

Having said this, we will soon see that predictions of criminal behavior beyond chance levels are not only possible, but that they add practical value to the management of offenders.

The Prediction of Dangerous Behavior: An Impossible Task?

The view that dangerousness cannot be predicted is not an isolated view:

> The more dangerous the behavior, the more difficult it is to predict. What the studies, taken in totality, actually show very clearly is the *you have to detain a much larger number of people than those who are actually dangerous in order to reach the dangerous* (Mathiesen, 1998: 461).

> It is clear from the research literature that we cannot, and will never be able to, predict with reasonable medical certainty future violence (Meloy, 1992: 949).

To understand the pessimistic assessments just quoted, we must consider: (1) the context and settings under which the negative conclusions were drawn, (2) what is being predicted, and (3) how the predictions are made (the predictors, models, and methods that are used). In answering these questions, we will show that the context was a special one, that the low base rates for what was being predicted (i.e., violence) made prediction a formidable task, and that the models of prediction were inadequate. Therefore, it is not surprising that so many were led to the conclusion that practically useful prediction is not possible.

In regard to the context under which "dangerousness" assessments were made, there were several notable features. First, the subjects of the debate were usually mentally disordered offenders. Second, the concern was (and still is) with the "doomsday" actions that authorities might initiate as a result of a person being found both mentally disordered and at risk for future violence. These doomsday actions were criminal and civil commitment laws that justified the confinement of offenders for periods longer than the typical sentence imposed upon offenders who were not mentally disordered. The justification for such actions is that the mentally disordered may profit from the care and security of a hospital setting and that society benefits from the removal of a potentially violent person from the community. The intrusiveness of the actions that might be taken upon a person judged both mentally ill and at the risk of future violence are extreme compared to the actions taken in the routine practice of criminal justice and corrections. The fact that much of the literature on dangerousness has dealt with mentally disordered individuals who were subject to extreme actions placed high expectations on predictive accuracy.

Referring back to the 2 x 2 accuracy tables, if we assess someone to be dangerous when he or she, in actuality, is not, and therefore incapacitate this individual, then we make a false positive error. This error is viewed by civil libertarians as a threat to individual rights and freedoms. In the first study of its kind, Steadman and Cocozza (1974) followed 98 patients from a hospital for the criminally insane who were judged by the psychiatric staff as a danger to the community but nevertheless were released by the courts. Upon follow-up, only 20 of 98 patients encountered an arrest, implying that in order to prevent one arrest we must imprison almost four people.

Since the Steadman and Cocozza (1974) study, there have been a number of similar reports from natural experiments (e.g., Fagan & Guggenheim, 1996, see also Chapter 9). In these studies, the false positive rate was always high (exceeding 50%) and attracted concern from critics of prediction. On the other side of the coin, we have the problem of false negatives. Just as the civil liberties of individuals are respected by avoiding unnecessary deprivation of liberties, so is protection of the community respected by the confinement of truly dangerous individuals. Individuals released into the community after they are judged not to be a threat may subsequently reoffend—sometimes with tragic results. These are the false negatives. Thus, the accuracy of prediction is not simply a technical concern but a concern that is meaningful in human and social terms. As we can see, the context for the assessment of dangerous and violent behavior is filled with extreme interventions and serious possible outcomes. As a consequence, the standards for predictive accuracy are very high. Almost any errors, whether false positive or false negative, are seen as unacceptable for critics of prediction.

The second reason for the pessimistic conclusions about prediction concerns what is being predicted: violent behavior. Violent behavior has a low base rate, in the 10 percent range with one- to three-year follow-ups. We have already seen that if the base rate is 10 percent for a behavior, then by predicting that no one will reoffend, we have a correct prediction of 90 percent. Thus, predicting violent behavior, especially in the short term, is difficult because the base rates are quite low.

The most important reason for the anti-prediction commentaries is that many studies of the prediction of violence and criminal behavior use methods and models that are, quite simply, inadequate. Prediction methods that rely on clinical judgments and approaches that do not consider the range of correlates related to criminal behavior perform poorly.

Obstacles to Effective Risk Prediction

The Reluctance to Abandon Clinical Judgment. In Bonta's (1996) review of the literature, he described three "generations" of offender risk assessments. The first generation referred to clinical judgments of risk, whereas the second- and third-generation assessments were actuarial or evidenced-based. First-generation clinical assessments are characterized by informal, nonobservable criteria for making decisions. The actuarial approach involves explicit criteria for decisions that are validated by research.

To illustrate the clinical approach, we present a scene that is all too typical. A professional, trained in the social sciences, interviews an offender in a relatively unstructured manner. The clinician may ask some basic questions of all offenders, but for the most part there is considerable flexibility in the questions asked from one offender to another. Sometimes psychological tests may be given; which ones are administered varies from person to person. Files may be reviewed, but what is attended to in these files is also at the discretion of the professional. At the end of the process of information-gathering, the staff member arrives at a judgment regarding the offender's risk to the community and his or her treatment needs. If the professional is unsure of his or her assessment, then a case conference is held with others who have used similar methods. The key feature of the clinical approach is that the reasons for the decision are subjective, sometimes intuitive, and guided by "gut feelings"—they are not empirically validated.

Although it may be flattering to clinical professionals to be viewed as having expertise in offender risk prediction, the evidence suggests that they are relatively poor prognosticians compared to objective, actuarial risk-prediction approaches. This conclusion is not limited to the correctional and forensic fields, nor to adult offenders (see Hoge, 2001, for a review of young offender assessment). Paul Meehl (1954) long ago criticized clinicians for using nonempirical and subjective methods for making clinical diagnoses and predictions. The poor predictive accuracy of clinical judgments is also evident in such diverse areas as the prediction of academic success, neuropsychological diagnosis, and business bankruptcy (Dawes, Faust & Meehl, 1993).

The better alternative to the prediction of offender behavior is the actuarial method. One of the earliest examples of the actuarial method comes from Burgess (1928). Burgess examined more than 3,000 parolees and found 21 factors that differentiated parole successes from parole failures. Burgess then gave to every offender one point for each factor. For the offenders scoring the maximum points, the recidivism rate was 76 percent; for those with the least points, the rate was 1.5 percent. The actuarial approach of summating items developed by Burgess, perhaps because of its simplicity, has been the preferred choice in risk assessment methodology. Recently, sophisticated techniques (e.g., multiple regression, iterative classification) have been applied to the prediction problem, but these newer techniques have shown little improvement in predictive power (Jones, 1996; Silver, Smith & Banks, 2000).

Narrative reviews of the literature have almost always concluded that actuarial methods outperform clinical methods in risk assessment. Recent meta-analyses have confirmed, in a much more convincing way, the power of empirical, statistical approaches over clinical approaches.

William Grove and his colleagues (Grove et al., 2000) conducted a meta-analysis of 136 studies that compared actuarial approaches to risk prediction with clinical approaches. These studies were drawn from general clinical psychology and psychiatry. The results showed that actuarial methods performed better than clinical procedures in 47 percent of the studies and equally as well in another 47 percent. In only 6 percent of studies did clinical judgment outperform actuarial prediction.

There are three other meta-analyses that support the superiority of actuarial approaches over clinical methods (summarized in Table 6.2). These meta-analyses focused on more specific criterion behavior and/or used offender samples. Bonta, Law, and Hanson (1998) compared objective risk measures with psychiatric judgments of risk in the prediction of general and violent recidivism among mentally disordered offenders. Objective risk measures were far superior to professional assessments of dangerousness in the prediction of both outcomes. Mossman (1994) provided a comparison of 17 studies using clinical methods and 13 studies using "behavior-based predictions" to predict violent behavior among psychiatric patients (not necessarily offenders). The behavioral (objective, empirically based) prediction strategy yielded a significantly higher AUC (.78 vs. .67). Finally, Hanson and Bussière (1998) also found statistical risk assessment procedures to predict sexual offenders better than clinical procedures.

Table 6.2
The Superiority of Actuarial Risk Assessment: Meta-analytic Evidence

Study	Criterion	Clinical	Actuarial
Bonta et al. (1998)	General Recidivism	$r = .03$	$r = .39$
	Violent Recidivism	$r = .09$	$r = .30$
Hanson & Bussière (1998)	Sexual Recidivism	$r = .11$	$r = .42$
Grove et al. (1995)	General Mix	favored 6%	favored 46%
Mossman (1994)	Violence	AUC=.67	AUC=.78

In our own review of the evidence on the predictive validity of first-generation clinical procedures to risk prediction, we can only echo Grove and Meehl's (1996) observation:

> Clinical experience is only a prestigious synonym for anecdotal evidence when the anecdotes are told by somebody with a professional degree and a license to practice a healing art (p. 302).

Why then do so many professionals in the criminal justice system still refuse to use empirical, actuarial methods for risk prediction and offender classification? The answer is complex and involves a number of factors. Resource Note 6.1 provides a listing of some of the possible "classification destruction techniques." We have heard many of these over the years, but the most important obstacle to actuarial, evidence-based prediction, in our view, is the training of professionals. How many criminal justice programs in North America educate graduate students in the psychometrics of risk prediction and methodologies to develop and evaluate risk scales? (And we mean more than a few introductory lectures.) In our experience, very few. This situation is not limited to criminology. Grove and Meehl (1996:318) estimated that "there are probably not more than two dozen American psychology departments whose clinical training programs strongly emphasize the necessity for scientific proof." Considering the weight of the evidence, continued reliance on clinical risk prediction methods verges on unethical and unprofessional practice.

Resource Note 6.1

Classification Destruction Techniques: Objections to Using Actuarial Risk Assessment

Objection	Reality
It is not "either/or"; I use both.	At the moment when a decision is made, if the two approaches do not agree, you have to use one or the other, you cannot use both.
The scale was developed on a different sample and does not apply to my sample.	There may be some slight statistical shrinkage on a new sample, but only when the sample is unique would this be an issue. Also, with the turnover of staff coming from different backgrounds, clinical predictions for the setting can also suffer. The relative advantage of actuarial prediction remains.
The research does not apply to me as the individual professional.	If there are more than 100 studies involving hundreds of professionals showing that they do not predict as well as actuarial instruments, then what makes you think you are so superior to others?
It is too expensive.	Possibly, but what of the time spent in team meetings, the cost of incarcerating someone needlessly, or placing the public at risk by not identifying the dangerous offender?
I want to change behavior, not just predict it.	If the goal is to change behavior, you need to know the probability of an outcome so you can judge whether your actions have an effect.
Predictions are based on group data; I deal with the unique individual.	Life is guided by probabilities. If the individual is similar to the reference group and there are no obvious differences, it would be foolish to ignore the data. If a doctor told you that surgery is successful in 90 percent of cases similar to yours, would you ignore it?
The important data is not measurable; people cannot be reduced to numbers.	*Anything* that is written can be coded. Further, being rational and empirical does not mean being cold and unfeeling with clients.

Adapted from Grove & Meehl, 1996

Theoretical Irrelevance. Second- and third-generation risk assessments are evidenced-based and represent improvements over clinical approaches (Bonta, 1996). Many of them, however, are limited in their usefulness partly because they lack a theoretical foundation. Nearly all second-generation risk assessments have no theoretical basis—they are atheoretical. These instruments are usually quite brief and consist almost entirely of static, historical items. Burgess's (1928) risk scale is the first recorded example of a second-generation offender assessment instrument. There are many other more recent examples of second-generation risk scales, but before we describe a few, we need to explain one of the major purposes of offender risk assessment: *classification.*

Correctional systems, whether prison, probation, or parole, need to manage large numbers of offenders in a safe and cost-efficient manner. Recognizing the fact that not all offenders are the same, a great deal of effort is invested in identifying subgroups of like offenders who can be dealt with in a similar fashion. The identification of similar subgroups and assigning them to certain interventions is called classification. The most common type of classification is based upon risk level. For example, the risk for violence or escape forms part of the decision in the classification of inmates to maximum-security prisons. The risk of reoffending is critical in assigning the frequency of contact in parole supervision. All of the risk instruments that we will describe provide guidelines separating offenders into low-, medium-, and maximum-risk levels for offender classification.

Three good examples of second-generation risk assessment can be found in the United States, Canada, and the United Kingdom. In the United States, there is the Salient Factor Score or SFS (Hoffman, 1994). This scale was developed to assist parole selection in the Federal Bureau of Prisons from 1972 until 1987, when federal parole was abolished for newly sentenced inmates. However, the SFS is still widely used in many jurisdictions at the state and county levels. Research with the SFS has demonstrated respectable predictive validity. Studies using a number of samples of parolees have found correlations with recidivism ranging from .27 (Hoffman & Beck, 1984) to .45 (Hoffman, 1994).

In Canada, the Statistical Information on Recidivism or SIR scale was developed by Joan Nuffield (1982) along similar lines. Parolees falling in the "very good" risk category had an 84 percent success rate, while offenders in the "poor" category had a success rate of 33.6 percent. Correlations with recidivism have ranged from .15 for violent recidivism to .42 for general recidivism (Bonta et al., 1996). The AUCs for the SIR scale were .64 for violent recidivism and .74 for general recidivism. Although the SFS and SIR were developed nearly 20 years ago, static risk scales continue to be developed. Recently, Copas and Marshall (1998) developed the Offender Group Reconviction Scale (OGRS) for use in the United Kingdom. These three second-generation risk scales are summarized in Table 6.3.

Table 6.3
Second-Generation Risk Scales

Item	SFS (U.S.)	SIR (Canada)	OGRS (U.K.)
Static			
Type of offense	Yes	Yes	Yes
Prior criminal history	Yes (2 items)	Yes (5 items)	Yes (3 items)
Age	Yes	Yes (2 items)	Yes
Prior parole failure	Yes	Yes	No
Gender	No	No	Yes
Security classification	No	Yes	No
Sentence length	No	Yes	No
Risk interval	Yes	Yes	No
Drug abuse history	Yes	No	No
Dynamic			
Unemployed	No	Yes	No
Marital status	No	Yes	No
Number of dependents	No	Yes	No
Total items	6	15	6

Noticeable in the risk scales that we have described is the predominance of items that are static or unchangeable. On the SFS scale, for example, all but one item is static. An offender who was imprisoned at the age of 16 for an auto theft while high on heroin will fall into the "poor" category even if this occurred 20 years ago and he has been straight ever since. The SIR and the OGRS also rely heavily on static variables. Recalling our social learning perspective of criminal conduct, these risk scales focus on criminal history (one of the Big Four) with a few nods to achievement (e.g., employment, marital status) and substance abuse. This illustrates the first disadvantage to second-generation risk assessments: the neglect of many factors theoretically relevant to criminal conduct (Bonta, 2002; Wormith & Olver, 2002). Antisocial peers, attitudes, and personality are noticeably absent in these risk scales.

The second significant disadvantage to these scales stems from a failure to appreciate the importance of dynamic predictors. These scales give little credit to the offender who changes for the better. Nor do they inform the practitioner or supervising staff as to what needs to be done to reduce the offender's level of risk. The predictability of recidivism may be greatly increased through the monitoring of changes in the person and situations of offenders. These dynamic risk variables or criminogenic need factors are prime candidates for selection as the targets of service programs. Offender assessment instruments that include the assessment of dynamic risk factors, or criminogenic needs, are represented in the third generation of offender assessment.

The second-generation risk scales described were developed in an era of "dustbowl empiricism." It did not matter whether the items made any sense as long as they showed significant correlations with the criterion. Moreover, *stable* items were considered preferable to information that changed with time (Wilkins, 1975). In many ways, these risk scales were not much of an improvement over Burgess's work 50 years earlier. There are, however, many other important predictors. Paul Gendreau, Tracy Little, and Claire Goggin (1996) conducted a meta-analysis of the predictors of recidivism. They reviewed 131 studies between 1970 and 1994 and used Pearson correlation coefficients as measures of the effect size. Their results are shown in Table 6.4.

Table 6.4.
The Predictors of Recidivism

Predictor	n	k	r
Companions	11,962	27	.21
Antisocial cognitions	19,089	67	.18
Antisocial personality	13,469	63	.18
Race	56,727	21	.17
Criminal history	171,159	282	.16
Parenting practices	15,223	31	.14
Social achievement	92,662	168	.13
Interpersonal conflict	12,756	28	.12
Age	61,312	56	.11
Substance abuse	54,838	60	.10
Intelligence	21,369	32	.07
Personal distress	19,933	66	.05
SES	13,080	23	.05

n = sample size; k = number of studies

From Gendreau et al., 1996

The most striking finding from the Gendreau et al. (1996) meta-analysis was the agreement with our social learning perspective of criminal conduct. The best predictors match the "Big Four" theoretical factors: antisocial associates, attitudes, personality, and criminal history. Other relevant, mid-range predictors of recidivism were also those described by PCC theory as part of the "Big Eight" factors (e.g., family factors and social achievement indices such as education and employment). The poorest predictors were social class and psychological discomfort (e.g., anxiety, feelings of loneliness, poor self-esteem). Noteworthy is the fact that many of the predictors are dynamic or changeable. Second-generation risk assessments measure criminal history and little else.

It seems clear to us that improvements to offender assessment can be made with a more comprehensive assessment of the factors—both static and dynamic—that are associated theoretically and empirically with criminal behavior. The single-minded focus on static variables (e.g., criminal history) without attention to other theoretically relevant variables places limits on the utility of risk assessment. Earlier we expressed the requirement that prediction should provide utility. The second-generation risk scales are useful for release decisions and security and supervision classification, but should we not demand more from prediction technology? Our answer is yes. The criminal justice system is also

charged with minimizing the offender's risk to the community, with rein-
tegrating inmates into society, and with healing the lives of those touched
by crime. To reach these goals, a better theoretical understanding is needed and should be applied to offender assessment technology.

Social Learning and Prediction

Theoretically, predictability improves when one uses a variety of predictors that include both static and dynamic variables. Gendreau et al.
(1996) found the dynamic factors ($r = .15$) to be slightly better predictors
of recidivism than the static factors ($r = .12$). One of the basic tenets of
PIC-R is that criminal behavior is a function of the number and variety
of incentives and disincentives for both criminal and noncriminal behavior. These incentives and disincentives arise from multiple sources (e.g.,
family, friends, work).

Methodologically, combining individual predictors may improve prediction beyond simply viewing them in isolation. Inspection of Table 6.4
shows that the best set of predictors did not exceed .21. Detractors of
criminological prediction frequently have pointed to the relatively low correlations between individual variables and criminal behavior, and have
neglected to point out the significant improvements in prediction when
these variables are combined (recall that Burgess was combining variables in the 1920s).

What would be the advantages if we combined static and dynamic factors in a theoretically and empirically meaningful manner? Static predictors, such as a prior criminal record, are good predictors; however,
once convicted, the record is a mark that stays. Dynamic predictors are
important because they are potentially functional or causal factors of
criminal behavior. For example, poor use of leisure time is a predictor
of recidivism (Bonta & Motiuk, 1985; Raynor et al., 2000). It is also
dynamic and subject to change (therefore, possibly causal). Furthermore,
this dynamic risk predictor makes sense from a social learning perspective. An individual with productive leisure pursuits receives rewards
for prosocial behavior (from others or from the activity itself). Someone
without hobbies and who has no involvement in organized prosocial activities has fewer costs associated with criminal conduct.

The preceding discussion outlines the importance of combining predictors. It also hints about the relevance of predictors derived from
social learning theory. Let us take a moment to explore how theories of
criminal behavior can influence offender assessment. There are many theories or explanations of criminal conduct. They can be grouped into the
following three general categories: (1) sociological, (2) psychopathological, and (3) social learning. Sociological theories explain crime as a product of social-economic-political forces; the psychopathological theories
see a psychological-personal deficit as the culprit; and social-learning

theories such as PIC-R hypothesize criminal conduct as the result of a learning experiences in interaction with biosocial and situational factors.

The three perspectives can lead to very different assessment strategies. For example, if we ascribe to a sociological formulation of criminal conduct, then our assessment may focus on gathering information relevant to the individual's position in the social structure. Note his or her social status, ethnicity, and a few other factors and the assessment is completed. Table 6.5 presents some examples of variables for assessment that can be derived from each theoretical perspective.

Table 6.5
The Relationship Between Theory and Offender Assessment

Theoretical Perspective	Derived Risk Factor
Sociological	Social status (e.g., age, gender)
	Race and ethnicity
	Financial status (e.g., poverty)
Psychopathological	Psychological discomfort (e.g., anxiety)
	Self-esteem
	Bizarre thoughts
General Personality & Social Psychological	Social support for behavior
	Employment instability
	Antisocial attitudes
	Antisocial personality
	Substance abuse
	Criminal history
	High-crime neighborhood

From Bonta, 2001

Note that the assessment variables associated with the three theoretical perspectives can be quite different in substance and usefulness. The variables derived from sociological theories tend to be static (e.g., SES, ethnicity). There are relatively few variables, and they suggest that changing criminal behavior requires intervention at the broad social level. In contrast, the other two theoretical perspectives place great value on individual characteristics, many of which are dynamic in nature and, therefore, suggest interventions at the individual level.

Which theoretical approach do we choose? The answer is that we choose the theoretical perspective that has the support of evidence. As shown in Table 6.4 and throughout the text, the social learning perspective wins quite handily. Thus, one important lesson to be learned is that good offender assessment instruments result from the use of theories that guide us in selecting *relevant* variables for the assessment (Bonta, 2002).

The major categories of predictive variables suggested by PIC-R may be summarized as *ties to crime* (tapping the density of rewards and costs for criminal behavior) and *ties to convention* (tapping the density of rewards and costs for noncriminal alternative behavior). Within each category, predictor variables may be further distinguished according to whether they reflect behavioral history, personal competencies, cognitive supports for behavior, or social support for behavior. These categories and subclasses of predictor variables are presented in Table 6.6.

Table 6.6
Major Predictors of Crime Classified by Ties to Convention and Ties to Crime

Ties to Crime:
1) A history of involvement in criminal behavior
2) Personal competencies (e.g., self-management deficit)
3) Cognitive supports (e.g., procriminal sentiments)
4) Social supports (e.g., antisocial associates)

Ties to Convention:
1) History of involvement in noncriminal alternative behavior
2) Personal competencies (e.g., self-management skills)
3) Cognitive supports (e.g., prosocial sentiments)
4) Social supports (e.g., anticriminal associates)

The social learning perspective strongly suggests the development of more comprehensive offender assessment instruments that tap static and dynamic risk factors. These instruments are described as the third-generation risk-needs assessments. The needs assessment component specifically refers to dynamic risk factors or criminogenic needs.

Third–Generation Risk–Needs Assessments

Third-generation offender assessments distinguish themselves from second-generation assessments in that they systematically and objectively measure offender needs. Two of the most widely used offender risk-needs instruments are: the Wisconsin Risk and Needs assessment instrument (Baird, Heinz & Bemus, 1979) and the Level of Service Inventory–Revised (LSI-R; Andrews & Bonta, 1995). Only the LSI-R is theoretically based and directly concerned with the measurement of dynamic risk factors.

The Wisconsin Risk and Needs Assessment

The Wisconsin classification system consists of three components: a risk scale, a needs scale, and client management classification (CMC). CMC is an assessment approach that suggests a certain type of treatment intervention for different types of offenders. The risk and needs scales are shown in Table 6.7. Evidence for the predictive validity of the risk scale has been positive (Baird, 1981, 1991; Baird et al., 1979; Bonta, Parkinson, Pang, et al., 1994). The only exceptions are a study by Wright,

Clear, and Dickson (1984), which used a New York City sample of adult probationers and research with juvenile offenders (Ashford & LeCroy, 1988; Bonta, Parkinson, Pang et al., 1994).

Table 6.7
The Wisconsin Risk and Needs Instruments

Risk Form:

    Number of Address Changes in Last 12 months

    Percentage of Time Employed in Last 12 Months

    Alcohol Usage Problems

    Other Drug Problems

    Attitude

    Age at First Conviction

    Number of Prior Probation/Parole Supervision

    Number of Prior Probation/Parole Revocations

    Number of Prior Felony Convictions

    Convictions or Juvenile Adjudications

    Conviction or Juvenile Adjudication for Assault

Needs Form:

    Academic/Vocational Skills

    Employment

    Financial Management

    Marital/Family Relationships

    Companions

    Emotional Stability

    Alcohol Usage

    Other Drug Involvement

    Mental Ability

    Health

    Sexual Behavior

    Agent's Impression of Client's Needs

What is lacking in the Wisconsin classification system is evidence for the predictive validity of the needs scale. The needs scale was developed without a full appreciation that some offender needs are actually risk factors. There are even two separate forms, one for risk and one for needs. The needs assessed by the Wisconsin scale were defined by staff as "problems," and the research consisted of tabulating how much time was devoted by staff in dealing with the problem. Whether these problems had anything to do with criminal behavior was never evaluated by the originators of the Wisconsin system. Bonta and his colleagues (Bonta, Parkinson &

Barkwell, 1994; Bonta, Parkinson, Pang et al., 1994) conducted the only known analysis of the predictive validity of the needs scale and found relatively low correlations, with recidivism ranging from .10 to .22 (compared to the risk scale with rs ranging from .22 to .33). A number of the needs items showed either no relationship to recidivism (e.g., health) or very unstable relationships (e.g., academic/vocational). The AUC for the Wisconsin risk and needs scales combined was .67.

The Level of Service Inventory-Revised

The Level of Service Inventory–Revised or the LSI-R (Andrews & Bonta, 1995) is a theoretically-based risk-needs offender assessment. It also has the most extensive research literature of any offender classification instrument. For these reasons, we give a more detailed description.

The origins of the LSI-R can be traced to a perceived need by probation and parole officers in the late 1970s to become more explicit about how decisions were made regarding level of supervision and the type of services their clients needed. There was a sense that scarce resources should be distributed according to level of risk and the need for service. A quantitative decision-aid was planned that would be easy to use and not too time-consuming. There was also a sense that it should constitute a reasonably comprehensive survey of the factors judged relevant to decisions on level of supervision in legal and professional terms. The resulting risk/need scale was the LSI-R. The LSI-R samples 54 risk and needs items, each scored in a zero-one format and distributed across 10 subcomponents. A summary of the record form of the LSI-R is presented in Table 6.8.

The items on the LSI-R are those that the research literature has found to be associated with criminal conduct and that are theoretically relevant. Thus, the "Big Four" are represented in the subcomponents of Criminal History, Companions, and Attitudes/Orientation, as well as in the items from the Emotional/Personal subcomponent. Additionally, other important risk factors from the "Big Eight" such as family, substance abuse, and social achievement are represented. Theoretically speaking, almost all of the items from the LSI-R can be derived from PIC-R. Take for example, the Companions subcomponent. Information is gathered on: (a) criminal associates (i.e., sources of interpersonal rewards for deviant behavior and costs for prosocial behavior), and (b) prosocial associates (i.e., interpersonal sources of rewards for prosocial behavior and costs for criminal behavior). The distinction between "acquaintances" and "friends" taps the density (quality and frequency) of rewards and costs.

Table 6.7
Level of Service Inventory–Revised

CRIMINAL HISTORY

_____ 1 Any prior convictions, adult/number (   )

_____ 2 Two or more prior convictions (   )

_____ 3 Three or more prior convictions

_____ 4 Three or more present offenses/number

_____ 5 Arrested under age 16

_____ 6 Ever incarcerated upon conviction

_____ 7 Escape history institution

_____ 8 Ever punished for institutional misconduct/number (   )

_____ 9 Charge laid or parole/probation suspended during prior community supervision

_____ 10 Official record of assault/violence

EDUCATION/EMPLOYMENT

_____ 11 Currently employed

_____ 12 Frequently unemployed

_____ 13 Never employed for full year

_____ 14 Ever fired

School or when in school:

_____ 15 Less than grade 10

_____ 16 Less than regular grade 12

_____ 17 Suspended or expelled at least once

When homemaker, pensioner: #18 _only_.
When school, work, unemployed: #18, #19, #20 apply

_____ 18 Participation/performance

_____ 19 Peer interactions

_____ 20 Authority interactions

FINANCIAL

_____ 21 Problems

_____ 22 Reliance upon social assistance

FAMILY/MARITAL

_____ 23 Dissatisfaction with marital or equivalent situation

_____ 24 Nonrewarding, parental

_____ 25 Nonrewarding, other relatives

_____ 26 Criminal—family/spouse

ACCOMMODATION

_____ 27 Unsatisfactory

_____ 28 3 or more address changes, last year

_____ 29 High-crime neighborhood

LEISURE/RECREATION

_____ 30 No recent participation in an organized activity

_____ 31 Could make better use of time

COMPANIONS

_____ 32 A social isolate

_____ 33 Some criminal acquaintances

_____ 34 Some criminal friends

_____ 35 Few anticriminal acquaintances

_____ 36 Few anticriminal friends

ALCOHOL/DRUG PROBLEM

_____ 37 Alcohol problem, ever

_____ 38 Drug problem, ever

_____ 39 Alcohol problem, current

_____ 40 Drug problem, current specify drug _____

Item #41-#45 scored only if #39 or #40 scored.

_____ 41 Law violations

_____ 42 Marital/Family

_____ 43 School/Work

_____ 44 Medical

_____ 45 Other clinical indicators Specify _____

EMOTIONAL/PERSONAL

_____ 46 Moderate interference

_____ 47 Severe interference

_____ 48 Psychiatric treatment, past

_____ 49 Psychiatric treatment, present

_____ 50 Psychological assessment indicated, Area _____

ATTITUDE/ORIENTATION

_____ 51 Supportive of crime

_____ 52 Unfavorable toward convention

_____ 53 Poor, toward sentence, past

_____ 54 Poor, toward supervision

RECOMMENDATION:

*LSI Total Score _____

Since the first report on the predictive validity of the LSI-R (Andrews, 1982b), there have been at least 20 articles published on the LSI-R in professional journals and a score of others in government and agency reports and university theses. The research has ranged from examination of the psychometric properties of the LSI-R, such as its reliability, convergent validity, and factor structure (e.g., Loza & Simourd, 1994; O'Keefe, 1999), to the predictive validity of the instrument (e.g., Raynor et al., 2000). The evidence on the predictive validity of the LSI-R is most consistent. Table 6.9 gives a sampling of the results from longitudinal studies on the predictive validity of the LSI-R.

Table 6.9
A Sampling of LSI-R Correlations with Recidivism

Study	Sample	Follow-up	Outcome	r
Andrews (1982b)	185 probationers (M/F)	3 years	Rearrest	.41
Bonta (1989)	52 Native inmates (M)	1 year	Reincarceration	.35
Bonta & Motiuk (1985)	89 halfway house residents (M)	1 year	Reincarceration	.28
Bonta & Motiuk (1992)	580 inmates (M)	1 year	Reincarceration	.35
Coulson et al. (1996)	526 inmates (F)	2 years	Rearrest	.51
Cumberland & Boyle (1997)	281 probationers (M/F)	4 years	Reconviction	.39
Harris et al. (1993)	613 mentally disordered (M)	81 months	Violent Rearrest	.25
Lowenkamp, Holsinger & Latessa (2001)	422 halfway house residents (M/F)	1.6 years	Reincarceration	.22
O'Keefe, Klebe & Hromas (1998)	174 parolees (M/F)	2 years	Rearrest	.36
Raynor et al. (2000)	964 probationers (M/F)	1 year	Reconviction	.35
Rettinger (1998)	239 probationers (F)	57 months	Reconviction	.42
	202 inmates (F)	57 months	Reconviction	.54
Rowe (1996)	392 parolees (M/F)	1 year	Reincarceration	.41
Wadel et al. (1991)	94 community ex-offenders	10 months	Reconviction	.22

Note: M (male), F (female).

As Table 6.9 indicates, LSI-R scores predict recidivism with varying offender populations (Aboriginal, mentally disordered, and female offenders) and in different settings (probation, prison, halfway houses). The studies come from countries beyond Canada and include the United States (Lowenkamp, Holsinger & Latessa, 2001; O'Keefe, Klebe & Hromas, 1998), the United Kingdom (Raynor et al., 2000), and Australia (Cumberland & Boyle, 1997). There have also been a number of comparisons of the LSI-R to other offender risk instruments. All of the comparisons have showed the LSI-R to predict as well or better than the other instruments (Kroner & Mills, 2001; Loza & Loza-Fanous, 2001; Motiuk, Bonta & Andrews, 1986; Raynor et al., 2000). In Gendreau et al.'s (1996) meta-analysis, the LSI-R was compared to the SFS and Wisconsin classification instruments. The fact that the LSI-R produced the higher correlation coefficients led Gendreau et al. (1996) to conclude that the LSI-R is "the current measure of choice"(p. 590). A more recent meta-analysis by

Gendreau, Goggin, and Smith (2002) compared the LSI-R with the Psychopathy Checklist–Revised (PCL-R; this instrument is described in more detail in Chapter 9). With respect to general recidivism, the average effect size was .39 for the LSI-R and .25 for the PCL-R; for violent recidivism, the LSI-R yielded an effect size of .28 and the PCL-R produced an effect size of .25.

With respect to the criterion of utility, a number of studies have examined the usefulness of the LSI-R to manage correctional costs by reducing the amount of control placed on low-risk offenders. A frequent problem in offender assessment is the problem of "overclassification" or, in the language of prediction, "false positives." Overclassification is extremely wasteful of resources. Correctional staff who rely on professional judgment tend to overclassify offenders (Schneider, Ervin & Snyder-Joy, 1996). Another potential application of the LSI-R includes the delivery of effective supervision and services to the higher-risk offenders who are likely responsible for most of the criminal activity in the community. By attending to criminogenic needs as well as static risk, the overall risk level of some offenders may be decreased. These two potential uses of the LSI-R—decreased correctional controls for those who do not require it and identifying dynamic risk factors for treatment targeting and monitoring—are evident in studies on the LSI-R.

Reducing Overclassification. Halfway houses for criminal offenders can serve a diversion function and/or a reintegration function. Many correctional halfway houses are used to house low-risk offenders and thereby avoid the costs and potential harmful consequences associated with imprisonment. For correctional systems that have available a range of secure settings, the classification challenge is to ensure that low-risk offenders are placed into minimum-security community settings instead of higher-security prisons. A number of studies with the LSI-R have found that inmates with low scores (usually between 0 and 14) who were placed into halfway houses showed successful completion rates exceeding 90 percent (Bonta & Motiuk, 1982, 1985). In the early studies, the LSI-R was not used to assist with decisions for halfway-house placement, but subsequent studies did evaluate the LSI-R for making classification decisions.

In 1987, Bonta and Motiuk reported the results of two studies examining the use of the LSI-R in classification decisions. The first study assessed whether the traditional classification procedures (mainly professional judgments) used by the prison staff were identifying minimum-risk offenders for halfway house placement. The LSI-R was administered to 114 inmates, and their security placements were monitored. Approximately 34 percent of the inmates had LSI-R scores of 14 or less. However, two-thirds of this group of seemingly ideal candidates for halfway houses were not placed into a house. They served their sentences in prison. Furthermore, examination of more than 100 variables did not uncover information as to why some low-scoring inmates went to a halfway house and others did not. The conclusion was that the traditional method of classification (using a nonquantitative, subjective interview) might be improved by introducing a more objective assessment of offender risk. In the second study, 270 inmates were administered the LSI-R. This time, if an inmate's LSI-R score was low (0-14) then the inmate was automatically referred to the halfway-house selection board. Approximately 58 percent of these inmates were placed into a house. Although not all low-scoring inmates were classified to a halfway house, significantly more offenders with longer sentences and even with violent offenses were so placed. Yet, the success rate remained high (91.7%).

In the clearest demonstration of the usefulness of the LSI-R in reducing overclassification decisions, inmates from three institutions were administered the LSI-R, but only two of the institutions used LSI-R scores for halfway house placement decisions (Bonta & Motiuk, 1990). The third institution did not release LSI-R scores to the halfway house selection board. The institutions that used the LSI-R placed 51.2 percent of the low-scoring offenders into the halfway houses, while the blind institution (which did not have LSI-R scores) placed 16.4 percent of low-risk inmates. All of the low-scoring inmates who were placed into halfway houses completed their placements without incident. For an illustration of the use of the LSI-R to reduce overclassification at the individual level, see Resource Note 6.2.

Resource Note 6.2

Clinical Case: Assessment of the Least Restrictive Custody

Across North America prisons are at an all-time population high. Cells built to accommodate one person now routinely house two, and it is not uncommon to find three or four people assigned to the same cell. Some states are under court order to reduce their prison populations, whereas other states have legislated caps for how many inmates they can have. Although both American and Canadian laws are based, in part, on the principle of the least restrictive alternative (i.e., do not restrict the freedom of an individual unless it is absolutely necessary), it has had a negligent impact upon the prison population.

Garcia received a five-year sentence for attempted murder. He came home early from work one day (he was scheduled to work a double shift but at the last minute the employer felt it was not necessary) and found his wife eating dinner in the kitchen with another man. The man was wearing Garcia's bathrobe. Impulsively and angrily, Garcia grabbed a knife from the table and stabbed his wife's lover six times.

Garcia immigrated with his wife to the United States three years ago from Central America. They had no family or friends, but he hoped that with time they could establish a new life, save some money, and eventually sponsor his wife's mother to come to America. Garcia worked as a general handyman in a nearby restaurant and he would often work overtime as a dishwasher when the regular staff failed to report to work.

This was Garcia's first criminal offense. During his 27 years of life, he never had any conflict with the law. In his home country, Garcia attended a technical college from which he received a diploma in engine mechanics. He worked as a machinist in a local factory. There was no history of mental disorder or substance abuse.

At the local jail, Garcia underwent the formal classification process. Convicted of a violent offense and serving a relatively lengthy jail sentence, classification to a maximum-security prison was likely. The LSI-R was part of the classification process and his score was

Resource Note 6.2 *(continued)*

11. Inmates with similar scores had a probability of recidivism of 11.7 percent with a
probability of 94 percent success if placed
into a halfway house. His score on the Gough
So scale was 33 (at the 88.3 percentile), indicating a high degree of sensitivity to society's
norms and expectations. Other tests confirmed the image of a predominantly prosocial
individual.

Despite the seriousness of the offense,
Garcia was placed into a halfway house. Placement into a halfway house was not seen as a
"break" but rather an appropriate use of
scarce prison resources. In addition, from a
human perspective, continued incarceration
was not seen as producing any deterrent benefit and, because Garcia was considered a

low-risk offender, it ran the risk of increasing
the likelihood of his recidivating.

Garcia spent 18 months in the halfway
house. He was described as a model resident
and he continued working at the restaurant.
Garcia and his wife followed a marital counseling program at which Garcia learned to
balance his desire to save money quickly with
spending more time with his wife in mutually rewarding activities. At the end of 18
months, he was paroled.

At the time of this writing, Garcia has been
released six years. He now works for a small
factory as a machinist. His mother-in-law
immigrated to the United States six years
ago. Garcia and his wife have a six-year-old
daughter who has entered grade one.

In addition to diverting inmates to community-based residential
facilities, a study by Bonta and Motiuk (1992) suggested that the use of
the LSI-R could potentially reduce overclassifications within a prison system. The LSI-R was administered to 467 inmates who were classified to
prisons with different security levels (minimum, medium, maximum).
Using statistical modeling techniques, they estimated that if the LSI-R
classification guidelines were used, overclassification could have been
reduced by up to 38 percent. That is, significant proportions of inmates
could have been placed in less secure, and less costly, institutions.

Criminogenic Needs and the Dynamic Validity of the LSI-R.
The majority of the items that comprise the LSI-R are dynamic. Thus, we
would expect that scores on the LSI-R would change with reassessments.
The change could result from naturally occurring events (e.g., the
offender finds a job) or as the result of treatment (e.g., stops drinking).
This information could prove useful for monitoring improvement and dete-
rioration in offenders if it could be shown that changes in LSI-R scores
are related to recidivism (that is, the LSI-R taps criminogenic needs).
Three studies have found evidence for the dynamic validity of the LSI-R.

In the first study, Andrews and Robinson (1984) administered the LSI-
R to 57 probationers at intake and then again six months later. They
found that changes in LSI-R scores were associated with changes in
recidivism. For example, probationers who tested in the moderate-risk
range at intake and showed no change six months later had a recidivism
rate of 33 percent. However, for those moderate-risk inmates who
showed a reduction in risk level (low-risk at retest), the recidivism rate
was 0 percent. The moderate-risk individuals who experienced more difficulties over the retest period and who increased their LSI-R scores
showed increased recidivism rates (40%).

High risk on GRAD items → Reed men/Revries
when rearrested what
used the GRAS
20 tho

In a second study, Motiuk, Bonta, and Andrews (1990) administered the LSI-R to 55 inmates who were released from prison and then reassessed while on probation. For the inmates who were low-risk on the first testing and remained low-risk when reassessed, none recidivated. The inmates who increased in risk level to moderate or high showed a 33 percent recidivism rate.

The largest evaluation of the dynamic validity of the LSI-R was conducted by Peter Raynor and his colleagues (2000). One hundred and fifty-seven probationers from the United Kingdom were assessed and reassessed with the LSI-R; recidivism was measured one year later. The average test-retest interval was six months. The results are shown in Table 6.10. Note that low-risk offenders who became worse (had higher LSI-R scores) showed higher recidivism rates, and high-risk offenders who showed decreased scores demonstrated lower recidivism rates.

Table 6.10
The Dynamic Validity of the LSI-R (% recidivated)

	Re-assessment	
Intake	Low-Risk	High-Risk
Low-Risk	26.2	54.8
High-Risk	55.3	78.4

(From Raynor et al., 2000)

The finding that changes in LSI-R scores are associated with changes in recidivism supports the hypothesis that the dynamic items and subcomponents of the LSI-R may be criminogenic. The importance of criminogenic needs will be addressed later in the chapter, but for now, we simply wish to point out that the dynamic aspects of the LSI-R could be useful for supervising and monitoring offenders. These dynamic risk factors identify areas in which service delivery is required if we are to minimize offender risk.

New Developments with the LSI-R. Almost all of the research on the LSI-R during the 1980s and early 1990s evaluated the instrument with general samples of offenders. In the prediction studies, the criterion or outcome measure was almost always general recidivism. Recent studies of the LSI-R have evaluated the LSI-R with more diverse samples and against violent outcome.

In a longitudinal study of mentally disordered offenders, Harris et al. (1993) found a correlation of .25 between LSI-R scores and rearrest for a violent offense. This study involved a large sample ($n = 613$) with a very long follow-up period (nearly seven years). The effect of a long follow-up for violent behavior is that it increases the base rate and, therefore, permits a more appropriate evaluation of the predictive validity of a risk instrument.

There are two reports suggesting that the LSI-R may be a useful assessment instrument for male batterers. Both reports are based on the same sample of men who attended treatment for partner assault. In the first report, Jennifer Rooney and Karl Hanson (2001) found LSI-R scores to be one of the best predictors of treatment dropout. In the second report, Hanson and Wallace-Capretta (2000) found LSI-R scores not only correlated with the *partner's* reports of past abuse ($r = .29$) but scores also predicted general (AUC = .76; $r = .39$) and violent recidivism (AUC = .73; $r = .32$). Recidivism was measured as a rearrest and the follow-up period was five years.

Finally, David Simourd and Bruce Malcolm (1998) administered the LSI-R to three groups of 216 sex offenders: (1) rapists, (2) child molesters, and (3) incest offenders. The LSI-R demonstrated similar psychometric properties as typically found with nonsexual offenders. In addition, the incest offenders showed lower LSI-R scores than the other two groups. This finding is consistent with the general sex offender literature that shows that incest offenders have lower sexual recidivism rates than rapists and nonfamilial pedophiles (Hanson & Bussière, 1998). As of yet, there are no direct tests of the predictive validity of the LSI-R with respect to sexual recidivism.

The prediction of violent behavior is especially important in terms of public safety. As we pointed out early in this chapter, predicting violent behavior is difficult given the low base rates. The general approach for dealing with the assessment of risk for violent behavior is to develop specialized risk scales. Underlying this approach is the idea that we need a different set of predictors because those who commit violent acts are significantly different from the run-of-the-mill offender. Two risk instruments that are considered by many to be especially good at predicting violence are the PCL-R (Hare, 1991) and the Violence Risk Appraisal Guide (VRAG; Harris, Rice & Quinsey, 1993). Other "violence" scales abound in the literature (Kroner & Mills, 2001; Loza & Loza-Fanous, 2000, 2001; Simourd & Mamuza, 2000; Ward & Dockerill, 1999).

These instruments however, do not appear to perform any better than the LSI-R when it comes to predicting violent recidivism. Table 6.11 shows the effect size estimates found in some recent studies of the LSI-R and violent recidivism. Meta-analytic summaries have found the LSI-R to predict violent recidivism as well as the PCL-R (Gendreau, Goggin & Smith, 2002). In a direct comparison of the VRAG, PCL-R, and the LSI-R, Daryl Kroner and Jeremy Mills (2001) found the following correlations (AUC in parentheses) with violent recidivism: $r = .12$ (.56) for the PCL-R, $r = .15$ (.60) for the VRAG, and $r = .19$ (.68) for the LSI-R.

Table 6.11.
The LSI-R and Violent Recidivism

Study	Sample	Follow-up	r
Andrews & Robinson (1984)	464 probationers (M)	3 years	.26
Hanson & Wallace-Capretta (2000)	275 batterers (M)	5 years	.32
Harris et al. (1993)	613 mentally disordered (M)	81 months	.25
Kroner & Mills (2001)	87 inmates (M)	26 months	.19
Loza & Loza-Fanous (2001)	68 inmates (M)	2 years	.23
Rettinger (1998)	239 probationers (F)	57 months	.24
	202 inmates (F)	57 months	.31
Rowe (1996)	340 parolees (M)	1 year	.31

Note: M (male), F (female).

The most recent development with the LSI-R is the movement toward a "fourth-generation" offender assessment instrument. Characteristics of the fourth-generation assessment are an increased attention to the links between assessment and case management. Personal strengths are noted so that staff can use these strengths to build a prosocial orientation. In addition, special responsivity factors are considered in order to maximize the benefits from treatment interventions (responsivity is described more fully at the end of this chapter). The most recent version of the LSI-R, the Level of Service/Case Management Inventory (LS/CMI; Andrews, Bonta & Wormith, in press) has been modified to follow more closely our general theoretical perspective of criminal behavior and to make it more relevant to case management. The items have been reorganized to reflect the eight best sets of predictors of criminal behavior, with antisocial personality pattern highlighted. Given that the LS/CMI is based on the items of the LSI-R, scores on the LS/CMI have been found to predict both general and violent recidivism (Girard, 1999; Rettinger, 1998).

Similarly, there is a youth version of the LSI-R called the Youth Level of Service/Case Management Inventory (YLSI/CMI). The YLSI/CMI (Hoge, Andrews & Leshied, 2002) consists of 42 items drawn from the LSI-R and the research on delinquency. Naturally, there are some important differences in the item composition between the LSI-R and the YLSI/CMI because of the target population. For example, the YLSI/CMI pays more attention to family and school issues and less to employment. Scores on the youth version of the LSI-R have predicted recidivism in a number of studies (see Hoge, 2001, for a general review). Furthermore, Jung and Rawana (1999) found the YLSI/CMI to predict equally well for aboriginal and caucasian youths (male and female).

Summary of the LSI-R. The LSI-R, a product of the available research and a social learning perspective of criminal behavior, has demonstrated considerable evidence as a predictor of criminal conduct (Andrews & Bonta, 1995; Clements, 1996; Gendreau et al., 1996; Gendreau, Goggin & Smith, 2002). The predictive validity of the LSI-R has been shown with adult offenders, male and female, and other antisocial groups (mentally disordered, partner abusers). Modification of the LSI-R for youths has also demonstrated positive association with relevant outcomes. Particularly important for case management is that *changes* in LSI-R scores have predicted correctional outcome. Together these findings suggest that when we consider some of the essential ingredients of effective prediction (variety, functional, and historical characteristics, etc.) within a sound theoretical context—as the LSI-R attempts to do—we are able to predict a wide variety of rule-violating behavior among different offender samples.

The Role of General Personality Assessment in Offender Classification

Psychologists have long held a special interest in the measurement of personality and cognitive functioning. In fact, there is a branch of psychology (i.e., psychometrics) that is devoted to psychological measurement. For more than a century, psychologists have developed and used a variety of tests that measure personality function. The assessment instruments that have been developed can be grouped into two general types: (a) atheoretical, and (b) theory-based. Unfortunately, regardless of the type, most of these tests have dubious worth when it comes to understanding and helping criminal offenders.

Atheoretical Assessments of Personality

Jennifer Boothby and Carl Clements (2000) asked 830 correctional psychologists what tests they used. We found the answers disquieting. More than one-half of the psychologists reported using tests that have no evidence that they predict recidivism (e.g., Rorschach, projective drawings). In another survey of mental heath directors in 25 state correctional systems, projective tests were used in 10 states for pre-parole evaluations, a context in which the assessment of risk is a priority (Gallagher, Somwaru & Ben-Porath, 1999). Nearly all the states reported using the Minnesota Multiphasic Personality Inventory (MMPI). It seems that for the most part, psychological assessment approaches are being used with little regard to the empirical evidence regarding risk.

The MMPI is one of the most widely used psychological instruments in the world and in corrections (Gallagher et al., 1999). It was initially developed to assess personality maladjustment and assist mental health workers in making clinical diagnoses (Hathaway & McKinley, 1951). The MMPI consists of 566 True-False items (e.g., "I am a good mixer") that form 10 clinical scales and three validity scales. The inventory was left unaltered for 40 years until 1989, when many of the statements were updated and standardized on a more representative sample (MMPI-2; Butcher et al., 1989). Thus far, most of the research with the MMPI-2 and offender samples has been of a descriptive nature (Heilbrun & Heilbrun, 1995; Lilienfeld, 1996; Shea & McKee, 1996; Shea et al., 1996), with only one predictive study (Duncan, Kennedy & Patrick, 1995).

The 10 clinical scales of the MMPI were initially constructed to differentiate known clinical groups from normals. Of interest to us are the psychopathic deviate or Pd scale on the MMPI and the Antisocial Practices scale on the MMPI-2. Evaluations of the predictive validity of the Antisocial Practices scale are unavailable. Therefore, our comments are limited to the MMPI's Pd scale (more commonly referred to as Scale 4). Although the research has shown that Scale 4 (Pd) discriminates offenders from nonoffenders (concurrent validity), predictive validity estimates have been modest (Simourd et al., 1991).

Efforts to improve the MMPI as a useful assessment tool for offenders have been varied and not particularly encouraging. Analysis of the subscales that comprise Scale 4 have found unimpressive predictive validity estimates (Bayer, Bonta & Motiuk, 1985), and experimental scales based on MMPI items, such as the overcontrolled hostility scale (Megargee, Cook & Mendelsohn, 1967), have demonstrated mixed validity. Another approach has been to examine the high and low points or profile of the scales. Megargee and Bohn (1979) administered the MMPI to more than 1,200 inmates in a Florida prison. The individual MMPI profiles were statistically reduced (via hierarchical profile analysis) to 10 distinctive profiles. Each of these profiles was given a nondescript label (e.g., Able, Baker, Charlie, etc.) and, using clinical and institutional file information, an accompanying description of each profile and a prescription for treatment was produced.

The Megargee MMPI-based system is empirically based. There is no underlying theory as to why, for example, a type Delta (Scale 4, Pd, is the highest and only elevated scale on the MMPI) would be intelligent, free from anxiety, and hedonistic. It is simply a matter of a significant correlation of the profile with various measures of intelligence, anxiety, and impulsiveness. Much of the research has focused on replicating the 10 profiles. For the most part, independent researchers have confirmed that the MMPI profiles can be classified along the 10 types described by Megargee and Bohn, with a few exceptions (Bohn, Carbonell & Megargee, 1995; Hutton & Miner, 1995; Zager, 1988). However, the reliability of the MMPI classifications with the MMPI-2 is problematic. Megargee (1994) compared profiles from the MMPI and the MMPI-2 and found that only 60 percent had identical classifications.

Predictive validity information on the MMPI types is mixed with respect to institutional behavior. Some studies (Edinger & Auerbach, 1978; Wright, 1986) found the types to predict prison misconduct and assault, while others failed to find a relationship with institutional maladjustment (Bohn et al., 1995; Hanson et al., 1983; Louscher, Hosford & Moss, 1983; Moss, Johnson & Hosford, 1984). With respect to recidivism, the prediction of postrelease criminal behavior with the Megargee MMPI has found either no support (Moss et al., 1984) or weak relationships, depending upon the type of outcome being predicted (Megargee & Bohn, 1979; Motiuk et al., 1986).

Another atheoretical, personality-based classification system for offenders was developed by Herbert Quay (1984). In earlier work on the personality of delinquents, Quay (1965) found four personality factors or types that could describe most delinquents (subsequent research identified a fifth type). Quay also developed assessment instruments that were to be used to classify offenders into one of the different types. The resulting Adult Internal Management System (AIMS) is a classification system that consists of five offender types. It uses two behavioral assessment instruments, the Life History Checklist and the Correctional Adjustment Checklist, to assign offenders into one of the types.

The Life History Checklist includes 27 items that describe behavioral patterns or traits (e.g., physically aggressive, expresses lack of concern for others). The Correctional Adjustment Checklist consists of 41 items covering behaviors within the prison setting (e.g., victimizes weaker inmates, talks aggressively to staff). All the items from the questionnaires reflect the characteristics of the five offender types. These two checklists are completed by correctional staff during a two- to four-week period of observation for each new inmate. Upon completion, the checklists are scored and converted into a group classification that is used to assign the inmate to specific living quarters.

The five offender types and a brief description of each are as follows:

I. Aggressive-Psychopathic (AP): Aggressive individuals who show little concern about their victims. Constantly violating rules and searching for excitement.

II. Manipulative (M): Similar to the AP group, but uses manipulation and conning rather than victimizing others through aggressive means.

III. Situational (S): Relatively trustworthy offenders with a short criminal history. Do not see themselves as criminals and view their conflict with the law as transitory.

IV. Inadequate-Dependent (ID): Passive individuals who are frequently victimized by Group I and II offenders. Generally submissive and form dependent, immature relationships with others.

V. Neurotic-Anxious (NA): The worriers. Usually tense and depressed and tend to blow up when under stress. This group is also easily victimized by Group I and II inmates.

AIMS was developed to manage inmates safely within a prison setting. The main goals were to separate the predators from their victims and to assign higher levels of supervision to those most likely to engage in institutional violence. Thus, the five groups all speak to the predator-prey relationship and hostility toward correctional staff.

Research on the validity of AIMS has emphasized the impact of AIMS classification on the reduction of prison violence. Quay (1984) reported that the use of AIMS in a United States federal prison reduced the inmate-staff and inmate-inmate assault rate by approximately 50 percent. Similar results have been reported by Levinson (1988). To our knowledge, only one study provides any data on the prediction of postrelease recidivism. Robert Levinson (1988) collapsed the five types into three groups and reported on a two-year follow-up of 220 inmates. The Heavy group (who were identified as both AP and M), as expected, had the highest rearrest rate.

In the late 1990s, a promising assessment instrument, the HCR-20, was developed (Webster et al., 1997). This is a 20-item instrument consisting of 10 historical items, five clinical items, and five risk management items. The five clinical items are: lack of insight, negative attitudes, active major mental illness symptoms, impulsivity, and unresponsiveness to treatment. The items were selected based on discussions with clinicians and the authors' reading of the risk prediction literature. The clinical items appear to tap an antisocial personality dimension. Although the HCR-20 appears to have significant face validity, there are very few studies of its predictive validity.

At the time of writing, there are three published studies on the predictive validity of the HCR-20. One study investigated only the H (history) subscale; this scale predicted violent recidivism (AUC = .68; Grann, Belfrage & Tengström, 2000). The second study used all three scales, but the sample consisted of *civilly* committed psychiatric patients (Douglas et al., 1999). The AUC was an impressive .76, but the clinical scale demonstrated the least predictive accuracy among the subscales (AUC = .63; for the history scale, the AUC was .72; for the risk management scale, it was .73). The only predictive study with criminal offenders using all three scales was by Kroner and Mills (2001). The AUC for the HCR-20 was .62 (for violent recidivism). Unfortunately, the AUCs for the individual scales were not reported. This indicates that more research on the HCR-20 is needed.

Theory-based Approaches to the Assessment of Personality

In contrast to the atheoretical personality assessment instruments, there are the theoretically based I-Level and Conceptual Level (CL) systems. Both assessment systems are used exclusively with juvenile delinquents. The I-Level (Interpersonal Maturity) system is based upon the theory that individuals develop in stages of emotional and social maturity (Sullivan, Grant & Grant, 1957). The seven stages or integration levels progress to increasingly sophisticated integrations between the person and his or her environment. These I-levels range from complete imma- turity (as the newborn infant) to total maturity (rarely achieved). Most delinquents fall between I-levels 2 and 4. The Conceptual Level system (Hunt & Hardt, 1965) places a greater emphasis on cognition and includes four stages (from egocentric thinking to an ability to think of problems from many different perspectives). In the Conceptual Level sys- tem, it is *how* the offender thinks rather than *what* the offender thinks that is important.

The assessment of I-Level is conducted in one of two ways. One method is an open-ended clinical interview (Harris, 1988). The other (less costly and more objective) method is the administration of the 155-item Jesness Inventory (Jesness, 1988). Conceptual level is usually assessed with the Paragraph Completion Method (Reitsma-Street & Leschied, 1988). This approach requires the subject to complete a paragraph with three or more sentences (e.g., When I am criticized . . .). The com- pleted responses are rated and categorized along one of the four con- ceptual level stages. Table 6.12 presents a summary of the two classi- fication systems.

Table 6.12
The I-Level and Conceptual Level Classification Systems

I-Level Stages		Conceptual Level Stages	
I-2:	Unsocialized Aggressive (physically aggressive) Unsocialized Passive (withdraws or complains)	I:	Egocentric (self-centered)
I-3:	Immature Conformist (unquestioning conformity to most powerful figure) Cultural Conformist (peer conformity) Manipulator	II:	Norm-Oriented (rules not questioned)
I-4:	Neurotic Acting-out (poor self image, overtly aggressive) Neurotic Anxious (poor self-image, inwardly aggressive)	III:	Independent
	Situational Reaction (crisis-oriented) Cultural Identifier (internalized criminal values)	IV:	Interdependent (can see many different perspectives)

Common to the two assessment systems, and also true for the MMPI and AIMS, is the idea of differential treatment. That is, rehabilitation is most effective when the treatment strategy and/or therapist is matched to the characteristics of the offender. For example, in the Preston typology study, Carl Jesness (1971) assigned institutionalized delinquents to one of six living units, depending upon their I-Level. The units differed in the personality characteristics of the staff and their approach to helping delinquents. Thus, for example, one that housed the manipulators (I-3) was comprised of staff sensitive to manipulation, used a token economy to shape prosocial interpersonal behavior, and held strict rules. Studies evaluating this matching principle have been quite encouraging for both the I-Level and Conceptual Level systems in terms of the in-program management of the delinquents and with respect to recidivism (although there are fewer studies) (Andrews, Bonta & Hoge, 1990).

Some Concluding Comments on Personality-Based Assessments

Beginning with Lombroso and Freud, there has continued a search for offender types. The four personality-based classification systems (MMPI, Quay, Conceptual Matching, and I-Level) have been influential in promoting and facilitating treatment efforts with offenders because of the emphasis placed on the matching of the intervention to the personality type of offender. The importance of this "matching" principle will become evident in the next section when the principles of risk, need, and responsivity are presented. What we conclude from this literature is that individuals differ along some important dimensions, and treatment will not be equally effective for all offenders. We need to recognize and assess the important personality factors related to the effectiveness of treatment.

Research on the personality-based classification systems needs to explore their predictive validity. Most of the studies of predictive validity have as their criteria institutional or in-program adjustment, and when these systems are compared, they all are able to predict (Van Voorhis, 1988). However, although having quiet and well-behaved prisoners may be important for the management of a correctional facility, it does not necessarily follow that these inmates will transfer this behavior into the community (Bonta & Gendreau, 1992). What is sorely lacking is evidence on the ability of the systems to predict recidivism; what little data does exist has not been impressive (e.g., Gendreau et al., 1996; Motiuk et al., 1986).

It appears that these various classification systems may be measuring the same types of offenders. Patricia Van Voorhis (1994) has conducted the most comprehensive evaluation of these classification systems to date. Inmates ($n = 369$) from two United States federal prisons (one minimum-security and one maximum-security) were assessed using the five classification systems (the Jesness was treated separately). For six months, a vast quantity of information was collected (prison misconduct, work performance and other measures of prison adjustment). No postrelease recidivism data were gathered.

Van Voorhis found that the five classification systems converged on the following four types of offenders: (1) committed criminal, (2) character disordered, (3) situational, and (4) neurotic anxious. Although the four types of offenders could be described in reliable ways, assessments of their relevance to correctional management were mixed. For example, the I-Level and CL classifications were unrelated to measures of misconduct in the maximum-security prison but predictive in the minimum-security setting. AIMS classification did not predict misconduct in either setting. As another example, two-thirds of the minimum-security inmates were classified by the AIMS as "situational." When the majority of inmates in a setting are viewed similarly, then what does classification accomplish?

One final but important comment concerns the general search for typologies. A type or a taxon implies that there are key characteristics associated with the type and that one type can be clearly differentiated from another type. If we take Quay's system as an example, an Aggressive-Psychopath (AP) offender has some specific characteristics that differentiate him or her from a Neurotic-Anxious (NA) offender. A typological system demands that individuals be classified as one type or another. Thus, for example, an offender who scores high on AP but has NA scores that are a close second must still be assigned to the AP category. Many of the subscales of these classification systems are intercorrelated, and there is overlap between the developmental stages. An offender who scores high on one scale or at a certain I-level may also have fairly high scores on another scale or produce responses typical of another I-level or Conceptual Level. Supporters of a taxon may argue that the problem is with the measurement instruments and, as these instruments become refined, a clearer identification of the type will be achieved. Others argue that it is ludicrous to attempt to force individuals into a pigeonhole. As Edwin Megargee and Martin Bohn (1979) so aptly put it:

> It is as if a parent whose child's report card indicated he was equally proficient in reading and writing demanded that the teacher decide whether the child was a reader or a writer (p. 66).

Classification for Treatment

Predictions of risk, as measured by the static risk scales (e.g., SFS, VRAG), provide valuable information that can facilitate release and placement decisions—decisions regarding the protection of the public. However, they provide little guidance about the treatment of the offender. What does the parole officer do with a high-risk offender assigned to his or her caseload? The items that comprise the nondynamic risk scales provide little help because they do not identify personal changeable characteristics.

For many years, correctional psychologists have psychological factors that may be the focus of treatment. Examples that we have seen are the I-Level, Conceptual Level matching, and the Megargee MMPI-based classification systems. These offender assessment systems are all used to guide differential treatment. However, here we focus on the value of three general principles of classification for purposes of effective correctional treatment: (1) risk, (2) need, and (3) responsivity (Andrews, Bonta & Hoge, 1990).

The Risk Principle

There are two aspects to the *risk principle*. The first is that criminal behavior can be predicted. Evidence that we have reviewed in this book should make it clear that there is no need to dispute this statement. The second aspect of the risk principle involves the idea of matching levels of treatment services to the risk level of the offender. At this point, we build the bridge between assessment and effective treatment. More precisely, as we are faced with a higher-risk offender, we need to deliver more intensive and extensive services if we are to hope for a significant reduction in recidivism. For the high-risk offender, we need intensive service; for the low-risk offender, minimal or no intervention is sufficient.

Although the risk principle appears to make a great deal of common sense, sometimes theory and practice do not always agree. For example, labeling theory warns against official intervention but fails to tailor this warning to minimum-risk offenders. Instead, it appears that all offenders would be better off if we provided less service. Furthermore, in many human service agencies, workers prefer to work with the motivated lower-risk clients rather than the high-risk, resistant clients. After all, it is personally reinforcing to work with someone who listens and tries to follow your advice. Table 6.13 provides some examples describing what happens when treatment is—or is not—matched to the risk level of the offender. In each of the studies, reductions in recidivism for high-risk offenders were found only when intensive levels of services were provided. However, when intensive services were provided to low-risk offenders, they either had a very minimal effect or a negative effect.

Table 6.13
Risk Level and Treatment (% Recidivism)

Study	Risk Level	LEVEL OF TREATMENT	
		Minimal	Intensive
O'Donnell et al. (1971)	Low	16	22
	High	78	56
Baird et al. (1979)	Low	3	10
	High	37	18
Andrews & Kiessling (1980)	Low	12	17
	High	58	31
Bonta et al. (2000)	Low	15	32
	High	51	32

The Need Principle

Many offenders, especially high-risk offenders, have multiple needs. They need places to live and work and/or they need to stop taking drugs. Some have poor self-esteem, chronic headaches, or cavities in their teeth. These all translate into needs. The *need principle* draws our attention to the distinction between criminogenic and noncriminogenic needs, a point that we introduced when discussing dynamic risk factors. Criminogenic needs are a subset of an offender's risk level. They are *dynamic* risk factors that, when changed, are associated with changes in the probability of recidivism. Noncriminogenic needs are also dynamic and changeable, but they are weakly associated with recidivism. Thus, instruments that measure criminogenic needs, such as the LSI-R, have direct relevance to the treatment of offenders.

Our argument is that if treatment services are offered with the intention of reducing recidivism, changes must occur on criminogenic need factors. Offenders also have a right to the highest-quality service for other needs, but that is not the focus of *correctional* rehabilitation. Addressing noncriminogenic needs is unlikely to alter future recidivism significantly unless it indirectly impacts on a criminogenic needs. We may help an offender feel better, which is important and valued, but this may not necessarily reduce recidivism.

The practical importance of criminogenic need factors is that they form the intermediate goals of treatment. Because we cannot often observe directly an offender's criminal behavior, we must be satisfied to try to change the aspects of the person and his or her situation that we think are linked to the criminal behavior. When these needs are successfully targeted in treatment, chances are increased that recidivism will be reduced.

Craig Dowden (1998) has tabulated a comprehensive listing of criminogenic need factors. He reviewed 225 treatment studies and coded for the type of need targeted in the treatment. His review produced 374 effect size estimates. Treatment targets that were coded as noncriminogenic (e.g., vague emotional problems, self-esteem, physical activity) showed either no relationship with recidivism or slight increases. Targeting criminogenic need factors was associated with reductions in recidivism. Some of the important criminogenic needs were antisocial attitudes, negative emotionality (anger, hostility), family affect and supervision, self-control, and social support for prosocial behavior.

One major set of criminogenic needs that is widely supported by theories of crime is criminal attitudes. All theories—labeling theory, control theory, differential association, and so forth—in some way or another give respect to the role of criminal attitudes in criminal behavior (Andrews, 1990). Assessments of procriminal attitudes have repeatedly evidenced significant associations with criminal behavior among adult criminals (Andrews, Wormith & Kiessling, 1985; Bonta, 1990; Simourd, 1997;

Simourd & Olver, 2002; Simourd & Van de Van, 1999; Walters, 1996) and young offenders (Shields & Ball, 1990; Shields & Whitehall, 1994).

As shown with the previous example of the LSI-R, there is also evidence for the dynamic validity of procriminal attitudes (see Table 6.14). Increases in procriminal attitudes are associated with increased recidivism, and recidivism decreases when the offender holds fewer procriminal beliefs and attitudes. In contrast, traditional clinical treatment targets, such as anxiety and emotional empathy, failed to demonstrate dynamic predictive validity. Continued research and development into the assessment of criminogenic needs will have enormous impact on the rehabilitation of offenders and the development of our conceptual understanding of criminal behavior.

Table 6.14
Three-Year Recidivism Rates by Six-Month Retest of Procriminal Attitude (N)

Risk Level	Retest Risk Level			
Intake	Low	Moderate	High	Overall
High (38)	7	43	40	29
Moderate (58)	10	37	57	33
Low (56)	10	20	67	16
Overall (152)	10	34	52	19
	(72)	(53)	(27)	(152)

From Andrews & Wormith, 1984

The Responsivity Principle

The *responsivity principle* refers to delivering treatment programs in a style and mode that is consistent with the ability and learning style of the offender. The general responsivity principle is quite straightforward: Offenders are human beings and the most powerful influence strategies available are cognitive-behavioral strategies. It matters little whether the problem is antisocial behavior, depression, smoking, overeating, or poor study habits—cognitive-behavioral treatments are more effective then other forms of intervention. Hence, one should use cognitive-behavioral styles of service to bring about change.

Additionally, there are more specific responsivity considerations. For example, an insight-oriented therapy delivered in a group format may not "connect" very well for a neurotic, anxious offender with limited intelligence. Offender characteristics such as interpersonal sensitivity, anxiety, verbal intelligence, and cognitive maturity speak to the appropriateness of different modes and styles of treatment service (Bonta, 1995). It is under the responsivity principle that many of the psychological approaches to offender assessment that were described earlier may have their value (Van Voorhis, 1997). By identifying personality and cognitive styles, treatment can be better matched to the client.

Table 6.15 summarizes a number of studies that found differential effects on outcome depending upon the type of treatment provided and the characteristics of the client. Client characteristics have ranged from anxious to amenable (i.e., verbal, anxious, and motivated) and treatment styles have ranged from the psychodynamic to the medical (e.g., drug therapy).

Table 6.15
The Responsivity Principle

PICO: Mean Follow-Up Months Incarcerated (Grant, 1965)

	PSYCHODYNAMIC CASEWORK		
Client Type	No	Yes	p
Amenable	4.8	2.1	*
Nonamenable	4.8	5.5	ns

Camp Elliott: Estimated Success Rates (Grant, 1965)

	LEVEL OF STRUCTURE		
Client Type	Low	High	p
High Maturity	.72	.60	*
Low Maturity	.46	.60	*

Recidivism Rates of Probationers (Andrews & Kiessling, 1980)

	SUPERVISION BY CITIZEN VOLUNTEERS		
Client Type	No	Yes	p
High Empathy	.80	.00	*
Low Empathy	.48	.42	ns

Mean # of New Offenses (Leschied: In Reitsma-Street, 1984)

	LEVEL OF STRUCTURE		
Client Type	Low	High	p
High Conceptual Level	nr	nr	nr
Low Conceptual Level	1.54	.47	*

p = probability; ns = not significant; nr = not reported

Table 6, p. 39, from D.A. Andrews, J. Bonta & R.D. Hoge (1990). Classification for effective rehabilitation: Rediscovering psychology. *Criminal Justice and Behavior, 17*(1), 19-52. Reprinted with permission.

Only a few of the possible variables that come under the responsivity principle have been studied. Theories of personality and crime suggest a host of possibilities that have barely been considered by researchers in corrections. The issue of amenability or motivation to treatment is an emerging area of research. James Prochaska and his colleagues (Prochaska, DiClemente & Norcross, 1992) describe methods that a therapist can use to increase the client's motivation to change. Their work has been in the area of addictions, but some of the principles of "motivational interviewing" have been applied to general offenders (Kennedy & Serin, 1999) and sex offenders (Wilson & Barrett, 1999). Increasing motivation may be particularly important with high-risk offenders who tend to drop out of treatment. If we are to adhere to the risk principle, then we must ensure that high-risk offenders remain in treatment (Wormith & Olver, 2002). We are curious about the differential effectiveness of rehabilitation programs with women, ethnic minorities, psychopaths, and mentally disordered offenders. We also want to know about the relative effectiveness of cognitive problem-solving, victim reconciliation programs, and other interventions upon different offenders. More work is required in this area.

The Role of the Professional and the Integrity of Assessment

Much rests on the assessment of offenders. Decisions are made in the delivery of services and the restriction of individual freedom. As we have noted many times, even under the best of conditions, risk-needs instruments make errors. Another source of error can be traced to the assessor. Rarely studied in the correctional assessment literature is whether the assessment instruments are used as they were designed to be used. That is, do classification and probation officers follow the instructions for completing the scales and do they make use of the information?

James Bonta, Brad Bogue, Michael Crowley, and Laurence Motiuk (2001) describe two general findings of importance with regard to the integrity of offender assessment. First, even after highly structured training in the use of a new classification system, there often remain high rates of errors. For example, soon after the introduction of the LSI-R in the State of Colorado, a review of LSI-R records found that 13 percent of 336 files had errors. Many of the errors were simple addition mistakes, but others dealt with misunderstandings of how some of the items were to be scored. To the credit of Colorado's correctional system, the administration of risk-needs assessment were monitored and steps taken to improve the assessment process. Many jurisdictions fail to monitor and correct the process.

There is also some indirect evidence suggesting that staff may not fully utilize the new instruments. A number of studies have reported that staff are often reluctant to change what they have done for years in order to adopt a new and better assessment procedure (Bonta et al., 2001). In a study by Schneider et al. (1996), staff were surveyed about their views of a newly introduced classification system (Wisconsin Risk and Need). Less than one-half of the probation officers thought it was a helpful instrument. Only 27 percent thought that the instrument was more accurate then their professional judgment. The major reason given for completing the instrument was expectation from their supervisors (78-83% range). Similar results have been reported by Maung and Hammond (2000), who asked probation staff in England about their views of the LSI-R and another risk instrument that was being pilot-tested.

We cannot help but suspect that the failure by staff to recognize the benefits of empirically based classification instruments would lead to errors and a resistance to use the results in case management. The problems that have been encountered point to a need for a high degree of training, personal professionalism, and managerial supervision. Staff who administer offender assessment instruments must conduct the assessments conscientiously, and manager's must actively assist and supervise.

Professionals often exercise discretion in making decisions—it is an important part of a fair and just system. Predictions of criminal activity are often at the heart of discretionary action. The principles of risk, need, and responsivity do not provide the final word on offender assessment. Although they provide an empirical basis to offender assessment, sooner or later there will always be a case that does not fit the formula. There is room (and a need for) professional judgment, which can serve to override these principles of assessment in the unique case. However, we must be careful that professional overrides are not used in a haphazard and irrational manner and that they do not become the preferred choice for making predictions. Rather, we should look on overrides as an opportunity to improve our assessments. This can be done by systematically monitoring our use of overrides and, if patterns emerge, incorporating (or perhaps discovering) a new principle of assessment. Simply put, science should be used in a constructive manner.

Summary

In the beginning of this chapter, we insisted upon demonstrations of predictions, clear statements of how predictions are made, and demonstrations of the utility of predictions. We found that theory and research in PCC may be translated into valid, objective, and practical assessment instruments. In addition, principles of effective intervention may be stated that suggest who may profit from treatment services (the risk principle), what should be targeted (the need principle), and the appropriate mode and style of treatment (the responsivity principle).

The Level of Service Inventory–Revised (LSI-R) is one instrument that samples both risk and need factors, links with a comprehensive theoretical perspective, and has relevance to offender treatment. In the last edition of this text, we were certain that this inventory would change as further experience with it accrues from community and institutional settings. We were right; the LS/CMI introduces modifications that we expect will lead to greater utility.

The research with the various offender assessment instruments has been informative to theory development. One of the recurring issues that arises in explanations of criminal conduct is whether a certain theoretical perspective is limited by age, gender, or race. From our consideration of developmental factors in the preceding chapter, certain variables (i.e., family, school, peers) may carry more weight with youthful offenders, but they are not necessarily unique to young offenders. For example, the YLS/CMI (Hoge & Andrews, 2001) often samples components similar to those from the adult LSI-R but may, for example, oversample the area of education and ask little about employment. In other words, the correlates of crime identified with adult offenders are similar for delinquents.

Correspondingly, the evidence suggests that the correlates of criminality are much the same for gender and race. The research thus far has found the correlates of criminal behavior to be highly similar for males and females (Loucks & Zamble, 1999; Simourd & Andrews, 1994). Risk assessment research has found parrellel results for males and females with the LSI-R (Coulson et al, 1996; Kirkpatrick, 1999; Rettinger, 1998) and with the youth version of the LSI-R (Jung & Rawana, 1999). With respect to race, our conclusions are more tentative because most of the offender risk research was conducted on Aboriginal offenders in Canada and one from the United States that included minority groups. However, the studies with the LSI-R (Bonta, 1989; Lowenkamp, Holsinger & Latessa, 2001), the Wisconsin (Bonta, LaPrairie & Wallace-Capretta, 1997), and the SIR (Hann & Harman, 1993) have shown these instruments to predict recidivism regardless of race.

There has been considerable progress in offender assessment over the past 20 years. The "professional judgment," first-generation approach to assessment is difficult to defend, but it is still used in some jurisdictions. Evidence-based, second-generation assessments are widely accepted, but many of them focus on static risk factors and thus limit their usefulness for offender risk management. The importance of the objective assessment of offender needs has been recognized for quite some time (Clements, 1986), but there was no appreciation of the distinction between criminogenic and noncriminogenic needs until recently. This is a distinction demanded by a general personality, social psychological perspective of criminal conduct. This theoretical perspective also warns us that certain psychological and intellectual dysfunctions are not necessarily risk factors. Thus, both theoretically and empirically, we see the use of general personality and intellectual tests (such as the MMPI and WAIS-R) for risk and criminogenic needs assessment as indefensible as clinical judgment.

We anticipate that the next 20 years will see continued improvements in the predictive accuracy of offender risk-needs instruments as more theoretically relevant and precise measures of the correlates of criminal behavior are included in the scales. There are two important directions for improving predictive accuracy. They involve using different methods for assessment and the assessment of a variety of domains. For example, the LSI-R samples a variety of areas or domains related to criminal behavior. However, the assessment of any one domain can use different methods. To illustrate, antisocial attitudes can be assessed through interviews, as with the LSI-R, but also through self-report questionnaires. Using multi-method, multi-domain sampling significantly improves predictive accuracy (see Resource Note 6.3).

Resource Note 6.3

Improving Predictive Accuracy: Multi-Method, Multi-Domain Sampling
(Andrews, Wormith & Kiessling, 1985)

Knowledge destruction is a pseudoscientific method used to discount research that does not support a favored theoretical position. This method employs two general arguments to dismiss research: (1) point out errors in conceptualization, and/or (2) point out errors in measurement. These approaches are honorable on their own but theoreticists apply the honorable approach of negative criticism only to research findings that are considered threatening to their personally, professionally, or ideologically pleasing positions. Moreover, they rarely ever actually explore the effects of these potential threats to validity but simply assert the existence of a threat. Here we explore some actual effects of some potential threats to validity.

An error in conceptualization often involves assertions that the theory underlying a study is "faulty." For example, a biology-crime linkage is declared illusionary because the "medical model" is wrong, or a personality-criminality linkage is dismissed because we already know that crime is socially based. Another aspect of an error in conceptualization is to invoke the concept of "construct validity." The evidence is not denied, but the "true" nature of either the predictor variable or the criterion is questioned. Thus, for example, level of education and attitudes, all measured at the individual level, are proclaimed to be primarily indicators of social class even though class is actually a weak correlate of criminality.

In the day-to-day operations of research, it is errors of measurement that produce most concern. Error-free assessments are an ideal unlikely to be achieved, and for purposes of knowledge construction, this means that another study is always a possibility. It means that any study can be dismissed because of potential errors of measurement. In this process, one points out the weakness of the measure and, in this way, dismisses any associations uncovered by research. However, what the destroyers of knowledge do not alert their audiences to is the fact that errors of measurement may have one of three effects on the predictor-criterion correlation. Measurement errors may (1) overestimate the relationship, (2) have no effect, or (3) underestimate the relationship. Knowledge destruction considers only the first possibility.

A study by Andrews, Wormith, and Kiessling (1985) explored what would happen when potential errors of conceptualization and measurement were systematically addressed. More specifically, does the relationship between personality and crime disappear as criminological theory would predict?

They explored errors of conceptualization in two ways. First, they compared the relative and incremental predictive criterion validities of six sets of personality variables that have some support in the theoretical and/or empirical literature. Second, they considered a variety of other measures (e.g., age and criminal history) to evaluate their incremental contributions to the prediction of criminal behavior.

Errors in measurement were explored by using multimethod assessments, repeated measurements, and multidomain sampling. Any particular method of assessment has a weakness (e.g., paper-and-pencil questionnaires are threatened by a tendency to respond in the socially desirable way or to check "true" more often than "false"; personal interviews may be threatened by interviewer-based sources of bias such as "halo" effects). Therefore, multimethod assessments of a particular trait may be more accurate

Resource Note 6.3 *(continued)*

than monomethod approaches. This issue was explored by comparing the magnitude of the R squares established when monomethod assessments were employed with the R squares achieved when multimethod assessments were employed.

A second issue is the effect of temporal instability in the assessment of variables. In the language of knowledge destruction, "we all know that assessments of attitudes and personality are highly unstable over time; hence, it is silly to expect predictive criterion validity." Technically stated, if scores are changing from one time to another, how can we possibly expect them to correlate with an external criterion? Thus, a solution is to conduct retests so that any movement may be tapped. Perhaps assessments of dynamic personality variables will yield increases in the magnitude of the personality-crime association.

The predictor domain may be undersampled by a failure to consider more than one domain or trait. Assessments of procriminal attitudes may have predictive validity in relation to criminal behavior, but that does not mean that other variables do not also have predictive validity. These other variables may even possess incremental predictive validity; that is, they may explain over and above that which is explained by procriminal attitudes. Thus, multidomain sampling may improve rather than decrease predictions.

Finally, this study also explored the effect of an extended follow-up period. One of the major ways of destroying knowledge regarding individual differences has been to note that the follow-up period was "only six months," "only a year," and so on. What, in fact, is the effect on R squares of an extended follow-up? Does predictive validity decrease as the knowledge destruction perspective suggests or does predictive validity improve as a sampling perspective would suggest?

A paper-and-pencil questionnaire battery was administered to probationers within the first few weeks of intake and readministered six months into probation. The battery included measures of six aspects of personality: (1) Alienation (feelings of isolation, powerlessness, normlessness, and an awareness of limited opportunity), (2) Conventional Suc-

cess Orientation, (3) Personal Distress (low self-esteem and anxiety), (4) Empathy, (5) Socialization (for which very low scores indicate an antisocial personality), (6) Criminal Personality, and (7) Criminal Attitudes.

Assessments were also available for age, criminal history, educational level, employment stability, delinquent associates, family dissension, and scholastic maladjustment.

Some of the Findings

1. *Multimethod assessments of the criterion (criminal behavior).* Recidivism was measured in two ways: self-reported criminal behavior and official records. The effect of simultaneously considering both measures of the criterion was examined by computing Canonical Rs. Logically, canonical correlations are an extension of multiple correlations. In the case of multiple correlations, two or more predictor variables are weighted in order to maximize the correlation with a single criterion variable. In canonical correlations, two or more predictor variables are weighted to maximize the correlation with two or more weighted criterion variables (in this case, self-reported criminal behavior and officially measured criminal behavior). The resulting correlation is called a Canonical Correlation (Can R).

   The R between Criminal Personality scores and unofficial recidivism was .40 (R square = .16). The Can R between Criminal Personality scores and the weighted combination of both measures of recidivism was .51 (R square = .26). The increase in the R squared was .10, and, thus, the proportional increase in validity associated with a multimethod assessment of the criterion was 60 percent (.10/.16). The mean increase in predictive validity was approximately 62 percent when similar analyses were conducted with the Criminal Sentiments measures. Thus, multimethod assessments of the criterion are associated with increases in the magnitude of estimates of predictive validity.

2. *Multimethod assessment of the predictor.* Assessments based on paper-and-pencil questionnaires and personal interviews

Resource Note 6.3 *(continued)*

were simultaneously examined. The correlation between the paper-and-pencil assessment of Criminal Sentiments and recidivism was .46 (R square = .21). The correlation with recidivism when both the paper-and-pencil and interview-based assessments were combined was .63 (.396). This represents an increase of 83 percent (.180/.216) in the validity estimate. Once again, multimethod assessment of the predictor was associated with dramatic gains in predictive validity.

3. *Multitrait assessments and the incremental validity of personality assessments.* We have seen that the Can R between recidivism and the two types of measures of Criminal Sentiments was .63. When Criminal Personality, age, and criminal history were added to the predictor list, the Can R was .74. The increase in explained variance was 37 percent. Multitrait or multidomain assessments of predictors may be associated with increased predictive validity, and furthermore, assessments of personality do contribute to the predictability of recidivism over and above the fact that they also share variance with criminal history and education.

4. *The effect of an extended follow-up.* Probationers were followed for up to three postprobation years. The R between Criminal Personality scores and reconvictions during the period of probation was .26. The R over the total follow-up period was .36 (an increase of .06). The proportional increase in validity associated with an increased follow-up period was 91 percent. The validity estimates for the assessments of Criminal Sentiments also increased, although by only 28 percent. Thus, the problem with short follow-up periods, when a problem at all, appears to be one of underestimation rather than overestimation.

5. *The effect of retests.* The correlation between intake Criminal Personality scores and recidivism was .44. When adding six-month retest scores to the prediction for-

mula, the R increased to .51. This was a 34 percent increase afforded by considering the fact that the probationers may have changed over a six-month period.

Assessments of attitudes are much more dynamic than fundamental personality variables. In fact, the increase in predictive validity associated with the introduction of retest scores on the paper-and-pencil measures of Criminal Sentiments was 76 percent. These results show that some attributes of people are more stable over time than are other attributes. The changes that do occur may well carry information that is relevant in the prediction of recidivism. Some changes that reassessments appear to detect are due to unreliability in our assessment instruments. However, some changes may be "real," and consideration of these changes will improve predictive accuracy.

A Final Comment

Procriminal attitudes and criminal personality were moderately to strongly related to the recidivism of probationers. However, procriminal attitudes and psychopathic personality do not exhaust the list of personal attitudes and personality characteristics that have been linked, in theory, to criminal behavior. Also examined were the predictive validities of Alienation (r = .29), Conventional Success Orientation (.24), Personal Distress (.26), and Empathy (.19). However, adding these variables did not increase the predictability of recidivism above that achieved by Criminal Sentiments and Criminal Personality.

Not all personal traits are equally relevant in the analysis of criminal behavior, just as not all situational variables are equally relevant. The task of research and theory is to uncover the relevant variables, to measure those variables in such a way that meaningful relationships may emerge, and to seriously explore threats to validity rather than engage in knowledge destruction.

The state of the research emboldens us to offer some general guidelines for the use of offender classification instruments (see Resource Note 6.4). We have learned a great deal in the last 20 years, and we expect the accumulation of knowledge to continue. The "fourth generation" of offender assessment instruments that are becoming available is an exciting new development that will offer new possibilities for research. We eagerly await the next developments.

Resource Note 6.4

Guidelines for Offender Assessment

The research on offender assessment has been impressive. Much has been learned, to the point at which specific suggestions can be made as to what would formulate good practice when it comes to assessment. The following are our "top 10" considerations when the task is to assess offenders:

1. *Use actuarial measures of risk.*

The evidence is unequivocal—actuarial assessments of risk are significantly superior to clinical assessments. This is true not only with general offenders but also for very specific offender groups such as the mentally disordered, sex offenders, and male batterers.

2. *Risk assessments should demonstrate predictive validity.*

There are many assessment instruments available for use, but sometimes the research on them is limited to psychometric properties such as internal reliability, face validity, interrater reliability, etc. Practitioners must ask about the predictive validity of the instruments they use because it is this type of validity that has the greatest utility in a correctional context.

3. *The assessment instruments should be directly relevant to the business of corrections.*

When dealing with offenders, we have interest in two general classes of behaviors: (1) rule violation and (2) psychological instability. They are both important and sometimes interrelated (e.g., paranoid delusions and violent assaults), but not always (e.g., depression is unrelated to recidivism). What we need to be clear about is that emotional

and psychological functioning is many times unrelated to criminal behavior. Thus, assessment of psychological instability *for purposes of assessing risk for criminal behavior* is largely irrelevant. Test administrators should be aware of what the test does predict and understand that assessments should be specific to the predicted outcome the situation demands.

4. *Use instruments derived from relevant theory.*

The correlates derived from traditional criminological and psychopathological theories of crime have proved to be minor. The social learning perspectives have the strongest empirical support. In these theories, criminal behavior is seen as a product of the interaction between cognitive-emotional-personality-biological factors and environmental reward-cost contingencies. Offender assessment instruments that are based on a general personality and social learning theory of criminal conduct offer robustness in their predictive accuracy and generalizability to a range of settings and samples.

5. *Assess criminogenic needs.*

Criminogenic needs are the dynamic risk factors that are highly important for risk management. For correctional staff who are concerned about how to intervene and reduce the risk posed by offenders, knowledge of criminogenic needs is vital. Assessing and reassessing criminogenic needs permits the evaluation of progress in treatment and changes in risk level during the course of normal supervision.

Resource Note 6.4 *(continued)*

6. *Use general personality and cognitive tests for the assessment of responsivity.*

The responsivity principle of offender classification states that the style and mode of treatment must be matched to the cognitive, personality, and sociocultural characteristics of the individual. There are a number of offender classification instruments and general personality measures that have utility for the assessment of personal characteristics that could affect the individual's responsiveness to treatment. Test administrators must be cognizant that many personality and cognitive tests offer little evidence regarding their ability to predict criminal behavior. However, they are excellent tools for assessing responsivity.

7. *Use multi-method assessment.*

No one test measures a single domain perfectly, and each method has a weakness. An important way for dealing with the shortcomings associated with a specific assessment methods is to use multiple, diverse methods. In this way, the weakness of one assessment method is compensated by the strength of another method.

8. *Use multi-domain sampling.*

There are many factors or domains that contribute to criminal behavior. Many of the tests used with offenders, however, measure relatively few domains. Therefore, offender assessment that incorporates multi-domain sampling should become a standard in offender risk assessments.

9. *Exercise professional and ethical responsibility.*

What is done with the results from assessments administered to offenders can have serious consequences. Therefore, those who conduct offender assessment have a responsibility to be well trained and knowledgeable of the strengths and weaknesses of the tests they use, and to apply the tests appropriately.

From Bonta, 2002

Chapter 7

Prevention and Rehabilitation

This chapter provides an overview of how mainstream criminology and criminal justice reached the conclusion that the literature on the effectiveness of correctional programming supported a "nothing works" position—and how that conclusion has shifted toward recognition of the value of human service in a justice context. It also summarizes the dynamic and functional significance of the theories on which the effective and ineffective intervention programs were based. Finally, an illustration of what effective correctional treatment looks and feels like in practice is provided.

A review of the effects of official punishment on reoffending is included in Chapter 8. The primary focus of the current chapter, however, is the effects of human service delivered within a justice context on reoffending. The justice context most often involves imposition of some type of judicial sanction. It is important to emphasize that the review in this chapter is speaking to human service programs often operating in a punishing justice context. Typically, our concern here is called "rehabilitation," "reintegration," or "correctional treatment," and the objective is reduced recidivism. Other, and often overarching, purposes of judicial sanctioning include retribution and/or restoration.

Retributive justice has to do with doing harm to offenders—harm was done to the victim (often defined abstractly as the "state") and justice entails harming the offender in turn. Just deserts theory adds that the severity of the penalty should be matched to the seriousness of the offense. Just deserts notions may place some upper limits on degree of harm, but it is difficult not to conclude that retribution and just deserts have played a major part in the explosion of punishment in the United States and an accompanying "mean spirit" (Cullen, 1995). Part of "being mean" includes not just more incarceration but a reduction of services and programs in prisons. Under retribution and just deserts, there is no expectation of reduced reoffending because holding the offender accountable is deemed sufficient. Thus, human service in the context of retributive service may be difficult, but many of the programs to be reviewed were offered under such conditions. Offering human services in the context of intensive supervision programs ("turning the heat up on offenders") provides a detailed discussion of how the promise resides not in the "heat" but in the human service (Gendreau, Cullen & Bonta, 1994).

Restorative approaches seek justice through efforts to repair harm done to the victim, to restore the community that may have been offended or disrupted by the criminal act, and to hold the offender accountable. Holding the offender accountable may involve, for example, requiring them to pay restitution or complete community service. The rhetoric of restorative justice is not always favorable to human service for the offender, but the restorative context may provide an easier setting for the delivery of human service. We will return to a more detailed discussion of restorative justice in Chapter 8.

An additional purpose of sanctioning is incapacitation. Here the primary concern is the control of reoffending during the period of imprisonment. The most obviously incapacitative type of sanctioning is a custodial sentence, although community sanctions involving intensive monitoring may also be considered to be in the interests of incapacitation. Sometimes, then, human service may be introduced under an incapacitation context with the hope that the control of recidivism may extend beyond expiration of the sentence. Sanctions based on general deterrence are intended to influence the criminal conduct of those nonoffenders (or offender "wannabees") who might be deterred by knowing that criminal activity has negative consequences. Once again, human service may be offered under conditions in which the primary purpose of sanctioning is general deterrence.

Specific deterrence, like rehabilitation, is intended to contribute to reduced recidivism. Specific deterrence, at the sanctioning stage, entails enhancing the offender's fear of official punishment. In criminal law, fear of official punishment is assumed to increase with the severity of the penalty imposed. Hence, reductions in reoffending are expected to increase with more severe penalties. It is possible that under conditions of a severe sentence handed down in order to reduce reoffending, human service may also be introduced with rehabilitation in mind.

As if the circumstances of rehabilitation were not complex enough to begin with, correctional agencies are subject to evaluation on a number of other considerations. Correctional agencies are asked to administer a sanction that may have been meted out for a variety of restorative, retributive, and other purposes. In addition, correctional agencies are asked to administer the sanction in ethical, legal, decent, humane, and cost-efficient ways. If the sanction involves restitution or community service, then agencies may additionally be evaluated in terms of restitution dollars paid and community service hours worked. Justice agencies within young offender systems additionally may be asked to keep child welfare concerns paramount and to attend to the special needs of the young person. In sum, correctional agencies are asked to do a lot of things. One of those things is to contribute to reduced reoffending, and that is to what we turn now.

From Idealism to "Nothing Works" and Back to Human Service: The How and Why of "Nothing Works"

The following is a critical summary of some of the influential reviews of the correctional treatment literature (many of which were briefly introduced in Chapter 2). Kirby (1954) classified "treatments" as follows: probation and parole, institution-based, capital punishment, psychotherapy, and noninstitutional. These classes of "treatment" may make some sense to administrators, bureaucrats, and policymakers, but they are of little direct relevance to the analysis of behavioral influence processes. At best, they are broad descriptions of the structures within which services are delivered, as opposed to descriptions of the content and processes of direct service. Kirby thereby set the stage for a continuing problem in the literature on the effectiveness of correctional treatment, namely, the failure to make a clear distinction between structural/setting variables and the clinical aspects of service (i.e., the behavior influence processes) that occur within that structure or setting.

The important variables determining the effectiveness of counseling are to be found within the broad setting conditions established by a criminal sanction. Restated in practical rather than methodological terms, correctional counselors have little immediate influence over the boundaries set by a criminal sanction. What they do influence are discretionary aspects of the management of a sentence and the specifics of services delivered (recall the discussion of knowledge through practice in Chapter 2).

Up to the 1990s, to our knowledge, not a single review of controlled studies on the effects of the criminal penalty (diversion, probation, custody, restoration) found consistent evidence of reduced recidivism. From the earliest to the latest reviews of the research literature, only the studies on the delivery of direct human service have shown promise—promise evident across a variety of settings, including nonjustice settings, diversion programs, probation, and custody. The conclusion "nothing works" may well be drawn from studies of official punishment, but it never made sense in terms of the effects of prevention and rehabilitation services.

Not surprisingly, Kirby (1954) found that the literature available in the early 1950s was methodologically weak. However, at least four studies of *direct* service included comparison conditions and objective measures of outcome. The studies were relevant because the broad setting conditions were roughly controlled within each of the studies. Three of the four better-controlled studies yielded findings favorable to counseling; they were Fox's study of a new training institution with an organized counseling service, Shulman's study of a community-based activity group, and Levy's study of therapy. The fourth (and less favorable) study was the grand Cambridge-Somerville Youth Study. (The latter will resurface in our detailed analyses of counseling processes, but for now note that the findings of three of four reasonably well-controlled studies were supportive of counseling.)

Kirby's conclusion was noncontroversial: "Most treatment programs are based on hope and perhaps informed speculation rather than verified information." He also made a plea for university-agency cooperation in research. Research was obviously required if the "treatment" of criminals was to have a solid empirical base.

Walter Bailey (1966) found 100 studies of correctional effectiveness; 22 of the studies approximated the experimental ideal. This was a considerable improvement over the state of the literature in the early 1950s. Sixty percent of the better-controlled studies reported "marked improvement" or demonstrated statistically significant gains relative to the comparison conditions; 23 percent reported "harm" or "no change." Approximately 50 of the 100 studies reported "considerable improvement" in the treatment group, and 10 of the total reported "harm" or "no difference."

Bailey's conclusions included a recognition that both the quality and quantity of studies had improved since the Kirby report. However, Bailey also stated that there had been no apparent progress in demonstrating the validity of correctional treatment. Bailey did not state the standard against which he assessed this lack of "progress." As Ted Palmer (1983) has noted, the standards set by the antitreatment forces were cloudy. By the mid-1960s, however, the proportion of well-controlled studies of correctional treatment that reported positive outcome was now 13 of 22, relative to Kirby's three of four. The proportion of "successes" had not increased, but the quantity of supportive studies certainly had.

Lest the reader begin to think positively in the glow of a "hit rate" of 50 to 60 percent, Bailey reminded his readers that it was the authors of the studies who wrote the reports. This gratuitous comment has since been enshrined in Michael Gottfredson's (1979) list of "treatment destruction techniques," and it is echoed in our sample of anti-rehabilitation themes (see Resource Note 2.5). In the same paragraph Bailey also stated that one could "substantially decrease the relative frequency of successful outcomes based upon reliably valid evidence" (p. 157).

What is "reliably valid evidence" (what standards are being set?) and why do these standards seem only to be applied to studies with findings favorable to counseling? Perhaps he meant that if one chooses to consider all potential threats to validity (e.g., external, construct validity) one could indeed find that each study reporting positive findings was limited. It would be amazing indeed if such limits could not be found, as it is inconceivable that any piece of research could be free of all potential threats to validity.

However, should not these absolute standards also be applied to those studies that failed to establish treatment effects? After all, it is equally likely that the "null effect" studies probably also failed to provide "reliably valid evidence" for treatment noneffectiveness. Bailey chose to accept the studies that found unfavorable results for direct human services. He concluded that the "evidence supporting the efficacy of correctional treatment is slight, inconsistent, and of questionable reliability" (1966:157). To be true to the anti-empiricism inherent in his unspecified "reliably valid" criterion, he might better have concluded that empirical investigations of effectiveness will forever yield evidence that is of questionable validity—no matter the quantity and consistency of the evidence produced.

In his last paragraph, Bailey returned to the empirical issues by providing four possible explanations for what he considered to be an overall negative situation for correctional treatment: (1) treatment is really ineffectual, (2) the treatments are being ineffectually applied, (3) the wrong treatments are being applied, or (4) the effectiveness of treatment is being hidden by Offender-by-Treatment interactions. These four "explanations" are true to the spirit of systematic empirical approaches in that there is an invitation—indeed a challenge—to explore both service and client variables further.

"Knowledge destruction" proliferated in the 1970s. Charles H. Logan (1972) examined 100 studies and summarized their findings as follows: High Success ($n = 20$), Good Success (35), Fair Success (15), Failure (16), and Can't Say (14). The latter category included three studies in which the success varied with particular combinations of clients and treatment. Overall, 73 studies provided some evidence of success, 16 were clear failures, and 11 had unclassifiable outcomes.

Logan set seven methodological criteria that he described as the minimal requirements for an adequate study of effectiveness. In an important advance for meta-evaluation, Logan listed his criteria and showed in tabular form how he had evaluated each of the 100 studies. Some standards were now at least open to inspection.

It is valuable to examine Logan's table in some detail. Eighteen studies of psychotherapy/counseling included a comparison condition based on random assignment and/or matching. We will accept Logan's judgment without arguing about the inappropriateness of registering the Cambridge-Somerville Youth Study twice in the "failure" category (two separate follow-ups of the same study found no evidence for the effectiveness of this program). Similarly, we will accept for now that the findings of the PICO project (recall Table 6.15) were assigned to the "uncertain outcome" category when they could have been represented twice in the "positive outcome" category (the PICO project found that "amenable" inmates responded best to personal counseling, while "nonamenable" inmates responded best to routine casework services). The success rates, as defined by Logan himself, showed that, minimally, 50 percent (9/18) of the better-controlled studies reported positive effects of counseling. If Offender-by-Treatment interactions (which suggest that treatment works for certain types of offenders) are considered, the success rate jumps to 78 percent (14/18).

However, Logan's interpretation of the findings was negative. Applying his methodological standards to the 100 studies, he found that not a single study was adequate (i.e., met all the criteria). Thus, his conclusion (p. 381) regarding the effectiveness of correctional treatment was presented by means of a quotation from Schur's summary from a few years earlier:

> No research has been done to date that enables one to say that one treatment program is better than another or that enables us to examine a man and specify the treatment he needs. There is no evidence that probation is better than institutions, that institutions are better than probation, or that being given a parole is better than escaping . . . much of what is now being done about crime may be so wrong that the net effect of the actions is to increase rather than to decrease crime.

With Logan's review, the effectiveness debate has broken with the discipline normally associated with scientific discourse. The most negative of the possibilities (i.e., human service does not work) is highlighted by a failure to differentiate between official punishment and treatment services. Yet, that most negative of possibilities in regard to effective human service is the one possibility least consistent with the evidence that he himself reviewed. It seems that any positive study that is limited (as all studies must be) may be dismissed.

Moreover, Logan goes a step beyond Bailey regarding the acceptance of the validity of the "null effect" studies. Bailey simply reminded us that the authors had themselves written the reports (i.e., you can't trust them). Logan implies that suspending the judgment that treatment had failed is a sign of character weakness: "[T]here is a strong current of optimism in these studies, with only a small minority (16%) *admitting* to failure" (p. 381; emphasis added). After describing all studies as inadequate according to "minimal" methodological criteria (and, hence, unworthy of serious consideration), Logan closed with a recommendation that experimental research be abandoned. The field was now ready for the next step in the destruction of correctional treatment: the recommendation that service efforts too should be abandoned.

The Martinson "Nothing Works" Debate

The reviews conducted by Martinson (1974) and his colleagues (Lipton, Martinson & Wilks, 1975) provided a summary of studies that was a major accomplishment. Two hundred and thirty-one controlled studies were reviewed, carefully described and tabulated. Depending upon how the studies are classified, some 40 to 60 percent of the studies included reports of positive effects on at least some types of offenders. Although the review consisted of 231 studies, Cullen and Gendreau (2000) remind us that the success outcome variable included measures such as institutional adjustment and substance abuse relapse. One hundred thirty-eight studies included measures of recidivism. Furthermore, if studies of probation, parole, and imprisonment are removed as "treatments," 83 studies are left (with 48% showing a reduction in recidivism).

The conclusions drawn by Martinson and his colleagues took various forms both in the original review articles and in subsequent commentaries, but the dominant message remained "nothing works." The Martinson review also served to demonstrate *knowledge destruction*:

1. Studies that reached negative conclusions regarding the effectiveness of treatment were accepted almost without question.

2. Studies that were supportive of treatment were subjected to intense criticism of a pseudoscientific variety that Gottfredson (1979) has called "treatment destruction" (see Resource Note 2.5). These techniques include "stressing the criterion problem," "contaminating the treatment," and "discounting the underlying theory."

3. What was almost never considered in these reviews was the possibility that the reasons provided for discounting the positive findings are often the very same factors that may be responsible for hiding or underestimating the effects of treatment (recall Resource Note 6.3). For example, unreliability in the measurement of outcome variables such as recidivism ("the criterion problem") should decrease, not increase, the chances of detecting the effects of treatment. Unreliability of measurement is a possible reason why effects are *not* found, and not a reason why effects *are* found. Similarly, errors in the conceptualization of crime and treatment should have the effect of preventing positive outcomes, not of promoting them. If the psychological model of crime is wrong ("discounting the underlying theory"), we would not expect to find any effects when service is guided by that model. A primary example of "contamination of treatment" is to suggest that the positive effects of counseling reflect nothing but the "natural interpersonal skills" of the counselor. If the findings are that counseling is effective when it is offered by interpersonally skilled therapists, so be it. Such a finding begins to say something about the conditions under which counseling is effective. It is not a reason for discounting treatment.

Stuart Adams (1975) and Ted Palmer (1975) reminded their readers of the nature of the evidence. Reports of success in the better-controlled studies (40% to 60%) compared favorably with research payoffs in medicine and industry. Moreover, as Bailey (1966) had suggested a decade earlier, there was now considerable evidence that the effectiveness of treatment may depend upon how the specifics of treatment are matched with the characteristics of offenders.

Ted Palmer's (1975) paper was a particularly strong document because his descriptions of effective programs were often direct quotes from the descriptions provided by Martinson et al. In response, Martinson (1976) made it clear that he was never really concerned about recidivism anyway. Rather, he said, there was no evidence that treatment programs influence aggregated crime rates. Although this was true, the issue of the impact of correctional intervention on aggregated crime rates was not being been explored by either Palmer or Martinson. Antipsychological criminologists often switch criterion variables from the psychological to the social. Martinson went on to attack Palmer personally: "To review one of Palmer's research projects is . . . something like translating the Moscow telephone book into Swahili." He attacked correctional treatment in general: "[it] is nine-tenths pageantry, rumination, and rubbish," and he revealed his position on the issue of Type-of-Offender-by-Type-of-Treatment interactions (matching): "a 'partly positive' result is probably akin to a partly pregnant girl friend." He summarized his evaluation of correctional research thus: "[with it] and thirty cents you can buy a cup of coffee in New York."

Depending upon where one stood on the correctional effectiveness issue, Martinson's (1976) response to Palmer (1975) marked either the ultimate end of the rehabilitative ideal or a source of embarrassment for those in the human and social sciences who maintained a respect for evidence. However, what remains unknown to many in both camps is that Martinson had the courage to recant and admit that while some programs did not work, others clearly did provide positive evidence of effectiveness ("I have often said that treatment...is "impotent"...the conclusion is not correct": Martinson, 1979:254).

Martinson's turnabout on the effectiveness issue was largely ignored. The "nothing works" perspective appeared to better serve the interests of various groups. Mainstream criminologists seemed pleased with "nothing works" because that conclusion fit with their general antipsychological bias. Moreover, as we shall see later in this chapter, many sociologists who had earlier been pro-intervention had become anti-intervention because many of the sociological theories had not translated into effective programs. Finally, the political left was becoming suspicious of state intervention in view of the events of the late 1960s and early 1970s. A conservative public seemed ready to promote the punishment of offenders, and scholars of the due process / just deserts schools could proceed with their agenda of "punishment with dignity" (as opposed to what they called the "tyranny of treatment").

As comfortable as "nothing works" was for many people, the fact remained that positive and promising evidence resided in the research literature. Indeed, positive evidence was growing at a fast rate. Paul Gendreau and Robert Ross prompted many people to look again at the evidence. Gendreau and Ross (1979; Ross & Gendreau, 1980) updated the reviews and directed attention to programs that did appear to "work." Their update was impressive: 95 experimental or quasi-experimental studies were published between 1973 and 1978; 86 percent of these reported positive outcomes. Not all of the 95 studies approximated the experimental ideal, but the evidence from studies published in the early 1970s was (like the earlier evidence) more supportive than nonsupportive of correctional counseling.

Gendreau and Ross provided a neat summary of the essential weakness of many of the "nothing works" arguments. They noted that rhetorical references to a "partly pregnant girl friend" could not dismiss the fact that Type-of-Offender-by-Type-of-Treatment interactions were frequently encountered in the research literature, and that the conclusions of studies that failed to uncover treatment effects were as subject to threats to validity as were the conclusions that treatment effects were found. Indeed, in science, acceptance of the null hypothesis is even more threatened than the rejection of the null hypothesis. They reminded readers that the effects of "treatment" were dependent upon the specifics, the "dosage," and the "integrity" of treatment. They concluded that the whole "nothing works" and antirehabilitation position implied that we were all too ready to escape some degree of responsibility for recidivistic crime.

The work of Francis Cullen and colleagues (Cullen & Gilbert, 1982; Travis & Cullen, 1984) was refreshing in that it asked whether the alternatives to rehabilitation are any more effective or humane than is rehabilitation. The answer was that without the rehabilitative ideal, one might expect increased use of incarcerative sentences for longer periods in less humane institutions, as well as increased recidivism (and as we will see in Chapter 8, the prophecy was realized). Cullen and his associates underscored the point that it was ludicrous to promote and justify theories of punishment over rehabilitation on the grounds that rehabilitation promoted punishment.

In the same time period, Ted Palmer (1983) provided a valuable update on the issue of the effectiveness of correctional rehabilitation. According to Palmer, some middle ground may eventually be found between the current camps of the "skeptics" and the "sanguines." Wherever that point may be located, Palmer perceived the current divisions to be less than those that separated the "nothing works" and "some things work" camps of the 1970s. Indeed, he anticipated that the justice system may soon reap benefits from the debate. He felt that points of agreement that had policy implications were appearing among the opposing camps. For example, effective programs must be appropriately intensive, multifocused when necessary, and matched to the needs and abilities of the clients.

Palmer postulated that the residual of the "nothing works" proponents was composed of two groups. The first group, Skeptics I, believed that the rehabilitation issue was settled. Sufficient research had been conducted to demonstrate that a few rehabilitation programs work, but they do not work very well. The other group, Skeptics II, felt that neither the research conducted to date nor the programs studied had been of sufficient quality to determine the degree to which rehabilitation has (or can) work. However, unlike the Skeptics I, they were open to (and encouraging of) the empirical exploration of well-implemented programs.

The Sanguine types believed that many programs and approaches have been shown to work for some types of offenders. Palmer noted that some believed that a proportion of offenders (the amenables) respond positively to a variety of approaches in a variety of settings. Others believed that success is a function of matching types of offenders with the appropriate approach. With an inappropriate match, neutral or even negative outcomes may be expected. Thus, some reasonable promise of rehabilitation resides in our ability to classify both clients and services, and to link those two sets of classes so that the chances of positive outcome are maximized. Palmer (1983) noted that the knowledge base for the Differential Intervention (DI) position is neither vast nor empirically flawless, and that the principles and processes of DI have not been systematically outlined.

In the mid-1980s, the authors of this text, and many of our colleagues and students, constituted a camp that we called "Sanguine Plus." We thought that the outcome literature was sufficiently strong to provide clinically workable hypotheses regarding the attributes of clients and services that are relevant to effective correctional counseling. Moreover, we thought that matching Type-of-Client-by-Type-of-Treatment interactions was an obvious consideration flowing easily from a broad social learning perspective on criminal conduct and on the situations of interpersonal influence (Andrews, 1980, 1983).

Our conclusions in the early 1980s were more radical than Palmer's (1983) view that criminologists and correctional professionals would, through debate and research, eventually converge into one camp that would be located somewhere between the skeptical and the sanguine. Our conclusion was that correctional counselors might best debate the possibility of breaking away from the field of criminology. They would find a more professionally rewarding environment in psychology and social work than they could expect to find in criminology. Criminology seemed to be preoccupied with social location, power, punishment, and the promotion of sociology and, as honorable as such interests might be, these areas of interest would not provide useful guidelines for human service professionals. Indeed, our pessimism regarding criminology was reinforced by the fact that while the reviews of the research evidence clearly supported the delivery of direct service, those same reviewers of the literature were contributing to a climate in which treatment was losing ground to variations on themes of official punishment.

Thus, we decided that in every presentation on the psychology of crime in which we were involved (whether in classrooms, symposia, criminal justice and correctional settings, professional conferences, or published articles), the antipsychological and prosociological biases of mainstream criminology would be noted and the contempt for evidence demonstrated. It was unacceptable to us that an influential discipline with strong ties to government policy units would so systematically deny the importance of human diversity (individual differences) and human service, while contributing directly to the implementation of variations on themes of official punishment.

Paul Gendreau and Robert Ross (1981, 1987) first underscored the theoretical and empirical weakness of official punishment. In 1987, they reported on studies of rehabilitation published between 1981 and 1987. The 1987 report revealed that findings favorable to rehabilitation were continuing to accrue, and findings for programs guided by labeling and deterrence theory yielded the least positive outcomes.

Andrews, Bonta, and Hoge (1990) restated the clinically relevant and psychologically informed principles of risk, need, responsivity, and professional discretion that had been in development at Carleton University for years. In addition to a restatement, this paper provided many examples of the validity of the principles. The Carleton University group then published their meta-analysis of the treatment literature (Andrews, Zinger et al., 1990a). The following section reports on that and more recent meta-analyses, but first we note how the criminal justice environment has changed since 1990.

In dramatic contrast to mainstream textbook criminology and criminal justice in the 1980s and early 1990s (which had changed almost not at all), the actual practice of corrections changed dramatically in many jurisdictions. Correctional Service Canada (CSC), under the leadership of Ole Ingstrup, embarked upon a major expansion of human service programs, with particular attention paid to the principles of risk, need, and responsivity. Within the Canadian province of Ontario, both the young offender and adult offender systems began to apply the principles of risk and need in a systematic manner. Another province, Newfoundland, permitted the release of moderate-risk inmates under electronic monitoring with the condition that the offenders attend an intensive cognitive behavioral program targeting criminogenic needs. The states of Colorado, Vermont, and Idaho, as well as counties in Minnesota and Oregon, introduced major reforms that took human service seriously. Moreover, California turned once again to treatment with Proposition 36. In Great Britain, risk/need assessments are entering probation, and sophisticated systems are being introduced to enhance the integrity of service delivery in a justice context (McGuire, 2001; McGuire & Priestly, 1995; Perry, 2001).

The dissemination of the evidence on treatment effectiveness has been widespread. The National Institute of Corrections (NIC), an arm of the U.S. Department of Justice, sponsored and organized training seminars with a focus on evidence-based correctional practice. Some of these sessions, through the use of satellite video communication technology, were able to reach thousands of correctional professionals at a time. In a conference organized by the Office of Justice Programs, senior representatives of the U.S. Department of Justice announced the marriage of corrections and human service. The International Community Corrections Association has sponsored annual conferences devoted to dissemination of the basic "what works" findings and has co-sponsored regional workshops along with NIC. At the annual conferences of the American Probation and Parole Association, American Corrections Association, and Canadian Psychological Association, sessions and seminars on assessment and treatment are approaching a dominant status. In 1996, the Conference Permanente de la Probation, an association of 12 European countries that provide probation services, held a seminar focusing on programs for reducing offending behavior. Similar "what works" conferences have been held in Denmark, Finland, The Netherlands, Norway, Sweden, New Zealand, Australia, Scotland, and Wales.

The systematic quantitative reviews of the correctional treatment literature have contributed to the turn-around in the shift from "nothing works" to "what works."

Meta-Analytic Reviews of Treatment Effectiveness

By 1990, the number of reports published in English on controlled evaluations of community and correctional interventions with offenders was fast approaching 500. Now it was clear that, on average, "treatment" reduced recidivism to at least a mild degree. Even some "skeptical" scholars agreed with this fact (e.g., Lab & Whitehead, 1990). As noted years before, even the most notorious of the critics of rehabilitation, Martinson (1979), acknowledged that some programs had positive effects, some had no effect, and some increased recidivism.

The most comprehensive review completed by the early 1990s was that by Mark Lipsey (1989). His was the most comprehensive not only of the qualitative reviews of the literature but of the systematic, quantitative, meta-analytic reviews of correctional treatment effectiveness. Recall that meta-analysis involves the derivation of a common quantitative estimate of the degree of association between treatment and reduced recidivism based upon a number of different studies. The meta-analytic approach is not without its own particular limitations, but it does allow a synthesis of the findings of many studies with a decreased likelihood that reviewers of the literature are applying different criteria of effectiveness in the different studies (Gendreau, Smith & Goggin, 2001; Glass, McGraw & Smith, 1981).

Lipsey found that 64 percent of 443 effect sizes found differences in recidivism that favored treatment over comparison conditions. This value of 64 percent is consistent with our reading of the earlier reviews of the literature, which concluded that 40 to 80 percent of the surveyed studies reported reduced recidivism. On average, according to Lipsey's (1989) meta-analysis, the treatment effect was equivalent to a reduction in recidivism from 50 percent for the control group to 45 percent in the treatment group [a 10 percent (5/50) reduction]. (Note that Lipsey was using neither the simple r nor the binomial effects size display outlined in Resource Note 1.1. Rather, Lipsey assumes a 50 percent recidivism rate in the control group and expresses the r in terms of how the recidivism rate of treatment groups deviates from that 50 percent value.) This positive (but very modest) effect was an underestimate in view of the well-known unreliability in the assessment of official recidivism (i.e., the offenses of many who reoffend may go unnoticed). Correcting for this unreliability, Lipsey estimated that the average effect of treatment more accurately represented a reduction from 50 percent to 40 percent (a reduction of 10 percentage points, or a 20% reduction, in that 10/50 = .20).

Estimates of the overall average effect of treatment (whether or not corrected for unreliability), however, do not recognize that methodological and treatment variables may be contributing to variation around the mean effect. In other words, are some types of studies and some types of treatment associated with larger effects on recidivism?

Appropriately, Lipsey adopted a conservative approach to determining the effect of type of treatment on recidivism. He insisted that any contributions of treatment variables to reduced recidivism would be considered only if they were evident after controls were introduced for methodological variables. As many reviewers of the treatment literature had suspected (but had not been able to demonstrate in a convincing way), Lipsey (1989) showed that the contribution of methodological variables to the magnitude of the effect of treatment was substantial (R square = .25, or an overall correlation of 0.50). To a considerable extent these methodological contributions reflected the following:

1. Small sample studies yielded larger effect size estimates;

2. Studies with the longest follow-up periods and with criterion variables of weak reliability and validity yielded the smaller estimates of effect size;

3. Less explicit reporting of methodological and statistical procedures was associated with higher estimates of effect size;

4. Initial nonequivalence of treatment and control groups was associated with larger or smaller effects depending upon the specifics of the nonequivalence;

5. Greater attrition from either the treatment or the control group was associated with smaller effect sizes;

6. Comparisons of treatment with "alternative treatment" yielded smaller estimates of effect size than did comparisons of treatment with "no treatment."

The last finding actually favors conclusions regarding the effectiveness of treatment, because, on average, it appears that even some form of "alternative" treatment (doing something) is better than no treatment (doing nothing). The first five methodological findings, however, demonstrate more clearly than ever that characteristics of the research design and procedures do influence estimates of the effects of treatment independently of the variations in treatment being studied. This is the systematic empirical tradition of PCC at its best. After asserting and empirically demonstrating the effects of various sources of error on estimates of the effects of treatment, Lipsey moved forward in the process of *knowledge construction.*

Lipsey (1989) found that, with methodological concerns controlled statistically, type of treatment made substantial incremental contributions to variation in effect size estimates (R square = .22, or 47 percent of the total explained variance). The major treatment variables associated with reduced recidivism included:

1. Longer duration of treatment and more meaningful contact (except for the continuous contact provided by institutional care);

2. Services provided outside of formal correctional settings and institutions;

3. Services under the influence of the evaluator;

4. Behavior-oriented, skill-oriented, and multimodal treatment;

5. Service for higher-risk cases;

6. Treatment that attends to extrapersonal circumstances (e.g., family).

The best treatments were structured and focused and, according to Lipsey, those treatments reduced recidivism rates by about 30 percent on average. Lipsey (p. 39) concluded that the best treatments (with few exceptions) were those that had been defined independently as most "clinically relevant" by the Carleton University group (Andrews, Bonta & Hoge, 1990). As many authors have been suggesting over the years (e.g., Andrews, 1979, 1980; Andrews & Kiessling, 1980; Gendreau & Ross, 1979, 1987; Glaser, 1974; Palmer, 1974; Ross & Fabiano, 1985), it appears that some approaches to treatment clearly are better than others, and to some extent, the effectiveness of treatment depends upon type of client.

Recall from Chapter 6 that the principles consistent with a psychology of crime and with the requirement of clinical relevance are as follows (Andrews, Bonta & Hoge, 1990; Andrews, Zinger et al., 1990a):

1. Treatment service is delivered to higher-risk (as opposed to lower-risk) cases.

2. Criminogenic needs are targeted for change (e.g., procriminal attitudes rather than self-esteem).

3. Styles and modes of treatment are employed that are capable of influencing criminogenic needs and are matched to the learning styles of offenders (i.e., cognitive behavioral and social learning approaches rather than nondirective, relationship-oriented counseling or psychodynamic, insight-oriented counseling; or specific matching according to responsivity systems such as I-Level, as described in the Chapter 6).

4. The professional reviews risk, need, and responsivity considerations as they apply to a particular person, and makes those treatment decisions that are most appropriate according to legal, ethical, humanitarian, cost-efficiency, and clinical standards.

These principles of effective treatment were hypothesized to apply regardless of the setting within which treatment was delivered. The settings themselves were hypothesized to be of minimal significance in the control of recidivism. That is, variation in criminal processing *without* systematic variation in the delivery of correctional treatment service is minimally related to recidivism. This reflected the view that variations in the type and severity of justice processing would have no systematic and positive effects on criminogenic need areas (e.g., antisocial attitudes, delinquent companions, family processes, school success, skill deficits, etc.). Fundamentally, none of the theories of criminal justice processing (labeling, deterrence, just deserts, or restorative justice) represent or reflect a well-developed social psychology of delinquency or crime.

Following these hypotheses, Andrews, Zinger et al., (1990a) undertook a meta-analysis of 154 treatment comparisons, 30 of which were assigned to the criminal sanction set. Criminal sanctions involved variations in the type or severity of judicial processing. These included: official processing versus police cautioning, probation versus informal adjustment, probation versus open custody, closed versus open custody, and probation versus closed custody. Two comparisons involved completors versus noncompletors of restitution programs. None of the comparisons involved variation in the duration of custody dispositions.

Analysis of the 30 comparisons revealed that not a single positive phi coefficient of .20 or greater was generated. Overall, the criminal sanction hypothesis was supported in that the mean phi coefficient was minimal: –.07. The fact that the phi coefficient was negative indicates that more, as opposed to less, criminal justice processing was associated with slightly increased recidivism rates. This finding was mildly consistent with labeling theory, and inconsistent with deterrence theory. In brief, if the type and severity of official punishment has any effect on recidivism, it appears to be that "less" is better than "more."

This negative effect of more severe judicial sanctions was maintained with statistical controls introduced for methodological variables and for particular treatment modalities. Additionally, Lipsey (1989) reported that nine specific tests of deterrence theory (shock incarceration and

"Scared Straight") yielded the most negative effects of all the treatment modalities tested (an average increase of 24% in recidivism rates).

Thus, meta-analysis confirmed what the earlier narrative reviews of the literature had uncovered. The mean effect of correctional treatment service, averaged across a number of dispositions, was clearly greater and more positive than that of criminal sanctioning without the delivery of treatment services [mean phi coefficients of 0.15 (N = 124) and −.07 (N = 30) for treatment and sanctioning, respectively]. Now we turn to differentiations within the treatment studies.

The 124 tests of treatment services were assigned to the categories of "appropriate," "unspecified," or "inappropriate" treatment according to the principles of risk, need, and responsivity. In fact, few studies differentiated clients according to risk, and not many studies were clear on the criminogenic need areas that were being targeted in treatment. Moreover, many studies were quiet on the specifics of the style and mode of service employed. Thus, the major criterion governing assignment to "appropriate correctional treatment service" proved to be the simple designation of a program as "behavioral," and 70 percent (38/54) of the "appropriate" treatments were behavioral.

Additional treatments in the "appropriate" set were those clearly delivered to higher-risk cases, structured programs that were specific and appropriate regarding criminogenic need (e.g., targeting criminal thinking), and a small set of treatments involving appropriate matching according to responsivity systems such as interpersonal maturity level.

Thirty-eight treatments were coded "inappropriate" because they employed deterrence methods (e.g., "Scared Straight"), nondirective client-centered/psychodynamic approaches, nonbehavioral milieu approaches, intensive nonbehavioral group interaction, or mismatched cases with treatment. Thirty-two comparisons entailed the delivery of some treatment service, but it was unclear whether that treatment was appropriate or inappropriate according to the clinical principles of effective service. These 32 comparisons were coded as "unspecified."

The average effect of appropriate treatment service (phi = .30) was significantly greater than unspecified treatment (.13), inappropriate treatment (-.06), and criminal processing without treatment (-.07). The mean phi coefficient of .30 for appropriate treatment represents an average reduction in recidivism of a little more than 50 percent from that found in comparison conditions. Using the binomial effect size display (see Resource Note 1.1), an average correlation of 0.30 represents an average recidivism rate of 65 percent in the comparison condition, compared to 35 percent in the appropriate treatment group.

Even with the dimensions of risk and need ignored, behavioral treatments had a substantially greater average effect on recidivism than did nonbehavioral treatments [.29 (N = 41) versus .04 (N = 113)]. However, the correlation between effect size estimates and the four-level type of treatment variable was much stronger than that between effect size and the simple behavioral/nonbehavioral variable. This suggests that the principles of risk and need were contributing to appropriate service. They will be reviewed in more detail.

The substantial correlation (which approached .70) between type of treatment and treatment effect size remained robust as controls were introduced for various methodological considerations. For example, consistent with Lipsey (1989), the evidence favorable to rehabilitation withstands controls for quality of the research design, sample size, length of follow-up, and ratings of therapeutic integrity. Indeed, Hill, Andrews, and Hoge (1991) reported that under higher-integrity conditions, the effects of inappropriate treatment tend to be particularly negative, while the effects of appropriate treatment are particularly positive. Small sample sizes as well as studies of treatments with evaluator involvement were associated with relatively large mean effect sizes. Even cynical interpretations of these findings (e.g., Lab & Whitehead, 1990) deserve serious attention, but it is important to note that the positive effects of appropriate treatment were also found in larger sample studies and in studies with less involved evaluators. At least in part, the amplification effect of small samples and involved evaluators may reflect therapeutic integrity. The robustness of the effect of appropriate treatment extends to tests conducted before and during the 1980s, to studies of young offenders and adult offenders, to samples varying in gender composition, and to programs offered in the community or in residential settings.

In regard to custody, there was a mild but detectable tendency for the effects of inappropriate service to be particularly negative in custody settings, and for the effects of clinically relevant service to be particularly positive in community settings. This finding, in combination with the mean negative effect of criminal sanctions, led Andrews and colleagues (Andrews, Zinger et al., 1990a) to conclude that they had initially underestimated the negative effect of custody. These research findings affirm a widely shared belief that custody is best viewed as the last resort. Moreover, it is important that the clinical appropriateness of service be attended to in residential settings.

Two additional aspects of custodial dispositions have not been addressed adequately in the correctional treatment literature. The first issue has to do with the possibility that failing to consider the incapacitation potential of custody has resulted in underestimates of the value of custody. The second issue has to do with the deliberate clinical use of custody.

First, the systematic research literature, including the reviews described above, does not deal with the issue of the control of recidivism through the incapacitation effects of custodial dispositions (Bonta & Gendreau, 1990, 1992). Our review of the treatment literature has not uncovered explorations of incapacitation effects sufficient to make strong statements on the relative in-program and postprogram effects on recidivism of custodial and noncustodial dispositions (for a discussion of this issue, see Andrews, 1983).

By way of illustration, Barton and Butts (1990) demonstrated that intensive supervision programs and custodial dispositions were statistically indistinguishable in their effects on recidivism over a two-year period. However, this was the dominant finding only when statistical adjustments of recidivism were made for the fact that the cases receiving the noncustodial dispositions were "at large" for significantly more time than the custody cases. When some unadjusted measures of recidivism (e.g., actual number of charges) were employed as the outcome measure, it was clear that over the two-year follow-up period the cases receiving a noncustodial disposition had significantly higher mean numbers of both status and criminal charges than the custody cases. The only finding that was clearly and unequivocally favorable to the noncustodial disposition was the fact that the mean seriousness of the recidivistic offenses of the custody cases was greater than that of the noncustodial cases.

Overall, determination of the relative value of noncustodial and custodial dispositions to the control of recidivism is a complex function of many considerations. Such considerations include in-program incapacitation effects and postprogram effects on recidivism; the quality of treatment services delivered within noncustodial and custodial settings; the seriousness of the offenses prevented through community-based treatment; and the human, social, and economic costs of official processing of less serious offenses. Interestingly, Barton and Butts (1990) concluded that, even considering the threat of net-widening (the application of sanctions to a wider group of offenders), the introduction of noncustodial alternatives was cost-efficient on a system-wide basis.

Second, the systematic research literature has not yet sufficiently explored the possibility that residential placements, based not on "just deserts" considerations but on the more immediate concern of the prevention of harm to self or others, may be just, ethical, decent, humane, and effective routes to reduced criminal recidivism. In our view, one of the outstanding contributions of the California research on the use of community versus residential placements is the evidence that correctional professionals may reduce recidivism through the exercise of discretionary short-term residential placements (Palmer, 1974). As much as we are ready to place severe restraints on the use of custody, many of us also feel that some young people may gain from the short-term protection, care, and service that a humane residential placement may provide.

Since the publication of Mark Lipsey's (1989), Carleton University's (Andrews, Zinger et al., 1990a), and John Whitehead and Steven Lab's (1989) meta-analytic reviews, there has been a tremendous amount of activity. The earlier work of Carol J. Garrett (1985) and Leah Gensheimer, Jeffrey P. Mayer, Rand Gottschalk, and William S. Davidson (1986) has been rediscovered. Others contributing to the expanding knowledge base include Robert Ross (Izzo & Ross, 1990; Ross, Antonowicz & Dhaliwal, 1995); Friedrich Lösel (1995), from Germany; and Santiago Redondo, and his colleagues, Vicente Garrido and J. Sanchez-Meca (1999), from Spain.

Douglas S. Lipton was the director of the Effective Correctional Treatment project in New York in the late 1960s, which led to the influential 1975 book by Lipton, Martinson, and Wilks (1975) on which the infamous Martinson (1974) paper was based. Douglas Lipton has re-entered the effectiveness debate as Principal Investigator on the huge CDATE project. CDATE, sponsored by the United States National Institute on Drug Abuse, has assembled, annotated, and subjected to meta-analytic review all treatment studies reported from 1968 to 1997. Douglas Lipton and colleagues Frank S. Pearson, Charles Cleland, and Dorline Yee (1997; Pearson & Lipton, 1999) detected trends more favorable to some types of treatment than to others (for example: cognitive behavioral/social learning strategies relative to deterrence-based programs). Mark Lipsey (1995, 1999) has continued to explore the effectiveness issue. His practical advice for practitioners continues to emphasize a focus on behavioral and skill issues in a structured manner, attention to integrity in implementation and delivery, and adequate dosage (100 or more contact hours, two or more contacts per week, over a period of 26 weeks or more).

All the activity has not been without criticism. Lab and Whitehead's (1990) response to the Carleton University meta-analysis continues to surface, most notably by persons committed to retributive or restorative justice. A few, but not many, continue to argue for models of justice that dismiss or discount the introduction of human service in a justice context. Andrews, Zinger and colleagues (1990b) addressed the 1990 critique but did not cover everything. Charles Logan, along with colleagues from the U.S. Federal Bureau of Prisons (Logan et al., 1991; Logan & Gaes, 1993), reaffirmed allegiance to just deserts and their antirehabilitation stance but, in the process, discounted the meta-analytic evidence, deplored the "missionary zeal" of "believers," and made reference to "smoke and mirrors." However, Gerald Gaes has recently moderated his earlier antirehabilitation stance and now accepts the fact that some offender treatment programs are effective in reducing recidivism (Gaes, 1998; Gaes et al., 1999). Lab and Whitehead (1990) also said that the findings were perhaps too conveniently consistent with our hypotheses in regard to risk, need, and responsivity, and where bias could not account for the findings, they noted that the explanation was probably due to a "tautology." The tautology, they suggested, reflected the fact that the principles themselves were derived from our pattern of findings in the particular group of studies reviewed (ignoring the fact that the principles were outlined prior to the meta-analysis). The fact remains, however, and as noted in our 1990 response to the critics, that some criticisms are simply beyond the realm of empirical exploration. For example, how do researchers respond to assertions that they are "wizards"?

The Carleton University data bank now includes more than 374 tests of the effects of judicial and correctional interventions on recidivism (Andrews, Dowden & Gendreau, 1999; Andrews & Dowden, 1999; Dowden, 1998; Dowden & Andrews, 1999a, 1999b, 2000: see Resource

Note 7.1 for a more detailed summary). The overall mean effect now is 0.08 ($N = 374$), which is close to the value revealed in Friederich Lösel's (1995) independent meta-analysis of the existing meta-analyses. That level of effect is mild, but clearly positive and utterly inconsistent with a blanket "nothing works" position. Using the binomial effect size display (recall Resource Note 1.1), an r of 0.08 reflects a difference of eight percentage points between the recidivism rates of the intervention and comparison groups: 46 percent reoffending in the intervention group compared with 54 percent reoffending in the comparison group.

The mean r of 0.08 is an average and the 95 percent confidence interval of .06 to .10 does *not* contain .00. In other words, correctional interventions do have an effect on recidivism. There is, however, a tremendous amount of variability around that mean. The poorest outcome within all 374 estimates is in the area of –0.40, while the best single outcome is in the area of +0.80. Perhaps the really interesting question is what are the sources of this variation? Note that increases in severity of the penalty continue to yield mild negative effects (mean $r = -0.03$, $k = 101$), while variation in human service delivery continues to yield modestly positive effects (mean $r = +0.12$, $k = 273$).

The mildly negative effect of increases in the severity of the criminal sanction is now so well established that specific deterrence may be declared to be empirically indefensible as a rationale for increases in the severity of the penalty. In Chapter 8, we present Paul Gendreau and colleagues' meta-analytic review of the effects on reoffending of the whole range of "innovative" and "traditional" punishments that were experimented upon in the 1980s and 1990s. These variations on themes of punishment included "turning the heat up on probationers," "turning the heat up on parolees," "boot camps," "Scared Straight," "more prison," "mandatory arrest of male batterers," and so on. Recall Mark Lipsey's negative findings regarding programs based on deterrence theory. Further, read Michael Tonry's (1994) commentary on the war on drugs in the United States. He reminds us that governments in Canada, Great Britain, and the United States, from the 1960s on, have repeatedly and consistently heard from blue-ribbon Commissions and expert advisory bodies that harsher penalties will not significantly increase public safety.

On the other hand, the evidence favoring the delivery of human service in a justice context continues to grow and deepen, albeit with many questions unanswered. As in the original sample, a simple coding of human service as behavioral or nonbehavioral yields striking differences in mean effect size (0.04, $k = 297$, for nonbehavioral treatment compared with 0.23, $k = 77$, for behavioral treatment). The shorthand phrase "behavioral" may be better described as "behavioral/social learning/cognitive behavioral." The coding of treatment programs was based on indication of the use of the following type of strategies: modeling (if you want to get a behavior going, demonstrate it), reinforcement (if you want to keep a behavior going, reward it), role-playing (set up opportunities for practice with corrective feedback), graduated practice (some behavior actually constitutes a complex skill that may best be broken down and practiced in smaller steps), extinction (assuring that antisocial styles of thinking, feeling, and acting are not inadvertently rewarded), and cognitive restructuring (pay attention to the risky content of thought and assist in trying out less risky thoughts). To our knowledge, every meta-analysis that has been reported upon, with the exception of Whitehead and Lab's (1989), has found the pattern noted above. As noted in the chapter on a general personality perspective (Chapter 4), the social learning models of criminal behavior have virtually no serious competitors when attention turns away from simple prediction and toward actually influencing criminal behavior.

The overall pattern of results favoring "clinically appropriate" human service continues in the expanded sample of studies. With the coding of risk, need, and responsivity once again defining "appropriate" treatment, the mean correlation coefficients with reduced reoffending were as follows: Criminal Sanctions (–.03, $k = 101$); Human Service inconsistent with each of risk, need, and responsivity (–.01, $k = 23$); Human Service consistent with only one of risk, need, and responsivity (+.02, $k = 106$); Human Service consistent with two of the three principles (+.18, $k = 84$); and Appropriate Service (consistent with all three principles: +.26, $k = 60$). The counting of number of principles adhered to was made possible by certain important changes in coding in the latest Carleton sample.

In our work with the expanded sample of tests of effective treatment, a more careful examination is being made of each of the three principles. One such look was described immediately above in the report on the social learning/cognitive behavioral aspect of responsivity. Separate explorations also were introduced for the risk and need principles. This allowed the counting of adherence with principles evident in the paragraph above.

In the Andrews et al. (1990a) report, the risk principle was explored within those particular studies that allowed such an exploration. That is, within any particular study of a particular treatment program, if the effects of treatment were reported separately for lower- and higher-risk cases, the separate estimates were placed in our meta-analysis (the estimate for the higher-risk subgroup was placed in the appropriate treatment category and the estimate for the lower-risk group in the inappropriate treatment category). The raw data in the appendix to the 1990 report reveals clear differences, with much larger effects found in the higher-risk subsamples relative to the lower-risk samples. Lab and Whitehead (1990) presented an intellectually serious criticism of our "within sample" approach; we agreed with some of their points. Overall, however, our "within sample" approach strongly supported the risk principle. We were more concerned with Mark Lipsey's finding that the risk principle indeed was supported but only to a minor degree. Lipsey (1989), unlike us, coded samples as a whole as either lower-risk or higher-risk. He used an aggregate approach wherein samples that included a predominant number of first offenders were coded as "lower-risk," while samples that included a predominant number of repeat offenders were coded as "higher-risk." We now employ the Lipsey approach when the more direct test of the risk principle is impossible because of insufficient data. What is found is that the risk principle continues to be supported for otherwise appropriate treatment, but the level of support is attenuated relative to the more direct "within sample" approach. Notably, Mark Lipsey and David Wilson (1998) endorsed the risk principle in their recent meta-analytic review of effective service for serious young offenders.

Lab and Whitehead (1990) were particularly negative about our tests of the need principle. Indeed, we did apply the need principle in a less-than-direct manner. Our applications of the need principle were basically reflected in the comments section of an appendix to the 1990 report. A graduate student at Carleton University, Craig Dowden, enthusiastically took on the task of systematically and objectively evaluating the validity of the need principle. Dowden (1998) took Figure 11.3 from this text (and earlier versions of this text) and applied it to the analysis of our expanded set of studies. Figure 11.3 rewords the dynamic risk factors supported by PCC in terms of more promising and less promising intermediate targets of change within programs concerned with the more ultimate target of reduced recidivism. Figure 11.3 dates back to the 1980s, and is not a summary of the findings of our earlier meta-analysis of correctional treatment.

Dowden counted the number of promising targets represented in treatment programs as well as the number of less promising targets represented in treatment programs. His counts agreed with the counts of an independent reader in more than 90 percent of the codes. The findings were strong: Across three samples of studies (Whitehead & Lab, 1989; Andrews et al. 1990a; new studies in Carleton University database), the mean effect size for studies of programs that targeted a greater number of the more promising targets than the less promising targets is +0.19 (k = 169), compared with a mean effect size of –.01 (k = 205) for studies of programs that emphasized less promising targets. The simple correlation between appropriate targeting and reduced recidivism was .47 in the Whitehead and Lab sample of studies (k = 87), .60 in the sample pulled together by Andrews, Zinger et al. (1990a: k = 67), .50 in our 1998 additional sample of studies (k =140), and .57 in the most recent set of studies added by Dowden (k = 80). Cross-sample findings as robust as the criminogenic need findings are inconsistent with a tautology argument. The importance of the criminogenic need principle should not be underestimated. Programs that placed an emphasis on less promising intermediate targets tended to increase reoffending rates. Not one program that targeted noncriminogenic needs was associated with reduced recidivism. The overall correlation between the number of criminogenic needs targeted and recidivism was .55.

This chapter has shown that the objective and quantitative findings of the existing literature on correctional effectiveness do not support a "nothing works" perspective. The "nothing works" perspective makes sense only if one limits one's view of the effects of treatment to that literature which deals with the effects of variations in the type and/or severity of official processing and sanctioning on recidivism. In dramatic contrast, the research literature on the effects of treatment service, offered under a variety of conditions of official processing, has revealed positive effects on average—and notably positive effects when the principles of risk, need, and responsivity have been applied.

These conclusions apply to the findings represented in the research literature. They do not apply to the vast majority of treatment programs that are being offered currently. Only a very small proportion of programs are evaluated, and few of these evaluations make their way into the published research literature. As noted elsewhere, over a recent 10-year period in which millions of young American and Canadian citizens came into contact with the justice system, the total number of published studies on what we have described as "appropriate" treatment was 21 (Andrews, Zinger et al., 1990a). We do not claim that this review provides a representative sample of current programming or that it speaks to the effectiveness of programs that have not been evaluated. Indeed, we are open to the possibility that the situation in juvenile justice is similar to that suggested by Miller and Hester (1986) in the field of addiction treatment, wherein lists of the most popular treatments and the best-validated treatments do not overlap at all. We are also open to the possibility that unvalidated but popular treatments may prove to be effective upon systematic exploration. The most important indication of this review is that there should be ongoing exploration and development of decent, humane, just, and effective means of introducing human service for purposes of reducing antisocial conduct.

In practical terms, what does clinically appropriate service look like? Summarizing the studies reviewed by Andrews and colleagues, the programs consistent with the principles of effective service were not at all mysterious. They included: (1) short-term behavioral/systems family counseling in which family process is targeted for change and/or in which relevant systems are expanded to include the school, peers, and other relevant settings in the community, (2) structured one-on-one paraprofessional programs in which the helpers were encouraged to be of active and direct assistance, (3) specialized academic/vocational programming, (4) intensive structured skill training, and (5) behaviorally-oriented individual counseling, group counseling, and structured milieu systems.

Most of the effective programs contained elements whose importance has been noted in this review. Additionally, Don Gordon, Don Andrews, James Hill, and Kevin Kurkowsky (1992) worked on an expanded and refined measure of therapeutic integrity in the delivery of family therapy. The measure of integrity reflects the specificity of the model that links intervention to outcome, the training and clinical supervision of direct service workers, adequate dosage, and monitoring of service process and intermediate gain. Their findings are so strong that they demand comment. The effects of therapeutic integrity may be incremental to the effects of appropriate treatment and to the methodological variables known to influence estimates of effect size. In brief, many of the programs that were found effective in our review are notable not only according to the principles of risk, need, and responsivity, but also according to their exceptional attention to the specifics of service delivery.

The latest Carleton University analyses (Resource Note 7.1) also suggest that a host of indicators of integrity are linked with positive outcome when the conditions are favorable to clinically and psychologically appropriate treatment. The latter types of treatment are human service programs consistent with the principles of risk, need, and responsivity. The problem with the meta-analytic findings is that so few primary studies report in detail on the indicators of integrity.

In summary, evidence to date suggests that the delivery of clinically relevant treatment service is a promising route to reduced recidivism. Whatever the social role of punishment, there is no evidence that a reliance on just deserts or deterrence-based sanctioning is followed by meaningful reductions in recidivism (see Chapter 8 for further evidence on sanctioning). The possibility of large reductions in recidivism resides in delivering appropriate treatment services to people at risk and in need. Notably, however, the meta-analyses reviewed here suggest that the use of community alternatives to custodial sanctions will enhance the effectiveness of appropriate treatment services.

Now we turn to linkages among the major theories of criminal conduct and the design and outcomes of correctional counseling programs.

Theory and Intervention

PIC-R stressed two fundamental principles of behavioral influence that are important whether interpersonal influence is occurring in family, peer, or formal treatment settings (Andrews, 1980):

1. *The Relationship Principle*: Interpersonal influence by antecedent and consequent processes is greatest in situations characterized by open, warm, enthusiastic, and nonblaming communication, and by mutual respect, liking, and interest. This principle is also known as the socio-emotional principle.

2. *The Structuring Principle*: The procriminal versus anticriminal direction of interpersonal influence is determined by the procriminal/anticriminal content of the messages communicated or by the procriminal/anticriminal nature of the behavior patterns that are modeled, rehearsed, and subject to reinforcement and punishment contingencies. This principle is also known as the con-

tingency, control, and/or training principle. The structuring dimension reflects the use of effective authority practices, anti-criminal modeling, differential approval and disapproval, problem-solving, skill building, advocacy, and brokerage (Andrews, 1980; Andrews & Carvell, 1997; Andrews & Kiessling, 1980).

These two fundamental dimensions of interpersonal exchanges have a long history in the general social psychology of interpersonal interaction (e.g., Bales, 1950), counseling theory (e.g., Rogers, 1961), and the social psychology of criminal conduct (e.g., Sutherland's theory of differential association). Indeed, we saw them in Chapter 3 in the discussion of Freudian models of parenting practices, in Chapter 4 in discussions of PIC-R, and in Chapter 5 in discussions of family process and family therapy.

The indicators of relationship and structuring are another way of expressing general responsivity practices. The indicators of a positive relationship establish the conditions favorable to modeling effects, favorable to effective interpersonal reinforcement and/or effective interpersonal disapproval, and to creating an attractive rather than aversive setting for intervention

The first set of conditions (relationship), if positive, tends to promote learning and enhance interpersonal influence. The second set (contingency) determines what is learned or the direction of influence. In correctional counseling, the structuring dimension is responsible for movement or changes that are favorable to criminal behavior or unfavorable to criminal behavior. If the content of interactions is irrelevant to criminal behavior, the effects on criminal conduct will be negligible.

Recall the overall model of programming (Chapter 2, Figure 2.1) that suggested that the design and operation of effective programs were contingent upon a number of sets of variables:

1. Selecting appropriate intermediate targets (focusing on attributes of people and their circumstances, which, if changed, are associated with shifts in the chances of criminal behavior);

2. Offering services that are able to produce the desired intermediate changes (the process and content of intervention on the relationship and contingency dimensions);

3. Building a program structure that will support effective process (for example, selecting and training counselors in ways compatible with desired process and outcome);

4. Matching cases and programs to clients according to risk, need, and responsivity;

5. Conducting programs with due concern for justice, ethicality, and cost-effectiveness.

We are ready to explore the relationship between intervention effectiveness and theories of criminal conduct. This discussion begins with psychodynamic theory and continues with the other theoretical perspectives of criminal conduct.

Psychodynamic Theory and Psychotherapy

The broad outlines of psychoanalytic theory received strong support from cross-sectional and longitudinal studies. Recall that parent-child conflict, poor parenting skills, early involvement in antisocial behavior, and the various indicators of a weak superego (generalized misconduct, egocentricism) were all among the best validated correlates and predictors of criminal conduct. It is clear that psychodynamic theory suggests a number of important need factors (or intermediate targets for intervention).

Psychoanalysis, however, does not provide a powerful technology of behavioral influence for correctional purposes. Without question, orthodox psychoanalysis appears to be geared to "freeing" people from neurotic misery as opposed to inhibiting antisocial behavior. Psychoanalytic "talking therapy" focuses on the past and involves the search for unconscious motivators and "insight." A prerequisite for success is a reasonable level of verbal intelligence and relatively strong motivation to sit through weekly (or more frequent) sessions over periods of a year or longer. Traditionally, it is assumed that the "good" client for psychoanalysis is one experiencing some level of internally generated neurotic misery. However, according to psychoanalytic theory, the majority of persistent and serious offenders are not bothered by misery because they act out rather than internalize conflict.

We are unaware of any explicitly psychoanalytic programs that have impacted positively on delinquency prevention or corrections. As noted by Glueck and Glueck (1950), long-term psychoanalysis may be too expensive and inefficient for wide-scale use in prevention and corrections. However, other powerful elements of psychoanalysis (e.g., the importance of transference relationships and the possibility of identification with the therapist) are found in other approaches to counseling.

Evaluations of more or less psychodynamic, yet unstructured, approaches to therapy, counseling, and casework are more plentiful. By "unstructured" we mean that the counselors appeared not to make use of direct training procedures such as behavioral rehearsal, systematic conditioning (classical or operant), role-playing, or coaching. What we refer to here are approaches to counseling that rely heavily upon "talk," "psychological interpretation," "emotional expression and ventilation," "emotional support," and "therapist-client relationships" in group or individual therapy. The published studies tend to have explored eclectic programs that draw on many different models of therapy and counseling. Because so few studies have systematically monitored the ongoing process of treatment, our descriptions of process are based on the declared orientations of the counselors studied.

Our reading of this literature suggests that these "insight-oriented," "evocative," and "relationship-dependent" approaches to correctional counseling and casework were either ineffective or criminogenic in their effects. This trend is particularly evident when such unstructured programs are offered to high-risk and/or interpersonally immature cases (e.g., Craft, Stephenson & Granger, 1966; Goodman, 1972; Grant, 1965; Grant & Grant, 1959; Harris, Rice & Cormier, 1994; Kassenbaum, Ward & Wilner, 1971; Murphy, 1972; Truax, Wargo & Volksdorf, 1970).

In summary, these studies suggest that focusing exclusively on the relationship dimension without a focus on establishing anticriminal contingencies is ineffective or harmful. They also illustrate intervention programs that were not closely tied to theories of criminal conduct in terms of either the intermediate targets selected or the intervention procedures employed.

From the earliest days of the "talking cure," Freud (1953) warned psychodynamic therapists that their highly verbal, evocative, relationship-dependent, and insight-oriented therapy was inappropriate for cases with poor verbal ability and/or cases displaying narcissistic and/or psychotic disorders. He stressed that some degree of experienced discomfort and an ability to enter into an emotional relationship with the therapist were crucial to success. He added that, without immediate social support for both treatment and personal change, the chances of successful treatment were minuscule. Freud went so far as to admit that once his therapeutic reputation was established, he accepted only cases that were personally and socially committed to service gains (Andrews, Bonta & Hoge, 1990:37-38).

The results of the above-noted programs contrast dramatically with the findings of studies that employed more structured approaches to counseling and focused upon influencing more theoretically relevant need factors (the "appropriate" set in Andrews, Zinger et al., 1990a).

Labeling, Conflict, and Due Process Theory

Labeling and conflict theory have not done well in the cross-sectional and longitudinal studies. A host of person-based measures has been found to distinguish between offenders and nonoffenders, while the favored variable (social class) of these theories was not prominent in this set of correlates. Nor have these theories performed well in studies of prevention and corrections. Indeed, it is now widely recognized (even by self-avowed friends of labeling and conflict theory such as Stanley Cohen, 1985) that a preoccupation with antitreatment and due process themes has contributed to current trends toward increased use of incarceration and punishment—and perhaps increased recidivism rates (Cullen & Gendreau, 1989; Cullen & Gilbert, 1982; Leschied, Austin & Jaffe, 1988).

Alan Leschied and his colleagues from the London Family Court Clinic have documented that reduced use of mental health services, increased court processing, and increased use of custody have followed the implementation of Canada's Young Offenders Act (Leschied, Jaffe & Willis, 1991). This act was very much a product of labeling theory of the 1960s and 1970s, in combination with due process and children's rights themes. The act was implemented in the early-1980s context of distrust of correctional treatment and discretion. The edited collection by Alan Leschied, Peter Jaffe, and Wayne Willis provides a fascinating glimpse of a piece of legislation that reached down into the immediate contingencies of action in many settings. Those contingencies included disincentives for active counseling or treatment on the part of probation officers and other youth workers, but incentives for offering young people restitution and other alternative actions that did not address their criminogenic needs. The contingencies included powerful incentives for lawyers to engage in due process activities that may postpone justice and delay high-need young people and their families in making contact with human service agencies.

Given that the psychology of criminal conduct is so peripheral to their main concerns, the labeling, conflict, and due process perspectives do not contain well formulated principles of behavioral influence. Indeed, these theorists tend to be among the most "antitreatment" in sentiment. Their primary treatment recommendation has been to "leave kids alone whenever possible" (e.g., the "radical nonintervention" of Schur, 1973). A second and related recommendation has been to divert people from the criminal and juvenile justice systems. Third, labeling and conflict theorists were among the major proponents of the view that criminal justice processing is (and should be) about punishment rather than rehabilitation. They spoke of the "tyranny of treatment" and the "dignity of punishment."

Based on the assumption that official labeling or processing is invariably criminogenic, diversion involves a preference for the least restrictive alternative (that is, lack of processing is preferred to processing, low levels of community supervision are preferred to higher levels of supervision, community-based supervision is preferred to incarceration, etc.). The diversion rhetoric has resulted in an explosion of alternatives to incarceration, and increasing numbers of people have been caught in the "widening net."

Returning to the individual level of analysis, a problem with the labeling and conflict perspectives' use of the principle of least restrictive processing is that they fail to consider explicitly the risk levels and needs of the offenders. Such a problem arises because labeling and conflict theorists deny individual differences in the propensity for criminal activity. The lowest levels of service and control may be quite appropriate for low-risk cases but inappropriate for higher-risk cases (see the "Buddy System" in Resource Note 2.3). Essentially unidimensional conceptualizations of both "treatment" and "offenders" are unlikely to lead to successful programming.

When programs must be offered, the labeling and conflict theorists have shown a preference for loosely structured group programs over one-to-one counseling. There is a distinct sense (not unlike the assumptions of the client-centered, nondirective, relationship-oriented therapy advocated by Carl Rogers) that the experience of interpersonal warmth and relationship dynamics within groups will have beneficial effects. Assumptions such as these are also found in our review of the treatment implications of subcultural theory.

Subcultural and Differential Association Theory

The subcultural, differential opportunity, and differential association perspectives led to a number of community-action interventions. The assumption was that the criminogenic subcultures (and/or isolation from legitimate opportunity) were a reflection of community disorganization, inadequate access to the services that make conformity possible, and gang membership. Thus, programs were initiated in various settings, including New York's Lower East Side (The Mobilization for Youth Project), Chicago (Chicago Area Project), and Boston (Midcity Youth Project).

These programs were reviewed in detail by Schur (1973) and by Klein (1971). Klein's book, *Street Gangs and Street Workers*, is particularly rich in the attention paid to the specific processes of intervention. The community-action components of the programs tended to focus not on individuals as the targets of service but on the development and strengthening of welfare agencies, neighborhood organizations, and inborn leadership. The focus on gang members was operationalized through the introduction of detached workers. These workers were to establish relationships with gang members and serve as advocates, brokers, sometime counselors, companions, and recreational agents.

The majority of the programs were not well evaluated. However, those that were explored systematically were found to have either no impact on delinquency or to *increase* delinquency. The latter finding deserves serious review. An increase in delinquent behavior as a consequence of intervention is not only practically significant but of tremendous theoretical value. Such a finding suggests that the programs were impacting upon variables of true causal significance, albeit inadvertently.

According to Klein's and Schur's reviews, the community development aspects of some programs were successful in terms of creating improved neighborhood conditions, new welfare agencies, and recreational opportunities. However, this intermediate change appeared irrelevant to the ultimate goal of reducing delinquency.

In Klein's review of the evidence, the increased delinquency was linked to the detached worker programs. In particular, increased delinquency was found when workers "succeeded" in increasing the cohesiveness of delinquent groups. In other words, prior to the introduction of workers, the gangs were relatively weak groups—disorganized, often lacking in leadership, composed of relatively few hard-core members, and often characterized by infighting. With the introduction of a worker, the gangs became more organized and cohesive, and delinquency increased. Klein's work also demonstrated that the removal of the worker could be associated with reduced gang cohesiveness and reduced delinquency. Specifically, Klein argued that the intermediate goal of work with street gangs should be to weaken the groups, not strengthen them.

This pattern of findings underscores the need to consider both the relationship and contingency aspects of interpersonal functioning. Facilitating and encouraging interaction within delinquent groups, without simultaneously establishing anticriminal contingencies, will have the effect of increasing delinquency. This is a direct implication of behavioral reformulations of differential association theory. Why, then, would delinquency prevention programmers deliberately offer programs that are bound to be either ineffective or detrimental?

The answer is twofold. One reason is that subcultural theory carries a lot of excess baggage with it. As Chapter 3 showed, the sociologists were determined to respect "culture"—not to tamper with it directly, but rather to open up legitimate opportunities. Similarly, the disorganization of the gangs must have looked like just another part of the disorganized lower-class areas. Thus, to organize was considered "good" because community disorganization caused powerlessness, poverty, and crime.

The second part of the answer is that subcultural theory did not have a solid theory of human behavior at its base. (The idea was that people merely conform to their cultures, and thus the focus must be on the culture.) Therefore, according to Klein, the goals of the program often had little to do with either the prevention or control of delinquency. Instead, the projects were intent on doing good for the disadvantaged. This meant offering help and assistance regardless of the intermediate value of that assistance in the control of delinquency. Moreover, a focus on reducing delinquent associations or an attempt to reduce procriminal values would imply that "their" culture was somehow inferior to "our" culture. The negative contribution of the concept of culture deflected attention away from the "causal variables"—personal attitudes, values and beliefs supportive of crime, personal problems in the area of self-management and cognitive control, antisocial associates, and distressed families with problems of cohesiveness and parenting practices.

The dual problem of not having a powerful model of human behavior to work from and not being willing to intervene actively at the level of associates, attitudes, and personal skills was evident in other major sociological intervention projects. Two examples follow. The first is Jim Hackler's (1966, 1978) Opportunities for Youth Program. The second involves tests of guided group interaction programs.

Hackler's program is one of the best formulated and best evaluated in the literature. Hackler carefully detailed the underlying model of human behavior, program structures, and outcomes. Well aware of the poverty of the personal psychology of labeling and subcultural theory, he attempted to formulate a psychological model that was compatible with sociological theory yet helpful in the design of intervention programs. Specifically, he (1978:35) postulated a complex causal chain in which being held in low esteem by others (and perhaps the self) leads to deviant behavior (see Figure 7.1).

1. Being lower-class, underprivileged, ethnic minority
   ↓
2. Being held in low esteem
   ↓
3. Teachers and others anticipate deviance from low-esteem persons
   ↓
4. Ego perceives that others anticipate deviance
   ↓
5. Ego perceives self as deviant
   ↓
6. Ego searches for roles consistent with deviant self-concept
   ↓
7. Ego adopts deviant role (i.e., engages in deviant behavior)
   ↓
8. Ego accepts deviant norms.

Figure 10.1
Hackler's Causal Chain

This is a somewhat dramatic symbolic interactionist integration of anomie, labeling, and subcultural theories. The model suggests that it is not useful to attempt to change prodelinquent attitudes and values because it is not deviant norms that cause delinquent behavior but delinquent behavior that causes delinquent norms. Similarly, the low esteem with which the lower class is held by representatives of the dominant culture is outside the realm of reasonable short-term intervention. Thus, Hackler decided to focus upon Step 4, that is, a boy's perception that others perceive him as delinquency-prone.

How might a program be structured to bring about the desired perception on the part of the boy? Hackler opted for two approaches: a "work group" experience and a "teaching machine testing" experience. Approximately 240 young boys (13-14 years old) who lived in Seattle housing projects were randomly assigned to either a "work program," a "teaching machine testing program," or no-treatment control groups. The experiences had no effects on attitudes as assessed by self-report questionnaires and no obvious effects on postprogram delinquency. Although the data are weak, the higher-risk cases ("bad" boys as rated by teachers, mothers, and peers) exposed to the work program performed more poorly postprogram than did the higher-risk controls.

What specifically were these programs? What were the details of the intervention processes that failed to influence intermediate attitudes and ultimate behavior? The teaching machine program was designed explicitly not to be a remedial education program. Rather, the boys were to test the machines and advise the teachers whether they found the machines interesting and/or useful and whether they discovered ways to cheat with the machines. The "teachers" were instructed *not* to reward the boys for good academic performance. The work program involved groups of boys engaging in community clean-up projects (e.g., in public parks) under the supervision of an adult leader. The leader was instructed *not* to reward the boys for good work performance, because direct reward contingencies would lead the boys to believe that the leader thought that they were irresponsible, lazy, or inadequate.

In all, it would be difficult to conceive of a less direct approach to behavioral influence than those employed in the Seattle Project. With hindsight, it is obvious that these programs were focusing on inappropriate intermediate targets in inadequate ways. Still, this project continues to be promoted as evidence that nothing works. Perhaps what it really shows is the poverty of anomie, labeling, and subcultural theory for designing effective intervention programs. We owe a great debt to Hackler for having the drive, tenacity, and respect for evidence to conduct and report on such a direct test of sociological notions of the 1960s.

The high levels of passivity of intervention in the Seattle Project are also evident in several evaluations of guided group interaction programs. Here the difficulty of sociologically based intervention programs is revealed in rather broad ways. LaMar Empey, like Hackler, rigorously outlined the rationale for what is known as the Provo Experiment (Empey & Erickson, 1972; Empey & Rabow, 1961). Stephenson and Scarpitti (1974) provide a useful review of a number of controlled-outcome evaluations of guided group interaction programs. As in the case of Hackler's work, these evaluation studies are classics in the psychology of crime. Stephenson and Scarpitti's conclusion was that the programs were not any more effective than regular probation.

Much can be learned from the evaluations of guided group interaction (though we wish there had been more attention to treatment process). We have no objection to group programs when their activities are structured so that real alternatives are provided to antisocial ways of thinking, feeling, and acting (Agee, 1986; Andrews, 1980; Bush, 1995; Bush & Bilodeau, 1993) and real opportunities are given for the acquisition of new cognitive and interpersonal skills, such as perspective-taking and self-regulation (Robinson & Porporino, 2001). However, at the heart of the clinical sociology version of guided group interaction was the belief that attitudes were not really properties of individuals but instead were properties of groups. There was also the notion that the "group" must adopt anticriminal values for the learning to transfer to the individual. Workers were encouraged to reinforce candor more than they did anticriminal expressions, and there was a fear that too much of an emphasis on the anticriminal would establish conditions of "rejection of the rejectors." We believe that to hope that collections of antisocial young people with some guidance will form anticriminal groups is hoping for too much. It is placing excessive reliance on the relationship principle and ignoring the contingency principle. Quite simply, it is not consistent with the psychology of human behavior.

Many programs are still operating on the basis of weakly formulated principles of group dynamics, often infused with a mishmash of Rogerian and existential notions of the underlying goodness of humankind (e.g., Cordess, 2001; Mobley, 1999), which would become evident if only the person or group could experience trust, openness, and noncontingent valuing. The work of Jack Bush (1995), along with his colleagues Brian Bilodeau and Mark Kornick, has made great strides in managing this problem. Candor must be encouraged when antisocial cognitions are being explored. In their Cognitive Self Change program, absolute candor without judgment and without "counseling" or "correction" is the practice when a "thinking report" is being prepared. At the stage of trying out less risky cognitions, however, guidance through modeling and encouragement is the norm, and the principle of respectful and caring communication is not violated.

Programs that concentrate on the relationship principle without attention to contingencies are disturbing. Equally disturbing are programs that take the contingency principle to the extreme and focus on confrontation with name-calling, humiliation, and abuse. Yelling at and otherwise abusing people contingent upon expressions of procriminal sentiments or behavior is not consistent with the relationship or structuring principles of effective interaction. In human service, people should be treated with respect, concern, and care.

Finally, helping to change the circumstances of at-risk people and changing their personal, interpersonal, familial, and community characteristics is a real challenge when the reduction of criminal recidivism is the goal. It does not happen magically, nor through the incidental learning opportunities provided by not being arrested and/or not going to court (diversion), nor through the incidental learning opportunities that might be provided by paying restitution, completing a community service order, or by a trip to court or somewhere even further into the system ("accountability" through just processing, restoration, or punishment). It does not happen in groups that are relationship-oriented, evocative, sensitive, and supportive but too respectful of the "subculture" to offer alternatives to antisocial styles of thinking, feeling, and acting. Nor does it happen in groups that employ oppressive and abusive techniques. It does not happen when neighborhoods get a new park or a new human service agency. It happens when well-developed, well-validated services focusing on criminogenic factors are delivered to at-risk individuals and their families.

Paraphrasing Andrews and Kiessling (1980:462-463), effective rehabilitative efforts involve workers who are interpersonally warm, tolerant, and flexible, yet sensitive to conventional rules and procedures. These workers make use of the authority inherent in their position without engaging in interpersonal domination (i.e., they are "firm but fair");

they demonstrate in vivid ways their own anticriminal-prosocial attitudes, values, and beliefs; and they enthusiastically engage the offender in the process of increasing rewards for noncriminal activity. The worker exposes and makes attractive the alternatives to procriminal attitudes, styles of thinking, and ways of acting. The worker does not depend upon the presumed benefits of a warm relationship with the offender and does not assume that offenders will self-discover these alternatives. The alternatives are demonstrated through words and actions, and explorations of the alternatives are encouraged through modeling, reinforcement, and specific guidance (Andrews, Bonta & Hoge, 1990:36-37).

Behavioral and Social Learning Approaches

As we outlined in Chapter 4 (PIC-R), and throughout this text, behavioral, cognitive-behavioral, and social learning approaches to treatment provide the greatest likelihood of success. This is not simply a technology of behavioral influence. It reflects an underlying psychology of human behavior that, in turn, offers an empirically defensible psychology of criminal conduct. Offenders, being human, seek pleasure and try to avoid pain. Their behavior is influenced by the immediate contingencies of action that are situationally induced and personally and interpersonally mediated. Stability in human behavior is evident because these contingencies are maintained by such personal variables as personality, attitudes, competencies, and incompetencies, and by important others such as parents and peers.

PIC-R suggests that if some of these contingencies can be changed, then the density of the incentives and disincentives for criminal acts and noncriminal acts may be shifted more in the favor of noncriminal alternatives. The research literature provides a number of reasonably well-validated program models for changing those contingencies so that the chances of criminal conduct are reduced.

Although there has been little rehabilitative work with a focus on antisocial attitudes, some direction is provided by Andrews (1980), Wormith (1984), and Bush (1995). Generally, well-trained and well-supervised paraprofessionals working within a well-formulated model of criminal conduct and service delivery can have demonstrably positive effects. The work of William S. Davidson and colleagues is outstanding in this regard (Davidson et al., 2001). They have produced detailed manuals for the training of paraprofessionals in one-on-one behavioral advocacy approaches and family system approaches. Similarly, Jack Bush's (1995) Cognitive Self Change program is supported by manuals and training opportunities along with research support (Henning & Frue, 1996).

Intensive, structured skill development programs with detailed models for service delivery and training of therapist/coaches are available (Goldstein & Glick, 1987; Hollin & Palmer, 2001; Ross & Fabiano, 1985). Similarly, the relationship and structuring aspects of short-term behavioral family system approaches (such as functional family therapy) have been implemented in many settings outside of their Utah origins. Multisystemic family service also has moved well beyond its South Carolina origins (see Chapter 5).

Cognitive-behavioral programs have been employed with sex offenders (Hanson et al., 2002) and with men who physically abuse their female partners (Dobash et al., 2000; Dutton, 1995). To date, the evidence is favorable to treatment. These two areas of work are producing detailed accounts of the specific antisocial attitudes, values, and beliefs that support the sexual and physical abuse of women and children. In particular, Hanson and Harris's (2000) ongoing work documenting, organizing, and assessing denial and minimization among offenders may provide a model for more general assessments of the "cognitive distortions" that support antisocial conduct and interfere with progress in treatment.

The sex offender literature, along with progress in the field of addictions, is also exploring the promise of relapse prevention approaches (e.g., Hanson, 1996). The cognitive and situational focus of relapse is interesting from the perspective of social learning: high-risk situations are identified for particular cases, and detailed cognitive and behavioral strategies are developed for those situations. Experimental evaluations on the effectiveness of relapse prevention with sexual and general offenders have not been reported as yet. However, a meta-analysis of the literature on the efficacy of relapse prevention for smoking, alcohol, and drug abuse suggests promise (Irvin et al., 1999). Jennifer Irvin and her colleagues found an overall effect size of $r = .12$ (based on 26 studies). For substance abuse, the r was .14; the r was .09 for smoking.

Indications are that we may be on the verge of an explosion of knowledge regarding the design and implementation of effective services of the cognitive-behavioral, social learning variety. Even within specialized school and vocational programs, it is the focused and structured programs that have been linked with reduced recidivism (e.g., Le Marquand & Tremblay, 2001). We expect that advances in prevention and rehabilitation will reflect developments of the cognitive-behavioral approaches. We envision community-based human service agencies that are staffed by well-trained and well-supervised persons able to deliver effective programs in the context of both prevention and corrections. Such agencies may receive referrals from the police and the courts with due consideration of just deserts. The expansion of community corrections may well deliver on these promises, with plenty of false starts and rerouting to be expected.

Examples of effective programs have been distributed throughout the text. We close this chapter not with more data but with material intended to induce the look and feel of effective correctional counseling. (The data on these core correctional practices is presented in Resource Note 7.1.)

Resource Note 7.1

Recent Findings from an Ongoing and Expanded Meta-Analysis of the Effects of Human Service in a Justice Context

The PCC perspective on effective correctional treatment is relatively straightforward. A general personality and social learning perspective on criminal behavior suggests that offenders may be differentiated according to their risk of reoffending; recognizes that these risk factors are personal, interpersonal, and tied to immediate situations in an array of behavioral settings such as home, work, school, and leisure; differentiates between major and minor risk factors; identifies the dynamic risk factors that may best be targeted if the objective is reduced reoffending; and— more than any alternative perspective—is very clear regarding some fundamental processes of behavioral influence and behavior change.

Thus, we hypothesize that: (1) human service in a justice context will have greater impact on reduced recidivism than will variation in retributive and/or restorative aspects of sanctioning, and (2) the positive impact of human service will increase with adherence to the principles of risk, need, and general responsivity. Reflecting Lipsey (1990) and Andrews, Zinger, et al. (1990a; Andrews, 1996), we hypothesize further that: (3) the positive impact of clinically appropriate and PCC-relevant human service will be enhanced when offered in community-based nonresidential settings and when delivered with integrity. The latter includes structured learning procedures, modeling, and reinforcement. Finally, we hypothesize that: (4) the crime reduction potential of clinically appropriate and PCC-relevant service will be evident across and within categories of control variables suggested by threats to internal, external, construct, and statistical conclusion validity.

Our extensions of the 1990 study (Andrews, Zinger et al., 1990a) incorporate considerations of a variety of research design, case,

study, and setting factors. Here, however, we focus upon the issues of human service versus criminal sanctioning and, within human service, upon applications of the principles of risk, need, and responsivity.

According to PCC as outlined in this text, deterrence, labeling, and other justice theories are so underdeveloped in psychological terms that any interventions based on those perspectives will have weak effects compared to the effects of human service interventions based on a general personality and social learning perspective. In an expanded set of 374 tests, this pattern of results continues. Inspection of Table 7.1.1 reveals that the mean effect size for criminal sanctions (-0.3) is lower than the mean effect size for human service (.12). Not presented in the table is the fact that human service in a restorative justice context was no more effective than human service in a nonrestorative justice context (a mean effect size of .17 in eight tests within a restorative context compared with a mean effect of .12 in 265 tests within a nonrestorative context). To date, evaluated restorative justice programs have not been very concerned with the introduction of human service.

In this report, only the general responsivity principle was coded, and no attempt was made to code for the personality responsivity systems or any of the other specific responsivity considerations. Thus, the single coding requirement for conformity with the responsivity principle is the use of behavioral, social learning, and/or cognitive behavioral strategies. Adherence to the responsivity principle was associated with enhanced effect sizes. Similarly, Table 7.1.1 also shows the significant contribution of adherence to the criminogenic need principle and to the risk principle. Table 7.1.2 summarizes the mean effect

Resource Note 7.1 *(continued)*

sizes found when personal and interpersonal domains are targeted appropriately and when they are targeted inappropriately. Personal targets such as self-control deficits and anti-social cognition yielded relatively large effect sizes while the targeting of personal distress and fear of official punishment yielded weak effects on reduced reoffending.

Clinically and Psychology Appropriate Treatment. Appropriate Treatment is a composite of Any Service, Risk, Need, and General Responsivity. The two levels of inappropriate service represented in Table 7.1.1 are "No" (criminal sanctions without human service, or human service that is not consistent with each of risk, need, and responsivity) and "Yes" (human service consistent with each of risk, need, and responsivity). The four levels of Appropriate Treatment shown in Figure 7.1.1. of this Resource Note are "0" (criminal sanctions without human service or human service inconsistent with each of risk, need, and responsivity) and "1," "2," and "3," representing human service consistent with one, two, or three of the human service principles. The corresponding mean effect sizes are -0.2 ($k = 124$), $.02$ ($k = 106$), $.18$ ($k = 84$), and $.25$ ($k = 60$) for the four levels of Appropriate Treatment.

Community/Nonresidential Settings. The mean effects size increased with level of Appropriate Treatment both in community settings and institutional/residential settings. However, the *positive* effects of appropriate treatment were enhanced in community settings (mean effect size = $+.35$, $k = 30$) while the *negative* effects of inappropriate service were augmented in residential settings (mean effects size = $-.10$, $k = 25$). Please see Figure 7.1.2 within this Resource Note.

Core Correctional Practices. Table 7.1.3 lists the basic elements of behavioral influence. We call them "core correctional prac-

tices" because they represent what we and others (e.g., Trotter, 1999) believe should be part of the essential skills and qualities for those who work with offenders. As shown in the table, indicators of a high-quality relationship and structuring are associated with enhanced effects sizes. The structuring indicators include modeling, reinforcement, problem-solving, structured learning, and others.

Exploration of a Variety of Study, Organizational, and Validity Considerations. Effect size increased to at least a mild degree with the following indicators of internal validity: an evaluator who was involved in the design and/or delivery of the service, small sample studies of less than 100, and studies of new or "fresh" programs. Statistical controls for threats to internal validity, however, did not eliminate the effect of Appropriate Treatment. Other factors related to effect size but not shown in Table 7.1.4 were random assignment (eta = .10) and follow-up periods of less than two years (eta = $-.12$). Once again, statistical controls for these considerations did not erase the positive effects of Appropriate Treatment. Similarly, considerations of age, gender, and ethnicity of cases did not influence the effects of Appropriate Treatment.

In the end, however, four variables were linked with effect size in a positive manner once controls for Appropriate Treatment were introduced. They were Community-Based Programs, Involved Evaluator, Non-Justice Ownership of the Program, and Referral to Program by Justice Officials. As presented in the main body of this chapter (Table 7.1), the strength of Appropriate Treatment was evident even when offered under the conditions least favorable to large effect sizes. Overall, however, the existence of limiting conditions does not negate the evidence to date in favor of clinically relevant and psychologically informed human service in a variety of justice contexts.

Resource Note 7.1 *(continued)*

Table 7.1.1
Mean Effect Size by Adherence to Principles of Effective Correctional Treatment in 374 Tests and Correlation of Adherence with Effect Size

Principle	Adherence to Principle No	Adherence to Principle Yes	Correlation with Effect Size (eta)
Human Service	−.03 (101)	.12 (146)	.35***
Risk: Services Delivered to Higher-Risk Cases	.03 (96)	.10 (278)	.17***
Criminogenic Needs: # of Criminogenic Needs Targeted Exceed Noncriminogenic	−.01 (205)	.19 (169)	.54***
General Responsivity: Social Learning/Cognitive Behavioral Strategies	.04 (297)	.23 (77)	.40***
Full Adherence: Clinically Appropriate Treatment (adheres to all of the above)	.05 (314)	.28 (60)	.42***
Community-Based Full Adherence: Clinically Appropriate Treatment	.06 (219)	.35 (30)	.49***
Residential-Based Full Adherence: Clinically Appropriate Treatment	.002 (95)	.17 (30)	.38***

k = number of tests of treatment
*** $p < .001$

Table 7.1.2
Mean Effect Size and Correlation of Need Targeted with Effect Size (k)

Need Area Targeted	%	Mean Effect Size Not Targeted	Mean Effect Size Targeted	Correlation with Effect Size
CRIMINOGENIC NEEDS				
Personal Criminogenic Targets: Antisocial Cognition and Skill Deficits	26	.04 (277)	.21 (97)	.39***
Interpersonal Criminogenic Targets: Family and Peers	19	.05 (392)	.22 (72)	.37***
Individualized Matching with Need (specific needs not identified)	17	.06 (313)	.21 (61)	.30***
School/Work	24	.06 (286)	.15 (88)	.21***
Substance Abuse	10	.08 (338)	.11 (36)	.06 (ns)
NONCRIMINOGENIC NEEDS				
Personal Noncriminogenic Needs (personal distress, fear of official punishment)	46	.11 (203)	.04 (171)	−.18**
Interpersonal Noncriminogenic Needs (e.g., family processing other than nurturance, supervision)	12	.09 (329)	.01 (45)	−.13*

k = number of tests of treatment
%: percentage of tests with need targeted
* $p < .05$; ** $p < .01$; *** $p < .001$
ns = nonsignificant

Resource Note 7.1 *(continued)*

Table 7.1.3
Mean Effect Size by Elements of Core Correctional Practice (CCP)

Element of CCP	Element Present (k) No	Element Present (k) Yes	Correlation with Effect Size
Relationship Skills	.07 (361)	.34 (13)	.26***
Structuring Skills	.06 (330)	.27 (44)	.37***
Effective Reinforcement	.07 (359)	.31 (15)	.25***
Effective Modeling	.06 (337)	.28 (37)	.36***
Effective Disapproval	.08 (366)	.30 (8)	.18***
Structured Skill Learning	.06 (336)	.30 (38)	.39***
Problem Solving	.06 (329)	.25 (45)	.33***
Advocacy/Brokerage	.08 (321)	.11 (53)	.10*
Effective Authority	.07 (359)	.26 (15)	.19***

* p < .05; *** p < .001
k = number of tests of treatment

Table 7.1.4
Mean Effect Size by Indicators of Integrity of Implementation and Service Delivery (k = 374)

Indicator	Indicator Present No	Indicator Present Yes	Correlation with Effect Size
Staff Selected for Relationship Skills	.07 (361)	.34 (13)	.26**
Staff Trained	.04 (206)	.13 (168)	.26**
Clinical Supervision of Staff	.06 (305)	.16 (69)	.21**
Number of Hours of Service	(metric nonbinary variable; k = 84)		.20**
Rated Appropriate Dosage	.07 (221)	.09 (153)	.05 (ns)
Printed/Taped Manuals	.05 (303	.20 (71)	.30**
Monitor Process and/or Intermediate Change on Targets	.07 (227)	.10 (147)	.07 (ns)
Specific Model	.03 (173)	.12 (201)	.23***
New/Fresh Program	.05 (250)	.13 (124)	.20**
Small Sample (100<)	.04 (340)	.15 (134)	.28***
Involved Evaluator	.04 (296)	.23 (78)	.41***

k = number of tests of treatment
** p < .01; *** p <.001
ns = nonsignificant

The Dimensions of Effective Correctional Counseling: The "What and How" of Effective Modeling and Reinforcement

An important role for the correctional worker is to serve as an anti-criminal model for clients and as a source of reinforcement for their clients' anticriminal expressions and efforts. This is consistent with the relationship and structuring role of family therapists, the nurturance and training roles of parents, and the communication and instruction-al roles of teachers. We are not referring here to the application of any particular program or technique but to how probation and parole officers, case managers, youth workers, and staff in residential settings interact with antisocial individuals. The manual from which the following notes were drawn was prepared to assist in the training of citizen volunteers for direct-contact, one-to-one roles with young adult probationers (Andrews, 1979). The following notes are also consistent with Chris Trotter's (1999) guidelines to probation officers working with involuntary clients. We are assuming that the agency (and its management and staff) value the objective of reduced recidivism. Thus, one task of agency staff and managers is to increase anticriminal expressions and decrease procriminal expressions of clients.

The first step is to ensure that managers and staff are able to recognize and distinguish between anticriminal and procriminal expressions. This knowledge and skill cannot be assumed to exist, just as parents of antisocial children cannot be assumed to be able to differentiate the deviant and nondeviant activities of their children (Patterson, 1997; Van Dieten, 1991). Similarly, in probation offices there are individual differences in the level of socialization among probation staff and volunteers, and we have found that the anticriminal expressions of officers in interviews with their probationers link with the recidivism of their probationers (Andrews, 1980). Consultation and clinical experience also tell us that staff and managers are sometimes not attentive to their own expressions of antisocial attitudes. For example, some staff may develop a cynicism regarding the criminal justice system that is readily reinforced by clients. Some staff or volunteers may adopt "con talk" to show their clients how "down-to-earth" they can be and to gain their acceptance.

Procriminal expressions include the antisocial attitudes/procriminal sentiments to which we have repeatedly referred: the specific attitudes, values, beliefs, rationalizations, and techniques of neutralization that imply that criminal conduct is acceptable. These include: (a) negative attitudes toward the law, courts, and police; (b) tolerance for rule violations in general and violations of the law in particular; (c) identification with offenders; and (d) endorsement of exonerating mechanisms. Anticriminal expressions include: (a) an emphasis on the negative consequences of law violations for the offender, the victim, and the community at large, (b) rejection of, or placing more realistic limits on, "rationalizations" or "justifications" for law violations, and (c) expressions of the risks involved in associating with criminal others or in accepting their belief systems. As discussed in the previous section, some specific criminal acts, such as sex offenses, violent sex offenses, spouse abuse, and violence in general, have their own supporting cognitions and vocabulary to which workers must be sensitive.

Procriminal expression includes association with criminal others; anticriminal expression is reduced association with criminal others and increased association with anticriminal others. Procriminal expressions include continuing to seek out risky situations or circumstances (e.g., the same old bar scene) rather than avoiding them. The following examples of anticriminal expressions are based on the links between self-management and problem-solving skills in relation to criminal behavior: (a) probationers examining their own conduct, making a judgment about how well their behavior corresponds to their anticriminal values and beliefs or how well they are attaining their goals, and making self-evaluative comments "good"–"bad" depending upon how well the standards are being met; (b) thinking before acting, pausing to consider consequences of a given action; and (c) weighing the merits of alternative ways of behaving in a given situation. Procriminal expressions in this area include: (a) a lack of self-observation, self-evaluation, or self-monitoring; (b) evaluation against standards that are too severe, too lax, or frankly procriminal; (c) an insensitivity to or denial of significant problems; and/or (d) an inability to consider new ways of behaving in problem situations.

Attending sessions and doing the homework exercises following the treatment plan are also anticriminal expressions to be encouraged. One should watch out in particular for clients supporting the anticriminal efforts of other clients. When front-line staff support, rather than ignore or even ridicule, the anticriminal efforts of clients, this is an example of anticriminal modeling and reinforcement. When both staff and clients support expressions of anticriminal efforts, a therapeutic community of some criminological potency has been created. This element of correctional counseling speaks clearly to group and residential programming.

Two studies have assessed the procriminal/prosocial direction and reward-cost contingencies in the social interactions of delinquents and nondelinquents. Buehler, Patterson, and Furniss (1966) directly observed and behaviorally analyzed inmate-inmate and inmate-staff interactions in an institutional setting, while Dishion et al. (1996) videotaped the interactions of 186 boys ages 13 to 14 years. Both studies were powerful demonstrations that the contingencies of interaction within delinquent groups were procriminal. Rule-breaking talk was followed by reinforcement, and prosocial talk was punished by delinquent associates. A construct such as "subculture" is not needed to understand that when procriminal people are brought together in groups what is created is differential modeling, reinforcement, and punishment that favors procriminal expressions. When volunteers, staff, and managers are selected, trained, supervised, and rewarded without reference to their value in the process of anticriminal modeling and reinforcement, we may expect that contingencies favoring procriminal expressions will be maintained. This is especially the case when the model of treatment explicitly demands that the volunteers, staff, and managers *not* attend to procriminal expressions. The way to create anticriminal groups and residences is to select, train, supervise, and reward the nonclients (volunteers, staff, and managers) according to their value in the modeling and differential reinforcement of anticriminal expressions.

In good correctional practice, procriminal and anticriminal expressions are determined not just by standardized risk, need, and responsivity assessments but through individualized assessments of the criminogenic factors and situations that apply to particular individuals. Many expressions that we may like or not like for various professional, political, and ideological reasons are not typically criminogenic. Correctional programs should not attempt to produce "perfect people" according to some standard of perfection.

Many expressions are neutral with regard to criminal activity. Criminally neutral expressions are often confused with procriminal expressions. They include thoughts, feelings, and actions that are not associated in any functional manner with future criminal conduct. Thus, in the absence of any evidence to the contrary, indicators of self-esteem, vague feelings of emotional distress, generalized anxiety, low self-confidence, little interest in interpersonal fun and games, or preferring to be alone at times should be considered to be such neutral expressions. A particular problem for residential programs is the tendency to focus on maintaining housekeeping duties and schedules. Thus, being neat, clean, quiet, willing to clean toilets, and/or willing to go along with a particular program's emphasis upon sports, religion, "12 steps," or whatever, may gain more attention than anticriminal expressions that actually transfer to the chances of criminal behavior in the community.

Effective Workers. Workers who are successful with their clients: (a) establish high-quality relationships with them, (b) demonstrate anticriminal expressions (modeling), (c) approve of the client's anticriminal expressions (reinforcement), and (d) disapprove of the client's procriminal expressions (punishment), while at the same time demonstrating alternatives.

High-Quality Relationship Conditions. A high-quality interpersonal relationship creates a setting in which modeling and reinforcement can more easily take place. Important to such a relationship is an open, flexible, and enthusiastic style wherein people feel free to express their opinions, feelings, and experiences. Also needed are mutual liking, respect, and caring. The expression of disapproval is meaningful against a background of attentiveness, expressions of understanding ("real," not "phony"), mutual enjoyment of recreational activities, pleasant discussion, use of humor, and frequent contact. Most high-quality relationships are characterized by a shared agreement on the limits of physical and emotional intimacy. Openness, warmth, and understanding are offered within those limits.

Effective Modeling. The effective model:

1. Demonstrates behavior in concrete and vivid ways;

2. Takes care to illustrate the behavior in some concrete detail when only a verbal description is being offered;

3. Is rewarded himself/herself for exhibiting the behavior and makes specific reference to the rewards if only a verbal illustration is offered;

4. Rewards the person for exhibiting the modeled behavior or some approximation of it;

5. Is generally a source of reinforcement rather than only of punishing or neutral events;

6. Makes evident the general similarities between himself/herself and the other person (e.g., "I had a similar problem at your age");

7. Recognizes that the other person may have good reason to fear or distrust the modeled behavior and hence will model a "coping" as opposed to a "master" style (Officer: "I too was afraid to approach the teacher about my grades but, scared as anything, I went up and asked her about it," versus "I just walked up to her and . . .").

Effective Reinforcement. With a behavioral approach, there is no reason to believe that any one set of events will always function as reinforcers for all persons at all times. Thus, it is important that one who is going to influence behavior through reinforcement has a wide variety of potential reinforcers at hand. The characteristics of a high-quality relationship constitute just such a collection of reinforcers. Sometimes simply eye contact and statements that show the person is listening will be sufficient; at other times, there must be emphatic expressions of support and agreement. Sometimes more concrete events (such as a shared movie or shopping trip) will be the reinforcers. Generally, what we have described as a high-quality relationship constitutes one of the most widely applicable and powerful sets of reinforcers.

High-level reinforcement in an interpersonal situation includes the following elements:

1. Strong, emphatic, and immediate statements of approval, support, and agreement with regard to what the probationer has said or done (nonverbal expression, eye contact, smiles, shared experiences);

2. Elaboration of the reason why agreement and approval are being offered (i.e., exactly what it is you agree with or approve of);

3. Expression of support should be sufficiently intense to distinguish it from the background levels of support, concern, and interest that you normally offer;

4. While less important than Items 1, 2, and 3, the worker's feedback should at least match the probationer's statement in emotional intensity (i.e., be empathic), and his or her elaboration of the reason for support should involve some self-disclosure (i.e., openness).

With high-level verbal and gestural approval and with elaboration on the reasons for approval, there is an opportunity to demonstrate anti-criminal expressions while offering feedback. The officer's statement of approval may close with a gentle probe that encourages the probationer to explore further the issues involved in the anticriminal expression.

Effective Disapproval. Just as a high-quality relationship sets the occasion for effective modeling and reinforcement, so does it establish the conditions necessary for effective disapproval. Within the context of an open and warm relationship, disapproval may be delivered with less fear that the offender will try to avoid or escape future contact with the officer, and less chance of an aggressive response by the client. Within such a relationship, a simple reduction in the normal levels of expressed interest and concern may function as a punisher. Expressed disapproval is more punishing within an open and warm relationship than it would be in a relationship characterized by distrust and dislike. Finally, we have the "4-to-1" rule: give at least four positive supportive statements for every punishing one. Someone who is routinely austere, judgmental, and "proper" is likely to be avoided.

High-level disapproval in an interpersonal situation is characterized by:

1. Strong, emphatic, and immediate statements of disapproval, nonsupport, and disagreement with what the client has said or done (including the nonverbal: a frown, or even an increase in the physical distance between you and the client);

2. Elaboration of the reason why you disagree and disapprove (this is an opportunity to model an anticriminal alternative);

3. The expression of disapproval stands in stark contrast to the levels of interest, concern, and warmth previously offered the probationer;

4. The levels of disapproval should be immediately reduced and approval introduced when the probationer begins to express or approximate anticriminal behavior.

From the point of view of most correctional clients (and most volunteers and professionals), it would be silly to communicate a blind support for the criminal justice system in all of its day-to-day operations, to accept the notion that there are no situations under which criminal activity is reasonable, or to state that "crime never pays." At the same time, correctional workers who have direct contact with clients will be ineffective if they are explicitly nonsupportive of the system, enamored with the positive aspects of criminal activity, or accepting of the rationalizations for law violations. The effective correctional worker exposes the client to anticriminal alternatives, is able to distinguish between specific negative instances within the criminal justice system and its general ideals (e.g., between a particularly obnoxious cop and the role of the police), and can explore with clients the limits of the common justifications for criminal activity. Resource Note 7.2 provides a case illustration of correctional treatment.

Resource Note 7.2

Treatment of a High-Risk Offender

David was the second of five children. His mother was a quiet, hardworking woman; his father, though regularly employed, drank alcohol every night. When he drank, he would become physically violent with the family. Since birth, David was a difficult child. Temper tantrums were frequent and the "terrible twos" seemed to come much earlier for David. He hated school, his teachers, and his classmates. David repeated two grades, was truant often, and was expelled twice for fighting. His parents never came to scheduled meetings with the principal and school counselor. According to David's father, "he's just a little energetic; he'll grow out of it. Anyway, the most important things are learned in the real world, not school." David started stealing, first from his parents at age 7, and then shoplifting from merchants at age 8. By age 11, he was drinking; by 12, in a juvenile facility; at 13, hooked on sniffing glue.

When the psychologist met David, he was serving a 12-month sentence for breaking and entering. He was 22 years old and addicted to cocaine. The results of testing were as follows:

LSI-R Score	44 (probability of recidivism of 76%)
Depression	19 (high)
Procriminal Attitudes	32.4 percentile
Gough's So	21.8 percentile
Psychopathy	63.5 percentile
Anxiety	60 percentile

David came to see the psychologist because he claimed to be upset with himself and his life. He felt suicidal and tense. He could not sleep at night and suffered from headaches. A program of relaxation training and cognitive-behavioral therapy targeting self-defeating thoughts and increasing competency skills was started immediately. Two months later,

David reported feeling much better. He was sleeping well, there were no headaches, and he felt good about himself. Test results showed that anxiety and depression levels had decreased significantly.

David started to thank the psychologist for all his help, but the psychologist suggested that there was still some work to do. After two months, David thought that this psychologist was not "all that bad" and maybe it was worth listening to him (relationship principle). The psychologist pointed out to David that there had been no movement in the other test scores. The LSI-R shifted a bit to a score of 41, but there was virtually no movement on the procriminal attitude scales and measures of psychopathy. Perhaps if treatment focused on criminogenic needs, enough progress could be made to keep David out of jail. David, somewhat reluctantly, agreed.

A highly structured program was outlined (directive principle). He would be seen three times a week (risk principle) on an individual basis. David was a very manipulative person, so treatment within a group format was seen as an occasion for him to grandstand and try to control the session. Also, his reading was marginal (grade 7) and he exhibited borderline intelligence (IQ of 82). An individual therapy format fitted with the responsivity principle. The psychologist could observe David closely, ensure that he understood the discussions, and help him with his behavioral homework lessons.

Treatment focused on his procriminal attitudes in general and his attitudes supportive of drug-taking. Also, prosocial skill training was given (avoiding jail talk, making appropriate requests to staff, etc.). Because he was in prison, more concrete behavioral homework assignments dealing with avoiding criminal associates and crime opportunities could

Resource Note 7.2 *(continued)*

not be given (recall from the meta-analysis of treatment programs that the impact of treatment in closed settings is not as great as in the community). Treatment sessions consisted of systematic reinforcement of prosocial attitudes and behaviors as well as delivering interpersonally mediated costs for procriminal expressions of attitudes and behaviors. Skill training involved the modeling of the behavior by the therapist and the imitation of the behavior by David along with corrective feedback from the psychologist.

Three months after the treatment targeting criminogenic needs began, David was retested. Treatment continued, and after another three months, the tests were readministered. The results were as follows:

Test	Treatment Begins	3 months	6 months
LSI	41	36	35
		(percentiles)	
Psychopathy	63.5	45.5	35.4
So	21.8	49.2	64.2
Procriminal			
Attitudes	32.4	87.0	87.0
Identification			
with criminals	91.2	14.6	2.2

How real were these changes? Was David just giving the responses the therapist wanted? There were two pieces of evidence that suggested a more fundamental change in behavior. First, reports from correctional staff and other inmates noted changes. For example, at the two-month mark in treatment, David received an institutional misconduct citation. He assaulted another inmate who was bragging about his crimes and the drugs he took ("I was just trying to teach him a lesson, that he was ruining his life"). Obviously, there was still some room for progress. The second piece of evidence came from his postrelease behavior. At the time of his parole, David fell from the very poor category (76% probability of recidivism) to the poor category (57.3% probability of recidivism). During the two-year postrelease period, David was returned to prison once on a technical violation. His parole officer thought that "he was in danger of reoffending" and a preventive detention was ordered. He was rereleased from prison one week later and there were no further incidences.

Effective Use of Authority. Most workers in corrections are in a position of power and authority relative to the offender. Ineffective use of authority relies on monitoring for compliance with the rules and initiating negative sanctions when violations are detected. The effective style for authority figures is "firm but fair." Effective practices include monitoring but also entail respectful guidance toward compliance. We see this pattern as consistent with John Braithwaite's (1989) idea of "reintegrative shaming," but without the "shaming."

Skill Building Through Structured Learning. The important skills to be taught include problem-solving and other aspects of self-management (recall Chapter 5 on development) including cognitive self-change (Bush, 1995). The elements of structured learning are those outlined by Arnold Goldstein (1986): (1) describe the components of the skill in detail; (2) model or demonstrate the skill components; (3) arrange for reinforced practice of the skill components through role playing with corrective feedback; (4) extend learning opportunities through homework assignment; and (5) generally, provide opportunities to enhance the skill.

When the pleasures of crime reside deep in the very act, one needs to work on changing the motivation and enhancing the costs of the activity. When a full analysis of the contingencies of action reveals a repeated history of disregard for the rights of others with resulting serious harm, and reveals no areas of intervention of reasonable promise, justice professionals should advise authorities (courts and parole boards) of the results of their comprehensive assessment and let justice be done in a pure just deserts, incapacitation, or restorative sense. Although rare, there may be some contexts in which human service will not contribute to reduced reoffending with high-risk cases.

Knowledge Construction and Knowledge Destruction in Three Parts

Part One: Can the Contributions of Appropriate Treatment Survive Controls for Competing Variables?

We have noted how Mark Lipsey's (1989) meta-analyses provided estimates of the impact of methodological issues, threats to validity, and treatment variables on effect size. His analysis is important in dealing with the ongoing criticism that treatment effects can be explained away by nontreatment variables. Recall the antirehabilitation and treatment destruction techniques listed in Resource Note 2.5. If critics did not agree with the findings surrounding offender rehabilitation, then they claimed that the results were due to the quality of the design, the treatment was tried with a particular group of offenders and could not work with others, and the evaluation was flawed because the researchers who designed the program did the evaluation. Against this backdrop of knowledge destruction, Lipsey's analyses actually showed that treatment effects survived controls for the effects of the methodological variables that he measured and tested.

The findings from the Carleton University meta-analyses confirm what Lipsey and others have found. When methodological and implementation factors are considered, the effectiveness of appropriate treatment remains a viable, practical approach for dealing with criminal behavior. In the remaining sections of this text, the evidence for this conclusion is presented. We leave it to our readers to decide whether they are convinced by the analyses. As noted in Resource Note 7.1, we found that clinically and psychologically appropriate treatment was the single strongest correlate of effect size (the correlation with effect size was .42, $k = 374$). The mean effect sizes at each level of the four-level appropriate treatment were −.02 ($k = 124$) for punishment only or human service inconsistent with each of risk, need, and responsivity), .02 (human service adhering with only one of risk, need, and responsivity), .18 (human service in adherence with two of risk, need, and responsivity), and .26 (human service consistent with risk, need, and responsivity).

With appropriate treatment controlled, and a host of competing variables considered, only four variables enhanced the prediction of effect size over and above appropriate treatment. The four were "an evaluator involved in the design and/or delivery of service," "community based setting," "nonjustice ownership of program," and "referral to program by a justice person." The question addressed here is how clinically relevant and psychologically appropriate treatment relates to outcome when the four most powerful control variables are considered. The first row in Table 7.1 gives the average effect size for the four levels of treatment (least appropriate to most appropriate) while controlling for the effects of the four extra-treatment variables. The next three rows reveal the effect of treatment when conditions favor the enhancement of effect size. For example, appropriate treatment (coded 3) was positive and strongest when three or four of the control variables favoring a large effect size were present (mean effect size of .38). The average effect of most appropriate treatment was reduced when only two of the four control variables favored a large effect size (.22), but the mean effect of most appropriate treatment remained greater than the mean effect of less appropriate treatment (-.01). The mean effect of most appropriate treatment is very low when none or only one control variable favors a large effect size but, once again, even that low mean effect of treatment (.11) is much greater than the mean effect of the least appropriate treatment (mean effect size -.09).

Table 7.1.
Mean Effect Size by Appropriate Treatment and the Major Control Variables (k)

	Inappropriate		Appropriate		Correlation
	0	1	2	3	with Effect Size
Effect Size Adjusted for Involved Evaluator, Community Setting, Nonjustice Ownership, and Justice Referral					
	−.02 (124)	.03 (106)	.17 (84)	.25 (60)	.53***
Number of Major Control Variables Favorable to Large Effect					
None/One	−.09 (27)	−.02 (28)	.07 (23)	.11 (13)	.48***
Two	−.01 (88)	.03 (55)	.17 (25)	.22 (21)	.56***
Three/Four	.04 (9)	.06 (23)	.25 (36)	.38 (26)	.60***

*** $p < .001$
k = number of tests of treatment

In summary, clinically and psychologically appropriate treatment—as specified by the general personality and social learning perspective—outperforms alternative treatments whether the background conditions are favorable or unfavorable to reduced reoffending. We expect there are conditions under which clinically relevant and psychologically informed human service will not prove superior to alternative interventions. We look forward to tests of those limits of human service in justice and primary prevention contexts.

Part Two: How Applicable Are the Findings Regarding Appropriate Treatment with Different Types of Cases?

There is no limit to the setting, case-based, and other conditions that may be found to raise questions about conclusions regarding appropriate treatment. For example, with reference to the Carleton databank, there is not a single experimental study that speaks to the effects of treatment on the violent reoffending of older female sex offenders who have spent 20 years in a maximum-security prison. There are not even many studies that have examined outcome with female offenders of any age. To date, however, the robustness of the findings regarding the effectiveness of human service is impressive across reviewers, settings, and types of cases.

Tables 7.2 through 7.4 provide a modest look at the applicability of the principles of effective service in the total Carleton sample and in subsamples defined by age (younger), gender (women), and ethnicity (minority group member, nonwhite). It is obvious that rates of adherence with principles of effective treatment were robust, as were the correlation coefficients of adherence with effect size (Table 7.2). The importance of school/work, personal distress, and noncriminogenic interpersonal targets (see Table 7.3) remains unclear with women and minorities. In exploration of elements of core correctional practice (Table 7.4), the only evidence of weak general applicability was with the weakest of the correlates (advocacy/brokerage and effective authority) and with the smallest subsamples (women and ethnic minorities). These findings suggest that statistical power issues must be explored in view of the combination of small sample sizes and weak estimated effect sizes. It is too early to conclude that advocacy/brokerage and authority are unimportant with women and minorities. In our view, the overall dominant finding is the robustness of the major correlates of positive program outcomes.

Table 7.2
Rate of Adherence with Principle and Correlation of Adherence to Principle with Effect Size (ES) by Subpopulation

Principle	Total sample (k = 374)	Young (k = 193)	Female (k = 45)	Minority (k = 106)
Human Service				
% Adherence	73	76	78	63
Correlation with ES	.35	.31	.31	.29
Risk: Services Delivered to Higher-Risk Cases				
% Adherence	74	74	80	80
Correlation with ES	.17	.20	.40	.18
Criminogenic Needs: # of Criminogenic Needs Targeted Exceed Noncriminogenic				
% Adherence	45	29	47	41
Correlation with ES	.54	.52	.49	.41
General Responsivity: Social Learning/Cognitive Behavioral Strategies				
% Adherence	21	29	33	22
Correlation with ES	.40	.43	.38	.43
Clinically Appropriate Treatment (adheres to all four of the above)				
% Adherence	16	21	27	17
Correlation with ES	.55	.46	.56	.46

k = number of tests of treatment

Table 7.3
Percentage of Tests with Need Areas Targeted and Correlation with Effect Size by Subpopulation

Need Area	Total Sample	Young	Female	Minority
Criminogenic Needs Targeted				
Personal Criminogenic Targets: Antisocial Cognition and Skill Deficits				
% Adherence	26	33	18	29
Correlation with ES	.39	.39	.32	.33
Interpersonal Criminogenic Targets: Family and Associates				
% Adherence	19	23	31	15
Correlation with ES	.37	.33	.45	.34
Individualized Matching with Need (specific criminogenic needs not identified)				
% Adherence	17	19	07	12
Correlation with ES	.30	.30	.26	.28
School/Work				
% Adherence	24	26	16	21
Correlation with ES	.21	.23	−.08 (ns)	.10 (ns)
Substance Abuse				
% Adherence	10	03	11	08
Correlation with ES	.06 (ns)	.04 (ns)	−.01 (ns)	−.02 (ns)
Noncriminogenic Needs Targeted				
Personal Noncriminogenic Targets (personal distress, physical activity)				
% Adherence	46	45	24	40
Correlation with ES	−.18	−.20	−.03 (ns)	−.18
Interpersonal Noncriminogenic Targets (family process, not affection/supervision)				
% Adherence	12	17	13	13
Correlation with ES	−.25	−.20	−.23	−.16 (ns)

s = nonsignificant

Table 7.4
Elements of Core Correctional Practice (CCP): Percent of Tests with CCP Element Present and Correlation of CCP Presence with Effect Size

CCP	Total Sample (k = 374)	Young (k= 193)	Female (k = 45)	Minority (k = 108)
Relationship Skills of Staff				
% of tests	03	03	02	02
Correlation with ES	.26	.31	.32	.27
Structuring Skills of Staff				
% of tests	12	12	16	08
Correlation with ES	.37	.34	.56	.36
Effective Reinforcement				
% of tests	04	04	02	06
Correlation with ES	.25	.22	.45	.40
Effective Modeling				
% of tests	10	12	11	11
Correlation with ES	.36	.35	.29	.23
Effective Disapproval				
% of tests	02	03	02	03
Correlation with ES	.18	.19	.32	.17
Structured Skill Learning				
% of tests	10	11	16	08
Correlation with ES	.31	.37	.56	.38
Problem-Solving				
% of tests	12	12	11	11
Correlation with ES	.33	.29	.29	.23
Advocacy/Brokerage				
% of tests	14	19	04	12
Correlation with ES	.10	.16	.14 (ns)	.26
Effective Authority				
% of tests	04	02	04	03
Correlation with ES	.19	.13	.24 (ns)	.08 (ns)

ns = nonsignificant

Part Three: How Practical are the Findings for the Real World?

We have just seen that the variable "an evaluator involved in the design and/or delivery of service" enhanced the prediction of effect size but that it did not eliminate the effect of appropriate treatment. Some antirehabilitationists have interpreted the finding that effect sizes are larger when a researcher is involved as evidence of an artificial inflation of the effectiveness of treatment. Because many "evaluator-involved" studies are one-shot, demonstration studies with extensive training and supervision of staff, the treatment literature does not accurately represent what is really "out there." Careful training and supervision are indeed important factors—they speak to program integrity. Quay (1977) observed 25 years ago that the widely touted failure of Kassebaum et al.'s (1971) prison treatment program was likely due to the inadequate conceptualization of the program and the fact that the staff was poorly trained and did not believe in the efficacy of the treatment. Program integrity refers to the extent to which treatment staff actually do what they say they are going to do. In order to ensure that the program is consistent with the therapeutic principles and techniques, we can ask the following questions:

1. Is staff selected to enhance the effectiveness of treatment?

2. Is there a clearly defined theoretical model underlying the program?

3. Is there written documentation that lays down what is to be done?

4. Is staff trained to follow the model?

5. Are staff supervised and monitored during the delivery of the program?

6. Is the program delivered with appropriate intensity and in the manner it was designed to be delivered?

An examination of the Carleton University databank shows that indicators of program integrity are related to outcome across a range of offender samples (Table 7.5). Staff selection, training, and supervision; structured programming manuals; and a clearly specified model of human behavioral influence were all related to effect size. The exception was the monitoring of change on the intermediate targets and hours of service with minorities. However, controlling for program integrity factors did not diminish the impact of clinically appropriate treatment.

Lipsey (1999) confirms our general conclusion that well designed treatments, regardless of whether they are experimental "demonstration" projects, are valuable. He selected from his database of 400 juvenile treatment studies only those studies that were "initiated and supervised by personnel *other* than the researcher and implemented in ordinary youth service or juvenile justice settings" (emphasis added, p. 620). Lipsey's (1999) analysis of 196 "practical rehabilitative programs" led him to conclude that "rehabilitative programs of a practical 'real world' sort clearly can be effective" (p. 641).

Table 7.5
Mean Effect Size by Indicators of Integrity of Implementation and Service Delivery for Total Sample, Young Offenders, Female Offenders, and Minorities

Integrity	Total Sample (k = 374)	Young (k = 193)	Female (k = 45)	Minority (k = 105)
Staff Selected for Relationship Skills				
% of tests	03	03	02	02
Correlation with ES	.26	.31	.32 (ns)	.27
Staff Trained				
% of tests	45	54	44	35
Correlation with ES	.26	.32	.33	.34
Clinical Supervision of Staff				
% of tests	19	21	29	12
Correlation with ES	.21	.22	.51	.28
Number of Hours of Service				
% of tests	(reduced samples because of missing values)			
Correlation with ES	.20	.41	.45	−.08
Rated Appropriate Dosage				
% of tests	41	40	40	32
Correlation with ES	.05 (ns)	.11 (ns)	.28	.22
Printed/Taped Manuals				
% of tests	19	24	16	17
Correlation with ES	.30	.32	.26	.22
Monitor Process and/or Intermediate Change on Targets				
% of tests	39	48	44	30
Correlation with ES	.07 (ns)	.07 (ns)	.22 (ns)	.12 (ns)
Specific Model				
% of tests	54	59	56	45
Correlation with ES	.23	.27	.36	.18
New/Fresh Program				
% of tests	33	40	38	28
Correlation with ES	.20	.19	.26	.33
Small Program/Sample				
% of tests	36	45	58	38
Correlation with ES	.28	.19	.26	.22
Involved Evaluator				
% of tests	21	26	18	21
Correlation with ES	.41	.42	.62	.53

k = number of tests
ns = nonsignificant

The finding that programs do not need to be driven by researchers under methodologically rigorous conditions in order to be effective should be encouraging for many practitioners, policymakers, and the public. These factors do help to improve success (MacKenzie, 2000). However, they may help because of their impact on the design and delivery of appropriate treatment. After all, researchers not only like to demonstrate the effectiveness of their intervention through methodologically sophisticated designs, but they also invest considerable time into thinking about what should comprise the treatment and spend a great deal of time training and supervising staff in the delivery of treatment. All this said, is the considerable investment in treatment still worth it?

By now, the reader probably knows that our answer is a resounding yes. Our affirmation of offender rehabilitation is based on a number of factors (e.g., reduction in recidivistic crime saves human misery for the offender and potential victims, the alternatives of punishment for deterrence purposes and just deserts are unsatisfactory, etc.). Another practical advantage is the cost-benefits associated with effective treatment.

Our focus here is cost-*benefit* studies of treatment rather than cost-*effectiveness*. Cost-effectiveness may estimate the probability of an outcome, but it does not assign an estimate of the monetary value for the outcome. The simple question is: "How much does it cost to treat an offender who does not recidivate?" In a cost-benefit study, a monetary value is placed on the benefits of successfully treating an offender. For example, by successfully treating an offender rather than incarcerating him or her, we may avoid lost wages, welfare costs that may be needed to support the family of an incarcerated offender, and the "pain and suffering" of potential victims. Even such intangible costs such as "pain and suffering" can be estimated by reviewing recent jury settlements. For readers who wish to learn more about the techniques of cost-benefit analysis, we recommend an excellent "how to" book chapter by Mark Cohen (2001) along with Brandon Welsh and David Farrington's (2000a) comprehensive summary of the difficulties surrounding cost-benefit analysis.

The number of studies that have directly applied cost-benefit analyses to controlled evaluations of treatment programs is few. The number of studies falls between seven (Welsh & Farrington, 2000b) and nine (Farrington, Petrosino & Welsh, 2001). However, the following sampling of conclusions clearly demonstrates that offender rehabilitation programs have substantial cost-benefits:

- "monetary value of saving a high-risk youth [is in the order] of $1.7 to $2.3 million" (Cohen, 1998, p. 5)

- "if a 14 percentage point reduction in recidivism is achieved...this could result in an economic gain of $39,870 per prisoner, or $3.98 million for 100 treated prisoners" (Donato & Shanahan, 1999, p. 1)

- "our lowest plausible estimate for the dollar benefits of avoided criminal activity . . . was $26.42 million, or $10,918 per treatment client" (based on an analysis of 2,242 drug abusers; Rajkimar & French, 1997, p. 318)

The most important analysis, to date, on the cost-benefits of prevention and treatment is found in a report by Steve Aos, Polly Phipps, Robert Barnoski, and Roxanne Lieb (2001). Aos and his colleagues applied a cost-benefit analysis to 305 studies ranging from early childhood intervention programs to adult offender treatment studies. Their meta-analytic review provided both a positive conclusion, "(some) programs are good bets both to lower crime rates and to lower the net costs of crime to tax payers" (p. 5) and also a wealth of cost-benefit data on individual programs. Table 7.6 gives a few examples of some of the treatment programs discussed .

Table 7.6
A Sampling of the Economic Benefits per Offender of Treatment Programs

Program	k	Average Benefit ($) per offender	Range ($)
Multi-Systemic Therapy	3	81,789	31,661 – 131,918
Functional Family Therapy	7	36,608	14,149 – 59,067
Aggression Replacement Training	4	20,715	8,287 – 33,143
Moral Reconation Therapy	8	5,134	2,471 – 7,797
Reasoning and Rehabilitation	6	4,653	2,202 – 7,104

k = number of studies

From Aos et al., 2001

This brief review demonstrates that effective treatments can be delivered in real world settings. Appropriate treatments delivered with high levels of integrity can have significant impacts on recidivism and cost-benefits. Our knowledge of the principles of effective treatment and the program integrity/implementation factors has been valuable for the delivery and monitoring of offender program systems. We know a great deal about the pitfalls in implementing treatment programs and how to avoid some of them (Gendreau, Goggin & Smith, 1999, 2001). Our knowledge has led to the development of quantitative methods such as the Correctional Program Assessment Inventory for assessing how well a certain program adheres to the "what works" principles (Gendreau & Andrews, 2001; Latessa & Holsinger, 1998). In addition, program accreditation systems in Canada and the United Kingdom draw heavily on the literature and principles outlined in PCC (Wozniak, 2001). It is clear that the research literature on offender rehabilitation has translated well into everyday practice.

Summary

No longer is it possible to conclude that the empirical evidence regarding intervention indicates that direct human service does not work or that official punishment is promising. The evidence favoring rehabilitation in a justice context over a reliance on variation in criminal processing is overwhelming. Still, the number of evaluative studies of correctional service should continue to increase. While millions of young people were processed by juvenile justice systems during the last decades, the total number of treatment papers in the Whitehead and Lab (1989) review involved only 21 systematic studies of *appropriate* service. Were it not for behavioral psychologists, the total number of papers involving appropriate service would have been nine. Negatively, our expanded sample of tests includes an overrepresentation of studies of punishment without variation in service.

From a positive perspective, there is renewed interest, vigor, and sensitivity in the psychology of criminal conduct (Cullen & Gendreau, 2001; Caspi et al., 1994; Loeber & Farrington, 1998) and in correctional service and prevention (e.g., Andrews et al., 2001; Cullen, 2002; Gibbons, 1999; Sherman et al., 1997). Support for offender rehabilitation can be found not only among researchers but also from the people who work with offenders on a day-to-day basis, such as correctional staff and the public at large (Cullen, Fisher & Applegate, 2000; Roberts & Stalans, 1998). There are solid reasons to focus on the client in ethical and humane ways and on the quality of service delivered within just dispositions (Andrews, Zinger et al., 1990a:386-387). Primary prevention studies are also positive but few in number, and the most promising prevention approaches are actually based on highly targeted human service efforts. The final chapter will highlight positive developments in this regard.

Chapter 8

Getting Mean, Getting Even, Getting Justice: Punishment and a Search for Alternatives

When someone is hurt or wronged, the common response is to strike back. It occurs at both the individual and societal levels. Hurts are to be punished, but not unduly so. Fairness and justice must also apply. In almost all societies, punishment is a consequence of breaking the law and the application of punishment or negative sanctions is highly regulated. There are many purposes for punishment within the criminal justice system. They include retribution, denunciation of the act, and deterrence. In this chapter, we touch upon these varying purposes, but our focus will be on the deterrent function of punishment. That is, does punishment effectively inhibit criminal behavior?

Criminal Justice Sanctions and Just Deserts

Laws define unacceptable behaviors and set the penalties for engaging in those behaviors. For the sake of simplicity, we will use the term "sanction" to refer to the official application of punishment for breaking the law (more generally, sanctions can refer to both the approval and disapproval of behavior). Sanctioning criminal behavior follows two simple ideas. First, it is anticipated that sanctions will deter the individual (specific deterrence) and other members of society (general deterrence) from behaving illegally. Second, the sanction must fit the crime or the hurt caused by crime (this is the retribution purpose of punishment). A punishment should not be overly harsh or too lenient; it must be fair and just.

The United States now accounts for approximately one-quarter of the world's prison population (Walmsley, 2002). The U.S. incarceration rate of 700 per 100,000 has now surpassed Russia's (665 per 100,000). In 1999, more than 6 million people, 3 percent of the U.S. adult population, were either in custody or on probation or parole (Bureau of Justice Statistics, 2001). In California, the corrections budget is only slightly less than the budget for higher education (Currie, 1998; Meehan, 2000). One-third of the inmates in California prisons are there for technical violations of community supervision rather than new criminal offenses (Miller, 1995). Not only is imprisonment a common penalty, but many jurisdictions have introduced measures to make prisons as unpleasant as possible. It is not enough to limit freedom and remove offenders from their families and communities. The "no frills" prisons in the United States appear to take pride in outdoing each other in the deprivation of television, cigarettes, library and exercise facilities, and other "perks."

The most severe penalty, capital punishment, is enjoying a renewed popularity. In the United States, there were 3,527 inmates on death row by the end of 1999 (Bureau of Justice Statistics, 2001). In Texas, three people are executed each month, while Oklahoma, with one-sixth the population of Texas, was to set a "record" of eight executions in one month (*Ottawa Citizen*, 2001). Moreover, the application of the death penalty is not reserved for adults. Approximately 2 percent of persons under sentence of death were arrested when they were 17 years of age or under (Bureau of Justice Statistics, 2001).

Even community sanctions have become "tougher." At one time, the range of sanctions available to the courts was relatively modest.Generally, it was a fine, probation, or prison. Now there is an array of "intermediate sanctions." In addition to regular probation, there are intensive supervision programs that use urine testing for drugs and electronic bracelets to track the whereabouts of offenders. Sometimes offenders are required to spend a brief period in prison before beginning a probation sentence. As Erwin (1986:17) wrote, probation should be as "punishing" as prison.

It is unclear when exactly we started "getting tough" on crime. Most scholars place the beginnings at some time in the 1970s (Clear, 1994; Cullen & Gilbert, 1982). Francis Cullen and Karen Gilbert (1982) give an excellent and thoughtful analysis of the social-political conditions that were fertile grounds for a toughening of attitudes toward crime. The Vietnam war, the prison riot at Attica where prison guards were killed by a storming state militia, and the Watergate scandal all contributed to a general distrust of government to do the right thing. Add to these events rising crime rates, Martinson's (1974) "nothing works" evaluation of offender treatment, and academic criminology's anti-individual position, and we can understand the shift away from individualized rehabilitation programs to a reliance on punishment to deal with crime.

Mainstream criminological theory supported utilitarian models of criminal behavior. That is, people engage in criminal acts because crime pays. Therefore, to rid us of crime, the costs for crime must increase. The utilitarian model would also hypothesize that reducing the rewards for crime (forget about increasing costs) should also alter the probability of crime. In fact, the utilitarian model is not entirely inconsistent with the multiple options offered by the PIC-R model of criminal behavior (see

Table 8.1). Reducing criminal behavior can be achieved by shifting the rewards and costs for criminal *and* prosocial behavior. However, for many reasons, increasing punishment or the costs to crime (Cell B) was the preferred choice in U.S. criminal justice policy.

Table 8.1.
Decreasing the Chances of Crime

Behavior		Rewards		Costs
Criminal	(A)	reduce	(B)	add
Prosocial	(C)	add	(D)	reduce

A report of the Committee for the Study of Incarceration authored by Andrew von Hirsch (1976) proved to be influential. The report questioned the effectiveness of rehabilitation, the ability to predict criminal behavior, and the whole idea of "individuation" within a criminal justice context. Consequently, incarceration, except for rare situations, should have nothing to do with the potential danger an offender might pose or his or her likelihood of rehabilitation. Parole and indeterminate sentences, which rested so much in the rehabilitation of offenders, were unnecessary. Punishment has one purpose: deterrence. Furthermore, punishment is morally justified because people who do wrong *deserve* to be punished. The role of sanctions is to give the offender his or her "just deserts."

Criminal sanctions that were tailored to fit the crime and not the offender were presumed to deter future criminal behavior and lead to a fair and just criminal justice system. The United States went on a spree of adding sanctions and increasing the severity of sanctions. Limits were placed on judicial discretion with the introduction of sentencing guidelines and minimum mandatory penalties (von Hirsch, 1987). The state of Washington introduced a "three strikes and you're out" law in 1993, making life imprisonment mandatory for a third felony conviction. Three-strikes laws followed in California and 24 other states (Turner et al., 1999). Not to be outdone, a number of states (e.g., Georgia, Montana, South Carolina) made two strikes sufficient to merit life in prison without parole (Austin et al., 1999). Discretion at the "back end" of the criminal justice system was also curtailed by the abolishment of parole boards and the introduction of "truth-in-sentencing" laws. A "penal harm movement" (Clear, 1994) emerged with little consideration as to whether the promise of safer communities and a fairer system was achieved.

The Effects of Imprisonment on Crime

The "get-tough" approach to crime is reflected in laws with mandatory minimum penalties, longer prison sentences, and other efforts to make sanctions more unpleasant. We have always had mandatory minimum penalties, but they were limited either to very serious crimes such as an intentional act of murder or to a few specific crimes (e.g., brief periods of incarceration for impaired driving). What changed was that the list of offenses for which mandatory penalties were prescribed increased dramatically and the penalties became more severe.

Three-strikes laws and truth-in-sentencing legislation are the most common examples of the get-tough legislation. Three-strikes laws basically require a judge to give a life prison term after the third offense. Truth-in-sentencing laws require offenders to serve a minimum amount of their sentence (approximately 85% of the sentence) before release on parole or some other form of conditional release. Both types of legislation are usually intended to target violent offenders but, as we will soon see, this is not always the case.

The 1978 report of the National Academy of Sciences (Blumstein, Cohen & Nagin, 1978) questioned the value of indiscriminately imprisoning offenders. The value of incapacitation rested with selectively incapacitating the high-risk, high-frequency offender (i.e., "career criminal"). As we saw in Chapter 2, a number of longitudinal studies found that approximately 6 to 15 percent of offenders commit 50 percent of all crimes. This small but highly active group of offenders is the group that requires incapacitation.

The effectiveness of selective incapacitation depends on the ability to identify that small segment of offenders who commit the majority of crimes. Peter Greenwood (1982) constructed a seven-item prediction scale that, he claimed, would identify high-frequency robbers. Furthermore, imprisoning this group of robbers for eight years would reduce the number of robberies by nearly 20 percent. Greenwood estimated that selectively incarcerating the high-frequency offenders would lead to an overall 5 percent reduction in the prison population.

Unfortunately, Greenwood's claims were too good to be true. Jan Chaiken and Marcia Chaiken (1982), fellow researchers at the RAND corporation, re-analyzed Greenwood's data and concluded that neither robberies nor the prison population would be significantly affected. In a subsequent study, Visher (1986) reached a similar conclusion. Greenwood (Greenwood & Turner, 1987) himself also later tempered his estimates. However, it was too late. Many academics and the U.S. federal and state governments embraced the concept of selective incarceration.

The three-strikes laws are clearly products of a belief in selective incapacitation. Putting aside the difficulty in identifying high-risk offenders (Chapter 6 gives a fuller discussion of this topic), the results from three-strikes laws have been disappointing. First of all, the laws do not always target the violent offender. For example, in California, any felony crime (violent or not) counts toward the three strikes. As a result, approximately 20 percent of third-strike offenses in the state are drug-related (Meehan, 2000) and 60 percent are for a nonviolent offense (Austin et al., 1999). Second, the application of the law varies considerably across states. In California, 40,000 offenders have been given 25 years to life under three-strikes legislation while Florida has used similar legislation on 116 offenders (Turner et al., 1999). Even within one state, California, there are significant discrepancies in the use of the legislation among the counties (Austin et al., 1999; Meehan, 2000). The fact that one county would use the law more frequently than another raises suspicions that prosecutors are having undue influence over sentencing (Austin et al., 1999).

Two arguments in support of get-tough legislation are that it restores faith in the criminal justice system and it deters people from committing crime. Political leaders argue that the consequences for law violation must be quick and severe in order to ensure law and order. Furthermore, they say, this is what the public expects and wants. Whether the public really wants a get-tough approach depends upon how the question is posed. Public opinion surveys that ask very general questions (e.g., "Do you favor tougher sentences for criminals?") do find the majority of respondents agreeing to a get-tough approach. The public thinks poorly of parole, that courts are too lenient, and that prisons are "country clubs." However, when the public is given *choices* or more factual and detailed information, a less punitive attitude emerges (Cullen, Fisher & Applegate, 2000; Hough & Roberts, 1999).

A number of factors moderate what Cullen et al. (2000) call the "mushy" get-tough attitudes of the public. First, when questions are posed that provide alternatives to the most serious penalty (e.g., death penalty versus life in prison or incarceration versus rehabilitation), it is the minority who endorses the harshest alternative. If more detail is given about the crime (e.g., the robbery did not cause physical harm) or about the offender (juvenile or mentally disordered), then the public appears to become more understanding and tolerant. When questioned specifically about three-strikes laws, only 17 percent of sampled residents in Ohio would give life sentences to *all* offenders after the third strike (Applegate et al., 1996). A survey of 641 prison wardens found that only 21 percent thought that their prison should be more austere (Johnson, Bennett & Flanagan, 1997). Nonetheless, get-tough policies abound. It is understandable that the public cannot be informed on all facts related to public policy. However, it appears inexcusable to us that so many political leaders are neither well informed nor interested in educating their constituents.

With respect to deterrence and the reduction of crime, there is little evidence supporting get-tough interventions such as three-strikes and truth-in-sentencing laws. Researchers have not ignored the opportunity to evaluate these major criminal justice policies. What they found was that crime rates have not been affected. In one study, states were grouped into whether or not they had three-strikes and truth-in-sentencing laws. Contrary to expectations, the lowest general and violent crime rates were found in states that did *not* have either type of legislation (Turner et al., 1999). In analyses of the data from California, no decreases in crime, violent or petty, have been found (Austin et al., 1999; Stolzenberg & D'Alessio, 1997).

The tough laws have had other unintended effects. Crime rates have been falling in the United States and Canada throughout the 1990s. However, the prison population in the United States continues to rise rather than fall (Blumstein, 1998). This leads to an increase in correctional costs. Greenwood and his colleagues (Greenwood et al., 1994) estimated that California's spending on corrections would double by 2002. Other states are also expected to use proportionately more of their budgets to fund three-strikes and truth-in-sentencing provisions—all of this at the expense of crime prevention programs (Greenwood, 1998). In many instances, the cost of incarceration far outweighs the cost of crime, especially drug offenses (Austin et al., 2000). Even more alarming is that African-Americans are 13 times more likely to be imprisoned on a third strike than Caucasians (Schiraldi & Ambrosio, 1997).

When we consider the *general* literature on the impact of imprisonment on recidivism, it is not surprising that we do not find a deterrent effect with the three-strikes laws. A narrative review of the literature found that the severity or length of the sentence was unrelated to crime (von Hirsch et al., 1999). In a meta-analytic review of the literature, Paula Smith, Claire Goggin, and Paul Gendreau (2002) found longer sentences associated with a 3 percent *increase* in crime (see Resource Note 8.1). Prisons can impact on crime if we incarcerate for life everyone who commits a crime. Even if we were willing to embark on such a questionable economic and social experiment, we would still have crime. There are always children who grow up delinquent and who can easily "replace" those whom we imprison.

Resource Note 8.1

The Effects of Prison Sentences on Recidivism
(Smith, Goggin & Gendreau, 2002)

As with all negative sanctions, the imprisonment of offenders is expected to deter the offenders from further crime. Incarceration curtails personal liberty and deprives one from the pleasures normally enjoyed in daily life. These are thought to be punishing enough that when experienced, individuals would avoid the behavior that led to the punishment. If imprisonment does not deter, then perhaps the period of deprivation was simply not long enough to give the full impact of punishment. Penal policy over the past decade has clearly followed this argument. Society needs to increase the length of incarceration for various crimes in order to reduce recidivism. However, does increasing the time spent in prison really reduce recidivistic crime?

Paula Smith, Claire Goggin, and Paul Gendreau tried to answer this question through a meta-analytic review of the prison literature. Two types of studies were selected. There were 27 studies that compared community-based offenders (e.g., probationers) to inmates and 23 studies that compared prisoners serving longer sentences to inmates serving shorter sentences (e.g., inmates released on parole with inmates who were ineligible for parole). To be included in the review, there had to be a minimum of a six-month follow-up. Moreover, as with all meta-analytical reviews, the results had to be reported in a way that permitted the calculation of a common effect size.

Altogether, 57 studies representing more than 350,000 offenders were identified for

Resource Note 8.1 *(continued)*

analyses. Almost all the studies had methodological weaknesses. Only one study used random assignment. Despite the methodological problems with the studies analyzed, the general results confirmed the findings reported in the narrative literature review by von Hirsch et al. (1999).

Smith and her colleagues used the phi coefficient (ϕ) as their effect size indicator. Phi is a measure of association used with dichotomous data and its interpretation is similar to the Pearson correlation coefficient. The 57 studies produced 337 effect sizes. A summary of the findings is presented in the following table.

Type of Comparison	Sample Size	ϕ
Prison vs. community	268,806	.07
Longer vs. shorter time in prison	107,165	.03
All combined	375,971	.03

Regardless of the type of comparison, imprisonment was not associated with any decreases in recidivism. In fact, the results were the contrary. Offenders who were imprisoned had recidivism rates approximately 7 percent (ϕ = .07) higher than community-based offenders, and inmates with longer sentences had recidivism rate 3 percent (ϕ = .03) higher than inmates with shorter sentences. Considering all the studies together, imprisonment was associated with a 3 percent increase in recidivism.

Some penologists have suggested that prisons may be "schools for crime." Prisons bring offenders together where individuals are given opportunities to learn the techniques for crime and rationalizations for antisocial behavior. Low-risk offenders may be particularly vulnerable to an "indoctrination" into criminal patterns of thinking and behaving. High-risk offenders, on the other hand, do not need to learn any new tricks of the trade or receive further encouragement for their antisocial ideas. Smith and her colleagues tried to code, as best as they could, the risk levels of the offender samples found in the studies. They found no differential association between type of sanction (prison or community) and offender risk level.

To be clear, neither the authors of the report nor we are saying that there should be no prisons. Our sense of justice requires imprisonment for serious violations against society. Society needs to encourage a respect for law and demonstrate that some acts will not be tolerated. There are also some offenders who pose such an extremely high risk to reoffend violently that the only way to prevent harm is to incarcerate these offenders. However, those offenders requiring lengthy periods of confinement are a small proportion of the offender population. Advocates of imprisonment may argue that even if imprisonment does not deter, it at least takes them out of circulation and public safety is achieved. One area of research rarely considered is the antisocial behavior that goes on within prisons. Inmates and guards are assaulted, rapes occur, possessions stolen, contraband smuggled, and drugs abused. Crime on the street may be simply shifted to a different environment hidden from the public view.

Before moving on to evaluations of noncustodial deterrents, we would like to make a few comments on the deterrent value of the most severe form of punishment—the death penalty. Researchers studying the effects of the death penalty all agree that there is no impact on homicide rates or other violent crimes (cf., Bailey & Peterson, 1998). The studies include various methodologies, but they all reach the same conclusion. There are studies comparing homicide rates before and after the introduction of the death penalty (e.g., Decker & Kohnfeld, 1984, 1987) and comparisons of neighboring states with and without the death penalty (e.g., Sellin, 1980). None find a deterrent effect.

In regard to the use of capital punishment, an unsettling finding was reported by John Cochran, Mitchell Chamlin, and Mark Seth (1994). They found that murders by strangers actually increased following the resumption of executions in Oklahoma after 25 years of no executions in that state. Homicides involving acquaintances, friends, and family showed no change. Rather than deterring others from killing, "the reactivation of capital punishment produces an abrupt and permanent increase in the likelihood that citizens of Oklahoma will die at the hands of a stranger " (pp. 123-124).

Cochran et al. (1994) interpreted the increase of stranger murder as due to a "brutalization" effect. Essentially, the execution of offenders by the state "brutalizes society by legitimating lethal violence" (p. 108). Consequently, a stranger who finds himself or herself in a volatile situation has fewer inhibitions to use lethal violence. People who know each other have emotional/personal inhibitory controls. A more recent analysis of homicide statistics in Oklahoma by William Bailey (1998) reconfirmed the brutalization hypothesis. Despite the evidence, the death penalty is enjoying a renaissance of sorts, with 38 states having the death penalty and executing more people in 1999 ($n = 98$) than any other year since the 1950s (Snell, 2000).

Evaluations of Intermediate Sanctions

Twenty-five years ago, judges had essentially two sentencing options: prison or probation. However, in the 1980s, because of the pressure of overcrowded prisons, alternatives to the two extremes of the punishment continuum were sought. Sanctions were needed that were harsher than probation but not as severe or costly as prison. Alternative punishments were to give judges more choices in order to properly fit the crime to the punishment and achieve a "rational" sentencing system (Canadian Sentencing Commission, 1987; Morris & Tonry, 1990; Tonry & Lynch, 1996).

The most well-known forms of intermediate sanctions are Intensive Supervision Programs (ISP), shock incarceration (e.g., boot camps, Scared Straight), and electronic monitoring programs. Georgia was the first state to introduce an ISP in 1982. At the time, Georgia had the highest incarceration rate in the United States. However, simple probation would not do. Instead what was needed were probation sentences "to increase the heat on probationers in order to satisfy the public demand for just punishment" (Erwin, 1986:17). The ISP in Georgia consisted of 25 offenders supervised by two officers—a probation officer who did the counseling and case management and a "surveillance" officer who checked curfews, conducted drug tests, and made unannounced home visits. There was a minimum of five face-to-face contacts. Within a decade, almost every state had an ISP (Cullen, Wright & Applegate, 1996).

Shock incarceration programs expose offenders to the harshness of prison life with the hope that it will shock them away from a criminal lifestyle. The most popular form of shock incarceration is the military-style boot camp. Once again, Georgia holds the distinction of opening the first shock incarceration/boot camp in the United States (a Special Alternative Incarceration program or SAI was opened in 1983). Georgia's SAI involved military-style drills and long hours of physical labor each day. There was no treatment. Although other boot camps had a counseling/treatment component, it was the drills, exercise, and labor that consumed eight or more hours of the day (Parent, Chaiken & Logan, 1989). By the mid-1990s, there were 35 states with boot camps (Camp & Camp, 1997). Boot camps were also established in the Canadian provinces of Manitoba and Ontario and in the United Kingdom (Farrington et al., 2000).

One variant of shock incarceration was New Jersey's Juvenile Awareness Project, more popularly known as "Scared Straight." Youths visited "lifers" in Rahway State Prison, where the inmates described to their audience, in colorful detail, the horrors of prison life. This "shock confrontation" approach was intended to show the youths what would happen if they followed a life of crime. A television documentary popularized the program and led to similar projects in other parts of the United States, Canada, and Europe (Finckenauer et al., 1999).

Electronic monitoring programs have an interesting origin. Judge Jack Love of New Mexico was reading a *Spiderman* comic book in which the villain attached an electronic monitoring device to track Spiderman. This allowed the criminal to carry out his crimes when Spiderman was not around. Why not, thought Love, turn the tables and put electronic bracelets on the criminals so that the authorities would know their whereabouts? Thus was born electronic monitoring (EM). Today, EM programs can be found throughout the United States, Canada, and Europe (Schmidt, 1998; Whitefield, 1999).

None of these intermediate punishments have demonstrated reductions in recidivism. Furthermore, under certain conditions, these programs have made matters worse by increasing recidivism and correctional costs. A brief summary of the evaluation literature follows.

Early evaluations of ISP often used prisoners as the comparison group and showed ISP participants in a favorable light. However, when ISP offenders were offenders under normal probation, the reconviction and rearrest rates were very similar. Joan Petersilia and Susan Turner (1993) conducted a large-scale evaluation of 14 ISP programs involving 2,000 adult offenders. Offenders were *randomly* assigned to an ISP, prison, or probation/parole group. A one-year follow-up found 37 percent of the ISP offenders rearrested compared to 33 percent of the controls. Not surprisingly, given the close monitoring of ISP participants, the ISP offenders were more likely breached with technical violations (65% vs. 38%). Reductions in recidivism in the range of 10-20 percent were found, however, in ISPs that provided treatment to the offenders. Finally, they found that ISPs cost more per offender than for the control group ($7,200 vs. $4,700 per year).

Evaluations of shock incarceration and boot camps have also found that treatment is required in order to find reductions in recidivism. Doris MacKenzie, Robert Brame, David McDowall, and Claire Souryal (1995) examined eight state boot camps. Although groups were not randomly assigned, additional statistical controls were introduced for factors that could have influenced recidivism. One-half of the programs evidenced lower re-arrest rates than the controls, but reductions in recidivism were associated with the boot camps that had a treatment component. Their conclusion: "military drill and ceremony, hard labor, physical training, and strict rules and discipline . . . in and of themselves do not reduce recidivism" (p. 351). More recent evaluations of boot camps have not altered this conclusion. In one study, new arrests were actually higher for the boot camp participants than for regular probationers (50.8% vs. 32.5%; Jones & Ross, 1997).

The New Jersey "Scared Straight" program was evaluated by James Finckenauer and his colleagues in the late 1970s. Forty-six juveniles who visited lifers in prison were compared to 35 control subjects. The first evaluation found no impact on attitudes to crime or the criminal justice system (Finckenauer & Storti, 1978). A six-month follow-up by Finckenauer (1979) found that the youths who attended the Rahway program had higher rearrest rates (41.3%) than the youths who were not exposed to the program (11.4%). Surprisingly, 19 of the 46 youths attending the program did not even have a prior criminal record, and their recidivism rate was 31.6 percent. Despite the contra-indicative findings, similar programs were developed in other U.S. jurisdictions and in the United Kingdom, Australia, and Norway. Evaluations of many of these programs have shown that none of them reduced recidivism and a few even produced harmful effects (Finckenauer et al., 1999; Petrosino, Turpin-Petrosino & Finckenauer, 2000).

Finally, there are the electronic monitoring (EM) programs. EM was supposed to be an "alternative" to imprisonment. Instead of a prison sentence, the offender was given a community sentence and required to stay at home ("house arrest"). An electronic signaling device, usually attached to the ankle, permitted monitoring of the offender's location from a probation office. Leaving the home, without permission, would set off an alarm and the authorities would seek the apprehension of the offender.

Research on EM has found three general results. First, most EM programs do not offer an alternative to prison. Offenders in these programs are often low-risk offenders who would have received a community-based sanction anyway. That is, EM programs, like many intermediate sanctions, appear to widen the correctional net applying more rather than less controls (Cullen et al., 1996). Second, EM does not reduce recidivism. For example, a quasi-experimental study of three Canadian EM programs by Bonta, Wallace-Capretta, and Rooney (2000b) found that it was offender risk factors that accounted for variations in recidivism; electronic monitoring had no effect. Third, and consistent with the findings reported earlier, adding a treatment component to EM appears associated with reduced recidivism (Bonta, Wallace-Capretta & Rooney, 2000a).

The Unfulfilled Promise of Fairness

Andrew von Hirsch and others have argued that the predictability of mandatory sentencing policy would reduce reliance on incarceration and bring fairness into the criminal justice system. Judges would be required to operate with set sentencing guidelines that matched the punishment to the crime and not the person. Thus, a similar act committed by different people would receive the same consequence. With respect to reducing the use of imprisonment, the evidence is mixed (D'Alessio & Stolzenberg, 1995; Moody & Marvell, 1996). When it comes to achieving fairness, one does not have to search for long to find examples in which fairness was clearly not achieved. Austin et al. (1999) presented a few "typical" cases from interviews with 100 three-strikes offenders. One offender received 27 years for attempting to sell stolen property valued at $90; another received 25 years for reckless driving (a police car chase). Currie (1993) describes a first-time offender who received life without parole for possession of 5.5 ounces of crack cocaine.

Some may see these examples as nothing more than exceptions to the rule and believe that for most offenders, fairness operates. Analyses of the racial composition of arrestees and prisoners suggest otherwise. With America's "war on drugs," drug crimes are targeted by the police, and this had differentially affected ethnic minorities. General arrest rates are four times higher for African-Americans than for whites, and the discrepancy widens for drug offenses (Daly & Tonry, 1997). In addition to differential arrest practices, mandatory prison sentences for most drug offenses have also affected minority groups. About one-half of the U.S. prison population is comprised of ethnic minorities.

Travis Pratt (1998) conducted a meta-analysis of the research on race and sentencing. The studies reviewed involved more than 48,000 offenders and produced 47 effect size estimates. His analysis is instructive in that it also partly explains why many early studies did not find a relationship between race and sentencing. When race was measured as "black/white," there was a nonsignificant correlation with length of sentence ($r = .07$). Seriousness of the offense was the best predictor of sentence length ($r = .36$). Thus, it appears racial discrimination plays a minimal role in court sentencing. However, African-Americans no longer represent the only significant minority group in the United States, Hispanic and Native Americans represent other important groups. When race was recoded as "white/nonwhite," then race became a significant factor in sentencing and the influence of criminal history and offense history disappeared (r values were not given for this analysis).

The importance of differentiating within racial/ethnic groups is reinforced in a study by Michael Leiber (1994). Leiber analyzed nearly 2,000 youth cases that passed through the courts in Iowa. He found that African-Americans received harsher sentences than whites. Native Americans also received more severe sentences than whites but not as severe as the African-American youths.

Racial bias has also been reported in the application of the death penalty. One-third of persons executed in 1999 and 40 percent of the inmates on death row were black (African-Americans represent approximately 12% of the population). Aguirre and Baker's (1990) review found that blacks, especially if the victim was white, were more likely to receive the death penalty.

Finally, it appears that mandatory sentencing policies have affected female offenders. Historically, female offenders have enjoyed leniency from the courts. Daly and Bordt (1995) found 45 percent of the 50 court data sets that they reviewed favored women in sentencing. Sentencing guidelines, however, require that criminal acts are treated equally and render personal factors (e.g., gender) inconsequential.

Daly and Tonry (1997) have noted that when sentencing guidelines are introduced, there are three possible options. First, sentences can be reduced for men to bring them more in line with the sentences women receive. Second, sentences for men and women can converge to some midpoint. Third, sentences can increase for women. It appears that our appetite for punishment has led to the third option. An early evaluation of Minnesota's sentencing guidelines found that the sentences for women increased under the guidelines (Knapp, 1984). A similar result has also been reported with implementation of Oregon's sentencing guidelines (Bogan & Factor, 1995).

Breaking Bad Habits

It is astonishing that in spite of the negative findings, criminal justice sanctions still remain wildly popular. Legislators trip over each other in trying to come up with harsher penalties, criminologists continue to conduct studies hoping to find that deterrence will work, and programs are made more demeaning. There is no shortage of ideas. In New Jersey, offenders were made to dress in woman's clothes in order to tear down macho attitudes (Wilson, Goldiner & Mickle, 1993). Graeme Newman (1995) has proposed to replace prisons with corporal punishment, preferably with electric shocks. Prisons would be a last resort and only after corporal punishment has failed to deter the offender—"there is no more getting off lightly with corporal punishment" (Newman, 1995:179).

A number of factors operate to keep punishment entrenched in criminal justice policy. First, people *believe* in the effectiveness of punishment (Thomas & Foster, 1975). Second, politicians and legislators, rightly or wrongly, think that being "tough on crime" is what the public wants. As a result, few politicians are willing to take the risk of losing elections by acting on evidence about what does reduce recidivism. Third, rehabilitation is seen as being soft on crime and not effective. Once again, few political leaders appear prepared to convince the public on the effectiveness of offender treatment. Finally, and borrowing from a point made by Finckenauer et al. (1999), the lack of awareness on the research facilitates program inertia. Many practitioners either do not have the time or the inclination to evaluate their programs or to keep abreast of the research. Once a politically popular program is up and running, it does not take much for it to keep going.

The get-tough approach has failed to deliver on the promises of improved public safety, cost efficiency, and social justice. We see a need for a Winston Churchill who, when he was Home Secretary and responsible for prisons and the police, was known as the "prisoner's friend" (Gardner, 2000). Churchill chastened judges for passing sentences that were too long, limited the use of solitary confinement, and ensured that prisoners were provided with entertainment, education, and meaningful work. Without such leadership it will indeed be difficult to diminish our dependence on get-tough policies.

Why Doesn't Punishment Work?

The answer to the question "why doesn't punishment work?" can be found in the hundreds of studies conducted by psychologists. We know a great deal about the conditions under which punishment inhibits behavior. This knowledge comes from laboratory and applied studies with animals and humans. Unfortunately, as our colleague Paul Gendreau points out, these studies are rarely cited in the criminological deterrence literature. If only the deterrence advocates would have read this literature, then we may not have embarked on such a frustrating course of criminal justice policy. To us, the ineffectiveness of get-tough policies reveals the need for a psychology of criminal conduct in the formulation of criminal justice policy.

In this section, we summarize what is known about the effectiveness of punishment. For a more detailed discussion, the interested reader is referred to other sources (Azrin & Holz, 1966; Johnston, 1972). Punishment is defined as a consequence to a behavior that decreases the likelihood of the behavior from reoccurring. There is no mention of pain or suffering, the feelings and emotions that most people associate with punishment. *Any* consequence to a behavior, obviously painful or not, that reduces the probability of the behavior is a punishment.

As we outlined earlier in PIC-R (see Chapter 4), there are two types of consequences to behavior: rewards and costs. Furthermore, rewards and costs consist of additive or subtractive stimuli. Additive costs are what come to mind when most people think about punishment. Adding a noxious or painful stimulus (e.g., spanking a child, yelling at an employee, delivering an electric shock to a rat) is expected to inhibit or reduce the probability of behavior. However, removing a reward or something valued (i.e., a subtractive cost) can also decrease the probability of behavior. Giving your partner "the cold shoulder" or sending a misbehaving child to his or her room ("time out") are examples of subtractive costs.

The literature on the effectiveness of punishment is rich and the types of punishments used in experiments are varied. The majority of studies use electric shock because of the high degree of control over its intensity and duration. However, there are studies using unpleasant odors, submerging a hand in freezing water, puffs of air to the eye, loud noises, removing money, placing children in a room away from rewards (time-out), forcibly repeating certain physical movements (overcorrection), and thinking of disgusting and unpleasant thoughts (Matson & Kazdin, 1981).

Based on this literature, we present a brief summary of the important conditions for effective punishment, along with a commentary on the relevance of the research to the crime problem.

Condition 1: Maximum Intensity

It is unclear whether the intensity of punishment is the most important factor in suppressing behavior, but it certainly ranks, along with immediacy, as one of the more important (Van Houten, 1983). At first blush, this last statement seems to say that if we simply "turn up the heat," then we can stop criminal behavior. However, it is not simply turning up the intensity dial. Studies suggest that we have to turn the dial to full to stop behavior effectively.

In general, low levels of punishment do show an immediate suppression of behavior; however, the effects are temporary (Azrin, 1956). The behavior not only returns to its original levels but it may even result in higher rates of responding. This then necessitates further increasing the intensity of punishment in order to suppress behavior. Once again, the inhibitory effect is temporary, and an escalating cycle of punishment is required. Apparently, the subject learns to tolerate punishment (Solomon, 1964). In most Western countries and for most offenders, sanctions are increased gradually. For example, the first-time offender who commits a minor nonviolent crime is likely to receive probation; only with return to the court for new crimes does the penalty increase.

Producing complete behavior suppression requires *immediate* delivery of *very intense* levels of punishment (Azrin, Holz & Hake, 1963; Johnston, 1972). Retributionists may propose to give offenders the maximum penalty right off the bat. As we have already seen, in some jurisdictions, we are already close to doing just that (e.g., three-strikes and two-strikes laws).

The problem with a policy of maximum punishment for a crime is that it offends our sense of justice and fairness. Imagine if we administer life imprisonment for the rapist, bank robber, pickpocket, income tax cheater, and jaywalker. Would most of us consider this to be fair punishment? Formalized systems of criminal justice try to follow a principle of proportionality (match level of punishment to the severity of the crime). The option of maximum punishment is unacceptable to most.

Condition 2: Immediacy

The sooner the punishment follows the behavior, the more likely that the behavior will be suppressed. Introducing a delay between the behavior and the punishment can significantly alter the effectiveness of the punishment (Deluty, 1978; Dinsmoor, 1998). Why is this? It is mainly because there are opportunities for the behavior to be reinforced prior to the delivery of punishment (Skinner, 1953). One has to think of behavior as a chain of responses. The last response in the chain may be punished, and this may have some effect on the preceding responses, but the suppression effect diminishes the further the response is from the punishment.

To illustrate what could happen, consider an offender who is caught breaking into a car (the behavior) and is arrested and placed in a police cell (the punishment). What has the offender learned? Perhaps he or she learned that it is not worth opening a car door with a crowbar. However, the punishment will unlikely affect the behaviors leading up to the crime (e.g., visiting criminal friends, smoking some drugs, and then going out for a little excitement). We can go one step further and imagine that the offender is released on bail. What happens then? While waiting for trial, he or she may still associate with criminal others, abuse drugs, and may even have occasion to commit undetected crimes.

Condition 3: Consistency

One theory regarding why punishment "works" is called avoidance theory (Dinsmoor, 1954, 1998). Simply stated, punishment elicits an undesirable emotional response (fear, anxiety) and by not engaging in the behavior that produces punishment, the organism avoids the unpleasant emotion. Behavior is inhibited because it avoids something unpleasant. However, anxiety and fear do not last forever. The physiological responses that we label as anxiety and fear (e.g., increased heart rate, sweating, etc.) dissipate. It is as though we forget how bad the punishment was; to be reminded, it is important that the undesirable behavior is punished every time it occurs.

Unlike rewards, with which infrequent or unpredictable reinforcement (referred to as variable ratio or interval schedules) lead to high-rate and stable behavior, allowing an undesirable behavior to go unpunished once in a while is counterproductive. People and animals *behave*; they rarely sit still. The criminal must be caught every time he or she commits a crime and not be allowed opportunities to engage in other unwanted behavior that may be reinforced.

Consistency is also important in the development of discriminative stimuli. A stimulus that is associated with the presence or absence of a reward or a punishment provides informational value regarding the outcome for a particular behavior. When a student walks into a classroom, he or she knows that looking attentive, taking notes, and asking reasonable questions will produce reinforcement (e.g., praise from the teacher, good marks, respect from fellow students). Engaging in other behaviors (e.g., sleeping, eating, talking) will probably be punished. Dealing drugs while a police cruiser is driving by increases the probability of punishment. Both the classroom and the police cruiser function as discriminative stimuli and *signal* the types of outcomes that are likely to occur given certain behaviors.

Stimuli acquire a discriminative function through associations with outcome. The more frequently behavior is paired with an outcome, the more likely that situational stimuli will cue the person to behave in a certain way. Take for example, a person who is allergic to seafood. Every time he or she eats seafood, vomiting ensues. After a few of these experiences, the mere sight of fish may trigger avoidance behavior. Of course, the intensity of the punishment will affect the speed of discrimination learning. Mild nausea to certain foods may take more trials than a violent physical reaction.

Condition 4: No Escape or Reinforced Alternatives

When an organism is punished, efforts are made to escape the situation. By escaping from an aversive situation the following two results are possible: (1) escape behavior is reinforced and (2) the original behavior may continue because the organism now finds itself in a nonpunishing situation (Van Houten, 1983). The behavioral outcome may be desirable (e.g., a child leaves a group of children who are teasing him about his interest in books to read in the library). Alternatively, the outcome could be undesirable (e.g., an inmate escapes from custody to rob again). Thus, a situation associated with punishment may serve as a cue to engage in escape behavior. To deal with such a situation, all routes to escape must be blocked.

We made the point earlier that people are behaving organisms. Behavior consists of a multitude of specific responses to our environment. Individuals have behavioral repertoires. For example, an individual may have the skills to read, cook an omelet, and paint murals. The activation of a certain set of behaviors depends upon whether the behavior is likely to be reinforced. It is unlikely that the person will read aloud a book to an empty classroom, cook a meal on an autobus, or paint a mural on the side of a stranger's house. The behaviors would not be reinforced in these situations. People choose behaviors that they think will produce rewards and if one behavior does not work, then they choose another from their bag of behavioral skills.

In any particular situation, an individual needs to make choices regarding what behavior to use. A young man who is introduced to an attractive woman may choose from his behavioral skill repertoire those behaviors that he thinks may gain her admiration. Should he smile, engage in polite conversation, or show her his tattoo of "Mom"? All of these behaviors may be in his repertoire, but they do not have equal chances of being rewarded. Psychologists talk of a hierarchy of behaviors. In any given situation, an organism has behaviors that form an ordering of their likelihood of being reinforced. The most likely behavior to occur in a specific situation is one that has the longest history of reinforcement in similar situations and the other behaviors follow according to their reinforcement histories. The young man in our example may start with the behavior that was most successful for him in the past. However, if the behavior is met with a frown, then he resorts to another behavior that was perhaps not as successful in the past but may work this time. Thus, a punished response is not simply eliminated; it is displaced by another response (Dinsmoor, 1955).

Antisocial behavior consists of many different specific acts. A chronic offender exhibits many different undesirable behaviors (e.g., dishonesty, physical aggression, thievery, etc.). Punishing one behavior (e.g., the dishonesty associated with fraud) leaves many other behaviors that could be used to achieve personal goals. As a consequence, unless reinforcement of alternative antisocial behaviors is unavailable, criminal behavior, in one form or another, will continue.

Condition 5: The Density of Punishment Must Outweigh the Density of Reinforcement

Very few behaviors produce only rewards or only costs. Most behaviors have both rewards and costs associated with them. Going to work everyday may produce money and workplace friendship, but it also involves getting up in the morning, fighting rush-hour traffic, and coping with other irritants. Azrin et al. (1963) observed that a behavior with a significant history of reinforcement was more resistant to the effects of punishment than a behavior with a limited history of reinforcement.

This has been observed many times and is reflected in PIC-R. The greater the density of reinforcement associated with behavior in terms of intensity, immediacy, consistency, and variety, the greater the density of punishment required to suppress behavior. High-risk offenders have high densities of reinforcement associated with their criminal behavior and, thus, their behaviors are highly resistant to punishment.

Condition 6: The Effectiveness of Punishment Interacts with Person Variables

Principle 4 of PIC-R states that the effects of reinforcement *and* punishment interact with a wide range of person factors (e.g., biological, cognitive, state conditions). In other words, people react differently to punishment (inter-individual differences) and even from one moment to another (intra-individual differences). A few days in jail may present very different costs for the individual who lives on the street versus the white-collar criminal. A verbal reprimand would have different effects depending upon whether an individual is intoxicated. Threats of future punishment would be relatively meaningless for the impulsive person with poor planning skills.

What does this say about the effectiveness of punishment with offenders? Many offenders evidence poor self-regulation skills (Gottfredson & Hirschi, 1990). Their thinking tends to be concrete and oriented to the present situation. A childhood history of erratic and frequent punishment is common and may produce a certain level of tolerance for punishment. Some offenders have biological-temperamental traits that make them unresponsive to punishment. Theories of psychopathy and antisocial personality hypothesize deficits in the physiological mechanisms underlying fear and anxiety (Eysenck, 1998; Lykken, 1995).

Inhibiting behavior requires judgments of the likelihood of certain outcomes. To the dismay of economic and rational choice theories of crime, offenders (and people in general) do not operate like computers. They do not always weigh the pros and cons of behavior carefully and accurately before making their choice. Studies of offenders show that they tend to underestimate the chances of being punished and overestimate the rewards of crime (Montmarquette & Nerlove, 1985; Piliavin et al., 1986). Finally, when we consider some of the developmental experiences of many offenders—abuse and neglect—where is the logic that more of the same will suppress antisocial behavior? For punishment to be effective, one of the necessary conditions is that it must be matched to characteristics of the offender. In our criminal justice system, a matching that depends on personal factors would violate the principles of fairness.

The Side Effects of Punishment

Even if we could replicate the conditions for effective punishment in the real world, we are still faced with what Skinner (1953:190) referred to as the "unfortunate by-products of punishment." Punishment may suppress behavior, but it can also lead to unintended and undesirable behaviors. A brief review of the "side effects" of punishment (Newsom, Favell & Rincover, 1983) should give us further reasons to consider non-punishment alternatives to deal with antisocial behavior.

Punishment is a noxious stimulus with usually painful physical, emotional, or psychological qualities. It is the avoidance of pain that explains why punishment suppresses behavior. A painful stimulus however, may produce other consequences than simply suppressing a certain behavior. First of all, a painful stimulus of sufficient intensity may interfere with other *desirable* behaviors. A severe beating suffered by woman at the hands of a male partner may prevent her from socializing with friends, going to work, and enjoying recreational activities. When punishment is pervasive during childhood, social and emotional development is often impaired.

Second, if intense punishment is coupled with a situation in which there is no escape, then there is the risk of developing "learned helplessness" (Seligman, 1975). Martin Seligman (1975) exposed dogs to frequent shocks in a box with an electric floor that provided no opportunity to escape. After a number of trials, the dogs in the experimental group were then placed in another box where a partition was low enough to permit them to jump to the other side and avoid the shocks. The dogs in the control group, which did not have the experience of unavoidable shock, quickly learned to jump over the partition and avoid further shocks. The dogs in the experimental group, however, whined and laid down in a corner, making no attempts to escape. They learned that there was nothing they could do to avoid the shocks. This learned helplessness forms the basis for some models of human depression (Joiner & Wagner, 1995; Seligman, 1975) and coping models of stress (Mikulincer, 1994).

The concept of learned helplessness highlights the importance of self-efficacy beliefs and cognitive attributions. In the learned helplessness paradigm, the individual learns that he or she has no control over the environment. Whatever happens is attributed to fate or luck. Nearly 50 years ago, Miller (1958) hypothesized a belief in fate as a "focal concern" for delinquents. By attributing consequences to fate, taking responsibility for behavior can be minimized. There are other attributional styles that can be triggered by punishment.

When people have pain inflicted upon them, they make attributions as to why they were punished. One attribution is that it is fate and there is nothing that can be done about it. Another attribution is that individuals may view their actions as inappropriate and the punishment as deserving. That is, they accept the fact that the behavior should be punished either for their own good or the good of maintaining social order.

This attribution is dependent upon a commitment to prosocial values and respect for the law, a problematic area for many offenders.

If the punishment is viewed as unfair and undeserving, then anger and hate toward the punisher or feelings of rejection may be elicited. These negative emotions facilitate undesirable behaviors such as aggression toward the punisher or ignoring any attempts at influence by the other (Church, 1963; McCord, 1997). Painful punishment is found associated with reflexive aggression in animals and humans. Children who judge the disciplining techniques of parents as harsh tend to avoid parental contact, which further interferes with socialization efforts (Deater-Deckard & Dodge, 1997).

Modeling is a highly important and effective process for learning new behaviors. Bandura and Walters (1959) demonstrated that children may imitate the aggressive disciplinary practices displayed by their parents. Watching parents and other authority figures (e.g., teachers) use physical punishment provides learning opportunities for young children. Children learn that using aggression to deal with offensive behavior is acceptable. In addition, the delay between a behavior and the punishment may provide occasion for other inappropriate behaviors to be reinforced. Joan McCord (1997) gives an example of a child who does something wrong. The child is faced with telling the truth or lying to avoid punishment. Which behavior is chosen depends upon the rewards and costs associated with each behavioral option. For many young children, the immediate costs associated with telling the truth may far outweigh the long-term rewards associated with honesty.

Psychology's Shift Away from Punishment

After reflecting upon the psychology of punishment, it seems that punishment creates more problems then it solves. In the 1960s and 1970s, punishment was frequently used as a technique to modify behavior (Leitenberg, 1976). Laboratory studies with animals showed that punishment can work, and its application to the suppression of undesirable behavior in people seemed a natural progression.

Many behavior modification studies employed electric shock, pugnacious odors, and other physically aversive procedures on a variety of behaviors. Bedwetting in children, self-injurious behaviors among autistic persons, and even homosexual orientation have been targeted. Antisocial behaviors such a pedophilic interest, sexual exhibitionism, and drug abuse were shocked or paired with noxious stimuli. Physical punishments were soon replaced by psychological punishments. Offenders were taught covert sensitization by which they *imagined* negative consequences to their behavior (Cautela, 1970; see Resource Note 8.2 for an example).

It soon became apparent to psychologists that if punishment was to be used, it had to be used sparingly and always coupled with the reinforcement of prosocial behavior. Punishments that are particularly effective with people tend to be interpersonal in nature. Hunt and Azrin (1973) provide an excellent illustration of combining interpersonal punishment (time out) with reinforcement. The families of alcoholics, employers, and other community agents were taught to systematically reinforce behaviors incompatible with drinking and ignore or discourage behaviors associated with alcohol abuse. An evaluation of the program found the experimental group spending considerable less time drinking (14%) than a comparison group who received more traditional treatment (79%).

Resource Note 8.2

Self-Directed Imagined Punishment: Covert Sensitization of Alcohol Abuse

Joseph Cautela (1970) developed a cognitive-behavioral intervention by which the therapist guides the client through imaginary scenes of aversive control over behavior. A behavior that needs to be suppressed is paired with thoughts of negative consequences. Association of the behavior with visualized punishment "sensitizes" the client to the negative consequences. The procedure is called covert sensitization and it has been applied to a variety of behaviors, most notably alcohol abuse (Rimmele, Howard & Hifrink, 1995) and sexual deviance (Perkins, 1991, 1993). The following is an example of covert sensitization with an alcoholic:

Therapist: "You are walking into a bar. You decide to have a glass of beer. You are now walking toward the bar. As you are approaching the bar you have a funny feeling in the pit of your stomach. Your stomach feels all queasy and nauseous. Some liquid comes up your throat and it is very sour. You try to swallow it back down, but as you do this, food particles start coming up your throat to your mouth. You are now reaching the bar and you order a beer. As the bartender is pouring the beer, puke comes into your mouth . . . As soon as your hand touches the glass, you can't hold it down any longer. You have to open your mouth and puke. It goes all over your hand; all over the glass and the beer. You can see it floating around in the beer . . ." (Cautela, 1970:37).

The therapist instructs the client to rehearse the covert sensitization scenes until the imagery is automatic. The client is then encouraged to use the procedure when tempted to drink. Today, covert desensitization is sometimes used in cognitive-behavioral therapies but is rarely used as the sole therapeutic technique.

In summary, experimental and applied studies over the years showed a shift from punishing undesirable behavior to reinforcing desirable behavior that was incompatible with the target behavior. Reinforcement, compared to punishment, has two important advantages. First, only reinforcement can shape new behaviors; punishment only suppresses existing behavior. For offender populations with limited prosocial skills, all the punishment in the world will not teach them new skills. Second, reinforcement procedures avoid the obvious ethical and professional dilemmas associated with purposefully inflicting pain (Matson & Kazdin, 1981). Psychologists have learned that there are more effective and efficient ways of changing behavior than using punishment.

Summary on Punishment

A general policy of punishment to inhibit undesirable behavior is wrought with difficulties. Yet, it is difficult to abandon the belief that punishment is an effective deterrent. The human belief in the efficacy of punishment is resilient to change. We are taught from childhood that punishment will suppress behavior. Years of socialization and anecdotal portrayals of how fear of punishment have "turned people around" are difficult to ignore. Add to this the political currency of get-tough rhetoric and it seems we have no option but to punish.

We are faced with a need to discourage inappropriate behaviors and express dissatisfaction with violation of law. Punishing to express disapproval of antisocial behavior is one thing; punishing to deter is another matter. Scholars aware of the psychology of punishment have noted that the necessary conditions for effective punishment are virtually impossible to meet for the criminal justice system (McCord, 1999; Moffitt, 1983). Police cannot be everywhere to ensure the certainty of detection, the courts cannot pass sentence quickly, and correctional officials have difficulties ensuring adequate supervision and monitoring.

What many criminal justice policies fail to consider is that there are other ways of eliminating antisocial behavior. Increasing the rewards associated with prosocial behavior would make the rewards associated with crime less attractive. Rewarding prosocial behavior would also simultaneously increase the costs of criminal behavior because there would be more to lose. A multi-pronged attack involving a shifting of the rewards and costs for both criminal and prosocial behavior rather than a one-sided attack would more likely produce the desirable result. As we saw in the last chapter, reductions in recidivism are found with offender rehabilitation programs that depend on reinforcement and not punishment.

The Rise of Restorative Justice: An Alternative to Retribution

Not everyone was pleased with the get-tough movement. Rehabilitationists (like ourselves) continued to research and build knowledge around the effectiveness of offender treatment. Then there were others who felt that the focus on offenders, whether to rehabilitate or punish, ignored a critical piece in the puzzle of crime: the victim. Victims were dissatisfied with the criminal justice system for many reasons. They felt insignificant in the criminal justice process (i.e., reduced mainly to providing witness testimony) and ignored in the delivery of services (i.e., offenders received treatment services while victims had to cope on their own). In the 1980s, victims became better organized and soon acquired an influential political voice (Carrington & Nicholson, 1984). Small improvements were made in service delivery to victims (e.g., women shelters, trauma counseling). Larger gains, however, were made in the political arena in terms of influencing legislative changes (e.g., more severe sentences, victim rights legislation).

The victim movement has largely been characterized by efforts to ensure that offenders received their just deserts. This usually translated into "getting tough." The dominant view among many victim advocacy groups was that the criminal justice system was too soft on offenders and that harsher penalties are needed to do justice to the harm suffered by victims. However, others with an interest in the harm suffered by victims saw things differently. In contrast to the just deserts and punitive views was the view that the hurts need to be *healed*. Moreover, the healing process requires an equal collaboration among offenders, victims, and the community to correct the wrongs committed by offenders. The concepts of healing, collaboration, and making amends are central to restorative justice. The introduction of restorative justice into the criminal justice system has been influenced by two traditions: (1) Judeo-Christian notions of justice (with an emphasis on understanding and forgiveness as opposed to the retributive "eye-for-an-eye") and (2) aboriginal/Indian approaches to justice.

The first restorative justice program can be traced to a small town in Kitchener, Ontario. In 1974, a probation officer with strong ties to the Mennonite church asked a judge to delay the sentencing of two adolescents convicted of vandalism while he tried something different (Peachy, 1989). He proposed to the judge that he would take the teenagers to meet their victims and offer to make amends. The youths would benefit by understanding how their behavior affected the victims, and the victims would have the opportunity to say what they needed to make things right. Surprisingly, most of the victims asked for restitution and not incarceration or probation. As for the young offenders, they reported better understanding of the harm that they caused. From this experiment grew what are called Victim/Offender Reconciliation Programs (VORPs).

Restorative justice programs like the VORP described have a number of characteristics (Zehr & Mika, 1998). Crime is seen as a violation of interpersonal relationships. All who are harmed, offender included, must take responsibility for "making right the wrong." This requires a dialogue between offender and victim wherein they discuss how the crime has affected them (if possible, through face-to-face meetings). The offender has the opportunity to show the victim that he or she is willing to make amends and offer an apology. The victim has the chance to tell the offender how he or she has been affected by the crime and what is needed to deal with the pain. Perhaps the victim may even forgive the offender. Together, often with the support of community members, they discuss how each of them can contribute to a resolution to alleviate the harm created from the crime.

In countries with significant indigenous populations (the United States, Canada, Australia, and New Zealand), aboriginal communities have been given increasing control over matters of justice. For example, on 170 reservations in the United States, policing is managed by Indian tribal governments (Luna, 1998). With greater responsibility over the delivery of justice, aboriginal communities have been given the freedom to apply some of their traditional ways of dealing with conflict. One view held by many indigenous peoples shares many of the values forwarded by restorative justice advocates. That is, crime is a community problem, and the responsibility for a solution rests with the community (Taraschi, 1998). Punishing the offender is one way to deal with crime, but it may not be what is best for the victim and other members of the community. Crime hurts many people, and punishing the offender does not make the hurt go away for the victim and others who have been affected by the crime. What is needed is a healing and a restoration of relationships within the community.

Family group conferences and sentencing circles are two examples of restorative justice practices that have been heavily influenced by aboriginal ideas of justice. Family group conferences began in 1989 in New Zealand (Morris & Maxwell, 1997, 1998). Influenced by Maori tradition, juvenile offenders and their parent(s) meet their victim(s) and any other interested member(s) of the community to discuss how best to deal with the hurts caused by the crime and to reintegrate the offender in the community. A police representative and a mediator also attend the conference. Sentencing circles began in the Yukon Territory of Canada, a region where the majority of the population is aboriginal (Stuart, 1996). In the presence of a judge, everyone who is affected by the crime works together in developing an appropriate response to the offender's antisocial behavior. The recommendations that result from a family group conference or a sentencing circle may include punishment, but the emphasis is on healing and encouraging everyone who is affected by the crime to create a "satisfying" justice.

Offender responsibility and victim participation in resolving conflict are the basic features of restorative justice. This said, however, there is controversy over how much victim involvement is required in order for a program to be called a restorative justice program (Braithwaite, 1999; McCold, 2000). Programs such as VORP, family group counseling, and sentencing circles are unambiguous restorative justice practices. On the other hand, there are programs in which there is little, if any, direct contact between the victim and the offender and agreements are brokered through an intermediary (Zehr & Mika, 1998). For example, a victim may not wish to meet the offender. Nevertheless, the victim may agree to an offer of restitution (either financial or through community service) from the offender, or to a written apology. Should court-ordered restitution or community service be considered "restorative" for the offender even though the victim provided no input? These are but two debatable illustrations of what could be considered restorative justice practices.

Restorative justice programs exist in North America, Australia, New Zealand, Europe, and parts of Asia (McCold, 1998). Restorative justice principles are also exerting an influence on legislative policy and the criminal justice system. In New Zealand, the Children, Young Persons, and their Families Act prevents the Youth Court from making a decision until a family group conference is held. Governmental agencies in Canada and the United States have initiated a dialogue on how restorative justice principles can be introduced into criminal law (Kurki, 1999; Llewellyn & Howse, 1999). South Africa's Truth and Reconciliation Commission was formed to deal with the human rights abuses during a period of apartheid (Villa-Vicencio, 1999). In addition, the state of Vermont has implemented a reparative probation program that works with Community Reparation Boards to help probationers make amends to their victims (Dooley, 1996).

As restorative justice programs have proliferated, so too has the research. Unfortunately, many of the evaluations have not used rigorous evaluation methodologies. Many studies are largely descriptive of processes, and the outcomes measured tend to deal with the participants' satisfaction with the process. In general, victims and offenders report being pleased with the process and the resolution to the conflict (Coates & Gehm, 1988; Galaway & Hudson, 1990; Umbreit, 1999). For example, 86 percent of the offenders and 88 percent of the parents of the offenders expressed satisfaction, whereas 51 percent of the victims who participated in a family group conference were satisfied with the results (Morris & Maxwell, 1998).

Interpreting the results from evaluation studies is difficult because of the significant attrition rates found in many restorative justice programs. Table 8.2 summarizes the participation rates in 13 studies that had attempted to bring victims and offenders together for face-to-face meetings. Participation in restorative justice programs is voluntary. It is clear from the table that not all victims want to meet their offender. Thus, the high levels of satisfaction could be due to a subject selection factor. It is also noteworthy that the majority of offenders have committed nonviolent crimes. Most programs typically exclude sex offenders, domestic violence cases, and other serious crimes although there are exceptions. For example, Mark Umbreit and Betty Vos (2000) presented two case studies in which surviving family members met the offenders who killed one of their family members. The two offenders were on death row.

Restorative justice is not only about repairing the harm done to the victim. Helping the offender address the factors that led to the conflict in the first place can contribute to the offender's restoration. Although some may not agree that recidivism is an important outcome measure by which to judge the value of a restorative justice program, most see enhanced public safety as important goal (Bazemore, 1996; Zehr & Mika, 1998). Bringing offenders to accept responsibility for their actions and repairing the harm to the satisfaction of all parties are the major goals. In addition, community involvement in the restoration process facilitates the acceptance and reintegration of the offender into the community.

Table 8.2
Participation in Victim-Offender Meetings

Study	Referred(n)	Meeting(%)	Sample
Bonta et al. (1983)	139	4	adult
Bonta et al. (1998)	243	10	
Coates & Gehm (1988)	196	50	youth/adult
Gehm (1990)	535	47	youth/adult
Marshall & Merry (1990)			
a) police-based	211	47	youth
b) court-based	162	51	adult
Maxwell & Morris (1994)	200	46	youth
McCold & Wachtel (1998)	189	43	youth
Nuffield (1997)	228	35	adult
Nugent & Paddock (1995)	296	65	youth
Perry et al. (1987)	1021	46	adult
Umbreit (1995)	4445	39	youth/adult
Umbreit & Coates (1992)	2799	40	youth
Umbreit (1988)	179	54	youth
Umbreit & Roberts (1996)			
a) Coventry	276	13	youth/adult
b) Leeds	535	8	youth/adult

We adopt the position that if restorative justice is to play more than a marginal role in the current criminal justice system, then demonstrating an effect on recidivism is vital. Table 8.3 presents a meta-analytic summary of restorative justice evaluations that used recidivism as an outcome measure. Studies were included if there was a comparison group and recidivism was measured post-program. The studies varied considerably in their methodological rigor. Only four studies used random assignment. The average r was .03, representing an overall reduction in recidivism of 3 percent. The Confidence Interval (CI) gives the range at which the true value may lie with 95 percent certainty (the effect size is an *estimate* of the true value). If the confidence interval includes zero, then there is a 95 percent chance that there is no association with recidivism. The average effect size of .03 across studies, although the CI does not include zero, is not an impressive result. Furthermore, the results with programs that are undeniably intended to be restorative (VORP and FGC), show no association with recidivism. However, though it is not shown in the table, there was considerable variability in effect sizes among the *individual* studies, ranging from −.45 to .39. This finding suggests that under certain conditions restorative justice may be associated with significant reductions in recidivism.

Table 8.3.
Meta-Analytic Results from a Review of Restorative Justice Programs

Type of Program	n	k	r	CI
All programs	22,685	44	.03	.02 – .04
Juvenile	19,666	32	.02	.01 – .03
Adult	2,521	11	.08	.04 – .12
VORP	3,686	19	−.02	−.05 – .01
Restitution	18,871	24	.08	.07 – .09
Community Service	20,663	37	.03	.02 – .04
FGC	1,386	4	−.05	−.10 – .00

Notes: n = total sample size; k = number of effect sizes; CI = 95% confidence interval; VORP = victim-offender reconciliation program; FGC = family group conference.

A study by James Bonta, Suzanne Wallace-Capretta, Jennifer Rooney, and Kevin McAnoy (in press) suggested that offender treatment delivered within a restorative justice context may work especially well in reducing recidivism. They used a quasi-experimental research design to evaluate a restorative justice program intended to divert offenders from prison and into the community. Staff from the program contacted victims and encouraged them to meet the offenders in order to develop a restorative plan for the court. Although only 14 percent of the victims agreed to face-to-face meetings, many victims contributed to the plan through the intermediary efforts of the staff.

Program staff helped offenders to identify their needs and obtain treatment services. More than 90 percent of the offenders participated in a cognitive-behavioral treatment program. The 72 offenders participating in the restorative justice program were matched to a group of 72 probationers along six factors. An important matching variable was the offender's risk of recidivism (as measured by a modified Wisconsin risk instrument). The reconviction rate for the restorative justice offenders at one year was 15.3 percent and the rate was 37.5 percent for the matched group of probationers ($r = .25$, $p < .01$). As the follow-up period increased, the differences in recidivism rates between the two groups also increased. At three years, the restorative justice offenders demonstrated a recidivism rate of 34.7 percent, while the probationers had a recidivism rate of 66.1 percent ($r = .31$, $p < .001$).

Theoretically, why should we expect restorative justice to impact on criminal behavior? Besides providing treatment to address offender needs, there are a number of other possible mechanisms specifically associated with restorative justice principles that may alter the chances of reoffending. Understanding the impact of a crime on a victim may challenge an offender's rationalizations for crime. Increased empathy for the victim may act to inhibit hurtful behaviors. The forgiving, nonpunitive context of the victim-offender encounter may nourish a more prosocial attitude. When community members participate in a restorative justice process, they may act as an informal support system providing concrete assistance in acquiring prosocial behaviors (Bazemore, Nissen & Dooley, 2000). At this point however, the mechanisms described are hypotheses that still need to be tested.

Summary

The American experiment of "getting tough" has failed miserably in achieving the goals of fairness, cost-effectiveness, and enhancing public safety. Politicians continue to forge ahead, thinking that increasing the severity of punishment is what the public wants. Yet, careful analyses of public opinion surveys demonstrate that if people are given more detailed information of crime and criminals and alternatives to imprisonment, they are open to less punitive interventions.

Academic criminology has been seduced by the simplistic deterrence arguments. Moreover, if scholars wanted research funding, ignoring the political interest in deterrence would have risked financial hardship. Professional myopia prevented many scholars from examining the psychological literature on the effectiveness of punishment. Knowledge of this literature may not have swayed the political leaders, but it may have softened support for get-tough approaches from the academic community. A *psychology* of criminal conduct must be part of the knowledge base that guides criminal justice policy.

In the new millennium, we are seeing a shift away from an obsession with punishing offenders to more humane approaches for dealing with offenders. The growing influence of restorative justice reflects dissatisfaction with the adversarial, punitive, offender orientation of the present justice system. How far the influence of restorative justice will reach remains to be seen. Offender rehabilitation appears to be returning in popularity. Twenty-five years ago, the "R" word (rehabilitation) would elicit ridicule and scorn. This reaction is no longer evident. The resurgence and importance of treatment in reducing recidivism was affirmed in the previous chapter and remains the most promising form of reducing recidivism.

Chapter 9

Exceptional Offenders

In this chapter, we look at offenders who distinguish themselves from the mainstream—and in this regard we call them "exceptional." These are the mentally disordered, the psychopaths, and human predators such as sex offenders, stalkers, and serial killers. In general, these offenders stand out through behavior considered by most people to be bizarre and, at times, abhorrent. Violence is often seen as one of their most frightful characteristics.

Our general approach in this chapter, and indeed in this text, is to emphasize the individual. Sometimes scholars begin with dissecting the criterion behavior, or the criminal act, and developing theories to explain the offense. Thus, there are theories of white-collar crime, vandalism, serial killers, and mass murderers. Instead of emphasizing these "mini-theories," we will take the stance that much can be learned from a more comprehensive theoretical base. That is, the correlates of general criminal behavior show remarkable similarities for specific forms of criminal deviance. Sometimes there are more similarities than there are differences.

The Mentally Disordered Offender (MDO)

When many people first hear the phrase "mentally disordered offender," the names that jump to mind are Charles Manson, David Berkowitz (Son of Sam), Albert de Salvo (the Boston Strangler), and Jeffrey Dahmer. Images of senseless, grotesque, and extremely violent behavior flood the mind. Lesser known but almost equally bizarre offenders are publicized daily in the news media, and even fictional television characters with mental illnesses are portrayed as highly violent (Diefenbach, 1997). To the average citizen, the prevalence of mentally disordered offenders appears high. Moreover, their behavior seems incomprehensible and almost always violent. Determining whether these views correspond to the facts is one of the purposes of this section.

Estimating the incidence of mental disorder among criminal offenders requires a clear definition of the "mentally disordered offender"(MDO). Unfortunately, a widely accepted definition is virtually nonexistent.

Part of the problem is that the two major social systems responsible for the MDO, the legal and the mental health systems, have varying interpretations of mental disorder. Furthermore, even within each system there is little agreement on the meaning of such terms as "insanity" and "mental illness."

One of the most influential taxonomies or classification systems for mental disorder today is the Diagnostic and Statistical Manual of Mental Disorders or DSM-IV (American Psychiatric Association, 1994). DSM-IV describes behavioral patterns and psychological characteristics that are clustered into diagnostic categories. For example, someone with auditory hallucinations, bizarre delusions (e.g., a pet dog controlling the behavior of the person), and a history of these delusions and hallucinations lasting more than six months is likely to be diagnosed as schizophrenic.

DSM-IV covers a wide range of disorders. Each person is evaluated on five different classes of information or axes. The first two axes deal directly with the mental disorders. Axis III describes medical conditions. Axis IV relates to severity of stressors. Axis V deals with general functioning. In addition to guiding clinicians as to the behavioral patterns that should be considered in making a diagnosis, DSM-IV also provides information (when available) on the prevalence of the disorder and the age of onset.

The first axis is what most would consider the truly clinical syndromes (i.e., schizophrenia, manic-depression, and major depression). Some of these clinical syndromes are considered psychotic disorders (e.g., presence of hallucinations and delusions, strange speech), with Axis I disorders often forming the basis for assessments of fitness to stand trial and pleas of not guilty by reason of insanity (NGRI).

Axis II describes some of the disorders of interest to the study of criminal behavior. It is here that we find the Personality Disorders and, in particular, Antisocial Personality Disorder (APD). The criteria for diagnosis of APD include: minimum age of 18, history of a conduct disorder (e.g., truant and uncontrollable at home), dishonesty, irresponsibility in work and social settings, lawbreaking, and lack of remorse.

Because the diagnostic process depends to a considerable degree upon clinical judgment, it is easy to label almost all serious offenders as having a mental disorder (e.g., APD). Recognizing the need for more objective assessments, researchers have developed structured interviews in which clinicians are trained to ask questions and evaluate the responses in a standardized format. Some structured interviews yield objective clinical diagnoses according to existing diagnostic systems such as DSM-IV or the World Health Organization's International Classification of Diseases (ICD). The Diagnostic Interview Schedule (DIS) is a good example of this methodology. The DIS yields a diagnosis according to the earlier DSM-III-R categories on Axes I and II (Robins & Helzer, 1994). Another diagnostic method, the Psychopathy Checklist developed by Robert Hare, is closely related to DSM-IV's Antisocial Personality Disorder. This instrument will be described later in the chapter.

Estimating the Prevalence of Mental Disorders

Table 9.1 presents a few studies on the incidence of mental disorders among criminal populations. Some of these studies have used structured interviews to arrive at a diagnosis, while others have relied upon professional clinical judgment. Considering the fact that the DIS has shown impressive inter-rater agreement, ranging from .79 to .96 (Helzer et al., 1985; Malgady, Rogler & Tryon, 1992) and that it is sufficiently objective to produce computerized versions (Robins & Helzer, 1994), we place more emphasis on findings using the DIS.

Table 9.1
The Prevalence of Mental Disorder (%)

Assessment Method/Study	DISORDER						
	Schizo	Manic-dep	Dep	APD	Alcohol	Drug	Any
DIS							
Hodgins & Cote (1990)							
495 inmates (Canada)	6.3	1.6	8.1	46.6	33.1	18.6	96.3
Teplin & Swartz (1989)							
728 inmates (U.S.)	3.3	3.3	4.9				
1,149 inmates (U.S.)	1.4	1.5	4.9				
Daniel et al. (1988)							
100 female inmates (U.S.)	7.0	2.0	17.0	29.0	10.0		90.0
1,802 general population	1.1	1.1	8.1	1.2			
ICD							
Webster et al. (1982)							
248 pretrial (Canada)	39.4			27.0	13.7		96.0
Inada et al. (1995)							
1,396 pretrial (Japan)	28.9	2.9	—	3.1	16.4	12.3	80.7
Psychiatric Diagnosis							
Guy et al. (1985)							
96 inmates (U.S.)	11.5	3.1	1.1	9.0	25.0	11.5	75.0
Cloninger & Guze (1970)							
66 female parolees (U.S.)	1.5		6.1	65.2	47.0	25.8	100.0
Andersen et al. (1996)							
228 inmates (Denmark)	7.0	2.0	5.0	17.0	11.0	29.0	64.0
Smith et al. (1996)							
235 inmates (Ireland)	4.3	1.7	—	—	26.8	19.5	57.8
Wormith & McKeague (1996)							
2,500 probationers (Canada)	1.7	2.9	—	2.7	5.6	–	18.9
Gunn (1993)							
1,365 inmates (U.K.)	2.4			8.8	22.7		

Schizo: Schizophrenia   Dep: Major depression
Manic-dep: Manic-depression   APD: Antisocial personality

There are two findings that emerge from Table 9.1. First, hardly anyone escapes a diagnosis of a mental disorder. Most studies found that anywhere from 23.1 to 100 percent of the offenders were diagnosed as having a mental disorder. The second and more important point is that the major psychiatric disorders are relatively rare. For the majority of studies, the prevalence of schizophrenia was less than 7 percent, and approximately 2 to 3 percent for manic-depression. Only in the pretrial settings, where there are issues of fitness to stand for trial and NGRI decisions, are the rates high (Inada et al., 1995; Webster et al., 1982). One of the most frequent diagnoses was APD, a mental disorder that lacks the unusual symptomatology associated with Axis I disorders. Moreover, it is important to keep in mind that some of these prevalence rates are based upon lifetime incidence, which inflates the figures. This does not minimize our concern for MDOs, but places the problem in perspective.

Dangerousness and the MDO

The mentally disordered offender has often been at the center of the debate surrounding dangerousness. Various criminal and civil commitment laws are used to confine MDOs for periods longer than the typical sentence given to non-MDOs for the same offense. The argument is that these offenders pose a risk for further violent behavior and that preventive confinement is needed until they are no longer "dangerous." One of the difficulties in making decisions about the individual's dangerousness is the lack of knowledge about the base rates of violent behavior for MDOs. Only a few studies provide such information.

One of the first studies in this area was Henry Steadman and Joseph Cocozza's (1974) evaluation of the "Baxstrom patients." The opportunity for this study arose when an inmate (Johnnie Baxstrom) took his case before the U.S. Supreme Court. Baxstrom was transferred from a prison to a hospital for the criminally insane because he was diagnosed as mentally disordered. Consequently, he was institutionalized beyond the end of his sentence. Baxstrom's lawyers argued that, without evidence of dangerousness, he must be released. The court agreed and not only was Baxstrom transferred from the hospital for the criminally insane to a regular psychiatric hospital, but so too were 976 other offenders who had been housed in similar hospitals. Presumably, the most dangerous offenders in New York state were transferred to regular psychiatric facilities, and some were duly released at the completion of their sentence. (Baxstrom was released after a new trial in which the jury decided that he was not mentally ill; he died two weeks later from an epileptic seizure.)

The Baxstrom patients were assessed by psychiatrists and psychologists as "dangerous mental patients"; thus, their transfer to a regular hospital and their eventual release provided an estimate of the base rate of violent behavior among this group of MDOs. Steadman and Cocozza (1974) traced 246 of these offenders through their stay in the psychiatric hospitals (via patient records) and 98 were tracked upon their release into the community. The follow-up period averaged two and one-half years. A review of the patient files showed that the offenders had very low assault rates while in the psychiatric hospitals—only 15 percent were assaultive.

Postrelease antisocial behavior also showed low base rates. Twenty (20.4%) were rearrested, 11 (11.2%) were reconvicted, and only two of the 98 offenders committed a violent offense (one assault and one robbery). Because patients released from psychiatric hospitals may be rehospitalized instead of arrested for a criminal offense, rehospitalizations were also examined in order to ascertain whether the behaviors initiating rehospitalization were violent (this would increase the base rate of the behavior). With the hospital data and community information taken together, the base rate of violent behavior was 14.3 percent. Steadman and Cocozza (1974) concluded: "The Baxstrom patients were not very dangerous. Only 14 of 98 releases ever displayed behavior that could be classified as dangerous" (p. 152).

Thornberry and Jacoby (1979) found almost identical results. They followed men who were ordered by the court to be transferred from a hospital for the "criminally insane" to regular psychiatric hospitals and eventually released. Of 432 mentally disordered offenders released into the community, only 14.5 percent committed another violent offense (the average follow-up period was two and one-half years).

Before concluding that the Baxstrom patients and those from the Thornberry and Jacoby (1979) study were not dangerous, we must be reminded that all of these patients had already committed a violent offense that led to their hospitalization. Additionally, we must ask: Not dangerous compared to whom? Compared to nonoffenders, a 14 percent base rate for violent behavior seems quite high, but what is the base rate of violent behavior for offenders who are not mentally disordered?

Lynette Feder (1991) conducted a follow-up of MDO offenders along with a matched group of nondisordered offenders. One hundred and forty-seven psychiatric inmates from New York state were compared to a representative sample of 400 nonpsychiatric inmates during an 18-month follow-up period. Rearrest and rehospitalization data were collected. The rearrest rate for the MDOs was 64 percent; it was 60 percent for the non-MDOs. Rearrests for violent offenses were 19 percent for the MDOs and 15 percent for the general offender population. These differences were not statistically significant.

With regard to the Feder (1991) study, almost one-half of the MDOs were rehospitalized at least once during the follow-up period, with 18 percent rehospitalized for criminal behavior. (None of the general inmates were hospitalized for criminal behavior.) At first glance, this suggests that the recidivism rate, with rehospitalization data included, is significantly higher for the MDOs and that they are more dangerous than the arrest data indicate. However, the vast majority of the rehospitalizations for criminal behavior were for "nuisance" and nonviolent offenses. Violent offenses were more likely dealt with by the criminal justice system.

Feder's (1991) findings do not mean that those with a mental illness pose no threat to the general public. Her study illustrates only that, among known criminal offenders, having a mental disorder does not increase the risk of criminal behavior. That is, the conclusions regarding the dangerousness of MDOs is relative to the comparison group (Arboleda-Flórez, Holley & Crisanti, 1996). There is, however, a substantial body of evidence (e.g., Brennan, Mednick & Hodgins, 2000; Tiihonen et al., 1997) showing that psychiatric patients have higher arrest rates than *non*patients. There is a need to explain why this is so. Teplin (1984) has suggested that the police have an arresting bias. Yet, a recent large-scale study involving five metropolitan police departments found no evidence for an arresting bias (Engel & Silver, 2001).

In a carefully controlled study, Bruce Link, Howard Andrews, and Francis Cullen (1992) compared various groups of mentally ill patients with a randomly selected sample of adults without any mental disorder. Table 9.2 summarizes the major criminal/violent behavior differences between the chronically disturbed patients and the nondisturbed adults.

Table 9.2
Criminal and Violent Behavior among Psychiatric and Nonpsychiatric Patients (%)

	OFFICIAL			SELF-REPORTED	
Group	All Arrests	Violent	Arrests	Weapon	Fighting
Patients	12.1	5.8	22.5	12.9	28.6
Nonpatients	6.7	1.0	9.9	2.7	15.1

Note: *N*s vary for patients (93-173) and nonpatients (185-386).

From Link et al., 1992

Whether the behavior was based upon official records or self-reports, the findings of the study were consistent. Chronically disturbed patients (having received treatment for at least one year) were more likely to be arrested and to have committed violent acts. Controls were added for sociodemographic variables, neighborhood conditions (e.g., homicide rates), and psychotic symptoms (e.g., delusions of the devil controlling behavior). When these controls were added, only psychotic symptoms could account for the differences (but the strength of this variable was modest).

In recent years, the role of psychotic symptomatology has been a focus of study. Link and Steuve (1994) have proposed that delusions of "threat/control-override" (TCO) are the critical links to violence. Thus, thoughts that people are trying to harm you or that your mind is being controlled by others increase the likelihood of responding violently to these perceived threats. Link and Steuve (1994) found that TCO delusions or thoughts were associated with violence in *both* a patient and a nonpatient population. That is, cognitions supportive of antisocial behavior were the key predictors of violence.

These results were replicated in a large study of more than 10,000 adults who were interviewed using the DIS as part of the Epidemiologic Catchment Area (ECA) survey (Swanson et al., 1996). The ECA survey is a large study of the prevalence of psychiatric disorders and mental health service utilization in five cities in the United States. Swanson and his colleagues (1996) examined three groups of respondents: (1) those with no major psychiatric disorder, (2) a major, Axis I disorder, and (3) a major disorder with substance abuse. They also examined the presence of TCO symptoms and non-TCO symptoms (hallucinations, feelings of grandeur). Each respondent was asked about the commission of violent acts during the past year and also since the age of 18. Although this was a retrospective analysis, a number of conclusions were drawn from their results (Table 9.3). First, TCO symptoms increase the likelihood of violence for mentally disordered and nondisordered individuals. Second, substance abuse greatly increases the chances of violence. In a further analysis of this finding, Swanson et al. (1996) found that the effects of TCO became statistically insignificant when substance abuse was entered into the statistical equation. Third, having psychotic and even non-TCO symptoms were still presented as a risk factor, although a modest one in comparison to substance abuse and TCO symptoms.

Table 9.3
Threat/Control-Override (TCO) Symptoms as a Risk Factor for Violence
(Probability of self-reported violent acts since age 18)

Symptom	Axis I Disorder		
	No Disorder	Axis I Only	Substance Abuse
None	.17	.26	.70
Non-TCO	.27	.39	.75
TCO	.40	.63	.86

From Swanson et al., 1996

Recent data from the MacArthur Violence Risk Assessment Study has raised doubts about the importance of the TCO-violence link. The MacArthur Violence Risk Assessment Study involved extensive interviewing of more than 1,100 acute psychiatric patients from three American cities. These patients were then followed after their release from the hospital. Paul Appelbaum, Pamela Robbins, and John Monahan (2000) interviewed the patients at 10-week intervals for a period of one year. Questions tapping TCO delusions were asked and a measure of violence was constructed based upon a composite of self-reports and hospital and police files. The researchers found no relationship between TCO delusions and violence.

The failure by Appelbaum et al. (2000) to replicate the earlier findings reported by Link and Steuve (1994) and Swanson et al. (1996) could not be accounted for by differences in how TCO delusions or violence were measured. However, the retrospective methodology and the self-reports of violence used in the earlier studies were important factors. When Appelbaum et al. (2000) reanalyzed their data using a retrospective approach and only self-reports of violent behavior, they found a TCO-violence association.

At first glance, it appears that Appelbaum et al.'s (2000) findings are inconsistent with our general theoretical views. However, closer examination of their results is congruent with predictions from a general personality and social psychology perspective. First of all, the screening questions for TCO delusions tapped paranoid cognitions (e.g., Have you believed people were spying on you?) and not specifically cognitions supportive of violent behavior. The researchers, as part of their interviews, did ask a specific question about violent behavior. Patients who responded positively to the question, "Do you sometimes think about hurting people?" were significantly more likely to be violent than patients who denied such a thought. Second, patients with TCO delusions all scored significantly higher on measures of anger and impulsivity (characteristics of antisocial personality), and this appeared to be a more important factor.

In summary, the existence of a mental disorder appears to be a mild risk factor compared to the general population, but only in the presence of characteristics common to many offenders (e.g., substance abuse, antisocial personality, cognitions supportive of violent behavior). Psychotic delusions may be less important then previously thought and may be understood by the possibility that psychotic delusions tend to be associated with social isolation. For many people, if they are confronted by someone with delusions, the reaction would be avoidance. There is some evidence that seriously disturbed individuals have very small social networks (Swanson et al., 1996). We would assume that this would naturally limit the individual's social supports for crime. The next question that we attempt to answer is whether having a mental disorder is a risk factor among offender populations, who already pose an elevated risk to the public.

The Prediction of Criminal Behavior Among MDOs

One of the major shortcomings in the prediction of criminal behavior among MDOs is a failure to examine critically the factors comprising assessments of risk. As we have pointed out, it is simply not enough to say that dangerous behavior cannot be predicted. We must ask why the predictors are so poor. The answer may have to do with a preoccupation with using the wrong factors in the prediction model. The variables usually investigated, namely mental health and psychopathological indicators, may not be the best predictors; the better predictors may be the very same ones found with general offender groups.

Concerned about the relevance of various theoretical models to explain the behavior of MDOs, James Bonta, Moira Law, and Karl Hanson (1998) conducted a meta-analysis of the predictors of general and violent recidivism. They asked whether factors considered important by psychopathological and clinical perspectives would predict recidivism and how these factors compared to predictors drawn from a general PCC. Bonta and his colleagues reviewed 64 longitudinal studies conducted between 1959 and 1995. The criterion of recidivism included both criminal justice and rehospitalization measures. The average follow-up period was 4.8 years, yielding base rates of 45.8 percent for general recidivism and 24.5 percent for violent recidivism.

Table 9.4 presents the results for general recidivism (the pattern was similar for violent recidivism) along with the results from the meta-analyses by Gendreau et al. (1996) and Hanson and Bussière (1998). We will say more about the Hanson and Bussière meta-analysis of sex offender recidivism later in this chapter. For now, our focus is on the MDO. What is clear from Table 9.4 is that the predictors of recidivism for MDOs follow a pattern very similar to the general offenders in Gendreau et al.'s meta-analysis. Criminal history and antisocial personality, two of the "Big Four," were among the best predictors of recidivism, whether violent or not. The other predictors—and their effect sizes—showed almost parallel results across the disordered and nondisordered samples.

Table 9.4
Predictors of Recidivism by Sample (r)

| Risk Factor | Sample | | |
	General	MDO	Sex
Antisocial Support	.21	nr	nr
Antisocial Personality	.18	.18	.14
Antisocial Cognitions	.18	nr	.09
Criminal History	.16	.22	.13
Social Achievement	.13	.04	.03
Family Factors	.10	.10	.08
Substance Abuse	.10	.11	.03
Intelligence	.07	.01	.09
Lower-Class Origins	.05	.00	.05
Personal Distress	.05	−.04	.01

Notes: General (Gendreau et al., 1996); MDO (Bonta et al., 1998); Sex (Hanson & Bussière, 1998). nr = not reported.

In the MDO meta-analysis, there were too few studies measuring antisocial supports and antisocial cognitions. This gap in the research can be traced, in our opinion, to the dominating influence of psychopathological models to explain MDOs. The training of clinical psychologists and psychiatrists naturally predisposes them to seek explanation in factors such as psychosis and other measures of psychological disturbance. However, the results from the Bonta et al. (1998) meta-analysis found these factors to be poor predictors of recidivism. In fact, a diagnosis of an Axis I disorder was *negatively* related to general ($r = -.05$) and violent ($r = -.04$) recidivism. Just as the clinical models contributed little to the prediction of criminal behavior, so did variables drawn from sociological criminology. Lower social class and race did not predict general recidivism (race was a moderate predictor of violent recidivism; $r = .09$).

Two other important findings from the Bonta et al. (1998) meta-analysis deserve comment. First, actuarial assessments of risk once again proved themselves superior to clinical judgments of risk (recall Chapter 6). For general recidivism, the average r was .39 for actuarial assessments and only .03 for clinical judgments; for the prediction of violent recidivism, the corresponding rs were .30 and .09. Second, studies that compared the recidivism of MDOs with nondisordered offenders showed that compared to general offenders, those with a mental illness were *less* likely to reoffend with any offense ($r = -.19$) or a violent offense ($r = -.10$).

In summary, those with a major mental disorder may pose an elevated risk for criminal behavior compared to the general population, but they represent less of a risk when compared to nondisordered offenders. Measures of clinical psychopathology are important for the humane treatment of human beings and for the management of the disturbing symptoms, but they do not appear to be significant correlates of criminal behavior for most MDOs. What we find instead is that many of the variables identified from a PCC are far more important. This knowledge prepares us for what we are to find when we review treatment programs for MDOs. Those programs dominated by a clinical perspective and focusing upon psychopathological variables would be expected to have little impact on the recidivism of MDOs.

Treatment of the MDO

Considering the sensationalism that often surrounds the mentally disordered offender both in real life and in the media (e.g., the movie *Hannibal*), it is surprising to find an almost complete absence of controlled treatment studies specifically targeting this population. Most treatment studies that use experimental designs target offenders who are not mentally disordered. To our knowledge, there is no study with MDOs, except for drug testing, that uses an experimental design (with random assignment, pre- and posttesting, control groups, and objective measurement).

Clinical treatment of the MDO usually involves treating psychological complaints or the behaviors that are disruptive to the functioning of the institution. Thus, a depressed offender may follow a cognitive-behavioral program for self-defeating thoughts or receive antidepressant medication; a manic-depressive is likely to receive Lithium; and a schizophrenic would likely be hospitalized and receive a major tranquilizer. Upon elimination of the symptoms (or, at the very least, management of the symptoms), the patient is considered "cured" and no further treatment follows. In other words, most treatment programs with MDOs are no different than those provided for nonoffending, psychiatric patients. The treatment targets are psychiatric symptomatology and psychological distress—variables that show a weak relationship to criminal behavior. It is rare to find the MDO undergoing treatment programs that target, for example, criminal attitudes and associates.

Treatment with MDOs is often a combination of medication and inpatient treatment programs (Harris & Rice, 1997; Müller-Isberner & Hodgins, 2000). Because most of the research deals with institutionalized MDOs, token economies and therapeutic communities have been popular approaches. However, neither approach has shown success in reducing recidivism among MDOs.

Marnie Rice and her colleagues have evaluated two treatment approaches that were used in Ontario's hospital for the criminally insane. Therapeutic communities are typically loosely structured groups in which patients assume an intense responsibility for each other's behavior. Thus, an individual's transgression may be vigorously confronted by the other patients, and through peer pressure, the offender is encouraged to comply with group standards. (The program was also noteworthy for experimenting with LSD therapy, Weisman, 1995.) A 10-year follow-up of 169 MDOs who participated in a therapeutic community (post-LSD phase) found no differences in recidivism rates compared to a matched group of untreated MDOs (Harris, Rice & Cormier, 1994; Rice, Harris & Cormier, 1992). However, the nonpsychopathic MDOs did show a reduction in recidivism, suggesting that this type of treatment may have had some effect for certain types of MDOs.

An evaluation of a token economy program for 92 MDOs in the same hospital also showed no effect on recidivism (Rice, Quinsey & Houghton, 1990). Token economy programs have been largely ineffective among criminal populations (Ross & Fabiano, 1985). The reasons for their ineffectiveness with MDOs appear to be the same. That is, token economy programs tend to target noncriminogenic needs. The treatment program in the Rice et al. study (1992) targeted compliance to staff, self-care skills, and participation in institutional work programs.

In these programs, the assumption has been that treating the psychological disorder or improving staff compliant behaviors will reduce the likelihood of criminality. As anticipated by our discussion of prediction, psychological factors (e.g., anxiety, depression, etc.), being poor predictors of recidivism, are unlikely to be criminogenic. Thus, targeting these factors in treatment is unlikely to alter the criminal behavior of the MDOs.

There have been two promising developments in the treatment of MDOs. First, there is a recognition that the treatment of MDOs should attend to the general offender rehabilitation literature (Harris & Rice, 1997; Müller-Isberner & Hodgins, 2000). Perhaps it is time for psychiatric staff to target criminogenic needs in a cognitive-behavioral treatment format. Second, the importance of providing treatment and support post-hospitalization is being given more attention. Specialized aftercare programs have been developed for MDOs released on conditional release in states such as California, Oregon, New York, and North Carolina with promising results (Bloom & Williams, 1994; Swanson et al., 2001; Wiederanders, Bromley & Choate, 1997; Wiederanders & Choate, 1994; Wiederanders, Choate & Bromley, 1993). We hope that these trends continue.

Antisocial Personality Disorder, Psychopathy, and Antisocial Personality Pattern

Axis II of DSM-IV (American Psychiatric Association, 1994) describes personality disorders and mental retardation. The personality disorders include, for example, obsessive-compulsive personality, paranoid personality, and narcissistic personality. Also included is Antisocial Personality Disorder (APD). Most of the personality disorders have an early onset, and APD is differentiated from the other personality disorders by a "pervasive pattern of disregard, and violation of, the rights of others" (p. 645). A summary of the diagnostic criteria for APD is given in Table 9.5.

Table 9.5
DSM-IV Criteria for Antisocial Personality Disorder

Criteria

I. Disregard for the rights of others. At least three of the following:
  a) behaves in a way that is grounds for arrest
  b) deceitful and manipulative
  c) impulsive
  d) aggressive
  e) irresponsible
  f) lack of remorse

II. Age 18 or more
III. A history of childhood conduct disorder
IV. Antisocial behavior not a product of a schizophrenic/manic episode.

The criteria for APD in DSM-IV stress *behavioral* characteristics. The public and some researchers view certain emotional factors as unique to some offenders (e.g., the "cold-blooded killer"). The DSM-IV criteria capture the aggressiveness and unremorsefulness but none of the emotional flatness of this individual. Think also of the self-centered company president who ingratiates himself or herself to employees only to fire them at the slightest questioning of authority. The personality construct that fits our general image of these people is psychopathy, in which we have the additional features of superficial charm, a lack of empathy, and an egocentric interpersonal position. Because the construct suggests a type of persona that interests us and because there is a sizeable body of good research, we will focus on psychopathy.

The term "psychopathy" is widely used by both professionals and the general public; it is firmly entrenched within our culture (see Resource Note 9.1 for a clinical illustration). The public's image of the psychopath is the smooth charmer who is also capable of violent and sadistic behavior. Variations of the concept have been within the professional domain for over a century, from Pinel's "mania without frenzy" to Prichard's 1835 description of "moral insanity" (Pichot, 1978) to Freud's underdeveloped superego. However, it was Hervey Cleckley (1982) who presented the contemporary clinical description of the psychopath.

Resource Note 9.1

A Case Study of a Psychopath

Everybody called him "Red." He was 30 years old, tall, and good looking, with red hair and a neatly trimmed red beard. Red came from a middle-class background. His father was a government civil servant and his mother was a journalist for the city newspaper. When Red was four years old, his parents divorced and he went to live with his father until he was six years old. From age six on, he was sent to boarding school.

Boarding school was difficult for Red. He hated the school ("It was like the army"), the work, and the teachers. He ran away many times and finally, at age 17, it was for good. Red ran to Florida, where he found his older sister. He told her that things were going so well in school and he was so advanced that the teachers said he could take a holiday and visit his sister. At his sister's house, Red began to drink by sneaking liquor from the cabinet and replacing it with colored water. Three weeks later, a telegram came to his sister. As she was not home, he opened the telegram and learned that their father died suddenly in a car accident.

Red returned to his home in New York state to claim his inheritance. He told authorities that his sister had committed suicide six months ago; he showed forged documents to support his claim. Red inherited everything. He lived in his father's house and began to party. Red's friends drank and took drugs. Most had been in juvenile detention homes at some time in their lives or in jail. Red enjoyed his life: no school, no work, and lots of excitement.

The party ended quickly. One night he was drunk and assaulted his "best friend" with a baseball bat. Although the friend suffered a broken wrist, he refused to press charges. The police came, but there were no formal charges. For the next five years, Red had numerous skirmishes with the law, was married one time, and became addicted to drugs.

At age 21, all the inheritance was spent. Red began moving from city to city. In each city, he met a woman who worked at a low-paying job and he moved in with her. Each woman learned after a few months that he brought trouble along with him. He continued to drink, injected cocaine, and committed "break and enters" and thefts to support his drug habit. Jail sentences rarely exceeded 60 days.

Then, at age 30, Red violently assaulted the woman with whom he was living. This time, the judge gave him two years. The day after he was brought into custody, Red began phoning his common-law wife pleading forgiveness. At first she would hang up, but this did not discourage Red. Within two weeks, she was accepting his calls. Within the month, she was visiting him in jail; she continued to do so until his release. While Red was receiving visits from his common-law wife and accepting the money she brought, he was also busy with other plans. He was not only lining himself up with women introduced by his fellow inmates, but he was also phoning the "companions" advertisements in the newspaper.

At the time of his release, Red had offers from three women for a place to live. Tests completed in prison showed the following results:

Level of Service Inventory-Revised (LSI-R):	48 (maximum possible 54)
Psychopathy Checklist-Revised (PCL-R):	36 (maximum 40)
Gough's Socialization Scale: (low score indicates a disregard for rules)	8 (maximum 25)
Attitude toward the Law, Courts, Police:	14 percentile
Identification with Criminal Others:	92 percentile
IPAT Anxiety Scale:	4 (maximum is 10)
Bennett's Self-Esteem:	81 percentile

Drawing upon his many years of experience as a psychiatrist, Cleckley (1982) noted patterns in the characteristics shown by his psychopathic patients. From his observations, Cleckley formulated a list of characteristics that is widely accepted today as the best picture of the psychopath (Figure 9.1).

Key features
   Manipulative
   Superficial charm
   Above-average intelligence
   Absence of psychotic symptoms (delusions, hallucinations)
   Absence of anxiety
   Lack of remorse
   Failure to learn from experience
   Egocentric
   Lacks emotional depth

Other characteristics
   Trivial sex life
   Unreliable
   Failure to follow a life plan
   Untruthful
   Suicide attempts rarely genuine
   Impulsive
   Antisocial behavior

Figure 9.1
Cleckley's Checklist for Psychopathy

Our summary description of Cleckley's psychopath in Figure 9.1 is intended to make three important points about psychopathy. First, psychopaths have all the outward appearances of normality. They do not hallucinate or have delusions, and they do not appear particularly encumbered by debilitating anxiety or guilt (Cleckley titled his book *The Mask of Sanity*). Second, psychopaths appear unresponsive to social control. For example, they continue to get into trouble despite punishment from society and those around them. Thirdly, Cleckley's view was that criminal behavior was not an essential characteristic. In fact, Cleckley presented many case examples of patients with no criminal record.

This last point is particularly important. If we accept the assumption that a psychopath is not necessarily a criminal, then a number of important corollaries follow:

1. Not all criminals are psychopathic.

2. An etiological explanation of crime may not serve as an explanation of psychopathy, and vice-versa.

3. Following from Corollary 2, assessment and treatment methods for psychopaths and criminals should be substantially different.

Hare's Psychopathy Checklist (PCL-R)

Robert Hare and his colleagues took the diagnostic criteria proposed by Cleckley and developed it into an objective assessment instrument based upon structured interviews and file reviews. Hare (1980) reduced more than 100 behaviors and characteristics listed by clinicians and researchers to 22 items, and then to 20 items (Hare, 1990), thought to represent the key indicators of psychopathy. The result was the Psychopathy Checklist-Revised or PCL-R (Figure 9.2). Each item is scored on a three-point scale: "0" (zero) for not applicable, "1" for uncertain, and "2" for definitely present. (Hare provides a training program to ensure reliable scoring.) The higher the score, the more likely the individual is a psychopath.

Glibness/superficial charm
Grandiose sense of self-worth
Need for stimulation/prone to boredom
Pathological lying
Conning/manipulative
Lack of remorse or guilt
Shallow affect
Callous/lack of empathy
Parasitic lifestyle
Poor behavioral controls
Promiscuous sexual relations
Early behavior problems
Lack of realistic, long-term goals
Impulsivity
Irresponsibility
Failure to accept responsibility for own actions
Many short-term marital relationships
Juvenile delinquency
Revocation of conditional release
Criminal versatility

Figure 9.2
The Psychopathy Checklist-Revised (PCL-R)

From Hare, 1990. Reproduced with permission of Multi-Health Systems, Inc., 908 Niagara Falls Blvd., North Tonawanda, NY 14120-2060 (800/456-3003) and Robert D. Hare, Ph.D.

The first comment that we need to make is on the differences between APD as defined in DSM-IV and psychopathy as measured by the PCL-R. When DSM-IV was being developed, the working group charged with overseeing the field trials for antisocial personality attempted to better integrate the affective and interpersonal aspects of psychopathy (e.g., empathy, arrogant self-appraisal) into the diagnostic category (Hare, 1996). However, results from the field trials were mixed, and these characteristics did not find themselves into DSM-IV (Widiger et al., 1996). As a result, the essential difference between DSM-IV's APD and the PCL-R's psychopathy is on the emotional-interpersonal dimension (Hare, 1998).

This difference has a number of implications. First, DSM-IV's APD is not the same as psychopathy; two separate sets of criteria are used in making the diagnosis. Clinicians and researchers, however, often tend to use the two terms interchangeably. Second, the DSM-IV diagnosis relying on behavioral antisocial history may measure persistent criminality more than a personality characteristic. This limits the usefulness of the APD diagnosis in forensic and correctional settings. For example, it is estimated that up to 80 percent of inmates in Canada's penitentiaries meet the criteria for APD (Correctional Services Canada, 1990). The problems with DSM-IV's APD (underinclusiveness and utility) have led many forensic and correctional researchers and clinicians to rely on the PCL-R for assessments of antisocial personality.

An important question is whether psychopaths are qualitatively different from other criminals or whether all criminals are psychopaths to some extent—some more so than others. That is, is psychopathy a discrete personality construct, a taxon, or a continuous dimension of personality?

Hare, among others (e.g., Harris, Rice & Quinsey, 1994; Skilling, Quinsey & Craig, 2001), has taken the position that psychopathy is a distinct personality construct with a constellation of affective, cognitive, and behavioral characteristics not shared by other disorders. One of the central features of psychopathy is the lack of guilt or concern about the effects of one's actions on others. Hans Eysenck (1964) and Ronald Blackburn (1975) have long argued for a distinction between "primary" psychopaths (the classical version) and "secondary" psychopaths (those who feel some guilt). Hare (1970, 1996) rejects the notion that some psychopaths feel guilty and anxious about their misbehavior. This debate is important because it touches upon the very notion of the treatability of psychopaths and their tendency for violence. Those with a capacity for emotionality and a "conscience" are more amenable to treatment (Blackburn, 1993; Eysenck, 1998) and less likely to act violently (Herpertz & Sass, 2000). Thus, Hare's model suggests an unresponsiveness to treatment and a pessimism about the futures of psychopathic persons.

Stephen Porter (1996) has adopted the position that psychopaths can be subdivided into primary and secondary groups. Behaviorally, both groups may appear similar. They act with indifference to others and in a harmful way. However, secondary psychopaths have the capacity to feel guilt and remorse, but they learn to "turn off" these feelings. This process bears a resemblance to Sykes and Matza's cognitive techniques of neutralization, but the goal is affective disinhibition. Despite all the research on possible subtypes of psychopaths and the role of guilt, remorse, and empathy, there is still no agreement (Porter, 1996; Schmitt & Newman, 1999).

Research with the PCL-R presents a confusing picture regarding the question of psychopathy as a taxon. Scores on the PCL-R can fall between 0 and 40. At what point does one become a psychopath? What is the cut-off score delineating psychopaths from others? Hare (1990) recommended a cut-off score of 30, but in practice, researchers have used scores varying from 25 (Harris et al., 1989) to 32 (Serin, Peters & Barbaree, 1990). In terms of practice, the PCL-R appears to follow a dimensional model of psychopathy.

Despite the seemingly dimensional nature of the PCL-R, Grant Harris, Marnie Rice, and Vernon Quinsey (1994) have suggested that the PCL-R does measure a discrete personality type or taxon. The problem is that the PCL-R, like any measurement instrument, is imperfect, and measurement error is masking the true assessment of psychopathy. By using taxonomic analyses (statistical procedures intended to identify discrete entities) on PCL-R data from 653 mentally disordered offenders, Harris, Rice, and Quinsey (1994) found evidence for the existence of a discrete personality construct that could be called psychopathy. They used a number of different statistical procedures that produced varying results, but the most powerful statistical procedures (MAXCOV analysis; Meehl, 1995) and the overall pattern of results supported the existence of a taxon. However, there has been only one replication (on a Scottish prison sample). This study was cited by Hare (1998), but details of the methodology have yet to be published. Until replications with other samples and methodologies are completed, a final verdict on the status of psychopathy as a taxon is left to the future.

PCL-R and the Prediction of Criminal Behavior

Since the first study in 1988 by Stephen Hart, Philip Kropp, and Robert Hare, there have been many more studies on the predictive validity of the PCL-R. The studies have been summarized in two major reviews. In the first review, Randall Salekin, Richard Rogers, and Kenneth Sewell (1996) conducted a meta-analysis of 18 studies that yielded 29 effect sizes. Salekin et al. (1996) included post-dictive studies in their analysis even though they recognized the limitations of this type of design. We will describe their results using only the 16 effective sizes calculated from predictive studies that investigated postrelease nonsexual recidivism (some studies used institutional behavior and sexual recidivism as outcomes). For general recidivism, after transforming Salekin et al.'s effect size measure of d of .57 (Table 3), we found an average r of .27. This effect size was almost identical to that reported by Gendreau et al. (1996; $r = .28$). For violent recidivism, the r was .32.

In a second review of the predictive validity of the PCL-R, James Hemphill, Robert Hare, and Stephen Wong (1998) calculated effect size estimates for 14 *prospective* studies. They found an r of .27 for general recidivism, .27 for violent recidivism, and .23 for sexual recidivism (based on one study). Hemphill et al. (1998) then compared the PCL-R with other actuarial scales (e.g., SFS, SIR, and LSI-R) and found that the PCL-R correlated with general and violent recidivism as well as the other scales. They concluded that because the predictive validity estimates for the PCL-R were as good and sometimes better than the other scales and the PCL-R was theoretically relevant, then "the PCL-R should be considered a primary instrument for guiding clinical appraisals of criminal recidivism and dangerousness" (p. 160).

The predictive validity of the PCL-R is impressive, but caution is advised in equating dangerousness with psychopathy. Not all violent and dangerous offenders are psychopaths as measured by the PCL-R. The prediction studies of Serin (1996) and Harris et al. (1991) found significant proportions of violent offenders who scored below 30 on the PCL-R. For example, Serin (1996) found a false positive rate of 35.8 percent for the PCL-R. In a study of offenders declared by Canadian courts as "dangerous offenders," only 39.6 percent were assessed as psychopaths by the PCL-R (Bonta, Harris, et al., 1996).

Claims that the PCL-R should be the "primary instrument for . . . appraisals of criminal recidivism and dangerousness" need to be viewed with caution in light of the research. First, there is some evidence that the PCL-R may be improved upon by including additional risk factors. This is the approach adopted by Grant Harris and his colleagues (Harris, Rice & Quinsey, 1993; Rice & Harris, 1997) in their development of the Violence Risk Appraisal Guide (VRAG). More than 600 MDOs released from a maximum-security hospital were followed for an average of 81.5 months. In addition to the PCL-R ($r = .34$), a number of other factors predicted violent recidivism. Examples were elementary school maladjustment, alcohol abuse, and separation from parents prior to the age of 16. Eleven additional predictors to the PCL-R were identified that, when combined to construct the VRAG, improved prediction beyond knowledge of only the PCL-R ($r = .44$).

Second, comparisons of the PCL-R do not always show the PCL-R to be a better predictor of other risk assessment instruments. In the Hemphill et al. (1998) meta-analysis, there was only one comparison of the LSI-R with the PCL-R and this was a study of mentally disordered offenders in which a *modified* LSI-R was scored from files. A number of other studies comparing the PCL-R with other actuarial assessment instruments have found the PCL-R neither superior nor inferior to them (see Chapter 6). Paul Gendreau and his colleagues have conducted two meta-analyses comparing the PCL-R and the LSI-R. In neither meta-analyses did the PCL-R outperform the LSI-R. In fact, in the latest meta-analyses (Gendreau, Goggin & Smith, 2002), the LSI-R actually performed better than the PCL-R when the outcome was general recidivism ($r = .39$ vs. $r = .25$) and as well as the PCL-R when the outcome was violent recidivism ($r = .28$ vs. $r = .25$; nonsignificant difference).

Cleckley was clear that he considered psychopathy to be entirely a personality construct. However, inspection of Figure 9.2 shows that the PCL-R has items that tap both personality factors (e.g., impulsivity) and criminal behavior (e.g., juvenile delinquency). Does the PCL-R measure two distinct factors and, if so, which factor is most relevant to risk prediction? Early studies using factor analysis (a statistical method designed to discover common "factors" among many variables) of the PCL-

R identified two major factors (Hare, Strachan & Forth, 1993; Harpur, Hakstian & Hare, 1988). Factor I is characterized by such descriptors as selfishness, a lack of guilt, and poor empathy for others, while Factor II describes an antisocial lifestyle (e.g., early behavior problems, impulsiveness, thrill-seeking). That is, one factor deals with personality characteristics while the other deals with factors more directly associated with criminal behavior. Recent attempts to replicate the two-factor model, however, have been mixed and, at this point, the stability of two distinct factors is unclear (Cooke & Michie, 2001).

In Hemphill et al.'s review (1998), there were five studies that examined the predictive validity of the factors with respect to general recidivism and three studies that used violent recidivism as the outcome criterion. Factor 2 (antisocial lifestyle) was a better predictor of general recidivism than Factor 1 (personality). There was no difference with respect to violent recidivism (but there were only three studies). These findings suggest that the personality features of psychopathy, as measured by the PCL-R, may have little to do with general criminality, although there is a possibility that the personality traits may be relevant to the prediction of *violent* recidivism.

Are There Noncriminal Psychopaths?

Are there individuals with the personality characteristics of psychopathy whose behavior does not bring them into conflict with the law? Cathy Widom (1977) reasoned that it is possible that perhaps the criminal psychopaths represent only the unsuccessful psychopaths (the ones that get caught). Perhaps there are many psychopaths who, although engaging in questionable behavior, are not clients of the criminal justice system. This is essentially the premise of Cleckley and others: that one can be a psychopath and not a criminal.

Widom (1977) developed a procedure of recruiting psychopaths from the general population. She placed an ad in the newspaper searching for people who were "adventurous," "exciting," "impulsive," and "willing to do anything for a dare." This procedure was replicated in 1985 (Widom & Newman). Neither of the two studies identified a significant proportion of the psychopaths who did not show evidence of criminal behavior. In the first study, 32.1 percent of the sample ($n = 28$) reported a history of incarceration as an adult. In the second study, although only 5.1 percent ($n = 40$) reported a history of incarceration, they had an arrest rate of 41 percent (the arrest rate for the first study was not reported). We can only suspect based on the incarceration rate that the arrest rate for the first study must have been as high—and probably much higher.

Finally, Belmore and Quinsey (1994) conducted interviews with subjects recruited from the community and scored them on a 16-item scale, of which eight items were taken from the PCL-R. Their 15 highest-

scoring subjects all had arrest histories. Thus, efforts thus far to identify a "pure" group of noncriminal psychopaths have not been particularly successful.

The Treatment of Psychopaths

Clinicians, in general, have viewed psychopaths as incurable (Phillips
& Gunderson, 1999; Reid & Gacono, 2000). Certainly, this has been
Cleckley's view. Their intractability has been attributed to a biological
deficit and/or early childhood experiences so severe that they are
beyond hope. Treatment methods supposedly tailored for psychopaths,
such as therapeutic communities (Blackburn, 1993; Hobson, Shine &
Roberts, 2000), have shown that psychopaths are not very motivated for
treatment and that they drop out of treatment programs quite early
(Ogloff, Wong & Greenwood, 1990). Unstructured treatment methods have
actually shown increases in recidivism for psychopaths (Harris, Rice &
Cormier, 1994). Despite the absence of evidence for unstructured, psychodynamic treatment, efforts continue to confront "psychopathic transference" and "paranoid regressions" (Kernberg, 1998) because it has "the
ring of truth" (Cox, 1998).

Clinical anecdotes and a few published studies may fuel the belief that
psychopaths are untreatable, but in our view, things may not be as dark
as they seem. A number of reviews of the treatment literature have all
come to the same conclusion: there is insufficient evidence to say
whether treatment does or does not make a difference (Garrido, Esteban
& Molero, 1996; Lösel, 1998; Wong, 2000). Part of the problem is that
almost all the treatment programs have been poorly conceived interventions and milieu therapies that permit psychopaths to con staff into
believing they are making progress (Hare et al., 2000; Hobson et al.,
2000). From what we know about effective correctional treatment, why
would we expect them to be effective? We would predict that with high-
risk offenders exposed to such treatments there would be the danger of
increased recidivism. Until we have studies that systematically apply the
risk, need, and responsivity principles and target the other dynamic risk
correlates of criminal behavior, it is too early to accept the view that "psychopaths" are unreachable.

Are There Psychopathic Children?

Psychopathy is usually seen as a stable personality pattern that
changes little from year to year. Although the criminal activity of psychopaths decreases around the age of 40, it is unclear whether the
reduction is due to avoiding apprehension or a real change in behavior
(Hare, 1998). The stability of the psychopathic construct also suggests
that the personality and behavioral traits must have started early in life.

In Chapter 5, we saw that the origins of an antisocial personality pattern characterized by impulsiveness, sensation-seeking, and restlessness could easily be identified in early childhood. With the recent incidents of children and young persons committing very violent crimes, some researchers have taken a special interest in exploring the possibility of extending the notion of psychopathy to children.

Adelle Forth and her colleagues (Forth, Hart & Hare, 1990; Forth, Kosson & Hare, in development) modified the PCL-R for use with adolescent offenders as young as age 13. The modifications involved deleting some items (e.g., "many short-term marital relationships") and altering the scoring criteria for some of the items (e.g., "criminal versatility). Frick et al. (1994) have gone one step further and modified the PCL-R for use with children as young as six years old. In this version, the items are scored based on information provided by parents and teachers. Donald Lynam (1997) began with the PCL-R as the model and then selected items from two child maladaptive behavior tests to "translate" the PCL-R constructs into a 41-item Childhood Psychopathy Scale for use with 12- and 13-year-olds. Research with these scales has been limited to reliability and normative data and some tests of their construct validity and factor structure (generally, two factors are found: Callous/Deceitful and Conduct Disorder). There has been only one predictive study of the youth version of the PCL-R. In a sample of 220 adolescent sex offenders (ages 12-18), scores on the youth version predicted general ($r = .25$) and violent re-offending ($r = .19$) but not sexual reoffending (Gretton et al., 2001).

Regardless of what the research will uncover in the coming years, we share the concerns of others about the utility of applying the construct of psychopathy to children and adolescents (Edens et al., 2001; Hoge, 2002). Basically, does it make sense to extend a personality construct that has always been limited to adults to children? Recall that the diagnostic criteria for Antisocial Personality Disorder require a minimum age of 18. John Edens and his colleagues (2001) provide a thoughtful analysis and critique of the assessment of "juvenile psychopathy." First, as we have already noted, the research on youth versions of the PCL-R has not included predictive validity data. Second, at times, the research has had serious methodological weaknesses. For example, the Frick et al. (1994) study was based on a small sample of 92 children, and Lynam (1997) was able to translate only 13 of the 20 PCL-R items for use with children. The most difficult problem, however, is that some of the items of the youth versions of the PCL-R may be normative or related to development. What adult has not chuckled at the adolescent's "grandiose sense of self-worth" or "failure to accept responsibility"? Are impulsiveness, the need for stimulation, and lack of realistic, long-term goals reflective of normal adolescence? Edens et al. (2001) suspect that modifications of the PCL-R may overestimate psychopathic features in adolescence. They conclude that "reliance on psychopathy measures to make decisions regarding long-term placements for juveniles is contraindicated at this time" (p. 53).

An Alternative to Traditional Clinical Diagnostics: The Antisocial Personality Pattern

The DSM-IV, the PCL-R, and other clinical classification systems operate on the assumption that certain behavioral patterns "hang together" to create categories that can be reliably differentiated from other classifications, and that they have their own etiologies and course of development. For example, someone who is diagnosed as schizophrenic has characteristics unlike a manic-depressive, with a different etiology and prognosis. The same can be said for antisocial personality disorder (APD) and psychopathy. The problem with APD and Psychopathy is that there is no consensus regarding their etiology and prognosis (Lykken, 1995).

Before outlining our position, we would like to reaffirm our admiration for the work of Robert Hare and his colleagues. The research surrounding the PCL-R has brought an empirical, actuarial perspective to the assessment of mental disorder and has saved forensic psychology from its dependence on professional judgment for decisionmaking. We also see the assessment of antisocial personality as critical for effective offender assessment. After all, antisocial personality is one of the "Big Four" theoretical correlates and best predictors of criminal behavior. However, we are not convinced by Hare's (1998, p. 197) statement that "the personality and social-psychological factors that explain antisocial behavior in general . . . may not be applicable to psychopaths." We think that PCC has much to say about antisocial personality and psychopathy.

An alternative perspective to the clinical diagnostic understanding of antisocial personality is to adopt a broad definition that encompasses behavioral and personality characteristics that are relevant to the assessment and treatment of criminal behavior. Antisocial personality is characterized by impulsiveness, sensation-seeking, fearlessness, egocentrism, hostile emotions, and law-violating behaviors. The list of descriptors can be expanded by drawing upon the item content of various assessment instruments used to assess antisocial personality (e.g., Gough's Socialization scale, Peterson et. al.'s measure of Psychopathy, Lilienfeld and Andrew's Psychopathic Personality, PCL-R).

By focusing on the characteristics that describe antisocial personality, we can avoid the pessimistic attitudes associated with the diagnostic approach. Diagnostic approaches, whether it is the DSM-IV or PCL-R, leave many with the impression that an individual labeled APD or psychopathic is untreatable. In many jurisdictions, a diagnosis of APD or psychopathy and the associated "unable to learn from experience" is used to justify added criminal justice sanctions (Bonta et al., 1998; Wong, 2000). As pointed out earlier, there is no evidence that psychopaths and APD offenders cannot learn from treatments that follow the principles of risk, need, and responsivity.

Psychopathy and APD are viewed as stable personality traits that change little with time. From a prediction perspective, they are static risk factors (Hare, 1998). However, viewing psychopathy/APD as a static risk factor may be a mistake. Examination of the items of the PCL-R finds that up to 14 of the 20 items are dynamic. There is no *a priori* reason to assume that re-administration of the PCL-R following appropriate treatment would not show changes in scores. In addition, a number of studies have reported correlations in the range of .64 to .86 with the LSI-R, a static-dynamic assessment instrument (Simourd & Hoge, 2000; Stevenson & Wormith, 1987). The assumption that antisocial personality is immutable has diverted researchers from studying the dynamic possibilities of the PCL-R.

Table 9.6 reconfigures the items of the PCL-R in accordance with a PCC (we take some liberty in categorizing the items). The PCL-R and the construct of psychopathy fit nicely into the principles of risk, need, and responsivity. The predictive power of the PCL-R reported from around the world (Hare et al., 2000) may be traced to the static criminal history and dynamic/criminogenic risk factors. By conceptualizing psychopathy as a broad antisocial personality pattern within a PCC, we not only understand the basis for the predictive accuracy of the PCL-R but also are provided a positive, proactive agenda for treatment. Treatment targets are identified (criminogenic needs) and responsivity considerations outlined.

Table 9.6
The PCL-R as Seen from a Psychology of Criminal Conduct

Static Criminal History
Parasitic lifestyle
Early behavior problems
Many short-term marital relationships
Juvenile delinquency
Revocation of conditional release
Criminal versatility

Dynamic Criminogenic Needs
Pathological lying
Conning/manipulative
Lack of remorse or guilt
Poor behavioral controls
Promiscuous sexual relations
Lack of realistic, long-term goals
Impulsivity
Irresponsibility
Failure to accept responsibility

Responsivity
Glibness/superficial charm
Grandiose sense of self-worth
Need for stimulation/prone to boredom
Shallow affect

Application of PCC to the PCL-R has been reported by David Simourd and Robert Hoge (2000). The LSI-R and PCL-R were administered to 321 inmates in a Canadian penitentiary. Approximately 11 percent scored 30 or above on the PCL-R. Comparing the psychopaths to the nonpsychopaths, the psychopaths scored higher on the LSI-R total score and on all of the dynamic subcomponents except for Financial. In other words, psychopaths are at high risk to reoffend and their risk is partly accounted for by higher levels of criminogenic needs.

Some readers may interpret our view as psychopathic offenders being nothing more than high-risk, high-need offenders. Perhaps, if researchers selected the top tenth percentile of LSI-R scores, all the physiological and learning experiments conducted with the PCL-R would be replicated. We are not sure if there is a substantive difference between PCL-R-defined psychopaths and the high-risk offenders identified by different offender risk measures. Future research will undoubtedly clarify our understanding of this special subset of offenders. Until then, we at least offer hypotheses for testing and exploration.

The Sex Offender

Along with mentally disordered and violent offenders, sex offenders elicit a great deal of public apprehension and fear. Most of their criminal acts are violent, involving rape and the use of force. (Sex offenses not involving force, such as exhibitionism, will not be dealt with in this chapter.) Although the fear is high, these offenses are less prevalent today than they were 10 to 20 years ago (Canadian Centre Criminal Justice Statistics, 1999; Maletzky, 1991). The public's apprehension and abhorrence toward sex offenders is compounded by the fact that their victims are, for the most part, women and children, and persons for whom the psychological impact of the crime is often very traumatizing (Resick, 1993).

Incidence of Sex Crimes

Accurate estimates of the incidence of sexual crimes are extremely difficult to obtain. Many victims fail to report such offenses for fear of reprisals or because of shame or embarrassment. Until recently, police and prosecutors have been reluctant to pursue certain types of complaints (e.g., domestic violence). Additionally, the legality of some sexual acts (e.g., homosexuality) has changed the "counting" or recording of these behaviors. Despite these limitations, aggregate statistics provide some valuable insights.

Crime statistics show incidence rates that vary depending on the particular sexual crime and the method of measurement. For example, the United States National Crime Victimization Survey gives a rape incidence rate of 0.8 percent per 1,000 women, whereas specialized surveys yield twice the rate (Koss, 1996). The incidence of child sexual abuse appears higher than the rape of adult women. David Finkelhor and his colleagues (Finkelhor et al., 1990) surveyed 2,626 American men and women and found that 16 percent of the men and 27 percent of the women reported a history of sexual abuse. The acts ranged from unwanted touching (4.5% of the men and 14.6% of the women) to unwanted sexual intercourse (9.5% of the men and 14.6% of the women).

Gene Abel, Mary Mittelman, and Judith Becker (1985) interviewed 411 adult sex offenders about their criminal histories. These 411 offenders reported 218,900 sex crimes. On average, this represents 533 sex crimes per offender. The average number of victims was 366. In a similar vein, a self-report questionnaire was administered to 485 juvenile sex offenders from different sites in the United States and Canada (Zolondek et al., 2001). They found that each juvenile offender (ages 11-17 years) reported between nine and 46 sex offenses. These figures indicate not only a high incidence of undetected sex crimes but that relatively few offenders are responsible.

How Unique are Sex Offenders?

Are sex offenders so different from nonsexual offenders that a fundamentally different approach to theory, assessment, and treatment is required? For example, besides the offense, how do sex offenders differ from other offenders in their behavioral histories, personalities, cognitions, and attitudes? Are their criminogenic needs limited to their sexual behavior, or are the criminogenic needs identified for the nonsexual criminal population (e.g., antisocial personality, drug addiction) just as relevant?

The commonly held view is that sex offenders are "specialists." That is, their crimes are almost exclusively sex crimes. If this is true, then treatment should focus on factors directly associated with the sexual behavior. For example, treatment should target sexual arousal, attitudes toward women, heterosexual social skills, and so forth. As we will soon see, these dynamic risk factors are important, but there is also evidence to suggest that nonsexual criminogenic variables may be more important than originally thought.

There are a number of studies demonstrating that sex offenders also commit many nonsexual crimes. Mark Weinrott and Maureen Saylor (1991) interviewed 99 institutionalized sex offenders who reported, during the year prior to incarceration, 19,518 offenses that were not sex-related ("nonsex" offenses). Some of these offenses were committed during the commission of a sexual offense (e.g., kidnapping a child), but it is unlikely that all of the nonsex offenses were limited to sexual crimes. The 37 rapists in the study, as expected, reported high rates of nonsex offenses (11,277 were reported). However, child molesters, who are generally considered to limit their deviance to children, also reported a very high number of nonsex offenses (8,219). Even the 21 incest offenders reported 2,080 nonsex crimes. Similarly, Maletzky (1991) found that of the 5,000 sex offenders treated at an outpatient clinic, 24 percent had histories of nonsex offenses. Finally, a review of the criminal records of more than 7,000 sex offenders in England and Wales revealed that approximately 60 percent of the offenders were convicted of a nonsexual offense (Soothill et al., 2000). That is, many sex offenders do engage in criminal behavior that is not limited to deviant sexual activity.

The previously described studies were all retrospective accounts of the criminal behavior of sex offenders. However, longitudinal studies also show the same general pattern. That is, many sex offenders go on to commit not only sexual crimes but also nonsexual crimes. Bench, Kramer, and Erickson (1997) followed 408 sex offenders who were treated for an average of four years. Although 24.6 percent recidivated with a sexual offense, they found a *non*sexual recidivism rate of 26.8 percent. In a meta-analysis by Hanson and Bussière (1998) the nonsexual recidivism rate for more than 23,000 sex offenders was 12.2 percent (the average follow-up was about four and one-half years). Child molesters showed a nonsexual, violent recidivism rate of 9.9 percent and rapists a rate of 22.1 percent.

These studies highlight the possibility that there may be important similarities between sex offenders and nonsex offenders. One example is the role of antisocial supports. Many clinicians see sexual offenders as social isolates, awkward in social interactions, and very introverted. Reports of sexual abuse by multiple offenders in day care clinics (Finkelhor, Williams & Burns, 1988), the growth of propedophilia organizations (Thorstad, 1991), and the use of the Internet for deviant sexual purposes (Delmonico, 1997) have painted a different portrait of an underworld of child pornography and sex rings.

There are only two studies that directly investigated the role of social supports in sex offending. In the first study, Karl Hanson and Heather Scott (1996) asked 126 sex offenders, 57 nonsex offenders, and 119 nonoffenders questions about their associations with others. Child molesters reported knowing other child molesters and rapists knowing other rapists. Nonoffenders reported having no sex offenders in their social networks. In the second study (Underwood et al., 1999), 113 child molesters were asked to report whether they molested a child in the presence of another adult (they were not asked if the other adult was a convicted sex offender). Thirty-eight percent reported that another adult was present during the commission of the offense.

This is not to say that sex offenders are no different from nonsex offenders. One consistent finding is that a sex offender is more likely to recidivate with a sexual crime than a nonsex offender (Bonta & Hanson, 1995; Hanson, Scott & Steffy, 1995; Soothill et al., 2000). From the evidence presented thus far, and based upon our broad theoretical perspective of criminal conduct, we would expect significant overlap in the risk factors for sex offenders and nonsex offenders. However, there will also be some traits unique to sexual deviance. To further develop this idea we consider the relative importance of variables specific to sex behavior and some of the other variables found predictive of criminal behavior.

Risk Factors for Sexual Offending

Clinicians and researchers have assessed many different factors thought relevant to sexual offending. Many assessments, driven by a psychopathological model of sexual deviance, have focused on general personality characteristics and indices of personal distress. These types of clinical assessments appear to have had little success in outlining the important personal factors associated with sexual deviant behavior.

For example, William Murphy and James Peters's (1992) review of MMPI literature with pedophiles found that the most frequent elevations were on the very same scales on which criminals score high (i.e., Scales 4/Pd and 9/Ma). Not only could they not identify any specific type of MMPI profile for pedophiles, but even in studies that show a "statistically" significant profile, the actual frequency of these profiles did not exceed 20 percent of the population. Results like these are all too common to make the MMPI a practically useful test for sex offenders (Marshall & Hall, 1995). An increasing number of researchers (Gordon, 1992; Marshall, 1996) have recognized the limitations of general personality and clinical factors, and they have promoted a multiple-factor approach to the understanding of deviant sexual behavior. That is, attention has been brought to factors such as psychopathy, drug abuse, unstable employment, and the other correlates of an antisocial lifestyle.

Deviant sexual fantasies have been regarded as an important correlate of sexual offending (Knight, Prentky & Cerce, 1994). Although such fantasies may be correlated with sexual deviance, it is unclear as to whether it plays a causal role. Fantasies are pleasurable ideations; they differ from the evaluative function of attitudes toward a behavior. Ron Langevin, Reuben Lang, and Suzanne Curnoe (1998) administered a sexual fantasy scale to 129 sex offenders and 77 controls (22 nonoffenders and 50 nonsex offenders). They found that the overall reported rate of deviant fantasies for the sex offenders was relatively low (33.3%), although it was higher than for the controls (11%). Furthermore, more of the controls reported some type of fantasy (deviant or not) than the sex offenders (90.9% vs. 62.5%). Langevin et al. (1998) concluded from the low rates of deviant fantasies and the finding that many of the sex offenders reported normal sexual fantasies that fantasies are unlikely to have etiological significance. Similarly, pornography may serve to stimulate deviant fantasies, but it does not appear to have an etiological role in sexual aggression (Seto, Maric & Barbaree, 2001).

One promising approach to understanding sexual deviance is the assessment of the cognitions that support and encourage sexual deviance. In the last decade, researchers have been speaking about attitudes tolerant of sexual assault (Hanson, 2001; Hanson, Cox & Woszczyna, 1991; Hanson, Gizzarelli & Scott, 1994) and cognitive distortions (Hall & Hirschman, 1992). Attitudes tolerant of sexual deviance and cognitive distortions are similar to the neutralizations and rationalizations discussed earlier (e.g., "Sometimes having sex with a child can be a way of showing love for the child"). The importance of these cognitions and attitudes, as we will soon explain, is that they represent dynamic risk factors. Dynamic risk factors are important for the supervision and treatment of offenders.

The literature on the risk factors of sexual recidivism has been summarized in a meta-analysis by Karl Hanson and Monique Bussière (1998). They reviewed 61 longitudinal studies with nearly 29,000 sex offenders (rapists and child molesters). The average follow-up was between four and five years. The sexual offense recidivism rate was 13 percent (the nonsexual rate was 12%). We refer the reader back to Table 9.4, in which Hanson and Bussière's ranking of risk predictors are compared to the results from general offenders and MDOs.

Two conclusions about sex offense recidivism can be drawn from Table 9.4. First, there was a fair amount of consistency in the ordering of predictors across all three meta-analyses. Antisocial personality was one of the best predictors, while measures of personal distress and social class fell at the bottom of the list. Criminal history showed the second highest effect size; antisocial cognitions came in third. The relatively low position of antisocial cognitions, in comparison to that found in Gendreau et al.'s (1996) meta-analysis, may reflect the state of development in the measurement of deviant sexual cognitions. The second conclusion drawn from Table 9.4 is the field's lack of attention to the potential importance of social supports for sexual deviance. There are only two studies in this area (Hanson & Scott, 1996; Underwood et al., 1999) and their results were congruent with our expectations based on a general PCC. Taking the results together, the overlap we predicted in the risk factors for sex and nonsex offenders was confirmed.

Hanson and Bussière (1998) also identified risk factors specific to sexual deviance. (These predictors are not shown in Table 9.4.) The single best predictor was a deviant phallometric assessment ($r = .32$). Phallometric assessment or penile plethysmography was developed by Kurt Freund (1965) to assess male sexual arousal to stimuli. A device that measures penile tumescence is attached to the penis and erections are measured as the subject is exposed to various stimuli. For example, in the case of a pedophile, slides that include pictures of nude children, nude adults, and neutral stimuli (e.g., a landscape) may be shown, then penile responses to the different stimuli are measured by physiological monitors, and differential arousal to the deviant stimuli is noted.

Considering its directness, plethysmographic measurement has considerable face validity. Moreover, sexual arousal is often assumed to be a mediating factor in sexual offending. Learning to control deviant sexual arousal is an important goal in sex offender treatment programs. Specific reviews of the phallometric literature are consistent with Hanson and Bussière's findings of the importance of sexual arousal in deviant sexual behavior (Lalumière & Quinsey, 1994; Malcolm, Andrews & Quinsey, 1993).

Hanson and Bussière (1998) found that a criminal history was a moderate predictor of sexual recidivism ($r = .13$). When *sexual* criminal history was measured, the r increased to .19. This finding was expected by us. The PIC-R perspective of behavior is derived from a broad personality and social-psychological theory of human behavior. In general terms, behavioral history, cognitions favorable to the behavior, social supports for the behavior, and certain personality factors make contributions to the production and maintenance of behavior. When we narrow our meaning of behavior to refer to criminal behavior, we narrow our definitions of the "Big Four" and we talk about *criminal history, antisocial cognitions, criminal associates*, and *antisocial personality*. As the Hanson and Bussière findings suggest, it is important to further subdivide our theoretical constructs. Thus, moving from *any* criminal history to *sexual* criminal history, our predictive estimates increase (from .13 to .19).

A few additional findings from the Hanson and Bussière (1998) meta-analysis are noteworthy. Many researchers consider a history of victimization as an antecedent to sexual violence as an adult. That is, being sexually victimized as a child leads to a maladjusted adult who is likely to repeat history by sexually abusing others. In an earlier study, Hanson and Slater (1988) questioned this view. They reviewed studies of pedophiles ($n = 1,717$) and found that 28.2 percent of offenders reported being sexually victimized in childhood. This rate of sexual victimization is higher than that found among nonoffender populations (which is about 10%, according to Peters, Wyatt & Finkelhor, 1986), but not significantly different from the rates observed in other clinical populations, nor between various offender groups. Thus, Hanson and Slater (1988) concluded that sexual abuse may increase the likelihood of general problems rather than specific problems such as sexual deviance. The results of the sex offender meta-analysis confirmed their earlier suspicions. A history of childhood sexual abuse was unrelated to sexual recidivism ($r = -.01$).

One of the practical benefits that arise from meta-analytic reviews of risk factors is that it permits the construction of actuarial risk scales based on evidence. Karl Hanson has used the results from the Hanson and Bussière (1998) meta-analysis to construct, validate, and refine actuarial measures of risk for sexual recidivism. Hanson (1997a) coded seven variables selected from the meta-analysis that were present in various data sets. The best four predictors (prior sex offense, age, victim gender, and relationship to victim) were retained to create the Rapid Risk Assessment for Sexual Offense (RRASOR). The correlation between scores on the RRASOR and sexual recidivism was .27 (AUC = .71). This result compared favorably to other actuarial risk scales for sex offenders. For example, the Minnesota Sexual Offender Screening Tool correlated .14 with sexual recidivism (AUC = .65) and the Sex Offender Risk Appraisal Guide showed a correlation of .17 (AUC = .68) with sexual recidivism (Barbaree et al., 2001).

In a collaborative effort, Hanson and Thornton (2000) combined the RRASOR with the risk scale used in the prison service in the United Kingdom to produce Static-99. The resulting 10-item scale produced a correlation of .33 with sexual recidivism (AUC = .71). In an independent validation on 1,400 sex offenders from Sweden, Sjöstedt and Långström (2000) found an AUC = .76 for Static-99 and .72 for the RRASOR.

The most important development in the assessment of sexual offenders has come from a recognition of the importance of dynamic risk factors. Most risk scales for sex offenders have relatively few items, and most of the items are of a static nature (Hanson, 1998, 2001). Furthermore, there has been very little research conducted on the dynamic factors that may be predictive of future recidivism. In a large-scale research program directed by the Ministry of the Solicitor General of Canada, the dynamic risk factors associated with sexual recidivism are gradually being identified.

In the first phase of the Dynamic Predictors of Sexual Reoffense Project, Hanson and Harris (2001) compared sex offenders who recidivated sexually with sex offenders who did not reoffend sexually. Particular attention was paid to stable and acute dynamic factors. Stable factors require months or years to change (e.g., alcoholism) and acute factors change within hours or days (e.g., a sudden drinking binge or a neighbor dropping off a child for babysitting). This retrospective, cross-sectional study identified a number of dynamic factors that differentiated the recidivists from the nonrecidivists. The best nine risk factors were subsequently organized to form a dynamic risk scale called the Sex Offender Need Assessment Rating (SONAR; Hanson & Harris, 2001).

The second phase of the research is in progress. This phase uses a longitudinal design and the research involves sites from Canada, the United States, and England. Probation and parole officers are administering risk scales including a modified SONAR and other measures of potentially dynamic risk factors. The dynamic measures are readministered on a regular basis (weekly for acute dynamic factors and every six months for stable dynamic factors). During the course of this three and one-half year project, sexual recidivism will be monitored and the dynamic factors will be evaluated as to their relationship with sexual recidivism. The findings from this study will be important for the ongoing supervision of sex offenders in the community.

The Treatment of Sex Offenders

As we have already said, efforts to manage sexual recidivism usually involve decreasing sexual arousal. Sexual arousal, in many programs, is the treatment target or dynamic risk factor that is assumed to lead to sexual offending. Various interventions are introduced, and measures such as phallometric assessments are used to measure success in decreasing deviant sexual arousal. Another direct, physiological indicator of sexual arousal is serum testosterone levels. High levels of the male hormone testosterone are assumed to be associated with high levels of sexual arousal and, in turn, sexual activity (Hucker & Bain, 1990; Prentky, 1985). Therefore, high testosterone levels are often viewed as synonymous with excessive sexual drives and sexual aggression.

If high testosterone levels increase the risk for sexual offending, then one obvious treatment approach is to decrease serum testosterone levels. Efforts to reduce sexual arousal and the linking of this reduction to decreases in sexual recidivism are crucial to establishing sexual arousal as a dynamic risk factor. Two interventions to reduce sexual arousal are physical castration and the so-called "chemical castrations." Both methods decrease testosterone levels and thereby are expected to affect sexual arousal.

Studies of physical castration have shown low rates of recidivism, many in the 2 to 4 percent range (Bradford, 1997). However, most of the studies have used pretest and posttest research designs without comparison groups. Across studies there is also extreme variability in the sexual recidivism rates. For example, approximately 10 percent of castrates continue to have erections (Brown & Courtis, 1977) and some have even shown higher rates of sexual activity after castration (Heim, 1981). Needless to say, this procedure involves serious ethical dilemmas as well as physical and psychological side effects. As a result, physical castrations have not been performed on any large scale for the past 20 years. With the advent of drugs that either block the release of the hormones (androgens) that stimulate testosterone secretion or compete with other hormones for the neurophysiological sites that release testosterone, physical castrations are not necessary. Drugs such as cyproterone acetate (CPA; Androcur) and medroxyprogesterone (MPA; Provera) have been hailed as the new treatments for sexual offenders.

Reductions in hormonal levels and general libido have followed with the administration of CPA and MPA. However, reductions in deviant sexual thoughts and masturbation rates have not been convincingly demonstrated (Marshall et al., 1991). While many sex offenders show reduced recidivism rates while under medication (Bradford, 1997; Walker et al., 1984), there has been no experimental demonstration that recidivism is reduced solely as a result of these drugs. John Bradford and Anne Pawlak (1993) evaluated CPA with 19 sex offenders in a double-blind study and found CPA associated with a reduction in testosterone levels, sexual fantasies, and masturbation. However, information on recidivism was not reported. Thus far, no study has investigated whether any reduced recidivism after medication is due to the counseling/treatment programs that almost all the offenders receive while on medication, or due to the long-term effect of the medication itself (Barbaree & Marshall, 1998).

In summary, sexual arousal has not yet been shown to be a dynamic risk factor, and there is little empirical evidence that physiological interventions targeting sexual arousal are essential to effective treatment. However, physiological interventions do have considerable face validity and may be useful adjuncts to the treatment of high-risk cases. Medication may provide early and immediate stabilization that heightens the client's responsiveness to treatment. Hopefully, future research will explore this role.

It is interesting how history in the social sciences repeats itself. We have seen how corrections in the 1960s was prorehabilitation and how the bubble burst with Martinson's review of the treatment literature. Like Martinson, researchers Lita Furby, Mark Weinrott, and Lyn Blackshaw (1989) reviewed studies (n = 42) that provided information on the recidivism of offenders (sex offenders in this case). They concluded that "there is as yet no evidence that clinical treatment reduces rates of sex reoffenses" (p. 27). This review was published in the influential *Psychological Bulletin* and caused a stir within the research community.

Furby et al. (1989) provided a review that was unusual in that it compared studies of untreated sex offenders to other independent studies of treated offenders. Only a minority of the comparisons came from the same study. Of the seven studies that provided data on both treated and untreated sex offenders, one showed treatment to be associated with reductions in sex offense recidivism. Six studies reported data on treated and untreated offenders and general criminal recidivism. Here, five of the six studies had lower recidivism rates for the treated offenders. At first glance, this seems to suggest that treatment may reduce general criminal recidivism but not sexual recidivism—that the criterion behaviors are independent of one another (the opposite of what we have been arguing). Most striking in this review paper, however, is the almost complete absence of any analysis of what actually composes treatment. Recall from our meta-analysis of the treatment literature (Andrews, Zinger et al., 1990a) that there can be appropriate and inappropriate treatments. Perhaps the failure of the treatment programs in this review was the result of inappropriate treatments.

The Furby et al. (1989) conclusion has not gone unchallenged (Becker & Hunter, 1992; Marshall & Barbaree, 1990; Marshall et al., 1991). Other researchers have provided a more optimistic outlook on the treatment of sex offenders (Barbaree & Marshall, 1998; Worling & Curwen, 2000). The clinical work of Barry Maletzky (1991) at the Sexual Abuse Clinic in Portland, Oregon, is illustrative of a multifaceted approach with sexual offenders. In the clinic, which has treated more than 5,000 sex offenders since 1971, treatment is individually tailored to the offender and may include aversive conditioning to reduce deviant sexual arousal, social skills training, orgasmic reconditioning (masturbating to nondeviant fantasies), and a range of other therapeutic techniques. Nearly 3,800 patients who have completed treatment were followed up for a period ranging from one to 17 years. The success rate was 91 percent.

Working with a more serious offender population, Janice Marques and Craig Nelson (1992) are applying cognitive-behavioral treatment and relapse prevention programming to incarcerated sex offenders. Relapse prevention involves teaching offenders to recognize the situations that increase the risk of offending and how to either avoid these high-risk situations or deal with them in a nondeviant fashion. This is a long-term study; preliminary postrelease outcome data are promising. Marques, Day, Nelson, and West (1994) found a sexual recidivism rate of 8.2 percent for the treatment group and 13.4 percent for the control group. The average follow-up time was 34.2 months.

There are two recent meta-analyses of the treatment literature with sex offenders. Catherine Gallagher and her colleagues (Gallagher et al., 1999) analyzed 25 studies and found a moderate reduction due to treatment (Cohen's $d = .43$ or $r = .21$). The cognitive-behavioral treatments were the most effective forms of intervention. In the late 1990s, the Association for the Treatment of Sexual Abusers (ATSA) created a committee of researchers to review the treatment literature. The resulting report is the most comprehensive review published to date (Hanson et al., 2002). Forty-three studies representing more than 9,000 sex offenders were analyzed. With an average follow-up of four years, treatment was associated with an 8 percent reduction in recidivism. Although the reduction is modest compared to the results from treatment programs with nonsexual offenders, the results from the two meta-analysis are much more optimistic than the Furby et al. (1989) review nearly 15 years ago. As Hanson et al. (in press) observed, the knowledge that has accumulated from the general offender treatment literature has not yet been fully applied to the treatment of sex offenders. Movement in this direction may result in larger reductions in sexual recidivism.

Human Hunters and Predators

Sex offenders, in order to carry out their acts, must select, follow, and "capture" their victims. Certainly, some offenders may take advantage of unexpected opportunities, but for the most part, there is a certain amount of planning required to complete the act undetected (remember, many sex offenders have committed far more sex offenses than those for which they were apprehended). This aspect of violent criminal behavior—the following, watching, and waiting—is one of the most fearful aspects of criminal behavior. When the goal of the behavior is to commit the most violent and gruesome acts, fear and concern is intensified. Serial murderers, sex offenders (who are in effect, serial sex offenders), and ex-partners who stalk their lovers appear to form a class of offenders unlike most criminals. We have already seen that sex offenders have some unique characteristics, but also that they share commonalities with nonsex offenders when we consider the broad theoretical constructs. For the remainder of this chapter, we summarize the emerging literature on stalkers and serial murderers.

Stalkers

In 1989, Rebecca Shaeffer, a television actress, was shot and killed on her doorstep; her murderer was a fan who had a two-year history of following her, writing letters, and trying to meet her. The murder resulted in the first of the anti-stalking laws in California (1993), laws that now can be found in all but one American state (Westrup & Fremouw, 1998). It also drew public attention to a behavior that had largely gone unnoticed. At first, the attention was directed to the stalking of celebrities and political figures, but later it broadened to include the far more prevalent stalking of a partner in a love relation that had soured. Legal definitions of stalking have two components: (1) attempts to gain physical proximity to the victim, and (2) the causing of fear.

Interest in stalking was evident long before the introduction of anti-stalking laws. In 1942, the French psychiatrist de Clérambault described a syndrome characterized by the delusional belief that another, higher-status, and unsuspecting person was in love with the patient (all six patients described by de Clérambault were females). This belief then served as the unrelenting motive for following and attempting to communicate with the victim. De Clérambault's syndrome eventually became a delusional disorder, erotomanic type in DSM-IV. Many of the early studies operated from the premise that stalking behavior was motivated by an obsessive love of the victim *and* a delusion that the victim loved the stalker. That is, stalking was a feature of an Axis I disorder such as paranoid schizophrenia (Goldstein, 1978).

Subsequent to de Clérambault's analysis, investigators began to differentiate types of stalkers according to the presence or absence of delusions and the type of delusion. There remained the erotomania marked with delusions of the victim loving the stalker, but also proposed was obsessional love without the delusion that the victim loves the stalker. For example, John Hinckley Jr. shot President Ronald Reagan to demonstrate to actress Jodie Foster the depth of his love, hoping that she would reciprocate (Perez, 1993). The delusional stalkers were also characterized by situations in which the victim had no prior relationship with the stalker. Kristine Kienlen (1995) noted that in most cases of delusional stalking, the victim and stalker had never met. The third type of stalker was nondelusional but highly obsessive (Zona, Sharma & Lane, 1993). The "simple obsessive" stalker, unlike the delusional stalker, often had a prior relationship with the victim (e.g., ex-intimate, coworker, neighbor).

Early descriptions of stalkers were based upon highly selective samples of celebrity and political stalkers who exhibited clinical symptomatology. We must note from the outset that these clinical cases are quite rare. Although millions may have adoration for movie stars, sports figures, and political leaders, very few give up their everyday lives to pursue relentlessly a certain celebrity. We also wish to affirm that we are not talking about the political assassin. Political assassins can be quite rational and their motives are easily explainable. They hold beliefs that harming the politician is valued, they associate with others who reinforce and facilitate stalking behavior, they have a history of dealing with political foes in a violent manner, and they likely exhibit an antisocial personality. Those charged with protecting political and world leaders know that assassins who hold a valued political ideology and organization are the most dangerous. From a PCC perspective, we can understand why.

When dealing with the delusional celebrity stalker, a question often asked is how likely are these stalkers to step beyond harassment and fear provocation to actual physical harm. There are certainly cases of delusional stalkers who have killed their victims (e.g., the case of Rebecca Shaeffer). In Kienlen's (1995) sample of 25 stalkers investigated at a forensic clinic, 84 percent of the stalkers had face-to-face contact with their victims and two resulted in murder. However, this sample had already been preselected for their violent actions—they all came from a forensic clinic.

There are also examples in which no physical harm has resulted. Take as an illustration the case of Margaret Ray. Margaret Ray invaded the home of television personality David Letterman on at least six occasions but committed nonviolent acts such as eating food from his kitchen (Perez, 1993). Harmon, Rosner, and Owens (1995) reviewed 48 cases of harassment and stalking that had been referred to a forensic clinic. They found that 21 percent exhibited aggressive behavior ranging from throwing bottles to physical assault. Studies on risk of violence with delusional stalkers who have not already been screened for violent behavior are almost nonexistent.

Park Dietz and his colleagues (Dietz, Matthews, Van Duyne et al., 1991) analyzed 1,800 "nut mail" letters written to Hollywood celebrities by 214 subjects. The letters were culled from those screened by a security firm specializing in services to entertainment figures. They found that only 17.3 percent of the individuals who wrote to celebrities actually attempted to make physical contact with them. Furthermore, they found no relationship between writing threats and the act of actually approaching the celebrities. In a similar study, but targeting members of the U.S. Congress, those who threatened government leaders were *less* likely to approach the politician (Dietz, Matthews, Martell et al., 1991).

Perhaps the best study to date that provides some answer to the potential dangerousness of delusional stalkers comes from Reid Meloy's (1996) review of three of the largest studies on stalking (n = 142). Fifty percent of the subjects made threats to their victims, but only one-quarter of those who made threats actually attempted to harm the victim. Although this is a high false-positive rate (75%), Meloy noted that those who did not threaten the victim were unlikely to harm the victim, leading him to conclude that the presence of threats was a risk factor.

In general, many delusional stalkers infrequently cause physical harm to their victims. They may cause emotional upset and harassment, but only the extreme cases physically harm or kill the individuals they are following (we will discuss the extreme cases in our section on serial killers). Why is this? The answer can be formulated by reflection on some of the major risk factors of criminal behavior. In the stalking cases described, the most salient feature is the presence of deviant cognitions, or "delusions." Let us consider the other major risk factors. With respect to behavioral history, the common pattern is a history of nonviolent "following behavior." Regarding social supports for the behavior, celebrity stalkers tend to operate alone—informing others of their behavior is likely met with efforts to discourage the behavior. Finally, Meloy (1996) found that erotomanic stalkers were *underrepresented* by antisocial personality disorder (APD), presumably because APD individuals cannot feel love and attachment to the victim. All this said, are there some stalkers who pose a more significant risk? Two likely candidates are domestic stalkers and serial murderers.

Domestic Stalkers

In the early 1990s, the feminist movement was successful in garnering public concern about violent domestic relationships. Surveys showed that a significant proportion of women, as well as men, have been stalked. In the United States, Patricia Tjaden and Nancy Thoennes (1996) found that 8 percent of 8,000 women surveyed in 1994 were stalked at least once in their lifetime, with 61 percent of the stalkers being an ex-intimate. The rate was 2 percent for the 8,000 men, with males more likely to be stalked by a coworker, neighbor, or stranger. In a survey of 348 British women, 24 percent reported at least one incident of stalking (Sheridan, Davies & Boon, 2001).

Although significant numbers of women have experienced being stalked by an ex-intimate, research is scant on the danger the stalker poses to the woman. A few studies have found that women who had experienced physical and verbal abuse during the relationship may be stalked by their ex-intimate after the relationship ends (Coleman, 1997). Thus, this history of conflict during the relationship can carry beyond the end of a relationship (Wright et al., 1996). In an in-depth study of the problem, Russell Palarea and his colleagues (Palarea et al., 1999) compared the Los Angeles police files of 223 intimate (married, cohabiting, dating) and 88 nonintimate stalking cases. Intimate stalkers were more likely to carry out threats of physical violence (80.6%) than nonintimate stalkers (19.4%). Further analysis showed that a general history of violence was the best predictor of assault to the victim ($r = .43$).

In addition to behavioral history, certain personality traits may play a role. At this point, we suspect that APD may be a minor personality factor in domestic stalking cases that are motivated by revenge (that is, "I'll teach you for leaving me"). Our guess is that the APD stalker is relatively uncommon, being easily distracted by other women and "getting over" the relationship quickly. However, a more prevalent personality constellation may be an obsessive attachment disorder (Abrams & Robinson, 1998). In Canada's Violence Against Women Survey, 35 percent of the women reported controlling behavior from their husbands (Johnson & Sacco, 1995). Examples of controlling behavior were limiting contact with her family and insisting on knowing her whereabouts at all times. Excessive and obsessive control over the partner has been hypothesized as an important precursor to spousal murder (Wilson & Daly, 1992).

Theoretical explanations of stalking are highly speculative because of the limited research on the topic. Research on stalking has only come into its own in the 1990s (Meloy, 1998). Explanations have centred around disrupted childhood attachments (Kienlen, 1998) and socio-cultural values that support male dominance through aggression (White et al., 2000). However, our theoretical perspective of crime suggests some plausible factors that are consistent with research on related topics such as family violence. Our theoretical perspective becomes relevant when we specify the "Big Four" in relation to stalking behavior. A history of interpersonal conflict within an intimate relationship, an obsessive personality, and delusions/cognitions supportive of following behavior become important. Antisocial supports for the behavior may not play as important a role because of the overall strength of the other "Big Four" factors and the cumulative effects of other variables such as alcohol abuse and employment stress.

Serial Killers

When it comes to a discussion of serial killers, we are forced once again to rely more on educated guesses than hard facts. Serial murderers are usually defined as murderers who have at least three victims over an extended period of time. This definition differentiates the serial murderer from the mass murderer who kills many people in a brief period of time. Examples of mass murderers are Marc Lépine, who entered a classroom in Montreal and opened fire, killing 14 women; Thomas Hamilton, responsible for shooting and killing 16 school children and their teacher in Dunblane, Scotland; and, more recently, Eric Harris and Dylan Klebold, who killed 12 students and a teacher at Columbine High School in Colorado. Both serial killers and mass murderers, to use Elliott Leyton's (1986:25) description, "appear to kill *for its own sake*." There are no other obvious goals as with the professional killer or the revenge-seeking individual. However, because very little is known about the psychology of mass murderers, we will limit our presentation to serial killers.

Serial murderers have been with us for a long time (e.g., Jack the Ripper) but the tremendous media interest in serial killers has made it the "crime of the 1990s" (Holmes & Holmes, 1994). There are no reliable measures of the prevalence of serial killers, but estimates from various scholars have ranged from 35 to 200 serial killers in the United States (Holmes & Holmes, 1994). When these figures are compared to homicide statistics, we find that serial murders are extremely rare, representing less than 1 percent of all homicides in the United States (Fox & Levin, 1998).

There is an emerging literature on the characteristics of serial killers (Fox & Levin, 1998; Gresswell & Hollin, 1994). First of all, serial killers are usually Caucasian males (approximately 15 percent are African-Americans; Jenkins, 1998). Female serial killers do exist but tend to be relatively rational and instrumental in their actions (Holmes, Hickey & Holmes, 1998). Keeney and Heide (1994) reviewed 14 female serial killing cases taken from various media sources and found that the most frequent motive was money and that the victims were well known to them (e.g., 37% of the victims were family members and another 43% were under care from the murderer). Also, there was no sexual assault, stalking, torture, or "overkill" of the 62 victims. Contrast these findings to the male serial killer and a different picture develops.

The male serial killer tends to stalk and seek out the victim, who is often a stranger. David Berkowitz ("Son of Sam") cruised the streets of New York and shot into cars occupied by unsuspecting women or couples. There was no sexual assault—only six people dead. Many male serial killers move in large geographical areas. For example, Ted Bundy began his string of 22 murders in Washington state, moved to Utah, then Colorado, and finally was apprehended permanently in Florida (Bundy had been arrested but escaped from a Colorado jail).

The most frightening aspect of some serial killers is the sexual and sadistic form of their murders. This type of serial killer is definitely the minority among serial killers (Fox & Levin, 1999). These "lust murderers" are noted for their violent fantasies (Holmes, 1989; Holmes & Holmes, 1998). Prentky, Burgess, Rokous, Lee, Hartman, and Ressler (1989) found that 86 percent of 25 serial sexual murderers reported sadistic fantasies prior to the crime. The rate for nonserial sexual murderers was 23 percent. The frequently observed sadistic fantasies of the serial sexual murderer led Holmes (1989) to hypothesize that these fantasies serve as a cognitive rehearsal for the act.

Sex offenders have been thought to lack empathy for their victims. If they had empathy, then the suffering of the victim would inhibit their behavior. In a study of rapists, Rice, Chaplin, Harris, and Coutts (1994) found that rapists showed the greatest sexual arousal, phallometrically measured, to stimuli in which the victim was raped as opposed to consenting to sex. A subsequent study with child molesters (Chaplin, Rice & Harris, 1995) found them to prefer depictions of sexual interactions in which the child suffered and was brutalized. The authors interpreted these findings as attributable to a lack of empathy—a view supported by the finding that the sex offenders in both studies scored lower on paper-and-pencil measures of empathy.

However, it is unlikely that sex offenders completely lack empathy. The exceptions may be the delusional, schizophrenic sex offender who commits extreme violence on the victim with little awareness of the consequences of his or her actions. Most sex offenders have some empathic capacity—they do not score zero on the paper-and-pencil measures of empathy. Two possibilities exist. The sex offender may engage in some form of cognitive "neutralization" technique to psychologically distance himself (or herself) from the victim (e.g., "she deserves it," "she likes it"). This cognitive distortion has been observed in generally violent offenders. The other possibility is that victim suffering is a goal of the assault. That is, the attacker is quite aware of the harm and hurt experienced by the victim and that is exactly what reinforces the behavior.

Karl Hanson (Hanson, 1997b; Hanson & Scott, 1995) has argued that empathy has two subcomponents: perspective-taking skills and sympathetic feelings toward others. As a consequence, sex offenders can vary with respect to their ability to take the perspective of their victim *and* their emotional reaction to the victim. For some sex offenders, accurately reading the cues from the victim is difficult. For others (an example may be a subgroup of sexual sadists), the offender knows full well the suffering that is being inflicted on the victim but either does not care or finds the victim's response reinforcing. For the serial killer who is also a sexual sadist, sexual pleasure *and* victim suffering can be powerful nonmediated rewards.

Although not a study of sexual serial killers, a report by Dietz, Hazelwood, and Warren (1990) is instructive. Dietz et al. (1990) described 30 cases from the FBI that involved sexual torture. Although more than one-half of the cases had no prior criminal record, nearly all of them had histories of deviant *sexual* behavior and all had grandiose, narcissistic personalities, with 40 percent having antisocial personality features. The maintenance of deviant sexual cognitions was evident in that most of the sexual sadists either saved something from the women (e.g., clothing, hair) or recorded their crimes in some manner (e.g., diaries, pictures). The sexual sadist had an accomplice in one-third of the cases studied, a finding noted in other studies of sexual sadists (Hucker, 1997). In Canada, the notorious case of Karla Homolka, who assisted Paul Bernardo in the abduction, torture, and rape of young girls (allegedly including Homolka's own sister) is an illustration of social support for even the most heinous crimes.

Sexual serial killers also vary as to their psychological stability. Granted, killing someone for no other reason than to kill them or for sexual gratification can hardly be accepted as psychologically normal. What we mean is that some sexual serial killers are clearly delusional and psychotic while others are more "in control." Ted Bundy showed sufficient charm and skill to lure women to his car and eventually to their rape and death. Others engage in definitely bizarre and grotesque acts, ranging from collecting "trophies" (Edmund Kemper decapitated and kept the heads of his victims) to cannibalism (Jeffrey Dahmer) to sexual desecration after the death of the victim.

So, what can explain repetitive and sadistic murder, a behavior that is the most severely sanctioned act in almost every society on earth? There have been many explanations, ranging from an XYY genotype in one case (Kraus, 1995), the obvious sexual gratification in sexual serial killers (they kill to eliminate witnesses), being sexually abused as a child (Ressler et al., 1986) and, of course, the layperson's pronouncement that they are "crazy." Leyton (1986:298) attributes it to society's tolerance of a wide range of social activities, thereby "releasing humans too much from their social contract" and a social class tension. Thus, the serial killer is often from the working class and the victim is from the middle or upper class.

In our opinion, Leyton (1986) is mistaken in his view that there is some sort of unconscious rebellion against the upper classes. However, he has a point regarding the lack of social controls over the serial killer. Almost all serial killers have had horrendous backgrounds marked by parental abuse and neglect. They were also social isolates during their development into adulthood. Even the smooth-talking Ted Bundy was an outcast in high school and had only one date. Finally, many serial killers, and especially the sadistic sexual killer, experience delusional worlds that further distance them from social controls. The lack of interpersonal controls and the failure to develop internal controls for prosocial behaviors "frees" the person to act according to idiosyncratic and bizarre fantasies. Coupled with a behavioral history of violent behavior, poor coping skills, and sadistic fantasies beginning in childhood (Gresswell & Hollin, 1994; Hale, 1998; Ressler et al., 1986), the results are not at all surprising.

Summary

One of the themes in this text is that our knowledge of criminal behavior can be forwarded by applying a psychology of criminal conduct (PCC) to the analysis. By a PCC, we do not simply mean taking research from the field of abnormal psychology and psychiatry and directly applying it to offenders. The offenders discussed in this chapter are a good example of the folly of this approach. Our present knowledge of MDOs, sex offenders, psychopaths, and other human predators is almost entirely founded upon the wholesale application of clinical models. The results have been unsatisfactory.

Instead, advances in this area will be made as researchers and clinicians begin to loosen their allegiance to clinical ideology and start to investigate the role of established correlates among these groups of offenders. Targeting one or two variables in treatment, such as sexual arousal (Rice, Harris & Quinsey, 1991), will have little effect on recidivism. Only when we start focusing on multiple targets (Hall, 1990) and functional correlates (Hale, 1998) can we expect change.

Chapter 10

PCC: Applications in Related Areas

In this chapter, we consider some of the principles derived from a Psychology of Criminal Conduct (PCC) and their relationship to two social problems: (1) domestic violence against women, and (2) substance abuse. We also consider how a PCC could be applied to a recent reform in policing—community policing. There are many possible topics that could be presented (e.g., crime prevention, child abuse), but reviewing the various possibilities would go beyond the scope of this text.

Our review of the three topics that we have chosen is not meant to represent comprehensive, state-of-the-art literature reviews. Such reviews are readily available in textbooks and journal articles. Our analysis of the topics is selective and intended to highlight how a PCC can be helpful and informative. This chapter is also speculative because direct testing of the validity of the "Big Four"; the principles of risk, need, and responsivity; and direct comparisons between appropriate treatment and sanctions are either rare or entirely nonexistent. We are ready to accept the criticism that this chapter is "armchair theorizing." Yet, we hope that it will lead to research that improves our understanding of a wide range of deviant behaviors.

Domestic Violence Against Women

Recent surveys in the United States and Canada reveal a disturbing picture of the prevalence and incidence of violence within families. In the 1998 National Crime Victimization Survey, American women reported more than one million violent victimizations committed by an intimate or ex-intimate partner (Rennison & Welchans, 2000). The survey also found that 1,830 murders were attributable to intimate partners. In Canada's Violence Against Women Survey, approximately one-quarter of Canadian women reported at least one incident of physical or sexual assault since age 16 from an intimate or ex-intimate (Johnson & Sacco, 1995).

The violence against adult women within intimate relationships is just one facet of the violence that exists in many families. The levels of child abuse are equally disturbing. It is estimated that 17,000 girls under the age of 12 were raped in the United States in 1992, with nearly one-half of the sexual assaults committed by a family member (Langan & Harlow, 1994). The statistics on physical abuse against children vary widely depending upon what constitutes physical abuse. If physical punishment is included in the definition, then nearly all parents would be described as physically abusive (Straus, 1991). Estimates of the rates of physical abuse that exclude "normal disciplining practices" and that have the potential of prompting the intervention of child welfare and criminal justice agencies range from 102 to 110 per 1,000 children (Wolfner & Gelles, 1993).

In this section, our attention is directed to the domestic assault of women. This focus does not minimize our concern over child abuse, for we believe that child abuse is especially disconcerting because of the extreme vulnerability of children. We choose the topic of spousal abuse only to illustrate the potential applications of a PCC. Many of our comments and views could be applied equally to the issues surrounding child welfare.

Studying the violence that occurs in families is important for a number of reasons. First, we are interested in learning what we can do to decrease the violent victimization within these families. The woman who is abused by her partner is not only at risk for her own personal safety but also for the safety of her children. A number of studies have demonstrated that a violent spouse is also likely to be violent toward children (McCloskey et al., 1995; Ross, 1996). Second, both the women and the children who witness the suffering are more likely to experience emotional, psychological, and behavioral problems (McCloskey et al., 1995; Wolfe & Jaffe, 1991). The study of violence against women begins with a concern for the well-being of the victims.

Third, we need to know who are the high-risk abusers and what interventions would be successful in stopping the violence. The accurate identification of violent men is needed to inform police and other social agents who are empowered to remove familial aggressors for the protection of other family members. Because the majority of women, for various reasons, do not leave abusive relationships, and violent men may continue their assaults in new relationships, social service providers require knowledge of effective interventions that will stop the cycle of family violence.

Finally, understanding family violence is important for the prevention of future violence. Although not conclusive, there is research suggesting that experiencing and witnessing family violence by children increases the risk that these children will grow up to be violent in both intimate and general interpersonal relationships (Kruttschnitt & Dornfeld, 1993; Straus & Kantor, 1994; Widom, 1989).

In this section, we pose the following questions derived from a PCC:

1. What are the characteristics of offenders who are likely to commit violence against their partners?

2. Are the risk factors similar to the predictors of general criminal behavior?

3. What are the characteristics of effective interventions for those who assault their spouses?

Men Who Batter Their Partners

Considering the prevalence of spousal violence, it is surprising how little research exists on the assessment of risk for spousal abuse, especially in comparison to the hundreds of studies with general criminal offenders. The reasons for this state of affairs are many. The first explanation that comes to mind is that spousal assault was only recently considered to be a serious criminal act. Prior to the 1970s, the police and the courts viewed the violence that occurred in families as a private problem. Domestic disputes were infrequently acted upon, doctors and nurses did not report suspicious bruises, and the victims themselves did not tell anyone about their sufferings. There was no visible problem and, therefore, there was no need for research.

The women's movement changed our perception about what goes on in homes across the country. It exposed the range of physical and sexual abuse suffered by women and children at the hands of men. Women can and do assault their male partners. In fact, a meta-analytic review by John Archer (2000) found that women are more likely to use physical aggression then men but the difference is in the *severity* of the injury. When men act aggressively, they inflict more injury. For example, compared to men, women are 22 times more likely to be raped and eight times more likely to be stalked by their partner (Tjaden & Thoennes, 2000). For these reasons and the fact that the literature deals almost exclusively with man-to-women violence, we will restrict our review to this literature. Public education and the establishment of social services such as women's shelters made it easier for victims to come forward and tell their stories. Nevertheless, risk assessment research did not flourish.

Many studies centered on the assessment of violent acts in intimate relationships. A good example of this type of research was the development of the Conflict Tactics Scale (CTS; Straus, 1979). The CTS measures the frequency of different "tactics" used by couples to make decisions and settle disputes. The items range from "discussed the issue calmly" to "used a knife or gun." The CTS highlights the physical abuse aspects of intimate relationships and has been criticized for ignoring verbal and emotional abuse within the relationship. Moreover, some sociological and feminist scholars (e.g., Dobash & Dobash, 1979, 1995) took the position that the patriarchal views held by most men accounted for the violence against women. The use of aggression for the control of women was "normal" within a male cultural context, and differentiating men along other dimensions had minimal value.

Patriarchal attitudes are undoubtedly important, but we agree with others (e.g., Dutton, 1994, 1995) that they are insufficient to explain the violence and that more complex social-psychological models of explanation are needed. We also accept the view that emotional and verbal abuse can be as hurtful as physical abuse. However, because of the lack of agreement as to what constitutes verbal and emotional abuse, for the present we prefer to deal only with physical abuse against women. The first lesson from a PCC is that we must begin with differentiating men in terms of their risk to abuse their partners. PCC emphasizes individual differences, so we would expect variability in the characteristics of men who batter. Not all men assault their partners, and those who do assault their partners vary in the severity of their assaults.

Information on risk factors for spousal abuse comes from two sources: (1) surveys of spousal violence, and (2) specific studies of conflictual relationships. Surveys provide prevalence and incidence information, but they also yield other important information. Some surveys may ask men to report on their behavior in domestic situations, and victimization surveys may ask victims to describe the characteristics of their assailants. From these surveys and studies, we can compose a list of potential risk factors. We remind the reader that surveys use cross-sectional research designs (i.e., abusers are compared to nonabusers) and not longitudinal designs that speak to the predictive validity of certain variables.

Analyzing data from the Canadian Violence Against Women Survey, Rhonda Lenton (1995) found that patriarchal values (jealousy and control over the women) were significantly correlated with abuse. These, however, were not the only correlates of violence against women. Another significant offender characteristic associated with physical assault was witnessing the father abuse the mother, a finding consistent with social learning theory. Factors that were found to bear no relationship to spousal violence were socioeconomic factors such as employment, income level, and education.

Pan, Neidig, and O'Leary (1994) administered a modified version of the Conflict Tactics Scale to more than 14,000 army personnel from 38 bases across the United States. As mentioned earlier, the CTS (Straus, 1979) measures different behaviors used to handle conflict (e.g., pushing and shoving, threatening). The findings showed, first of all, that there was variation in the level of husband-to-wife violence. Nearly 70 percent of the respondents reported *no* physical aggression against their spouse, 24.4 percent reported "mild" physical aggression (e.g., slapped or threw something), and 5.6 percent reported "severe" aggressive acts (e.g., choked or used a knife on the spouse).

Pan et al. (1994) reported the results only from multivariate analysis and did not provide effect size estimates for the individual correlates of spousal abuse. We can only approximate from their analysis a ranking of the risk factors. This ranking is as follows:

1. Marital stress

2. Alcohol/drug abuse

3. Depressive symptomatology

4. Age (being younger)

5. Income (lower)

Interestingly, job stress was unrelated to spousal aggression, further adding to the mix of results with respect to this variable (Barling & Rosenbaum, 1986; Lenton, 1995). The finding by Pan et al. (1994) may have been an artifact of sampling a military population with its own unique culture and environment.

In a 30-month longitudinal study of 393 recently married couples, O'Leary, Malone, and Tyree (1994) found that three variables predicted physical aggression toward the spouse. They were: (1) marital discord (r = .22), (2) witnessing the father abuse the mother during childhood (r = .21), and (3) an aggressive personality (r = .18). Some consistencies emerge when we compare the results to earlier studies. First, and not surprisingly, marital dissatisfaction is related to spousal abuse. That is, factors within the immediate situation (i.e., victim-offender interactions) are reliably associated with intimate violence. Second, being raised in a family in which the father physically assaulted the mother is a risk factor. From a social learning perspective, the father is a model for the son in how to deal with interpersonal conflict. Finally, an aggressive (antisocial) personality appears associated with spousal assault.

The similarities between male batterers and criminal offenders are further strengthened in a study by Andrew Klein (1996). Klein examined 663 cases of male batterers that passed through a Massachusetts court. All the cases had a restraining order imposed on the men. Twelve offender characteristics were examined with respect to recidivism (re-abuse) over a two-year period. It is interesting that 90 percent of the cases came before the court at the victim's request. That is, the majority of the offenders were involved in civil cases, and police intervention accounted for only a minority of cases. Yet, a significant proportion of the offenders had extensive criminal records that included offenses other than spousal assaults. Nearly all of the men had a prior criminal record (80%) with, on average, six prior court appearances that included offenses as serious as murder. Nearly one-quarter of these men (23.4%) had also committed violent crimes against males.

Within one year, one-half of the women returned to court to have the restraining order removed, citing reconciliation. During the two-year follow-up, 56.4 percent of the men were rearrested for a new crime; the rearrest rate for spousal assault was 34 percent. Only two offender characteristics predicted new abuse: age and prior criminal history (rs were not given). One other factor predicted domestic violence recidivism: the court order of "no contact." In cases in which the court ordered no contact with the woman, the re-abuse rate was 35.7 percent; it was 27.3 percent in cases in which contact was allowed.

Klein (1996) drew two major conclusions from his study. First, male batterers, at least the ones for whom a restraining order is sought, "look like criminals, act like criminals, and re-abuse like criminals" (p. 207). Second, the failure of restraining orders may be explained by the finding that these abusers were relatively high-risk offenders for whom a civil restraining order is nothing more than a nuisance.

Donald Dutton and Stephen Hart (1992) also work from the premise that spouse assaulters and "regular" criminals are very similar groups. Their study focused on known criminal offenders. Dutton and Hart (1992) reviewed 597 inmate files and interviewed 70 inmates and 29 female partners. The files were categorized into nonviolent ($n = 74$), violent stranger ($n = 346$), and violent family ($n = 177$). Although both violent groups were more likely than the nonviolent offenders to have come from a family in which there was violence, the family violent group had more abuse in the family of origin than the stranger violent group (54.6% vs. 38.7%). In other words, exposure to violence in childhood that was specifically directed to family members yielded more precise identification of men who assault their present partners.

Psychiatric diagnoses were also obtained from the file reviews. Antisocial Personality Disorder (APD) was the most frequent diagnosis for the violent group, with no statistically significant differences between the family violent and stranger violent subgroups (21.5% vs. 20.7%). Further analysis identified the following risk factors: Axis I disorder, APD, abuse in family of origin, substance abuse, poor marital relationship, employment instability, and age. The interview component of Dutton and Hart's (1992) study did not provide offender risk information, but it did offer one finding relevant to our discussion. More than two-thirds (35.7%) of the partners of the stranger violent offenders reported being abused by the men. Even in the absence of an official record of violence, a significant proportion of violent offenders posed a physical risk to their partners.

APD and psychopathic features appear to be common characteristic of men who batter (Huss & Langhinrichsen-Rohling, 2000). In a large cross-sectional study of nearly 1,000 men, Karl Hanson and his colleagues (Hanson et al., 1997) found APD evident in 63 percent of severely abusive men compared to a rate of 28 percent among nonabusive men. Similar findings have been reported by others (Magdol et al., 1997). However, there may be other personality characteristics specific to wife battering. Donald Dutton (1995) has proposed a theory in which a "borderline personality" is central to the abusive individual. Such a personality is characterized as impulsive and quick to anger and has such an intense fear of being abandoned that he or she uses violence to maintain control over the relationship.

The role of attitudes toward women and violence is central in most theories of male batterers, and the research supports its relevance (Hanson et al., 1997; Holtzworth-Monroe & Stuart, 1994). What has recently been recognized as important is social support for the behavior. As the reader may observe, we are covering the "Big Four." In fact, a number of social learning models have been applied to understanding the male batterer. For example, Holtzworth-Munore and Gregory Stuart's (1994) model describes "distal correlates" (genetics, childhood family, and peer experiences) and "proximal correlates" (attitudes, impulsivity, attachment to others). In a direct test of social learning theory, Deborah Reitzel-Jaffe and David Wolfe (2001) administered a battery of measures to 611 male university students. The two best predictors of abuse were negative attitudes toward women and association with peers who shared similar beliefs and who were also abusive in their relationships.

Murray Straus (1996), who is often credited with bringing family violence to the research forum, has presented a "checklist" for identifying high-risk male batterers based on his extensive experience and review of the research. The checklist includes items that we know are reliable predictors of criminal behavior (e.g., drug abuse, history of violence, rationalizations for abuse). However, the checklist is silent on social supports for the behavior and only indirectly taps potential personality factors ("extreme dominance," "extreme jealousy"). Other experts in the area have presented similar lists and guides based upon their reviews of the literature (Kropp et al., 1995; Saunders, 1995; Thompson, Saltzman & Johnson, 2001). From our own cursory review, we too can construct a list of factors that are correlated or predictive of spousal abuse. However, it is only recently that these "lists" have been formalized into objective assessment instruments.

In the previous edition of this text, we reported that we knew of no validated, actuarial risk scale developed for the assessment of men who assault their partners. Within four years, the picture has changed. Donald Dutton and Randall Kropp (2000) describe three categories of risk scales being used for the assessment of domestic violence. Astonishingly enough, the first category consists of instruments that have absolutely no empirical research guiding their development or any "attempts to establish validity" (p. 174). The second group of instruments consists of measures being currently evaluated but not yet published. Thus, we limit our discussion to the third category of risk scales that have either published validity data or are in press.

The Danger Assessment Scale gathers information on the batterer's history of violence, use of alcohol and drugs, psychological abusiveness, and availability of a gun. The information is taken from the reports of partners of abusive men. The only predictive validity study on this scale is based on a very small sample of women ($n = 49$) who were contacted by telephone during a three month follow-up (Goodman, Dutton & Bennett, 2000). Despite the small sample and short-follow-up, the Danger Assessment Scale predicted re-abuse ($r = .61$).

The Spousal Assault Risk Assessment (SARA; Kropp et al., 1995) is a 20-item scale broken down into the following four subcomponents: criminal history, psychosocial adjustment, spousal assault history, and current offense. The psychometric properties of the scale (e.g., internal reliability, convergent and divergent validity) have been satisfactory and ratings differentiate spousal assaulters from nonassaulters (Kropp & Hart, 2000). However, predictive validity data is still sparse. In a seven year follow-up of 88 abusive men, SARA demonstrated modest predictive accuracy, with AUCs ranging from .52 to .65 (Grann & Wedin, 2002). We suspect that the relatively poor predictive data may be due to some of the item content. For example, the item "severity of the index offense" was *negatively* related to outcome and would detract for predictive accuracy. The best predictor items were past history, personality disorder, and minimization/denial of assault, variables consistent with a PCC.

Finally, we offer a few comments on the use of actuarial risk instruments validated on general offenders and applied to male batterers. According to Dutton and Kropp (2000), there have been two, as of yet, unpublished reports of the PCL-R and spousal assault. Both studies used the 12-item, screening version of the PCL-R and cross-sectional designs. The results from the two studies were contradictory and led Dutton and Kropp (2000, p. 178) to conclude that "the PCL may not be the best instrument to use." As we observed in Chapter 6, the LSI-R may have some utility in the assessment of male baterers. Scores on the LSI-R have predicted treatment dropout (Rooney & Hanson, 2001) and partner's reports of abuse and violent recidivism (Hanson & Wallace-Capretta, 2000).

Risk assessment research in the area of spousal assault is in its infancy. We see progress in this area as important for laying the foundation for effective interventions and the protection of women. There is, however, resistance to this type of research from the antiprediction position of feminist perspectives of domestic violence. Take, for example, Stark's (1996:139) comment: "the major determinant of a woman's future risk is *her* present capacity for autonomy, *not* the personal characteristics or history of the batterer" (emphasis in original). Another explanation for the lack of risk prediction development is the general tendency of professionals working in one area (i.e., domestic violence) to ignore another area (i.e., criminal behavior). We have seen this tendency operate with respect to mentally disordered offenders, an area in which psychopathological and clinical models of explanation prevail. From descriptions of treatment programs for male batterers, it appears that professionals dealing with domestic violence also limit themselves to clinical theorizing.

In Chapters 6 and 7, we emphasized the point that effective rehabilitation programs begin with reliable assessments of risk and criminogenic needs. Effective programs are those that follow the risk and need principles. Without risk-needs assessments, the effectiveness of treatment becomes less likely. As we turn to the treatment literature on men who assault their partners, and knowing that the field lacks systematic risk-needs assessment, we prepare ourselves to find relatively few demonstrations of effective interventions.

Treatment of Male Batterers

In 1984, Lawrence Sherman and Richard Berk published a study that established the approach to domestic violence for the next decade. In Minneapolis, police who responded to calls of domestic disputes were randomly assigned to one of the following three conditions: (1) arrest the suspect, (2) remove the offender from the home for eight hours, or (3) advise the offender and victim to seek help.

A six-month follow-up found a lower recidivism rate for the arrest condition (13%, according to police data) compared to removal from the home (26%) and providing advice (18%). Similar differences in favor of the arrest condition were found when victim reports of re-abuse were used. Within a few years, 15 states had passed mandatory arrest legislation in domestic violence incidents and, where it was not mandated in law, most police forces in the United States and Canada adopted mandatory arrest policies.

Are mandatory arrest legislation and policies the solutions for controlling the recidivism of men who assault their spouses? In our meta-analysis of the offender rehabilitation literature, we found that sanctions did not decrease recidivism; instead, criminal justice sanctions were associated with small increases in recidivism. Could it be that, despite the similarities between male batterers and criminals, there is a difference in the type of intervention that is effective?

One of the cornerstones of science is replication. While the police, politicians, and the public quickly accepted mandatory arrests as the solution to spousal violence, a number of replication studies were being conducted. There have been five published replications of the Minneapolis Domestic Violence Experiment. All of the studies used randomized assignment, all had arrest as one of their conditions (alternative conditions varied among sites), and all had sample sizes large enough so that interaction effects could be evaluated. The results from the replications were mixed.

In some sites, arrest reduced re-abuse according to victim reports taken at six months (Colorado Springs and Miami). However, *increases* in re-abuse were reported in Charlotte, Milwaukee, and Omaha when the follow-up was extended to one year (Garner, Fagan & Maxwell, 1995; Schmidt & Sherman, 1996). Garner et al. (1995) concluded that no definitive statement could be made because of methodological problems with the various replications. Schmidt and Sherman (1996) took the position that the studies were sufficiently well conducted so that the results justified repealing mandatory arrest laws.

The results from the arrest programs remain consistent with our general findings from the offender rehabilitation literature. Criminal sanctions without direct services to higher-risk offenders and without treatments targeting criminogenic needs have minimal impact on recidivism. The only time that arrest "worked" in the replication studies was for employed offenders. Apparently, employed assaulters have a "stake in conformity" and, therefore, have much to lose by being arrested. Similar findings were reported by Thistlethwaite, Wooldredge, and Gibbs (1998), using a broader definition of "stake in conformity." Stake in conformity was defined by employment, stability of residence, college education, SES, and being married at time of arrest. Nearly 700 men arrested for domestic violence were followed over a period of one year. Severe sanctions (i.e., jail sentence) were associated with reduced recidivism only for those scoring high on the "stake in conformity" scale.

Drawing upon PIC-R, we can explain both the inhibition of aggression among spousal assaulters with a "stake in conformity" and the continued violence from the unemployed, less educated, and poorer offenders. Arrest and the threat of losing employment, residence, and status would be subtractive costs. Consequently, for the offender with a "high stake in conformity," arrest or another type of sanction is a sufficient cost to inhibit the behavior. For the offender who has accumulated little (e.g., job, residence, stable relationship), the subtractive cost of a sanction has a diminished value and is less likely to inhibit behavior. Why, though, does the behavior *increase*? The answer may be found in the other major factors involved in criminal behavior. The behavioral habit of assaulting one's partner (history) continues to have reinforcing value. The other maintaining factors for the abuse (attitudes, personality, social supports, and the immediate situation) continue unabated and become further consolidated into the individual's behavioral repertoire. Recall that higher-risk offenders are often impulsive and not future-oriented. Although abusers, particularly those with prior criminal justice experience, know quite well the likelihood of arrest and punishment, this knowledge shows no deterrent effect on their behavior (Heckert & Gondolf, 2000).

Employment is also associated with other activities and situations that increase the density of reinforcement for prosocial (nonabusive) behavior. An employed individual is more likely to have prosocial companions and to have a stable residence with fewer financial concerns, is less likely to abuse alcohol and drugs, and so on. An employed individual is also absent from the home for greater periods of time and therefore is in less contact with his partner. In other words, it is likely that the offenders who were deterred by arrest were relatively low-risk offenders for whom even a small increase in the density of costs (brief arrests) was sufficient to control their behavior.

Another possible operating factor is that the low-risk offenders may be more likely to seek help for their abuse. High-risk offenders with a low "stake in conformity" tend to drop out of batterer treatment programs

(Daly & Pelowski, 2000). That is, official recognition of the low-risk offender's private deviance may have initiated participation in treatment programs. We know little from the arrest and sanction studies how many offenders sought treatment or what outcomes resulted from any treatment. In the one study that provides this information (Gondolf, 1999), program length and the comprehensiveness of services were significantly related to reduced recidivism.

In 1989, Daniel Saunders and Sandra Azar conducted a review of treatment programs and approaches for dealing with spousal violence. There were three major approaches in use: (1) self-help groups (e.g., Batterers Anonymous), (2) family therapy, and (3) individual cognitive-behavioral therapy. At the time of Saunders and Azar's (1989) review, there were no evaluations of self-help groups. However, two years later, Mark Hamm and John Kite (1991) reported on a comparison of the recidivism rates of 166 spouse abusers who attended Batterers Anonymous (BA) with the rates of 245 abusers *selected from other studies* (e.g., Sherman & Berk, 1984) who were only arrested. The recidivism rate for the BA group was 11.4 percent; it was 13.5 percent for the arrest-only comparison groups. The differences were hardly dramatic.

Evaluations of family systems or couples interventions have not employed comparison groups, but the results have been in the direction of decreases in abuse (Tolman & Bennett, 1990). However, these interventions are infrequently used in domestic violence cases and usually limited to cases in which the violence is minor (Gelles, 1997). The most common criticisms of this approach are that the goal of reconciliation and the underlying assumption that the victim shares some responsibility for the violence serve to revictimize the women and further jeopardize their safety.

Most of the cognitive-behavioral interventions reviewed by Saunders and Azar (1989) had small sample sizes (average of 57; Hamm & Kite, 1991) and used pretest and posttest research designs or compared treatment completers with treatment dropouts. The problem with pretest and posttest research designs is that reductions in domestic violence can occur without formal interventions (Jacobson et al., 1996; Margolin & Fernandez, 1987; Quigley & Leonard, 1996). Keeping the methodological limitations in mind, the majority of the studies find reduced spousal abuse for those who received cognitive-behavioral treatment.

The earliest well-designed evaluation of a treatment intervention is a study by Donald Dutton (1986). Fifty men who attended a four-month cognitive-behavioral program were compared to 50 men who were not treated because either their probation terminated before space was available in the program (n = 42) or they were judged "unsuitable" for the program. Analyses were conducted to ensure that both groups were similar on factors that could affect outcome. Both groups displayed nearly equivalent assault histories (general and spouse specific) and personal demographics (e.g., unemployment rates). Dutton reported the post-program recidivism rates for both groups, a first for a treatment evaluation at the time. Previous studies limited their reports to changes on the Conflict Tactics Scale, victim reports of violence during treatment, or changes on other personality and attitudinal factors. Official measures of recidivism/re-abuse were not reported.

Dutton (1986) found a recidivism (re-abuse) rate of 4 percent for the treated men and 16 percent for the untreated group at a six-month follow-up. These treatment results compared favorably to Sherman and Berk's (1984) arrested men (13%), who showed similar criminal histories and personal demographics to Dutton's subjects. At two and one-half years, the treated group maintained the benefits of the treatment while the recidivism rate for the untreated group increased to 40 percent. These findings demonstrate the long-term impact that treatment can have, while arrests provide only a brief suppression of the abuse (recall from the Minneapolis replication studies that for a number of sites recidivism increased with longer follow-up).

In a less well controlled study, but noteworthy for the length of follow-up, Dutton and his colleagues (Dutton et al., 1997) reported an average 5.2 year follow-up of men who were treated for spousal abuse. Officially recorded criminal acts served as the outcome measure. The recidivism rate for men who completed at least 12 treatment sessions was significantly lower (17.9%) than for offenders who dropped out prematurely from treatment (22.2%). Although the results may be explained by differences in motivation, they are in the anticipated direction shown by most treatment research with offenders.

Dobash and her colleagues (Dobash et al., 2000) have described an evaluation of a profeminist, cognitive-behavioral program. The program was highly structured and delivered on a weekly basis. The cases of 84 abusive men who attended the treatment were compared to 229 cases that went through the regular criminal justice services. One year later, the female partners of the men were asked to report on the men's violence. For the men who completed the treatment program, the violence rate was 33 percent; it was 70 percent for the men who did not receive treatment.

Daniel Saunders (1996) reported an evaluation of a spousal abuse treatment program that speaks to the issue of responsivity. Saunders compared two types of treatments: a "feminist, cognitive-behavioral treatment" (FCBT) and a "process-psychodynamic treatment" (PPT). FCBT was described as "typical of many programs throughout the country" (p. 394). Abusive men (*n* = 178) were randomly assigned to one of two groups (the random assignment ran into some problems, but they were minor). The average follow-up was two years. Saunders found no differences in arrest rates or women's reports of their partner's abuse (23.2% were arrested in the FCBT group and 20.3% for PPT).

Saunders (1996) also conducted a detailed analysis of program processes. Audiotaping of group sessions was conducted, and the tapes were analyzed in terms of content and focus of discussions. As expected, the PPT groups spent more time on childhood abuse and past behavior and emphasized self-disclosure. Modeling and role-playing were almost nonexistent. PPT did not ignore the issue of abuse; group sessions did include some discussions of the present abuse. With the FCBT, role-playing and modeling were far more frequent, group leaders were more willing to give advice, and efforts were made to use "coping thoughts."

From our PCC perspective, we expected to find that the cognitive-behavioral intervention would provide significantly better outcomes than the psychodynamic approach. Perhaps the impressively high success rates of approximately 80 percent placed a "ceiling effect" on the ability to differentiate the two treatment groups. This ceiling effect is similar to the high base rate problem that limits prediction research (Chapter 6).

Saunders (1996), however, found an interaction effect. That is, the type of treatment affected different types of offenders. Personality questionnaires were administered to the men, allowing an analysis of the differential impact of treatment on different personalities. Men with dependent personalities showed lower recidivism rates when assigned to PPT (33%) and higher rates after completing FCBT (52%). Offenders with antisocial personality disorder and substance abuse, which may fit the majority of male batterers, did better in the FCBT (36% recidivism rate) and poorer in the PPT (53%). These results are consistent with the general offender rehabilitation literature and remind us of the deleterious effects of unstructured psychodynamic therapy with psychopaths (Harris, Rice & Cormier, 1994).

Saunders (1996) interpreted the results within the context of the responsivity principle. That is, a certain style of treatment worked best with certain types of individuals. We agree that this is a possible explanation, but we would also suggest that inattention to the principles of risk and need are alternative explanations. There was no differentiation in risk level. All the men, regardless of treatment type, received approximately the equivalent number of sessions. The risk levels of the men in the study are difficult to judge because no criminal and abuse history information was given. The men may have been a relatively low-risk group (the majority were described as Euro-American, with higher income and more education than the average agency population).

With respect to criminogenic needs, no information was presented on the content of the behavioral rehearsals and modeling. That is, what skills were being trained and encouraged? Although social skills training is common in cognitive-behavioral programs with male batterers, the assumption that these men have social skills deficits has been challenged (Holtzworth-Munroe, 1992). Saunders (1996) reported that the FCBT group spent a significant amount of time on relaxation training, supposedly to learn to manage anger. Apparently, anger, rationalizations for abuse, and discussions of cultural norms supportive of male dominance were the major targets of treatment. Success in effecting change on these variables was not reported.

The outlook for research on abusive men is promising. Our forecast is that within the next few years considerable progress will be made on clarifying the personalities of male batterers and introducing actuarial-based risk assessments. Treatment providers will gradually abandon ideology in favor of empirical demonstrations of what works. Structured, behavioral interventions will become the norm because they demonstrate observable effects (Edleson & Syers, 1991; Dobash & Dobash, 2001). The unstructured format promoted by Jennings (1987) will be left for the uninformed or those who are more committed to ideology than evidence.

Finally, we see treatment becoming more integrated with criminal justice controls. Whether this will be a positive development remains to be seen. Dutton (1995) has commented that the use of arrest or the threat of criminal justice sanctions may serve as a temporary suppressor of abuse and a window of opportunity for the introduction of treatment. Even fairly mild interventions, such as a simple social work visit following a police call, appear to have some positive effects with the more serious abuser (Davis & Taylor, 1997). However, Barry Rosenfeld's (1992) review of court-ordered treatment questions the effectiveness of this approach. Hopefully, continued research will guide the development of an equitable balance between criminal justice controls and offender treatment.

Substance Abuse

In 1996, we were invited along with our colleague Paul Gendreau to speak at a conference called "Criminal Conduct and Substance Abuse Treatment." The conference was intended to bring together substance abuse counselors and correctional professionals to discuss how the two fields can learn from each other and improve the delivery of services to their respective clients. From the addictions field, Reid Hester, Alan Marlatt, Harvey Milkman, and Kenneth Wanberg were the invited speakers. The proceedings from the conference clearly highlighted the overlap in issues, clientele, and intervention techniques used in corrections and the field of substance abuse. What surprised many in the audience was why it took so long for the two fields to come together.

Alcohol abuse affects millions of people in North America. The DSM-IV (American Psychiatric Association, 1994) estimates that 7 percent of adults in the United States have an alcohol dependence disorder and approximately 800,000 are receiving services for alcohol abuse in any given year (Greenfeld, 1998). Reliable estimates of the prevalence of other drug abuse are more difficult to come by because of the variety of drugs that may be considered for inclusion in surveys (e.g., over-the-counter drugs, tobacco, etc.). However, the 1997 National Survey on Drug Abuse found 11.2 percent of Americans over the age of 12 reported using an illicit drug in the past year (Substance Abuse and Mental Health Services Administration, 1998). Substance abuse has far-reaching consequences. It disrupts the social, economic, emotional, and physical well-being of the abuser and his or her family and friends. Alcohol abuse accounts for enormous health costs as a result of alcohol-related diseases and accidents. Add drug abuse to the problem, and the social and economic costs appear insurmountable.

Surveys of offender populations find that significant proportions have substance abuse problems. In the 1997 survey of state inmates, 51 percent of the offenders reported being under the influence of alcohol or an illegal substance during the commission of the offense (Office of National Drug Control Policy, 1999). Using urinalysis testing, surveys find 51 to 80 percent of male arrestees testing positive for an illicit drug (Hser, Longshore & Anglin, 1994; Office of National Drug Control Policy, 1999).

An important aspect of the widespread abuse of substances among offenders is the relationship between substance abuse and violence (Bushman & Cooper, 1990; Pernanen, 1991). Alcohol is suspected of contributing to the disinhibition of controls over aggressive behavior. Some illicit drugs such as cocaine may trigger paranoid ideations that lead to aggressive behavior. Finally, obtaining the money to purchase illicit drugs often requires unlawful behavior and bringing the individual into direct contact with criminals.

Substance abuse has been found associated with violent crimes among adults (Valdez et al., 1995) and young offenders (Cookson, 1992). In a longitudinal study of 1,265 children followed to the age of 21, alcohol abuse was associated with both violent and property crime (Fergusson & Horwood, 2000). Substance abuse has been especially implicated in murders (Smith & Zahn, 1999). For example, in a study of 251 homicides committed in Copenhagen, 55 percent of the murderers were intoxicated at the time of the offense (Gottlieb & Gabrielsen, 1992). Victimization surveys that include victim reports on the condition of the offender find intoxication a factor in 30 percent of violent crimes (U.S. Department of Justice, 1995). Finally, substance abuse is a predictor of recidivism among general offenders (Gendreau, Little & Goggin, 1996) and mentally disordered offenders (Bonta, Law & Hanson, 1998). Whether we examine the results from cross-sectional surveys or longitudinal studies, it is indisputable that substance abuse is a correlate of criminal behavior that is more important than class and race.

So what was to be done to cope with Elliott Currie's (1993) "American nightmare"? For many, the answer was to declare "war" on drugs. Spending for the war on drugs increased from less than one-quarter of a million dollars during the Nixon administration to $13 billion by 1992 (Currie, 1993). What was all this money buying? Seventy percent was directed to the police, courts, and prisons. Controlling the problems associated with substance abuse was to be achieved through increasing the punishment for the behavior.

Simply getting tough on the substance-abusing offender has had a limited impact on reoffending. Police crackdowns have shown mixed results in controlling drug availability and drug-related crimes (Worden, Bynum & Frank, 1994). Increasing prison sentences has not deterred drug crimes (Fagan, 1994). Enhanced monitoring through urine screening has also failed to influence misconduct (Belenko, Mara-Drita & McElroy, 1992). Instead, the increased dependence on sanctions has produced overworked police officers, clogged courts, and overcrowded prisons. Some question whether the increased emphasis on punishment and control is merely a disguised effort to control the poor and the minorities in the inner cities of America (Byrne & Taxman, 1994; Currie, 1993; Daly & Tonry, 1997).

During the "war on drugs," treatment programs continued to operate and evaluations were conducted. There were actually increases in the number of drug treatment programs offered in prisons (Chaiken, 1989). However, the demand far outstripped the supply. Falkin, Wexler, and Lipton (1992) estimated that approximately 90 percent of state prisoners with a drug problem were *not* in treatment. In the study of arrestees in Los Angeles described earlier (Hser et al., 1994), more than 274,000 offenders were judged to be in need of treatment, but there were only 38,602 admissions to treatment programs during the year the estimates were conducted.

Many treatment programs for substance-abusing offenders use a variety of objective assessment instruments. The scales usually focus on the assessment of substance abuse and the severity of the abuse. A few of the best validated scales are the Addiction Severity Index (ASI; McClellan et al., 1980), the Alcohol Dependence Scale (ADS), and the Drug Abuse Screening Test (DAST; Hester & Miller, 1995). These instruments are either interview-based (ASI) or self-administered paper-and-pencil tests (ADS and DAST). Sometimes, but not routinely, offender risk scales are also administered.

The State of Colorado introduced one of the most comprehensive and systematic classification systems for drug-abusing offenders in the United States. The Colorado Standardized Offender Assessment Program (CSOAP) was enacted into law and developed under the leadership of Vern Fogg and Brad Bogue (1996). At the presentencing level, offenders are screened for substance abuse using the ADS and the DAST. Offenders identified by these brief screening instruments as having potential substance abuse problems are further assessed with more detailed assessments of substance abuse. In addition, the Level of Service Inventory-Revised (LSI-R) is administered. The results of the assessment of general risk and needs (LSI-R) and specific assessments of substance abuse are then used to guide classification to the various treatment programs offered in the state (Lauen, 1997).

Some of the substance abuse treatment programs offered in Colorado appear to have the ingredients for effective intervention. The program developed by Kenneth Wanberg and Harvey Milkman (1995) is a structured, cognitive-behavioral intervention that attends to the principles of risk, need, and responsivity. The program also includes elements of motivational interviewing and relapse prevention (discussed in the following paragraphs). Evaluations of the assessment of risk for drug-abusing offenders and the effects of matching offenders to programs based upon needs and risk levels are presently underway.

In 1980, Alan Marlatt and Judith Gordon wrote a paper that had a major influence in the treatment of alcoholism. They noted that behavior therapy was effective in producing changes in behavior, but the *maintenance* of the changes was problematic. Reviewing the results of interventions with a variety of addictions (alcohol, cigarettes, and heroin), they observed that within a matter of months after completing treatment, the treatment participants returned to their former addiction. Marlatt and Gordon (1980) reasoned that the avoidance of relapse was not to be found in "bigger and better treatment packages" but rather in providing clients direct training in recognizing the situations that trigger failure and teaching them how to cope with these situations.

An illustration of how relapse prevention works is drawn from the research by Helen Annis and her colleagues on alcohol abuse. Treatment for alcohol addiction begins with an analysis of the situations in which drinking is likely to occur. To facilitate this assessment, Annis developed the Inventory of Drinking Situations (IDS; Annis, 1982). This paper-and-pencil test has eight scales measuring high-risk situations for alcoholics. Examples of the scales are Unpleasant Emotions (drink to forget about worries), Social Pressure to Drink ("out on the town" with friends), and Testing Personal Control ("I have changed and can handle a few drinks").

For the individual in treatment, specific high-risk situations can be identified and the person trained to recognize and avoid these high-risk situations and thus prevent relapse (Annis & Davis, 1989; Annis & Martin, 1995). Relapse prevention is a cognitive-behavioral program in which the client practices alternative responses to high-risk situations (e.g., refusing a drink, planning an alternative activity for Saturday night). The relapse prevention model has considerable intuitive appeal. Early research on its effectiveness was mixed (Carroll, 1996; Ito, Donovan & Hall, 1988; Saunders & Houghton, 1996; Stephens, Roffman & Simpson, 1994). However, a recent meta-analysis of 26 studies ($n = 9,504$) found relapse prevention strategies generally effective for alcohol problems (Irvin et al., 1999). Today, relapse prevention forms an essential component in the treatment of a wide range of addictive behaviors (Marlatt, 1996; McCrady, 2000), including sexual deviance (Hanson, 1996; Ward & Hudson, 1996).

Annis and Davis (1989) observed that introducing treatment and relapse prevention may be premature with clients who have "generalized" profiles on the IDS (that is, the client's drinking has generalized across all eight risk situations). The therapist is then faced not only with the problem of where to begin, but also must ask if the client is ready for treatment. Where is the motivation for change if drinking (or other drug abuse) is so common and reinforcing? These generalized profiles and the associated "unreadiness" to participate in treatment is common among offender samples in which multiple substance abusers are found. Therefore, structured treatment and relapse prevention may be unsuitable for many clients at the beginning of treatment (Annis, Schober & Kelly, 1996; Marlatt, 1996). To deal with the resistant client, research-practitioners have developed a technique referred to as "motivational interviewing."

Motivational interviewing originated out of the need to deal with the client who either denies or does not recognize that he or she has an addiction. This is a situation not foreign to those who treat sex and nonsex offenders. Thus, correctional professionals are well advised to consider the role of motivational interviewing in their own work. The general premise is that clients seeking treatment are at different stages of readiness to change. James Prochaska and Carlo DiClemente (1982) have formulated a model that outlines the stages of change during the treatment process. The first two stages, Precontemplation and Contemplation, are where motivational interviewing can be valuable.

At the Precontemplation and Contemplation stages, the client does not see that he or she has a problem that requires a change. Behavior is rationalized or denied, or the client is "thinking about it." The goal of motivational interviewing is to move the client from "I am thinking about it" to "I am going to do something about it." William Miller and Stephen Rollick (1991) advocate a therapeutic technique that motivates the client to progress beyond the contemplation stages. The therapist engages the client in a nonthreatening relationship, builds rapport, and gently and cautiously nudges the client in the direction of accepting that there is a problem that must be faced.

On the surface, motivational interviewing looks like client-centered therapy. The sessions appear unstructured, and the therapist engages in active listening with little advice-giving. Behavioral homework assignments may be assigned (e.g., write in a log book what your family does and says after you have a drink), but the relatively unstructured approach directs the client toward problem identification. Motivational interviewing is preparation for formal, structured treatment and relapse prevention training. This technique recognizes that not all people referred to treatment are equally motivated to engage in treatment. Considering that many offenders come to treatment because of external motives (e.g., mandated by court, applying for parole), motivational interviewing provides a way of enhancing personal motivation.

Motivational interviewing appears to be a counseling technique that is congruent with the responsivity principle. The therapist's style of intervention is adjusted to the client's cognitive and affective characteristics at a particular point in time. At the precontemplative stage of therapy, a confrontative or highly structured intervention may have no impact (or a negative impact) on the client who does not *think* there is a problem or does not *care* about the impact of his or her behavior on others. Introducing such a client directly into a structured cognitive-behavioral program could invite dropout or failure. The first step is to engage the client. The therapist attempts to do this by adopting a nonthreatening, friendly, and helpful style. As the client becomes committed to a process of change and his or her cognitive-affective views change, then the therapist's style of interaction and the treatment modality is modified. Reviews of the motivational interviewing literature find the technique effective in keeping clients in treatment and reducing their alcohol intake (DiClemente, Bellino & Neavins, 1999; Walitzer, Dermen & Conners, 1999). However, evidence supporting reductions in recidivism is still lacking (Ginsburg et al., 2002).

There are numerous evaluations of individual treatment programs indicating positive effects (Falkin et al., 1992; Lipton, 1995; Swartz, Lurigio & Slomka, 1996). However, Frank Pearson and his colleagues are conducting a meta-analysis of the drug (and correctional) treatment literature. The project is called the Correctional Drug Abuse Treatment Effectiveness (CDATE) project. It promises to be an informative and useful review of the literature. It is a massive undertaking involving a team of researchers collecting and reviewing both published and unpublished studies conducted between 1968 and 1996 from around the world. In some preliminary analyses, treatment appropriateness was evaluated, as much as possible, according to the definition provided by Andrews, Zinger et al. (1990a).

Table 10.1 presents some of the findings reported by the CDATE researchers (Pearson & Lipton, 1999; Pearson, Lipton & Cleland, 1996). We also inserted our 1998 meta-analysis of the offender rehabilitation literature (Andrews & Bonta, 1998). The most important finding from the Pearson et al. (1996) meta-analysis is that treatment is more effective in reducing recidivism than sanctions or other unspecified forms of intervention. Although Pearson et al. (1996) reported a lower effect size for appropriate treatment than found in our meta-analysis (.22 vs. .30), we think that this may be explained by their difficulty in separating studies that treated higher-risk drug abusers from lower-risk offenders.

Table 10.1
Effectiveness of Drug Abuse and Offender Treatment (phi)

Study	Sanction	Inappropriate	Unclear	Appropriate
Andrews et al. (1998)	−.02	−.03	.13	.25
Pearson et al. (1996)	.03	.06	.09	.22
Pearson & Lipton (1999)				
Boot camp	.05			
Unstructured group		.04		
Therapeutic community			.13	

The CDATE meta-analysis is consistent with a PCC. Treatment programs that are cognitive-behavioral and that target criminogenic needs are effective in reducing the problem behavior. Two studies described below further illustrate effective substance abuse treatment programs that are based upon a general social learning perspective of behavior.

The first example is the classic study of the Community-Reinforcement program by George Hunt and Nathan Azrin (1973). Although the treatment targeted alcoholic nonoffenders, it demonstrated the application of social learning principles to the treatment of substance abuse. The Community-Reinforcement program (Azrin et al., 1982; Hunt & Azrin, 1973) has shown some of the largest effects in the alcohol abuse treatment literature (Miller, 1990). The general approach involved rearranging the density of rewards and costs associated with drinking behavior. Eight alcoholics were assigned to receive Community-Reinforcement counseling and another matched group of eight alcoholics received the regular treatment regime available from a local state hospital.

The Community-Reinforcement program helped the client find a job and provided family counseling as well as counseling aimed at increasing social interactions with those who discouraged drinking. All of these interventions were based on the premise that interpersonal rewards for being sober had to be increased and the rewards for drinking had to be decreased. For example, maintaining a satisfying job and interacting with nondrinking companions increased the density of rewards for sobriety (and simultaneously increased the costs for drinking). The results showed that for the participants of the Community-Reinforcement program, the amount of time spent drinking was halved compared to the control group.

Our second example of an effective treatment program is selected from the prison literature. As we observed earlier, the war on drugs did not eliminate treatment programs for drug abusers. There was actually an increase in the number of treatment programs available for substance-abusing inmates. Douglas Lipton (1994) has even suggested that incarceration provides an opportunity for treating those who would not come to treatment on their own. Most of the prison-based programs are therapeutic communities; a few have demonstrated success (Falkin et al., 1992; Wexler, Falkin & Lipton, 1990). We will not examine these programs. Instead, we will look at one that was developed from a social learning perspective of criminal behavior.

The Rideau Treatment Centre prevention program has been offered as a core program to substance-abusing inmates in an Ontario prison for the past decade. A recent evaluation demonstrates the effectiveness of the treatment approach for these incarcerated offenders (Marquis et al., 1996). Two groups of inmates who participated in the substance abuse relapse prevention group were compared to a waiting list comparison group. The second treatment group also received anger management training. Both treatment programs were highly structured, cognitive-behavioral treatments. The targets for treatment were relevant criminogenic needs (specifically, substance abuse and anger/aggressive behavior). Attention was also given to the risk level of the offenders as measured by the LSI-R. Upon follow-up from prison, the recidivism rate was 41 percent for the treatment subjects and 62 percent for the comparison group. When type of recidivism was analyzed (violent versus nonviolent), substance abuse treatment alone had no impact. However, the inmates who also received anger management training showed significantly lower violent recidivism rates compared to the nontreated group (34% vs. 59%).

Our discussion of the addiction treatment field suggests that the effective ingredients are similar to those found in the general treatment of offenders. Programs that promote a positive therapist-client relationship but follow a structured format are associated with decreased relapse rates (Project MATCH Research Group, 1997). Moreover, cognitive-behavioral styles of interventions appear to be more effective with higher-risk substance-abusing offenders. Community support and specific training on relapse prevention techniques may also enhance the long-term success of treatment.

From a theoretical perspective, offsetting the rewards associated with substance abuse involves altering many reinforcement contingencies. Shifting the reward balance to favor nonabuse requires the assistance of the individual's social community, as well as changes in attitudes and feelings of competency and self-control (see also Petraitis, Flay & Miller, 1995). Family members, employers, and friends can systematically learn to reinforce sobriety and express disapproval for substance abuse. Individuals can learn cognitive skills to cope with high-risk situations and stop themselves when they begin to rationalize their substance abuse or think in a way that supports substance abuse. The behavioral changes do not come easily. For many substance-abusing offenders, the behavior is frequent (often daily) and has a long history. The automatic, habitual nature of substance abuse presents a serious challenge. However, as the evidence suggests, there are interventions that can overcome these obstacles.

Community Policing

In this chapter, we have provided two examples (spousal assault and substance abuse) of areas in which a PCC can make a contribution. Much of the research cited throughout this text is from the corrections sector of the criminal justice system, in which prediction and treatment are important activities. In closing this chapter, we would like to comment on a criminal justice sector outside of corrections. We think that a PCC may offer some potential applications in police work, and we would like to reflect on some of these possibilities.

The public tends to think of policing in fairly narrow terms. The everyday citizen sees the main goal of the police as the protection of citizens. The police attempt to achieve this goal by acting as a visible deterrent and by apprehending and bringing to justice those who violate the law. There is no doubt that the apprehension of criminals is an important activity of the police officer. For the most part, a PCC says little about this aspect of policing. Observant and careful detective work is the critical factor that leads to the arrest of offenders. However, knowledge of the risk factors associated with criminal offending and the interventions that decrease recidivism may be helpful in other aspects of police work.

One possible area in which PCC may be able to make a contribution is in community policing. Community policing started in the late 1970s as a new approach that embraced a philosophy of the police officer working with the community to solve the problem of crime (Trojanowicz & Bucqueroux, 1990). The traditional function of arresting suspects is seen as too restrictive and ineffective in preventing crime or decreasing the public's fear of crime. In community policing, alternatives to arrest are encouraged in situations in which it is not mandated by virtue of a violent or otherwise very serious offense. Community policing has become extremely popular. Community policing programs have been implemented throughout the United States and in many parts of the world. In 1999, 64 percent of American police departments had full-time community police officers (U.S. Department of Justice, 2001).

Community policing can mean many different things, and this is one of the problems that arise when people come together to talk about this reform in policing (Rosenbaum & Lurigio, 1994). In order to give the reader an idea of the variety of activities encompassed under the umbrella of community policing, we present a few of the results from Maguire, Kuhns, Uchida, and Cox's (1997) survey of nonurban police agencies (Table 10.2). Although Maguire et al.'s (1997) survey focused on police agencies serving communities with populations of less than 50,000, it gives one of the few quantified analyses of community policing activities available.

Table 10.2
A Sampling of Community Policing Activities

Activity	% of Agencies
Antidrug programs	68
Neighborhood Watch	53
Meeting community leaders	52
Door-to-door visits of businesses	43
Foot and bike patrols	41
Use of citizen volunteers	36
Neighborhood stations	20

From Maguire et al., 1997

Table 10.2 shows the variety of activities represented by community policing. Some of these activities even involve providing programs (we will say more about police involvement in antidrug programs). However, the common thread throughout these activities is the heightening of police presence in the community. Meeting community leaders and business owners and walking about neighborhoods are practices that are promoted. These activities are expected to produce a number of benefits. The important advantages cited by supporters of community policing are that victims may find it easier to come forward and report a crime and citizens may feel safer in their community. Notice how this approach is so different from traditional policing. Whether one approach is more effective than the other in reducing crime is unclear. In a comparison of New York City's "zero tolerance" policing policy and San Diego's "neighborhood policing philosophy," Judith Greene (1999) reported no difference in crime reduction. However, she found that the traditional policing approach was associated with far more complaints of police brutality and lawsuits against the police.

Another potential benefit of community policing (and this is where a PCC enters the picture) is that the increased contact with residents may enhance knowledge of the offenders in the community and their victims. The community police officer who is in direct contact with the residents of a neighborhood comes to know the people and their problems. The more detailed knowledge of the residents in the neighborhood, as opposed to the knowledge that can be gleaned from a patrol car, encourages the police officer to consider alternatives to arrest. After all, it is generally more difficult to arrest someone who is not a stranger.

Let us review some of the key findings from a PCC. First, individuals differ in their personal characteristics and their reasons for acting in a certain way. As a consequence, there is no "across the board" method that will be effective for dealing with people. The traditional policing approach has been to arrest the lawbreaker. Although police have always had some discretion in the use of arrest, discretion has become limited in recent years due to changes in laws and policies toward certain behaviors (e.g., spousal assault, substance abuse). Community policing encourages alternatives to arrest and thereby returns some discretion to the police. It is an interesting commentary that community policing has become popular in a time when legislators are taking discretion away from the police and courts.

If community policing is to be successful, then the police must exercise their discretion judiciously and effectively. In our opinion, decisions affecting the offender and the community can be improved by knowledge of the factors controlling criminal behavior. When choosing whether to arrest a suspect, the officer at a basic level must make an assessment of offender risk. We do not expect officers to walk around with an LSI-R or some other risk-needs instrument to help them make risk assessments, but it may not be unreasonable to train officers to make assessments "in their heads" using information that is supported by research.

The community police officer may be in a good position to become familiar with the offenders who operate in a neighborhood. This familiarity may come from direct experience with the offender and from information provided by others in the community. From these sources the officer may be able to evaluate the offender on the "Big Four" correlates of criminal behavior: criminal history, social support, antisocial personality features, and procriminal attitudes. Other risk information (e.g., substance abuse, unemployment) may also be available.

The research also indicates that sanctions are not effective in reducing the likelihood that the offender will reoffend. Thus, the long-term deterrent effect of arrest on the offender is questionable. Arresting an offender would certainly prevent crime in the short term through its incapacitative impact. An arrest would also show that justice is being served, but the police officer should be under no illusion that arresting the offender will keep him or her from repeating crimes after he or she is released into the community. Only direct services targeting the criminogenic needs of the offender have consistently demonstrated reductions in recidivism.

The ineffectiveness of punishment and sanctions to control recidivism may be disheartening to some police officers. However, the alternative—treatment—could provide an opportunity for the police to build upon the first part of their motto: "to *serve* and protect." In order to best serve the public, being in the position to make a brief assessment of the criminogenic needs of offenders could help the community police officer take the most appropriate course of action. Often the criminogenic needs of offenders are obvious, as when a drug addict is arrested in an alley while self-injecting with a needle. Sometimes the situation may not be so clear. For example, the police may enter a house during a domestic dispute and find the man speaking incoherently and the woman too upset to explain the situation to the police. Should the man be arrested or taken to a detoxification center or a psychiatric facility? The police confront many different situations, offenders, and victims. All of these factors influence their decisions (Finn & Stalans, 1995).

We are not advocating that police officers become counselors. We do, however, encourage the training of police officers in general psychology as well as the psychology of criminal conduct. Most police academies already provide recruits with courses in the social psychology of interpersonal relationships. They teach police cadets the cues that signal imminent danger from an individual and how to talk to an angry or intoxicated suspect (i.e., responsivity considerations). General psychological principles are used in such areas as hostage negotiations (Butler, Leitenberg & Fuselier, 1993) and criminal profiling (Holmes & Holmes, 1996; Wilson & Soothill, 1996). Our major message is that including the study of PCC in the training curriculum of police academies would enhance their daily work. We would make the same argument for the training of probation officers, prison guards, judges, and lawyers.

One of the interesting developments in community policing is that some police forces have become involved in providing prevention and treatment services (Fleissner & Heinzelmann, 1996). An example is the use of police officers in school-based drug education programs. Project DARE is the largest program of this type in the United States. Well-trained uniformed police officers provide a 17-week program of drug education to students in grades five and six. The goal is to teach young children to say "no" to drugs. The curriculum includes providing knowledge about the harmful effects of drugs, building self-esteem, and dealing with gang pressure.

In the most rigorous evaluation of Project DARE to date (Rosenbaum, & Hanson, 1998), schools in the state of Illinois were randomly assigned to either an experimental condition (Project DARE) or to a no-treatment condition. Nearly 1,800 students were involved and followed over a six-year period. There were no differences in alcohol or cigarette use between the children who participated in Project DARE and those who did not. Rosenbaum and Hanson (1998) also calculated a delinquency index (items included stealing, group fighting, and damage to property) but found no impact due to DARE. In a 10-year follow-up of DARE participants, Donald Lynam and his colleagues founed no differences with a comparison group in outcomes (Lynam et al., 1999).

A possible explanation of the failure of Project DARE may be found in our knowledge of effective offender rehabilitation. First, consider the risk principle, and then ask if Project DARE matched the level of intervention to the risk students pose for engaging in substance use. We do not think that the risk principle operated in the program intervention. All school children who participate in Project DARE, whether they are high risks for substance abuse or not, receive the same structured program. In an earlier evaluation, Rosenbaum, Flewelling, Bailey, Ringwalt, and Wilkinson (1994) provided a limited subgroup analysis suggesting a differential impact of the program as a function of risk. They found that the girls in Project DARE showed decreased alcohol use but there was no change for the boys. These findings suggest that the intensity of the program and its comprehensiveness in targeting criminogenic needs was insufficient for dealing with higher-risk (male) cases.

Next, we can consider the program results with respect to the need principle. Some of the treatment targets in the DARE program may not be dynamic risk factors for substance abuse. For example, self-esteem may not be an important precursor to alcohol use and cigarette smoking. There is also considerable evidence that knowledge of the harmful effects of substance use does not deter addictive behavior. One only needs to look at the millions who smoke cigarettes to see the limitation of drug education programs that stress the harmful effects of substance abuse.

One of the most telling findings of the Rosenbaum and Hanson (1998) evaluation was that the program had no effect on attitudes toward alcohol and drugs, self-esteem, and resistance to peer pressure—factors thought by the authors to be associated with substance abuse. Although we may question the importance of self-esteem, we would hypothesize attitudes supportive of substance abuse (one of the "Big Four") as being highly relevant. It may well be that the style of education provided to young children may not match the learning capabilities of the children (responsivity). Resisting peer pressure may be a valuable skill, but perhaps the program needs to spend more time on learning how to change peer groups that support substance use. Finally, we can only wonder why exposure to a uniformed police officer over a 17-week period did not influence attitudes toward the police.

We hope that the failure of Project DARE to demonstrate an impact does not discourage school boards from offering substance abuse programs for children. We also hope that police agencies continue to try innovative methods for engaging the public in dealing with crime. There have been some reports that a significant proportion of front-line police officers is resistant to community policing and some of the initial enthusiasm has waned (Dicker, 1998; Schneider et al., 2000). We hope that they do not retreat to their more traditional roles. Rather, the results of research evaluations should be used to modify and improve programs that have good intentions. In our analysis of Project DARE, we can submit reasons why no impact was observed and suggest how improvements can be made. This, above all, is the value of research.

Closing Remarks

Our analysis in this chapter of spousal assault, substance abuse, and community policing explored some of the potential value a PCC can add to understanding social problems and developing services to deal with them. We may be completely wrong and accused of stretching our theoretical constructs to the point of distortion. However, without contrary evidence, our suggestion of expanding the explanatory role of a PCC to study more than the thief, rapist, and murderer has some merit.

Behavior, whether it is socially defined as prosocial, antisocial, mad, or just problematic, is developed and maintained by the same general principles of learning and conditioning. If PCC can be helpful in understanding criminal behavior, then it is a small step to explain related behaviors such as spousal assault and substance abuse. We invite researchers from other fields to explore and empirically test hypotheses generated from a PCC.

Chapter 11

A General Personality and Social Psychology of Criminal Conduct

There exists now an empirically defensible general psychology of criminal conduct (PCC) that is of practical value in prevention, judicial processing, and corrections. It also speaks to young people, adjudicated offenders, victims, parents, teachers, employers, and anyone interested in predicting and reducing antisocial behavior. It also speaks to those who may wish to increase antisocial behavior in the interest of some higher loyalty, such as saving human life (burning abortion clinics), enhancing the status of women (burning video shops that sell pornography), or supporting colleagues stressed by their employer (blocking traffic during a labor strike). A generally applicable PCC indeed will speak to many notions of what constitutes antisocial behavior.

Moreover, it should speak to policy advisors, policymakers, and legislators who must come to see that respect for human diversity, human service, and human science is not just a relic of a positivistic past (as asserted by critical/Marxist criminology). Politically, PCC asks, who is against promoting an understanding of the criminal behavior of individuals that may contribute to reduced victimization and reduced costs of public protection? PCC applies to the antisocial behavior of the more privileged and the less privileged, as well as to a wide range of antisocial acts.

Although not always clearly stated, the social science of crime has been most concerned with aggregated crime rates. What social science has not done well is acknowledge that accurately measured, community-wide crime rates reflect the behavior of individuals. Furthermore, effective policy must reach down and impact on the immediate contingencies of action for people in the natural settings of home, school, work, play, boardroom, neighborhood, street corner, and farmer's field. Perhaps the most immediate recommendation involves an insistence that policy encourage rather than discourage the delivery of high-quality direct service to people and families at risk. It is no longer acceptable that criminology simply recommend that social services be expanded. We know that one of the characteristics of those at risk for criminal behavior is that they have made more use of social services than those less at risk, and we have known this since the 1950s (Glueck & Glueck, 1950). There is a need for promotion of the development of agencies that offer *clinically appropriate* services.

From a social science perspective, a challenge is the development of social systems wherein the need for social service agencies is reduced. With this, PCC agrees. For example, when system-wide family disruption rates, school dropout rates, and unemployment rates are lowered, the need for agencies focusing on familial, educational, and vocational issues decreases dramatically. Once again, PCC suggests that such broad structural interventions must reach down and impact on individuals in their immediate situations of action. Insofar as they do not, the need for clinically relevant direct service remains a very real priority. The only morally and politically acceptable alternative to this position is to assume that the agencies will work toward organizing the offspring of dysfunctional families, the school dropouts, and the unemployed into political units that can exercise power in ways supportive of their prosocial interests.

What about those portions of mainstream sociological criminology that still have antipsychological bias as a fundamental element of their discipline? As reported more than a decade ago (Andrews & Wormith, 1989), we continue to find sociologists and criminologists claiming "not me." The fact that there is now denial by individual scholars that they ever denied PCC indicates some progress. Professionally rooted conceptual enemies of PCC, such as anomie, subcultural, and labeling theorists, are reformulating their theories, and thus becoming indistinguishable from a general social psychology of crime in all but their choice of language, their continuing distrust of personality, and (sometimes) their lack of contact with the powerful principles of behavioral influence found within the social learning approach.

Differential association theory, whose creator also constructed the sociological outlines of antipsychological bias, was reformulated with the help of radical behaviorism and now has a powerful psychology of action at its base. Even the Marxists recognize that romantic images of lower-class Robin Hoods redistributing the wealth of the nation were not consistent with human nature, nor with the substantial body of research on the psychology of crime. Professional proponents of PCC have always respected individual differences while reformulating psychoanalytic theory into theories of control through bonding and self-control. As the Yale school of psychologists, sociologists, and anthropologists suggested years ago, the contributions of psychodynamic and control theories may also be advanced by a social learning and cognitive-behavioral perspective on criminal conduct. At the very least, a cognitive-behavioral psychology would allow the recognition of highly stable individual differences from slipping into antitreatment themes.

Similarly, in the area of forensic mental health, strong ties to psychiatric traditions and personal distress variables are being weakened. The signaled rewards for adopting a more general psychology of criminal behavior are becoming strong. In psychiatry itself, large-scale surveys of young people have established that (in terms of incidence and costs accrued) the primary mental health problem is antisocial behavior rather than internalization or psychotic disorders (Beitchman, Inglis & Schacter, 1992; Breton et al., 1999; Verhulst et al., 1997).

Social work has been more central to criminal justice and corrections practice than to theory and research. Casework approaches were important parts of many of the early controlled explorations of prevention and rehabilitation but were not part of the 40 to 80 percent of the studies reporting reduced recidivism. Thus, social work also had its "nothing works" period and, as in criminology, the attention of many in the field turned to "big picture" concerns that devalued direct service. Now, empirically based, effective casework models are available that integrate what we have called the relationship principle with the structuring of behavioral techniques (e.g., Hilarski & Wodarski, 2001). Within social work, strong statements of support for direct service exist regarding families (e.g., Geismar & Wood, 1986) and concerning clients more generally (e.g., McIvor, 1995).

We are less certain of those professionals and scholars who concentrate on theories of official punishment. This particular heterogeneous camp of labeling, deterrence, just deserts, and restorative justice proponents seems to work with an underlying psychology of human behavior that is of limited value. Some believe, for example, that being held accountable for one's behavior through judicial processing somehow makes one more responsible (deterrence/just deserts) or less responsible (labeling). Which it is depends not on considerations of individual differences but on whether the proponents want to push "alternatives," "intermediate sanctions," or "lock 'em up" viewpoints. When asked to account for their readiness to dismiss human diversity and the potential of human service, they reply with "big picture" concerns of justice, aggregated crime rates, and even preventing the breakdown of society. Offering human treatment services to offenders and their families seems to threaten proponents of punishment and incapacitation. At this time, we think restorative justice holds the most promise for maintaining accountability while encouraging the delivery of services to higher-risk cases. Restorative justice approaches may serve the victim and the broader community while contributing to reduced victimization through support of effective service for offenders.

We think that the following factors contribute to the "faith" in punishment that is so strong within the just deserts community:

1. Propunishment attitudes and values acquired at home and in schools of law and criminal justice;

2. Propunishment associates of similar background and inclination;

3. Isolation from others who take human diversity, human service, and human science more seriously;

4. A disregard for evidence, because their approach is moral and not utilitarian;

5. Governments that distribute rewards to those policy units that best justify their political agenda of the moment.

While the public may not have given up on rehabilitation to the degree that mainstream criminology and criminal justice have, citizens still appear to vote for "law and order"—particularly when human service and "peace and security" alternatives are not articulated.

In Canada, human service, rehabilitation, and prevention are no longer on the back burner in many of the research and policy units. The debates around the Young Offender Act and the report of the Canadian Sentencing Commission, both products of anti-service and "back to justice" sentiments, were interesting because they were informed by evidence and because the voluntary and professional sectors made their views known in a clear, and sometimes even coordinated, manner. The opinions of the nongovernmental agencies were sought actively, and presentations were facilitated by government officials. In the case of the debate around the just deserts recommendations of the Sentencing Commission, the federal correctional agency already had embarked on a protection of the public agenda that incorporated both secure management of the sentence and the delivery of correctional treatment services. The apparent inconsistency of the Commission's underplaying of rehabilitation and Correctional Service Canada's official commitment to assisting offenders in change may have played a role in the government's rejection of the antirehabilitation themes in the Commission's report. Not unrelated, in a very short period of time, criminal justice psychology has emerged as a major component of undergraduate and graduate programs in several Canadian universities. Federal government research offices are currently major players in correctional policy, and their research findings are well represented in major criminology and psychology journals. For all of this, many politicians continue to talk about "getting tough" on offenders, and simultaneously are taking steps that are weakening the voluntary sector agencies that may help them attain the objective of reduced reoffending.

It appears that current debate on family violence will also be responsive to evidence and not dismissive of human service. Once again, the voluntary and professional associations are active participants. One emerging theme is viewing the arrest and detention of male batterers as the occasion for direct services focusing on: (1) the safety of the victim, and (2) the initiation of tightly focused antibattering treatment for the offender. Here a model may be developing for a more effective criminal justice response to many types of crime. Consistent with some interpretations of community policing (see Chapter 10), the police response may well become one aimed at the resolution of the immediate crisis, the healing and future safety of the victim, and the mobilization of community resources in the interest of reduced future victimization.

What is happening at the legislative and policy level in the United States, Europe, and elsewhere? We know that protreatment documents are being produced and initiatives undertaken by several major national institutes and professional associations in the United States. Recall the brief references to the National Institute of Corrections (NIC), the Office of Justice Programs, and the International Community Corrections Association (ICCA) in Chapter 7, as well as the developments in a variety of states and counties. Rehabilitation is being discussed once again in policy units in Europe. The Conférence Permanente Européenne de la Probation, an association of probation agencies representing most of the European Union, sponsored a seminar on offender rehabilitation in 1996. "What works" conferences followed in Sweden (1997), Norway (1998), The Netherlands (2001), and Finland (2001). The British Home Office and HM Inspectorate of Probation have initiated a system-wide "what works" initiative based on the principles of risk-need-responsivity and other feature of evidence-based practice (Chapman & Hough, 1998; Home Office Communication Directorate, 1999; Underdown, 1998). Similar policy and practice statements can be found in The Netherlands (Netherlands, 2001), Australia (Arthur Andersen Consulting, 2000; Howells & Day, 1999), and New Zealand (McLaren, 1992; New Zealand, 1999). The importance of objective offender risk-needs assessment has been recognized in many countries spanning the globe (e.g., United Kingdom, Puerto Rico, Singapore).

At the Eighth United Nations Conference on the Prevention of Crime and the Treatment of Offenders (1990), direct human service received less attention than did alternatives to incarceration, community service orders, and intermediate sanctions. However, the Canadian delegation managed to have "services to offenders while under sanction" inserted into a resolution on the need for research that links type of offender, type of sanction, and recidivism (Cormier, 1991). The Ninth and Tenth conferences focused on "safe and effective alternatives to incarceration," and there was no further endorsement of rehabilitation.

The traditional concerns of the psychology of crime are back in the forefront of criminology and are reentering criminal justice and corrections. Indeed, the largest body of well-established research findings in criminology has always resided in the psychology of criminal conduct, inherent in the consistency of findings in the voluminous prediction literature and in the literature on controlled evaluations of criminal justice processing, prevention, and treatment.

Is it possible to move beyond risk/need assessments (now common in corrections) to revitalize direct human service programming in prevention and corrections? If our objective is a reduction in antisocial and criminal behavior, we must. The first step is to disseminate the basic empirical, theoretical, and practical knowledge that exists now in the general personality and social psychology of crime—particularly the social learning and cognitive-behavioral statements of that knowledge. If human service approaches are to be revitalized, it is crucial that the underlying psychological model of crime and its prevention be one that not only organizes knowledge but is also fruitful, powerful, and self-correcting. Social learning and cognitive-behavioral approaches have no competitors on these points.

First we summarize what we think is known about individual differences in criminal conduct, then we turn to who should be in touch with that knowledge.

What is Known Within the General Social Psychology of Crime

The rational-empirical roots of the psychology of crime induce a healthy skepticism when summarizing research findings. They also feed a respect for evidence. The public that supports the development of a PCC has a right to hear what has been learned, and the people in positions to influence the revitalization of human service should know why they should support direct treatment services.

The first finding, now well-established within PCC, is that there are substantial individual differences in criminal conduct. People differ in their frequency of criminal activity and in the number, type, and variety of criminal acts in which they engage. In addition, while accounting for a disproportionate amount of the total criminal activity, the more criminally active offenders tend not to be specialists. These findings are apparent across methods of measurement and particular types of offense, and they are found within the typical indicators of social location such as geography, age, race/ethnicity, gender, and social class.

The current state of empirical knowledge can be summarized in a few illustrations. Figure 11.1 provides a summary of reasonably well-established correlates of criminal behavior. Figure 11.2 orders these factors into classes of major and minor risk factors. For the weakest risk factors, the average correlation coefficients are estimated to be in the range of .05 to .10. The average coefficients for the stronger of the risk factors are estimated to be in the range of .20 to .30.

1) LOWER-CLASS ORIGINS, as measured by neighborhood characteristics or indices of parental education/occupation.

2) FAMILY OF ORIGIN
Long-term reliance on welfare (as opposed to occasional use of welfare services).
Criminality in family of origin (parents, siblings, other relatives).
Multiple psychological handicaps (low verbal intelligence, emotional instability, alcoholism, parenting skill deficits).
Antisocial attitudes.

3) PERSONAL TEMPERAMENT, APTITUDE, AND EARLY BEHAVIORAL HISTORY
Restlessly energetic, impulsive, adventurous, pleasure-seeking, a taste for risk.
Below-average verbal intelligence.
Response to frustration more likely to involve resentment and anger rather than composure or anxiety/guilt/depression.
Lack of conscientiousness.
Egocentricism (below age-based norm for perspective-taking).
Moral immaturity (below age-based norm for moral thinking).
Poor problem-solving/coping skills.
If diagnosed as a child, more likely to be diagnosed externalizing (conduct disorder) than internalizing (neurotic/depressive/withdrawn).
Early and generalized misconduct (lying, stealing, aggression, early experimentation with sex and drugs—including tobacco).

4) EARLY AND CONTINUING FAMILY CONDITIONS
Low levels of affection/cohesiveness within home.
Low levels of supervision and poor discipline within home.
Neglect/abuse.

5) SCHOOL-BASED RISK FACTORS
Below-average effort.
Lack of interest/being bored.
Not worrying about occupational future.
Conduct problems (truancy).
Poor schools.

6) PERSONAL EDUCATIONAL/VOCATIONAL/SOCIOECONOMIC ACHIEVEMENT
Low level of achieved education.
Long periods of unemployment (rather than low levels of occupational prestige).
Reliance on welfare (as opposed to occasional use of welfare services, and rather than low income).

7) INTERPERSONAL RELATIONSHIPS
Generalized indifference to opinion of others.
Unstable marital history.
Rejected/rejecting.

8) SOCIAL SUPPORT FOR CRIME
Association with antisocial others.
Isolation from noncriminal others.

9) PERSONAL ATTITUDES/VALUES/BELIEFS SUPPORTIVE OF CRIME
High tolerance for deviance in general.
Rejection of the validity of the law in particular.
Applies rationalizations for law violations to a wide variety of acts and circumstances.
Interprets a wide range of stimuli as reasons for anger.
Thinking style and content is generally antisocial.

10) BEHAVIORAL HISTORY
Criminal history, juvenile and adult (look for an uninterrupted history, beginning at a young age, including a variety of different types of offenses and violations that continue even while under sentence).
Alcohol and drug abuse.
Aimless use of leisure time.
Disorganized lifestyle.

11) PSYCHOPATHOLOGY
High scores on measures of "antisocial personality/psychopathy." Many forms of emotional/behavioral disturbance when combined with a history of antisocial behavior (e.g., conduct problems plus shyness).

12) OTHER RISK FACTORS
Being male.
Being a member of some minority groups.
Being young (16-22 years).
A host of apparent biological anomalies that as yet have not been pulled together in a theoretically interesting, empirically convincing, or practically useful way.
Other risk factors, as yet undiscovered or completely missed in our reviews of the literature.

Figure 11.1
A Brief Survey of Risk Factors from the Cross-Sectional and Longitudinal Studies
From Andrews, 1989; Andrews, Leschied & Hoge, 1992

The Major Factors:

1) Antisocial/procriminal attitudes, values, beliefs, and cognitive-emotional states (i.e., personal cognitive supports for crime);

2) Procriminal associates and isolation from anticriminal others (i.e., interpersonal supports for crime);

3) Temperamental and personality factors conducive to criminal activity, including psychopathy, weak socialization, impulsivity, restless aggressive energy, egocentrism, below-average verbal intelligence, a taste for risk, and weak problem-solving/self-regulation skills;

4) History of antisocial behavior evident from a young age, in a variety of settings, and involving a number and variety of different acts;

5) Familial factors that include criminality and a variety of psychological problems in the family of origin and, in particular, low levels of affection, caring, and cohesiveness; poor parental supervision and discipline practices; and outright neglect and abuse;

6) Low levels of personal educational, vocational, or financial achievement and, in particular, unstable employment;

The Minor Factors:

7) Lower-class origins as assessed by adverse neighborhood conditions and/or parental education/vocational/economic achievement;

8) Personal distress, whether assessed by way of the sociological constructs of anomie, strain, and alienation or by way of the clinical constructs of low self-esteem, anxiety, depression, worry, or officially labeled "mental disorder";

9) A host of biological/neuropsychological indicators that have yet to be integrated in a convincing manner by way of either theory or the construction of practical risk/need assessment instruments.

Figure 11.2
Risk/Need Factors within the General Personality and Social Psychology of Criminal Conduct

When a number and variety of risk factors are sampled, the multiple correlations with crime reach the .70 level. This is particularly so when a multidomain sampling of predictors is supplemented by multimethod assessment and when temporal changes on the more dynamic risk factors are included in the prediction formula.

The same sets of risk factors appear to be involved within categories of geography, class, age, gender, and ethnicity. Furthermore, the correlations with crime of these biological and social location variables is reduced, if not eliminated, when controls are introduced for the stronger of the personal, interpersonal, and familial risk factors. Remaining to be documented is whether the correlation between gender/ethnicity/race/class and crime that remains after controlling for the major personal and interpersonal factors is actually a result of the processing effects suggested by the social inequality versions of social location theories. PCC does not deny inequality and does not deny bias in both official and unofficial responses to rule violation.

The same risk factors apply across different types of criminal behavior, though crime-specific indicators of antisocial attitudes, associates, and behavioral history may be most useful when the focus is on violence or sex offenses (see the meta-analytic results with mentally disordered offenders and sex offenders in Chapter 9). For example, laboratory assessments of deviant sexual arousal may enhance predictive validity when working with pedophiles.

The establishment of risk factors is one step on the road to an increased understanding of criminal conduct. Empirically derived knowledge also may contribute to increased effectiveness and efficiency in the design and delivery of effective prevention and rehabilitation programs. Knowledge of risk factors facilitates the construction of practical risk assessment instruments, which in turn makes it possible to identify individuals and families who are at risk for criminal conduct. This ability has been well-established at levels well above chance (and at a level that will assist in programming). Intensive and otherwise appropriate services, as defined according to the psychology of criminal conduct, are most effective when delivered to higher-risk as opposed to lower-risk cases. This principle, like any other, requires additional study—in particular with the highest-risk cases (e.g., "psychopaths"). Experimental tests with the highest-risk groups simply have not been conducted. We are confident, however, that the existing body of experimental evidence regarding the relative effectiveness of clinically relevant and psychologically informed intervention does not reflect a "creaming" of offenders (i.e., treatment groups were not composed of clients who were at low-risk for criminal recidivism from the start).

The more dynamic risk factors are relevant to prevention and rehabilitation also in that they suggest promising intermediate objectives of programming, which when achieved should be followed by reductions in criminal behavior. This is the criminogenic need principle of effective prevention and treatment. Thus, Figure 11.3 contains many of the same variables listed in Figures 11.1 and 11.2, but in Figure 11.3, potential risk/need factors are sorted into promising and less promising intermediate targets of human service programming. Here the listing of knowledge in PCC is much more dependent upon clinical experience, theoretical inference, and common sense than was the list of risk factors.

Consumers of PCC should be aware that multiwave longitudinal studies and controlled treatment studies are few in number compared to investigations of prediction studies and simple differentiation between offenders and nonoffenders. In addition, very few studies that may contribute to convincing knowledge regarding criminogenic need factors have reported upon what changes in personal characteristics and circumstances actually enhanced predictive validity relative to initial assessments (multiwave longitudinal studies). Nor have many reported upon what personal and circumstantial factors mediated the effects of intervention on recidivism (controlled studies of intervention that approximated experimental ideals). With all of these caveats, Figure 11.3 provides a useful guide for agencies struggling to identify what they should be focusing upon if their mandate includes the reduction of criminal conduct.

Promising Targets for Change

- Changing antisocial attitudes
- Changing antisocial feelings
- Reducing antisocial peer associations
- Promoting familial affection/communication
- Promoting familial monitoring and supervision
- Promoting child protection (preventing neglect/abuse)
- Promoting identification/association with anticriminal role models
- Increasing self-control, self-management, and problem-solving skills
- Replacing the skills of lying, stealing, and aggression with more prosocial alternatives
- Reducing chemical dependencies
- Shifting the density of the personal, interpersonal, and other rewards and costs for criminal and noncriminal activities in familial, academic, vocational, recreational, and other behavioral settings so that the noncriminal alternatives are favored
- Providing the chronically psychiatrically troubled with low-pressure, sheltered living arrangements
- Ensuring that the client is able to recognize risky situations and has a concrete and well-rehearsed plan for dealing with those situations
- Confronting the personal and circumstantial barriers to service (client motivation; background stressors with which clients may be preoccupied)
- Changing other attributes of clients and their circumstances that, through individualized assessments of risk and need, have been linked reasonably with criminal conduct

Less Promising Targets

- Increasing self-esteem (without simultaneous reductions in antisocial thinking, feeling, and peer associations)
- Focusing on vague emotional/personal complaints that have not been linked with criminal conduct
- Increasing the cohesiveness of antisocial peer groups
- Improving neighborhood-wide living conditions without touching the criminogenic needs of higher-risk individuals and families
- Showing respect for antisocial thinking on the grounds that the values of one culture are as equally valid as the values of another culture
- Increasing conventional ambition in the areas of school and work without concrete assistance in realizing these ambitions
- Attempting to turn the client into a "better person," when the standards for being a "better person" do not link with recidivism.

Figure 11.3
Promising and Less Promising Intermediate Targets in Prevention and Rehabilitation
From Andrews, 1989; Andrews, Bonta & Hoge, 1990; Andrews, Leschied & Hoge, 1992

We view our list as more promising than the Sutherland tradition, within which it seemed almost everything in the universe contributed to differential association (antisocial attitudes and associates). We also view our list of criminogenic factors as more promising than perspectives that begin and end with a framework within which human beings pursue pleasure and avoid pain according to: (1) opportunities for easy and simple gratifications through force and/or fraud, and (2) a level of self-control that had been established at an early age through parenting practices. Accepting or rejecting any of the above discussion, the need to revise Figure 11.3 in empirical or otherwise helpful ways currently is a major concern within PCC. This should be communicated to others who may come to support direct service.

The general personality and social psychology of criminal conduct also supports explorations of responsivity considerations. These considerations are fundamental in that they have to do with what styles and modes of behavioral influence actually impact upon behavior. First and foremost, the responsivity principle suggests that behavior—criminal or non-criminal—is influenced by the outcomes of particular acts, signaled by the incentives and disincentives of the immediate situation of action. Second, behavior is influenced by the personally and interpersonally mediated sources of these signaled rewards and costs for criminal versus non-criminal action. Accepting these suggestions, the most empirically defensible and powerful theory of criminal activity is a broadly based social learning perspective that suggests how both self-control and interpersonal influence occur.

Drawing upon Andrews and Kiessling (1980) and Andrews and Carvell (1997), the five dimensions of effective correctional supervision and counseling entail:

1. *Relationship*: relating in open, enthusiastic, caring ways.

2. *Authority*: "firm but fair"; distinguishing between rules and requests; monitoring; reinforcing compliance; no interpersonal domination or abuse.

3. *Anticriminal modeling and reinforcement*: demonstrating and reinforcing vivid alternatives to procriminal styles of thinking, feeling, and acting.

4. *Concrete problem-solving*: skill-building and removal of obstacles toward increased reward levels for anticriminal behavior in settings such as home, school, and work.

5. *Advocacy and brokerage*: seeking and obtaining the most appropriate correctional services for the client.

At the same time, theory and research suggest that some styles and modes of treatment have poor track records in prevention and correction. Group programs designed according to the principles of clinical sociology were outright failures. These programs involved creating intense group interactions without the leader of the group gaining control over the expression and rewarding of antisocial sentiments. In addition, as yet, there is no convincing evidence that programs designed according to the principles of either deterrence or labeling theory have been successful. "Yelling at people" is inconsistent with the relationship factor described above, and fear of punishment is not a major predictor of criminal conduct. Similarly, "radical nonintervention" (i.e., doing nothing in the face of antisocial potential) is simply inconsistent with the risk principle (on the other hand, though, radical nonintervention makes sense for the lowest-risk cases). There is no evidence that innovative alternative punishments such as community service orders, electronic monitoring, or restitution are rehabilitative in any important sense, although they may be excellent alternatives to criminal processing as long as the net is not widened and failure to comply does not result in further processing. Nondirective, client-centered counseling and unstructured psychodynamic therapy also have yet to prove themselves in corrections. The more interpersonally and cognitively mature offenders, however, may respond to these less structured, more evocative, and more relationship-dependent styles of service.

To date, the findings regarding the effectiveness of various treatments have been robust across categories of gender, age, ethnicity, and class (Andrews, Dowden & Rettinger, 2001). Such variables, however, may prove to be important responsivity factors for some types of treatment. Other potential responsivity factors include interpersonal anxiety, psychopathology, verbal intelligence, language, and motivation, which all await systematic study in the context of prevention and correctional treatment.

Finally, there is no consistent evidence that variation in criminal sanctions is capable of significant reductions in criminal recidivism (recall Chapter 8). The most we can say is that there is an incapacitation effect of incarceration but a slight increase in post-penalty criminal recidivism. Appropriate treatment services appear to work best in the community. Diversion, probation, custody, intensive supervision, boot camps, and electronic monitoring are not human service interventions. They are settings within which rehabilitation programs may operate.

Figure 11.4 provides a brief summary of the elements of effective human service in a justice context.

- Deliver the more intensive human services to higher-risk cases
- Target criminogenic needs
- Use behavioral/social learning/cognitive-behavioral influence strategies
- Sensitivity to specific responsivity considerations
- Service reflects a theory that links practice, intermediate objectives, and reduced reoffending
- Workers are trained in the delivery of the specific service
- Clinical supervision is provided to the workers
- Training/program manuals available
- Service process and intermediate gain are monitored
- Adequate dosage is provided (duration and frequency of sessions appropriate)
- Enthusiastic and caring workers
- Authority is exercised in firm and fair ways
- Workers demonstrate and reinforce clear alternatives to antisocial styles of thinking, feeling, and acting
- Workers engage in and demonstrate concrete problem-solving, as well as other relevant skill-building
- Workers are advocates for the offender and broker clinically appropriate services

Figure 11.4
Elements of Effective Human Service Programming

Who Has the Power to Promote Human Service in Prevention and Corrections?

Professors in university-based departments of psychology, psychiatry, sociology, social work, criminology, and criminal justice are powerful in that they teach others, who in turn go into the field. Some consult with government and other social agencies. It would be helpful if the social psychology of crime was taught in those departments and referenced in consultations. There were few strong voices in the university setting when respect for human diversity and human service was being denied and the punishment agenda expanded.

The more clinically oriented schools may come to teach their students that the criminological objective of reduced antisocial conduct is at least as worthy as the traditional clinical objective of reduced personal distress. Existing child, youth, and family services also should be exposed to the general social psychology of crime. They are natural settings from which both prevention and rehabilitation programming may flow.

School officials, teachers, and guidance counselors also may gain from a general social psychology of crime. Schools are natural settings for prevention and rehabilitation efforts. Most of the research on schools has examined means and ways to boost IQ and scholastic scores. We know that academic achievement and the peer associations often formed in school are correlates of crime. PCC should be applied in these settings to achieve more than academic goals.

In addition, judges, defense attorneys, prosecutors, probation and parole officers, and other correctional officials should become knowledgeable in the psychology of crime. Perhaps lawyers should argue in favor of effective service for their clients as often as they argue for variations on themes of punishment. The major point here is that correctional agencies are human service agencies, and correctional professionals are human service professionals.

These notions of evidence-based practice require changes in roles and resource allocation strategies along the following lines:

1. The case management role is important and valued but may be too passive for effective treatment. An emphasis must be put on systematic assessment aimed at treatment.

2. Correctional managers must be offered rewards for implementing and documenting treatment programs.

3. With regard to status within the agency, managers and workers can be rewarded more for treatment-related efforts than for case monitoring.

4. Agencies or programs that deal with low-risk cases in nonintrusive and efficient ways are highly valued, but a greater proportion of the total resource pie may be best allocated to agencies and agents working with higher-risk cases.

5. A simple caseload mentality is no longer warranted. Rather, resource allocation strategies might better weigh service efforts by the risk/need levels of clients served and by programs matched to risk/need.

6. Arranging alternatives to custody, with service provision for higher-risk cases, may once again come to be seen as a major role for probation officers.

7. A major aspect of the agency will come to involve ongoing research, evaluation, and informed program change.

8. A new position of clinical supervisor to be introduced in many agencies.

9. Community-based noncorrectional agencies in the domains of child, youth, family, substance abuse, employment, education, mental health, and other services may become engaged as full partners with correctional agencies in the delivery of "effective" service. Interestingly, in some communities, these noncorrectional agencies involved in service delivery include direct service programs operated by the police, courts, and the offices of prosecuting attorneys. This means that formal correctional agencies, such as police, probation, parole, and community-based residential settings, must themselves be a vital part of the community.

The challenge for correctional agencies is great. Not only must correctional workers and managers be brought into contact with "what works," they must be trained in the skills that effective service requires—and supported in the practice of those skills. With the involvement of noncorrectional agencies, the task becomes even more complex. Many of those community-based agencies are as committed to service strategies that are ineffective with offenders as are correctional agencies to surveillance and negative sanctioning. The need is not just for information and skill training but also for high-quality feedback about where any given agency or program may stand relative to what is suggested as promising by PCC. Toward this end, the Correctional Program Assessment Inventory is being developed to assist agencies and programs to establish where they are now relative to where they may wish to go in the development of effective service (Andrews, 1995: Gendreau & Andrews, 2001; Latessa & Holsinger, 1998). The working hypothesis is that just as surveying the best-established risk/need factors developed effective risk/need instruments, so may programs be assessed with reference to the presence or absence of the best-validated service elements.

Finally, we need political support for the design, delivery, and evaluation of human services with some integrity and decency. A few guidelines for political activity and public education are outlined in Figure 11.5. The final element in Figure 11.5 notes the importance of forming partnerships with groups committed to primary prevention. Insofar as PCC is a truly interdisciplinary social psychology of crime, we know that criminal conduct is a reflection of a variety of factors, including the immediate situational, personal, interpersonal, familial, and the broader social arrangements that may be defined in geographic, economic, political, cultural, and social structural terms. As a discipline of crime prevention develops (Ekblom, 1996), a contribution of PCC will be to maintain a focus on ensuring that the broader interventions reach down and influence the contingencies under which individuals and families at risk actually live. Another contribution will be the ability to point to many successful efforts in the domain of human service in the more limited context of justice. We look forward to learning much more about aggregated crime rates through systematic primary prevention efforts that attend to individuals in their immediate situations of action.

Conclusion

There now is a human science of criminal conduct. There are empirically defensible theories of criminal conduct that may be helpful in designing and delivering effective service. The literature is reasonably strong and supports vigorous pursuit of ethical, decent, humane, and cost-efficient approaches to prevention and rehabilitative programming for higher-risk cases under a variety of conditions of just sanctioning—and under primary prevention conditions. The active and effective human service agency may contribute to a still more powerful knowledge base by building assessment, reassessment, and research into the agency.

Right from the first edition of this book we stated that a major issue, one on which work was only beginning, entailed dissemination and implementation: how to make use of what works. The implementation issues continue to be huge (see Bernfeld, Farrington & Leschied, 2001). However, the dissemination issues have changed. In a few short years, the basics of PCC have been widely disseminated within corrections (if not as effectively within the domains of the courts and the public). The mainstream textbooks aside, the interests of PCC are now prominent in the major journals of psychology and criminology. The tireless efforts of Paul Gendreau, Robert Ross, Elizabeth Fabiano, Frank Porporino, Larry Motiuk, Steven Wormith, James McGuire, Philip Priestly, Vern Fogg, Brad Bogue, John Gorschuk, Marc Carry, and many others (including, we

- Do not "oversell" treatment and rehabilitation—there is no cure for crime (but cutting recidivism rates by 30% to 60% is not a trivial accomplishment).

- Recognize that we are all interested in protection of the public, and we are all interested in protecting people from abuse.

- Find ethical, legal, fair, humane, decent, and cost-efficient ways of providing effective treatment services to those in need, whatever the just sanction.

- Prevention and rehabilitation concern protection of the public and, unlike official punishment, have research support.

- Recognize that many professionals are antitreatment because they have been trained in intellectual traditions that are antitreatment. They are not evil and they are not stupid. They merely suffer from "socially constructed repression" or "motivated not seeing." Their training, attitudes, and differential association patterns make it difficult for them to recognize the evidence. (However, all but the highest-risk authoritarian among them can be rehabilitated.)

- Do not be confused by charges of being "too right-wing" or "too left-wing" or "no wing at all" (wishy-washy liberal/apolitical). The antitreatment rhetoric, politically, is all over the map in terms of political orientation:
  —treatment is punishment in disguise (the left)
  —treatment lets hardened criminals off too easily (the right)

- Watch out in particular for the vision of the just deserts theorists. These punishment experts have merged the concerns of the left and the right into a grand and seductive position wherein consideration of rehabilitation represents a threat that Canadian and American young people will not receive the precise dose of punishment they deserve by virtue of their misdeeds.

- Remind punishment experts that treatment is subject to peer review, informed choice, ethical standards, civil suits, and criminal processing in cases in which treatment is abusive.

- Confront, neutralize, and destroy the simple-minded versions of "nothing works," "labeling," "deterrence," and "just deserts" positions. Similarly, neutralize and/or destroy theories that deny human diversity (e.g., that lower-class origins causes most crime).

- Challenge every politician, senior bureaucrat, and academician who engages in rhetoric that is unfavorable to the delivery of high-quality services to young people in need.

- Promote legislation and government/agency policy that support rather than discourage the delivery and development of high-quality clinical service. Change the political and social structure so that it supports service.

- Keep an eye on the price of reduced antisocial behavior, reduced harm, and reduced costs of criminal justice processes. Promote evaluative efforts and learn from the evaluations.

- Do not become trapped in arguments with primary prevention advocates who believe that a society-wide focus on unemployment, sexism, or racism will eliminate crime. Be against inequality, but recognize the value of direct service.

Figure 11.5
Political Activity and Public Education
From Andrews, Leschied & Hoge 1992

think, ourselves) in the domains of conference presentations and consultations have had some effect. The efforts of the National Institute of Corrections of the U.S. Department of Justice (NIC Community, NIC Academy, NIC Information Center) are most noteworthy in that the "what works" committee (led by the late David Dillingham with Ron Breschani and Nancy Shomaker) has sponsored many training programs across the United States. Some of these trainings, with the work of Ed Wolohan, through satellite technology have reached thousands of practitioners and managers at a time. In the United Kingdom, David Perry's "what works" group has dramatically changed the national probation service aligning the service with evidence-based practice (Perry, 2001). Among professional associations, the International Community Corrections Association (ICCA, formerly IARCA) has led the way in promoting ready access to the "what works" material.

With the exception of target groups such as the police, courts, students of mainstream criminology, and the broader public, dissemination of the basics of PCC is proceeding at a good pace. Otherwise, implementation and ongoing development of effective programming is the priority.

Finally, perhaps (as the conflict/Marxist theorists claimed), a psychology of crime does inevitably lead to "correctionalism." But we ask: What is wrong with working toward increased knowledge that may speak to reduced harm to self and others?

References

Abel, G.G., M.S. Mittelman & J.V. Becker (1985). Sexual offenders: results of assessment and recommendations for treatment. In M.H. Ben-Aron, S.J. Hucker & C.D. Webster (eds.), *Clinical Criminology* (pp. 191-205). Toronto: M & M Graphics.

Abrams, K.M. & G.E. Robinson (1998). Stalking part I: An overview of the problem. *Canadian Journal of Psychiatry*, 43, 473-476.

Adams, S. (1975). *Evaluation: A way out of the rhetoric*. Paper presented at the Evaluation Research Conference, Seattle, WA.

Agee, V.L. (1979). *Treatment of the violent incorrigible adolescent*. Lexington, MA: Lexington Books.

Agee, V.L. (1986). Institutional treatment programs for the violent juvenile. In S. Apter & A. Goldstein (eds.), *Youth Violence: Program and Prospects* (pp. 75-88). New York: Pergamon Press.

Agnew, R. (1992). Foundation for a general strain theory of crime and delinquency. *Criminology*, 30, 47-87.

Agnew, R. (1994). The techniques of neutralization and violence. *Criminology*, 32, 555-580.

Agnew, R. (1995). Testing the leading crime theories: An alternative strategy focusing on motivational processes. *Journal of Research in Crime and Delinquency*, 32, 363-398.

Agnew, R. (1997). Stability and change in crime over the life course: A strain theory explanation. In T.P. Thornberry (ed.), *Developmental theories of crime and delinquency* (pp. 101-132). New Brunswick, NJ: Transaction Publishers.

Aguirre, A. & D.V. Baker (1990). Empirical research on racial discrimination in the imposition of the death penalty. *Criminal Justice Abstracts*, March.

Ajzen, I. (1996). The directive influence of attitudes on behavior. In P.M. Gollwitzer & J.A. Bargh (eds.), *The psychology of action: Linking cognition and motivation to behavior* (pp. 385-403). New York: Guilford Press.

Ajzen, I. & M. Fishbein (1980). *Understanding attitudes and predicting social behavior*. Englewood Cliffs, NJ: Prentice Hall.

Akers, R.L. (1973). *Deviant behavior: A social learning approach*. Belmont, CA: Wadsworth.

Akers, R.L. (1985). *Deviant behavior: A social learning approach* (3rd ed). Belmont, CA: Wadsworth.

Akers, R.L. (1994). *Criminological theories: Introduction and evaluation*. Los Angeles: Roxbury.

Akers, R.L. & J.K. Cochran, (1985). Adolescent marijuana use: A test of three theories of deviant behavior. *Deviant Behavior*, 6, 323-346.

Alexander, J.F. (1973). Defensive and supportive communications in normal and deviant families. *Journal of Consulting and Clinical Psychology*, 40, 223-231.

Alexander, J.F. & C. Barton (1976). Behavioral systems therapy for families. In D.H.L. Olson (ed.), *Treating Relationships* (pp.167-188). Lake Mills, IA: Graphic.

Alexander, J.F., C. Barton, R..S. Schiavo & B.V. Parsons (1976). Systems-behavioral intervention with families of delinquents: Therapist characteristics, family behavior, and outcome. *Journal of Consulting and Clinical Psychology*, 44, 656-664.

Alexander, J.F. & B.V. Parsons (1973). Short-term behavioral intervention with delinquent families: Impact on family process and recidivism. *Journal of Abnormal Psychology*, 81, 219-225.

Allen, J.P., S.T. Hauser & E. Borman-Spurrell (1996). Attachment theory as a framework for understanding sequelae of severe adolescent psychopathology: An 11-year follow-up study. *Journal of Consulting and Clinical Psychology*, 64, 254-263.

American Psychiatric Association. (1994). *Diagnostic and statistical manual of mental disorders—DSM IV*. Washington, DC: The American Psychiatric Association.

Andersen, H.S., D. Sestoft, T. Lillebaek, G. Gabrielsen & P. Kramp (1996). Prevalence of ICD-10 psychiatric morbidity in random samples of prisoners on remand. *International Journal of Law and Psychiatry*, 19, 61-74.

Anderson, B.J., M.D. Holmes & E. Ostresh (1999). Male and female delinquents' attachments and effects of attachments on severity of self-reported delinquency. *Criminal Justice and Behavior*, 26, 435-452.

Andrews, D.A. (1979). *The dimensions of correctional counseling and supervision process in probation and parole*. Toronto: Ontario Ministry of Correctional Services.

Andrews, D.A. (1980). Some experimental investigations of the principles of differential association through deliberate manipulations of the structure of service systems. *American Sociological Review*, 45, 448-462.

Andrews, D.A. (1982a). *A personal, interpersonal and community-reinforcement perspective on deviant behaviour (PIC-R)*. Toronto: Ontario Ministry of Correctional Services.

Andrews, D.A. (1982b). *The Level of Supervision Inventory (LSI): The first follow-up*. Toronto: Ontario Ministry of Correctional Services.

Andrews, D.A. (1983). The assessment of outcome in correctional samples. In M.L. Lambert, E.R. Christensen & S.S. DeJulio (eds.), *The measurement of psychotherapy outcome in research and evaluation* (pp. 160-201). New York: Wiley.

Andrews, D.A. (1989). Recidivism is predictable and can be influenced: Using risk assessments to reduce recidivism. *Forum on Corrections Research*, 1(2), 11-18.

Andrews, D.A. (1990). *Role of antisocial attitudes in the psychology of crime*. Paper presented at the Annual Conference of the Canadian Psychological Association, Ottawa, Ontario.

Andrews, D.A. (1995). *Assessing program elements for risk reduction: The Correctional Program Assessment Inventory*. Paper presented at the Research to Results Conference of the International Community Corrections Association, October, Ottawa, Ontario.

Andrews, D.A. (1996). Criminal recidivism is predictable and can be influenced: An update. *Forum on Corrections Research*, 8, 42-44.

Andrews, D.A. & J. Bonta (1995). *The Level of Service Inventory – Revised*. Toronto: Multi-Health Systems.

Andrews, D.A., J. Bonta & R D. Hoge (1990). Classification for effective rehabilitation: Rediscovering psychology. *Criminal Justice and Behavior*, 17, 19-52.

Andrews, D.A., J. Bonta & S.J. Wormith (in development). *The Level of Service/Case Management Inventory (LS/CMI)*. Toronto: Multi-Health Systems.

Andrews, D.A. & C. Carvell (1997). *Core correctional treatment - Core correctional supervision and counseling: Theory, research, assessment and practice.* Carleton University, Ottawa, Canada.

Andrews, D.A. & C. Dowden (1999). A meta-analytic investigation into effective correctional intervention for female offenders. *Forum on Corrections Research*, 11(3), 18-21.

Andrews, D.A., C. Dowden & P. Gendreau (1999). *Clinically relevant and psychologically informed approaches to reduced re-offending: A meta-analytic study of human service, risk, need, responsivity and other concerns in justice contexts.* Carleton University, Ottawa, Canada.

Andrews, D.A., C. Dowden & J.L. Rettinger (2001). Special populations within Canada. In J.A. Winterdyck (ed.), *Corrections in Canada: Social reactions to crime* (pp. 170-212). Toronto: Prentice Hall.

Andrews, D.A., W. Friesen & J.J. Kiessling (1980). *A three year postprogram follow-up of the CaVIC probationers: The effects of selection of officers, supervision by volunteers and supervision practices on recidivism.* Final report submitted to the Solicitor General Canada, Ottawa, Ontario.

Andrews, D.A. & J.J. Kiessling (1980). Program structure and effective correctional practices: A summary of the CaVIC research. In R.R. Ross & P. Gendreau (eds.), *Effective correctional treatment* (pp. 439-463). Toronto: Butterworth.

Andrews, D.A., A.W. Leschied & R.D. Hoge (1992). *A review of the classification and treatment literature.* Toronto: Ministry of Community and Social Services.

Andrews, D.A. & D. Robinson (1984). *The Level of Supervision Inventory: Second report.* Report to Research Services (Toronto) of the Ontario Ministry of Correctional Services.

Andrews, D.A. & J.S. Wormith (1984). *Criminal sentiments and criminal behaviour.* Programs Branch User Report. Ottawa: Solicitor General Canada.

Andrews, D.A. & J.S. Wormith (1989). Personality and crime: Knowledge destruction and construction in criminology. *Justice Quarterly*, 6, 289-309.

Andrews, D.A., J.S. Wormith & J.J. Kiessling (1985). *Self-reported criminal propensity and criminal behavior: Threats to the validity of assessment and personality.* Programs Branch User Report. Ottawa: Solicitor General Canada..

Andrews, D.A., I. Zinger, R.D. Hoge, J. Bonta, P. Gendreau & F.T. Cullen (1990a). Does correctional treatment work? A psychologically informed meta-analysis. *Criminology*, 28, 369-404.

Andrews, D.A., I. Zinger, R.D. Hoge, J. Bonta, P. Gendreau & F.T. Cullen (1990b). A human science approach or more punishment and pessimism-rejoinder. *Criminology*, 28, 419-429.

Andrews, K.H. & D.B. Kandel (1979). Attitude and behavior: A specification of the contingent consistency hypothesis. *American Sociological Review*, 44, 298-310.

Annis, H.M. (1982). *Inventory of Drinking Situations (IDS-100)*. Toronto: Addiction Research Foundation.

Annis, H.M. & C.S. Davis (1989). Relapse prevention. In R.K. Hester & W.R. Miller (eds.), *Handbook of alcoholism treatment approaches* (pp. 170-182). New York: Pergamon Press.

Annis, H.M. & G.J. Martin (1995). Profile types on the Inventory of Drinking Situations: Implications for relapse prevention counseling. *Psychology of Addictive Behaviors*, 9, 176-182.

Annis, H.M., R. Schober & E. Kelly (1996). Matching addiction outpatient counseling to client readiness for change: The role of structured relapse prevention counseling. *Experimental and Clinical Psychopharmacology*, 4, 37-45.

Aos, S., P. Phipps, R. Barnoski & R. Lieb (2001). *The comparative costs and benefits of programs to reduce crime.* Olympia, WA: Washington State Institute for Public Policy. http://www.wa.gov/wsipp

Applebaum, P.S., P.C. Robbins & J. Monahan (2000). Violence and delusions: Data from the MacArthur Violence Risk Assessment study. *American Journal of Psychiatry*, 157, 556-572.

Applegate, B.K., F.T. Cullen, M.G. Turner & J.L. Sundt (1996). Assessing public support for three-strikes-and-you're-out laws: Global versus specific attitudes. *Crime & Delinquency*, 42, 517-534.

Arboleda-Flórez, J., H.L. Holley & A. Crisanti (1996). *Mental illness and violence: Proof or stereotype?* Ottawa: Health Canada.

Arbuthnot, J. & D.A. Gordon (1986). Behavioral and cognitive effects of a moral reasoning development intervention for high-risk, behavior-disordered adolescents. *Journal of Consulting and Clinical Psychology*, 54, 208-216.

Archer, J. (2000). Sex differences in aggression between heterosexual partners: A meta-analytic review. *Psychological Bulletin*, 126, 651-680.

Arthur Andersen Consulting (2000). *Review of community correctional services in Victoria.* Melbourne: Department of Justice.

Ashford, J.B. & C.W. LeCroy (1988). Predicting recidivism: an evaluation of the Wisconsin Juvenile Probation and Aftercare Risk Assessment Instrument. *Criminal Justice and Behavior*, 15, 141-151.

Austin, J., J. Clark, P. Hardyman & A.D. Henry (1999). The impact of "three strikes and you're out." *Punishment and Society*, 1, 131-162.

Ayers, C.D., J.H. Williams, J.D. Hawkins, P.L. Peterson, R.F. Catalano & R.D. Abbott (1999). *Journal of Quantitative Criminology*, 15, 277-306.

Azrin, N.H. (1956). Some effects of two intermittent schedules of immediate and non-immediate punishment. *Journal of Psychology*, 42, 3-21.

Azrin, N.H. & W.C. Holz (1966). Punishment. In W.K. Honig (ed.), *Operant behavior: Areas of research and application* (pp. 380-447). New York: Appleton-Century-Crofts.

Azrin, N.H., W.C. Holz & D. Hake (1963). Fixed-ratio punishment. *Journal of the Experimental Analysis of Behavior*, 6, 141-148.

Azrin, N.H., W. Sisson, R. Meyers & M. Godley (1982). Alcoholism treatment by disulfiram and community reinforcement therapy. *Journal of Behavior Therapy and Experimental Psychiatry*, 13, 105-112.

Bailey, W.C. (1966). Correctional outcome: An evaluation of 100 reports. *Journal of Criminal Law, Criminology and Police Science*, 57, 153-160.

Bailey, W.C. (1998). Deterrence, brutalization, and the death penalty: Another examination of Oklahoma's return to capital punishment. *Criminology*, 36, 711-733.

Bailey, W.C. & R.D. Peterson (1998). Capital punishment, homicide, and deterrence: An assessment of the evidence. In D.M. Smith & M.A. Zahn (eds.), *Studying and preventing homicide: Issues and challenges* (pp. 223-245).

Baird, C. (1981). Probation and parole classification: The Wisconsin model. *Corrections Today*, 43,36-41.

Baird, C. (1991). *Validating Risk Assessment Instruments Used in Community Corrections.* Madison, WI: National Council on Crime and Delinquency.

Baird, S C., R C. Heinz & B.J. Bemus (1979). *Project Report #14: A two year follow-up.* Madison, WI: Department of Health and Social Services, Case Classification/Staff Deployment Project, Bureau of Community Corrections.

Bales, R.F. (1950). *Interaction process analysis.* Reading, MA: Addison-Wesley.

Bandura, A. (1989). Human agency in social cognitive theory. *American Psychologist*, 44, 1175-1184.

Bandura, A., C. Barbaranelli, G.V. Caprara & C. Pastorelli (1996). Mechanisms of moral disengagement in the exercise of moral agency. *Journal of Personality and Social Psychology*, 71, 364-374.

Bandura, A. & R.H. Walters (1959). *Adolescent aggression.* New York: Ronald.

Bank, L., J.H. Marlowe, J.B. Reid, G.R. Patterson & M.R. Weinrott (1991). A comparative evaluation of parent-training interventions for families of chronic delinquents. *Journal of Abnormal Child Psychology*, 19, 15-33.

Barbaree, H.E. & W.L. Marshall (1998). Treatment of the sexual offender. In R.M. Wettstein (ed.), *Treatment of offenders with mental disorders.* New York: Guilford.

Barbaree, H.E., M.C. Seto, C.M. Langton & E.J. Peacock (2001). Evaluating the predictive accuracy of six risk assessment instruments for adult sex offenders. *Criminal Justice and Behavior*, 28, 490-521.

Barling, J. & A. Rosenbaum (1986). Work stressors and wife abuse. *Journal of Applied Psychology*, 71, 346-348.

Bartol, C.R. (1996). Police psychology: Then, now, and beyond. *Criminal Justice and Behavior*, 23, 70-89.

Barton, C. & J.F. Alexander (1980). Functional family therapy. In A.S. Gurnam & D.P. Kniskern (eds.), *Handbook of family therapy* (pp. 403-443). New York: Brunner/Mazel.

Barton, C., J.F. Alexander, H., Waldron, C.W. Turner & J. Warburton (1985). Generalizing treatment effects of functional family therapy: Three replications. *American Journal of Family Therapy*, 13, 16-26.

Barton, W.H. & J.A. Butts (1990). Viable options: Intensive supervision programs for juvenile delinquents. *Crime & Delinquency*, 36, 238-256.

Bartusch, D.R.J., D.R. Lynam, T.E. Moffitt & P.A. Silva (1997). Is age important? Testing a general versus a developmental theory of antisocial behavior. *Criminology*, 35, 13-48.

Battin, S.R., K.G. Hill, R.D. Abbott, R.F. Catalano & J.D. Hawkins (1998). The contribution of gang membership to delinquency beyond friends. *Criminology*, 36, 93-115.

Baxter, D.J., L.L. Motiuk & S. Fortin (1995). Intelligence and personality in criminal offenders. In D.H. Saklofske & M. Zeidner (eds.), *International handbook of personality and intelligence* (pp. 673-686). New York: Plenum.

Bayer, B.M., J. Bonta & L.L. Motiuk (1985). The Pd subscales: An empirical evaluation. *Journal of Clinical Psychology*, 41, 780-788.

Bazemore, G. (1996). Three paradigms for juvenile justice. In B. Galaway & J. Hudson (eds.), *Restorative justice: International perspectives* (pp. 37-67). Monsey, NY: Criminal Justice Press.

Bazemore, G., L.B. Nissen & M. Dooley (2000). Mobilizing social support and building relationships: Broadening correctional and rehabilitative agendas. *Corrections Management Quarterly*, 4, 10-21.

Becker, H.S. (1963). *Outsiders: Studies in the sociology of deviance.* New York: Free Press.

Becker, J.V. & J.A. Hunter, Jr. (1992). Evaluation of treatment outcome for adult perpetrators of child sexual abuse. *Criminal Justice and Behavior*, 19, 74-92.

Beitchman, J.H., A. Inglis & D. Schachter (1992). Child psychiatry and early intervention: IV. The externalizing disorders. *Canadian Journal of Psychiatry*, 37, 245-249.

Belenko, S., I. Mara-Drita & J.E. McElroy (1992). Drug tests and the prediction of pretrial misconduct: Findings and policy issues. *Crime & Delinquency*, 38, 557-582.

Belmore, MF. & V.L. Quinsey (1994). Correlates of psychopathy in a noninstitutional sample. *Journal of Interpersonal Violence*, 9, 339-349.

Bench, L.L., S.P. Kramer & S. Erickson (1997). A discriminant analysis of predictive factors in sex offender recidivism. In B.K. Schwartz & H.R. Cellini (eds.), *The sex offender: New insights, treatment innovations and legal developments* (pp. 15.1-15.15). Kingston, NJ: Civic Research Institute.

Berkowitz, L. (1962). *Aggression: A social psychological analysis.* New York: McGraw-Hill.

Bernfeld, G.A., D.P. Farrington & A.W. Leschied (eds.) (2001). *Offender rehabilitation in practice: Implementing and evaluating effective programs.* Chichester, England: Wiley.

Berrueta-Clement, J.R., L.J. Schweinhart, W.S. Barnett & D.P. Weikart (1987). The effects of early educational intervention on crime and delinquency in adolescence and early adulthood. In J.D. Burchard & S.N. Burchard (eds.), *Prevention of delinquent behavior* (pp. 220-240). Newbury Park, CA: Sage.

Blackburn, R. (1975). An empirical classification of psychopathic personality. *British Journal of Psychiatry*, 127, 456-460.

Blackburn, R. (1993). Clinical programs with psychopaths. In K. Howells & C.R. Hollin (eds.), *Clinical approaches to the mentally disordered offender* (pp. 179-208). West Sussex, England: Wiley.

Blasi, A. (1980) Bridging moral cognition and moral action: A critical review of the literature. *Psychological Bulletin*, 88, 1-45.

Bloom, J.D. & M.H. Williams (1994). *Management and treatment of insanity acquittees: A model for the 1990s.* Washington, DC: American Psychiatric Press.

Bloom, B. & S. Covington (1998). *Gender specific programming for female offenders: What is important and why it is important.* Paper presented at the annual meeting of the American Society of Criminology, Washington, DC, November.

Blumstein, A. (1998). U.S. criminal justice conundrum: Rising prison population and stable crime rates. *Crime & Delinquency*, 44, 127-135.

Blumstein, A., J. Cohen & D. Nagin (1978). *Deterrence and incapacitation: Estimating the effects of criminal sanctions on crime rates*. Washington, DC: National Research Council.

Blumstein, A., J. Cohen, J.A. Roth & C.A. Visher (1986). *Criminal careers and "career criminals."* Washington, DC: National Academy of Sciences.

Bogan, K. & D. Factor (1995). Oregon guidelines 1989-1994. *Overcrowded Times*, 6, 1, 13-15.

Bohn, M.J., J.L. Carbonell & E. Megargee (1995). The applicability and utility of the MMPI-based offender classification system in a correctional mental health unit. *Criminal Behaviour and Mental Health*, 5, 14-33.

Bolen, R. (2000). Validity of attachment theory. *Trauma, Violence and Abuse*, 1, 128-153.

Bonta, J. (1989). Native inmates: Institutional response, risk, and needs. *Canadian Journal of Criminology*, 31, 49-62.

Bonta, J. (1990). *Antisocial attitudes and recidivism*. Paper presented at the Annual Convention of the Canadian Psychological Association, Ottawa, Ontario.

Bonta, J. (1995). The Responsivity Principle and offender rehabilitation. *Forum on Corrections Research*, 7, 34-37.

Bonta, J. (1996). Risk-needs assessment and treatment. In A.T. Harland (ed.), *Choosing correctional options that work: Defining the demand and evaluating the supply* (pp. 18-32). Thousand Oaks, CA: Sage.

Bonta, J. (2001). Offender assessment: General issues and considerations. In D. Jones & C. Deluf (eds.), *Compendium 2000 on effective correctional programming*. Ottawa: Correctional Services Canada.

Bonta, J. (2002). Offender risk assessment: Guidelines for selection and use. *Criminal Justice and Behavior*, 29, 355-379.

Bonta, J., B. Bogue, M. Crowley & L. Motiuk (2001). Implementing offender classification systems: Lessons learned. In G.A. Bernfeld, D.P. Farrington & A.W. Leschied (eds.), *Offender rehabilitation in practice: Implementing and evaluating effective programs* (pp. 227-245). Chichester, England: Wiley.

Bonta, J.L., J. Boyle, L.L. Motiuk & P. Sonnichsen (1983). Restitution in correctional halfway houses: Victim satisfaction, attitudes, and recidivism. *Canadian Journal of Criminology*, 20, 140-152.

Bonta, J. & P. Gendreau (1990). Reexamining the cruel and unusual punishment of prison life. *Law and Human Behavior*, 14, 347-372.

Bonta, J. & P. Gendreau (1992). Coping with prison. In P. Suedfeld & P.E. Tetlock (eds.), *Psychology and social policy* (pp. 343-354). New York: Hemisphere.

Bonta, J. & R.K. Hanson (1995). *Violent recidivism of men released from prison*. Paper presented at the 103rd Annual Convention of the American Psychological Association, New York.

Bonta, J., W.G. Harman, R.G. Hann & R.B. Cormier (1996). The prediction of recidivism among federally sentenced offenders: A re-validation of the SIR scale. *Canadian Journal of Criminology*, 38, 61-79.

Bonta, J., A. Harris, I. Zinger & D. Carriere (1996). *The crown files research project: A study of Dangerous Offenders.* Ottawa: Solicitor General Canada.

Bonta, J., C. LaPrairie & S. Wallace-Capretta (1997). Risk prediction and re-offending: Aboriginal and non-Aboriginal offenders. *Canadian Journal of Criminology,* 39, 127-144.

Bonta, J., M. Law & R.K. Hanson (1998). The prediction of criminal and violent recidivismamong mentally disordered offenders: A meta-analysis. *Psychological Bulletin,* 123, 123-142.

Bonta, J. & L.L. Motiuk (1982). *Assessing incarcerated offenders for halfway house.* Unpublished report, Ottawa-Carleton Detention Centre, Ottawa, Ontario.

Bonta, J. & L.L. Motiuk (1985). Utilization of an interview-based classification instrument: A study of correctional halfway houses. *Criminal Justice and Behavior,* 12, 333-352.

Bonta, J. & L.L. Motiuk (1987). The diversion of incarcerated offenders to correctional halfway houses. *Journal of Research in Crime and Delinquency,* 24, 302-323.

Bonta, J. & L.L. Motiuk (1990). Classification to correctional halfway houses: A quasi-experimental evaluation. *Criminology,* 28, 497-506.

Bonta, J. & L.L. Motiuk (1992). Inmate classification. *Journal of Criminal Justice,* 20, 343-353.

Bonta, J., B. Pang & S. Wallace-Capretta (1995). Predictors of recidivism among incarcerated female offenders. *Prison Journal,* 75, 277-294.

Bonta, J., R. Parkinson & L. Barkwell (1994). *Revising the Wisconsin classification system.* Paper presented at the Annual Meeting of the American Society of Criminology, Miami, Florida.

Bonta, J., R. Parkinson, B. Pang, L. Barkwell & S. Wallace-Capretta (1994). *The revised Manitoba Classification System for probationers.* Report available from Ministry Secretariat, Solicitor General Canada, Ottawa.

Bonta, J., S. Wallace-Capretta & J. Rooney (1998). *Restorative justice: An evaluation of the Restorative Resolutions project* (User Report 1998-05). Ottawa, Ontario: Solicitor General Canada. Also at http://www.sgc.gc.ca

Bonta, J., S. Wallace-Capretta & J. Rooney (2000a). A quasi-experimental evaluation of an intensive rehabilitation supervision program. *Criminal Justice and Behavior,* 27, 312-329.

Bonta, J., S. Wallace-Capretta & J. Rooney (2000b). Can electronic monitoring make a difference? An evaluation of three Canadian programs. *Crime & Delinquency,* 46, 61-75.

Bonta, J., S. Wallace-Capretta, J. Rooney & K. McAnoy (in press). An outcome evaluation of a restorative justice alternative to incarceration. *Contemporary Justice Review.*

Booth, A. & D.W. Osgood (1993). The influence of testosterone on deviance in adulthood: Assessing and explaining the relationship. *Criminology,* 31, 93-117.

Boothby, J.L. & C.B. Clements (2000). A national survey of correctional psychologists. *Criminal Justice and Behavior,* 27, 716-732.

Borduin, C.M., S.W. Henggeler, D.M. Blaske & R. Stein (1990). Multisystemic treatment of adolescent sex offenders. *International Journal of Offender Therapy and Comparative Criminology,* 34, 105-113.

Borduin, C.M., B.J. Mann, L.T. Cone, S.W. Henggeler, B.R. Fucci, D.M. Blaske & R.A. Williams (1995). Multisystemic treatment of serious juvenile offenders: Long-term prevention of criminality and violence. *Journal of Consulting and Clinical Psychology*, 63, 569-578.

Born, M., V. Chevalier & I. Humblet (1997). Resilience, desistance and delinquent career of adolescent offenders. *Journal of Adolescence*, 20, 679-694.

Bowlby, J. (1971). *Attachment and loss, Vol. 1: Attachment*. Harmondsworth, England: Penguin Books.

Bowlby, J. (1988). *A secure base: Clinical implications of attachment theory*. London: Routledge & Kegan Paul.

Boyd, N. (ed.). (1986). *The social dimensions of law*. Toronto: Prentice Hall.

Bradford, J.M.W. (1997). Medical interventions in sexual deviance. In D.R. Laws & W. O'Donohue (eds.), *Sexual deviance: Theory, assessment, and treatment* (pp. 449-464). New York: Guilford.

Bradford, J.M.W. & M.A. Pawlak (1993). Double-blind placebo crossover study of cyproterone acetate in the treatment of the paraphilias. *Archives of Sexual Behavior*, 22, 383-402..

Braithwaite, J. (1981). The myth of social class and criminality reconsidered. *American Sociological Review*, 46, 36-47.

Braithwaite, J. (1989). *Crime, shame and reintegration*. Cambridge, England: Cambridge University Press.

Braithwaite, J. (1999). Restorative justice: Assessing optimistic and pessimistic accounts. In M. Tonry (ed.), *Crime and Justice: A Review of Research, Vol. 25* (pp. 1-127). Chicago: University of Chicago Press.

Brennan, P.A., E.R. Grekin & S.A. Mednick (1999). Maternal smoking during pregnancy and adult criminal outcomes. *Archives of General Psychiatry*, 56, 215-219.

Brennan, P.A. & S.A. Mednick (1993). Genetic perspectives on crime. *Acta Psychiatrica Scandinavica*, 87, 19-26.

Brennan, P.A., S.A. Mednick & S. Hodgins (2000). Major mental disorders and criminal violence in a Danish birth cohort. *Archives of General Psychiatry*, 57, 494-500.

Breton, J.J., L. Bergeron, J.P. Valla, C. Berthiaume, N. Gaudet, J. Lambert, M. St. Georges, L. Houde & S. Lepine (1999). Quebec Child Mental Health Survey: Prevalence of DSM-III-R mental health disorders. *Journal of Child Psychology and Psychiatry and Allied Disciplines*, 40, 375-384.

Broidy, L.M. (2001). A test of general strain theory. *Criminology*, 39, 9-33.

Brown, R.S. & R.W. Courtis (1977). The castration alternative. *Canadian Journal of Criminology and Corrections*, 19, 196-205.

Buehler, R.E., G.R. Patterson & J.M. Furniss (1966). The reinforcement of behavior in institutional settings. *Behavioral Research and Therapy*, 4, 157-167.

Bureau of Justice Statistics. (2001). *Corrections statistics*. Washington, DC: Department of Justice. See http://www.ojp.usdoj.gov/bjs/correct.htm

Burgess, E.W. (1928). Factors determining success or failure on parole. In A.A. Bruce, A.J. Harno, E.W. Burgess & J. Landesco (eds.), *The workings of the indeterminate-sentence law and the parole system in Illinois* (pp. 221-234). Springfield, IL: State Board of Parole.

Burgess, R.L. & R.L. Akers (1966). A differential association-reinforcement theory of criminal behaviour. *Social Problems*, 14, 128-147.

Bush, J. (1995). Teaching self-risk management to violent offenders. In J. McGuire
(ed.), *What works: Effective methods to reduce re-offending* (pp. 139-154). Sussex, England: Wiley.

Bush, J. & B. Bilodeau (1993). *Options: A cognitive change program.* Longmont, CO: National Institute of Corrections.

Bushman, B.J. & H.M. Cooper (1990). Effects of alcohol on human aggression: An integrative research review. *Psychological Bulletin*, 107, 342-354.

Buss, A.H. (1966). *Psychopathology.* New York: Wiley.

Butcher, J.N., W.G. Dahlstrom, J.R. Graham, A. Tellegen & B. Kaemmer (1989). *The Minnesota Multiphasic Personality Inventory-2: Manual for Administration and Scoring.*
Minneapolis: University of Minnesota Press.

Butler, W.M., H. Leitenberg & G.D. Fuselier (1993). The use of mental health professional
consultants to police hostage negotiation teams. *Behavioral Sciences and the Law*,
11, 213-221.

Byrne, J.M. & F.S. Taxman (1994). Crime control policy and community corrections practice: Assessing the impact of gender, race, and class. *Evaluation and Program Planning*, 17, 227-233.

Cadoret, R.J. & C. Cain (1980). Sex differences in predictors of antisocial behavior in
adoptees. *Archives of General Psychiatry*, 37, 1171-1175.

Camp, C. & G. Camp (1997). *The corrections yearbook.* South Salem, NY: Criminal Justice Institute.

Campbell, D.T. & J.C. Stanley (1963). *Experimental and quasi-experimental designs for
research.* Chicago: Rand McNally.

Canadian Centre for Justice Statistics. (1992). *Characteristics of federal inmates who recidivate.* Working paper. Ottawa: Statistics Canada.

Canadian Centre for Justice Statistics. (1999). Sex offenders. *Juristat*, 19(3), 1-15.

Canadian Sentencing Commission. (1987). Community punishments as sanctions in their
own right. In Canadian Sentencing Commission, *Sentencing reform: A Canadian
approach* (pp. 338-343). Ottawa: Canadian Government Publishing Centre.

Carey, G. (1992). Twin imitation for antisocial behavior: Implications for genetic and family environment research. *Journal of Abnormal Psychology*, 101, 18-25.

Carey, G. & D. Goldman (1997). The genetics of antisocial behavior. In D.M. Stuff, J. Breiling & J.D. Maser (eds.), *Handbook of antisocial behavior* (pp. 243-254). New York:
Wiley.

Carrington, F. & G. Nicholson (1984). The victim's movement: An idea whose time has
come. *Pepperdine Law Review*, 11, 1-13.

Carroll, K.M. (1996). Relapse prevention as a psychosocial treatment: A review of controlled
clinical trials. *Experimental and Clinical Psychopharmacology*, 4, 46-54.

Caspi, A., T.E. Moffitt, D.L. Newman & P.A. Silva (1996). Behavioral observations at age
3 years predict adult psychiatric disorders. *Archives of General Psychiatry*, 53,
1033-1039.

Caspi, A., T.E. Moffitt, P.A. Silva, M. Stouthamer-Loeber, R.F. Krueger & P.S. Schmutte (1994). Are some people crime-prone? Replications of the personality-crime relationship across countries, genders, races, and methods. *Criminology*, 32, 163-195.

Cautela, J.R. (1970). The treatment of alcoholism by covert sensitization. *Psychotherapy: Theory, Research and Practice*, 7, 83-90.

Chaiken, J.M. & M.R. Chaiken (1982). *Varieties of criminal behavior: Summary and policy implications*. Santa Monica, CA: RAND Corporation.

Chaiken, J.M. & M.R. Chaiken (1983). Crime rates and the active criminal. In J.Q. Wilson (ed.), *Crime and public policy* (pp. 11-29). San Francisco: Institute for Contemporary Studies.

Chaiken, M.R. (1989). *Prison programs for drug-involved offenders*. Washington, DC: National Institute of Justice.

Chamberlain, P. (1996). Intensified foster care: Multi-level treatment for adolescents with conduct disorders in out-of-home care. In E.D. Hibbs & P.S. Jensen (eds.), *Psychosocial treatments for child and adolescent disorders: Empirically based strategies for clinical practice* (pp. 475-495). Washington, DC. American Psychological Association.

Chamberlain, P. & P.C. Friman (1997). Residential programs for antisocial children and adolescents. In D.M. Stoff, J. Breiling & J.D. Maser (eds.), *Handbook of antisocial behavior* (pp. 416-424). New York: Wiley.

Chamberlain, P. & J.B. Reid (1994). Differences in risk factors and adjustment for male and female delinquents in treatment foster care. *Journal of Child and Family Studies*, 3, 23-39.

Chandler, M. (1973). Egocentrism and antisocial behavior: The assessment and training of social perspective-taking skills. *Developmental Psychology*, 44, 326-333.

Chaplin, T.C., M.E. Rice & G.T. Harris, (1995). Salient victim suffering and the sexual responses of child molesters. *Journal of Consulting and Clinical Psychology*, 63, 249-255.

Chapman, T. & M. Hough (1998). *Evidence based practice: A guide to effective practice*. London: Home Office Publications Unit.

Chess, S. & A. Thomas (1984). *Origins and evolution of behavior disorders: From infancy to early adult life*. New York: Brunner/Mazel.

Chess, S. & A. Thomas (1990). The New York Longitudinal Study (NYLS): The young adult periods. *Canadian Journal of Psychiatry*, 35, 557-561.

Christiansen, K.O. (1977). A preliminary study of criminality among twins. In S.A. Mednick & K.O. Christiansen (eds.), *Biosocial basis of criminal behavior* (pp. 89-108). New York: Gardner.

Church, R.M. (1963). The varied effects of punishment on behavior. *Psychological Review*, 70, 369-402.

Clarke, S.H. & F.A. Campbell (1998). Can intervention early prevent crime later? The Abecedarian Project compared with other programs. *Early Childhood Education Quarterly*, 13, 319-343.

Clear, T. (1994). *Harm in American penology: Offenders, victims and their communities*. Albany, NY: State University of New York Press.

Cleckley, H. (1982). *The mask of sanity* (4th ed.). St. Louis: Mosby.

Clements, C.B. (1986). *Offender Needs Assessment.* College Park, MD: American Correctional Association.

Clements, C.B. (1996). Offender classification: Two decades of progress. *Criminal Justice and Behavior,* 23, 121-143.

Cloninger, C.R. & S.B. Guze (1970). Psychiatric illness and female criminality: The role of sociopathy and hysteria in the antisocial woman. *American Journal of Psychiatry,* 127, 79-87.

Cloward, R.A. & L.E. Ohlin (1960). *Delinquency and opportunity: A theory of delinquent gangs.* New York: Free Press.

Coates, R.B. & J. Gehm (1988). An empirical assessment. In M. Wright & B. Galaway (eds.), *Mediation and Criminal Justice: Victims, Offenders and Community* (pp. 251-263). Newbury Park, CA: Sage.

Cochran, J.K., M.B. Chamlin & M. Seth (1994). Deterrence or brutalization? An impact assessment of Oklahoma's return to capital punishment. *Criminology,* 32, 107-134.

Cohen, A.K. (1955). *Delinquent boys: The culture of the gang.* Glencoe, IL: Free Press.

Cohen, M. (1998). The monetary value of saving a high-risk youth. *Journal of Quantitative Criminology,* 14, 5-33.

Cohen, M. (2001). To treat or not to treat? A financial perspective. In C.R. Hollin (ed.), *Handbook of offender assessment and treatment* (pp. 35-49). Chichester, England: Wiley.

Cohen, S. (1985). *Visions of social control.* Cambridge, England: Polity Press.

Coleman, F.L. (1997). Stalking behavior and the cycle of domestic violence. *Journal of Interpersonal Violence,* 12, 420-432.

Coleman, J.S., T. Hoffer & S. Kilgore (1982). *High school achievement: Public, Catholic, and Protestant schools compared.* New York: Basic Books.

Coles, C.D. & K.A. Platzman (1993). Behavioral development in children prenatally exposed to drugs and alcohol. *International Journal of Addictions,* 28, 1393-1433.

Collingwood, T.R., A.F. Douds & H. Williams (1976). Juvenile diversion: The Dallas Police Department Youth Services Program. *Federal Probation,* 40, 23-27.

Conger, R.D. & R.L. Simons (1997). Life-course contingencies in the development of adolescent antisocial behavior: A matching law approach. In T.P. Thornberry (ed.), *Developmental theories of crime and delinquency* (pp. 55-99). New Brunswick, NJ: Transaction.

Cooke, D.J. & C. Michie (2001). Refining the construct of psychopathy: Towards a hierarchical model. *Psychological Assessment,* 13, 171-188.

Cookson, H.M. (1992). Alcohol use and offence type in young offenders. *British Journal of Criminology,* 32, 352-360.

Cookston, J.T. (1999). Parental supervision and family structure: Effects on adolescent problem behaviors. *Journal of Divorce and Remarriage,* 32, 107-122.

Coombs, M. (1999). A brave new crime-free world? In J.R. Botkin, W.M. McMahon & L.P. Francis (eds.), *Genetics and criminality: The potential misuse of scientific information* (pp. 227-242). Washington, DC: American Psychological Association.

Cordess, C. (2001). Forensic psychotherapy. In C.R. Hollin (ed.), *Handbook of offender assessment and treatment* (pp. 309-329). Chichester, England: Wiley.

Cormier, R.B. (1981). Canadian recidivism index. *Canadian Journal of Criminology*, 23, 103-104.

Correctional Services Canada. (1990). A mental health profile of federally sentenced offenders. *Forum on Corrections Research*, 2 (1), 7.

Costa, P.T., Jr. & T.A. Widiger (eds.) (1994). *Personality disorders and the five-factor model of personality*. Washington, DC: American Psychological Association.

Coulson, G., G. Ilacqua, V. Nutbrown, D. Giulekas & F. Cudjoe (1996). Predictive utility of the LSI for incarcerated female offenders. *Criminal Justice and Behavior*, 23, 427-439.

Cox, M. (1998). A group-analytic approach to psychopaths: "The ring of truth." In T. Millon, E. Simonsen, M. Birket-Smith & R.D. Davis (eds.), *Psychopathy: Antisocial, criminal, and violent behavior* (pp. 393-406). New York: Guilford.

Craft, M., G. Stephenson & C. Granger (1966). A controlled trial of authoritarian and self-governing regimes with adolescent psychopaths. *American Journal of Orthopsychiatry*, 34, 543-554.

Craig, R.D. & K. Truitt (1996). Moral problem solving among inmates in a maximum security correctional institution. *International Journal of Offender therapy and Comparative Criminology*, 40, 243-252.

Crawford, C., T. Chiricos & G. Kleck (1998). Race, racial threat, and sentencing of habitual offenders. *Criminology*, 36, 481-511.

Cressey, D.R. (1955). Changing criminals: The application of the theory of differential association. *American Journal of Sociology*, 61, 116-120.

Cressey, D.R. & D.A. Ward (1969). *Delinquency, crime, and social control*. New York: Harper and Row.

Crews, F. (1986). In the big house of theory. *The New York Review of Books*, 29 (May), 36, 41.

Crocker, A.G. & S. Hodgins (1997). The criminality of noninstitutionalized mentally retarded persons: evidence from a birth cohort followed to age 30. *Criminal Justice and Behavior*, 24, 432-454.

Cullen, F.T. (1995). Assessing the penal harm movement. *Journal of Research in Crime and Delinquency*, 32, 338-358.

Cullen, F.T. (2002). Rehabilitation and treatment programs. In J.Q. Wilson & J. Petersilia (eds.), *Crime and public policy* (2nd ed.)(pp. 253-289). Oakland, CA: ICS Press.

Cullen, F.T., B.S. Fisher & B.K. Applegate (2000). Public opinion about punishment and corrections. In M. Tonry (ed.), *Crime and justice: A review of research, Vol. 27* (pp. 1-79). Chicago: University of Chicago Press.

Cullen, F.T. & P. Gendreau (1989). The effectiveness of correctional rehabilitation. In L. Goodstein & D.L. MacKenzie (eds.), *The American prison: Issues in research policy* (pp.23-24). New York: Plenum.

Cullen, F.T. & P. Gendreau (2001). From nothing works to what works: Changing professional ideology in the 21st century. *The Prison Journal*, 81, 313-338.

Cullen, F.T., P. Gendreau, G.R. Jarjoura & J.P. Wright (1997). Crime and the bell curve: Lessons from intelligent criminology. *Crime & Delinquency*, 43, 387-411.

Cullen, F.T. & K.E. Gilbert (1982). *Reaffirming rehabilitation.* Cincinnati: Anderson.

Cullen, F.T., M.T. Larson & R.A. Mathers (1985). Having money and delinquent involvement: The neglect of power in delinquency theory. *Criminal Justice and Behavior*, 12, 171-192.

Cullen, F.T., J.P. Wright & B.K. Applegate (1996). Control in the community: The limits of reform? In A.T. Harland (ed.), *Choosing correctional options that work: Defining the demand and evaluating the supply* (pp. 69-116). Thousand Oaks, CA: Sage.

Cumberland, A.K. & G.J. Boyle (1997). Psychometric prediction of recidivism: Utility of the Risk Needs Inventory. *Australian and New Zealand Journal of Criminology*, 30, 72-86.

Currie, E. (1993). *Reckoning: Drugs, the cities, and the American future.* New York: Hill and Wang.

Currie, E. (1998). *Crime and punishment in America.* New York: Holt/Metropolitan.

Curry, G.D. (2000). Self-reported gang involvement and officially recorded delinquency. *Criminology*, 38, 1253-1274.

Dadds, M.R., S. Schwartz & M. Sanders (1987). Marital discord and treatment outcome in behavioral treatment of child conduct disorders. *Journal of Consulting and Clinical Psychology*, 55, 396-403.

D'Alession, S.J. & L. Stolzenberg (1995). The impact of sentencing guidelines on jail incarceration in Minnesota. *Criminology*, 33, 283-302.

Dalgaard, O.S. & E. Kringlen (1976). A Norwegian twin study of criminality. *British Journal of Criminology*, 16, 213-233.

Dalteg, A. & S. Levander (1998). Twelve thousand crimes by 75 boys: a 20-year follow-up study of childhood hyperactivity. *Journal of Forensic Psychiatry*, 9, 39-57.

Daly, J.E. & S. Pelowski (2000). Predictors of dropout among men who batter: A review of studies with implications for research and practice. *Violence and Victims*, 15, 137-160.

Daly, K. & R.L. Bordt (1995). Sex effects and sentencing: An analysis of the statistical literature. *Justice Quarterly*, 12, 141-175.

Daly, K. & M. Tonry (1997). Gender, race, and sentencing. In M. Tonry (ed.), *Crime and justice: A review of research* (pp. 201-252). Chicago: University of Chicago Press.

Daniel, A.E., A.J. Robins, J.C. Reid & D.E. Wifley (1988). Lifetime and six month prevalence of psychiatric disorders among sentenced female offenders. *Bulletin of the American Academy of Psychiatry and the Law*, 16, 333-342.

Darlingotn, R.B. (1996). On race and intelligence: A commentary on affirmative action, the evolution of intelligence, the regression analysis in The Bell Curve, and Jensen's two-level theory. *Psychology, Public Policy, and Law*, 2, 635-645.

Davidson, W.S., S.D. Jefferson, A. Legaspi, J. Lujan & A.M. Wolf (2001). Alternative interventions for juvenile offenders: History of the adolescent diversion project. In C.R. Hollin (ed.), *Handbook of offender assessment* (pp. 221-236). Chichester, England: Wiley.

Davis, R.C. & B.G. Taylor (1997). A proactive response to family violence: the results of a randomized experiment. *Criminology*, 35, 307-333.

Dawes, R.M., D. Faust & P.E. Meehl (1993). Statistical prediction versus clinical prediction: Improving what works. In G. Karen & C. Lewis (eds.), *A handbook for data analysis in the behavioral sciences* (pp. 351-367). Hillsdale, NJ: Lawrence Erlbaum Associates.

Day, K. (1993). Crime and mental retardation. In K. Howells & C.R. Hollin (eds.), *Clinical approaches to the mentally disordered offender* (pp. 111-144). Chichester, England: Wiley.

Deater-Deckard, K. & K.A. Dodge (1997). Externalizing behavior problems and discipline revisited: Nonlinear effects and variation by culture, context, and gender. *Psychological Inquiry*, 8, 161-175.

Decker, S.H. & C.W. Kohfeld (1984). A deterrence study of the death penalty in Illinois, 1933-1980. *Journal of Criminal Justice*, 12, 367-377.

Decker, S.H. & C.W. Kohfeld (1987). An empirical analysis of the effect of the death penalty in Missouri. *Journal of Crime and Justice*, 10, 23-46.

de Clérambault, G.G. (1942). *Les psychoses passionelles, oeuvre psychiatrique.* Paris: Presses Universitaires de France.

DeKeseredy, W.S. & M.D. Schwartz (1996). *Contemporary Criminology.* Belmont, CA: Wadsworth.

Delmonico, D.L. (1997). Cybersex: High tech sex addiction. *Sexual Addiction and Compulsivity*, 4, 159-167.

Deluty, M.Z. (1978). Self-control and impulsiveness involving aversive events. *Journal of Experimental Psychology: Animal Processes*, 4, 250-266.

Dembo, R., K.A. Cervenka, B. Hunter & W. Wang (1999). Engaging high risk families in community based intervention services. *Aggression and Violent Behavior*, 4, 41-58.

Dembo, R., J. Schmeidler, B. Nini-Gough, C.C. Sue, P. Borden & D. Manning (1998). Predictors of recidivism to a juvenile assessment center: A three year study. *Journal of Child and Adolescent Substance Abuse*, 7, 57-77.

Denkowski, G.C. & K.M. Denkowski (1985). The mentally retarded offender in the state prison system: Identification, prevalence, adjustment, and rehabilitation. *Criminal Justice and Behavior*, 12, 55-70.

Denno, D.W. (1990). *Biology and violence: From birth to adulthood.* Cambridge, England: Cambridge University Press.

Dicker, T.J. (1998). Tension on the thin blue line: Police officer resistance to community-oriented policing. *American Journal of Criminal Justice*, 23, 59-82.

DiClemente, C.C., L.E. Bellino & T.M. Neavins (1999). Motivation for change and alcoholism treatment. *Alcohol Research and Health*, 23, 86-92.

Diefenbach, D.L. (1997). The portrayal of mental illness on prime-time television. *Journal of Community Psychology*, 25, 289-302.

Dietz, P.E., R.R. Hazelwood & J. Warren (1990). The sexually sadistic criminal and his offenses. *Bulletin of the American Academy of Psychiatry and the Law*, 18, 163-178.

Dietz, P.E., D.B. Matthews, D.A. Martell, T.M. Stewart, D.R. Hrouda & J. Warren (1991). Threatening and otherwise inappropriate letters to members of the United States Congress. *Journal of Forensic Sciences*, 36, 1445-1468.

Dietz, P.E., D.B. Matthews, C. Van Duyne, D.A. Martell, C.D.H. Parry, T. Stewart, J. Warren & D.J. Crowder (1991). *Journal of Forensic Sciences*, 36, 185-209.

Digman, J.M. (1990). Personality structure: Emergence of the five factor model. *Annual Review of Psychology*, 41, 417-440.

Dinsmoor, J.A. (1955). Punishment: II. An interpretation of empirical findings. *Psychological Review*, 62, 96-105.

Dinsmoor, J.A. (1998). Punishment. In W. O'Donohue (ed.), *Learning and behavior therapy* (pp. 188-204). New York: Allyn & Bacon.

Dinwiddie, S.H. (1994). Psychiatric genetic and forensic psychiatry: A review. *Bulletin of the American Academy of Psychiatry and the Law*, 22, 342-327.

Dishion, T.J. & G.R. Patterson (1997). The timing and severity of antisocial behavior: Three hypotheses within an ecological framework. In D.M. Stoff, J. Breiling & J.D. Maser (eds.), *Handbook of antisocial behavior* (pp. 205-217). New York: Wiley.

Dishion, T.J. & J. Poe (1993). *Parent antisocial behavior as an antecedent to deviancy training among adolescent boys and their peers*. Paper presented at the annual meeting of the American Society of Criminology, Phoenix, AZ.

Dishion, T.J., K.M. Spracklen, D.W. Andrews & G.R. Patterson (1996). Deviancy training in male adolescent friendships. *Behavior Therapy*, 27, 373-390.

Dobash, R.E. & R. Dobash (1979). *Violence against wives*. New York: Free Press.

Dobash, R.E., R.P. Dobash, K. Cavanagh & R. Lewis (2000). *Changing violent men*. Thousand Oaks, CA: Sage.

Dobash, R.P. & R.E. Dobash (1995). Reflections on findings from the Violence Against Women Survey. *Canadian Journal of Criminology*, 37, 457-484.

Dobash, R.P. & R.E. Dobash (2001). Criminal justice programmes for men who assault their partners. In C.R. Hollin (ed.), *Handbook of offender assessment and treatment* (pp. 379-389). New York: Wiley.

Dollard, J., L. Doob, N. Miller, O. Mowrer & R. Sears (1939). *Frustration and aggression*. New Haven: Yale University Press.

Donato, R. & M. Shanahan (1999). The economics of implementing intensive in-prison sex-offender treatment programs. *Australian Institute of Criminology: Trends and issues* (No. 134). Canberra, Australia.

Dooley, M. (1995). Restorative justice in Vermont: A work in progress. In National Institute of Corrections, *Community justice: Striving for safe, secure, and just communities*. Washington, DC: National Institute of Corrections.

Douglas, K.S., J.R.P. Ogloff, T.L. Nicholls & I. Grant (1999). Assessing risk for violence among psychiatric patients: The HCR-20 violence risk assessment scheme and the Psychopathy Checklist: Screening version. *Journal of Consulting and Clinical Psychology*, 67, 917-930.

Dowden, C. (1998). *A meta-analytic examination of the risk, need and responsivity principles and their importance within the rehabilitation debate*. Unpublished master's thesis, Psychology Department, Carleton University, Ottawa.

Dowden, C. & D.A. Andrews (1999a). What works for female offenders: A meta-analytic review. *Crime & Delinquency*, 45, 438-452.

Dowden, C. & D.A. Andrews (1999b). What works in young offender treatment: A meta-analysis. *Forum on Corrections Research*, 11, 21-24.

Dowden, C. & D.A. Andrews (2000). Effective correctional treatment and violent reoffending. *Canadian Journal of Criminology*, 42, 449-467.

Dugdale, R.L. (1877/1970). *The Jukes: A study of crime, pauperism, disease, and heredity*. New York: Arno Press (originally published by G.P. Putnam).

Duncan, R.D., W.A. Kennedy & C.J. Patrick (1995). Four-factor model of recidivism in male juvenile offenders. *Journal of Clinical Child Psychology*, 24, 250-257.

Dutton, D.G. (1986). The outcome of court-mandated treatment for wife-assault: A quasi-experimental evaluation. *Violence and Victims*, 1, 163-175.

Dutton, D.G. (1994). Patriarchy and wife assault: The ecological fallacy. *Violence and Victims*, 9, 167-182.

Dutton, D.G. (1995). *The domestic assault of women: Psychological and criminal justice perspectives*. (2nd ed). Boston: Allyn & Bacon.

Dutton, D.G., M. Bodnarchuk, R. Kropp, S.D. Hart & J.R.P. Ogloff (1997). Wife assault treatment and criminal recidivism: An 11-year follow-up. *International Journal of Offender Therapy and Comparative Criminology*, 41, 9-23.

Dutton, D.G. & S.D. Hart (1992). Risk markers for family violence in a federally incarcerated population. *International Journal of Law and Psychiatry*, 15, 101-112.

Dutton, D.G. & P.R. Kropp (2000). A review of domestic violence risk instruments. *Trauma, Violence, and Abuse*, 1, 171-181.

Edelson, J.L. & M. Syers (1991). The effects of group treatment for men who batter: An 18 month follow-up study. *Research on Social Work Practice*, 1, 227-243.

Edins, J.F., N.G. Poythress & S.O. Lilienfeld (1999). Identifying inmates at risk for disciplinary infractions: A comparison of two measures of psychopathy. *Behavioral Sciences and the Law*, 17, 435-443.

Edens, J.F., J.L. Skeem, K.R. Cruise & E. Cauffman (2001). Assessment of "juvenile psychopathy" and its association with violence: A critical review. *Behavioral Sciences and the Law*, 19, 53-80.

Edinger, J.D. & S.M. Auerbach (1978). Development and validation of a multidimensional multivariate model for accounting for infractionary behavior in a correctional setting. *Journal of Personality and Social Psychology*, 36, 1472-1489.

Edwards, D.L., S.K. Schoenwald, S.W. Henggeler & K.B. Strother (2001). A multilevel perspective on the implementation of multisystemic therapy (MST): Attempting dissemination with fidelity. In G.A. Bernfeld, D.P. Farrington & A.W. Leschied (eds.), *Offender rehabilitation in practice* (pp. 97-120). Chichester, England: Wiley.

Ekblom, P. (1996). Towards a discipline of crime prevention: A systematic approach to its nature, range and concepts. In T. Bennett (ed.), *Preventing crime and disorder: Targeting strategies and responsibilities* (pp. 43-97), Cropwood Series. Cambridge, England: University of Cambridge, Institute of Criminology.

Elkins, I.J., W.G. Iacono, A.E. Doyle & M. McGue (1997). Characteristics associated with the persistence of antisocial behavior: Results from recent longitudinal research. *Aggression and Violent Behavior*, 2, 101-124.

Elliott, D.S., D. Huizinga & S.S. Ageton (1985). *Explaining delinquency and drug use*. Beverly Hills: Sage.

Elliott, D.S., W.J. Wilson, D. Huizinga, R.J. Sampson, A. Elliott & B. Rankin (1996). The effects of neighborhood disadvantage on adolescent development. *Journal of Research in Crime and Delinquency*, 33, 389-426.

Ellis, L. & H. Hoffman (1990). Views of contemporary criminologists on causes and theories of crime. In L. Ellis & H. Hoffman (eds.), *Crime in biological, social, and moral contexts* (pp. 50-58). New York: Praeger.

Ellis, L. & A. Walsh (1997). Gene-based evolutionary theories in criminology. *Criminology*, 229-276.

Empey, L.T. & M.L. Erickson (1972). *The Provo Experiment: Evaluating community control of delinquency*. Lexington, MA: D.C. Heath.

Empey, L.T. & J. Rabow (1961). The Provo Experiment in delinquency rehabilitation. *American Sociological Review*, 26, 679-695.

Engel, R.S. & E. Silver (2001). Policing mentally disordered suspects: A rexamination of the criminalization hypothesis. *Criminology*, 39, 225-252.

Erwin, B.S. (1986). Turning up the heat on probationers in Georgia. *Federal Probation*, 50, 17-24.

Esbensen, F-A. & D.W. Osgood (1999). Gang resistance education and training (GREAT): Results from a national evaluation. *Journal of Research in Crime and Delinquency*, 36, 194-225.

Esbensen, F-A., L.T. Winfree, L. He & T.J. Taylor (2001). Youth gangs and definitional issues: When is a gang a gang, and why does it matter? *Crime & Delinquency*, 47, 105-130.

Eysenck, H.J. (1964). *Crime and personality*. London: Routledge and Kegan Paul.

Eysenck, H.J. (1977). *Crime and personality* (2nd ed.). London: Routledge and Kegan Paul.

Eysenck, H.J. (1998). Personality and crime. In T. Millon, E. Simonsen, M. Birket-Smith & R.D. Davis (eds.), *Psychopathy: Antisocial, criminal, and violent behavior* (pp. 40-49). New York: Guilford.

Eysenck, H.J. & G.H. Gudjonsson (1989). *Causes and cures of criminality*. New York: Plenum Press.

Eysenck, S.B.G. & H.J. Eysenck (1978). Impulsiveness and venturesomeness: Their position in a dimensional system of personality description. *Psychological Reports*, 43, 1247-1255.

Fagan, J.A. (1994). Do criminal sanctions deter drug crimes? In D.L. Mackenzie & C.D. Uchida (eds.), *Drugs and crime: Evaluating pubic policy initiatives* (pp. 188-214). Thousand Oaks, CA: Sage.

Fagan, J. & M. Guggenheim (1996). Preventive detention and the judicial prediction of dangerousness for juveniles: A natural experiment. *The Journal of Criminal Law and Criminology*, 86, 415-448.

Falkin, G.P., H.K. Wexler & D.S. Lipton (1992). Drug treatment in state prisons. In D.R. Gerstein & H.J. Harwood (eds.), *Treating drug problems* (pp. 89-131). Washington, DC: National Academy Press.

Farnworth, M., T.P. Thonrberry, M. Krohn & A.J. Lizotte (1994). Measurement in the study of class and delinquency. *Journal of Research in Crime and Delinquency*, 31, 32-61.

Farrington, D.P. (1995). The development of offending and antisocial behaviour from childhood: Key findings from the Cambridge Study in delinquent development. The Jack Tizard Memorial Lecture. *Journal of Child Psychology and Psychiatry*, 36, 929-964.

Farrington, D.P. (1997). Early prediction of violent and non-violent youthful offending. *European Journal on Criminal Policy and Research*, 5, 51-66.

Farrington, D.P. (1998). Youth crime and antisocial behavior. In A. Campbell & S. Muncer (eds.), *The social child* (pp. 353-392). East Sussex, England: Psychology Press.

Farrington, D.P., G.C. Barnes & S. Lambert (1996). The concentration of offending in families. *Legal and Criminological Psychology*, 1, 47-63.

Farrington, D.P., G. Hancock, M. Livingston, K. Painter & G. Towl (2000). *Evaluation of intensive regimes for young offenders. Research Findings No. 121*. London, England: Home Office Research, Development and Statistics Directorate.

Farrington, D.P., S. Lambert & D.J. West (1998). Criminal careers of two generations of family members in the Cambridge study in delinquent development. *Studies on Crime and Crime Prevention*, 7, 85-106.

Farrington, D.P. & A.M. Morris (1983). Sex, sentencing, and reconviction. *British Journal of Criminology*, 23, 229-248.

Farrington, D.P., A. Petrosino & B.C. Welsh (2001). Systematic reviews and cost-benefit analyses of correctional interventions. *The Prison Journal*, 81, 339-359.

Feder, L. (1991). A comparison of the community adjustment of mentally ill offenders with those from the general prison population. *Law and Human Behavior*, 15, 477-493.

Fergusson, D.M., J.K. Fifield & S.W. Slater (1977). Signal detectability theory and the evaluation of prediction tables. *Journal of Research in Crime and Delinquency*, 14, 237-246.

Fergusson, D.M. & L.J. Horwood (1995). Early disruptive behavior, IQ, and later school achievement and delinquent behavior. *Journal of Abnormal Child Psychology*, 23, 183-199.

Fergusson, D.M. & L.J. Horwood (2000). Alcohol abuse and crime: A fixed-effects regression analysis. *Addiction*, 95, 1525-1536.

Fergusson, D.M., L.J. Horwood & D.S. Nagin (2000). Offending trajectories in a New Zealand birth cohort. *Criminology*, 38, 525-551.

Feshbach, N.D. (1984). Empathy, empathy training and the regulation of aggression in elementary school children. In R.M. Kaplan, V.J. Konecni & R.W. Novaco (eds.), *Aggression in children and youth* (pp. 192-208). The Hague: Martinus Nijhoff.

Feshbach, N.D. (1989). Empathy training and prosocial behavior. In J. Groebel & R.A. Hinde (eds.), *Aggression and war: Their biological and social basis* (pp. 101-111). Cambridge, England: Cambridge University Press.

Finckenauer, J.O. (1979). *Juvenile awareness project: Evaluation report No. 2*. School of Criminal Justice, Rutgers, Newark, NJ.

Finckenauer, J.O., P.W. Gavin, A. Hovland & E. Storvoll (1999). *Scared Straight: The panacea phenomenon revisted*. Prospect Heights, IL: Waveland Press.

Finckenauer, J.O. & J.R. Storti (1978). *Juvenile awareness project help: Evaluation report No. 1*. School of Criminal Justice, Rutgers, Newark, NJ.

Finkelhor, D., G. Hotaling, I.A. Lewis & C. Smith (1990). Sexual abuse in a national survey of adult men and women: Prevalence, characteristics, and risk factors. *Child Abuse and Neglect*, 14, 19-28.

Finkelhor, D., L.M. Williams & N. Burns (1988). *Nursery crimes: Sexual abuse in day care*. Newbury Park, NJ: Sage.

Finn, M.A. & L.J. Stalans (1995). Police referrals to shelters and mental health treatment: Examining their decisions in domestic assault cases. *Crime & Delinquency*, 41, 467-480.

Fishbein, M. (1997). Predicting, understanding, and changing socially relevant behaviors: Lessons learned. In C. McGarty & S.A. Haslam (eds.), *The message of social psychology: Perspectives on mind in society* (pp. 77-91). Oxford, England: Blackwell.

Fleissner, D. & F. Heinzelmann (1996). *Crime prevention through environmental design and community policing*. Washington, DC: National Institute of Justice.

Fogg, V. & B. Bogue (1996). *The Colorado standardized offender assessment program: A learning organization system for managing measurement, meaning and methods in community corrections*. Denver: Office of Probation Services.

Fonagy, P., M. Target, M. Steele, H. Steele, Leigh, A. Levinson & R. Kennedy (1997). Morality, disruptive behavior, borderline personality disorder, crime, and their relationships to security attachment. In L. Atkinson & K.J. Zucker (eds.), *Attachment and psychopathology* (pp. 223-274). New York: Guilford Press.

Forth, A.E., S.D. Hart & R.D. Hare (1990). Assessment of psychopathy in male young offenders. *Psychological Assessment: A Journal of Consulting and Clinical Psychology*, 2, 342-344.

Forth, A.E., D.S. Kosson & R.D. Hare (in development). *The Hare Psychopathy Checklist: Youth version*. Toronto: Multi-Health Systems.

Fox, J.A. & J. Levin (1998). Multiple homicide: Patterns of serial and mass murder. In M. Tonry (ed.), *Crime and justice: A review of research, Vol. 23* (pp. 407-455). Chicago: University of Chicago Press.

Fox, J.A. & J. Levin (1999). Serial murder: Myths and realities. In M.D. Smith & M.A. Zahn (eds.), *Studying and preventing homicide: Issues and challenges*. Thousand Oaks, CA: Sage.

Freud, S. (1953). *A general introduction to psychoanalysis*. New York: Permabooks.

Freund, K. (1965). Diagnosing heterosexual pedophilia by means of a test for sexual interest. *Behaviour Research and Therapy*, 3, 229-234.

Frick, P.J., C.T. Barry & D.S. Bodin (2000). Applying the concept of psychopathy to children: Implications for the assessment of antisocial youth. In C.B. Gacono (ed.), *The clinical and forensic assessment of psychopathy: A practitioner's guide* (pp. 3-24). Mahwah, NJ: Lawrence Erlbaum Associates.

Frick, P.J., B.S. O'Brien, J.M. Wootton & K. McBurnett (1994). Psychopathy and conduct problems in children. *Journal of Abnormal Psychology*, 103, 700-707.

Furby, L., M. Weinrott & L. Blackshaw (1989). Sex offender recidivism: A review. *Psychological Bulletin*, 105, 3-30.

Gaes, G. (1998). Correctional treatment. In M. Tonry (ed.), *The handbook of crime and punishment* (pp. 712-738). New York: Oxford University Press.

Gaes, G., T.J. Flanagan, L.L. Motiuk & L. Stewart (1999). Adult correctional treatment. In M. Tonry & J. Petersilia (eds.), *Prisons. Crime and justice: A review, Vol. 26* (pp. 361-426). Chicago: University of Chicago Press.

Galaway, B. & J. Hudson (eds.) (1990). *Criminal justice, restitution, and reconciliation.* Monsey, NY: Criminal Justice Press.

Gallagher, C.A., D.B. Wilson, P. Hirschfield, M.B. Coggeshall & D.L. MacKenzie (1999). A quantitative review of the effects of sex offender treatment on sexual reoffending. *Corrections Management Quarterly*, 3, 19-29.

Gallagher, R.W., D.P. Somwaru & Y.S. Ben-Porath (1999). Current usage of psychological tests in state correctional settings. *Corrections Compendium*, 24, 1-3, 20.

Gardner, D. (2000). Managing crime and punishment. *The Ottawa Citizen*, November 17.

Garner, J., J. Fagan & C. Maxwell (1995). Published findings from the Spousal Assault Replication Program: A critical review. *Journal of Quantitative Criminology*, 11, 3-28.

Garret, C.J. (1985). Effects of residential treatment of adjudicated delinquents: A meta-analysis. *Journal of Research in Crime and Delinquency*, 22, 287-308.

Garrido, V., C. Esteban & C. Molero (1996). The effectiveness in the treatment of psychopathy: A meta-analysis. In D.J. Cooke, A.E. Forth, J. Newman & R.D. Hare (eds.), *International perspectives on psychopathy* (pp. 57-59). Leicester, England: British Psychological Society.

Gehm, J. (1990). Mediated victim-offender agreements: An exploratory analysis of factors related to victim participation. In B. Galaway & J. Hudson (eds.), *Criminal justice, restitution, and reconciliation* (pp. 177-182). Monsey, NY: Criminal Justice Press.

Geismar, L.L. & K. Wood (1986). *Family and delinquency: Resocializing the young offender.* New York: Human Sciences Press.

Gelles, R.J. (1997). *Intimate violence in families* (3rd ed). Thousand Oaks, CA: Sage.

Gendreau, P. & D.A. Andrews (2001). *The Correctional Program Assessment Inventory - 2000 (CPAI 2000).* University of New Brunswick, Saint John, New Brunswick.

Gendreau, P., D.A. Andrews, C. Goggin & F. Chanteloupe (1992). *The development of clinical and policy guidelines for the prediction of criminal behavior in criminal justice settings.* Unpublished manuscript available from the Department of Psychology, University of New Brunswick, St. John, New Brunswick.

Gendreau, P., F.T. Cullen & J. Bonta (1994). Intensive rehabilitation supervision: The next generation in community corrections? *Federal Probation*, 58, 72-78.

Gendreau, P., C. Goggin & F.T. Cullen (1999). *The effects of prison sentences on recidivism.* Ottawa, Ontario: Solicitor General Canada. Also http://www.sgc.gc.ca

Gendreau, P., C. Goggin & P. Smith (1999). The forgotten issue in effective correctional treatment: Program implementation. *International Journal of Offender Therapy and Comparative Criminology*, 43, 180-187.

Gendreau, P., C. Goggin & P. Smith (2001). Implementation guidelines for correctional programs in the "real world." In G.A. Bernfeld, D.P. Farrington & A.W. Leschied (eds.), *Offender rehabilitation in practice* (pp. 247-268). Chichester, England: Wiley.

Gendreau, P., C. Goggin & P. Smith (2002). Is the PCL-R really the "unparalleled" measure of offender risk? A lesson in knowledge cumulation. *Criminal Justice and Behavior*, 29, 397-426.

Gendreau, P. & M. Leipciger (1978). The development of a recidivism measure and its application in Ontario. *Canadian Journal of Criminology*, 20, 3-17.

Gendreau, P., T. Little & C. Goggin (1996). A meta-analysis of the predictors of adult offender recidivism: What works! *Criminology*, 34, 575-607.

Gendreau, P. & R.R. Ross (1979). Effective correctional treatment: Bibliotherapy for cynics. *Crime & Delinquency*, 25, 463-489.

Gendreau, P. & R.R. Ross (1981). Correctional potency: Treatment and deterrence on trial. In R. Roesch & R.R. Corrado (eds.), *Evaluation and Criminal Justice Policy* (pp. 29-57). Beverly Hills: Sage.

Gendreau, P. & R.R. Ross (1987). Revivication of rehabilitation: Evidence from the 1980s. *Justice Quarterly*, 4, 349-408.

Gendreau, P., P. Smith & C. Goggin (2001). Treatment programs in corrections. In J.A. Winterdyk (ed.), *Corrections in Canada: Social reactions to crime* (pp. 238-263). Toronto: Prentice Hall.

Gensheimer, L.K., J.P. Mayer, R. Gottschalk & W.S. Davidson (1986). Diverting youth from the juvenile justice system: A meta-analysis of intervention efficacy. In S.J. Apter & A. Goldstein (eds.), *Youth violence: Programs and prospects* (pp. 39-57). Elmsford, NY: Pergamon.

Gibbons, D.C. (1986). Breaking out of prisons. *Crime & Delinquency*, 32, 503-514.

Gibbons, D.C. (1999). Review essay: Changing lawbreakers—what have we learned since the 1950s? *Crime & Delinquency*, 45, 272-293.

Gibbs, J.C. (1995). EQUIP: A peer-group treatment program for delinquents. In R.R. Ross, D.H. Antonowicz & G.K. Dhaliwal (eds.), *Going straight: Effective delinquency prevention and offender rehabilitation* (pp. 179-192). Ottawa: Air Training and Publications.

Gibbs, J.C., K.D. Arnold, H.H. Ahlborn & F.L. Cheesman (1984). Facilitation of sociomoral reasoning in delinquents. *Journal of Consulting and Clinical Psychology*, 52, 37-45.

Gibbs, J.C., G.B. Potter, A.K. Liau, A.M. Schock & S.P. Wightkin (2001). Peer group therapy. In C.R. Hollin (ed.), *Handbook of offender assessment and treatment* (pp. 259-268). Chichester, England: Wiley.

Gilligan, C. (1982). *In a different voice: Psychological theory and women's development.* Cambridge, MA: Harvard University Press.

Ginsburg, J.I.D., R.E. Mann, F. Rotgers & J.R. Weekes (2002). Using motivational interviewing with criminal justice populations. In W.R. Miller & S. Rollnick (eds.), *Motivational interviewing: Preparing people for change* (pp. 333-346). New York: Guilford Press.

Girard, L. (1999). *The Level of Service Inventory-Ontario revision: Offender classification and recidivism.* Unpublished doctoral dissertation, University of Ottawa, Ottawa, Ontario.

Gjone, H. & J. Stevenson (1997). A longitudinal twin study of temperament and behavior problems: Common genetic or environmental influences? *Journal of the American Academy of Adolescent Psychiatry*, 36, 1148-1456.

Glaser, D. (1974). Remedies for the key deficiency in criminal justice evaluation research. *Journal of Research in Crime and Delinquency*, 10, 144-154.

Glass, G.V., B. McGraw & L. Smith (1981). *Meta-analysis in social research.* Beverly Hills: Sage.

Glueck, S. & E.T. Glueck (1950). *Unraveling juvenile delinquency.* Cambridge, MA: Harvard University Press.

Goetz, M.J., E.C. Johnstone & S.G. Ratcliffe (1999). Criminality and antisocial behaviour in unselected men with sex chromosome abnormalities. *Psychological Medicine,* 29, 953-962.

Goldstein, A.P. (1986). Psychological skill training and the aggressive adolescent. In S. Apter & A. Goldstein (eds.), *Youth violence: Program and prospects* (pp. 89-119). New York: Pergamon Press.

Goldstein, A.P. & B. Glick (1987). *Aggression replacement training: A comprehensive intervention for aggressive youth.* Champaign, IL: Research Press.

Goldstein, A.P. & B. Glick (1994). *The prosocial gang: Implementing aggression replacement training.* Thousand Oaks, CA: Sage.

Goldstein, A.P., M. Sherman, N.J. Gershaw, R.P. Sprafkin & B. Glick (1978). Training aggressive adolescents in prosocial behavior. *Journal of Youth and Adolescents,* 7, 73-92.

Goldstein, R.L. (1978). De Clérambault in court: A forensic romance. *Bulletin of the American Academy of Psychiatry and the Law,* 6, 36-40.

Gondolf, E.W. (1999). A comparison of four batterer intervention systems: Do court referral, program length, and services matter? *Journal of Interpersonal Violence,* 14, 41-61.

Goodard, H.H. (1920). *Human efficiency and levels of intelligence.* Princeton, NJ: Princeton University Press.

Goodman, G. (1972). *Companionship therapy.* San Francisco: Jossey-Bass.

Goodman, L.A., M.A. Dutton & L. Bennett (2000). Predicting repeat abuse among arrested batterers: Use of the Danger Assessment Scale in the criminal justice system. *Journal of Interpersonal Violence,* 15, 63-74.

Gordon, A. (1992). *Psychopathy in sexual offenders.* Paper presented at the 11th Annual Research and Treatment Conference for the Behavioral Treatment of Sexual Abusers, Portland, OR.

Gordon, D.A. (1995). Functional family therapy for delinquents. In R.R. Ross, D.H. Antonowicz & G.K. Dhaliwal (eds.), *Going straight: Effective delinquency prevention and offender rehabilitation* (pp. 163-178). Ottawa: Air Training and Publications.

Gordon, D.A. (2001). Parent training via CD-ROM: Using technology to disseminate effective prevention practices. *The Journal of Primary Prevention,* 21, 227-251.

Gordon, D.A., D.A. Andrews, J. Hill & K. Kurkowsky (1992). *Therapeutic integrity and the effectiveness of family therapy: A meta-analysis.* Unpublished manuscript available from D.A. Andrews, Carleton University, Ottawa, Ontario.

Gordon, D A., J. Arbuthnot, K.E. Gustafson & P. McGreen (1988). *Home-based behavioral systems family therapy with disadvantaged juvenile delinquents.* Unpublished manuscript, Psychology Department, Ohio University, Athens, OH.

Gordon, D.A., K. Graves & J. Arbuthnot (1995). The effect of functional family therapy for delinquents on adult criminal behavior. *Criminal Justice and Behavior,* 22, 60-73.

Gordon, D.A., G. Jurkovic & J. Arbuthnot (1998). Treatment of the juvenile offender. In R.M. Wettstein (ed.), *Treatment of offenders with mental disorders* (pp. 365-428). New York: Guilford Press.

Gottfredson, D.C. (1986). An empirical test of school-based environmental and individual interventions to reduce the risk of delinquent behavior. *Criminology*, 24, 705-731.

Gottfredson, M.R. (1979). Treatment destruction techniques. *Journal of Research in Crime and Delinquency*, 16, 39-54.

Gottfredson, M.R. & T. Hirschi (1990). *A general theory of crime.* Stanford, CA: Stanford University Press.

Gottlieb, P. & G. Gabrielsen (1992). Alcohol-intoxicated homicides in Copenhagen, 1959-1983. *International Journal of Law and Psychiatry*, 15, 77-87.

Gough, H.G. (1965). Cross-cultural validation of a measure of asocial behavior. *Psychological Reports*, 17, 379-387.

Gould, S.J. (1981). *The mismeasure of man.* New York: Norton.

Grann, M., H. Belfrage & A. Tengström (2000). Actuarial assessment of risk for violence: Predictive validity of the VRAG and the historical part of the HCR-20. *Criminal Justice and Behavior*, 27, 97-114.

Grann, M. & I. Wedin (2002). Risk factors for recidivism among spousal assault and spousal homicide offenders. *Psychology, Crime and Law*, 8, 5-23.

Grant, J.D. (1965). Delinquency treatment in an institutional setting. In H.C. Quay (ed.), *Juvenile delinquency: Research and theory.* Princeton, NJ: Van Nostrand.

Grant, J.D. & M.Q. Grant (1959). A group dynamics approach to the treatment of non-conformists in the Navy. *Annals of the American Academy of Political and Social Science*, 322, 126-135.

Greene, J.A. (1999). Zero tolerance: A case study of police policies and practices in New York City. *Crime & Delinquency*, 45, 171-187.

Greenfeld, L.A. (1998). *Alcohol and crime: An analysis of national data on the prevalence of alcohol involvement in crime.* Washington, DC: Bureau of Justice Statistics.

Greenwood, P.W. (1982). *Selective incapacitation.* Santa Monica, CA: RAND Corporation.

Greenwood, P.W. (1998). Investing in prisons or prevention: The state policy makers' dilemma. *Crime & Delinquency*, 44, 136-142.

Greenwood, P.W., P. Rydell, A.F. Abrahamse, J.P. Caulkins, J. Chiesa, K.E. Model & S.P. Klein (1994). *Three strikes and you're out: Estimated benefits and costs of California's new mandatory-sentencing law.* Santa Monica, CA: RAND Corporation.

Greenwood, P.W. & S. Turner (1987). *Selective incapacitation revisited: Why the high rate offenders are hard to predict.* Santa Monica, CA: RAND Corporation.

Grekin, E.R., P.A. Brennan, S. Hodgins & S.A. Mednick (2001). Male criminals with organic brain syndrome: Two distinct types based on age at first arrest. *American Journal of Psychiatry*, 158, 1099-1104.

Gresswell, D.M. & C.R. Hollin (1994). Multiple murder: A review. *British Journal of Criminology*, 34, 1-14.

Gretton, H.M., M. McBride, R.D. Hare, R. O'Shaughnessy & G. Kumka (2001). Psychopathy and recidivism in adolescent sex offenders. *Criminal Justice and Behavior*, 28(4), 427-449.

Griffin, K.W., G.J. Botvin, L.M. Scheier, T. Diaz & N.L. Miller (2000). Parenting practices as predictors of substance abuse, delinquency, and aggression among urban minority youth: Moderating effects of family structure and gender. *Psychology of Addictive Behaviors*, 14, 174-184.

Grove, W.M., E.D. Eckert, L. Heston, T.J. Bouchard, Jr., N. Segal & D.T. Lykken (1990). Heritability of substance abuse and antisocial behavior: A study of monozygotic twins reared apart. *Biological Psychiatry*, 27, 1293-1304.

Grove, W.M. & P.E. Meehl (1996). Comparative efficiency of informal (subjective, impressionistic) and formal (mechanical, algorithmic) prediction procedures: The clinical-statistical controversy. *Psychology, Public Policy, and Law*, 2, 293-323.

Grove, W.M., D.H. Zald, B.S. Lebow, B.E. Snitz & C. Nelson (2000). Clinical versus mechanical prediction: A meta-analysis. *Psychological Assessment*, 12, 19-30.

Gunn, J. (1993). Lecture: Epidemiology and forensic psychiatry. *Criminal Behaviour and Mental Health*, 3, 180-193.

Gurling, H.M.D., B.E. Oppenheim & R.M. Murray (1984). Depression, criminality and psychopathology associated with alcoholism: Evidence from a twin study. *Acta Geneticae Medicae Gemellologiae: Twin Research*, 33, 333-339.

Guttridge, P., W.F. Gabrielli, Jr., S.A. Mednick & K.T. Van Dusen (1983). Criminal violence in a birth cohort. In K.T. Van Dusen & S.A. Mednick (eds.), *Prospective studies of crime and delinquency* (pp. 211-224). Hingham, MA: Kluwer Nijhoff.

Guy, E., J.J. Platt, I. Zwerling & S. Bullock (1985). Mental health status of prisoners in an urban jail. *Criminal Justice and Behavior*, 12, 29-53.

Haapasalo, J. & E. Pokela (1999). Child-rearing and child abuse antecedents of criminality. *Aggression and Violent Behavior*, 4, 107-127.

Hackler, J.C. (1966). Boys, blisters, and behavior: The impact of a work program in an urban central area. *Journal of Research in Crime and Delinquency*, 4, 155-164.

Hackler, J.C. (1978). *The prevention of delinquency: The great stumble forward*. Toronto: Methuen.

Hagan, J. (1989). *Structural criminology*. New Brunswick, NJ: Rutgers University Press.

Hagan, J. (1992). The poverty of a classless criminology—The American Society of Criminology 1991 Presidential Address. *Criminology*, 30, 1-19.

Hagan, J., A.R. Gillis & J. Simpson (1985). The class structure of gender and delinquency: Toward a power-control theory of common delinquent behavior. *American Journal of Sociology*, 90, 1151-1177.

Hale, R. (1998). The application of learning theory to serial murder, or "You too can learn to be a serial killer." In R.M. Holmes & S.T. Holmes (eds.), *Contemporary perspectives on serial murder* (pp. 75-84). Thousand Oaks, CA: Sage.

Halverson, C.F., Jr., G.A. Kohnstamm & R.P. Martin (eds.) (1994). *The developing structure of temperament and personality from infancy to adulthood*. Hillsdale, NJ: Lawrence Erlbaum Associates.

Hall, G.C.N. (1990). Prediction of sexual aggression. *Clinical Psychology Review*, 10, 229-245

Hall, G.C.N. & R.C. Hirschman (1992). Sexual aggression against children: A conceptual perspective of etiology. *Criminal Justice and Behavior*, 19, 8-23.

Hamm, M.S. & J.C. Kite (1991). The role of offender rehabilitation in family violence policy: The Batterers Anonymous experiment. *Criminal Justice Review*, 16, 227-248.

Hann, R.G. & W.G. Harman (1993). *Predicting Release Risk for Aboriginal Penitentiary Inmates. User Report 1993-12*. Ottawa: Solicitor General Canada.

Hannah-Moffat, K. (1999). Moral agent or actuarial subject: Risk and Canadian women's imprisonment. *Theoretical Criminology*, 3, 71-94.

Hannah-Moffat, K. & M. Shaw (2001). Taking risks: Incorporating gender and culture into the classification and assessment of federally sentenced women in Canada. *Policy Research Report*, Ottawa, Ontario: Status of Women Canada.

Hanson, R.K. (1996). Evaluating the contribution of relapse prevention theory to the treatment of sex offenders. *Sexual Abuse: A Journal of Research and Treatment*, 8, 201-208.

Hanson, R.K. (1997a). T*he development of a brief actuarial risk scale for sexual offense recidivism*. Ottawa, Ontario: Solicitor General Canada (also http://www.sgc.gc.ca).

Hanson, R.K. (1997b). Invoking sympathy—assessment and treatment of empathy deficits among sexual offenders. In B.K. Schwartz & H.R. Cellini (eds.), *The sex offender: New insights, treatment innovations and legal developments* (pp. 1.1.-1.12). Kingston, NJ: Civic Research Institute.

Hanson, R.K. (1998). What do we know about sex offender risk assessment? *Psychology, Public Policy, and Law*, 4, 50-72.

Hanson, R.K. (2001). Sex offender risk assessment. In C.R. Hollin (ed.), *Handbook of offender assessment and treatment* (pp. 85-96). Chichester, England: Wiley.

Hanson, R.K. & M.T. Bussière (1998). Predicting relapse: A meta-analysis of sexual offender recidivism studies. *Journal of Consulting and Clinical Psychology*, 66, 348-362.

Hanson, R.K., O. Cadsky, A. Harris & C. Lalonde (1997). Correlates of battering among 997 men: Family history, adjustment, and attitudinal differences. *Violence and Victims*, 12, 191-208.

Hanson, R.K., B. Cox & C. Woszczyna (1991). Assessing treatment outcome for sexual offenders. *Annals of Sex Research*, 4, 177-208.

Hanson, R.K., R. Gizzarelli & H. Scott (1994). The attitudes of incest offenders: Sexual entitlement and acceptance of sex with children. *Criminal Justice and Behavior*, 21, 187-202.

Hanson, R.K., A. Gordon, A.J.R. Harris, J.K. Marques, W. Murphy, V.L. Quinsey & M.C. Seto (2002). First report of the Collaborative Outcome Data Project on the effectiveness of psychological treatment for sex offenders. *Sexual Abuse: A Journal of Research and Treatment*, 14, 167-192.

Hanson, R.K. & A.J.R. Harris (2000). Where should we intervene? Dynamic predictors of sexual offense recidivism. *Criminal Justice and Behavior*, 27, 6-35.

Hanson, R.K. & A.J.R. Harris (2001). A structured approach to evaluating change among sex offenders. *Sexual Abuse: A Journal of Research and Treatment*, 13, 105-122.

Hanson, R.K. & H. Scott (1995). Assessing perspective-taking among sexual offenders, nonsexual criminals, and nonoffenders. *Sexual Abuse: A Journal of Research and Treatment*, 7, 259-277.

Hanson, R.K. & H. Scott (1996). Social networks of sexual offenders. *Psychology, Crime and Law*, 2, 249-258.

Hanson, R.K., H. Scott & R.A. Steffy (1995). A comparison of child molesters and non-sexual criminals: Risk predictors and long-term recidivism. *Journal of Research in Crime and Delinquency*, 32, 325-337.

Hanson, R.K. & S. Slater (1988). Sexual victimization in the history of sexual abusers. *Annals of Sex Research*, 1, 485-499.

Hanson, R.K. & D. Thornton (2000). Improving risk assessments for sex offenders: A comparison of three actuarial scales. *Law and Human Behavior*, 24, 119-136.

Hanson, R.K. & S. Wallace-Capretta (2000). *Predicting recidivism among male batterers (User Report 2000-06)*. Ottawa: Solicitor General Canada.

Hanson, R.W., C.S. Moss, R.E. Hosford & M.E. Johnson (1983). Predicting inmate penitentiary adjustment: An assessment of four classificatory methods. *Criminal Justice and Behavior*, 10, 293-309.

Hare, R.D. (1970). *Psychopathy: Theory and research*. New York: Wiley.

Hare, R.D. (1978). Electrodermal and cardiovascular correlates of psychopathy. In R.D. Hare & D. Schalling (eds.), *Psychopathic behavior: Approaches to research* (pp. 107-143). Toronto: Wiley.

Hare, R.D. (1980). A research scale for the assessment of psychopathy in criminal populations. *Personality and Individual Differences*, 1, 111-119.

Hare, R.D. (1982). Psychopathy and physiological activity during anticipation of an aversive stimulus in a distraction paradigm. *Psychophysiology*, 19, 266-271.

Hare, R.D. (1990). *The Hare Psychopathy Checklist – Revised*. Toronto: Multi-Health Systems.

Hare, R.D. (1996). Psychopathy: A clinical construct whose time has come. *Criminal Justice and Behavior*, 23, 25-54.

Hare, R.D. (1998). Psychopaths and their nature: Implications for the mental health and criminal justice systems. In T. Millon, E. Simonsen, M. Birket-Smith & R.D. Davis (eds.), *Psychopathy: Antisocial, criminal, and violent behavior* (pp. 188-212). New York: Guilford.

Hare, R.D., D. Clark, M. Grann & D. Thornton (2000). Psychopathy and the predictive validity of the PCL-R: An international perspective. *Behavioral Sciences and the Law*, 18, 623-645.

Hare, R.D., C.E. Strachan & A.E. Forth (1993). Psychopathy and crime: A review. In K. Howells & C.R. Hollin (eds.), *Clinical approaches to the mentally disordered offender* (pp. 165-178). Chichester, England: Wiley.

Harmon, R.B., R. Rosner & H. Owens (1995). Obsessional harassment and erotomania in a criminal court population. *Journal of Forensic Sciences*, 40, 188-196.

Harpur, T.J., R. Hakstian & R.D. Hare (1988). Factor structure of the psychopathy checklist. *Journal of Consulting and Clinical Psychology*, 56, 741-747.

Harpur, T.J. & R.D. Hare (1990). Psychopathy and attention. In J. Enns (ed.), *The development of attention: Research and theory* (pp. 429-444). New York: Holland.

Harris, G.T. & M.E. Rice (1997). Mentally disordered offenders: What research says about effective service. In C.D. Webster & M.A. Jackson (eds.), *Impulsivity theory: Assessment and treatment* (pp. 361-393). New York: Guilford.

Harris, G.T., M.R. Rice & C.A. Cormier (1989). *Violent recidivism among psychopaths and nonpsychopaths treated in a therapeutic community*. Research report from the Penetanguishene Mental Health Centre VI(1), April, Penetanguishene, Ontario.

Harris, G.T., M.E. Rice & C.A. Cormier (1994). Psychopaths: Is a therapeutic community therapeutic? *Therapeutic Communities*, 15, 283-299.

Harris, G.T., M.E. Rice & V.L. Quinsey (1993). Violent recidivism of mentally disordered offenders: The development of a statistical prediction instrument. *Criminal Justice and Behavior*, 20, 315-335.

Harris, G.T., M.E. Rice & V.L. Quinsey (1994). Psychopathy as a taxon: Evidence that psychopaths are a discrete class. *Journal of Consulting and Clinical Psychology*, 62, 387-397.

Harris, P.W. (1988). The Interpersonal Maturity Level classification system: I-Level. *Criminal Justice and Behavior*, 15, 58-77.

Hart, S.D. & R.D. Hare (1997). Psychopathy: Assessment and association with criminal conduct. In D.M. Stoff, J. Breiling & J.D. Maser (eds.), *Handbook of antisocial behavior* (pp. 22-35). New York: Wiley.

Hart, S.D., P.R. Kropp & R.D. Hare (1988). Performance of male psychopaths following conditional release from prison. *Journal of Consulting and Clinical Psychology*, 56, 237-232.

Hartnagel, T.F. (1992). Correlates of criminal behaviour. In R. Linden (ed.), *Criminology: A Canadian perspective* (2nd ed.) (pp. 91-126). Toronto: Harcourt Brace.

Hartung, F.E. (1965). A vocabulary of motives for law violations. In F.E. Hartung, *Crime, law and society* (pp. 62-83). Detroit: Wayne State University Press.

Haskins, R. (1989). Beyond metaphor: The efficacy of early childhood education. *American Psychologist*, 44, 274-282.

Hastings, R. (1991). Corrections with class. *Forum on Corrections Research*, 3, 36.

Hathaway, S. & J.C. McKinley (1951). *Minnesota Multiphasic Personality Inventory*. New York: Psychological Corporation.

Hawkins, J.D., T. Herrenkohl, D.P. Farrington, D. Brewer, R.F. Catalano & T.W. Harachi (1998). In R. Loeber & D.P. Farrington (eds.), *Serious and violent juvenile offenders: Risk factors and successful interventions.* (pp. 106-146). Thousand Oaks, CA: Sage.

Hayes, S.C. & W.L. Walker (1986). Intellectual and moral development in offenders: A review. *Australian and New Zealand Journal of Criminology*, 19, 53-64.

Heckert, D.A. & E.W. Gondolf (2000). The effect of perceptions of sanctions on batterer program outcomes. *Journal of Research in Crime and Delinquency*, 37, 369-391.

Heilbrun, K. & A.B. Heilbrun (1995). Risk assessment with the MMPI-2 in forensic evaluations. In Y.S. Ben-Porath, J.R. Graham, G.C.N. Hall, R.D. Hirschman & M.S. Zaragoza (eds.), *Forensic Applications of the MMPI-2* (pp. 160-178). Thousand Oaks, CA: Sage.

Heim, N. (1981). Sexual behavior of castrated sex offenders. *Archives of Sexual Behavior*, 10, 11-19.

Helzer, J.E., L.N. Robins, L.T. McEvoy, E.I. Spitznagel, R.K. Stoltzman, A. Farmer & I.F. Brockington (1985). A Comparison of Clinical and Diagnostic Interview Schedule diagnoses: Physician reexamination of lay-interviewed cases in the general population. *Archives of General Psychiatry*, 42, 657-666.

Hemphill, J.F., R.D. Hare & S. Wong (1998). Psychopathy and recidivism: A review. *Legal and Criminological Psychology*, 3, 139-170.

Henggeler, S.W., P.B. Cunningham, S.G. Pickrel & S.K. Schoenwald (1995). Multisystemic therapy for serious juvenile offenders and their families. In R.R. Ross, D.H. Antonowicz & G.K. Dhaliwal (eds.), *Going straight: Effective delinquency prevention and offender rehabilitation* (pp.109-133). Ottawa: Air Training and Publications.

Henggeler, S.W., G.B. Melton & L.A. Smith (1992). Family preservation using multisystemic therapy: An effective alternative to incarcerating serious juvenile offenders. *Journal of Consulting and Clinical Psychology*, 60, 953-961.

Henggeler, S.W., G.B. Melton, L.A. Smith, S.K. Schoenwald & J. Hanley (1993). Family preservation using multisystemic therapy: Long-term follow-up to a clinical trial with serious juvenile offenders. *Journal of Child and Family Studies*, 2, 283-293.

Henggeler, S.W., S.K. Schoenwald, C.M. Borduin, M.D. Rowland & P.B. Cunningham (1998). *Multisystemic treatment of antisocial behavior in children and adolescents*. New York: Guilford Press.

Henggeler, S.W., S.G. Pickrel, M.J. Brondino & J.L. Crouch (1996). Eliminating (almost) treatment dropout of substance abusing or dependent delinquents through home-based multisystemic therapy. *American Journal of Psychiatry*, 153, 427-428.

Henggeler, S.W., S.K. Schoenwald & S.G. Pickrel (1995). Multisystemic therapy: Bridging the gap between university- and community-based treatment. *Journal of Consulting and Clinical Psychology*, 63, 709-717.

Henning, K.R. & B.C. Frueh (1996). Cognitive-behavioral treatment of incarcerated offenders. *Criminal Justice and Behavior*, 23, 523-541.

Henry, B., A. Caspi, T.E. Moffitt & P.A. Silva (1996). Temperamental and familial predictors of violent and nonviolent criminal convictions: Age 3 and age 18. *Developmental Psychology*, 32, 614-623.

Henry, F. (1986). Crime—A profitable approach. In B.D. MacLean (ed.), *The political economy of crime* (pp. 182-203). Scarborough, Ontario: Prentice Hall.

Herpertz, S.C. & H. Sass (2000). Emotional deficiency and psychopathy. *Behavioral Sciences and the Law*, 18(5), 567-580.

Herrenkohl, T.I., B. Huang, R. Kosterman, D.J. Hawkins, R.F. Catalano & B.H. Smith (2001). A comparison of social development processes leading to violent behavior in late adolescence for childhood initiators and adolescent initiators of violence. *Journal of Research in Crime and Delinquency*, 38, 45-63.

Herrnstein, R.J. & C. Murray (1994). *The bell curve: Intelligence and class structure in American life*. New York: Free Press.

Hersen, M. & D.H. Barlow (1976). *Single case experimental designs: Strategies for studying behavioral change*. New York: Pergamon Press.

Hester, R.K. & W.R. Miller (1995). *Handbook of alcoholism treatment approaches*. Boston: Allyn & Bacon.

Hilarski, C. & J.S. Wodarski (2001). The effective social worker. *Journal of Human Behavior in the Social Environment*, 4, 19-39.

Hill, J., D.A. Andrews & R.D. Hoge (1991). Meta-analysis of treatment programs for young offenders: The effect of clinically relevant treatment on recidivism with controls for various methodological variables. *Canadian Journal of Program Evaluation*, 6, 97-109.

Hill, K., J.C. Howell, D.J. Hawkins & S.R. Battin-Pearson (1999). Childhood risk factors for adolescent gang membership: Results from the Seattle social development project. *Journal of Research in Crime and Delinquency*, 36, 300-322.

Hindelang, M.J. (1972). The relationship of self-reported delinquency to scales of the CPI and MMPI. *Journal of Criminal Law, Criminology and Police Science*, 63, 75-81.

Hindelang, M.J. (1981). Variations in sex-race-age-specific incidence rates of offending. *American Sociological Review*, 46, 461-474.

Hinshaw, S.P. (1992). Externalizing behavior problems and academic underachievement in childhood and adolescence: Causal relationships and underlying mechanisms. *Psychological Bulletin*, 111, 127-155.

Hirschi, T. (1969). *Causes of delinquency*. Berkeley: University of California Press.

Hirschi, T. & M.J. Hindelang (1977). Intelligence and delinquency: A revisionist review. *American Sociological Review*, 42, 571-587.

Hobson, J., J. Shine & R. Roberts (2000). How do psychopaths behave in a prison therapeutic community? *Psychiatry, Crime and Law*, 6, 139-154.

Hodgins, S. & G. Cote (1990). Prevalence of mental disorders among penitentiary inmates in Quebec. *Canada's Mental Health*, 38, 1-4.

Hoffman, P.B. (1982). Females, recidivism, and salient factor score: A research note. *Criminal Justice and Behavior*, 9, 121-125.

Hoffman, P.B. (1994). Twenty years of operational use of a risk prediction instrument: The United States Parole Commission's Salient Factor Score. *Journal of Criminal Justice*, 22, 477-494.

Hoffman, P.B. & J.L. Beck (1984). Burnout—Age at release from prison and recidivism. *Journal of Criminal Justice*, 12, 617-623.

Hoffman, P.B., B. Stone-Meierhoefer & J.L. Beck (1978). Salient factor score and release behavior: Three validational samples. *Law and Human Behavior*, 2, 47-63.

Hoge, R.D. (2001). *The juvenile offender: Theory, research, and application*. Norwell, MA: Kluwer.

Hoge, R.D. (in press). Standardized instruments for assessing risk and need in youthful offenders. *Criminal Justice and Behavior*.

Hoge, R.D. & D.A. Andrews (1986). A model for conceptualizing interventions in social service. *Canadian Psychology*, 27, 332-341.

Hoge, R.D. & D.A. Andrews (2001). *The Youth Level of Service/Case Management Inventory and manual (YLS/CMI)*. Ottawa: Ontario: Department of Psychology, Carleton University.

Hollin, C.R. & E.J. Palmer (2001). Skills training. In C.R. Hollin (ed.), *Handbook of offender assessment and treatment* (pp. 269-280). Chichester, England: Wiley.

Holmes, R.M. (1989). *Profiling violent crimes: An investigative tool*. Newbury Park, CA: Sage.

Holmes, R.M. & S.T. Holmes (1994). *Murder in America.* Thousand Oaks, CA: Sage.

Holmes, R.M. & S.T. Holmes (1996). *Profiling violent crimes: An investigative tool.* Thousand Oaks, CA: Sage.

Holmes, R.M. & S.T. Holmes (1998). *Serial murder* (2nd ed.). Thousand Oaks, CA: Sage.

Holmes, S.T., E. Hickey & R.M. Holmes (1998). Female serial murderesses: The unnoticed terror. In R.M. Holmes & S.T. Holmes (eds.), *Contemporary perspectives on serial murder* (pp. 59-70). Thousand Oaks, CA: Sage.

Holosko, M.J. & T.M. Carlson (1986). Recidivism among ex-offenders residing at a CRC in St. John's, Newfoundland. *Canadian Journal of Criminology*, 28, 385-396.

Holtzworth-Munroe, A. & G.L. Stuart (1994). Typologies of male batterers: Three subtypes and the differences among them. *Psychological Bulletin*, 116, 476-497.

Home Office Communication Directorate. (1999). *The What Works initiative.* London, England: Home Office Communication Directorate.

Hotlzworth-Munroe, A. (1992). Social skills deficits in maritally violent men: Interpreting the data using a social information processing model. *Clinical Psychology Review*, 12, 605-617.

Hough, M. & J.V. Roberts (1999). Sentencing trends in Britain: Public knowledge and public opinion. *Punishment and Society*, 1, 11-26.

Howells, K. & A. Day (1999). *The rehabilitation of offenders: International perspectives applied to Australian correctional systems (No. 112).* Canberra: Australian Institute of Criminology.

Hser, Y.-I., D. Longshore & M.D. Anglin (1994). Prevalence of drug use among criminal offender populations: Implications for control, treatment, and policy. In D.L. MacKenzie & C.D. Uchida (eds.), *Drugs and crime: evaluating public policy initiatives* (pp. 18-41). Thousand Oaks, CA: Sage.

Hucker, S.J. (1997). Sexual sadism: Psychopathology and theory. In D.R. Laws & W. O'Donohue (eds.), *Sexual deviance: Theory, assessment, and treatment* (pp.194-224). New York: Guilford Press.

Hucker, S.J. & J. Bain (1990). Androgenic hormones and sexual assault. In W.L. Marshall, D.R. Laws & H.E. Barbaree (eds.), *Handbook of sexual assault: Issues, theories, and treatment of the offender* (pp. 93-102). New York: Plenum.

Huff, R.C. (1998). *Comparing the criminal behavior of youth gangs and at-risk youths.* Washington, DC: National Institute of Justice, Research in Brief.

Hunt, D.E. & R.H. Hardt (1965). Developmental stage, delinquency, and differential treatment. *Journal of Research in Crime and Delinquency*, 2, 20-31.

Hunt, G.M. & N.H. Azrin (1973). A community-reinforcement approach to alcoholism. *Behavior Research and Therapy*, 11, 91-104.

Huss, M.T. & J. Langhinrichsen-Rohling (2000). Identification of the psychopathic batterer: The clinical, legal, and policy implications. *Aggression and Violent Behavior*, 5, 403-422.

Hutton, H.E. & M.H. Miner (1995). The validation of the Megargee-Bohn typology in African American and Caucasian forensic psychiatric patients. *Criminal Justice and Behavior*, 22, 233-245.

Inada, T., F. Minagawa, S. Iwashita & T. Tokui (1995). Mentally disordered criminal offenders: Five years' data from the Tokyo district public prosecutor's office. *International Journal of Law and Psychiatry*, 18, 221-230.

Irvin, J.E., C.A. Bowers, M.E. Dunn & M.C. Wang (1999). Efficacy of relapse prevention: A meta-analytic review. *Journal of Consulting and Clinical Psychology*, 67, 563-570.

Ito, R.J., D.M. Donovan & J.J. Hall (1988). Relapse prevention in alcohol aftercare: Effects on drinking outcome, change process, and aftercare attendance. *British Journal of Addiction*, 83, 171-181.

Izzo, R.L. & R.R. Ross (1990). Meta-analysis of rehabilitation programs for juvenile delinquents. *Criminal Justice and Behavior*, 17, 134-142.

Jacobs, P.A., M. Brunton, H.M. Melville, R.P. Brittain & W.F. McClemont (1965). Aggressive behavior, mental subnormality and the XYY male. *Nature*, 208, 1351-1352.

Jacobson, N.S., J.M. Gottman, E.T. Gortner, S.B. Berns & J.W. Shortt (1996). Psychological factors in the longitudinal course of battering: When do couples split up? When does the abuse decrease? *Violence and Victims*, 11(4), 371-392.

Janson, C.G. (1983). Delinquency among metropolitan boys: A progress report. In K.T. Van Dusen & S.A. Mednick (eds.), *Prospective studies of crime and delinquency* (pp. 147-180). Hingham, MA: Kluwer Nijhoff.

Jarjoura, G.R. (1993). Does dropping out of school enhance delinquent involvement? Results from a large-scale national probability sample. *Criminology*, 31, 149-172.

Jarvik, L.F., V. Klodin & S.S. Matsuyama (1973). Human aggression and the extra Y chromosome. *American Psychologist*, 28, 674-682.

Jeffery, C.R. (1979). *Biology and crime*. Beverly Hills: Sage.

Jenkins, P. (1998). African-Americans and serial homicide. In R.M. Holmes & S.T. Holmes (eds.), *Contemporary perspectives on serial murder* (pp. 17-32). Thousand Oaks, CA: Sage.

Jennings, J.L. (1987). History and issues in the treatment of battering men: A case for unstructured group therapy. *Journal of Family Violence*, 2, 193-213.

Jennings, W.S., R. Kilkenny & L. Kohlberg (1983). Moral development theory and practice for youthful and adult offenders. In W.S. Laufer & J.M. Day (eds.), *Personality theory, moral development, and criminal behavior* (pp. 281-355). Toronto: Lexington Books.

Jenson, G.F. (1972). Parents, peers and delinquent action: A test of the differential association perspective. *American Journal of Sociology*, 78, 562-575.

Jesness, C.F. (1971). The Preston typology study: An experiment with differential treatment in an institution. *Journal of Research in Crime and Delinquency*, 8, 38-52.

Jesness, C.F. (1988). The Jesness Inventory classification system. *Criminal Justice and Behavior*, 15, 78-91.

Jessor, R. & S.L. Jessor (1977). *Problem behavior and psychosocial development: A longitudinal study of youth*. New York: Academic Press.

Jessor, R., S.L. Jessor & J. Finney (1973). A social psychology of marijuana use: Longitudinal studies of high school and college youth. *Journal of Personality and Social Psychology*, 26, 1-15.

Johnson, H. & V.F. Sacco (1995). Researching violence against women: Statistics Canada's national survey. *Canadian Journal of Criminology*, 37, 281-304.

Johnson, R.E. (1979). *Juvenile delinquency and its origins: An integrative theoretical approach.* Cambridge, England: Cambridge University Press.

Johnson, W.W., K. Bennett & T.J. Flanagan (1997). Getting tough on prisoners: Results from the National Corrections Executive survey, 1995. *Crime & Delinquency,* 43, 24-41.

Johnston, J.M. (1972). Punishment of human behavior. *American Psychologist,* 27, 1033-1054.

Joiner, T.E. & K.D. Wagner (1995). Attribution style and depression in children and adolescents: A meta-analytic review. *Clinical Psychology Review,* 15, 777-798.

Jones, M. & D.L. Ross (1997). Is less better? Boot camp, regular probation and rearrest in North Carolina. *American Journal of Criminal Justice,* 21, 145-161.

Jones, P.R. (1996). Risk prediction in criminal justice. In A.T. Harland (ed.), *Choosing correctional options that work: Defining the demand and evaluating the supply* (pp. 33-68). Thousand Oaks, CA: Sage.

Juby, H. & D.P. Farrington (2001). Disentangling the link between disrupted families and delinquency. *British Journal of Criminology,* 41, 22-40.

Jung, S. & E.P. Rawana (1999). Risk and need assessment of juvenile offenders. *Criminal Justice and Behavior,* 26, 69-89.

Kaemingk, K. & A. Paquette (1999). Effects of prenatal alcohol exposure on neuropsychological functioning. *Developmental Neuropsychology,* 15, 111-140.

Kassenbaum, G., D. Ward & D. Wilner (1971). *Prison treatment and parole survival: An empirical assessment.* New York: Wiley.

Kassin, S.M., A.V. Tubb, H.H. Hosch & A. Memon (2001). On the "general acceptance" of eyewitness testimony research. *American Psychologist,* 56, 405-416.

Katz, J. & W.J. Chambliss (1995). Biology and crime. In J.F. Sheley (ed.), *Criminology: A contemporary handbook* (pp. 275-303). Belmont, CA: Wadsworth.

Keeney, B.T. & K.M. Heide (1994). Gender differences in serial murders: A preliminary analysis. *Journal of Interpersonal Violence,* 9, 383-398.

Kennedy, S. & R. Serin (1999). Examining offender readiness to change and the impact on treatment outcome. In P.M. Harris (ed.), *Research to results: Effective community corrections* (pp. 215-230). Lanham, MD: American Correctional Association.

Kernberg, O.F. (1998). The psychotherapeutic management of psychopathic, narcissistic, and paranoid transferences. In T. Millon, E. Simonsen, M. Birket-Smith & R.D. Davis (eds.), *Psychopathy: Violence, criminal, and violent behavior.* New York: Guilford.

Kienlen, K.K. (1995). *An obsessive and potentially dangerous pursuit: A case study approach to the phenomenon of stalking.* Unpublished doctoral dissertation, Minnesota School of Professional Psychology, Minneapolis, MN.

Kienlen, K.K. (1998). Developmental and social antecedents of stalking. In J.R. Meloy (ed.), *The psychology of stalking: Clinical and forensic perspectives* (pp. 51-67). New York: Academic Press.

Kirby, B.C. (1954). Measuring effects of treatment of criminals and delinquents. *Sociology and Social Research,* 38, 368-374.

Kirkpatrick, B.L. (1999). Exploratory research of female risk prediction and the LSI-R. *Corrections Compendium,* 24, 1-3, 14-17.

Klein, A.R. (1996). Re-abuse in a population of court-restrained male batterers: Why restraining orders don't work. In E.S. Buzawa & C.G. Buzawa (eds.), *Do arrests and restraining orders work?* (pp. 192-213). Thousand Oaks, CA: Sage.

Klein, M.W. (1971). *Street gangs and street workers.* Englewood Cliffs, NJ: Prentice Hall.

Klein, M.W. (1995). *The American street gang: It's nature, prevalence, and control.* New York: Oxford University Press.

Klein, N.C., J.F. Alexander & B.V. Parsons (1977). Impact of family systems intervention on recidivism and sibling delinquency: A model of primary prevention and program evaluation. *Journal of Consulting and Clinical Psychology*, 3, 469-474.

Kliewer, W., S.J. Lepore, D. Oskin & P.D. Johnson (1998). The role of social and cognitive processes in children's adjustment to community violence. *Journal of Consulting and Clinical Psychology*, 60, 199-209.

Knight, R.A., R.A. Prentky & D.D. Cerce (1994). The development, reliability, and validity of an inventory for the multidimensional assessment of sex and aggression. *Criminal Justice and Behavior*, 21, 72-94.

Kohlberg, L. (1958). *The development of modes of moral thinking and choice in the years ten to sixteen.* Unpublished doctoral dissertation, University of Chicago, IL.

Koss, M.P. (1996). The measurement of rape victimization in crime surveys. *Criminal Justice and Behavior*, 23, 55-69.

Kratzer, L. & S. Hodgins (1999). A typology of offenders: A test of Moffitt's theory among males and females from childhood to age 30. *Criminal Behaviour and Mental Health*, 9, 57-73.

Kraus, R.T. (1995). An enigmatic personality: Case report of a serial killer. *Journal of Orthomolecular Medicine*, 10, 11-24.

Kroner, D.G. & W. Loza (2001). Evidence for the efficacy of self-report in predicting nonviolent and violent criminal recidivism. *Journal of Interpersonal Violence*, 16, 168-177.

Kroner, D.G. & J.F. Mills (2001). The accuracy of five risk appraisal instruments in predicting institutional misconduct and new convictions. *Criminal Justice and Behavior*, 28, 471-489.

Kropp, P.R. & S.D. Hart (2000). The Spousal Assault Risk Assessment (SARA) guide: Reliability and validity in adult male offenders. *Law and Human Behavior*, 24, 101-118.

Kropp, P.R., S.D. Hart, C.D. Webster & D. Eaves (1995). *Manual for the Spousal Assault Risk Assessment Guide* (2nd ed.). Vancouver: British Columbia Institute of Family Violence.

Krueger, R.F., B.M. Hicks & M. McGue (2001). Altruism and social behavior: Independent tendencies, unique personality correlates, distinct etiologies. *Psychological Science*, 12, 397-402.

Krueger, R.F., T.E. Moffitt, A. Caspi, A. Bleske & P.A. Silva (1998). Assortative mating for antisocial behavior: Developmental and methodological implications. *Behavior Genetics*, 28, 173-186.

Krueger, R.F., P.S. Schmutte, A. Caspi, T.E. Moffitt, K. Campbell & P.A. Silva (1994). Personality traits are linked to crime among men and women: Evidence from a birth cohort. *Journal of Abnormal Psychology*, 103, 328-338.

Kruttschnitt, C. & M. Dornfeld (1993). Exposure to family violence: A partial explanation for initial and subsequent levels of delinquency? *Criminal Behaviour and Mental Health,* 3, 61-75.

Kumpfer, K.L., V. Molgaard & R. Spoth (1996). The Strengthening Families Program for the prevention of delinquency and drug use. In R. DeV Peters & R.J. McMahon (eds.), *Preventing childhood disorders, substance abuse, and delinquency* (pp. 241-267). Thousand Oaks, CA: Sage.

Kurki, L. (2000). Restorative and community justice in the United States. In M. Tonry (ed.), *Crime and justice: A review of research, Vol. 27* (pp. 235-303). Chicago: University of Chicago Press.

Lab, S.P. & J.T. Whitehead (1990). From "Nothing Works" to "The Appropriate Works": The latest stop on the search for the secular grail. *Criminology,* 28, 405-417.

Lahey, B.B. & R. Loeber (1997). Attention-deficit/hyperactivity disorder, oppositional defiant disorder, conduct disorder, and adult antisocial behavior: A life span perspective. In D.M. Stoff, J. Breiling & J.D. Maser (eds.), *Handbook of antisocial behavior* (pp. 51-59). New York: Wiley.

Lahey, B.B., R.R. Gordon, R. Loeber, M. Stouthamer-Loeber & D.P. Farrington (1999). Boys who join gangs: A prospective study of predictors of first gang entry. *Journal of Abnormal Child Psychology,* 27, 261-276.

Lalumière, M.L. & V.L. Quinsey (1994). The discriminability of rapists from non-sex offenders using phallometric measures: A meta-analysis. *Criminal Justice and Behavior,* 21, 150-175.

Langan, P.A. & C.W. Harlow (1994). Child rape victims, 1992. *Crime Data Brief.* Washington, D.C: U.S. Department of Justice, June.

Lange, J. (1929). *Crime as destiny* (translated 1931). London: Unwin.

Langevin, R., R.A. Lang & S. Curnoe (1998). The prevalence of sex offenders with deviant fantasies. *Journal of Interpersonal Violence,* 13, 315-327.

Latessa, E.J. & A. Holsinger (1998). The importance of evaluating correctional programs: Assessing outcome and quality. *Corrections Management Quarterly,* 2, 22-29.

Latimer, J. (2001). A meta-analytic examination of youth delinquency, family treatment, and recidivism. *Canadian Journal of Criminology,* 43, 237-253.

Laub, J.H. & R.J. Sampson (1988). Unraveling families and delinquency: A reanalysis of the Gluecks' data. *Criminology,* 26, 355-380.

Laub, J.H. & R.J. Sampson (1991). The Sutherland-Glueck debate: On the sociology of criminological knowledge. *American Journal of Sociology,* 96, 1402-1440.

Lauen, R.J. (1997). *Positive approaches to corrections: Research, policy, and practice.* Lanham, MD: American Correctional Association.

Le Blanc, M. & N. Lanctôt (1998). Social and psychological characteristics of gang members according to the gang structure and it's subcultural and ethnic make up. *Journal of Gang Research,* 5, 15-28.

Le Blanc, M. & R. Loeber (1998). Developmental criminology updated. In M. Tonry (ed.), *Crime and justice: A review of research. Vol. 23* (pp. 115-198). Chicago: University of Chicago Press.

Le Blanc, M., M. Ouimet & R.E. Tremblay (1988). An integrative control theory of delinquent behavior: A validation 1976-1985. *Psychiatry,* 51, 164-176.

Lee, M. & N.M. Prentice (1988). Interrelations of empathy, cognition, and moral reasoning with dimensions of juvenile delinquency. *Journal of Abnormal Child Psychology*, 16, 127-139.

Leiber, M.J. (1994). A comparison of juvenile court outcomes for Native Americans, African Americans, and Whites. *Justice Quarterly*, 11, 257-279.

Leitenberg, H. (1976). *Handbook of behavior modification and behavior therapy*. New York: Prentice Hall.

LeMarquand, D. & R.E. Tremblay (2001). Delinquency prevention in schools. In C.R. Hollin (ed.), *Handbook of offender assessment and treatment* (pp. 237-258). Chichester, England: Wiley.

Lenton, R.L. (1995). Power versus feminist theories of wife abuse. *Canadian Journal of Criminology*, 37, 305-330.

Leschied, A.W., G.W. Austin & P.G. Jaffe (1988). Impact of the Young Offenders Act on recidivism and special needs youth: Clinical and policy implications. *Canadian Journal of Behavioural Science*, 20, 322-331.

Leschied, A.W., A. Cummings, M. Van Brunschot, A. Cunningham & A. Saunders (2001). Aggression in adolescent girls: Implications for policy, prevention, and treatment. *Canadian Psychology*, 42, 200-215.

Leschied, A.W. & A. Cunningham (2001). Intensive community-based services can influence re-offending rates of high-risk youth: Preliminary results of the multisystemic therapy clinical trials in Ontario. *Empirical and Applied Criminal Justice Research*, 1, 1-24.

Leschied, A.W., P.G. Jaffe & W. Wills (1991). *The Young Offenders Act: A revolution in Canadian juvenile justice*. Toronto: University of Toronto Press.

Leventhal, T. & J. Brooks-Gunn (2000). The neighborhoods they live in: The effects of neighborhood residence on child and adolescent outcomes. *Psychological Bulletin*, 126, 309-337.

Levinson, R.B. (1988). Developments in the classification process: Quay's AIMS approach. *Criminal Justice and Behavior*, 15, 24-38.

Leyton, E. (1986). *Hunting humans*. Toronto: McClelland and Stewart.

Lilienfeld, S.O. (1996). The MMPI-2 antisocial practices content scale: Construct validity and comparison with the Psychopathic Deviate scale. *Psychological Assessment*, 1996, 8, 281-293.

Linden, R. (ed.) (1987). *Criminology: A Canadian perspective*. Toronto: Holt, Rinehart and Winston.

Linden, R. & K. Fillmore (1981). A comparative study of delinquency involvement. *Canadian Review of Sociology and Anthropology*, 18, 343-361.

Lindesmith, A.R. (1947). *Opiate addiction*. Bloomington, IN: Principles Press.

Link, B.G., H. Andrews & F.T. Cullen (1992). The violent and illegal behavior of mental patients reconsidered. *American Sociological Review*, 57, 275-292.

Link, B. & C. Steuve (1994). Psychotic symptoms and the violent/illegal behavior of mental patients compared to community controls. In J. Monahan & H. Steadman (eds.), *Violence and mental disorder*. (pp. 137-159). Chicago: University of Chicago Press.

Lipsey, M.W. (1989, November). *The efficacy of intervention for juvenile delinquency: Results from 400 studies.* Paper presented at the 41st annual meeting of the American Society of Criminology, Reno, NV.

Lipsey, M.W. (1995). What do we learn from 400 research studies on the effectiveness of treatment with juvenile delinquency? In J. McGuire (ed.), *What works: Reducing reoffending, guidelines from research to practice* (pp. 63-78). West Sussex, England: Wiley.

Lipsey, M.W. (1999). Can rehabilitative programs reduce the recidivism of juvenile offenders? An inquiry into the effectiveness of practical programs. *Virginia Journal of Social Policy and the Law*, 6, 611-641.

Lipsey, M.W. & J.H. Derzon (1998). Predictors of violent or serious delinquency in adolescence and early adulthood: A synthesis of longitudinal research. In R. Loeber & D.P. Farrington (eds.), *Serious and violent juvenile offenders: Risk factors and successful interventions* (pp. 86-105). Thousand Oaks, CA: Sage.

Lipsey, M.W. & D.B. Wilson (1998). Effective intervention for serious juvenile offenders: A synthesis of research. In R. Loeber & D.P. Farrington (eds.), *Serious and violent juvenile offenders: Risk factors and successful interventions* (pp. 313-345). Thousand Oaks, CA: Sage.

Lipsitt, P.D., S.L. Buka & L.P. Lipsitt (1990). Early intelligence scores and subsequent delinquent behavior: A prospective study. *American Journal of Family Therapy*, 18, 197-208.

Lipton, D.S. (1994). The correctional opportunity: Pathways to drug treatment for offenders. *Journal of Drug Issues*, 24, 331-348.

Lipton, D.S. (1995). *The effectiveness of treatment for drug abusers under criminal justice supervision.* Washington, DC: National Institute of Justice.

Lipton, D., R. Martinson & J. Wilks (1975). The effectiveness of correctional treatment: A survey of treatment evaluation studies. New York: Praeger.

Lipton, D., F.S. Pearson, C. Cleland & D. Yee (1997). *Synthesizing correctional treatment outcome: Preliminary CDATE findings.* Paper presented at the 5th Annual National Institute of Justice Conference on Research and Evaluation in Criminal Justice, July, Washington, DC.

Little, G.L. & K.D. Robinson (1989). Relationship of DUI recidivism to moral reasoning, sensation seeking, and MacAndrew alcoholism scores. *Psychological Reports*, 65, 1171-1174.

Llewellyn, J.J. & R. Howse (1999). *Restorative justice—A conceptual framework.* Ottawa: Law Commission of Canada.

Loeber, R. (1991). Risk factors and the development of disruptive and antisocial behavior in children. *Forum on Corrections Research*, 3, 22-28.

Loeber, R. & T.J. Dishion (1983). Early predictors of male delinquency. *Psychological Bulletin*, 94, 68-99.

Loeber, R. & D.P. Farrington (eds.) (1998). *Serious and violent juvenile offenders: Risk factors and successful interventions.* Thousand Oaks, CA: Sage.

Loeber, R., D.P. Farrington & D.A. Waschbusch (1998). Serious and violent juvenile offenders. In R. Loeber & D.P. Farrington (eds.), *Serious and violent juvenile offenders: Risk factors and successful interventions* (13-29). Thousand Oaks, CA: Sage.

Loeber, R. & M. LeBlanc (1990). Toward a developmental criminology. In M. Tonry & N. Morris (eds.), *Crime and justice: A review of research, Vol. 12* (pp. 375-473). Chicago: University of Chicago Press.

Loeber, R. & M. Stouthamer-Loeber (1986). Family factors as correlates and predictors of juvenile conduct problems and delinquency. In M. Tonry & N. Morris (eds.), *Crime and justice: An annual review, Vol. 7* (pp. 29-149). Chicago: University of Chicago Press.

Loeber, R. & M. Stouthamer-Loeber (1987). Prediction. In H.C. Quay (ed.), *Handbook of juvenile delinquency* (pp. 325-382). New York: Wiley.

Loeber, R. & M. Stouthamer-Loeber (1996). The development of offending. *Criminal Justice and Behavior*, 23, 12-24.

Logan, C.H. (1972). Evaluation research in crime and delinquency: A reappraisal. *Journal of Criminal Law, Criminology and Police Science*, 63, 378-387.

Logan, C.H. & G.G. Gaes (1993). Meta-analysis and the rehabilitation of punishment. *Justice Quarterly*, 10, 245-263.

Logan, C.H., G.G. Gaes, M. Harer, C.A. Innes, L. Karacki & W.G. Saylor (1991). *Can meta-analysis save correctional rehabilitation?* Report available from the Federal Bureau of Prisons, Washington, DC

Lösel, F. (1995). The efficacy of correctional treatment: A review and synthesis of meta-evaluations. In J. McGuire (ed.), *What works: Reducing reoffending* (pp. 79-111). Chichester, England: Wiley.

Loucks, A. & E. Zamble (1999). Predictors of recidivism in serious female offenders. *Corrections Today*, 61, 26-32.

Louscher, P.K., R.E. Hosford & C.S. Moss (1983). Predicting dangerous behavior in a penitentiary setting using the Megargee typology. *Criminal Justice and Behavior*, 10, 269-284.

Lowenkamp, C.T., Holsinger & E.J. Latessa (2001). Risk/need assessment, offender classification and the role of child abuse. *Criminal Justice and Behavior*, 28(5), 543-563.

Loza, W. & A. Loza-Fanous (2000). Predictive validity of the self-appraisal questionnaire (SAQ): A tool for assessing violent and nonviolent release failures. *Journal of Interpersonal Violence*, 15, 1183-1191.

Loza, W. & A. Loza-Fanous (2001). The effectiveness of the self-appraisal questionnaire in predicting offenders' postrelease outcome: A comparison study. *Criminal Justice and Behavior*, 28, 105-121.

Loza, W. & D.J. Simourd (1994). Psychometric evaluation of the Level of Supervision Inventory (LSI) among male Canadian federal offenders. *Criminal Justice and Behavior*, 21, 468-480.

Luengo, M.A., M.T. Otero, M.T. Carrillo-de-la-Peña & L. Mirón (1994). Dimensions of antisocial behaviour in juvenile delinquency: A study of personality variables. *Psychology, Crime and Law*, 1, 27-37.

Luna, E. (1998). The growth and development of tribal police: Challenges and issues for tribal sovereignty. *Journal of Contemporary Criminal Justice*, 14, 75-86.

Lykken, D.T. (1995). *The antisocial personalities*. Hillsdale, NJ: Lawrence Erlbaum.

Lynam, D.R. (1996). Early identification of chronic offenders: Who is the fledgling psychopath? *Psychological Bulletin*, 120, 209-234.

Lynam, D.R. (1997). Pursuing the psychopath: Capturing the fledgling psychopath in the nomological net. *Journal of Abnormal Psychology*, 106, 425-438.

Lynam, D.R., R., Milich, R. Zimmerman, S.P. Novak, T.K. Logan, C. Martin, C. Leukefeld & R. Clayton (1999). Project DARE: No effects at 10-year follow-up. *Journal of Consulting and Clinical Psychology*, 67, 590-593.

Lynam, D., T. Moffitt & M. Stouthamer-Loeber (1993). Explaining the relation between IQ and delinquency: Class, race, test motivation, school failure, or self-control? *Journal of AbnormalPsychology*, 102, 187-196.

Lyons, M.J., W.R. True, J. Goldberg, J.M. Meyer, S.V. Faraone, L.J. Eaves & M.T. Tsuang (1995). Differential heritability of adult and juvenile antisocial traits. *Archives of General Psychiatry*, 52, 906-915.

Lyons-Ruth, K. (1996). Attachment relationships among children with aggressive behavior problems: The role of disorganized early attachment patterns. *Journal of Consulting and Clinical Psychology*, 64, 64-73.

MacKenzie, D.L., R. Brame, D. McDowall & C. Souryal (1995). Boot camp prisons and recidivism in eight states. *Criminology*, 33, 327-357.

MacLean, B.D. (1986). Critical criminology and some limitations of traditional inquiry. In B.D. MacLean (ed.), *The political economy of crime*. Scarborough, Ontario: Prentice Hall.

MacPhail, D.D. (1989). The moral education approach in treating adult inmates. *Criminal Justice and Behavior*, 16, 81-97.

Magdol, L., T.E. Moffitt, A. Caspi, D.L. Newman, J. Fagan & P.A. Silva (1997). Gender differences in partner violence in a birth cohort of 21-year-olds: Bridging the gap between clinical and epidemiological approaches. *Journal of Consulting and Clinical Psychology*, 65, 68-78.

Maguire, E.R., J.B. Kuhns, C.D. Uchida & S.M. Cox (1997). Patterns of community policing in nonurban America. *Journal of Research in Crime and Delinquency*, 34, 368-394.

Main, M. (1996). Introduction to the special section on attachment and psychopathology: 2. Overview of the field of attachment. *Journal of Consulting and Clinical Psychology*, 64, 237-243.

Mak, A.S. (1990). Testing a psychological control theory of delinquency. *Criminal Justice and Behavior*, 17, 215-230.

Mak, A.S. (1991). Psychosocial control characteristics of delinquents and nondelinquents. *Criminal Justice and Behavior*, 18, 287-303.

Mak, A.S. (1996). Adolescent delinquency and perceptions of parental care and protection: A case control study. *Journal of Family Studies*, 2, 29-39.

Malcolm, P.B., D.A. Andrews & V.L. Quinsey (1993). Discriminant and predictive validity of phallometrically measured sexual age and gender preference. *Journal of Interpersonal Violence*, 8, 486-501.

Maletzky, B.W. (1991). *Treating the sexual offender*. Newbury Park, CA: Sage.

Malgady, RG., L.H. Rogler & W.W. Tryon (1992). Issues of validity in the Diagnostic Interview Schedule. *Journal of Psychiatric Research*, 26, 59-67.

Mannheim, H. (1965). *Comparative criminology*. Boston: Houghton Mifflin.

Margolin, G. & V. Fernandez (1997). The "spontaneous" cessation of marital violence: Three case examples. *Journal of Marital and Family Therapy*, 13, 241-250.

Marlatt, A. & J. Gordon (1980). Determinants of relapse: Implications for the maintenance of behavior change. In P.O. Davidson & S.M. Davidson (eds.), *Behavioral medicine: Changing health lifestyles*. (pp. 410-452). New York: Bruner-Mazel.

Marlatt, A.G. (1996). Models of relapse and relapse prevention: A commentary. *Experimental and Clinical Psychopharmacology*, 4, 55-60.

Marques, J.K., D.M. Day, C. Nelson & M.A. West (1994). Effects of cognitive-behavioral treatment and sexual recidivism: Preliminary results of a longitudinal study. *Criminal Justice and Behavior*, 21, 28-54.

Marques, J.. & C. Nelson (1992). The relapse prevention model: Can it work with sex offenders? In R.D. Peters, R.J. McMahon & V.L. Quinsey (eds.), *Aggression and violence throughout the life span* (pp. 222- 243). Newbury Park, CA: Sage.

Marquis, H.A., G.A. Bourgon, B. Armstrong & J. Pfaff (1996). Reducing recidivism through institutional treatment programs. *Forum on Corrections Research*, 8, 3-5.

Marshall, T.F. & S. Merry (1990). *Crime and victim accountability: Victim/offender mediation in practice*. London: Home Office.

Marshall, W.L. (1996). Assessment, treatment, and theorizing about sex offenders: Developments during the past twenty years and future directions. *Criminal Justice and Behavior*, 23, 162-199.

Marshall, W.L. & H. Barbaree (1990). Outcome of comprehensive cognitive-behavioral treatment programs. In W.L. Marshall, D.R. Laws & H.E. Barbaree (eds.), *Handbook of sexual assault: Issues, theories, and treatment of the offender* (pp. 363-385). New York: Plenum.

Marshall, W.L., R. Jones, T. Ward, P. Johnston & H.E. Barbaree (1991). Treatment outcome with sex offenders. *Clinical Psychology Review*, 11, 465-485.

Mathiesen, T. (1998). Selective incapacitation revisited. *Law and Human Behavior*, 22, 455-469.

Martinson, R. (1974). What works?—Questions and answers about prison reform. *The Public Interest*, 35, 22-54.

Martinson, R. (1976). California research at the crossroads. *Crime & Delinquency*, 22, 178-191.

Martinson, R. (1979). New findings, new views: A note of caution regarding prison reform. *Hofstra Law Review*, 7, 243-258.

Mason, D.A. & P.J. Frick (1994). The heritability of antisocial behavior: A meta-analysis of twin and adoption studies. *Journal of Psychopathology and Behavioral Assessment*, 16, 301-323.

Matseuda, R.L. & K. Anderson (1998). The dynamics of delinquent peers and delinquent behavior. *Criminology*, 36, 269-308.

Matson, J.L. & A.E. Kazdin (1981). Punishment in behavior modification: Pragmatic, ethical, and legal issues. *Clinical Psychology Review*, 1, 197-210.

Matza, D. (1964). *Delinquency and drift* (2nd ed.). New York: Wiley.

Maung, N.A. & N. Hammond (2000). Risk of re-offending and needs assessment: The user's perspective. *Home Office Research Study 216*. London: Home Office.

Maxwell, G.M. & A. Morris (1994). The New Zealand model of family group conferences. In C. Adler & J. Wundersitz (eds.), *Family conferencing and juvenile justice: The way forward or misplaced optimism?* (pp. 15-43). Canberra: Australian Institute of Criminology.

Mayer, R.R. (1972). *Social planning and social change.* Englewood Cliffs, NJ: Prentice Hall.

Mazerolle, P., R. Brame, R. Paternoster, A. Piquero & C. Dean (2000). Onset age, persistence, and offending versatility: Comparisons across gender. *Criminology*, 38, 1143-1172.

McClaren, K. (1992). *Reducing reoffending: What works now.* Auckland, New Zealand: Penal Division, Department of Justice.

McCarthy, J.G. & A.L. Stewart (1998). Neutralisation as a process of graduated desensitisation: Moral values of offenders. *International Journal of Offender Therapy and Comparative Criminology*, 42, 278-290.

McClellan, A.T., L. Luborsky, C.P. O'Brien & G.E. Woody (1980). An improved diagnostic instrument for substance abusing patients: The Addiction Severity Index. *Journal of Nervous and Mental Disease*, 168, 26-33.

McClosky, L.A., A.J. Figueredo, J. Aurelio & M.P. Koss (1995). The effects of systemic family violence on children's mental health. *Child Development*, 66, 1239-1261.

McCold, P. (1998). *Restorative justice handbook.* New York,: Alliance of Non-Governmental Organizations (NGOS) Crime Prevention and Criminal Justice.

McCold, P. (2000). Toward a holistic vision of restorative juvenile justice: A reply to the maximalist model. *Contemporary Justice Review*, 3, 357-414.

McCold, P. & B. Wachtel (1998). *Restorative policing experiment: The Bethlehem Pennsylvania police family group conferencing project.* Pipersville, PA: Community Service Foundation.

McCord, J. (1997). Discipline and the use of sanctions. *Aggression and Violent Behavior*, 2, 313-319.

McCord, J. (1999). Interventions: Punishment, diversion, and alternative routes to crime prevention. In A.K. Hess & I.B. Weiner (eds.), *The handbook of forensic psychology* (2nd ed.) (pp. 559-579). New York: Wiley.

McCord, J., R.E. Tremblay, F. Vitaro & L. Desmarais-Gervais (1994). Boys' disruptive behaviour, school adjustment, and delinquency: The Montreal prevention experiment. *International Journal of Behavioral Development*, 17, 739-752.

McCrady, B.S. (2000). Alcohol use disorders and the division 12 task force of the American Psychological Association. *Psychology of Addictive Behaviors*, 14, 267-276.

McGuire, J. (2001). *Methods to reduce the risk of re-offending: International perspectives.* Invited address to the "What Works" seminar, Helsinki, Finland, October.

McGuire, J. & P. Priestly (1995). Reviewing what works: Past, present and future. In J. McGuire (ed.), *What works: Reducing reoffending—Guidelines from research and practice* (pp. 3-34). Chichester, England: Wiley.

McIvor, G. (1995). Practitioner evaluation in probation. In J. McGuire (ed.), *What works: Reducing reoffending—Guidelines from research and practice* (pp. 209-219). Chichester, England: Wiley.

Mears, D.P., M. Ploeger & M. Warr (1998). Explaining the gender gap in delinquency: Peer influence and moral evaluations of behavior. *Journal of Research in Crime and Delinquency*, 35, 251-266.

Mednick, S.A. (1977). A bio-social theory of the learning of law-abiding behavior. In S.A. Mednick & K.O. Christiansen (eds.), *Biosocial basis of criminal behavior* (pp. 1-8). New York: Gardner Press.

Mednick, S.A., W.F. Gabrielli & B. Hutchings (1983). Genetic influences in criminal convictions: Evidence from an adoption cohort. In K.T. Van Dusen & S.A. Mednick (eds.), *Prospective studies of crime and delinquency* (pp. 39-56). Hingham, MA: Kluwer Nijhoff.

Mednick, S.A., W.F. Gabrielli & B. Hutchings (1984). Genetic influences in criminal convictions: Evidence from an adoption cohort. *Science*, 234, 891-894.

Mednick, S.A., W.F. Gabrielli & B. Hutchings (1987). Genetic factors in the etiology of criminal behavior. In S.A. Mednick, T.E. Moffitt & S.A. Stack (eds.), *The causes of crime: New biological approaches* (pp. 74-91). Cambridge, England: Cambridge University Press.

Mednick, S.A., T. Moffitt, W. Gabrielli & B. Hutchings (1986). Genetic factors in criminal behavior: A review. In D. Olweus, J. Block & M. Radke-Yarrow (eds.), *Development of antisocial and prosocial behavior: Research, theories, and issues* (pp. 33-50). New York: Academic Press.

Meehan, K.E. (2000). California's three-strikes law: The first six years. *Corrections Management Quarterly*, 4, 22-33.

Meehl, P.E. (1954). *Clinical versus Statistical Prediction*. Minneapolis: University of Minnesota Press.

Meehl, P.E. (1995). Bootstraps taxometrics: Solving the classification problem in psychopathology. *American Psychologist*, 50, 266-275.

Megargee, E.I. (1972). *The California Psychological Inventory handbook*. San Francisco: Jossey-Bass.

Megargee, E.I. (1982). Psychological determinants and correlates of criminal violence. In M.E. Wolfgang & N.A. Weinder (eds.), *Criminal Violence* (pp. 81-170). Beverly Hills: Sage.

Megargee, E.I. (1994). Using the Megargee MMPI-based classification system with MMPI-2s of male inmates. *Psychological Assessment*, 6, 337-344.

Megargee, E.I. & M.J. Bohn, Jr. (1979). *Classifying criminal offenders: A new system based on the MMPI*. Beverly Hills: Sage.

Megargee, E.I., P.E. Cook & G.A. Mendelsohn (1967). Development and validation of an MMPI scale of assaultiveness in overcontrolled individuals. *Journal of Abnormal Psychology*, 72, 519-528.

Meichenbaum, D.A. (1977). *Cognitive-behavior modification: An integrative approach*. New York: Plenum.

Meloy, J.R. (1992). Discussion of "On the predictability of violent behavior: Considerations and guidelines." *Journal of Forensic Sciences*, 37, 949-950.

Meloy, J.R. (1996). Stalking (obsessional following): A review of some preliminary studies. *Aggression and Violent Behavior*, 1, 147-162.

Meloy, J.R. (1998) (ed.). *The psychology of stalking: Clinical and forensic perspectives.* New York: Academic Press

Menard, S. (1995). A developmental test of Mertonian anomie theory. *Journal of Research in Crime and Delinquency,* 32, 136-174.

Merton, R.K. (1938). Social structure and anomie. *American Sociological Review,* 3, 672-682.

Merton, R.K. (1957). *Social theory and social structure.* New York: Free Press.

Mikulincer, M. (1994). *Human learned helplessness: A coping perspective.* New York: Plenum Press.

Miller, J. (1995). Criminal justice policy as social policy. In J. McGuire & B. Rowson (eds.), *Does punishment work?* London: Institute for the Study and Treatment of Delinquency, King's College.

Miller, W.B. (1958). Lower class culture as a generating milieu of gang delinquency. *Journal of Social Issues,* 14, 5-19.

Miller, W.R. (1990). Alcohol treatment alternatives: What works? In H.B. Milkman & L.I. Sederer (eds.), *Treatment choices for alcoholism and substance abuse* (pp.253-264). Lexington, MA: Lexington Books.

Miller, W.R. & R.K. Hester (1986). The effectiveness of alcoholism treatment: What research reveals. In W.R. Miller & N. Heather (eds.), *Treating addictive behaviors: Process of change* (pp. 121-174). New York: Plenum.

Miller, W.R. & S. Rollick (1991). *Motivational interviewing: Preparing people to change addictive behavior.* New York: Guilford.

Mobley, M.J. (1999). Psychotherapy with criminal offenders. In A.K. Hess & I.B. Weiner (eds.), *The handbook of forensic psychology* (2nd ed.) (pp. 603-639). New York: Wiley.

Moffitt, T.E. (1983). The learning theory model of punishment: Implications for delinquency deterrence. *Criminal Justice and Behavior,* 10, 131-158.

Moffitt, T.E. (1987). Parental mental disorder and offspring criminal behavior: An adoption study. *Psychiatry,* 50, 346-360.

Moffitt, T.E. (1990). The neuropsychology of juvenile delinquency. In M. Tonry & N. Morris (eds.), *Crime and justice: A review of research, Vol. 8* (pp. 99-169). Chicago: University of Chicago Press.

Moffitt, T.E. (1993). "Life-course-persistent" and "adolescent-limited" antisocial behavior: A developmental taxonomy. *Psychological Review,* 100, 674-701.

Moffitt, T.E. (1997). Adolescence-limited and life-course-persistent offending: A complementary pair of developmental theories. In T.P. Thornberry (ed.), *Developmental theories of criminal behavior* (pp. 11-54). New Brunswick, NJ: Transaction Publishers.

Moffitt, T.E. & P.A. Silva (1988). IQ and delinquency: A direct test of the differential detection hypothesis. *Journal of Abnormal Psychology,* 97, 330-333.

Moffitt, T.E., D.R. Lynam & P.A. Silva (1994). Neuropsychological tests predicting persistent male delinquency. *Criminology,* 32, 277-300.

Monahan, J. (ed.). (1980). *Who is the client?: The ethics of psychological intervention in the criminal justice system.* Washington, DC: American Psychological Association.

Montmarquette, C. & M. Nerlove (1985). Deterrence and delinquency: An analysis of individual data. *Journal of Quantitative Criminology*, 1, 37-58.

Moody, C.E. & T.B. Marvell (1996). The uncertain timing of innovations in time series: Minnesota sentencing guidelines and jail sentences—a comment. *Criminology*, 34, 257-267.

Morash, M. (1983). An explanation of juvenile delinquency: The integration of moral-reasoning theory and sociological knowledge. In W.S. Laufer & J.M. Day (eds.), *Personality theory, moral development, and criminal behavior* (pp. 385-409). Lexington: MA: Lexington Books.

Morris, A. & G. Maxwell (1997). *Family group conferences and convictions.* Occasional Papers in Criminology New Series, No. 5. Wellington, New Zealand: Institute of Criminology.

Morris, A. & G. Maxwell (1998). Restorative justice in New Zealand: Family group conferences as a case study. *Western Criminology Review*, 1. Online at http://wcr.sono ma.edu/v1n1/morris.html

Morris, N. & M. Tonry (1990). *Between prison and probation: Intermediate punishment in a rational sentencing system.* New York: Oxford University Press.

Moss, C.S., M.E. Johnson & R.E. Hosford (1984). An assessment of the Megargee typology in lifelong criminal violence. *Criminal Justice and Behavior*, 11, 225-234.

Mossman, D. (1994). Assessing predictions of violence: Being accurate about accuracy. *Journal of Consulting and Clinical Psychology*, 62, 783-792.

Motiuk, L.L., J. Bonta & D.A. Andrews (1986). Classification in correctional halfway houses: The relative and incremental predictive criterion validities of the Megargee-MMPI and LSI systems. *Criminal Justice and Behavior*, 13, 33-46.

Motiuk, L.L., J. Bonta & D.A. Andrews (1990). *Dynamic predictive criterion validity in offender assessment.* Paper presented at the Canadian Psychological Association Annual Convention, June, Ottawa.

Müller-Isberner, R. & S. Hodgins (2000). Evidence-based treatment for mentally disordered offenders. In S. Hodgins & R. Müller-Isberner (eds.), *Violence, crime and mentally disordered offenders* (pp. 7-38). New York: Wiley.

Murphy, B.C. (1972). *A quantitative test of the effectiveness of an experimental treatment program for delinquent opiate addicts.* Ottawa: Information Canada.

Murphy, W.D. & J.M. Peters (1992). Profiling child sexual abusers: Psychological considerations. *Criminal Justice and Behavior*, 19, 24-37.

Netherlands (2001). *Guidebook for effective criminal justice interventions.* Amsterdam: Directorate Prevention, Youth and Sanction Policy, Ministry of Justice.

Nettler, G. (1989). *Criminology lessons: Arguments about crime, punishment and the interpretation of conduct, with advice for individuals and prescriptions for public policy.* Cincinnati: Anderson.

New Zealand (1999), *Straight thinking: Interventions to reduce re-offending.* Auckland, New Zealand: Department of Corrections.

Newman, G. (1976). *Comparative deviance: Perception and law in six cultures.* New York: Elsevier.

Newman, G. (1995). *Just and painful: A case for the corporal punishment of criminals* (2nd ed.). New York: Harrow and Heston.

Newman, J.P. (1989). *Response modulation deficits in psychopaths: A matter of perspective*. Paper presented at the meeting of the International Society for the Study of Individual Differences, Heidelberg, Germany.

Newman, J.P., C.M. Patterson & D.S. Kosson (1987). Response perseveration in psychopaths. *Journal of Abnormal Psychology*, 96, 145-148.

Newsom, C., J.E. Flavell & A. Rincover (1983). The side effects of punishment. In S. Axelrod & J. Apsche (eds.), *The effects of punishment on human behavior* (pp. 285-316). New York: Academic Press.

Novaco, R. (1975). *Anger control: The development and evaluation of an experimental treatment*. Lexington, MA: Lexington Books.

Nuffield, J. (1982). *Parole decision-making in Canada*. Ottawa: Solicitor General of Canada.

Nuffield, J. (1997). *Evaluation of the adult victim-offender mediation program Saskatoon community mediation services*. Regina, Saskatchewan: Saskatchewan Justice.

Nugent, W.R. & J.B. Paddock (1995). The effect of victim-offender mediation on severity of reoffense. *Mediation Quarterly*, 12, 353-367.

O'Donnell, C.R., T. Lydgate & W.S.O. Fo (1971). The buddy system: Review and follow-up. *Child Behavior Therapy*, 1, 161-169.

Office of National Drug Control Policy (1999). Drug data summary. See www.white housedrugpolicy.gov

Ogloff, J.R.P., S. Wong & A. Greenwood (1990). Treating criminal psychopaths in a therapeutic community program. *Behavioral Sciences and the Law*, 8, 181-190.

O'Keefe, M. (1999). *Reliability and construct validity of the LSI for Colorado inmates*. Paper presented at the annual conference of the American Society of Criminology, November, Toronto, Canada.

O'Keefe, M., K.J. Klebe & C.S. Hromas (1998). "Validation of the Level of Supervision Inventory (LSI) for community-based offenders in Colorado: Phase II. Colorado Springs, CO: Colorado Department of Corrections.

O'Leary, K.D., J. Malone & A. Tyree (1994). Physical aggression in early marriage: Prerelationship and relationship effects. *Journal of Consulting and Clinical Psychology*, 62, 594-602.

Ottawa Citizen (2001). Record 8 executions set in Oklahoma. *The Ottawa Citizen*, January 2, 2001.

Pagani, L., R.E. Tremblay, F. Vitaro, M. Kerr & P. McDuff (1998a). The impact of family transition on the development of delinquency in adolescent boys: A 9-year longitudinal study. *Journal of Child Psychology and Psychiatry and Allied Disciplines*, 39, 489-499.

Pagani, L., R.E. Tremblay, F. Vitaro & S. Parent (1998b). Does preschool help prevent delinquency in boys with a history of perinatal complications? *Criminology*, 36, 245-268.

Palarea, R.E., M.A. Zona, J.C. Lane & J. Langhinrichsen-Rohling (1999). The dangerous nature of intimate relationship stalking: Threats, violence, and associated risk factors. *Behavioral Sciences and the Law*, 17, 269-283.

Palmer, E.J. & C.R. Hollin (1998). A comparison of patterns of moral development in young offenders and non-offenders. *Legal and Criminological Psychology*, 3, 225-235.

Palmer, T. (1974). The Youth Authority's community treatment project. *Federal Probation*, (March): 3-14.

Palmer, T. (1975). Martinson revisited. *Journal of Research in Crime and Delinquency*, 12, 133-152.

Palmer, T. (1983). The effectiveness issue today: An overview. *Federal Probation*, 46, 3-10.

Pan, H.S., P.H. Neidig & K.D. O'Leary (1994). Predicting mild and severe husband-to-wife physical aggression. *Journal of Consulting and Clinical Psychology*, 62, 975-981.

Parent, D.G., M. Chaiken & W. Logan (1989). *Shock incarceration: An overview of existing programs*. Washington, DC: Office of Justice Programs, U.S. Department of Justice.

Parker, R.N. & K. Auerhaln (1999). Drugs, alcohol, and suicide: Issues in theory and research. In D.M. Smith & M.A. Zahn (eds.), *Homicide: A sourcebook of social research* (pp. 176-191). Thousand Oaks, CA: Sage.

Passas, N. & R. Agnew (eds) (1997). *The future of anomie theory*. Boston: Northeastern University Press.

Patterson, G.R. (1982). *Coercive family process*. Eugene, OR: Castalia.

Patterson, G.R. (1997). Performance models for parenting: A social interactional perspective. In J.E. Grusec & L. Kuczynski (eds.), *Parenting and children's internalization of values: A handbook of contemporary theory* (pp. 193-226). New York: Wiley.

Patterson, G.R., D.S. DeGarmo & N. Knutson (2000). Hyperactive and antisocial behaviors: Comorbid or two points in the same process? *Development and Psychopathology*, 12, 91-106.

Patterson, G.R. & K. Yoerger (1999). Intraindividual growth in covert antisocial behaviour: a necessary precursor to chronic juvenile and adult arrests? *Criminal Behaviour and Mental Health*, 9, 24-38.

Peachy, D.E. (1989). The Kitchener experiment. In M. Wright & B. Galaway (eds.), *Mediation and criminal justice: Victims, offenders and community* (pp. 14-26). Newbury Park, CA: Sage.

Pearson, F.S. & D.S. Lipton (1999). A meta-analytic review of the effectiveness of corrections-based treatments for drug abuse. *The Prison Journal*, 79, 384-410.

Pearson, F.S., D.S. Lipton & C.M. Cleland (1996). *Some preliminary findings from the CDATE project*. Paper presented at the annual meeting of the American Society of Criminology, Chicago, Illinois.

Perez, C. (1993). Stalking: When does obsession become a crime? *American Journal of Criminal Law*, 20, 263-280.

Perkins, D. (1991). Clinical work with sex offenders in secure settings. In C.R. Hollins & K. Howells (eds.), *Clinical approaches to sex offenders and their victims* (pp. 151-177). Chichester, England: Wiley.

Perkins, D. (1993). Psychological perspectives on working with sex offenders. In J.M. Ussher & C.D. Baker (eds.), *Psychological perspectives on sexual problems: New directions in theory and practice* (pp. 168-205). London: Routledge.

Perry, D. (2001). *What works in England and Wales*. Invited address to the International Congress on the Effectiveness of Criminal Justice Sanctions, Amsterdam, The Netherlands, October.

Perry, L., T. Lajeunesse & A. Woods (1987). *Mediation services: An evaluation*. Winnipeg, Manitoba: Manitoba Attorney General.

Peters, S.D., G.E. Wyatt & D. Finkelhor (1986). Prevalence. In D. Finkelhor (ed.), *A sourcebook on child sexual abuse* (pp. 15-59). Beverly Hills: Sage.

Petersilia, J. (1998). *A decade of experimenting with intermediate sanctions: What have we learned?* Washington, DC: National Institute of Justice.

Petersilia, J. & S. Turner (1993). *Evaluating intensive supervision probation/parole: Results of a nationwide experiment*. Washington, DC: National Institute of Justice, Research in Brief.

Peterson, D.R., H.C. Quay & G.R. Cameron (1959). Personality and background factors in juvenile delinquency as inferred from questionnaire responses. *Journal of Consulting Psychology*, 23, 395-399.

Petraitis, J., B.R. Flay & T.Q. Miller (1995). Reviewing theories of adolescent substance use: Organizing pieces in the puzzle. *Psychological Bulletin*, 117, 67-86.

Petrosino, A., C. Turpin-Petrosino & J.O. Finckenauer (2000). Well-meaning programs have harmful effects! Lessons from experiments of programs such as Scared Straight. *Crime & Delinquency*, 46, 354-379.

Phillips, K.A. & J.G. Gunderson (1999). Personality disorders. In R.E. Hales, S.C. Yudofsky & J.A. Talbot (eds.), *Textbook of Psychiatry* (3rd. ed.) (pp. 795-805). Washington, DC: American Psychiatric Press.

Pichot, P. (1978). Psychopathic behavior: A historical overview. In R.D. Hare & D. Schalling (eds.), *Psychopathic behavior* (pp. 55-70). New York: Wiley.

Piliavin, I.M., J.A. Hardyck & A.G. Vadum (1968). Constraining effects of personal costs on the transgressions of juveniles. *Journal of Personality and Social Psychology*, 10, 227-231.

Piliavin, I.M., C. Thornton, R. Gartner & R.L. Matsueda (1986). Crime, deterrence, and rational choice. *American Sociological Review*, 51, 101-119.

Piquero, A.R. & T. Brezina (2001). Testing Moffitt's account of adolescence-limited delinquency. *Criminology*, 39, 353-370.

Platt, J., G.M. Perry & D.S. Metsge (1980). The evaluation of a heroin addiction treatment program within a correctional environment. In R.R. Ross & P. Gendreau (eds.), *Effective correctional treatment* (pp. 419-463). Toronto: Butterworth.

Platt, J.J. & M.F. Prout (1987). Cognitive-behavioral theory and interventions for crime and delinquency. In E.K. Morris & C.J. Braukmann (eds.), *Behavioral approaches to crime and delinquency: A handbook of applications, research, and concepts* (pp. 477-497). New York: Plenum.

Plomin, R. (1989). Environment and genes: Determinants of behavior. *American Psychologist*, 44, 105-111.

Porter, S. (1996). Without conscience or without active conscience? The etiology of psychopathy revisited. *Aggression and Violent Behavior*, 1, 179-189.

Pratt, T.C. (1998). Race and sentencing: A meta-analysis of conflicting empirical research results. *Journal of Criminal Justice*, 26, 513-523.

Pratt, T.C. & F.T. Cullen (2000). The empirical status of Gottfredson and Hirschi's general theory of crime: A meta-analysis. *Criminology*, 38, 931-964.

Prentky, R. (1985). The neurochemistry and neuroendocrinology of sexual aggression: Review and metatheory. In D.P. Farrington & J. Gunn (eds.), *Aggression and dangerousness* (pp.7-55). Sussex, England: Wiley.

Prentky, R.A., A.W. Burgess, F. Rokus, A. Lee, C.R. Hartman & R. Ressler (1989). The presumptive role of fantasy in serial sexual homicide. *American Journal of Psychiatry*, 146, 887-891.

Priest, B.J., S.T. Kordinak & T.F. Wynkoop (1991). Type of offense and level of moral development among adult male inmates. *Journal of Addictions and Offender Counseling*, 12, 2-11.

Prochaska, J.O. & C.C. DiClemente (1982). Transtheoretical therapy: Toward a more integrative model of change. *Psychotherapy: Theory, Research and Practice*, 19, 276-278.

Prochaska, J.O., C.C. DiClemente & J.C. Norcross (1992). In search of how people change: Applications to addictive behaviors. *American Psychologist*, 47, 1102-1114.

Project MATCH Research Group (1997). Matching alcoholism treatments to client heterogeneity: Project MATCH posttreatment drinking outcomes. *Journal of Studies in Alcohol*, 58, 7-29.

Putnins, A.L. (1997). Victim awareness programs for delinquent youths: Effects on moral reasoning maturity. *Adolescence*, 32, 709-714.

Quay, H.C. (1965). Psychopathic personality as pathological stimulus-seeking. American *Journal of Psychiatry*, 122, 180-183.

Quay, H.C. (1977). The three faces of evaluation: What can be expected to work. *Criminal Justice and Behavior*, 4, 341-354.

Quay, H.C. (1984). *Managing adult inmates: Classification for housing and program assignments*. College Park, MD: American Correctional Association.

Quigely, B.M. & K.E. Leonard (1996). Desistance of husband aggression in the early years of marriage. *Violence and Victims*, 11, 355-370.

Quinsey, V.L., G.T. Harris, M.E. Rice & C.A. Cormier (1998). Violent offenders: Appraising and managing risk. Washington, DC: American Psychological Association.

Quinsey, V.L., G. Coleman, B. Jones & I.F. Altrow (1997). Proximal antecedents of eloping and reoffending among mentally disordered offenders. *Journal of Interpersonal Violence*, 12, 794-813.

Raine, A. (1997). Antisocial behavior and psychophysiology: A biosocial perspective and a prefrontal dysfunction hypothesis. In D.M. Stoff, J. Breiling & J.D. Maser (eds.), *Handbook of antisocial behavior* (pp. 289-304). New York: Wiley.

Raine, A., T. Lencz, S. Bihrle, L. LaCasse & P. Colletti (2000). Reduced prefrontal gray matter volume and reduced autonomic activity in antisocial personality disorder. *Archives of General Psychiatry*, 57, 119-129.

Rajkumar, A.S. & M.T. French (1997). Drug abuse, crime costs, and the economic benefits of treatment. *Journal of Quantitative Criminology*, 13, 291-323.

Rankin, J.H. & R. Kern (1994). Parental attachments and delinquency. *Criminology*, 32, 495-515.

Raynor, P., J. Kynch, C. Roberts & S. Merrington (2000). *Risk and need assessment in probation services: an evaluation*. Home Office Research Study No. 211. London: Home Office

Raynor, P., D. Sutton & M. Vanstone (1995). The STOP program. In R.R. Ross & R.D. Ross (eds.), *Thinking straight: The reasoning and rehabilitation program for delinquency prevention and offender rehabilitation* (pp. 313-339). Ottawa: Air Training and Publications.

Raynor, P. & M. Vanstone (2001). "Straight thinking on probation": Evidence-based practice and the culture of curiosity. In G.A. Bernfeld, D.P. Farrington & A.W. Leschied (eds.), *Offender rehabilitation in practice* (pp. 189-203). Chichester, England: Wiley

Reckless, W.C. (1967). *The crime problem.* New York: Appleton-Century-Crofts.

Reckless, W.C. & S. Dinitz (1972). *The prevention of delinquency.* Columbus: Ohio State University Press.

Redondo, S., V. Garrido & J. Sanchez-Meca (1999). The influence of treatment programs on the recidivism of juvenile and adult offenders: A European meta-analytic review. *Psychology, Crime, and Law*, 5, 251-278.

Reid, W.H. & C. Gacono (2000). Treatment of antisocial personality, psychopathy, and other characterologic antisocial syndromes. *Behavioral Sciences and the Law*, 18, 647-662.

Reiss, D., M. Hetherington, R. Plomin & G.W. Howe (1995). Genetic questions for environmental studies: Differential parenting and psychopathology in adolescence. *Archives of General Psychiatry*, 52, 925-936.

Reitsma-Street, M. & A.W. Leschied (1988). The conceptual-level matching model in corrections. *Criminal Justice and Behavior*, 15, 92-108.

Reitzel-Jaffe, D. & D. Wolfe (2001). Predictors of relationship abuse among young men. *Journal of Interpersonal Violence*, 16, 99-115.

Rennison, C.M. & S. Welchans (2000). *Intimate partner violence.* Washington, DC: Bureau of Justice Statistics, Special Report.

Resick, P.A. (1993). The psychological impact of rape. *Journal of Interpersonal Violence*, 8, 223-255.

Ressler, R.K., A.W. Burgess, C.R. Hartman, J.E. Douglas & A. McCormack (1986). Murderers who rape and mutilate. *Journal of Interpersonal Violence*, 1, 273-287.

Rettinger, L.J. (1998). *A recidivism follow-up study investigating risk and need within a sample of provincially sentenced women.* Unpublished doctoral dissertation, Carleton University, Ottawa, Canada.

Rice, M.E., T.C. Chaplin, G.T. Harris & J. Coutts (1994). Empathy for the victim and sexual arousal among rapists and nonrapists. *Journal of Interpersonal Violence*, 9, 435-449.

Rice, M.E. & G.T. Harris (1997). Cross validation and extension of the Violence Risk Appraisal Guide with child molesters and rapists. *Law and Human Behavior*, 21, 231-241.

Rice, M.E., G.T. Harris & C.A. Cormier (1992). An evaluation of a maximum security therapeutic community for psychopaths and other mentally disordered offenders. *Law and Human Behavior*, 16, 399-412.

Rice, M.E., G.T. Harris & V.L. Quinsey (1991). Evaluation of an institution-based program for child molesters. *Canadian Journal of Program Evaluation*, 6, 111-129.

Rice, M.E., V.L. Quinsey & R. Houghton (1990). Predicting treatment outcome and recidivism among patients in a maximum security token economy. *Behavioral Sciences and the Law*, 8, 313-326.

Rimmele, C.T., M.O. Howard & M.L. Hilfrink (1995). Aversion therapies. In R.K. Hester & W.R. Miller (eds.), *Handbook of alcoholism treatment approaches: Effective alternatives* (2nd ed.) (pp. 134-147). Boston: Allyn & Bacon.

Roberts, J.V. & L.J. Stalens (1998). Crime, criminal justice, and public opinion. In M.H. Tonry (ed.), *The handbook of crime and punishment* (pp. 31-57). London: Oxford Press.

Robins, L. (1966) *Deviant children grown up: A sociological and psychiatric study of sociopathic personality.* Baltimore: Williams and Wilkins.

Robins, L. & J E. Helzer (1994). The half-life of a structured interview: The NIMH Diagnostic Interview Schedule (DIS). *International Journal of Methods in Psychiatry Research*, 4, 95-102.

Robinson, D. (1995). *The impact of cognitive skills training on post-release recidivism among Canadian federal offenders (R-41).* Ottawa: Correctional Service of Canada.

Robinson, D. & F.J. Porporino (2001). Programming in cognitive skills: The reasoning and rehabilitation programme. In C.R. Hollin (ed.), *Handbook of offender assessment and treatment* (pp. 179-193). Chichester, England: Wiley.

Rogers, C. (1961). *On becoming a person.* Boston: Houghton Mifflin.

Rogers, S. (1981). *Factors related to recidivism among adult probationers in Ontario.* Toronto: Ontario Ministry of Correctional Services.

Rooney, J. & R.K. Hanson (2001). Predicting attrition from treatment programs for abusive men. *Journal of Family Violence*, 16, 131-149.

Rosenbaum, D.P., R.L. Flewelling, S.L. Bailey, C.L. Ringwalt & D.L. Wilkinson (1994). Cops in the classroom: A longitudinal evaluation of drug abuse resistance education (DARE). *Journal of Research in Crime and Delinquency*, 31, 3-31.

Rosenbaum, D.P. & G.S. Hanson (1998). Assessing the effects of school-based drug education: A six-year multilevel analysis of project D.A.R.E. *Journal of Research in Crime and Delinquency*, 35, 381-412.

Rosenbaum, D.P. & A.J. Lurigio (1994). An inside look at community policing reform: Definitions, organizational changes, and evaluation findings. *Crime & Delinquency*, 40, 299-314.

Rosenfeld, B.D. (1992). Court-ordered treatment of spouse abuse. *Clinical Psychology Review*, 12, 205-226.

Rosenstein, D.S. & H.A. Horowitz (1996). Adolescent attachment and psychopathology. *Journal of Consulting and Clinical Psychology*, 64, 244-253.

Rosenthal, R. (1984). *Meta-analytic procedures for social research.* Beverly Hills: Sage.

Ross, R.R. (1995). The reasoning and rehabilitation program for high-risk probationers and prisoners. In R.R. Ross, D.H. Antonowicz & G.K. Dhaliwal (eds.), *Going straight: Effective delinquency prevention and offender rehabilitation* (pp. 195-222). Ottawa: Air Training and Publications.

Ross, R.,R., D.H. Antonowicz & G.K. Dhaliwal (eds.) (1995). *Going straight: Effective delinquency prevention and offender rehabilitation.* Ottawa: Air Training and Publications.

Ross, R.R. & E.A. Fabiano (1985). *Time to think: A cognitive model of delinquency prevention and offender rehabilitation.* Johnson City, TN: Institute of Social Science and Arts.

Ross, R.R., E.A. Fabiano & C.D. Ewles (1988). Reasoning and rehabilitation. *International Journal of Offender Therapy and Comparative Criminology, 32,* 29-35.

Ross, R.R. & P. Gendreau (eds.) (1980). *Effective correctional treatment.* Toronto: Butterworth.

Ross, R.R. & R.D. Ross (1995). The R & R program. In R.R. Ross & R.D. Ross (eds.), *Thinking straight: The reasoning and rehabilitation program for delinquency prevention and offender rehabilitation* (pp. 83-120). Ottawa: Air Training and Publications.

Ross, S.M. (1996). Risk of physical abuse to children of spouse abusing parents. *Child Abuse and Neglect, 20,* 589-598.

Rothbart, M.K. & S.A. Ahadi (1994). Temperament and the development of personality. *Journal of Abnormal Psychology, 103,* 55-66.

Rowe, D.C. (1983). Biometrical models of self-reported delinquent behavior: A twin study. *Behavior Genetics, 13,* 473-489.

Rowe, D.C. & D.P. Farrington (1997). The familial transmission of criminal convictions. *Criminology, 35,* 177-201.

Rowe, D.C. & D.W. Osgood (1984). Heredity and sociological theories of delinquency: A reconsideration. *American Sociological Review, 49,* 526-540.

Rowe, R.C. (1996). *Parole Decision Making in Ontario.* Report for the Ontario Ministry of the Solicitor General and Correctional Services, Toronto, Ontario.

Rubington, E. & M.S. Weinberg (1973). *Deviance: the interactionist perspective.* New York: Macmillan.

Rutter, M., B. Maughan, P. Mortimore & J. Ouston (1979). *Fifteen thousand hours: Secondary schools and their effects on children.* Cambridge, MA: Harvard University Press.

Salekin, R.T., R. Roger & K.W. Sewell (1996). A review and meta-analysis of the Psychopathy Checklist and Psychopathy Checklist-Revised: Predictive validity of dangerousness. *Clinical Psychology: Science and Practice, 3,* 203-215.

Sampson, R.J. & J.H. Laub (1990). Crime and development over the life course: The salience of adult social bonds. *American Sociological Review, 55,* 609-627.

Sampson, R.J. & S.W. Raudenbush (2001). *Disorder in urban neighborhoods—Does it lead to crime?* Washington, DC: National Institute of Justice, Research in Brief.

Sandberg, A.A., G.F. Koepf, T. Ishihara & J.S. Hauschka (1961). An XYY human male. *Lancet, 2* (August), 488-489.

Saudino, K.J., S. McGuire, D. Reiss, M.E. Hetherington & R. Plomin (1995). Parent ratings of EAS temperaments in twins, full siblings, half siblings, and step siblings. *Journal of Personality and Social Psychology, 68,* 723-733.

Saunders, B. & M. Houghton (1996). Relapse revisited: A critique of current concepts and clinical practice in the management of alcohol problems. *Addictive Behaviors, 21,* 843-855.

Saunders, D.G. (1995). Prediction of wife assault. In J.C. Campbell (ed.), *Assessing dangerousness: Violence by sexual offenders, batterers, and child abusers* (pp. 68-95). Thousand Oaks, CA: Sage.

Saunders, D.G. (1996). Feminist-cognitive-behavioral and process-psychodynamic treatment for men who batter: Interaction of abuser traits and treatment models. *Violence and Victims*, 11, 393-414.

Saunders, D.G. & S.T. Azar (1989). Treatment programs for family violence. In L. Ohlin & M. Tonry (eds.), *Family violence* (pp. 481-546). Chicago: University of Chicago Press.

Sawle, G.A. & J. Kear-Colwell (2001). Adult attachment style and pedophilia: A developmental perspective. *International Journal of Offender Therapy and Comparative Criminology*, 45, 32-50.

Schiraldi, V. & T.-J. Ambrosio (1997). *Striking out: The crime control impact of "three strikes" laws*. Washington, DC: The Justice Policy Institute.

Schmidt, A.K. (1998). Electronic monitoring: A review of the empirical literature. *Journal of Contemporary Criminal Justice*, 5, 141-153.

Schmidt, J.D. & L.W. Sherman (1996). Does arrest deter domestic violence? In E.S. Buzawa & C.G. Buzawa (eds.), *Do arrests and restraining orders work?* (pp. 43-53). Thousand Oaks, CA: Sage.

Schmitt, W.A. & J.P. Newman (1999). Are all psychopathic individuals low-anxious? *Journal of Abnormal Psychology*, 108, 353-358.

Schneider, A.L., L. Ervin & Z. Snyder-Joy (1996). Further exploration of the flight from discretion: The role of risk/need instruments in probation supervision decisions. *Journal of Criminal Justice*, 24, 109-121.

Schneider, F.W., P. Pilon, B. Horrobin & M. Sideris (2000). Contributions of evaluation research to the development of community policing in a Canadian city. *Canadian Journal of Program Evaluation*, 15, 101-129.

Schuessler, K.F. & D.R. Cressy (1950). Personality characteristics of criminals. *American Journal of Sociology*, 55, 476-484.

Schuler, M.E., M.M. Black & R.H. Starr, Jr. (1995). Determinants of mother-infant interaction: Effects of prenatal drug exposure, social support, and infant temperament. *Journal of Clinical Child Psychology*, 24, 397-405.

Schur, E.M. (1973). *Radical nonintervention: Rethinking the delinquency problem*. Englewood Cliffs, NJ: Prentice Hall.

Schwartz, C.E., N. Snidman & J. Kagan (1996). Early childhood temperament as a determinant of externalizing behavior in adolescence. *Development and Psychopathology*, 8, 527-537.

Schweinhart, L.J. & D.P. Weikart (1995). The high/scope Perry preschool study through age 27. In R.R. Ross, D.H. Antonowicz & G.K. Dhaliwal (eds.), *Going straight: Effective delinquency prevention and offender rehabilitation* (pp. 57-75). Ottawa: Air Training Publications.

Seligman, M.E.P. (1975). *Helplessness: On depression, development, and death*. San Francisco: Freeman.

Sellin, J.T. (1980). *The penalty of death, 1980*. Beverly Hills: Sage.

Serin, R.C. (1996). Violent recidivism in criminal psychopaths. *Law and Human Behavior*, 20, 207-217.

Serin, R. & J.S. Lawson (1987). Prediction of temporary absence outcome for penitentiary inmates. *Canadian Journal of Criminology*, 29, 35-49.

Serin, R.C., R.D. Peters & H.E. Barbaree (1990). Predictors of psychopathy and release outcome in a criminal population. *Psychological Assessment: A Journal of Consulting and Clinical Psychology*, 2, 419-422.

Seto, M.C., A. Maric & H.E. Barbaree (2001). The role of pornography in the etiology of sexual aggression. *Aggression and Violent Behavior*, 6, 35-53.

Shaw, D.S. & J.I. Vondra (1995). Infant attachment security and maternal predictors of early behavior problems: A longitudinal study of low-income families. *Journal of Abnormal ChildPsychology*, 23, 335-357.

Shea, S.J. & G.R. McKee (1996). MMPI-2 profiles of men charged with murder or other offenses. *Psychological Reports*, 78, 1039-1042.

Shea, S.J., G.R. McKee, M.E. Craig Shea & D.C. Culley (1996). MMPI-2 profiles of male pre-trial defendants. *Behavioral Sciences and the Law*, 14, 331-338.

Sheridan, L., G.M. Davies & J.C.W. Boon (2001). Stalking: Perceptions and prevalence. *Journal of Interpersonal Violence*, 16, 151-167.

Sherman, L.W. & R.A. Berk (1984). The specific deterrent effect of arrest for domestic assault. *American Sociological Review*, 49, 261-272.

Sherman, L.W., D.C. Gottfredson, D.L. MacKenzie, J. Eck, P. Reuter & S.D. Bushway (1997). *Preventing crime: What works, what doesn't, what's promising*. Washington, DC: National Institute of Justice.

Shields, I.W. & M. Ball (1990). *Neutralization in a population of incarcerated young offenders*. Paper presented at the annual meeting of the Canadian Psychological Association, Ottawa, Ontario.

Shields, I.W. & G.C. Whitehall (1994). Neutralizations and delinquency among teenagers. *Criminal Justice and Behavior*, 21, 223-235.

Short, J.F., Jr. (1957). Differential association and delinquency. *Social Problems*, 4, 233-239.

Short, J.F., Jr. (1991). Poverty, ethnicity, and crime: Change and continuity in U.S. cities. *Journal of Research in Crime and Delinquency*, 28, 501-518.

Shure, M.B. (1988). How to think, not what to think: A cognitive approach to prevention. In L.A. Bond & B.M. Wagner (eds.), *Families in transition: Primary prevention programs that work* (pp. 170-199). Newbury Park, CA: Sage.

Shure, M.B. (1993). I can solve problems (ICPS): Interpersonal cognitive problem solving for young children. *Early Childhood Development and Care*, 96, 49-64.

Shure, M.B. (1997). Interpersonal cognitive problem solving: Primary prevention of early high-risk behaviors in the preschool and primary years. In G.W. Albee & T.P. Gullotta (eds.), *Primary prevention works* (pp. 167-188). Thousand Oaks, CA: Sage.

Silver, E., W.R. Smith & S. Banks (2000). Constructing actuarial devices for predicting recidivism: A comparison of methods. *Criminal Justice and Behavior*, 27, 733-764.

Simons, R.L., C. Johnson, R.D. Conger & G. Elder (1998). A test of latent trait versus life course perspectives on the stability of adolescent antisocial behavior. *Criminology*, 36, 217-244.

Simourd, D.J. (1997). The Criminal Sentiments scale-modified and Pride in Delinquency scale: Psychometric properties and construct validity of tow measures of criminal attitudes. *Criminal Justice and Behavior*, 24, 52-70.

Simourd, D., J. Bonta, D.A. Andrews & R.D. Hoge (1991). *The assessment of criminal psychopathy: A meta-analysis.* Unpublished paper, Department of Psychology, Carleton University, Ottawa, Ontario.

Simourd, D.J. & R.D. Hoge (2000). Criminal psychopathy: A risk-and-need perspective. *Criminal Justice and Behavior*, 27, 256-272.

Simourd, D.J. & P.B. Malcolm (1998). Reliability and validity of the Level of Service Inventory-Revised among federally incarcerated sex offenders. *Journal of Interpersonal Violence*, 13, 261-274.

Simourd, D.J. & J.M. Mamuza (2000). The Hostile Interpretations Questionnaire: Psychometric properties and construct validity. *Criminal Justice and Behavior*, 27, 645-663.

Simourd, D.J. & M. Olver (2002). The future of criminal attitude research and practice. *Criminal Justice and Behavior*, 29, 427-446.

Simourd, D.J. & J. Van De Ven (1999). Assessment of criminal attitudes: Criterion-related validity of the Criminal Sentiments Scale-Modified and Pride in Delinquency scale. *Criminal Justice and Behavior*, 26, 90-106.

Simourd, L. & D.A. Andrews (1994). Correlates of delinquency: A look at gender differences. *Forum on Corrections Research*, 6, 26-31.

Sjöstedt, G. & N. Långström (2000). *Actuarial assessment of risk for criminal recidivism among sex offenders released from Swedish prison 1993-1997.* Paper presented at the 19th Annual ATSA Research and Treatment conference, November, San Diego, CA.

Skilling, T.A., V.L. Quinsey & W.M. Craig (2001). Evidence of a taxon underlying serious antisocial behavior in boys. *Criminal Justice and Behavior*, 28, 450-470.

Skinner, B.F. (1953). *Science and human behavior.* New York: Macmillan.

Skinner, W.F. & A.M. Fream (1997). A social learning theory analysis of computer crime among college students. *Journal of Research in Crime and Delinquency*, 34, 495-518.

Smith, C., H. O'Neill, J. Tobin, D. Walshe & E. Dooley (1996). Mental disorders detected in an Irish prison sample. *Criminal Behaviour and Mental Health*, 6, 177-183.

Smith, C. & T.P. Thornberry (1995). The relationship between childhood maltreatment and adolescent involvement in delinquency. *Criminology*, 33, 451-481.

Smith, D.A. & R. Brame (1994). On the initiation and continuation of delinquency. *Criminology*, 32, 607-629.

Smith, M.D. & M.A. Zahn (eds.) (1999). *Homicide: A sourcebook of social research.* Thousand Oaks, CA: Sage.

Smith, S.M. & C. Braun (1978). Necrophilia and lust murder: Report of a rare occurrence. *Bulletin of the American Academy of Psychiatry and the Law*, 6, 259-268.

Smith, W.R. & D.R. Smith (1998). The consequences of error: Recidivism prediction and civil-libertarian ratios. *Journal of Criminal Justice*, 26, 481-502.

Snell, T.L. (2000). *Capital punishment 1999.* Washington, DC: Bureau of Justice Statistics Bulletin.

Snyder, H.N. (1998). Serious, violent, and chronic juvenile offenders—An assessment of the extent of and trends in officially recognized serious criminal behavior in a delinquent population. In Loeber, R. & D.P. Farrington (eds.), *Serious and violent juvenile offenders: Risk factors and successful interventions* (pp. 428-444). Thousand Oaks, CA: Sage.

Sobell, M.B. & L.C. Sobell (1972). *Individualized behavior therapy for alcoholics: Rationale, procedures, preliminary results and appendix.* Sacramento: State of California Department of Mental Hygiene.

Sokol-Katz, J., R. Dunham & R. Zimmerman (1997). Family structure versus parental attachment in controlling adolescent behavior: A social control model. *Adolescence,* 32, 199-215.

Solomon, R.L. (1964). Punishment. *American Psychologist,* 19, 239-253.

Soothill, K., B. Francis, B. Sanderson & E. Ackerley (2000). Sex offenders: Specialists, generalists—Or both? *British Journal of Criminology,* 40, 56-67.

Spivack, G. & M.B. Shure (1982). The cognition of social adjustment: Interpersonal cognitive problem-solving thinking. In B.B. Lahey & A.E. Kazdin (eds.), *Advances in clinical child psychology,* Vol. 5 (pp. 323-372). New York: Plenum.

Spivack, G. & M.B. Shure (1989). Interpersonal cognitive problem-solving (ICPS): A competence building primary prevention program. *Prevention in Human Services,* 6, 151-178.

Spivack, G. & N. Cianci (1987). High-risk early behavior pattern and later delinquency. In J.D. Burchard & S.N. Burchard (eds.), *Prevention of delinquent behavior* (pp. 44-74). Newbury Park, CA: Sage.

Stark, E. (1996). Mandatory arrest of batterers: A reply to its critics. In E.S. Buzawa & C.G. Buzawa (eds.), *Do arrests and restraining orders work?* (pp. 115-149). Thousand Oaks, CA: Sage.

Stattin, H. & I. Klackenberg-Larsson (1993). Early language and intelligence development and their relationship to future criminal behavior. *Journal of Abnormal Psychology,* 102, 369-378.

Statistics Canada (2001). Crime statistics in Canada, 2000. *Juristat,* 21 (8), 1-22.

Steadman, H.J. & J.J. Cocozza (1974). *Careers of the criminally insane: Excessive social control of deviance.* Lexington, MA: Lexington Books.

Stephens, R.S., R.A. Roffman & E.E. Simpson (1994). Treating adult marijuana dependence: A test of the relapse prevention model. *Journal of Consulting and Clinical Psychology,* 62, 92-77.

Stephenson, R.M. & F.R. Scarpitti (1974). *Group interaction as therapy: The use of the small group in corrections.* Westport, CT: Greenwood Press.

Sternberg, R.J. (1986). Inside intelligence. *American Scientist,* 74, 137-143.

Sternberg, R.J., R.K. Wagner, W.M. Williams & J.A. Horvath (1995). Testing common sense. *American Psychologist,* 50, 912-927.

Stevenson, H.E. & S.J. Wormith (1987). *Psychopathy and the Level of Supervision Inventory.* User Report #1987-25. Ottawa, Canada: Solicitor General Canada.

Stolzenberg, L. & S.J. D'Alessio (1997). "Three strikes and you're out": The impact of California's new mandatory sentencing law on serious crime rates. *Crime & Delinquency,* 43, 457-469.

Stoolmiller, M. (1999). Implications of the restricted range of family environments for estimates of heritability and nonshared environment in behavior-genetic adoption studies. *Psychological Bulletin,* 125, 392-409.

Straus, M. (1979). Measuring intrafamily conflict and violence: The Conflict Tactics (CT) scales. *Journal of Marriage and the Family*, 41, 75-88.

Straus, M.A. (1991). Discipline and deviancy: Physical punishment of children and violence and other crime in adulthood. *Social Problems*, 38, 133-154.

Straus, M.A. (1996). Identifying offenders in criminal justice research on domestic assault. In E.S. Buzawa & C.G. Buzawa (eds.), *Do arrests and restraining orders work?* (pp. 14-29). Thousand Oaks, CA: Sage.

Straus, M.A. & G.K. Kantor (1994). Corporal punishment of adolescents by parents: A risk factor in the epidemiology of depression, suicide, alcohol abuse, child abuse, and wife beating. *Adolescence*, 29, 543-561.

Stuart, B. (1996). Circle sentencing: Turning swords into ploughshares. In B. Galaway & J. Hudson (eds.), *Restorative justice: International perspectives* (pp. 193-206). Monsey, NY: Criminal Justice Press.

Substance Abuse and Mental Health Services Administration (1998). *Preliminary results from the 1997 NHSDA, August 1998*. See http://www.samhsa.gov/oas/nhsda/nhsdafls.htm

Sullivan, C., M.Q. Grant & J.D. Grant (1957). The development of interpersonal maturity: Applications to delinquency. *Psychiatry*, 20, 373-385.

Sutherland, E.H. (1939). *Principles of criminology* (3rd ed.). Philadelphia: Lippincott.

Sutherland, E.H. (1947). *Principles of criminology* (4th ed.). Philadelphia: Lippincott.

Sutherland, E.H. & D.R. Cressey (1970). *Principles of criminology* (6th ed.). New York: Lippincott.

Svrakic, N.M., D.M. Svrakic & R.C. Cloninger (1996). A general quantitative theory of personality development: Fundamentals of a self-organizing psychobiological complex. *Development and Psychopathology*, 8, 247-272.

Swanson, J.W., R. Borum, M.S. Swartz, V.A. Hiday, H.R. Wagner & B.J. Burns (2001). Can involuntary outpatient commitment reduce arrests among persons with severe mental illness? *Criminal Justice and Behavior*, 28, 156-189.

Swanson, J.W., R. Borum, M.S. Swartz & J. Monahan (1996). Psychotic symptoms and the risk of violent behaviour in the community. *Criminal Behaviour and Mental Health*, 6, 309-329.

Swartz, J.A., A.J. Lurigio & S.A. Slomka (1996). The impact of IMPACT: An assessment of the effectiveness of a jail-based treatment program. *Crime & Delinquency*, 42, 553-573.

Swenson, C.C., S.W. Henggeler & S.K. Schoenwald (2001). Family-based treatments. In C.R. Hollin (ed.), *Handbook of offender assessment and treatment* (pp. 205-221). New York: Wiley.

Swenson, C.C., S.W. Henggeler, S.K. Schoenwald, K.L. Kaufman & J. Randall (1998). Changing the social ecologies of adolescent sexual offenders: Implications of the success of multisystemic therapy in treating serious antisocial behavior in adolescents. *Child Maltreatment: Journal of the American Professional Society on the Abuse of Children*, 3, 330-338.

Sykes, G.M. & D. Matza (1957). Techniques of neutralization: A theory of delinquency. *American Sociological Review*, 22, 664-670.

Taraschi, S.G. (1998). Peacemaking criminology and aboriginal justice initiatives as a revitalization of justice. *Contemporary Justice Review*, 1, 103-121.

Taylor, I., P. Walton & J. Young (1973). *The new criminology: For a social theory of deviance*. London: Routledge and Kegan Paul.

Taylor, T.K., J.M. Eddy & A. Biglan (1999). Interpersonal skills training to reduce aggressive and delinquent behavior: Limited evidence and the need for an evidenced-based system of care. *Clinical Child and Family Psychology Review*, 2, 169-182.

Tehrani, J.A., P.A. Brennan, S. Hodgins & S.A. Mednick (1998). Mental illness and criminal violence. *Social Psychiatry and Psychiatric Epidemiology*, 33, 81-85.

Tehrani, J.A. & S.A. Mednick (2000). Genetic factors and criminal behavior. *Federal Probation*, 64, 24-27.

Tennenbaum, D.J. (1977). Personality and criminality: A summary and implications of the literature. *Journal of Criminal Justice*, 5, 225-235.

Teplin, L.A. (1984). Criminalizing mental disorder: The comparative arrest rate of the mentally ill. *American Psychologist*, 39, 794-803.

Teplin, L.A. & J. Swartz (1989). Screening for severe mental disorder in jails. *Law and Human Behavior*, 13, 1-18.

Thistlethwaite, A., J. Wooldredge & D. Gibbs (1998). Severity of dispositions and domestic violence recidivism. *Crime & Delinquency*, 44, 388-398.

Thompson, M.P., L.E. Saltzman & H. Johnson (2001). Risk factors for physical injury among women assaulted by current or former spouses. *Violence Against Women*, 7, 886-899.

Thomas, A. & S. Chess (1977). *Temperament and development*. New York: Brunner/Mazel.

Thomas, A., S. Chess, H.G. Birch, M.E. Hertzig & S. Korn (1963). *Behavioral individuality in early childhood*. New York: New York University Press.

Thomas, C.W. & S.C. Foster (1975). A sociological perspective on public support for capital punishment. *American Journal of Orthopsychiatry*, 45, 641-657.

Thornberry, T.P. & J.E. Jacoby (1979). *The criminally insane: A community follow-up of mentally ill offenders*. Chicago: University of Chicago Press.

Thorstad, D. (1991). Man/boy love and the American gay movement. *Journal of Homosexuality*, 20, 251-274.

Tibbetts, S.G. & A.R. Piquero (1999). The influence of gender, low birth weight, and disadvantaged environment in predicting early onset of offending: A test of Moffitt's interactional hypothesis. *Criminology*, 37, 843-878.

Tiihonen, J., M. Isohanni, P. Räsänen, M. Koiranen & J. Moring (1997). Specific major mental disorders and criminality: A 26-year prospective study of the 1966 Northern Finland birth cohort. *American Journal of Psychiatry*, 154, 840-845.

Tinklenberg, J.A., H. Steiner, W.J. Huckaby & J.R. Tinklenberg (1996). Criminal recidivism predicted from narratives of violent juvenile delinquents. *Child Psychiatry and Human Development*, 27, 69-79.

Tittle, C.R. & H.G. Grasmick (1998). Criminal behavior and age: A test of three provocative hypotheses. *The Journal of Criminal Law and Criminology*, 88, 309-342.

Tittle, C.R. & R.F. Meier (1990). Specifying the SES/delinquency relationship. *Criminology*, 28, 271-299.

Tittle, C.R. & R.F. Meier (1991). Specifying the SES/delinquency relationship by social characteristics of contexts. *Journal of Research in Crime and Delinquency*, 28, 430-455.

Tittle, C.R., W.J. Villimez & D.A. Smith (1978). The myth of social class and criminality: An empirical assessment of the empirical evidence. *American Sociological Review*, 43, 643-656.

Tjaden, P. & N. Thoennes (2000). Prevalence and consequences of male-to-female and female-to-male intimate partner violence as measured by the National Violence Against Women Survey. *Violence Against Women*, 6, 142-161.

Tolman, R.M. & L.W. Bennett (1990). A review of quantitative research on men who batter. *Journal of Interpersonal Violence*, 5, 87-118.

Tomada, G. & B.H. Schneider (1997). Relational aggression, gender, and peer acceptance: Invariance across culture, stability over time, and concordance among informants. *Developmental Psychology*, 33, 601-609.

Tonry, M. (1994). Racial politics, racial disparities, and the war on crime. *Crime & Delinquency*, 40, 475-494.

Tonry, M. & M. Lynch (1996). Intermediate sanctions. In M. Tonry (ed.), *Crime and justice: A review of research, Vol. 20.* (pp. 99-144). Chicago: University of Chicago Press.

Tjaden, P. & N. Thoennes (1996). *Stalking in America: How big is the problem?* Paper presented at the annual meeting of the American Society of Criminology, Chicago, November.

Travis, L.F., III & F.T. Cullen (1984). Radical nonintervention: The myth of doing no harm. *Federal Probation*, 48, 28-32.

Temblay, R.E. (2000). *The origins of youth violence. ISUMA*, 1, 19-24.

Tremblay, R.E., B. Masse, D. Perron, M. LeBlanc, A.E. Schwartzman & J.E. Ledingham (1992). Early disruptive behavior, poor school achievement, delinquent behavior, and delinquent personality: Longitudinal analysis. *Journal of Consulting and Clinical Psychology*, 60, 64-72.

Trojanowicz, R. & B. Bucqueroux (1990). *Community policing: A contemporary perspective*. Cincinnati: Anderson.

Trotter, C. (1999). *Working with involuntary clients: A guide to practice*. Thousand Oaks, CA: Sage.

Truax, C.B., D.G. Wargo & N.R. Volksdorf (1970). Antecedents to outcome in group counseling with institutionalized juvenile delinquents. *Journal of Abnormal Psychology*, 76, 235-242.

Turner, S., P.W. Greenwood, E. Chen & T. Fain (1999). The impact of truth-in-sentencing and three strikes legislation: Prison populations, state budgets, and crime rates. *Stanford Law and Policy Review*, 11, 75-91.

Ullmann, L. & L. Krasner (1976). *A psychological approach to abnormal behavior* (2nd ed.). Englewood Cliffs, NJ: Prentice Hall.

Umbreit, M.S. (1988). Mediation of victim-offender conflict. *Journal of Dispute Resolution*, 85-105.

Umbreit, M.S. (1995). *Mediation of criminal conflict: An assessment of programs in four Canadian provinces.* St. Paul, MN: Center for Restorative Justice and Mediation.

Umbreit, M.S. (1999). Restorative justice: What work. In P.M. Harris (ed.), *Research to results: Effective community corrections.* Lanham, MD: American Correctional Association.

Umbreit, M.S. & R.B. Coates (1992). *Victim offender mediation: An analysis of programs in fours states of the U.S.* Minneapolis: Citizens Council Mediation Services.

Umbreit, M.S. & A.W. Roberts (1996). *Mediation of criminal conflict in England: An assessment of services in Coventry and Leeds.* St. Paul, MN: Center for Restorative Justice and Mediation.

Umbreit, M.S. & B. Vos (2000). Homicide survivors meet the offender prior to execution. *Homicide Studies,* 4, 63-87.

Underdown, A. (1998). *Strategies for effective offender supervision: Report of the HMIP What Works project.* London: Home Office Publications Unit.

Underwood, R.C., P.C. Patch, G.G. Cappelletty & R.W. Wolfe (1999). Do sexual offenders molest when other persons are present? A preliminary investigation. *Sexual Abuse: Journal of Research and Treatment,* 11, 243-247.

United States Department of Justice (1995). *Drugs and crime facts, 1994.* Washington, DC: Bureau of Justice Statistics.

United States Department of Justice (1997). *Highlights of the 1995 National Youth Gang Survey.* Washington, DC: Office of Juvenile Justice and Delinquency Prevention.

United States Department of Justice (2000). *Crime in the United States 1999.* Washington, DC: Federal Bureau of Investigation.

United States Department of Justice (2001). *Community policing in local police departments, 1997 and 1999.* Washington, DC: Bureau of Justice Statistics, Special Report, February.

Valdez, A., C.D. Kaplan & E. Codina (2000). Psychopathy among Mexican American gang members: A comparative study. *International Journal of Offender Therapy and Comparative Criminology,* 44, 46-58.

Valdez, A., C.D. Kaplan, R.L. Curtis & Z. Yin (1995). Illegal drug use, alcohol and aggressive crime among Mexican-American and white male arrestees in San Antonio. *Journal of Psychoactive Drugs,* 27, 135-143.

Van Dieten, M. (1991). *Individual, family, and community correlates of child problematic behaviour in disadvantaged families.* Unpublished doctoral dissertation, University of Ottawa, Ottawa, Ontario.

Van Dusen, K.T. & S.A. Mednick (eds.). (1983). *Prospective studies of crime and delinquency.* Hingham, MA: Kluwer Nijhoff.

Van Houten, R. (1983). Punishment: From the animal laboratory to the applied setting. In S. Axelrod & J. Apsche (eds.), *The effects of punishment on human behavior* (pp. 13-44). New York: Academic Press.

van IJzendoorn, M.H. (1995). Adult attachment representations, parental responsiveness, and infant attachment: A meta-analysis of the predictive validity of the adult attachment interview. *Psychological Bulletin,* 117, 387-403.

van IJzendoorn, M.H. (1997). Attachment, emergent morality, and aggression: Toward a developmental socioemotional model of antisocial behaviour. *International Journal of Behavioral Development*, 21, 703-727.

Van Voorhis, P. (1988). A cross classification of five offender typologies: Issues of construct and predictive validity. *Criminal Justice and Behavior*, 15, 109-124.

Van Voorhis, P. (1994). *Psychological Classification of the Adult Male Prison Inmate*. Albany, NY: State University of New York Press.

Van Voorhis, P. (1997). An overview of offender classification systems. In P. Van Voorhis, M. Braswell & D. Lester (eds.), *Correctional Counseling and Rehabilitation* (pp. 81-108). Cincinnati: Anderson.

Venables, P.A. (1987). Autonomic nervous system factors in criminal behavior. In S.A. Mednick, T.E. Moffitt & S.A. Stack (eds.), *The causes of crime: New biological approaches* (pp. 110-136). Cambridge, England: Cambridge University Press.

Verhulst, F.C., J. van der Ende, R.F. Ferdinand & M.C. Kasius (1997). The prevalence of DSM-III-R diagnosis in a national sample of Dutch adolescents. *Archives of General Psychiatry*, 54, 329-336.

Villa-Vicencio, C. (1999). *A different kind of justice: The South African Truth and Reconciliation Commission*, 1, 407-428.

Virkkunen, M. (1987). Metabolic dysfunction among habitually violent offenders: Reactive hypoglycemia and cholesterol levels. In S.A. Mednick, T.E. Moffitt & S.A .Stack (eds.), *The causes of crime: New biological approaches* (pp. 292-311). Cambridge, England: Cambridge University Press.

Visher, C.A. (1986). The RAND inmate survey: A reanalysis. In A. Blumstein, J. Cohen, J.A. Roth & C.A. Christy (eds.), *Criminal careers and career offenders*. Washington, DC: National Academy Press.

Vold, G.B. & T.J. Bernard (1986). *Theoretical criminology* (3rd ed.). New York: Oxford University Press.

von Hirsch, A. (1976). *Doing justice: The choice of punishments*. New York: Hill and Wang.

von Hirsch, A. (1987). *Past or future crimes: Deservedness and dangerousness in the sentencing of criminals*. New Brunswick, NJ: Rutgers University Press.

von Hirsch, A., A.E. Bottoms, E. Burney & P.-O. Wikström (1999). *Criminal deterrence and sentence severity: An analysis of recent research*. Oxford, England: Hart.

Wadel, D., J. Hawkins, D.A. Andrews, P. Faulkner, R.D. Hoge, L.J. Rettinger & D. Simourd, (1991). *Assessment, Evaluation and Program Development in the Voluntary Sector*. (User Report 1991-14). Ottawa: Solicitor General Canada.

Waldo, G.P. & S. Dinitz (1967). Personality attributes of the criminal: An analysis of research studies, 1950-1965. *Journal of Research in Crime and Delinquency*, 4, 185-202.

Walitzer, K.S., K.H. Dermen & G.J. Conners (1999). Strategies for preparing clients for treatment: A review. *Behavior Modification*, 23, 129-151.

Walker, P.A., W.J. Meyer, L.E. Emory & A.L. Ruben (1984). Antiandrogen treatment of the paraphilias. In H.C. Stancer, P.E. Garfinkel & V.M. Rakoff (eds.), *Guidelines for the use of psychotropic drugs: A clinical handbook* (pp. 427-444). New York: SP Medical & Scientific Books.

Walmsley, R. (2000). *World prison population list* (2nd ed.). Research Findings No. 116. London: Home Office Research, Development and Statistics Directorate.

Walsh, A. (2000). Behavior genetics and anomie/strain theory. *Criminology*, 38, 1075-1108.

Walters, G.D. (1992). A meta-analysis of the gene-crime relationship. *Criminology*, 30, 595-613.

Walters, G.D. (1996). The Psychological Inventory of Criminal Thinking Styles: Part III. Predictive validity. *International Journal of Offender Therapy and Comparative Criminology*, 40, 105-112.

Wanberg, K.W. & H.B. Milkman (1995). *Strategies for self-improvement and change: A cognitive behavioral approach for treatment of the substance abusing offender*. Denver: Center for Interdisciplinary Studies.

Ward, A. & J. Dockerill (1999). The predictive accuracy of the violent offender treatment program risk assessment scale. *Criminal Justice and Behavior*, 26, 125-140.

Ward, D.A. & C.R. Tittle (1994). IQ and delinquency: A test of two competing explanations. *Journal of Quantitative Criminology*, 10, 189-212.

Ward, T. & Hudson, S.M. (1996). Relapse prevention: A critical analysis. *Sexual Abuse: A Journal of Research and Treatment*, 8, 177-200.

Warr, M. (1993). Age, peers, and delinquency. *Criminology*, 31, 17-40.

Waters, E., D. Hay & J. Richters (1986). Infant-parent attachment and the origins of prosocial and anti-social behavior. In D. Olweus, J. Block & M. Radke-Yarrow (eds.), *Development of antisocial and prosocial behavior: Research, theories, and issues* (pp. 97-125). New York: Academic Press.

Watt, M.C., S. Frausin, J. Dixon & S. Nimmo (2000). Moral intelligence in a sample of incarcerated females. *Criminal Justice and Behavior*, 27, 330-355.

Webster, C.D., K.S. Douglas, D. Eaves & S.D. Hart (1997). *The HCR-20: Assessing Risk for Violence* (Version 2). Burnaby, BC: Simon Fraser University.

Webster, C.D. & M.A. Jackson (eds) (1997). *Impulsivity: Theory, assessment, and treatment*. New York: Guilford.

Webster, C.D., R.J. Menzies, M.D. Butler & R.E. Turner (1982). Forensic psychiatric assessment in selected Canadian cities. *Canadian Journal of Psychiatry*, 27, 455-462.

Webster-Stratton, C. & M. Hammond (1997). Treating children with early-onset conduct problems: A comparison of child and parent training interventions. *Journal of Consulting and Clinical Psychology*, 65, 93-109.

Weinrott, M.R. & M. Saylor (1991). Self-report of crimes committed by sex offenders. *Journal of Interpersonal Violence*, 6, 286-300.

Weisman, R. (1995). Reflections on the Oak Ridge experiment with mentally disordered offenders, 1965-1968. *International Journal of Law and Psychiatry*, 18, 265-290.

Wellford, C. (1975). Labeling theory and criminology: An assessment. *Social Problems*, 22, 332-345.

Wells, L.E. & J.H. Rankin (1991). Families and delinquency: A meta-analysis of the impact of broken homes. *Social Problems*, 38, 71-93.

Welsh, B.C. & D.P. Farrington (2000a). Monetary costs and benefits of crime prevention programs. In M. Tonry (ed.), *Crime and justice: A review of research, Vol. 27* (pp. 305-361). Chicago: University of Chicago Press.

Welsh, B.C. & D.P. Farrington (2000b). Correctional intervention programs and cost-benefit analysis. *Criminal Justice and Behavior*, 27, 115-133.

Werner, E.E. (1987). Vulnerability and resiliency in children at risk for delinquency: A longitudinal study from birth to adulthood. In J.D. Burchard and S.N. Burchard (eds.), *Prevention of delinquent behavior* (pp. 16-43). Beverly Hills: Sage.

West, D.J. & D. Farrington (1977). *Who becomes delinquent?* London: Heinemann Educational Books.

Westrup, D. & W.J. Fremouw (1998). Stalking behavior: A literature review and suggested functional assessment technology. *Aggression and Violent Behavior*, 3, 255-274.

Wexler, H.K., G.P. Falkin & D.S. Lipton (1990). Outcome evaluation of a prison therapeutic community for substance abuse treatment. *Criminal Justice and Behavior*, 17, 71-92.

White, J., R.M. Kowalski, A. Lyndon & S. Valentine (2000). An integrative contextual developmental model of male stalking. *Violence and Victims*, 15, 373-388.

Whitefield, D. (1999). Electronic monitoring in Europe: A conference report. *The Journal of Offender Monitoring*, 12, 15, 18-19.

Whitehead, J.T. & S.P. Lab (1989). A meta-analysis of juvenile correctional treatment. *Journal of Research in Crime and Delinquency*, 26, 276-295.

Widiger, T.A., R. Cadoret, R. Hare, L. Robbins, M. Rutherford, M. Zanarini, A. Alterman, M. Apple, E. Corbitt, A. Forth, S. Hart, J. Kultermann, G. Woody & A. Frances (1996). DSM-IV antisocial personality disorder field trial. *Journal of Abnormal Psychology*, 105, 3-16.

Widom, C.S. (1977). A methodology for studying non-institutional psychopaths. *Journal of Consulting and Clinical Psychology*, 45, 674-683.

Widom, C.S. (1989). Child abuse, neglect, and violent criminal behavior, *Criminology*, 27, 251-271.

Widom, C.S. & M.G. Maxfield (2001). An update on the "cycle of violence." Washington, DC: National Institute of Justice, Research in Brief.

Widom, C.S. & J.P. Newman (1985). Characteristics of non-institutional psychopaths. In D.P. Farrington & J. Gunn (eds.), *Aggression and Dangerousness* (pp. 57-80). New York: Wiley.

Wiederanders, M.R., D.L. Bromley & P.A. Choate (1997). Forensic conditional release programs and outcomes in three states. *International Journal of Law and Psychiatry*, 20, 249-257.

Wiederanders, M.R. & P.A. Choate (1994). Beyond recidivism: Measuring community adjustments of conditionally released insanity acquittees. *Psychological Assessment*, 6, 61-66.

Wiederanders, M.R., P.A. Choate & D.L. Bromley (1993). *The effectiveness of the conditional release program: Second report.* Sacramento: California Department of Mental Health.

Wigdor, A.K. & W.R. Gardner (eds.) (1982). *Ability testing: Uses, consequences, and controversies.* Washington, DC: National Academy Press.

Wikström, P-O.H. & R. Loeber (2000). Do disadvantaged neighborhoods cause well-adjusted children to become adolescent delinquents? A study of male juvenile serious offending, individual risk and protective factors, and neighborhood context. *Criminology*, 38, 1109-1142.

Wilkins, L.T. (1975). Inefficient statistics. In W.E. Amos & C.L. Newman (eds.), *Parole: Legal issues/decision-making/research* (pp. 211-229). New York: Federal Publications.

Wilson, J.Q. & R.J. Herrnstein (1985). *Crime and human nature.* New York: Simon and Schuster.

Wilson, M. & M. Daly (1992). Who kills whom in spouse killings? On the exceptional sex ratio of spousal homicides in the United States. *Criminology*, 30, 189-215.

Wilson, P. & K. Soothill (1996). Psychological profiling: Red, green or amber. *The Police Journal*, 69, 12-20.

Wilson, R.J. & M. Barrett (1999). Responsivity and motivation to change in sexual offenders. Paper presented at the annual conference of the American Society of Criminology, Toronto, Ontario

Wilson, T., D. Goldiner & P. Mickle (1993). Prisoner finds rehab a drag. *The Trentonian*, April 13.

Witkin, H.A., S.A. Mednick, F. Schulsinger, E. Bakkestrom, K.O. Christiansen, D.R. Goodenough, K. Hirschhorn, C. Lundsteen, D.R. Owen, J. Philip, D.B. Rubin & M. Stocking (1976). Criminality in XYY and XXY men. *Science*, 193, 547-555.

Wolfe, D.A. & P. Jaffe (1991). Child abuse and family violence as determinants of child psychopathology. *Canadian Journal of Behavioral Science*, 23, 282-299.

Wolfgang, M. (1983). Delinquency in Two Birth Cohorts. In K.T. Van Dusen & S.A. Mednick (eds.), *Prospective studies in crime and delinquency* (pp. 7-16). Hingham, MA: Kluwer Nijhoff.

Wolfner, G.D. & R.J. Gelles (1993). A profile of violence toward children: A national study. *Child Abuse and Neglect*, 17, 197-1993.

Wood, P.R., W.R. Gove, J.A. Wilson & J.K. Cochran (1997). Nonsocial reinforcement and habitual criminal conduct: An extension of learning theory. *Criminology*, 35, 335-366.

Wong, S. (2000). Psychopathic offenders. In S. Hodgins & R. Müller-Isberner (eds.), *Violence, crime and mentally disordered offenders* (pp. 87-112). Chichester, England: Wiley.

Worden, R.E., T.S. Bynum & J. Frank (1994). Police crackdowns on drug abuse and trafficking. In D.L. Mackenzie & C.D. Uchida (eds.), *Drugs and crime: Evaluating public policy initiatives* (pp. 95-113). Thousand Oaks, CA: Sage.

Worling, J.R. & T. Curwen (2000). Adolescent sexual offender recidivism: Success of specialized treatment and implications for risk prediction. *Child Abuse and Neglect*, 24, 965-982.

Wormith, J.S. (1984). Attitude and behavior change of correctional clientele: A three year follow-up. *Criminology*, 22, 595-618.

Wormith, J.S. (2001). Assessing offender assessment: Contributing to effective correctional treatment. *ICCA Journal*, 10, 12-23.

Wormith, J.S. & M. Olver (2002). Offender treatment attrition and its relationship with risk, responsivity and recidivism. *Criminal Justice and Behavior*, 29, 447-471.

Wormith, J.S. & F. McKeague (1996). A mental health survey of community correctional clients in Canada. *Criminal Behaviour and Mental Health*, 6, 49-72.

Wozniak, E. (2001). Program accreditation: Perceptions and realities. *ICCA Journal*, 10, 6-11.

Wright, B.R.E., A. Caspi, T.E. Moffitt & P.A. Silva (2001). The effects of social ties on crime vary by criminal propensity: A life-course model of interdependence. *Criminology*, 39, 321-352.

Wright, J.A., A.G. Burgess, A.W. Burgess, A.T. Laszlo, G.O. McCrary & J.E. Douglas (1996). A typology of interpersonal stalking. *Journal of Interpersonal Violence*, 11, 487-502.

Wright, K., T. Clear & P. Dixon (1984). Universal applicability of probation risk-assessment instruments: A critique. *Criminology*, 22, 113-134.

Wright, K.N. (1986). An exploratory study of transactional classification. *Journal of Research in Crime and Delinquency*, 23, 326-348.

Zager, L.D. (1988). The MMPI-based criminal classification system: A review, current status, and future directions. *Criminal Justice and Behavior*, 15, 39-57.

Zamble, E. & F.J. Porporino (1988). *Coping, behavior, and adaptation in prison inmates*. New York: Springer-Verlag.

Zamble, E. & V.L. Quinsey (1997). *The criminal recidivism process*. New York: Cambridge University Press.

Zehr, H. & H. Mika (1998). Fundamental concepts of restorative justice. *Contemporary Justice Review*, 1, 47-57.

Zhang, L. & S.F. Messner (1995). Family deviance and delinquency in China. *Criminology*, 33, 359-387.

Zolondek, S.C., G.G. Abel, W.F. Northey & A.D. Jordan (2001). The self-reported behaviors of juvenile sex offenders. *Journal of Interpersonal Violence*, 16, 73-85.

Zona, M.A., K.K. Sharma & J. Lane (1993). A comparative study of erotomanic and obsessional subjects in a forensic sample. *Journal of Forensic Sciences*, 38, 894-903.

Zuckerman, M. (1984). Sensation seeking: A comparative approach to a human trait. *Behavioral and Brain Sciences*, 7, 413-471.

Zukerman, M. (1993). P-impulsive sensation seeking and its behavioral, psychophysiological and biochemical correlates. *Neuropsychobiology*, 28, 30-36.

Author Index

Rollick, S. 414
Rooney, J. 251, 260, 354, 355, 404
Rosenbaum, A. 401
Rosenbaum, D.P. 418, 421
Rosenfeld, B.D. 410
Rosenthal, R. 6
Rosner, R. 391
Ross, D.L. 338
Ross, S.M. 398
Ross, R.R. 92, 163, 174, 202, 203, 280,
        281, 283, 286, 290, 367
Rotgers, F. 415
Roth, J.A. 180
Rothbart, M.K. 186
Rowe, D.C. 29, 152, 181, 182
Rowe, R.C. 246, 252
Ruben, A.L. 387
Rubington, E. 154
Rutherford, M. 371
Rutter, M. 198
Rydell, P. 334

Saas, H. 372
Sacco, V.F. 393, 397
Salekin, R.T. 373
Saltzman, L.E. 403
Sampson, R.J. 31, 76, 101, 119, 131,
        147, 209
Sanchez-Meca, J. 290
Sandburg, A.A. 184
Sanders, M. 219
Sanderson, B. 382, 413
Saudino, K.J. 186
Saunders, D.G. 403, 407-409
Saunders, G.A. 211
Sawle, G.A. 206
Saylor, M. 381
Saylor, W.G. 291
Scarpitti, F.R. 154, 304
Schacter, D. 425
Scheier, L.M. 206, 219
Schiraldi, V. 334
Schmidt, A.K. 337
Schmidt, J.D. 405
Schmitt, W.A. 372
Schmutte, P.S. 83
Schneider, A.L. 264
Schneider, B.H. 211
Schneidder, F.W. 422
Schock, A.M. 214
Schober, R. 414
Schoenwald, S.K. 219-221
Schuessler, K.F. 79
Schuler, M.E. 190
Schulsinger, F. 185
Schur, E.M. 85, 142, 300, 301

Schwartz, C.E. 186
Schwartz, M.D. 30, 39, 74
Schwartz, S. 219
Schweinhart, L.J. 197
Scott, H. 382-384, 395
Sears, R. 9, 132, 133, 135, 175, 222
Segal, N. 183
Seligman, M.E.P. 347
Sellin, J.T. 335
Serin, R.C. 231, 263, 373, 374
Sestoft, D. 359
Seth, M. 336
Seto, M.C. 307, 383, 385, 389
Sewell, K.W. 373
Shanahan, M. 325
Sharma, K.K. 390
Shaw, D.S. 188
Shaw, M. 29, 31, 32
Shea, C. 254
Shea, S.J. 254
Sheridan, J. 392
Sherman, L.W. 327, 405, 408
Sherman, M. 174
Shields, I.W. 262
Shine, J. 376
Short, J.F. Jr. 76, 148
Shortt, J.W. 407
Shure, M.B. 202, 203
Sideris, M. 422
Silva, P.A. 71, 72, 77, 179, 181, 188,
        190, 191, 194, 196, 208, 212, 213,
        327, 402
Silver, E. 234, 362
Simons, R.L. 211
Simourd, D.J. 82, 83, 246, 251, 254,
        261, 262, 379
Simourd, L. 74, 83, 266
Simpson, E.E. 413
Simpson, J. 23, 24, 77
Skeem, J.L. 377
Skilling, T.A. 372
Skinner, B.F. 101, 343, 347
Slater, S. 385
Slater, S.W. 231
Slomka, S.A. 415
Smith, B.H. 224
Smith, C. 359
Smith, D.A. 71, 72, 77, 135, 200, 208
Smith, L. 284
Smith, L.A. 219
Smith, P. 246, 252, 252, 284, 326, 334,
        374
Smith, S.M. 57
Smith, W.R. 234
Snell, T.L. 336
Snidman, N. 187

Subject Index